MOBILE PASTORALISM AND THE FORMATION OF NEAR EASTERN CIVILIZATIONS

In this book, Anne Porter explores the idea that mobile and sedentary members of the ancient world were integral parts of the same social and political groups in greater Mesopotamia during the period 4000 to 1500 BCE. She draws on a wide range of archaeological and cuneiform sources to show how networks of social structure, political organization, religious ideology, and everyday as well as ritual practice worked to maintain the integrity of those groups when the pursuit of different subsistence activities dispersed them over space. These networks were dynamic, shaping many of the key events and innovations of the time, including the Uruk expansion and the introduction of writing; so-called secondary state formation and the organization and operation of government; the literary production of the Third Dynasty of Ur and the first stories of Gilgamesh; and the emergence of the Amorrites in the second millennium BCE.

Anne Porter was an assistant professor in the School of Religion, Departments of Classics and Anthropology at the University of Southern California. She served as co-director of excavations at the Tell Banat Settlement Complex, Syria. She has been a visiting research Fellow at both the Institute for the Study of the Ancient World at New York University and the Institute for the Transregional Study of the Contemporary Middle East, North Africa, and Central Asia at Princeton University.

MOBILE PASTORALISM AND THE FORMATION OF NEAR EASTERN CIVILIZATIONS

Weaving Together Society

ANNE PORTER
University of Southern California

CAMBRIDGE
UNIVERSITY PRESS

CAMBRIDGE UNIVERSITY PRESS
Cambridge, New York, Melbourne, Madrid, Cape Town,
Singapore, São Paulo, Delhi, Mexico City

Cambridge University Press
32 Avenue of the Americas, New York NY 10013-2473, USA

Published in the United States of America by Cambridge University Press, New York

www.cambridge.org
Information on this title: www.cambridge.org/9781107666078

First published 2012
First paperback edition 2013

A catalogue record for this publication is available from the British Library

Library of Congress Cataloguing in Publication Data
Porter, Anne, 1957–
    Mobile pastoralism and the formation of Near Eastern civilizations : weaving together society /
    Anne Porter.
        p.   cm.
    Includes bibliographical references and index.
    ISBN 978-0-521-76443-8 (hardback)
        1. Iraq – Antiquities.   2. Middle East – Antiquities.   3. Iraq – Civilization – To 634.
    4. Middle East – Civilization – To 622.   5. Pastoral systems – Middle East – History – To 1500.
    6. Migration, Internal – Middle East – History – To 1500.   7. Sedentary behavior – Middle
    East – History – To 1500.   8. Social archaeology – Iraq.   9. Social archaeology – Middle
    East.   10. Archaeology – Methodology.   I. Title.
    DS73.1.P67   2011
    939'.4–dc22   2010052225

ISBN 978-0-521-76443-8 Hardback
ISBN 978-1-107-66607-8 Paperback

CONTENTS

FIGURES

TABLES

ACKNOWLEDGMENTS

This book has been a long time coming. The fundamental premise was generated when I was a Visiting Research Fellow at the Institute for the Transregional Study of the Contemporary Middle East, North Africa, and Central Asia in the Center for International Studies at Princeton University in 2002. Interaction with scholars in a very different field, political science, was not only stimulating but brought a different kind of rigor to my work and gave me the courage to take the next steps in breaking free of the paradigms that confine my own field. The final form of the book fell into place when I had the very great honor of being invited by Jean-Marie Durand to give the annual four lectures for Assyriology at the Collège de France in 2007. The completed product is a much expanded version of those lectures. Conversations in Paris with Dominique Charpin, Jean-Marie Durand, Jean-Jacques Glassner, Berthille Lyonnet, and Catherine Marro certainly invigorated too many aspects of this work to list. I am not an Assyriologist, although the last chapter of the book is devoted to matters of text and language, an endeavor much facilitated by the time I spent at the Institute for the Study of the Ancient World, New York University, in 2007–8. Several of the ideas in this book owe their genesis to work on another, related, project funded by the University of Southern California's Zumberge Award. I thank all of these institutions for their generous support.

I would also like to express my gratitude to the anonymous reviewers of the manuscript for their very valuable critiques, which gave definition to the end result, and to Thomas McClellan, Glenn Schwartz, and Dan Fleming for their repeated close readings of parts or the whole. I especially thank Marcella Frangipane for her graciousness in allowing me to reproduce illustrations of so much of her extraordinary work at Arslantepe.

The project would never have come to fruition, however, and I would not have been able to stay in archaeology, if not for the unstinting personal, professional, and especially intellectual support of a number of people over the years.

I thank them from the bottom of my heart. In alphabetical order they are: Clem Arrison, Marco Bonechi, Daniel Fleming, Thomas McClellan, Ian Morris, Thomas Payne, Glenn Schwartz, and Kathy St. John.

The book is dedicated to Clem Arrison for his truly altruistic support of junior scholars and artists. This isn't the project you funded, Clem; that one is still coming (soon). But this one wouldn't have happened without you nevertheless.

INTRODUCTION

This book is an act of permuting, which Merriam-Webster's online dictionary defines as "to change the order or arrangement of; to arrange in all possible ways."[1] It takes a wide range of archaeological and cuneiform sources – some well discussed in ancient Near Eastern scholarship, some less thoroughly treated – and extracts them from current paradigms in order to put them in a fresh relationship with each other. In order to do this, I start from a different perspective: that of mobile pastoralism. But the book is not about mobile pastoralists themselves. There is no search for the material traces of herders' lifeways or study of animal husbandry practices. Instead, the book is about the ways in which archaeologists and historians construct models and reconstruct the past, and it is also about the other possibilities always implicit in the evidence.

I choose the lens of mobile pastoralism because while it is increasingly recognized as a significant component in the economic systems of the ancient Near East, especially in the formative period of 4000–1500 BCE (when cities, governments, writing, law, and art all came into being), mobile pastoralism has often been relegated to a cultural, if not geographic and environmental, periphery by the very nature of the period's innovations. That periphery, however, is in actuality the dominant landscape of the region, and the thought that it was not particularly relevant bears examination. Sometimes reconstructions of this period convey, unintentionally no doubt, an image of beleaguered groups of people clinging somewhat desperately to narrow ribbons of land constituted by river valleys and circumscribed by a vast and frightening terra incognita. And yet hostile environments everywhere – untenable climates and arid landscapes – are full of people doing things and living ordinary human lives. To think that these people have no impact on the nature of the worlds in which they live is to

---

1   http://mw2.merriam-webster.com/dictionary/permuting.

deny them not only agency but also connections with those who live in more congenial climes.

If there are two theoretical perspectives that undergird this work, therefore, they are that human beings in all times and places do have agency (if agency is consciousness, the ability to make choices, and some degree or kind of power) and that there are very few groups of people in this world, past or present, who are completely isolated. Indeed, most of us are networked together in multiple series of relationships that render us – that *should* render us – resistant to classification. And all sorts of sometimes surprising things are interconnected. I do not explicitly develop these positions, which by now are rather well-worn in any case, but they are woven, and demonstrated, I hope, throughout a narrative that addresses one fundamental question: what happens to our reconstructions of the past when the mobile[2] and sedentary components of the ancient world are thoroughly interrelated parts of the same societies?

Asking this question requires the rearrangement of a number of matters. Instead of looking at pastoralists in the steppe, I look for ways we may see their presence in the settlements of the societies of which they were part. This, of course, at some level becomes a hypothetical exercise. There are no signs saying "pastoralists live here." But there are signs, at various points in time and space, indicating that certain kinds of issues and certain kinds of relationships are at stake that would seem to transcend a fully sedentary existence; so instead of delineating sociopolitical organization, I search for evidence of the practices that establish those relationships or speak to those issues. The outcome of these tasks is a rearrangement of some deeply embedded principles of Near Eastern archaeology and history: instead of understanding that sedentary agriculture, and specifically cereal cultivation, is the source of civilization, I find that some of the key attributes of this period – the development of urbanism, the nature of political organization and structure, the origins of writing – arise from the tensions implicit in societies that have significant mobile components. Those tensions, however, lie not in an incipient violence created when two fundamentally different ways of life are forced to exist side-by-side, but in the constant risk of fragmentation and dispersal of a social group when large parts of it constantly move.

So, on another level, this book is about structures and practices of integration and differentiation; it is about the nature of kinship, boundaries and identities – the things people do to maintain and change them and the forces that act on them that are beyond anyone's control. It is about how the way people

---

2   Of course mobility is not restricted to pastoralists, nor are pastoralists necessarily mobile (Bernbeck 2008a: 45–6). However, this book is restricted to mobile pastoralists as both the dominant mobile group and the dominant form of pastoralism during the periods under study.

think about the world and its organization and operation – cosmology – shapes what they do, whether ancient Mesopotamian or modern scholar. It is concerned with archaeological and historical methodologies and the blurring of domains of existence, as well as study. No doubt it is a little unwieldy at times, but I wish to maintain the interconnectedness of all the various elements that comprise the record of the past.

I begin this project, then, by arguing that the pervasive sense of a profound social as well as physical separation between mobile pastoralists and sedentary farmers/urban citizens is a theoretical construct and not an inevitable condition of animal husbandry. It is sometimes a political construct as well, a product of specific historical circumstances and/or of intellectual histories. Chapter 1 traces the origins of various archaeological interpretations of the role of mobility in the ancient world and the various ways in which certain fundamental tenets guide the reconstructions of Near Eastern scholarship. Dominant among these ideas is the relationship between mobility and sociopolitical organization, between pastoralist and tribe. An uncritical use of sociological theory and anthropological analogy has led practitioners of archaeology and Near Eastern studies into a corner in this regard, at the same time as some of the foundational premises of anthropology itself are under review. The pivotal question is this: if pastoralists and farmers belong to the same sociopolitical entities, how is the existence of these two apparently divergent political forms, tribe and state, to be reconciled? An answer requires the delineation of the long history of use and abuse of these two terms, "tribe" and "state."

There is another dimension to the problem. For fragmentation not to occur within groups dispersed over time and space, it would seem that something happens to counter the disintegrating potential of mobility. The structures and processes that inhibit disintegration are in and of themselves dynamic and have an impact on the eventuation of what we consider the fundamentals of civilization, so that not only do the empirical specifics of the origin of civilization change, but there is a larger theoretical outcome. Basic evolutionary precepts are undermined and other approaches to thinking about these shifts have to be developed, because if pastoralists and farmers belong to the same sociopolitical entities, organizational and administrative systems and structures must transcend – indeed counter – distance and separation or soon there is no group to administer; they must stretch.

Chapter 2 brings these approaches to the fore when considering the role of pastoralism in the context of a prominent problem in Near Eastern archaeology, the Uruk expansion. In the mid-fourth millennium BCE, a distinctive material culture argued to have disseminated from the very first city, Uruk of southern Mesopotamia, is found spread throughout a broad swath of the Near East. Long thought to be the material residue of the processes of colonization by a superior civilization of lesser ones, pastoralism may be demonstrated to have played a far more critical role in the expansion than any desire to appropriate land, raw materials, or political power. The complex distribution patterns of Uruk material culture speak to a specific set of problems wrought by the increasing mobility of significant sections of the populace – how to combat the disintegrating forces of fragmentation and dispersal so that key primary producers would remain an integral part of the sociopolitical system from which they originally derived. The means employed to this end shaped the ways in which some of the key transformations of this time took place and the forms they assumed, just as other transformations contributed to this new mobility by shifting how traditional subsistence practices worked in Mesopotamia and how the people who practiced them interacted. Religion and kinship emerge as dual and interconnected means of configuring sociopolitical relationships that transcend time and space.

But the dynamic significance of pastoralism is not confined to this one time of change; it is of enduring power in the ancient world. In order to demonstrate this, Chapter 4 focuses on a specific historical problem: the origins of those most famous of supposed nomads in the ancient Near East, the Amorrites,[3] the people who gave us Hammurabi and who dominated Mesopotamia in the early second millennium BCE. This chapter, however, is based on literary analysis rather than traditional historical methodologies and is offered as a complement to the rigorous studies of linguistic and textual detail more commonly utilized to understand this problem. Again, externality is the central issue: the Amorrites seem by all accounts to have been alien to the river valleys of Mesopotamia that they eventually came to dominate, because pastoralism is a key component of their economic and hence, to many scholars, political system, and at certain points some Amorrites actively claimed a history of mobility. And yet there are anomalies that confound us, hints of a long historical presence in Mesopotamia and associations with the sedentary world, at the same time as there is no trace of an indigenous Amorrite culture, since they did not even use their own language to write the official documents of their rule. This lack of written Amorrite, the fact that the Amorrites employed Akkadian, the language of their predecessors in political dominance, has led many to view them as cultureless nomads greedy for the superior civilization of the sedentary world. Such views impede our ability to realize fully the political nature of social and ethnic identities, and especially the activities of history making and storytelling – all factors that play into the construction of the sometimes enigmatic sources on the Amorrites.

However, a thousand years intervene between the end of the Uruk expansion and the emergence of the Amorrites, a thousand years in which all we think we know about the nature of society, polity, and culture is the antithesis of mobile

---

3   Following Fleming (2004), I use the Akkadian spelling with doubled "r," also thereby distinguishing the second-millennium group from the biblical Amorites.

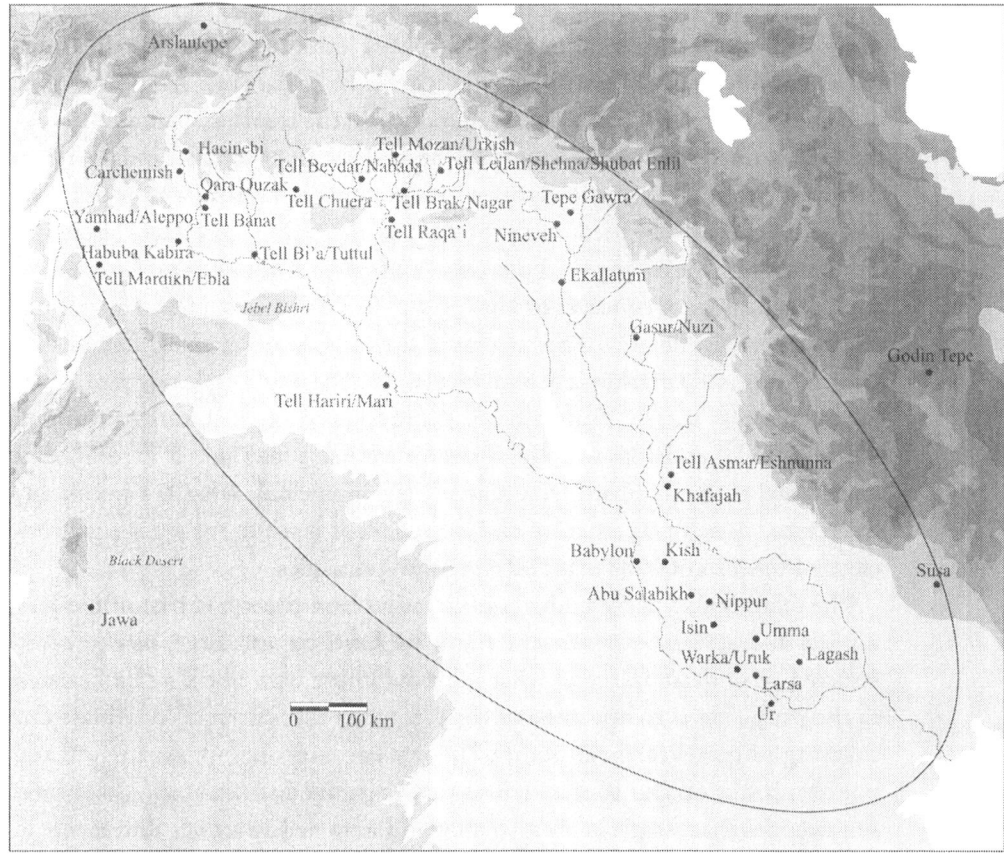

1. Map of the "land of the four riverbanks" with key sites.

pastoralism. This is the time of urban explosion across the land of the four riverbanks, the area around and between the Euphrates and Tigris from their headwaters in Turkey through to the Persian Gulf. It is the time when complex polities become more than that, when even "empires" are said to come into being. At the same time this was not a uniform process. There were regional differences in sociopolitical organization, usually characterized as between north and south, which seem to have had something to do with differences in environment and landscape, as long ago argued by Robert McCormack Adams (1974, 1981). An examination in Chapter 3 of settlement during the third millennium in the northern part of the land of the four riverbanks,[4] in Syria and Turkey (Fig. 1), shows how, rather than diverging trajectories resulting not

4   I have adapted the term "the four riverbanks" from Buccellati (1990a), since it expresses the geographic focus of this discussion without implying in any way the cultural or political priority of one region over the other and is thus to be preferred to terms such as Northern and Southern Mesopotamia, or Mesopotamia and the Jazireh. I extend its compass a little farther than Buccellati, however, to include all of the land between the rivers and, for their outer perimeters, the steppe beyond only the river valley itself as far as Ebla to the west

only in unlike organization but in differential levels of complexity, the third-millennium histories of north and south arose from the same set of processes, and more particularly, practices, set in motion in the fourth millennium. There are further outcomes to this situation: the association of certain kinds of structure with political form or levels of complexity; that is, kinship with tribes, civic ties with state, are obviated. In the ancient world, "tribe" and "state" were not fundamental oppositions, for both were configured through actual and philosophical/ideological concepts of kinship and had much in common operationally and organizationally. They operated similarly, in order to achieve similar ends. Significant variation is found, however, in the way social structure is perpetuated across society. Sometimes it is hidden and implicit, carried through and within the social knowledge of the individual; sometimes it is codified as an external entity, imposed from outside the individual. What are commonly interpreted as self-perpetuating and independent institutions are simply concretized versions of otherwise abstract social principles.

The relationship really under consideration here though is that of modern models and ancient experience. I think we have, by and large, nicely reconstructed an understanding of what life would have been like if *we* had existed in the past. That is to say, none of the categories that currently dominate our thinking are quite real for antiquity. They are based on our own experiences and our own histories. Our sources tell us that there are distinctions in these sorts of categories that people in the ancient world were well aware of – differences in ethnicity perhaps, differences in subsistence, differences in political functioning and organization. But are those differences the same as ours? In terms of the political categories we apply to the past, I will venture to say they are not. "Tribe" and "state" are both inappropriate frameworks, at least as we currently comprehend these words, to use in understanding the sociopolitical organization of the period from 4000 to 1500 BCE (Table 1).

and the Diyala on the east because, in emic terms, these regions constitute key parts of the interconnected world this study is about – an interconnectedness that is facilitated by pastoralism.

Table 1. Chronology 4000–1500 BCE.

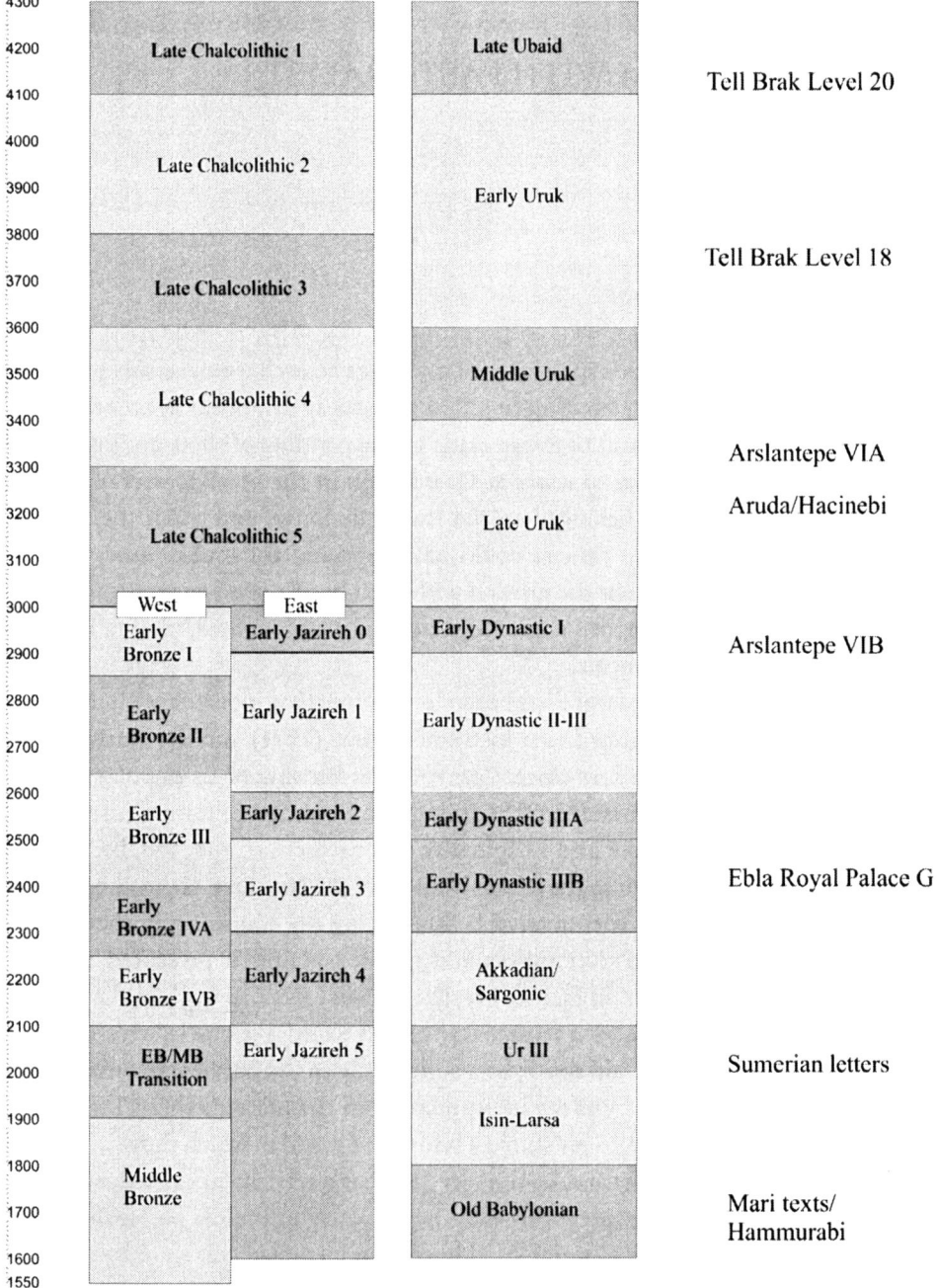

4300	Northern Mesopotamia		Southern Mesopotamia	
4200	Late Chalcolithic 1		Late Ubaid	
4100				Tell Brak Level 20
4000	Late Chalcolithic 2			
3900			Early Uruk	
3800				Tell Brak Level 18
3700	Late Chalcolithic 3			
3600				
3500	Late Chalcolithic 4		Middle Uruk	
3400				
3300				Arslantepe VIA
3200	Late Chalcolithic 5		Late Uruk	Aruda/Hacinebi
3100				
3000	West	East		
2900	Early Bronze I	Early Jazireh 0	Early Dynastic I	Arslantepe VIB
2800	Early Bronze II	Early Jazireh 1	Early Dynastic II-III	
2700				
2600	Early Bronze III	Early Jazireh 2	Early Dynastic IIIA	
2500				
2400	Early Bronze IVA	Early Jazireh 3	Early Dynastic IIIB	Ebla Royal Palace G
2300				
2200	Early Bronze IVB	Early Jazireh 4	Akkadian/ Sargonic	
2100				
2000	EB/MB Transition	Early Jazireh 5	Ur III	Sumerian letters
1900			Isin-Larsa	
1800	Middle Bronze			
1700			Old Babylonian	Mari texts/ Hammurabi
1600				
1550				

CHAPTER ONE

THE PROBLEM WITH PASTORALISTS

One of the most exotic experiences of my life as an archaeologist was presaged by a faint susurration swelling to a slow yet steady drumbeat in an otherwise eerie silence, a drumbeat that was made by the padding of thousands of camel feet wending their way to water at Qasr Burqu in the Black Desert of Jordan (Fig. 1). The camels belonged to the Rwala Bedouin, and when they finally came within sight, no camera could have captured the multisensory experience of dust rising from the ground with each hoof's thud to merge with the heat's haze through which these enigmatic creatures loomed, then faded, in a rhythm timed to their gait.

But my interest in pastoralists began long before that moment, with the book *Jawa: Lost City of the Black Desert* by Svend Helms (1981) and the reason I was at Qasr Burqu in the first place. Controversial because of its popular nature, where technical discussions of hydrology and stratigraphy were interwoven with personal anecdote and imaginative reconstruction, and, too, because of the connections drawn to the biblical stories of the Israelites, Helms's book did something I had not encountered before during my education in the archaeology of well-watered river valleys and rain-fed plains. It presented a world *without* much water or, in fact, as I realized when I went to work in the region, without anything at all – a remarkably barren world, yet one in which people lived. A world, one would think, best suited only to the hardiest of mobile pastoralists. At least, that was my interpretation in the master's thesis I wrote on the topic. But Helms also presented a bifurcated world in which those who built the settlement of Jawa were, by the very fact that a settlement existed, necessarily at odds in every respect with what he/we knew of mobile pastoralists and therefore could not *be* pastoralists.[1] I have been intrigued ever since by the relationship of pastoralists not only to settlement but to all aspects of materiality.

---

1 For an example of the continuing prevalence of this view, see Meyer 2010a.

The reader might, then, expect a study of Bedouin material culture to follow, as is often the case with archaeologists considering pastoralism. But my concerns here are instead with why we think what we do about pastoralism, in the mental constructs that enable model to defy not only logic but all too often evidence. Because it seemed to me then, in 1984 when I wrote the thesis on Jawa, and still today, that Helms was far from alone in his understanding that pastoralists were simply not capable of doing the things that settled people do, if only because they lacked the ability to organize in the same way. The reasons for that lack were thought somehow inherent in the nature of pastoralism itself, so that a situation observable in the modern world was, naturally, in place in the ancient world. Of course many factors contribute to this view, but the essential line of argument, deriving from anthropological research, was that animal husbandry and mobility both preclude the accumulation of differentials in wealth that leads to social stratification and that in turn leads to complexity. Mobility also constrains social interactions and organization so that to be pastoralist is essentially to be tribal.[2] And tribe is always something other than the state.

The reasoning goes as follows: as the tribe is based on kinship, the group is considered to have a low level of integration and centralization, is egalitarian in organization (Swidler 1972: 119; Gellner 1969, 1984: xiii; cf. Digard 1990: 97–8), and lacks institutional structure (Khoury and Kostiner 1990: 10) intrinsic to its very nature as an aggregation of small, self-contained groups of families bound together by a system of blood relationships that determine loyalties, degree of connection, and the nature of interaction (Evans-Pritchard 1969 [first published 1940]; Sahlins 1968) and that give rise to a moral economy of sharing (McGuire 1992: 182; Yoffee 1993: 69). But such groups are also divided by self-interest because the individual family controls the means of production (Khazanov 1978: 122; Lefébure 1979: 6; Johnson and Earle 1987: 241; Cribb 1991: 49), and pastoralism is such an unstable basis for an economy (Kuznar and Sedlmeyer 2008: 561) that it cannot generate the long-term reserves necessary for the development of social inequality (Childe 1951 [1936]; Asad 1979: 420; Cole 1981: 130; Gellner 1984: xi). There is no larger institutional entity that ensures connections through collection and/or redistribution of production. Tribally organized pastoralists are therefore usually unable or unwilling to sustain the concerted action necessary for state formation and state continuance. Successful and long-term state formation occurs primarily through conquest and only when large components of the pastoralist group, particularly the elite, settle and adopt institutions of leadership transmission, administration (Khazanov 1978: 124–5; Nissen 1980: 289; Kafadar 1995; Khoury and Kostiner 1990: 11; Postgate 1992: 86), and especially formalized militarization (Gellner 1990) from sedentary society. And, of course, a classic aspect of most theories of state formation is still – and above

---

2   See Porter 2000 for comprehensive discussion.

all else, as recently reiterated (Ur 2010) – the dissolution or suppression of the kinship ties that are the essence of the tribe. Explanations for the success or failure of the transition from tribe to state rely upon characteristics of the tribal system, such as its militaristic, expansionist nature (Sahlins 1961; Beck 1986: 14; Lapidus 1990: 34; Digard 1990: 102–3), bonds of loyalty (Digard 1990: 104), egalitarianism (Hall and Ikenberry 1989: 31), and, often, greed (Seaman 1991) or brutality (Gellner 1984: xii; Kuznar and Sedlmeyer 2008).[3]

As can be seen from the extensive references in the above passage, this understanding was developed through the explosion of ethnographic work on pastoralist groups that took place primarily from the late 1960s through mid-1980s, when certain issues dominated because of the larger geopolitical situation, one of which was the conflictual relationship between tribes and the states that were seeking to subordinate them. This material is very influential in archaeological interpretations, especially in the evolutionary archaeology still ascendant in the United States, and it sets the tone for that work in two ways, one material and one conceptual. In the first instance, the search for traces of ancient pastoralist presence is presumed rather fruitless, if only because nomads possess little material culture and have but an ephemeral presence in the landscape, and thus do not leave behind detectable residues of their existence.[4] In the second, pastoralism, and especially its political corollary, the tribe, is seen as either an earlier *stage* in the development of human societies, one that is then sidelined as the state develops, or as a *type* of society that is less sophisticated in its workings than the state. Either as stage or type, then, pastoralist tribes are not included as part of the physical or ideological environment of the state.

The upshot of both these positions, material and conceptual, is that archaeologists rarely consider the possibility that pastoralists were present in, or had any part in shaping, the settlements they excavate and the societies that inhabited them, especially once urbanism is present. Pastoralist and settlement are assumed to be mutually exclusive in every way. If for some reason pastoralists are recognized as intrinsic to the urban record, then they are thought to have sedentarized, which by definition means they have abandoned pastoralism (while perhaps claiming a lingering pastoralist identity) and, by implication, have chosen civilization.

But while ethnographic analogy is very useful for understanding some aspects of pastoralism, it is highly problematic for characterizing the nature and place of pastoralists in the ancient world (Bernbeck 2008a; Khazanov

---

3   For an explanation of the Islamic state that incorporates all these attributes, see Hall and Ikenberry 1989.

4   The alternative too often takes the form of simplistic correlations of material culture attributes such as crude handmade pottery (e.g., Alizadeh 2008: 103) or circular architecture with mobile ways of life, but see Berelov 2006 for an exception.

2009: 122).[5] There are several reasons for this, not least of which is the transmission of authority in academic practice, where certain ideas have considerable, and unwarranted, longevity (delineated, and challenged, by Marx 2006). Another reason is the marginalization of pastoralists in the *modern* world (exemplified in Claudot-Hawad 2006). Even the writings of Ibn Khaldoun, an early Islamic commentator often considered the first ethnographer of pastoralists, are inappropriate for characterizing the ancient situation, because they present his sociopolitical environment as a series of idealized dichotomies, a view later subscribed to by anthropologists (as Eickelman 1998 notes) and historians who still treat his work as if it were an unassailable source in no need of deconstruction (e.g., Kuznar and Sedlmeyer 2008). Certainly no contemporary ethnography describes pastoralists who exist in a context uninfluenced by a modern state and modern economy, entities very different from their ancient counterparts, although, because paradigms derived from modern examples are applied to ancient polities to determine whether or not they constitute a state, this is rarely evident. But ancient Near Eastern sources exist in a time, and a situation, before the anthropological materials are altogether relevant, and they needs must speak for themselves. When they do, it soon emerges that pastoralism is in no way separate from the urbanized, sedentary world more traditionally the focus of Near Eastern studies because it is in this environment that the fundamental features of the contemporary Western world - civilization, urbanism, public interest, government - are presumed to have come into existence.

Traditional discourse on the agricultural origins of civilization has always been accomplished, however, by the abnegation of other forms of sociopolitical organization and practice, and an entire segment of the population has simply been left out of this reconstruction: namely, the mobile groups that exploited the area outside the river valleys in pursuit of animal husbandry - the "nomads" of popular imagination, the pastoralists of anthropological discourse. Pastoralists are not part of these reconstructions because they have long been understood as existing outside civilization, even as against the very idea of civilization. It seems obvious. Whether approached from an environmental, social, or political perspective, pastoralists occupy different spaces than those occupied by farming villages, class-based cities, and urban government and so are intrinsically separate from them. That separation is furthered by mobility, which carries within it the potential for constant social readjustment according to the ways decisions are reached by the group (Salzman 1971: 107, 1972: 67; Gulliver 1975: 373; Marx 1978: 46; Dupire in Burnham 1979: 351-2; Lancaster and Lancaster 1986: 44). Individual families may determine where, and with whom, to go with their herds, or leaders of larger units such as lineage heads may control these

5   Bernbeck (1992, 2008a) provides strong empirical evidence of this in two different situations.

choices, choices that are often shaped by factors such as climatic conditions (for example, in times of drought pastoralist groups might disperse) and availability of pasturage. Other considerations also play a role; the political environment through which the group is to pass (Irons 1974), where differing assessments of risk in times of conflict may prompt temporary fission; or social issues such as family disagreements, where herding strategies enable association and disassociation between people without unpleasant public rupture (Gulliver 1975: 379; Tapper 1979: 46; Salzman 1980: 3; Glatzer 1983: 219; Lancaster and Lancaster 1991: 135; Cribb 2008: 547–8).

Such fluidity is charged with the risk of fracture, as families split from the larger community and even divide within themselves, not just for a season but sometimes for decades, maybe generations. But there is something puzzling here, for even if there is some shifting of constituents, with various members of the group perhaps choosing different affiliations or sedentarizing, individual pastoralist communities appear to maintain their essential integrity over long periods of time (Bonte 1979: 212–13; Kelly 1985; Cribb 1991: 54). That is, they do not fall apart or cease to exist because of the frequent reconfiguration of relationships that occur in the regular process of mobility. Not only that, individuals far removed from their pastoralist origins may still claim their original pastoral identity as real and current, and may activate the rights and obligations due them as members of the group, because various structures, ideologies, and practices exist that perpetuate personal and communal identities and relationships across time, and across space, as I will argue. These structures, ideologies, and practices are far more complex, however, than what is usually meant when people call mobile pastoralists "tribal."

The same risk of fracture is surely present when mobility is a tactic through which a community maximizes its opportunities, subsistence or social, by sending some of its members on peregrinations far from home while the rest remain in place. This, of course, is a global phenomenon today. Migrant workers leave their country of origin for better job opportunities and living conditions all over the world, the best known examples of which, perhaps, are the Latin American population in the United States, or the Turkish workforce in Germany. But it is also argued to have been the process by which pastoralism itself, as something other than village-based herding[6] and as an alternative way of life, originated. As sedentary agriculture expanded, especially with the use of irrigation, animal husbandry was pushed farther and farther away from the settled zone (Lees and Bates 1974; Bates and Lees 1977; Nissen 1980; Abdi 2003)[7] into peripheral areas

---

6 Whether called (incorrectly) transhumance, seminomadism, nomadic pastoralism, or any other of the myriad terms in use.

7 And see Chapter 2, where I will put forward a similar argument – though with different outcomes. This development in Mesopotamia does not constitute the origins of mobile pastoralism in general, but only of this practice in southern Mesopotamia. There is evidence that locates the beginnings of pastoralism in the seventh millennium (Garrard,

where it stayed, becoming in essence a new culture, a separate sociopolitical system (Buccellati 2008). In a very few generations, because of a simple physical separation brought about by mobility, all social connections with, along with any sense of obligation to, the community of origin are assumed to have been lost.

Yet as consideration of the contemporary migrant experience shows, there are numerous possible outcomes of spatial dispersal within a society: the emigrant group loses its ties to its place of origin, assimilating rapidly into the new society to the degree that new society permits,[8] sometimes repudiating their former communities outright;[9] the immigrant group maintains the integrity of its original community but in a new place, and it may operate in such a case independently of, or as a satellite to, the community's original home; or it straddles the two, more or less comfortably depending on the situation. These are but some of the possibilities that have played out in recent history, and while it may be assumed that communication technologies available only in the modern world allow for the maintenance of connection in diasporic situations, this is not the case. There are multiple ways of transcending time and space that do not need to be technologically based, nor even tangible, to be effective.

So the question is not whether multiple outcomes to dispersal were possible in ancient history as well, since multiple outcomes to any situation are always possible, but rather, why do they not appear to have been in evidence? Why does the pursuit of animal husbandry in the ancient world seem, at least as far as the scholarly literature goes, to have had but one result: separation, and an essential alienation, of mobile groups from sedentary society,[10] economic symbiosis notwithstanding, and yet within mobile groups themselves dissolution was somehow avoided?

The answer is: it does not. Until a particular moment in time, pastoralists in the ancient Near East were the same social, political, and familial entities as farmers, and so to consider them different in terms of culture, civilization, and complexity is therefore illogical. Rather than a picture of two separate entities coming together at certain points for certain reasons, we should envisage *one* entity splitting *apart* from time to time; or better, as a series of single entities diverging and merging in a myriad of combinations over time. This framework then necessitates a completely different understanding of the dynamics of sedentary–pastoralist interaction, and moreover reveals those dynamics to be critical factors in the

      Colledge and Martin 1996) in the Levant, while Alizedah (2009) places its origins in the highlands of Iran in the fifth millennium.

8   Until recently, Germany did not allow children of foreigners born in Germany to become citizens; Latino populations may be marginalized, if not ghettoized, by public attitudes of the community in which they find themselves, and the nature of their reception no doubt influences the nature of their relationship with their place of origin, as well as with their host situation.

9   Depending on why they left in the first place.

10   Which in turn gives rise to the hostility that pastoralists feel to their sedentary neighbors.

nature and organization of the world of the four riverbanks,[11] the region from Anatolia to southern Iraq encompassed and defined by the lands on either side of the Tigris and Euphrates, and the focus of this book.

This proposal, that pastoralists and farmers form unitary sociopolitical groups, not only runs counter to prevailing ideas of social and political organ-ization in the fourth, third, and second millennia BCE,[12] it seems deeply counter-intuitive to scholar and interested bystander alike, because the data seem surely to indicate that pastoralists *are* different *and* separate, and to prove the contrary will surely require radical new evidence. But my project here is not to present fresh discoveries that will overturn all our closest-held notions, nor to unearth novel ways of finding ephemeral populations in the archaeological record, so much as it is to discuss different ways of thinking about the evidence we have long had at our disposal. Separation is not, I would argue, a product of the data, but of specific historical events in conjunction with a deeply entrenched intel-lectual history (ancient and modern) that has on certain occasions been delib-erately constructed, or deployed, to effect desired outcomes.

Once such event was the Peace of Westphalia in 1648, which led to the creation of the nation-state through the delineation of territorial and sovereign boundar-ies. This ultimately had a major impact on interactions between pastoralists and the state, putting them at odds because of now divergent relationships to space, a situation that still has major resonance, often with violent outcomes, today. The state, in order to exert control over the boundaries that define it, cannot tolerate groups it perceives as transgressing those boundaries, for those groups threaten to destabilize it by demonstrating their ability to escape the means of control exercised within, and limited to, those boundaries.[13] Mobile pastoralists require easy passage to and from pasturage wherever it might be located, and an invisible line that divides traditional territories (as well as group members) and allocates them to separate states serves only to impede the normal function-ing of the group (e.g., Claudot-Hawad 2006; and Lancaster and Lancaster 2006: 346-9). Pursuit of these conflicting interests colors pastoralist-state relations in very particular respects, but is only one of the many ways the modern state has shaped the nature of pastoralist existence (e.g., Chatty 2006b).

The intellectual history influenced by centuries of colonialism – in that coloni-alist acts shaped the nature of pastoralism in Africa and South Asia in particular, and in that colonialist views of such groups portrayed them as merely backward or as outright criminal (Casimir and Rao 2003: 65) – also served a purpose. The work of scholars such as E. Evans-Pritchard (1969 [1940]) in his enormously

---

11 See Introduction, n. 4.
12 See, for example, A. T. Smith 2003: 153, n. 7.
13 See Marx 2006: 88-9 for a discussion of how the state perceives nomads (also Chatty 2006a); Chatty 2006b for how the state portrays nomads; and Lancaster and Lancaster 1986 for the way nomads see boundaries.

influential studies of the Nuer for example, which defined the organization and workings of the tribe for a long time and which still frames some of the research issues,[14] was undertaken explicitly in order to figure out how the British might rule their colonial subjects.[15] That very mission, in fact, has been argued to have created the tribe as a sociopolitical formation (Fried 1968, 1975; Hobsbawm and Ranger 1983). Whether one subscribes to this position or not, it is certain that colonial rule changed much, ranging from the minutiae of actual pastoralist subsistence practices (who moved where and why, how the move was organized and negotiated), to pastoralist social and political functioning, both internal (who ruled and how) and external (one pastoralist group's interactions with others). It is the colonialist view that has been the dominating discourse; we have hardly heard from pastoralists themselves.[16] And if we think that in the writings of their ethnographers we have, then the role of anthropology as the handmaiden of the colonialist endeavor must be recognized.

Furthermore, our understanding of the place of pastoralism in the economic, social, and political realms of the ancient Near East stems from a dual attraction to, and repulsion by, a highly alien landscape. Early explorers and artists were entranced by the romance of the desert and the mystique of the bedouin (Chatty 2006a: 1–3; see van der Steen and Saidel 2007 for references), while scholars focused on those thin strips of green that were familiar and safe, but more particularly, most resembled the world they came from, and therefore seemed to be the logical source of that world. The concept of Orientalism is well known, but the degree to which it created this seemingly unbridgeable chasm in Near Eastern studies between pastoralist and farmer has yet to be explored to its fullest extent; it dictates, for example, the entire research agenda of the great transformations – sedentarization, agriculture, and especially the emergence of city and state.

Finally, at least for my purposes here, these forces are bolstered by a pervasive materialist sensibility that perceives a lack of goods as a manifestation of a lack of complexity (Buchli 2004: 189), because of both the nature of our own social and intellectual environment, in which well-being is measured by wealth (Meskell 2005: 11), and the role played by historical materialism in academic formulations. A fundamentally Marxist outlook underpins evolutionary anthropology and archaeology: explicitly in the works of a number of writers from V. Gordon Childe (1951) to Charles Maisels (1990) and Randall McGuire (1992), and implicitly in studies such as that of Guillermo Algaze (1989, 2005, 2008) on

---

14   As seen in Salzman 1999 and the commentaries to that paper.
15   See Richards 1960 on the establishment of the East African Institute.
16   Perhaps this is a little disingenuous, because I might also argue that in fact we have heard from pastoralists – in the rebellions against colonial domination that contributed to the pervasive idea that pastoralists were/are inherently violent. As will be argued further, however, such rebellions are not a structural condition of existence vested in kinship systems as outlined by Evans-Pritchard, but a reaction to invasion, usurpation, and domination.

the Uruk expansion and Sumerian state formation and urbanization.[17] Indeed, it could be argued that historical materialism underpins any evolutionary perspective where economic and technical factors are the driving force of change. Yet, while it might be thought inescapable for archaeologists who are reliant on the material for their existence, there are new routes of interpretation to material culture that may escape any sort of Marxist foundation. We have moved from an understanding of material culture as a direct outcome of what people do to survive, to attempts to understand its complex relationship with what people think about themselves and about each other. No longer are we confined to a comparison of physical objects in the deployment of archaeological data; we are able to compare the social values, worldviews, and ritual practices that objects embody. Very different patterning in material culture may end up containing the same meaning in these terms, so that complexity need no longer be seen only as a function of quantity. That is, while in some cases complex societies manifest material wealth and monumental display, in other cases they may not.

Similarly, the fundamental materialism of the assumption in much archaeology, that subsistence practices dictate social practices, is giving way to the realization that although changes in subsistence practices are more readily explained than changes in social organization, the reverse may be true: changes in social relations may give rise to changes in subsistence practices. In either case, the relationship between subsistence and society is complicated and as likely to be indirect as it is to be direct. It cannot be presented as the outcome of assumed argumentation – that sedentism or mobility, farming or pastoralism, are sufficient explanations in themselves for the sociopolitical organization of any one group – but should instead be the central subject of investigation. For while the distance between desert and sown might be diminishing in recent discussions of pastoralism (Marx 2005, 2006; Berelov 2006; Saidel and van der Steen 2007; Barnard and Wendrich 2008),[18] attributions of tribalism as defining and determinative are increasing (Parkinson 2002; Meeker 2005; L. Cooper 2006; Alizadeh 2008; Lyonnet 2009; van der Steen 2009; Meyer 2010b; Lönnqvist 2010). Those few instances where the potential for an organic integration, or at least a range of complex intersections, of pastoralists and farmers, nomads, and urbanites in the ancient world is considered (van der Steen and Saidel 2007; Marx 2007; Buccellati 2008) do so from a single perspective: the linkages between people practicing different lifeways and different subsistence activities are dependent on a substate tribal organization (although cf. Lancaster and Lancaster 1998: 24) over which the state is superimposed and to which the state is largely meaningless.

17 As recognized in a commentary to Algaze's seminal 1989 article by Brentjes 1989.
18 Unfortunately, though, only among a specialist, academic audience and not widely enough even there.

How this intellectual history plays out may be seen in a number of discussions of pastoralism in all the regions mentioned above, but since my focus in this book is the region between and around the Euphrates and Tigris rivers in what is now Iraq and Syria, the heartlands of sedentary urbanism, I will concentrate on works that invoke pastoralism in that area. The first is Joy McCorriston's 1997 article on the impact of changes in textile production; the second, Gil Stein's 2004 synthetic comparison of econo-social[19] organization in Syria and Mesopotamia. These two works, in their different ways, are highly cogent presentations that incorporate pastoralists as a central component and a key dynamic of the Mesopotamian world in the fourth and third millennia.[20] It is not my intention here to critique either paper. Both bring us closer to new understandings of what life was like and how things worked in the ancient world. In both articles, however, descriptions of the integral value of pastoralism to the economies of the four riverbanks are followed by histories predicated on a fundamental separation in the social interactions between people who undertake cereal cultivation and those who undertake animal husbandry. This has the unintended consequence of negating the very insights provided by these studies.

In her investigation of the larger impact of the shift from flax to wool in textile production of the fourth to third millennia BCE, McCorriston (1997: 525) describes the options available to households no longer producing flax, apparently a highly labor-intensive enterprise. Flax fields were placed under less demanding cereal cultivation and women and men were now free, or perhaps forced, to develop additional subsistence activities. Women turned to weaving (528), while men turned to animal husbandry (525), thus altering both the organization of family and labor, as some members of the household would then be absent for prolonged periods. Women, however, were ultimately disadvantaged by this shift, for rather than weaving providing a source of income over which they might have had some sort of discretion, women "would have experienced diminished access to economic resources" (McCorriston 1997: 528) and "for those who wove, wool may have been obtained from sheep over which they had little or no control" (McCorriston 1997: 532).

McCorriston argues that because the woolen fiber women were weaving was not produced on land they owned or had rights to,[21] women were increasingly

---

19   In fact the traditional term "socioeconomic" is a misnomer in the approach of these, and indeed most, archaeologists in this field, for there is no question that, as McCorriston quotes Giddens, social relations are treated as a by-product of, and subordinate to, economic relations.

20   Whereas Abdi (2003), while directly reliant on Lees and Bates for the explanation of his archaeological findings, is focused on Iran and is concerned only to explain the emergence of "nomadic" pastoralism.

21   There is considerable variation in women's property rights, access to resources, and role in animal husbandry in pastoralist societies attested ethnographically. See, for example, Obeid 2006: 482 and n. 15; Bettini 2006: 967; Chatty 2006a: 11.

separated from the means of production, and hence they increasingly declined in social status and economic well-being (528), resulting in the alienation of their labor from the family and their subsequent indentured attachment to the large temple estates. She states: "I reiterate that within the complex, multiple, simultaneous courses of intensification, one strategy for marginal, land-poor households would have been to extensify wool production and that it is these households in particular in which women would have become increasingly alienated" (McCorriston 1997: 542). There are two conundrums here that are essential to the validity of McCorriston's argument. They are, first, that land-poor households would either not have been engaged in flax production in the first place or would have been working on fibers that they did not produce in exactly the same way as postulated for wool production. In either case therefore, the shift to wool should have made no difference to the organization of labor and the status of women. Second, even if this division of labor is so specifically gendered, itself a major question, it presumably takes place at least in part at the household level (as McCorriston does indeed indicate in the above quote) with the men of the family taking care of the sheep that produce wool and the women of the household turning that wool into fabric. Why, then, would women have any more or less access to the means of production than when involved in flax? Surely if the production of flax and wool were both cooperative family enterprises, then the same family relationships that determined access, status, and so on in terms of flax would prevail in terms of wool? What is it about wool production that might be thought to negate the obligations of male family members to female ones?

Perhaps it was the use of professional shepherds,[22] possibly a new phenomenon in the Uruk period, as argued by Green (1980) but accepted by few. If this were indeed the case, it seems unlikely to have contributed in any significant way to a change in women's labor or status in the estate context (i.e., the temple), where women did not control the means of their production in any case. In the domestic context, such shepherds would be under contract to families, and women would have the same access to raw materials as before. Moreover, just as families might split in order to manage herds, it seems equally possible that they might adopt pastoralism as a whole unit, with women as mobile as men and just as involved in animal husbandry. Modern analogy here does not serve to make either case, as both scenarios are frequently attested, but it does serve to demonstrate that families that are divided across subsistence tasks do not of necessity collapse. In a situation where the reverse process was in play, where due to the collapsing economy mobile pastoral families settled in villages and men turned to external labor, women assumed their men's responsibilities as

---

22 The term "specialized pastoralism" (Zeder 1991, 1998; Bates and Lees 1977) is to be avoided as it may mean many things, ranging from a distinct subsistence strategy to a category of worker.

well as those of their own, taking care of household, herds, other subsistence activities, and maintaining social networks (Marx 2006: 79).

That the same family relationships are thought *not* to prevail once flax shifts to wool, that there is assumed some fundamental difference (albeit not explicitly stated by McCorriston) once pastoralism enters the picture, derives from a particular, deeply embedded, and widespread understanding that pastoralism, especially the *non*-estate-controlled form of pastoralism, is in some innate way separate from the world of farmers and weavers to the degree that even close familial interactions and obligations become so attenuated that they result in the essential abandonment of women. This separation pertains not so much to the *physical* distance that mobility brings, but encompasses a profound *social* segregation.

The same understanding is evident in Gil Stein's (2004) comparison of the developmental trajectories of southern and northern Mesopotamian urbanism in the third millennium. The cities of northern Iraq, Syria, and southeastern Anatolia are characterized as "ephemeral" when juxtaposed with the cities of Mesopotamia proper (Stein 2004: 61) because they were not occupied consistently over millennia, in part because of environmental constraints that gave rise to economic particularities, that is, the dominance in the north of pastoralism. The organization of this pastoralism as of the mid-third millennium at least was what Stein terms "multicentric": "The state authorities clearly controlled large herds, which were often scattered in surrounding villages (Archi 1990). Secondary centers and towns provided the centers with animals and their products as a form of staple finance (Wattenmaker 1998). At the same time, it is clear that many (probably smaller) herds were in the hands of independent sedentary producers (both urban and rural), who raised them for their own subsistence needs (Stein 1987)" (Stein 2004: 70). Stein (2004: 69–70) cites Gelb, one of the foremost Assyriologists of his generation, but not an Ebla specialist, to demonstrate that herding was far more important in the north than in the south, especially his (Gelb 1986: 158) statement that sheep were the foundation of the Eblaite economy, an understanding that Matthiae (1988) and Archi (2006: 99) are at pains to reject, although they accept that textiles are well attested at Ebla and were of critical importance (Archi 1993: 12).

Stein goes on to say (2004: 70) that "we can reasonably assume that mobile herders maintained an uneasy relationship with the sedentary states, trading pastoral products with them in good years and raiding them when drought conditions weakened the cities while stressing their normal grazing lands" and that

in times of low rainfall the cities were unable to feed themselves even with rural surpluses. The northern cities attempted to buffer against these problems by relying heavily on herding, by both sedentarists and nomads. However the yields of sedentary pastoralism are quite low.... At the same time, the herds of sedentarists are vulnerable to raiding by nomadic pastoralists. Finally, a reliance on nomadic pastoralists ... would have been risky since pastoralists are notoriously quick to shift from trading to raiding when drought places pressure on their own grazing land. (Stein 2004: 77)

According to current climatological data, much of Syria would have experienced drought, sometimes severe, on a fairly regular basis (Wilkinson 1994: 499; 2003; and in Stein 2004: 62–3; for some of its consequences, see Lewis 1987).

A series of assumptions is evident throughout Stein's analysis (and the analyses of others). One, if *textiles* were of major importance to the southern economy, as a variety of texts from different sources seem to indicate throughout the third millennium (Waetzoldt 1972, 1987; Maekawa 1980, 1987; Adams 1981: 11; Algaze 2008: 77–82), then surely *herding* was also important in the south at that time, and perhaps as important as cereal cultivation, but not, because of its distribution vis-à-vis settlement, as visible. In the north, pastoralism in various forms wound around the cities spread thinly across the landscape (at least compared to southern Mesopotamia), using the broader spaces between them for grazing as much as more distant areas (illustrated in Wilkinson 2000). In the south, settlements were far more proximate to each other, and the space between them was mostly filled with irrigated fields and the canals that watered them, so that large-scale herding was located outside the entire region and even domestic herding was very constrained. Fallow fields and the patches of unfarmable land in the interstices of fields and towns were insufficient to support any significant quantity of sheep/goats (although it is often claimed otherwise) and, given the quantities of cattle kept (Englund 1995: 428), would primarily have been grazed by the latter. But while these different patterns themselves *might* have given rise to different levels of connection and integration between pastoralists and farmers in the two situations, it cannot be *assumed* that they did.[23]

Two, and more important, the idea that, in either the north or the south, the community – whether in reference to the state, estate or domestic – would have no direct control over one of its primary means of production, is problematic.[24] For despite Stein's highly feasible rendition of a complex mix of herding strategies, he also in the end visualizes a division between sedentary animal husbandry and mobile pastoralists, with the latter intrinsically separate from the state[25] at the same time that the state was intrinsically reliant on the latter. If textiles were a major component of the Eblaite economy, let alone its foundation, then does it seem reasonable that the weavers of Ebla would be dependent on an erratic source of supply such as frequently hostile pastoralists? The same question most certainly applies to the south.

Neither Stein nor McCorriston is to be especially criticized for these positions. They reflect what most Near Eastern scholars would assume to be the case, both

---

23   Sallaberger (2007: 418), for example, argues that similar relationships between pastoralism and central administration pertained in the north and south at this time.

24   Nissen (1980: 288) makes a similar point about control, although for different reasons.

25   As indeed does Sallaberger (2007: 418).

about pastoralism itself and the legitimacy of the path to this understanding. This idea of separation is deeply embedded in the psyche of modern scholars, despite periodic claims to the contrary, and derives from two essential chains of transmission, originating on the one hand in textual attestations of certain groups, and on the other, in anthropological approaches based in ethnography and applied in understanding these attestations. The key links in this chain are the seminal works of Michael Rowton and the two powerfully influential publications of Susan Lees and Daniel Bates (Lees and Bates 1974 and Bates and Lees 1977), which have given rise to corresponding traditions – Rowton to the epigraphical and Bates and Lees to the archaeological. Interestingly, the projects of both Rowton and Lees and Bates represented at the time innovative and transformative approaches to the problem, and both were "interdisciplinary." Rowton, an Assyriologist, employed ethnographies throughout his work, increasing his reliance on anthropological thinking during the 1970s when anthropological discussions of pastoralism were at their peak; Bates and Lees, anthropologists, brought contemporary anthropological understandings to archaeological discussions of an historical problem, the origin of so-called specialized pastoralism. Interestingly, neither cites the other, although both studies take some fundamental understandings from the same place: the pioneering work of Owen Lattimore (1962 [1940]) on nomad–sedentary relations in China.

Lees and Bates claimed in 1974 that the introduction of canal irrigation into southern Mesopotamia gave rise to specialized pastoralism at the expense of mixed farming strategies. Canal irrigation has higher labor needs than rain-fed farming, needs incompatible with the exigencies of both small-scale domestic (or in Stein's term "sedentary") herding and cereal cropping; and as well it reconfigured the space available for pasturing animals (Lees and Bates 1974: 189). Household units therefore chose to pursue one subsistence strategy or the other, and those who pursued herding were forced to graze their herds farther away from the core irrigated zones, and therefore farther away from their social group. The reduction of land open to pasture because it was now irrigated and the greater population densities supported by irrigation, in conjunction with the redistribution of population centers, contributed to the increasing physical marginalization of animal husbandry.

What happens next however is more problematic. Once households have made their subsistence choice and become nomads, they become "politically discrete and potentially predatory" (Lees and Bates 1974: 191) after only a very few generations. Although initially pastoralists would have kin ties with the sedentary farmers with whom they exchanged goods, distance and mobility, fragmentation and dispersal, serve to sever those social ties. By implication, then, Lees and Bates would seem to assume that social integration is maintained only by face-to-face interaction. This might be the case in the modern world (although I would suggest only in specific circumstances) – and the state has undoubtedly interfered with traditional practices and ideologies, often deliberately in order to break down such integration as inimical to its own interests – but it was not necessarily the case in the ancient world.

In addition, pastoralists would encounter strangers whom they would have no compunction about raiding or conquering (Lees and Bates 1974: 191). Bates and Lees (1977) list various reasons why raiding might be an expected systemic outcome for pastoralists, even though nomads and farmers are economically symbiotic, but the assumption on which their analysis is founded here is that pastoralists have no affective, that is social and/or emotional, ties beyond the boundaries of their own immediate group – a group, what is more, created through blood. This is a critical point, and it is the basis of almost every writer's characterization of nomad–sedentary relations in the ancient world, a relationship consistently qualified with phrases such as "uneasy interaction" and "incipient conflict."

This idea itself derives from a major stream of anthropological thought on kinship that is now rather contentious. On the one hand, anthropologists such as Marilyn Strathern (1992a, 1992b) and Janet Carsten (2000, 2004) delineate considerable variability in conceptions of kinship and ways of its construction; on the other, segmentary opposition theory, especially in discussions of "pastoralist tribes" (Baştuğ 1998; Salzman 2008a, 2008b), persists as a determinative of exclusionary group definition. This has profound repercussions for many related discussions, such as the nature of mobile pastoralism and the development of approaches to the early complex polity in the ancient Near East. Here I will only point out that social boundaries created through blood underlie the notion of endemic hostility in discussions of pastoralism in the ancient Near East and beyond, so that, while much is made – in these and other works (such as those of Rowton) – of pastoralists' need for agricultural products, the emphasis on raiding as a means of obtaining those goods obscures one critical point: though pastoralists need agricultural products, they also, and equally, need an outlet for their own production (Marx 2006), an outlet that raiding destroys. They need access to supplementary resources, too, access that is often best accomplished through the construction of social ties (Galvin 2008; Claudot-Hawad 2006: 659).

There is a common perception that, as animals are "banks on the hoof," pastoralists can maintain economic stasis whenever conditions are unfavorable, that is, simply withdraw and wait them out. But the precariousness of any viable balance achieved between factors such as carrying capacity, herd size, and labor renders this difficult, to say the least (Khazanov 2009: 120). In the case of drought, cited as a cause of hostile relations by Stein (2004), economic interdependence between pastoralists and farmers might be at its greatest. If crop production is low, farmers might be more dependent, rather than less, on the milk and meat provided by pastoralists for food sources (and see Nissen 1980: 288). Pastoralists might therefore sell off their herds because of higher demand and take up paid labor in the sedentary sector. Farmers might abandon their fields temporarily and move out to the steppes, themselves becoming pastoralists (e.g., Adams 1974; Nissen 1980: 286). Or pastoralists might choose to cash in their animals rather than lose them to starvation if unable to move them to adequate pasture or if the cost of that move is too high. The reduction of herd size in times of stress, especially when that stress is a result of insufficient resources, is a prime strategy (Marx 2006: 92), as is the intensification of animal husbandry (Galvin 2009). Moreover, in times of drought what little adequate pasture is available may be contested by a number of groups, sedentary and mobile, with the potential for stock and labor losses through violent conflict high. And while undoubtedly such conflict occurs, this is in the end not an optimal outcome for pastoralists any more than it is for farmers, and it is an outcome that they may choose to avoid if there are alternatives perceived as viable.

Raiding, therefore, is neither the easy solution nor a natural expression of hostile tendencies,[26] nor yet the result of structural segmentation, but is rather the product of contingent circumstances where regularized access to sources of agricultural products and outlets for pastoralist products has for some reason been curtailed – by the state, by prohibitive prices, by competition (Kuzner and Sedlmeyer 2008). It is also a "political instrument" (Lewis 1987: 12) used by pastoralists or deliberately provoked by the very powers to whom pastoralist raiding might seem inimical. Therefore, when raiding does occur it is itself of explanatory interest because it points to certain kinds of conditions, particularly conditions of disequilibrium.

From these kinds of circumstances can come an institutionalization of raiding as economic strategy, but if many of the classic examples of such pastoralist behavior commonly cited were tracked over time (and not even necessarily over *la longue durée*), the shifts in this behavior, and the relationship of those shifts to larger socioeconomic and historical circumstances, would become more evident. Despite popular opinion, pastoralist societies possess no innate nature that causes them to behave in any particular way. Even the type of structural dynamics imputed by Evans-Pritchard (about which, see below) is neither original nor inevitable, but a product of the time and place in which Evans-Pritchard encountered his subject group, the Nuer, as well as a product of the particular prior history of that group (Hutchinson 1996). As the periodic revisitation of the Nuer (Gough 1971; Holy 1979a; Kelly 1985; Hutchinson 2000) highlights, Nuer society, and indeed Nuer subsistence, are highly responsive to shifts in circumstances both immediate and distant.

I am not arguing that ancient pastoralists were immune to conflict, for "hostility" ran rampant among all political entities in the ancient Near East

---

26   The idea that pastoralists have an inherently militant nature and innate hostility to the sedentary world persists and is highly influential in political and media discourse. See, for example, Keegan 1993: 161.

(see, for example, Archi and Biga 2003; Sallaberger 2007), but that conflict was neither endemic nor a simplistic pastoralist/farmer antipathy. It is appropriate here to note also that conflict is always understood to stem from pastoralists, either as a result of active aggression on their part or because they transgress the rules of sedentary society (such as grazing on crops), prompting retaliation. It is almost never seen to be at the instigation of the sedentary population or the state, even when it is argued that the weakness of the state allows for pastoralist incursions. Conflict, deriving from either group, was more likely the last solution, not the first, to any problem or disruption encountered in subsistence routine. Yet even if every single pastoralist group known to scholarship were to demonstrate hostility to sedentary farmers at certain times and for certain reasons, this would not negate the understanding proposed in this book – that pastoralists and farmers were more than symbiotically connected in the ancient Near East,[27] for they were in fact *integral components of the same social entities and political systems* – because every single one of those groups is a product of circumstances that simply did not pertain in antiquity, be those circumstances political, economic, environmental, or even structural.

Raiding also characterizes the nature of conflict between pastoralist and sedentarist, tribe and state, as described by Rowton (1969c: 311), who, in his attempts (1973a, 1973b, 1974) to counter the view of polarized subsistence and geographical distance that prevailed at the time he wrote, perpetuated an equally pervasive dichotomization of sociopolitical organization (Adams 1970: 119) in his concept of dimorphism, a dichotomization that has come to obscure the evidence of a quite different relationship evident in the ancient literature with which he was concerned. Dimorphism describes a situation where tribal and urban institutions are in evidence side-by-side, usually within the same polity, sometimes only spatially proximate, and is to be explained as result of the economic interdependence of the two systems when tribal nomads live in the spaces between cities. Indeed, Rowton saw the pastoralist tribe as standing frequently as an autonomous political unit *within* states, which he iterated in almost every article he wrote. However, the term "dimorphism" seems to have taken on a life of its own, used in ways often far from Rowton's original intent. Dimorphism is more commonly understood now as bifurcated ways of life and sociopolitical organizations that are simply geographically adjacent (Wiggermann 2000: 182; Bonechi 2001; Steinkeller 2004: 36; Archi 2006: 99; van der Steen and Saidel 2007: 1; Rosen 2009: 63).

27 Although I confine myself to the land of the four riverbanks, Mesopotamia and beyond, this situation is equally applicable at certain times to other regions of the Near East such as the Levant (Berelov 2006, and see the collected works in Saidel and van der Steen 2007) and Iran (cf. Alizedeh 2009), or even the Eurasian steppes (Frachetti and Mar'yashev 2007: 221–3). The generally held assumption that it cannot be applicable to central Asia requires further examination.

This view coincides with the ways many scholars, especially in the English-language literature, understand one of the two most influential bodies of evidence for ancient pastoralism (apart from ethnographic analogy): the textual material from Mari.[28] Mari, located on the Euphrates River just before the modern border with Iraq and founded at the beginning of the third millennium BCE, was the seat of a succession of major polities in the north, including, in the early second millennium, two Amorrite kingdoms, one under the control of Samsi-Addu[29] and administered by his son, Yasmah-Addu, the other led by Zimri-Lim. Amorrites are seen as the paradigmatic nomads of the ancient world, sweeping in from the desert to destroy the settled kingdoms of the northern land at the end of the third millennium and infiltrating the southern lands, so that by the second quarter of the second millennium they ruled the heartland of civilization, Mesopotamia. The precise point of origin of the Amorrites and the path they took to power, literally and figuratively, are questions to which much attention has been given (e.g., Charpin 2003; Jahn 2007; Lönnqvist 2008; and see Chapter 4). By an accident of history we have considerable documentation of these two early Amorrite rulers, because when Zimri-Lim was defeated by his arch-rival and erstwhile ally, Hammurabi, his archive containing some twenty thousand texts (including selected records of his predecessors and approximately three thousand letters between himself, his foreign counterparts, and his administrators) was packed for shipment to Babylon, a move that did not, in the end, transpire (van Koppen 2006: 111–13). We are left with an archive shaped in two ways: by Zimri-Lim's administration and its choices of which tablets of its predecessors to keep, and by Hammurabi's administration and its choices of what to send. It is not therefore a comprehensive survey of the nature of existence at that time, but does reflect what was deemed important in these two contexts.

The letters in particular revealed the activities of mobile pastoralists to be a critical concern of the administration of Zimri-Lim and, moreover, not only did Zimri-Lim have very close ties to them, but they somehow had a privileged position under him. Although now all of Mesopotamia was under Amorrite control, the situation at Mari, where pastoralists were very present, seemed markedly different from the situation in the south, where the only traces of pastoralism to be found were a vague memory of nomadic origins in a genealogically remote past. The difference is often attributed to the "fact" that Zimri-Lim, unlike Hammurabi, say, who was the fifth in the line of dynastic succession, was a first-generation city-dweller. What is more, the situation under Zimri-Lim seemed very different from that under his predecessor

28   The other body of evidence, the neo-Sumerian texts of the end of the third and beginning of the second millennia, BCE will be discussed at length in Chapter 4.

29   Samsi-Addu is more commonly known by the Akkadianized version of his name – Shamshi-Addad.

Samsi-Addu (e.g., van Driel 2000), also Amorrite, and also, if *his* genealogies are to be believed, nomadic in origin. But, like the southerners, Samsi-Addu seems to have been further removed from his mobile origins as there is apparently little evidence that he had a particular attachment to any mobile group, and various factors have led scholars to believe he aspired to the cultural sophistication of the settled world.

Zimri-Lim, then, was an exception, and for a long time the evidence of two equally central components of his kingdom was simply filtered through the understanding that two separate groups, one nomadic, one sedentary, came together at this juncture, with the pastoralist chief Zimri-Lim appropriating the urban splendors of the sedentary world, much like the models proposed by Lattimore (1962 [1940]) for China. But while Zimri-Lim adopted palatial life, his tribesmen did not, and any integration between urban and mobile worlds was simply that of economic symbiosis as Rowton delineated it, or seminomadism as described by anthropology of the time; Zimri-Lim, the king of Mari and the *mat Hana*,[30] governed two independent worlds joined uniquely under him, and it is no wonder he struggled to keep them together.

For many, this view of the evidence from the Mari letters typifies the nature of ancient pastoralism as opposed to state-controlled herding (Sallaberger 2007: 418; Stein 2004). There is a real problem here, because a good portion of this scholarship is based on an earlier and very preliminary summation of a small percentage of the Mari texts (exemplified in Schwartz 1995; van Driel 2000; Stein 2004; Van de Mieroop 2004: 82–5; Nichols and Weber 2006) as transmitted in Kupper (1957), Luke (1965), Matthews (1978), and Rowton (see Bibliography) and does not avail itself of the voluminous work done by the current generation of French Mari scholars under the direction of Jean-Marie Durand and Dominique Charpin, and as well the essential contributions of Americans Jack Sasson and Daniel Fleming.

Now there is a very different picture in place. Rather than three mobile pastoralist tribes encompassed by the kingdom of Mari, the Yaminites, Simalites,[31] and Hana, there are but two, the Yaminites and Simalites, *hana* being a word that literally means "tent-dwellers" (Durand 1998: 417–18). *Hana* in Zimri-Lim's letters was used primarily to refer to his own tent-dwellers (Fleming 2004), who are now understood to be the Simalites (Charpin and Durand 1986), so that several of the conundrums about the place of mobile pastoralists in the kingdom of Mari – sometimes they seemed to be internal, sometimes external, sometimes they seemed to provide the basis of political power, sometimes they appeared to be bitter enemies – are resolved. The differences are in part between

30 Epigraphic convention has in the past rendered Sumerian words in uppercase while syllabic languages such as Akkadian are written in italics, although it is increasingly common to find Sumerian in boldface and I will follow suit.
31 I follow Fleming 2004: 13 in this usage.

those pastoralists who are of Zimri-Lim's own kith and kin and those who are not, and corresponding differences in sociopolitical organization, intergroup affiliations and histories, and geographic location of the several "tribal" groups named in the texts, groups that incorporated sedentary farmers who lived along the riverbanks (Fleming 2004).

Admittedly, the sheer quantity of very detailed work now published on Mari makes it difficult to put together a comprehensive, and comprehensible, synthesis (although for the historical narrative see Charpin 2004a), and the forthcoming publication of a compendium of Charpin's work in English[32] in particular will surely change the current level of engagement with this material.[33] Nevertheless, a close study of Mari yields great rewards, because its documents offer a far better source for understanding the place of mobile pastoralism in the land of the four riverbanks of the fourth through second millennia BCE than any modern ethnography. The worlds in which contemporary mobile pastoralists were and are encountered are not the worlds of antiquity, first and foremost because each of these pastoralist groups thus described is embedded in circumstances inevitably influenced, as previously noted, by the modern state.

This might not seem a particularly cogent objection to the use of modern analogies for ancient pastoralism, for it seems generally assumed that the state will function similarly, no matter the time and place, because it has very specific needs, namely the arrogation of power unto itself. It also seems generally assumed that pastoralists will function similarly, no matter the time and place, because they have a very specific nature.[34] But first, this is an inappropriate use of analogy. Ethnographies simply provide examples of possible behaviors in a range of circumstances, and ethnographers are very often unaware of what all those circumstances might have been until historical distance has been achieved. When the ethnographer has been trained to understand that economic factors are paramount, then he or she will see economic factors as the cause of observed behavior. When the ethnographer has been trained to understand that social factors predetermine the system, then it is hardly surprising that he or she understands those to be the explanation of the phenomenon at hand. When trends in anthropological scholarship shift, older ethnographies are revisited and new circumstances discovered.[35]

---

32 It is to be hoped that a similar collection of Durand's work in English will shortly follow.
33 Although the English translation of a selection of Mari letters by Heimpel (2003) and the comprehensive study of the organization of the Simalites and Yaminites by Fleming (2004) have yet to make the impact they should.
34 Such as Bienkowski and van der Steen 2001: 29, who suggest that it is possible to extract that which is "timeless and unchanging" from the modern, because certain behaviors have a Darwinian imperative.
35 Again, the Nuer provide an excellent case in point.

Second, such comparisons are feasible only if the ancient and modern states are based on the same principles in the first place. This is rather a difficult issue, because the very premise of a research topic such as state formation is that there is a defined entity that may be observed to come into existence. Whether or not a definition based on the modern state is explicit in such research, a "common armature of conceptualizations" (Gledhill 1988: 1) undergirds it: it is predicated on the presence or absence of agreed-upon traits that are currently in existence. We then go back in time to detect their first appearance. But I would argue that the first "states," those of the fourth and third millennia BCE, are in no way comparable to the early Islamic state, let alone to the post-Westphalian one of our own experience, to the extent that we should change the entire vocabulary of the discussion. One of the reasons they are profoundly different is the very nature of the social, economic, and political organization on which each state is predicated. In an unfortunate piece of circularity, however, we assume that the ancient state is based on the same principles of hierarchy and power that dominate the history of our own states, at least in part because our assumptions as to the nature of pastoralism and agriculture preclude any alternative. We know agriculture to be the locus of innovation and change, therefore we only look in agricultural situations for innovation and change. The consensus definition of state formation is that kinship gave way to class, inclusiveness gave way to exclusiveness, and the corporate gave way to the king, because we know the state to be based on highly unequal relations of power configured through social hierarchies. And therefore we look for the point at which those features are first evident to identify the beginning of the state (cf. Liverani 2006: 10). The Uruk period, discussed in Chapter 2, is currently the locus of the search in the ancient Near East (Rothman 2004).

And yet the primary evidence offers a very different picture of the ancient polity, especially of tribe/state, pastoralist/farmer, kin/class distinctions and dichotomies, or lack thereof, and especially where it is most detailed – that is, at Mari. I say Mari and not Ebla, contrary to general perception, as the Mari letters encompass personal interactions that declare the multiple sociopolitical groupings and identities, both self- and externally imposed (the very reason they are so difficult to deal with) of the parties involved, as opposed to the archival texts of Ebla, which delineate primarily the economic activities of certain kinds of transactions, many of which involve just one section of the system, the "palace." Information as to the self-conception and perception of the identities of the participants is only indirectly obtained from lists of the administration's income and expenditure. I say Mari, because there is sufficient, although less detailed, information from other contexts to show that the kingdom of Mari under Zimri-Lim (Table 2) was not the anomaly it is still thought to be. Its very particular nature was the product of contingent circumstances that apply only in part to other examples. Nevertheless, certain trends observable at Mari – that

Table 2. Isin-Larsa and Old Babylonian King Lists.

	Isin	Larsa	Babylon	Mari
30				
20		Naplanum (2025-2005)		
10	Ishbi-Erra (2107-1985)			
2000		Emisum (2004-1977)		
90	Shu-ilishu (1984-1975)			
80				
70	Iddin-Dagan (1974-1954)	Samium (1976-1942)		
60				
50	Ishme-Dagan (1953-1935)			
40		Zabaja (1941-1933)		
30	Lipit-Ishtar (1934-1924)			
20	Ur-Ninurta (1923-1896)	Gungunum (1932-1906)		
10				
1900		Abi-Sare (1905-1895)		
90	Bur-Sin (1895-1874)	Sumu-el (1894-1866)	Sumuabum (1894-1881)	
80			Sumulael (1880-1845)	
70	Lipit-Enlil (1873-1869)			
60	Erra-imitti (1868-1861)	Nur-Adad (1865-1850)		
50	Enlil-bani (1860-1837)			
40		Sin-Iddinam (1849-1843) Sin-iribam (1841-1842)	Sabium (1844-1831)	
30	Zambija (1836-1834) Iter-pisha (1833-1831) Ur-dukuga (1830-1828)	Sin-iqisham (1840-1836) Warad-Sin(1834-1823)	Apil-Sin (1830-1813)	Samsi-addu (1833?-1775)
20	Sin-magir (1827-1817)	Rim-Sin I (1822-1763)		
10	Damiq-ilishu (1816-1794)		Sin-muballit (1812-1793)	Yahdun-Lim (1810-1794)
1800				
90			Hammurabi (1792-1750)	Sumu-Yamam (1793-1792)
80				Yasmah-Addu (1785-1776)
70				
60				Zimri-Lim (1775-1762)
50			Samsuiluna (1749-1712)	
40				
30				
20				
10			Abi-eshuh (1711-1684)	
1700				
90				
80			Ammiditana (1683-1647)	
70				
60				
50				
40			Ammisaduqa (1646-1626)	
30				
20			Samsuditana (1625-1595)	
10				
1600				

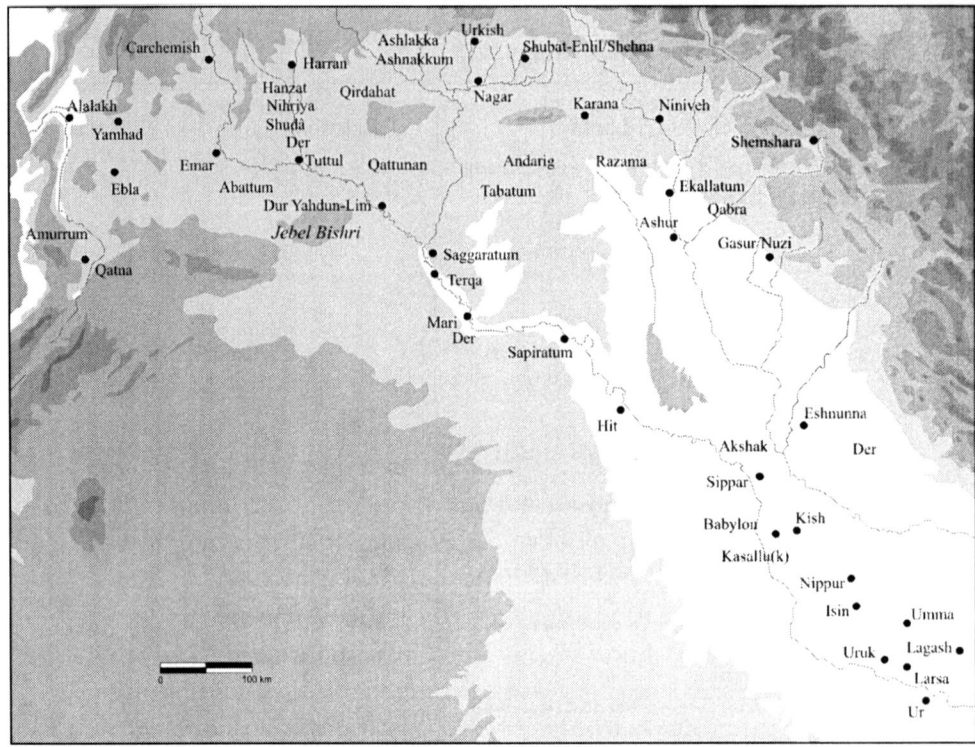

2. Map of second millennium sites.

sedentary farmer and mobile pastoralist may each claim the same sociopolitical identity, that those identities may be differentially defined by various groupings of farmer and pastoralist (Fleming 2004), that civic allegiance and bonds of kin coexist and are both equally held by the same person, that bonds of kinship are socially as well as biologically produced through a range of ideologies and practices (Durand 2004; Durand and Guichard 1997; Porter 2009a) – are also true of other polities in both north and south. If nothing else Mari offers something that few ethnographic examples can – historical depth, not just of the twenty years into which most of its tablet collections fit, but of the thousand-odd years of its existence (Margueon 2004).

It is not my task here, though, to summarize the whole history of Mari, but rather to demonstrate through a somewhat more restricted survey that the nature of the Mari kingdom under Zimri-Lim, about which there is so much detail, may, when fully contextualized, be illustrative of similar relationships in evidence across the land of the four riverbanks from the fourth to mid-second millennium BCE, in periods for which there is far less detailed information available. For one thing, when Zimri-Lim assumed control of Mari in 1775 BCE (Charpin 2004a: 192), he was not a newcomer to the settled world (Fig. 2), arriving fresh from the desert, but was retaking a city with which his family had had a long and perhaps integral relationship, one in fact interrupted by another pastoralist king, Samsi-Addu. Indeed, this was but the last act in a history of competition and conflict between two families that can be traced back to Zimri-Lim's (great)grandfather, Yaggid-Lim,[36] and Samsi-Addu's father, Ila-kabkabu (Charpin 2004a: 132–4; van Koppen 2006: 113–14), whose respective spheres of influence lay, initially, west and east – the Lim family dominated the region of the Euphrates while Samsi-Addu's family belonged to the land of the Tigris (Durand 1998: 107). The only information available about the origins of this battle royal comes from a later letter prayer from Samsi-Addu's son, Yasmah-Addu (Durand 2000: 72–4; see van Koppen 2006: 113 for his version in English). Yaggid-Lim and Ila-kabkabu swore a treaty that Yaggid-Lim broke. In response, Ila-kabkabu captured Yaggid-Lim's son, Yahdun-Lim.[37] Of course this description is highly partisan and we do not know the actual course of events. What is important to note, however, is that a history of rivalry over this region of the Euphrates is already in play; Mari was an essential gateway between east and west, and indeed to the north and south (Horowitz and Wasserman 2004; Joannès 1996; Lafont 2001).

Although it is not clear that Yaggid-Lim, who survived Ila-Kabkabu, ever ruled Mari, nor what happened there in the putative century or so between the last evidence for the *shakkanaku*, or "governors," and the first evidence for the Lim leadership (Charpin 2004a: 134–5)[38] during which time Mari was abandoned, it is certain that his son, Yahdun-Lim, did rule the city. Establishing his control as far as the Balikh and up to the western Habur it was perhaps inevitable that Yahdun-Lim would end up face-to-face with Samsi-Addu, who, when Ila-Kabkabu died, had assumed control of Ekallatum, only to be defeated and exiled by Eshnunna. Taking advantage of the king of Eshnunna's subsequent death some years later, Samsi-Addu recaptured Ekallatum, defeated Assur, which he then controlled for decades, and cast his eyes westward toward the Habur (Van de Mieroop 2004: 101). He then established a new administrative center at Shehna, now renamed Shubat-Enlil.

The Habur region at that time was more or less divided between Samsi-Addu and Yahdun-Lim (Charpin 2004a: 144), and eventually the two kings met in battle at Tell Brak, ancient Nagar (Charpin 2004a: 138), located near the confluence

---

36   See following for the discussion of Zimri-Lim's origins.

37   Durand (2010: 260) has recently stated that Yahdun-Lim was a recent arrival in the region of Mari, finding there a declining *shakkanaku* kingdom, which he easily took.

38   This single sentence in fact glosses over a considerable debate about (1) the nature of *shakkanaku* rule, with one school of thought seeing it as a southern governorship of Mari, the other as independent; and (2) the length of time between the *shakkanaku* period and the rebirth of Mari under Yahdun-Lim. See Butterlin 2007 for a summary and the current state of affairs. I myself am inclined to see the interlude between the *shakkanaku* and Amorrite periods as briefer than most, on archaeological grounds, and am willing to entertain the possibility that Yaggid-Lim might indeed fall within the last gasp of that period. It seems unlikely to me that Mari was abandoned for long after the end of the *shakkanaku* rule.

of the Habur and the eastern arm of its candelabra-like group of tributaries. While Yahdun-Lim was that day victorious, the contest was far from over, and he was forced to make an alliance with Eshnunna that caused him problems with the power to his west – Yamhad.[39] Eventually Samsi-Addu won by default, for Yahdun-Lim seems to have been assassinated by his son, Sumu-Yamam, who did not last long on the throne but was in turn assassinated by his subordinates (Charpin 2004a: 145–6).

Samsi-Addu appears not to have been very interested in Mari for some years after he took it (Charpin 2004a: 157) and eventually divided the administration of his kingdom between himself and his sons. Yasmah-Addu, famously a bitter disappointment to his father, became king of Mari; Ishme-Dagan, the favored child, ruled at Ekallatum; while Samsi-Addu, quite old by now, ensconced himself at Shubat Enlil. One crisis after another then ensued, at least from the point of view of international relations.[40] The administration was faced with a number of wars an all fronts. Samsi-Addu eventually died while Mari was under attack by pastoralists led by a person called Bannum who "restored the scion of Yahdun-Lim to his place" (Fleming 2004: 11, n. 30), that is, Zimri-Lim. Yasmah-Addu soon fled the city. Ishme-Dagan survived a while longer at Ekallatum but was sorely pressed by Eshnunna under Ibal-pi-Il, and eventually his kingdom, too, collapsed.

The question of Zimri-Lim's origins has long been a complicated one.[41] We have no direct evidence of his background, and no knowledge of him before he appears at Mari. Yet his personal history, if not actual parentage, is vital to this discussion because the relationships between polity and pastoralist, mobile groups and sedentary ones, that emerge in his correspondence are assumed to be unique to this particular concatenation of circumstances. Indeed, the fact that pastoralists figure so prominently in his documentation is the very thing that shades interpretations of him as alien to the urban, sedentary world.

Zimri-Lim was initially assumed to be Yahdun-Lim's biological son, although there was a school of thought that considered Yarim-Lim of Aleppo his father on the grounds of letters from Zimri-Lim in which he was addressed as such. But discoveries in the 1980s prompted Charpin and Durand (1985, 1986) to argue another scenario. In this proposal Zimri-Lim was born to a Simalite father, Hadni-Addu,[42] and a Yaminite mother, Addu-Duri, but passed as a son

---

39 Charpin (2004a: 140) notes that thereby eastern, particularly Eshnunnan, political and cultural influences became widely felt at Mari.

40 See Charpin 2004a for details of events in the reign of Samsi-Addu and Eidem 1994 for events after his death.

41 For a history of the divergent views, see Sasson 1998: 467–8.

42 Whereas the suffix "Lim," meaning to many assyriologists "tribe" or "clan," may be understood here as a patronymic or family name, Hadni-Addu should not be read as a member of Samsi-Addu's family because "Addu" refers to the storm god, Haddad, and is frequently included in names, as in fact is *lim* (Bonechi 1997).

of Yahdun-Lim when he took the throne, probably for the sake of legitimation. Now, however, Hadni-Addu is thought to have been a son or brother of Yahdun-Lim on the grounds that Zimri-Lim could have assumed command of neither the Simalites nor Mari if he had not been of royal blood, and it is the connection to the Simalites that is considered a little more attenuated, with Durand (2004: 185–6) cautioning against seeing Zimri-Lim as a nomad who took over "one of the great cities of the age" (cf. Fleming 2004: 162). Yahdun-Lim himself was however a Simalite, and was called father of the Hana (Charpin 2004a: 142), and both Zimri-Lim and Yahdun-Lim were called king of Mari and the land of the Simalites (Charpin and Durand 1986; Charpin 2004b; Heimpel 2003) as well as king of Mari and the land of the Hana (van Koppen 2006: 96–7). One wonders if this slight disassociation of Zimri-Lim from his Simalite heritage is sufficient to negate the continued tendency to take this background as proof of Zimri-Lim's combined tribal and mobile status and its hidden pejorative – that a nomad is somehow foreign to urban rule. But most leaders at this time seem to have been able to at least call on the allegiance of various mobile groups: the kings of Yamhad (modern-day Aleppo), Yarim-Lim (Zimri-Lim's father-in-law), and *his* father, Sumu-epuh, deployed Yaminites against Samsi-Addu; Samsi-Addu exists within a duality of "town and tribe" since Ekallatum is associated with the Yahruru[43] (Durand 1997: 215, letter 84) and he himself may have been a member of the Numha; the kings of Uruk were also kings of the Amnanum (Charpin 2003: 16, 2004a: 108), a Yaminite group, while the kings of Larsa had particular ties to the Emutbal (Steinkeller 2004), as indeed did various kings of the Habur (Charpin 2003; Porter 2009a and same letter as above). There is one other point: Zimri-Lim is often assumed to have taken over an urban administrative system essentially alien to his pastoralist background, yet either that administration was established by his father/grandfather, if they rebuilt a Mari that had previously stood empty, or, as seems increasingly possible, there was no substantial gap between the two periods and Yaggid-Lim was part of the previous system of the *shakkanaku*. In either case, the sedentary urban administration is as much a part of Zimri-Lim's background and inheritance as is his mobile network of kin.

What we know of Samsi-Addu's origins, in contrast, is presented as directly related to a town, Ekallatum, where his father is thought to have ruled (Charpin 2004a: 148; Van de Mieroop 2004: 101), although this too is contested (Durand 1998: 107). In fact we know less about Samsi-Addu's forebears than we do of Zimri-Lim's. Samsi-Addu's identity is further confounded by a text of a mortuary ritual for him found in the palace at Mari. This text includes mention of Sargon and Naram-Sin, the great kings of Akkad, implying that they were

---

43   This group may be the same as the Amnanum, since Amnanun-Yahruru is attested (Fleming 2004: 124, n. 61).

to be treated as his ancestors. There are also references to Akkad in two other contexts, leading Durand (1998: 108; Durand and Guichard 1997: 28) to suggest that Akkad is the dynastic homeland of this family. In Chapter 4 I explain how this ritual is in fact not a fictive genealogy purveyed so that Samsi Addu's connection to Akkad may be better perceived, nor an attempt to cast himself as the heir to Akkad for his own self-aggrandizement (Archi 2001: 10), but a manifestation of a particular ethos of rule in which he adopted, and adapted, local practices (Charpin 2004a: 151–2).[44]

Samsi-Addu also journeys to Akkad, and, in one inscription, is called the king of Akkad (Charpin 1984: 44–5). In fact the land that was once Akkad fell within the purview of Eshnunna and Babylon, and Samsi-Addu's trip there seems to have been made in the context of a peace treaty contracted with Eshnunna after a great war (Charpin 2004a: 162). It should therefore be seen not so much as a pilgrimage to an ancestral place or ideological homeland, but, depending on the contents of the treaty, as a journey to a meeting for the ratification of the pact itself, as Charpin (2004a: 163) has suggested. It need imply little about Samsi-Addu's origins or self-image. As for the title, if there was any sense that Samsi-Addu was indeed heir to Akkad or thought himself so, or was even merely from that region (let alone that anyone else viewed his kingdom as Akkad), it seems likely that this title would have been used frequently rather than in a single instance on a votive object.

And here is where the ideological discrepancies in academic frameworks become apparent, because, interestingly, the title "King of Akkad" is also attributed to Zimri-Lim at least once (Durand 1998: 484, letter 732), and if this is to be explained away as not a literal situation but a reference, say, to the settled component of his kingdom in the *Ah Purattim*, that is, the banks of the Euphrates river (Fleming 2004: 162), or, as Heimpel (2003: 23) prefers it, to the "palatial culture" of the far south,[45] surely the same is just as likely to be true of Samsi-Addu?

I dwell on this subject because these references are the mainstay of the argument that Samsi-Addu's situation in life was *qualitatively* different from that of Zimri-Lim (Fleming 2004: 161–2). There is one other regard in which these two kings are seen to have been at variance, and that is in their relationships to pastoralists and what that means for the sociopolitical worlds they inhabited. This is a complex question, the answer to which lies partly in the nature of the archives, which are overwhelmingly the documents of Zimri-Lim's reign,[46] partly in the

---

44 Charpin indeed notes throughout his discussion of Samsi-Addu this tendency to invoke local authority through a variety of means. Cf. Eidem 2000: 256.

45 Perhaps harking back to Margueron's (1982) understanding of Mari in the third millennium as a southern implant.

46 We have little understanding of the grounds on which his predecessors' texts were selected for preservation, so cannot predict what aspects of the earlier archives are adequately represented and what not.

nature of the relationship each king had to the place of the archives, Mari, and partly with the particular problems they faced. Samsi-Addu was concerned with the administration of a vast area comprised of independent major powers, petty kinglets, and mobile populations, all distributed over a mosaic of river valleys, rain-fed plains, dry steppes, and deserts. Zimri-Lim's territory, no matter what his ambitions, was rather more restricted to the Euphrates zone from Mari to Tuttul (Tell Bi'a) and its steppic environment, and much of his attention was directed toward keeping that intact (Eidem 2000: 256). But really the answer is both short and simple. This was not Samsi-Addu's place, and these were not Samsi-Addu's people.

Whatever picture the texts convey of interaction between the Addus, father and son, and the local pastoralist population will therefore be markedly different from the picture that would emerge from the family's own archives at Ekallatum. The texts from Tell Leilan (ancient Shubat Enlil) postdate the period of the Mari archives and so offer us little about Samsi-Addu in any case (Eidem 2000); but even here, as an appropriated place, the relationship would not parallel that of Zimri-Lim with his constituency, who could claim not only prior heritage at Mari, but who was in every way a homegrown boy. Nevertheless, the matter of Samsi-Addu's census (Durand 1998: 337–47) is informative. This must have been a vast undertaking, since the three points of the triangle that formed the kingdom of Upper Mesopotamia – Ekallatum, Mari, and Shubat Enlil – were to register the mobile contingents that fell within the polity, probably in order to have them swear an oath of fealty. Those groups, however, belonged to a number of other polities, both as members of kingdoms that had been incorporated by Samsi-Addu and as members of polities bordering the kingdom of Upper Mesopotamia but that moved within that region as part of their seasonal migrations. The letters on the topic show that Samsi-Addu and Yasmah-Addu administer pastoralists, may even be able to command them, and certainly have a greater connection with the Yaminites than the Simalites, but they seem to have no deep affiliation with/affection for any of these groups, although Samsi-Addu does elsewhere wax nostalgic for the outdoor life. They are aware that their control of at least some of the pastoralists in their territory is highly tenuous, if the letter from Samsi-Addu to Yasmah-Addu is anything to go by. The father warns his son not to count the Yaminites because then the Rabeeans will be angry and they won't go home (Durand 1998: 342, letter 641). In another such letter (Durand 1998: 345, letter 644) Samsi-Addu himself confesses he has not counted the Hana because they "showed repugnance to the idea." There are several issues implicit in this situation. Since the census is understood as prior to an oath of fealty, presumably being counted implies allegiance to Samsi-Addu, and this is unacceptable to those who may be within his territory but whose affiliations lie elsewhere. It also reflects the delicate balance that the ruler had to maintain, not because one pastoralist group was inimical to another but because in a time of hostility – such as that created by an expan-sionist king who has conquered a number of smaller polities and who is in turn faced with being gobbled up by other, equally expansionist powers – resources might be depleted and normal movements impeded, so that competition would be intensified and one's peers thus sensitive to the slightest intimation that one had designs upon their territory.

Ultimately, however, this sense of separation between Samsi-Addu and the mobile component that appears in the Mari texts of his time is, I think, because Samsi-Addu's people are the Numha,[47] who with the Yamutbal formed something of an eastern counterpart to the Yaminite/Simalite duality of the west (Heimpel 2003: 18; Durand 2004: 134–5), with a zone of overlap midway between the Tigris and Euphrates. They are therefore not present as the active base in the discourse between Yasmah-Addu and his father, which concerns pri-marily the western part of the Kingdom of the Upper Euphrates, and they are not present in the titulary of Samsi-Addu because his grandiose political ambi-tion transcends the kind of localized polity that is Zimri-Lim's fate. Such ambi-tion does not in itself make Samsi-Addu less of a pastoralist. It merely makes pastoralism one of many other concerns. Samsi-Addu is king of several places and several groups of Hana.

Differences between Samsi-Addu and Zimri-Lim – their situation and the organization of their constituencies, as well as differences between the various mobile and sedentary groups with whom they are associated – are therefore not differences of kind, but differences of, on the one hand, visibility, and, on the other (to a lesser extent), degree. The essential point is this: the Mari let-ters as now understood reveal multiple and interlocking sets of relationships between groups and individuals, lifestyles, and subsistence practices that cer-tainly transcend space, albeit their relationship to time is not especially visible in the fourteen-odd years covered by the archive. In this light, then, the very task of sorting out who is a pastoralist, who an Amorrite, who really a town dweller, and who a king rather than a tribal chief, is an exercise in frustration, and moreover rather misses the point. The Old Babylonian texts represent a complex network of connections and identities that *should* defy categorization; in a world were mobility is a major factor, those networks allow the group to persist. Fleming (2004: 24) captures the situation well when he says that the Mari team (and, I would add, his own work) have shown that "far from being set in irrevocable opposition as nomads and townspeople, or even in comple-mentary opposition, this large group considered itself part of one social fabric,

47   See Chapter 4 for a discussion of the evidence that Samsi-Addu was a Numha. Durand and Guichard (1997: 64) see the Numha as a Simalite group located in the northeast but related to Hammurabi of Babylon, while Fleming (2004: 10) states that at the time of Zimri-Lim the Numha were the constituent population of the kingdom of Kurda and not part of the Yaminite/Simalite construct.

divided not by mode of life or place of residence, but according to traditional associations of kin."

Several issues that emerge from the above discussion are in desperate need of further scrutiny: the very idea of "tribe," which has been roundly rejected within many branches of anthropology, yet is reemerging in many quite varying contexts[48] with no further theorization than what was accomplished (and then abandoned) in the evolutionary frameworks of the twentieth century; the slippage that has occurred between tribalism and pastoralism whereby they are now virtually synonymous to many users; the relationship between this form of organization and what we call the state; whether "forms" of organization are in any case useful heuristic devices; the applicability of notions of either tribe or state, however they are defined, to the ancient evidence; the different intellectual traditions from which these notions are derived; the nature of the evidence itself, archaeological and textual, and the methodologies used to retrieve it. I touch on all of them in this book but focus on only two: the interlocking complex of structure, discourse, and practice vested in kinship, religion, and the dead, which allows for groups spread over time and space to maintain cohesion and identity; and the interlocking complex of structure, discourse, and practice – in this case the construction of intellectual history, in the service of an actual historical situation – that created, and continues to create, separation.

Fleming's expression of the fact that kinship is the unifying feature of the variously named and located groups that populate the documents of the Mari archive can be extended much further. Durand (2004: 184) states that in the Old Babylonian period (or the first third of the second millennium BCE) everyone belonged to a tribe, and, within that, a clan, whether one is speaking of Mari or the Akkadians, the heartlands of southern Mesopotamia or the Jebel Sinjar. With this I also agree (with terminological reservations), but would go further still and argue that everyone in the ancient world (at least until the end of my remit at 1500 BCE) was so situated. The fact that this is not immediately apparent is the product of two intersecting tangents: the historical and the anthropological–archaeological. From this last comes the deeply ingrained idea that kinship was superseded by the state, and therefore when we see such clear evidence of kinship it must derive from that form of organization of which it is the defining characteristic, tribalism; and if tribalism is present within the state after it has long been superseded, then it can only have arrived there from somewhere else. And history has the answer: the Amorrites. These tribal characteristics must have been brought in from elsewhere to become mingled with the civil attachments that modern political theory demands of the state. Even among Mari scholars there remains a true Rowtonian dimorphism, where tribes exist

---

48   I cite as a representative, but somewhat random, sample the following: Parkinson 2002; Galaty 2002; various entries in Otto et al. 2006; Cooper 2006; Schulting n.d.

within states at the same time as the state, in the person of the king, is a member of the tribe. It all boils down to a single factor that overcomplicates these and other relationships for me: the conflation of social interactions/identities with political organization under the rubric "tribe." Extract the political from the equation once and for all and it becomes clear that many of the dualities and oppositions that persist readily disappear.

To do this, however, requires some examination of the anthropological (and to a lesser extent, sociological) materials on which fundamental ideas about the relationships between kinship, tribe, and state are based. The starting point is of necessity anthropological archaeology as the dominant form of discourse in the American practice of Mesopotamian and Syrian archaeology. A modified version of evolutionary archaeology, itself now so thoroughly critiqued (Yoffee 2005; Liverani 2006; Pauketat 2007) that it would be redundant to comment further here, anthropological archaeology in essence replaced the state as the central topic of concern[49] with the rubric "complex society," in recognition of the bankruptcy of the stage typologies of the past. And yet there is sometimes little difference between this approach and that of earlier work on state formation. If the "city-state" remains a reified form imbued with "historical inevitability" (A. T. Smith 2003: 96, on Yoffee 1997) and is repeatedly used in reference to the southern Mesopotamian polity, anthropological archaeologists still speak of chiefdoms (Pauketat 2007: 4) as the pre-state form of polity visible in the Near East (Stein 2001b; Matthews 2003) – and the chiefdom is simply but one form, an evolutionary higher form, of the tribe. More worrisome, though, is the fact that the tribe is increasingly described as that form of polity in place in at least parts of the north (L. Cooper 2006) long after the state has been established elsewhere – so much so that there now seems to be emerging a distinct "Syrian model" of sociopolitical organization (Steinkeller 1999a: 300; Schloen 2001: 268; Stein 2004; Oates and Oates 2006a: 410; Peltenburg 2007/8; Nishiaki 2010; Fuji and Adachi 2010; see Porter 2010a for a summary). In this model, the autocracy that is understood from the ancient record as the basic political system of the north, where the king had almost total control over both resources and people, is seen as having emerged from an essentially tribal background rooted in systems of kinship and descent that in turn correlates in some way with pastoralism as a necessary exploitation of the open steppes of that region (and see also Klengel 1992; van Driel 2000; Stein 2004; L. Cooper 2006; Lyonnet 2009). In contrast, in this view, the sociopolitical organization of the south derived in one way or another from the entrenchment of sedentary farming there, where the population was distributed across villages small enough to facilitate face-to-face interaction (Stone 2007: 221) as the basis of decision making. Mesopotamian sociopolitical organization, then, was communal

---

49   See Rothman 2004 for an overview of this change and Ur 2010 for an example.

in origin (Steinkeller 1999a). The difference between north and south in this framework is clearly related to the long-standing academic tradition that the particularities of the landscapes in each place must have something to do with the shape of their development (Adams 1981; Stein 1994a, 1994b; Renger 1995: 281; van Driel 2000; Rothman 2004; Wilkinson et al. 2007), especially in terms of those two outcomes that had such a profound impact on subsequent human history: urbanism and state formation.

Moreover, even if the ancient state is distinguished from the modern by labels such as archaic (Feinman and Marcus 1998), segmentary (Southall 1988; Frangipane 2001: 315; Stephen and Peltenburg 2002; Parkes 2003), incipient, nascent, or transitional (Trigger 2003), or replaced by the term "polity," the understandings that dominate this archaeological discourse, including very recent treatments, are in fact modern ones, applied to and not derived from, the ancient world; and the influence of Weber, profound in adducing the state, is little abated (see, for example, Ur 2010). Weber (1978: 54–6) defined the state by certain criteria: monopoly of control over the means of violence; authority based in legality rather than tradition; an administrative system, that is, bureaucracy, to execute its requirements; sovereign territorial boundaries; and class rather than kinship as the basis of social as well as political functioning. These parameters translate into the dominant reconstructions of the ancient Near Eastern polity in two different ways.

One way is in archaeological focus – certain topics are deeply embedded in this formulation and are very prominent because of it, especially the study of cylinder seals and sealings (Pittman 2001; Reichel 2002; Mazzoni 2006; Rothman 2007; Frangipane 2007). Seals and sealings constitute administrative technology and therefore their presence is widely accepted as indicative of the presence of bureaucracy. Bureaucracy is one of the most fundamental characteristics of the Weberian state – or, in current parlance, complex society. This remains the case despite the fact that seals were used as early as the sixth millennium in contexts that few would argue approach a state (Akkermans and Duistermaat 1997; Rothman 2007: 242; Ur 2010) and that the conceptual difference between the functions of a stamp and a cylinder seal is small (the technological and iconographic differences are another matter).

The other way is less direct, but equally pervasive: the elision between the Weberian state and the currency of complex society, "the elite." The state is seen as somehow separate from its members: it is that which governs them from above. A monolithic actor that operates with complete autonomy, the elite in the Mesopotamian/Syrian world is self-sequestered from the subordinate population it controls. The utter dominance and autonomy of the elite come from its control of the means of violence, to which is added control of ideology as another form of hegemony (Pollock and Bernbeck 2000: 151); class segregates the population into those with power and those without, again contributing to the autonomy and authority of the elite; and the check to this that the centrifugal pull of kinship would bring to bear in dispersing the interests and allegiances of its members to a network of other interactions is absent. In a form of rational-choice theory, all actions taken by the state/elite are in self-aggrandizement – to get and keep control (Baines and Yoffee 1998); similarly in history-based research, where the term "kingdom" rather than "state" usually pertains. There is no question, however, that the kingdom's nature parallels that of the state in anthropological archaeology: the kingdom is in essence a political autocracy derived from intense, yet very simple, social hierarchy (Archi 1982, 2006; Dolce 1998). A small elite – the royal family and their entourage – dominate an undifferentiated subordinate mass, especially through the control of luxury goods.

A general discomfort with the lack of fit between the evidence and this model (and its equal lack of explanatory power) has led to the proliferation of alternative approaches, which are nevertheless essentially variations on the Weberian theme rather than radical reenvisionings of the idea of the state. Adam Smith (2003: 11–12), for example, is concerned with "the production, maintenance and overthrow of sovereign authority" and assumes that early complex polities are "predicated on radical social inequality, legitimated in reference to enduring representations of order and vested in robust institutions of centralized governance" (Smith 2003: 30). Lisa Cooper (2006) understands archaeological indications of decentralization (themselves poorly theorized) as synonymous with lack of complexity, because the state is itself the centralized control of all its functions. Ergo decentralization equals tribalism.

And even though now it is widely recognized that certain elements of Weber's formulation are problematic or inapplicable to the ancient polity, in all these constructs, rather than concentrating on how people experienced and understood their lives, the focus instead is on the organizational frames in which they lived them. This focus (and where organization is perilously similar to form) derives from the implicit sense that the groups, status, or situation into which people are organized, or to which they are allocated, conditions the nature of their existence, and this in turn is a further legacy of the writings of Weber (Pierson 1996: 7). The end result of all this is ultimately a problem of agency: only the elite have it. This view of the world is encapsulated by statements such as that of Bretschneider (2007: 11): "If we consider the spatial organization, architectural implantation and structure of a city as the result of human interaction, then we are dealing in the first place with patterns of relationship and strategies of action of the socially and economically higher classes, i.e. the elite. It is after all the needs and aspirations of the powerful that monumentality must fulfill."

Agency and practice, whatever versions one subscribes to (Dobres and Robb 2000 provides a variety), are not just passing trends in social theory but the enduring recognition that the actions of all people, insignificant as they might be, are yet consequential because they all, past and present, make up the world in which each person acts, thinks, believes, and simply is (Porter 2010b). Such pronouncements as that above take no account of the complexity of human interactions nor of the possibilities of a dialectic of control, where every human being has some form of, or access to, power (Giddens 1984). As important, it fails to recognize the fact that in any world, power is vested in multiple, heter-archical, groups (albeit different kinds of power), while in the ancient world it was also vested in multiple beings – specifically, the dead and the divine, the latter a denomination that includes more entities than the gods alone (Pongratz-Leisten 2011). While many Near Eastern anthropological archaeologists are reluctant to engage with this idea, because they suppose it to fall within the realm of the cognitive, and therefore the immaterial, this is hardly the case. At the most basic level of analysis, the dead are present in burials, the gods in architecture and objects. Even when problematized, and the role of otherworldly beings included as in Baines's and Yoffee's 1998 study of "order, legitimacy and wealth" in Egypt and Mesopotamia, the Weberian underpinnings of this work still result in a monocular view whereby the elite are the sole subject of consideration. How those who fulfill the offices of rule are constituted by their situation within a larger system, and how their actions are enabled and constrained by the actions of others, remain unexamined.

The debt to Weber is explicit, and the underpinnings ultimately the same, in David Schloen's "patrimonial household model" (2001). Running parallel to the "tribal model" but mercifully avoiding its terminological quagmire, the patrimonial household (or the "house of the father") is argued to be both the fundamental structure of Near Eastern society and the model on which social and political relationships were built. Yet while I find myself in some sympathy with Schloen's (2001: 255) basic proposition that "familiar household relationships provided the pattern not only for governmental authority and obedience but also for the organization of production and consumption and for the integration of the gods with human society," and agree that there is little reality to the dualities so commonly held in Near Eastern studies between public and private, urban and rural, state and subject (Schloen 2001: 51), this model nevertheless carries its own hazards. Schloen ultimately duplicates the same hierarchical and authoritarian structure as any positivist archaeologist in his understanding of the household, despite the presentation of the model in a sophisticated and insightful theoretical frame.

One of the key problems lies in Schloen's conceptualization of the household as highly authoritarian and only vertically, and not also horizontally, integrated. The ubiquitous use of relationship terminology such as father, son, brother, master, and slave to represent interactions between people on multiple levels that Schloen asserts frequently as evidence of the applicability of the model is both more concrete and more organically embedded than simply a representation of how things worked, "because alternative conceptions of social hierarchy were not readily available" (Schloen 2001: 255). They are also more complex than he allows, for the deployment of such terminologies is very frequently the product of an actual, if socially constructed (Porter 2009a: 218), kinship that is as valid as any biologically engendered relationship, even when such kinship includes beings on other planes of existence. This is no mere ideological construct but the very real "native understanding" that Schloen extols. Kinship could be, and very often was, *created* for social, economic, and political reasons, and it was done through duplicating idioms of blood – sacrifice and incorporation into the ancestral (familial) group through the assumption of responsibility for funerary and post-funerary mortuary traditions (Foxvog 1980; Porter 2000, 2002a, 2002b), sometimes executed together (Durand 2004, 2005; Durand and Guichard 1997).

So here, too, the role of the subordinate is merely to do the master's bidding; and yet relationships configured through kinship work in a multiplicity of directions and on a multiplicity of levels that produce a dialectic whereby no member of the kin-group, ruling elite or otherwise, is unconstrained by the desires, actions, and existence of the others. What happens at the top, whether in tension with, in outright opposition to, or conformity with, those below, is as much a product of the nature of the bottom as it is the self-determination of the elite. For all "subjects are active elements in the reproduction of their authority" (Smith 2003: 155) – so much so that the very idea of top and bottom, elite and subordinate, becomes a gross distortion of the complexity of the social group. Such times as when authoritarian power is so complete and so oppressive that that dialectic is not in evidence are, as recent history has shown, ultimately short-lived.

The evidence speaks to something else again: a different set of practices, processes, and structures that constitute the polity, rendering it "complex" indeed, even if I would reject the use of that word in anthropological archaeology. Theoretical archaeology needs to address this specifically – not by simply shifting the discussion to another subject, but by examining anew the very notion of the polity. The considerations of power that have come to replace discussions of the state, while valuable in and of themselves, do not challenge the fundamental definitions that still pervade empirical studies in several regions – specifically in the ancient Near East. In a self-perpetuating circularity, new theoretical work builds on evidence that is erroneously adduced in the first place. However, there is another (and to me more cogent) reason not to abandon theoretical discussions of the state, and that is the fact that the state itself is still the defining political structure of the modern and hypermodern world, even as the state is itself challenged by alternative sociopolitical constructs and practices of power (Gledhill 2000). Study of the ancient state has a role to play beyond highlighting that which is new about modernity (Anderson 1974a, 1974b; Giddens 1981, 1987; Mann 1986). It offers us ways to think about these alternative and sub-state powers, many of which are understood to be based in traditional if not archaic ways of being, as well as ways to think about what the state could, even should, look like in the future. But these ends cannot be accomplished if the ancient state is not properly comprehended in its own terms, as encompassing a complete entity – all those who lived within it, not just those who appear to have controlled and run it.

Continuing for the moment the discussion of pitfalls, yet another of these, more immediate to my purpose, is vested in the synchronic analyses that characterize recent theoretical discussions of power. Synchronic studies, especially comparative works (such as Trigger 2003) that seek to expose conformity and regularity rather than variability (Stein 1998, 2005b), run the risk of falling into exactly the same traps as earlier anthropology by losing sight of both the historical specificity of how things work and the historical processes (Webster 1997: 324–5; Pauketat 2007; Boivin 2008) that give rise to them, often working at a level of generalization in both time and space that obscures fundamental divergences within the deployed examples that prove critical to understanding both theoretical and empirical problems (contra Renger 1995: 270).

This is evident in two examples discussed by both A. T. Smith (2003) and Yoffee (2005), the resolution of which would fundamentally alter the outcomes of their analyses. Both writers use materials from the Old Babylonian period in southern Mesopotamia to reveal greater complexity[50] and diversity in the Mesopotamian world than is commonly portrayed (a view I certainly endorse) – Yoffee as a discrete chronological and sociocultural entity across space in southern Mesopotamia; Smith as interwoven with the preceding Ur III period within a single space, the city of Ur. But a critical question is the relationship between the production of the material and epigraphic record and the situation that defines the Old Babylonian period, the emergence of a new political authority: the Amorrites (Stone 2002). Thought to have entered Mesopotamia at the end of the third millennium and contributing to, if not causing, the widespread collapse both of urban settlement in the north and of the empire of the Third Dynasty of Ur in the south (Van de Mieroop 2004; Jahn 2007), the Amorrites are almost always assumed to have adopted Mesopotamian culture – including administrative structures and political practices – lock, stock, and barrel. Yet any bits of evidence not in accord with established understandings of what is Mesopotamian are attributed to the culture of the invaders. Neither Smith nor Yoffee questions this situation, which suggests that they see the features they describe as entirely indigenous. But for many writers, certain aspects of sociopolitical organization and practice in evidence in the Old

---

50   In the original, not archaeological, sense of the word.

Babylonian period – multiple and parallel systems of authority, such as wards, assemblies, and elders (Seri 2005); the relationship of such systems of authority to corporate political behavior; the kin basis of substate social organization – might all be considered "tribal" and therefore unique to the Amorrites as well as intimately tied to their nomadic nature. Given the deep-seated belief that southern Mesopotamia is anything but tribal, while the north is increasingly seen as just that, it is hardly surprising that Syrian origins for the Amorrites are increasingly postulated (Weiss and Courty 1993; Charpin 2003; Lyonnet 2009; cf. Porter 2007a).

Equally central as conceptions of the state, therefore, but far more problematic in its use and misuse, is the notion of "the tribe" that is beginning to reemerge in a range of archaeological contexts. While applied to those societies not sufficiently developed to warrant the designation of "complex," the word "tribe" is itself the epitome of complexity. It is so complicated that it is virtually indefinable, yet its common usage is such that it would seem that everyone knows exactly what it means, and it might be assumed that it is a word even better understood in its technical and analytical contexts within anthropology. After all, anthropology as a discipline originated in the study of the tribe (Kuper 1988). But in fact anthropology does not hold any special privilege here, in large part because it has given up thinking reflexively in terms of the tribe for a number of reasons, not least because anthropologists were simply unable to come up with consensus on a working definition of it that was not fraught with controversy (e.g., Mafeje 1971; Colson 1986: 5). This was because, despite long-standing academic tradition, there was/is no one set of common features derivable from multiple ethnographic examples that can give rise to a core meaning of this label. In addition, the word "tribe" has been abandoned in studies especially of Africa, because of certainly pejorative, if not outright racist, implications (Southall 1970; Ekeh 1990; Lentz 1995). It was so fundamental to colonialist discourse as the devaluing of "the other" that it could not be used as an academic designation without perpetuating this practice (Peletz 1995: 345), although neither anthropologists, archaeologists, nor political scientists (such as Tapper 1979; Khoury and Kostner 1990; Salzmann 2008b) working in the Middle East seem to have had any such qualms.

On the other hand, the use of the term "complex" to describe ancient society has given rise to a set of value judgments that are as pejorative and hegemonic as any implicit in the idea of tribe, because although only one term is used, it still denotes a binary opposition embedded in a Western teleology in which increased complexity is more like "us" and, what is more, undeniably better. Whatever language is used – be it tribe and state, or complex and (ipso facto) simple/noncomplex society – there is no evolutionary relationship between these entities. In fact, I will go much further: tribe and state are not even similar categories. They may not be likened to two varieties of oranges, they are not even two kinds of fruit. Rather, they are a fruit and a vegetable. Whether in the various theoretical frameworks of academics or in practical diplomacy, what the tribe is, how it works, and what its history is, are seriously misapprehended. And where the task has gone off the rails is in understanding the tribe as a set of political structures, or as a set of social structures that operate in lieu of, or as if they were, political structures.

This situation, particularly insidious in terms of mobile pastoralists (Khazanov 1984: 151; Fleming 2004: 206, n. 33), goes back to the origins of anthropology and the role it played as a handmaiden of colonialism. The search for functional principles and a comprehensive definition of the tribe has traditionally been vested in figuring out how tribes maintain stability and order in the absence of the institutions of rule that the West (Gledhill 2000; Carsten 2004: 10) – especially as it was embodied in academic researchers working as tools of the colonial powers (Richards 1960; Trigger 1996) – recognizes as essential for those tasks.

One of the first ethnographic works, Lewis Henry Morgan's (1985 [first published 1877]) description of the North American Iroquois in the 1870s, showed how kinship in primitive societies provided order in the absence of recognizable forms of government, by establishing a set of obligations for members of the group according to relationships created by birth. This issue became the guiding question for E. Evans-Pritchard in the 1930s, in his study of the Nuer of the Sudan. Evans-Pritchard observed structural patterns in the social relationships of the Nuer, based in descent groups, that in succeeding decades have come for many to answer the question of how *all* such groups around the world and throughout time – all simple societies – form political organization and maintain order (Parkinson 2002). Evans-Pritchard believed that segmentary structures inhibited the development of social hierarchies so as to prevent one lineage from accumulating power at the expense of others, thus not merely promoting, but *ensuring*, egalitarianism (Gledhill 2000: 2) and simplicity, because it is in differentials of power and wealth that complexity is achieved.

From the beginning, then, attempts to understand the political formations of non-Western societies were framed in terms of contrasts to the state, especially the Weberian state, and nowhere more so than in archaeology. Pregnant still with the functional/structural implications of the groundbreaking work of Evans-Pritchard, Fortes, and other anthropologists of the 1930s through the 1950s, and hijacked by the neo-evolutionists of the sixties through eighties, archaeological treatments of the tribe have progressed little from the early days of neo-evolutionary theory, when the tribe was understood as a level of organization – that is, an early stage in the development of civilization through which human societies passed on their way to their ultimate goal, the state – or as a type of organization – the kin-based, segmentarily structured social system as developed by Evans-Pritchard.[51]

In reaction, nonevolutionists in anthropology and political theory proposed the tribe as an artificial formation in reaction to modern history (Fried 1968, 1975; Lonsdale 1977; Hobsbawm and Ranger 1983;[52] Colson 1986), created by colonial powers as a tool of administration or by indigenous peoples as a reaction to colonialism, and as having, therefore, no indigenous reality. There is good evidence in certain times and places to support this position, particularly in regard to those situations in which the tribe seems to function as a political system, but it is not universal. Nor should the significance of the tribe be delegitimized as an instrumentalist invention,[53] for this is ultimately counterproductive. To deny the authenticity of the tribe because its definition is incorrect or inappropriate is to deny not just whole avenues of analysis, but what is in fact a social reality for large numbers of people (Friedman 1975, 1996; Mauzé 1997), whether that reality was attributed or appropriated, constructed or primordial, recent or ancient, indigenous or exogenous. Just as the debate over the reality of segmentary lineage theory has obscured the significance of indigenous practices (Salzman 1978b, 1999), so a focus on "invention," while offering insight on one level, can impede investigation of the outcome of that invention, for the invention itself assumes a meaningful and forceful (if impalpable role) in self-definition and/or its definition by others. The invention itself becomes a factor of agency and history.

All these views have a common characteristic: the tribe is understood as something less than – and other than – the state, and is invariably associated with preindustrial forms of economy such as swidden agriculture and mobile pastoralism. It is considered traditional, if not outright regressive, in social and cultural terms. In contrast to the state, which has borders, the tribe has no true territorial definition but is nevertheless a "bounded autonomous political unit" (Colson 1986: 5). It is formed by blood ties and sentiments of affinity, whereas membership in the state is elective and maintained by sentiments of nationalism: the former are "real" and biological at root; the latter "imagined," created, and subscribed to voluntarily.

Much is made of this idea of an "imagined" unity, initially proposed by Benedict Anderson (1991 [first published 1983]). It is what transcends the biological determinism of the tribe and its inherent propensity to conflict and, in elevating the notion of the state to a conceptual level, an intellectual construct,

---

51   Although the first description of a segmentary system is attributed to W. Robertson Smith (Meeker 2005: 81).
52   Subsequently reconsidered in Ranger 1993.
53   Where the tribe, in the same way as ethnicity, is a creation of those who would manipulate group allegiance for their own political ends. Lentz 1995 summarizes the various scholars who have taken this position.

ennobles it. But this dichotomy is false. The social structures, ideologies, and practices that are taken to characterize the tribe are as much imagined as any idea of the civic community embodied in ideas of the state. This is the essence of kinship. Kinship constructs are imagined in that they are carried in the social knowledge of the person across vast distances of time and space, and, as well, in that the basis of the social relationships founded in kinship are as often what is increasingly termed "fictional"[54] as biological. Kinship, rather than being a maladapted and necessarily closed system, is extraordinarily malleable and elastic.

Indeed, ideas of kinship have changed radically since the earlier years of anthropological practice, when the focus was on sorting out indigenous kinship labels and classificatory systems. Kinship is now understood in "terms of social relations among variably situated actors engaged in the practice of social reproduction" (Peletz 1995: 366) and as multidimensional. Yet while terms such as "kin-based," "lineage," and "descent" are increasingly redeployed in describing and interpreting the origins of the early polity (Peltenburg 1999; Porter 2002a; Lisa Cooper 2006) and are a large part of the reason academic discourse is returning to the tribe as a descriptor, it is necessary to remember that these are purely academic constructs with a particular history of their own, a history that has produced and reproduced not only the modern world, comprised of unequal sociopolitical relations between tribe and state, but those we read into the ancient record as well. It is therefore important to understand exactly what these terms mean now and what they have meant in the past.

The centrality of kinship to anthropology as a discipline goes back, again, to Morgan (1966 [1871]; 1985 [1877]), who was concerned with the role of descent and kinship terminology in the evolution of social organization. Foreshadowing the work of Evans-Pritchard and Fortes (Fortes 1969: 4, 17), Morgan and his contemporaries, Maine (1986 [1861]) and McLennan (1970 [1865]), all argued aspects of the idea that extended familial ties provided both the organizing principle of primitive societies and the means of integrating individuals into political communities or corporations. These bonds were seen as chronologically prior to territorial attachment and provided ways of attributing group membership on the basis of descent (Verdon 1980: 129–30; Kuper 1982: 73–4). The ensuing debate revolved around the existence of primitive communism, whether maternal or paternal descent took precedence, and whether territorial ties were more determinative than kin ones (Swanton 1905; Goldenweiser 1910, 1914; Rivers 1924). It was with the establishment of field research as the central activity of the British school of social anthropology under the auspices of Malinowski and Radcliffe-Brown that the topic of kinship took on such a significant dimension and a particular role as a means of analysis, because the

---

54   Although see Porter 2009a: 218 for an argument as to why the term "socially constructed" is to be preferred.

theoretical concepts of earlier times could be assessed in the detailed study of practices of living groups (Kuper 1973, 1988; Holy 1996: 2). Radcliffe-Brown in particular took the central aspect of Morgan's work to be the recognition of a synchronic system of kinship relations expressed in terminological classifications (Fortes 1969: 27-8) and went on to develop concepts of kinship as the regulation of patterns of interaction between people (Radcliffe-Brown 1930/31) and as the regulation of transmission of rights through succession (Radcliffe-Brown 1935). Thus the focus passed from the evolutionary sequences of Maine and Morgan to the synchronic studies of actual "primitive" groups (much as is now occurring in archaeological contexts), with very specific outcomes. But the lack of historical depth in these studies obscured certain salient factors, notably variability in practice and organization over time, so that how these groups appeared at the time they were encountered came to be understood both as how they always had been and as how indeed they were supposed to be.

Some of the most influential descriptions of specific kinship systems and structures were provided by Evans-Pritchard in his study of the Nuer (1969 [1940]; 1956,) and Meyer Fortes (1945, 1949) for the Tallensi, both of whom distinguished the public domain of kin systems from the domestic, thereby bringing the connection between kin relations and political organization to the fore (Fortes 1969: 72). These two spheres, the public and the domestic, were in general characterized by the different ways kin structures operated. The domestic sphere was identified by horizontal ties linking members of the community; the public, by vertical ones. That is, horizontal linkages relate to the individual, and the living people to whom the individual is connected by blood and marriage, forming groups of "kindred." Holy (1996) depicts kinship as a series of concentric circles with ego, or the individual, at the center, and outer-circle kin relations increasingly distant. But as every ego is potentially a member of a number of different kindreds, and different kindreds overlap, this type of structure does not provide for group integration and group boundedness, nor does it provide for a satisfactory means of analysis (Holy 1996: 40–42). Marriage can render the group boundless by establishing so many kin connections with external groups (Schneider 1967: 66; Fortes 1969: 104) that webs of kinship "stretch out indefinitely, and result in a kaleidoscopic fluidity of social relations" (Fortes 1969: 108).

This is actually a good thing, and highly relevant for understanding the nature of interactions in ancient societies, but at the time it was considered extremely problematic, because it was believed that, as membership of the social group had to be delimited in some way, there was something missing in the construct. Vertical linkages, on the other hand, were thought to provide all of the above – integration, boundaries, and meaningful units of analyses – and these were formed through systems of descent or genealogical relationships structured through time rather than space. Membership in the group or corporation was granted on the basis of the individual's connection to a common ancestor. It was considered that there were three ways in which to recognize membership on the basis of descent: agnatic (patrilineal) descent traced through the father, the father's father, and so on; uterine (matrilineal) descent, from the daughter to the daughter's daughter; and cognatic, using either male or female lines, or a combination of both. Agnatic and uterine descent form unilineal descent systems; cognatic, multilinear ones (Holy 1996: 44).

But it was the development of segmentary lineage theory as proposed by Evans-Pritchard in his study of the Nuer within the framework of structural anthropology and as mediated by Aiden Southall (1970) that has proved perhaps the most influential model of all, especially in the reemergence of the tribe in archaeological discourse. Parkinson (2002: 7), for example, in attempting to derive an operational definition for archaeological purposes, lists the four attributes traditionally associated with the tribe: segmentation, the tendency to entropy, the tribe as a bounded group, the tribe as a "transitional" political form; and although this is not acknowledged, all four have their basis in a functionalist view of kinship. Parkinson dismisses all but segmentation as falsely derived from the synchronic limitations of traditional ethnographic practices, yet segmentation has no more "reality" than any of the other factors. Although now largely discredited or abandoned in much of anthropology (Holy 1979a, 1979b, 1996; Kuper 1982; Marx 2006), the debate on segmentary lineage theory has nevertheless been extraordinarily powerful (Fortes 1979: vii) in determining not only our understanding of tribes, but especially of mobile pastoralists (see, for example, Bonte 1979; Digard 1990). No model is more ubiquitous than that of Evans-Pritchard (in Service 1962, 1975; Goldschmidt 1979; Lancaster 1981; Digard 1990; Maisels 1990; Salzman 1999, 2008a). Concepts such as the centrality of the blood feud, group unity, and loyalty – the factors that are thought to create innate and structural antipathies between tribes and "the outside world" – also are heavily embedded in this debate.

In seeking to explain how a stateless society could operate in the absence of obvious mechanisms of centralized leadership, Evans-Pritchard was influenced both by Durkheim's principles of mechanical and organic solidarity and by Morgan's evolutionary sequence, whereby primitive political systems were seen as based on kinship, the state on territory, with the transition from one to the other marked by an intervening stage that combined the two – although by the time *The Nuer* was published, Evans-Pritchard had abandoned any diachronic interests in favor of a synchronic sociology of the tribe wherein these three types were coexistent (Kuper 1973: 109–10, 117–19, 1982: 82). *The Nuer* was a conscious attempt to abstract structural principles of sociopolitical organization from the actions of a tribal people, based upon the notion of the corporate group as first proposed by Morgan and transformed by Radcliffe-Brown. But whereas for Radcliffe-Brown corporate descent groups were understood as manifested in collective action and control of property, and in which people were arranged in fixed social segments, to Evans-Pritchard it was the relationship of such groups to other units in the larger political society that gave rise to the organization of corporation. Two interconnected structures in Nuer organization were described: one was territorial and governed the allocation of residences and resources; the other, social (Evans-Pritchard 1969 [1940]: 122).

Evans-Pritchard's use of territory may be understood as coresidence, or locality, and as a circumscribed and defined body of land that represents the dimensions of a political entity. Locality was integrated through the social structure of agnatic descent, which equated with the political entity. The territorial system was based around the tribe as the largest unit, but the tribe was in turn divided into smaller, more cohesive sections, or segments. The social articulation of this construction was the lineage system, which was also segmented, the largest section being the dominant clan, or major lineage, which was progressively subdivided until it reached the smallest section, or minimal lineage, which more or less corresponded to the level of village community (Evans-Pritchard 1969 [1940]: 203). As the divisions were patrilinear units, the smaller the segment, the closer the genealogical relationship, the more compact its territory, and the stronger its "sentiment of unity" (Evans-Pritchard 1969 [1940]: 142–3). Small lineages would combine to form larger ones in certain situations. The raison d'être for this segmentary lineage system was "balanced opposition" wherein the different sections operated only in opposition to other like sections. Sometimes all members of a major lineage would identify themselves as one against another major lineage; sometimes minor or minimal lineages might so cohere. In Evans-Pritchard's words, "Each segment is itself segmented and there is opposition between its parts. The members of any segment unite for war against adjacent segments of the same order and unite with these adjacent segments against larger sections" (Evans-Pritchard 1969 [1940]: 142); and "These fights between tribal sections and the feuds that result from them, though based on a territorial principle, are often represented in terms of lineages, since there is a close relation between territorial segments and lineage segments, and Nuer habitually express social obligations in a kinship idiom.... This principle of segmentation and the opposition between segments is the same in every section of the tribe and extends beyond the tribe to relations between tribes" (Evans-Pritchard 1969 [1940]: 143).

Thus the segmentary lineage system was the major integrative force in social organization even though it provided mechanisms of both fission and fusion. The functioning of the system was primarily evident in cases of blood feud, for "vengeance is the most binding obligation of paternal kinship and an epitome of all its obligations" (Evans-Pritchard 1969 [1940]: 152). By the same token, some means of maintaining social relationships through settlement of the feud was required, particularly when feuding occurred within a village community, and this could be achieved through the payment of blood-wealth and mediation. Blood feud was to become, and in many circles remains, one of the defining attributes of the tribe.

The first challenge to Evans-Pritchard's theory of segmentary opposition, which had rapidly come to be seen as diagnostic of all tribal, and certainly tribal pastoral, groups, came initially from the results of fieldwork done in Oceania and New Guinea, where it was found that lineage theory could not readily be applied as an analytical tool to the sociopolitical organization of tribes in these areas (Kuper 1982; Verdon 1980; Holy 1996). There were various problems, but one of the most important for this discussion is that there seemed to be a vast gulf between the rules of group membership as described by tribespeople and the various ways individuals were incorporated into the group in reality; groups living in one place contained elements unrelated by any discernible kin connections, yet were self-identified as a group and possessed a concept of lineage as definition of membership (Meggitt 1965; Strathern 1973: 24–5). Since the essence of kinship to anthropologists in this period was the discernment of rules of group membership (Peletz 1995: 349–50), and "the status of anthropology as a generalizing discipline" was at stake (La Fontaine 1973: 35), the question of which took precedence, territory or lineage, became a central issue.

Meyer Fortes also adopted the concept of the lineage system in his work on the Tallensi (1945, 1949), but pointed out that a major difference between its use among the Nuer and among the Tallensi lay in the types of subsistence strategy and population distributions characteristic of the two groups. The Nuer lineage system was understood as a mechanism for integration in the absence of a stable sedentary system or centralized political control, but for the Tallensi the lineage system operated as a means of differentiation within a dense population (1979: x). For them it provided a determinative framework of political and economic organization as well as social relationships (Fortes 1945: 30). For both the Tallensi and the Nuer, lineage systems were worked out through unilinear descent constructs of agnatic relations. But unlike Evans-Pritchard, Fortes gave greater weight to domestic or horizontal bonds of kinship, seeing them as overlapping and crosscutting lineage structures. These bonds formed principles of filiation or siblingship. Domestic and public kin structures each had a function in the integration and segregation of society as well as in the determination of rights and duties accruing to members: the domestic provided moral strictures for the constraint of conduct; the public, politico-jural obligations, privileges, and sanctions (Fortes 1953). Ultimately the two systems were "interdigitated" within society as a whole (Fortes 1969: 76).

But despite Fortes's recognition of the operation of the two types of kin structures in Tallensi society, it was the jural aspect of descent (Leach 1954; Smith 1956; Keesing 1975) that dominated the subsequent bifurcation of kinship studies into alliance theory, with its focus on delineations of marriage rules and patterns as forms of exchange (Lévi-Strauss 1969;[55] Goody 1969; Strathern 1969; Leach 1954; cf. Bourdieu 1995 [first published 1977]) and descent theory, using genealogical rules and patterns – a bifurcation that has recently been revitalized (Gillespie 2000a, 2000b; cf. Carsten and Hugh-Jones 1995). Archaeologists in particular have turned to Lévi-Strauss's concept of the house society (the collected entries of Joyce and Gillespie 2000; Chesson 2003; González-Ruibal 2006), in which marriage is more determinative than descent, in large part because there is a material component to this formulation with which archaeologists may engage, in contrast to kinship. The house is the integrative link between its members because it contains and possesses both physical and spiritual property that its members consume and to which they contribute, but whose overriding task it is to perpetuate. While there *need* not be a physical property (Joyce 2000), there in fact usually is. The house lives on long beyond the allotted span of any individual member or generation.

However, several studies have shown the operational integration of horizontal (marriage) and vertical (descent) structures (for example, Friedman 1975; Marx 1977; Kelly 1985), and it is becoming increasingly apparent that the two axes of kinship are not mutually exclusive (Leach 1954; Fortes 1969: 80; Bonte 1979: 214–15). It is not a matter of one or the other, kin-based society or house society, descent or residence, fact or fiction – even emic or etic views. These different ways of constituting social life, and academic analyses, may be interwoven with each other in unpredictable ways.

The second line of argument regarding segmentary opposition focused on the concept of descent, for it seemed undeniable that descent figured in the organization of most non-state societies in one form or another. If in large part the problem was one of divergence between what became known as the African model and empirical reality in other places, then some kind of reconciliation could be found in broadening the definition of descent. Fortes's version of descent as a unilinear genealogical entitlement to group membership was enlarged to include any social unit with genealogies constructed in any way as only one of the possible means of attributing membership and, further, the function of kinship was expanded to include other roles (Goody 1961; Leach 1962; Scheffler 1966; Kaberry 1967). Alternatively, the definition of descent could be narrowed by delegating aspects of kinship to the province of another school of anthropology altogether, if one could distinguish between actors' models and academic models, or between actors' models and actors' actual practices.

Scheffler (1966) and Keesing (1971) did just that by separating the conceptual world from the pattern of events and transactions in which people engage. They concluded that the first is ideological and therefore belongs to culture, more

---

55 Lévi-Strauss acknowledged his own debt to Morgan in the dedication of *The Elementary Structures of Kinship* (1969).

properly the concern of cultural anthropology; the second belongs to behavior and social structure, the legitimate concern of social anthropology (Strathern 1973: 22). And it is here that emerges a most pervasive and problematic dichotomy: between ideology and practice. The ideological cannot be separated from social structure on either practical or theoretical grounds, because the two are in essence components of a dialectic, as both Scheffler (1966: 550) and Keesing (1971: 126) eventually acknowledged (Strathern 1973: 26) and Salzman (1978a, 1978b) has demonstrated. Nor may behavior and culture be divorced, for behavior constitutes culture and culture is manifest in behavior (Bloch 1971: 218; Bourdieu 1990 [first published 1980]), a conundrum with which archaeologists in particular must come to terms. In this case, if a group is constituted by residence but has an ideology based on descent, then the question is, first and foremost, not which is more important, or which is followed in practice, but rather why is there a departure between the two? Why employ descent-based ideologies at all (Strathern 1969: 38-9; Salzman 1978a, 1978b)? Explanations - that these are merely folk ideologies with no basis in behavioral reality (Peters 1967), or that behavioral reality is correct and indigenous folk ideology incorrect - are now understood to have serious methodological, not to mention theoretical, shortcomings (Salzman 1978b: 54-7; Kraus 1998: 3-4).

These issues were also explicitly developed within studies of mobile pastoralists (Asad 1979: 421; Bonte 1979), where because of the materialist underpinnings of approaches to pastoralism current at that time - that is, as a mode of production determined by environmental constraints, whereby movement as adaptation was the primary consideration - behavioral reality was considered more significant than ideological constructs. Peters's concern was the conflict between the notion of segmentary lineage as represented to him by the bedouin of Cyrenacia, which was more or less appropriate to the theoretical framework devised by Evans-Pritchard, and the actual social practice of the bedouin, which was quite contrary to the model and in which territory was paramount. Peters's response to this dichotomy was, first, to argue that the segmentary lineage model did not exist in reality and, second, to dismiss indigenous models as only constituting a useful device employed by the bedouin for understanding their own social organization - employed incorrectly, for they explain the divergence in practice as exceptions based on unusual circumstances. Peters, in contrast, understood the real social practices to be necessary and permanent responses to environmental and demographic circumstances. Only two general comments need be reiterated here, for Salzman (1978a, 1978b) has dealt with the problems of Peters's analysis in detail. One, it is hard to imagine how an ideology that not only does not relate to actual practice but in fact is argued to conflict with it, can help anyone, observer or participant, to understand that practice. Two, an indigenous ideology is neither correct nor incorrect, and obviously has meaning in some capacity as far as its holders are concerned, and it is that meaning with which we should be concerned. Peters's failure to adequately understand the relationship between practice and ideology stems to some degree from the approach applied to the problem (the test of segmentary lineage theory), and one remedied to a certain extent by Salzman's broader view of both lineage systems and ideology.

Salzman (following Geertz 1973) argued that ideology should be conceived of as having a multiplicity of social roles. While it may be employed to serve the interests of a particular subgroup by, say, its reinforcement of social hierarchy or by differential access to resources, ideology is also something larger – it is a system of symbols that "provides guidelines for organization and action in socio-political matters" (Salzman 1978a: 622-3). In a similar fashion, lineage may also be something larger than segmentary lineage theory as we know it, being augmented both by the invocation of different types of descent, and in some cases residence (Salzman 1978b: 60), and by functioning in a variety of ways. In cases where there is a disparity between ideologies as espoused and actual social practice, ideology is then "asserted ideology," and its significance in understanding social organization is equal to that of behavioral reality.

Salzman's "asserted ideologies" are conceptions of social structure that are maintained by the actors but not necessarily practiced by them (Salzman 1978a, 1978b and cf. Bourdieu 1995 [1977]: 30-52). They exist as a model of behavior that is adaptive to certain circumstances – circumstances that do not always pertain, but that through historical experience are known to be possible – facilitating change. Descent-based ideologies allow for disincorporation and reincorporation of members of the group over vast distances in time and space. Therefore the correspondence between model and reality is contingent on the situation of the group: in some groups one will find a high degree of correspondence between ideology and actuality because circumstances are conducive to the implementation of the practices perpetuated by the model; in other cases, such as that of the bedouin of Cyrenacia at the time of Peters's study, they are not. For Salzman (1978a: 676), such circumstances are ongoing population mobility and interpenetration, which are a function of territorial stability. Territorial stability in turn may fluctuate due to environmental, political, or social conditions, and when this occurs, social structures that supersede structures built on residence or territory come into play.

The significance of this rather lengthy summary of anthropological research will play out over the next three chapters, where shifting practices that reproduce social interactions bear witness to changing contingent circumstances in the relationship between the social group and space. The upshot for now is that the tribe was, and unfortunately still is, understood as a bounded socio-political entity based on and organized through some version of interaction between horizontal and vertical ties of kinship that at best substitute for, at worst actually are, real political structure. This belief in kinship as real political structure is unquestionably present in the guise of the chiefdom, much beloved of archaeology of previous decades, where, because power is vested in the hands of a single individual bulwarked by his immediate kin-group, it is a logical precursor to fully fledged autocracy in the despotic rulers of the Mesopotamian state (kingdom).

Now there is no question that the archaeological constructs of tribe and chiefdom (Yoffee 1993, 2005; Pauketat 2007), or tribe and state (Schloen 2001) have recently been overtly rejected. But here's the problem. Such treatments are nevertheless still based on the understanding of tribe and state outlined above. Those who reject this framework do not do so because they have thought differently about these categories; they simply discard them as they stand. But the rendition of various elements that lay behind ideas of the tribe, in particular kinship, in *anthropology* have changed considerably, and the impact of those changes needs to be considered in the archaeological context before these ideas can be accepted or rejected.

For one thing, it is now recognized that ethnographic snapshots such as that of Evans-Pritchard are framed by the circumstances of the period in which they are taken. The deliberately ahistorical nature of early ethnography, a nature changed largely by the work of Maurice Bloch, indeed the inevitably ahistorical nature of any study based on the observations of short and specified periods of time (see also Boivin 2008), contribute to the idea that tradition means reification, that an example is axiomatic. *The Nuer* is the case in point – on the one hand, a single snapshot came to frame a set of rules for the tribe and how it is organized, and, on the other, the revisitation of the Nuer and the consequent historical dimension that this has brought to the discussion show just how much a product of contingency any ethnography is. Evans-Pritchard's acephalous Nuer were not independent entities without the state, but were studied by him during a particular point in time (Gledhill 2000: 42) – the peak of colonialism. Colonial overlordship, although not visible to Evans-Pritchard, actually fragmented the Nuer political system and accentuated the centrality of feuding at the same time as it diminished ritual mediation of conflicts (Hutchinson 1996: 131–2).[56] But this was not the only limitation to Evans-Pritchard's model. In fact the Nuer themselves did not apparently think in lineage idioms, conceiving of connections as construed through the hearth, and often failed to comprehend Evans-Pritchard's questions on the topic (Carsten 2004: 40). Despite the fact that there is still a small group of dedicated proponents of segmentary lineage, or balanced opposition, theory (such as Salzman 2008a, 2008b), subsequent research indicates that people in fact act and ally according to mutual interests and not necessarily according to position in descent structure (Marx 2006: 89).

---

56   See also Colson 1986 for similar understanding of other groups.

If in terms of how order is maintained and authority exercised – that is, political terms – the picture provided by earlier studies of the Nuer is false. So too is the deep conviction of a biological imperative to membership of the group, in social terms. Critiques of this view are now so numerous it is impossible to summarize them, and the study of kinship, once the very bedrock of anthropology, is considered "in crisis" (Sandstrom 2000: 35) – and perhaps rightly so, if the significance of kinship is confined to the delineation of lines of descent, marriage rules, kin-naming practices, and questions such as "what rules determine coresidence?" But if kinship is understood as relatedness (Carsten 2000) created by the sharing of substances (Schneider 1980; Parkes 2003), it may then equally be created by sharing the substance of food as much as the substances of semen and blood. David Schneider indeed proposed that the biological imperative that everyone assumed was fundamental to the way in which primitive society worked in fact originated in "folk concepts" of reproduction and a cognitive separation between "Western" and "non-Western" modes of social being that could no longer be considered valid (Schneider 1984; Yanagisako and Collier 1987; Latour 1993; Lamphere 2005). Relationships created through nurturing and centered on the hearth (Weismantel 1995; Carsten 2004) are as valid as any created through blood. Now, with the development of modern reproductive technologies, it is clear that conceptual boundaries between nature and culture are thoroughly dissolved (Strathern 1992a, 1992b; Edwards and Strathern 2000) and that there is an extraordinary variety of ways of conceiving and creating kinship.

The primordial and biologically deterministic nature of kinship is to be challenged therefore, even, or perhaps especially, in that period when it is thought to be the defining mode of existence – the world before the state. Some of the earliest texts are documents that attribute membership in the group on the basis of socially constructed kinship. Land-sale documents of the third millennium BCE (Gelb, Steinkeller, and Whiting 1991; Foxvog 1980) and records of adoption from diverse places in the second millennium BCE (such as Stone and Owen 1991), all show that in order to maintain the inextricable links between family identity, community membership, and land tenure, nonbiological kin relations may be constructed through socially validated practice. The alienation of land, which is ostensibly the subject of these documents, must take place within a framework that maintains an ideology of kinship. In order to do this, one may "de-ancestralize" the land by symbolically compensating the whole family, including previous generations, all of whom concur and participate in the sale. An alternative method is to avoid this "de-ancestralization" on an ideological if not actual level, by adopting the buyer into the family, which is perhaps to be seen as the reverse process, ancestralization. The ancestral nature of these transactions and their relation to the larger society are often made clear by prescriptions as to funerary matters (Foxvog 1980). To become adopted means one has responsibility for the continued ritualized care of the dead, because it is in healthy ancestral ties that group identity is maintained. In many parts of the world (for example, see Keesing 1970; Bloch 1971, 1986; Glazier 1984; McAnany 1995), this ancestral relationship between family and land is made abundantly clear by the placement of said ancestors in said land, and the way in which this is done can say much about the nature of both family and the family's relationship to the larger social entity.

The main point to make, though, is this: if the tribe – or any social grouping for that matter – is not bound by biology, then it is the tribe at some level that *chooses* what defines it, whom it lets in, and whom it does not, and these choices are both flexible and contingent. This point also applies to descent. It has long been recognized in anthropology that kinship ties are an ever-expanding circle that requires some other method of delimitation[57] and systems of descent, or genealogical relationships structured through time rather than space, have been attributed this function. Yet this is a Western construct that bears little relationship to how descent works in indigenous conceptions, where it performs a multiplicity of offices (Porter 2002a) and descent does not form social boundaries in and of itself. It is in fact often a means to the contrary – a means to *extend* boundaries to include the unknown other. Descent is a strategy to be manipulated as a means of inclusion or exclusion depending on what is deemed appropriate to the situation at hand. If, as Benedict Anderson (1991 [1983]) claims, the spread of modern nationalism is based on an imagined community of people who can conceive of a common identity with others even though they do not have a face-to-face relationship (cf. Bernbeck 2008a: 65), then descent – genealogy and the community of ancestors – accomplishes just that. It stretches time and space. It enables the conception of common identity with unknown others. Two strangers from different areas and different groups may encounter each other in a situation where they wish to engender a connection. A glass of tea and a genealogical discussion will bring them to a point where they discover a common ancestral link that allows them to consider themselves as kin. Once that happens then a whole blueprint of interaction is open to the participants in which rights and obligations are framed. Or not: it is equally possible that no such link is discoverable, and the participants in the discussion need have no obligation to each other.

What I hope is clear here is that genealogies should not be understood as reified social structures but as opportunities to create certain kinds of relationships and are therefore often shaped by, or deployed in the service of, other issues, so that social practices of inclusion or exclusion are the outcome, and not necessarily the cause, of any given situation. This has enormous significance for the explanation of a number of problems, because

---

57 If only for academic purposes (Holy 1996: 40–42; Edwards and Strathern 2000: 158).

social boundaries, themselves an academic construction rather than empirical reality (Amselle 1990; Carsten 2004: 12), are believed to inhibit the ability of the tribe to incorporate unknown others and hence to contribute directly to violence on the one hand and to inhibit the successful formation of the state on the other. Yet no tribe, or any other social group, is bound by a single set of delimiting relationships but consists rather of a series of relationships, these being, in the case of the ancient world, kinship, descent, residence, shared substances, tradition, and ritual (among other possibilities), that may be regarded as a web of integrative structures that form a system or network that is open-ended, as Elman Service in fact argued in 1962 (and cf. Giddens 1981; Amselle 1990) – unless something happens to close that network (Lesser 1961: 42; Dyson-Hudson 1972: 9; Marx 1977: 358; Dyson-Hudson and Dyson-Hudson 1980: 35–6; Giddens 1981: 160; and, for an operative example, Lancaster and Lancaster 1986: 43–4). To invoke the nature of the tribe, to assume its exclusionary basis as explanation, is to miss the essential research question of interest – what is going on that prompts the group to behave in an exclusionary, or inclusionary, way?

Kinship, descent, residence, shared substances, tradition, and ritual all provide rules and resources, as well as principles of organization, upon which actors draw in the constitution of society (Giddens 1984: 185). They are the rules and resources of social integration, they provide the basis of normative sanctions and a moral value system, and are therefore socio-civic rather than political in operation (contra Mafeje 1991: 14; Lentz 1995: 316, and indeed too many anthropologists to list), but they also create the identity of the individual and the group – although not necessarily in the bounded or monolithic way we assume. They are, in short, the way that tribes maintain social stability and order *apart from* the political institutions of government that *we* recognize as essential for those tasks, and they may vary immensely. The *political* organization so very often assumed as ensuing from those social relationships is in fact not consequent from them, but is contingent on a vast array of factors that are evident in the variety of political forms associated with ethnographic examples of the tribe, and the reason why a satisfactory definition was ever elusive (Mafeje 1971) and the quest for it ultimately abandoned.

New research, then, or the reexamination of older material,[58] shows that, if belonging to the tribe may be elective, crosscutting racial, linguistic, cultural, or religious ties; if delineations of group membership and boundaries are flexible and contingent while kinship itself encompasses social structures, ideologies, and practices in ways that are by no means necessarily coterminous and moreover only sometimes, and under very specific circumstances, substitute for political structure and practices; while the state embodies crosscutting networks of

---

58   For indeed Barth demonstrated this in 1961.

agents complicit[59] in the production of their society and government, then we are left not with any real forms that can be labeled tribe and state, but with disparate ideologies, practices, and principles that have connected and combined in widely variable ways, functioning equally variably (Porter 2010a). Certainly there is no necessary political outcome to the presence of kinship in any society, although the polity may be based in, use, or exploit kinship. Therefore the traditional dichotomy of tribe and state is in no way a valid heuristic device. And yet some of the concepts contained within these entities are unquestionably still pertinent and cannot be entirely abandoned.

The tribe, if one were to retain this term, should be defined as a set of *social* relationships based on idioms and/or practices of kinship and descent as the means through which people understand their place in society and the nature of their relationships with others. No necessary nature to that place, no necessary nature to those relationships, should be assigned, however, for each group may define both the rules that create their social relationships and the various ways in which they practice them as they wish. One may obviously therefore belong to a tribe and a state at the same time.[60]

And there is a point at which one does have to retain this term, if only because many groups that self-identify as tribes persist, however they came into being. Indeed, the United States has decreed by law that tribes exist (Colson 1986: 5), and what is more, the disparate features subsumed under this rubric show up so frequently that there seems little else that could describe those groups that carry them. This, I think, explains not only why the tribe has never left public, let alone popular, discussions, but also why it has crept back into academic discourse, especially that of archaeology. Nonetheless, the difficulties of this

59 "Complicit" here should not be read as willingly acceding to, or agreeing with, the political system in which people live. Rather, it indicates that how people live their lives, what they do, and what they think, all produce, directly and indirectly, consciously and unconsciously, the world in which they exist.

60 Notwithstanding academic convention that assumes the predominance of the latter obviates the former. The form of the state does not in any way dictate the forms of interaction that pertain between the people who live within it, even in the evolutionist models of anthropological archaeology, where political hierarchies not only coincide with social ones but are argued to be caused by them. This convergence, however, is the outcome of a history of Marxist thought on class. In any case, such hierarchies are not mutually exclusive to kinship, despite a popular equation of kinship with egalitarianism, nor with descent structures or practices, and descent may in fact contribute to them. Nearness to the eponymous ancestor of the tribe itself may be enough to afford higher status to one lineage branch over another. The other line of argument that renders kinship and state mutually exclusive, where state formation is assumed to be synonymous with urbanization, maintains that the increased population sizes and densities of cities in conjunction with the cohabitation of unrelated groups, either necessitated, or caused, the breakdown of kinship ties (e.g., Frangipane 2007/8: 174). As many ethnographic examples show, as discussed above, kinship and co-location are not mutually exclusive systems of attributing membership to the group.

terminology for the ancient world seem insuperable, both because the construct as applied to that world is itself false, and because to work with it even as redefined would require constant and too cumbersome qualification in order to prevent the specter of the old ways from reappearing. In any case, those relationships that are supposed to give evidence of the tribe in the ancient world, especially in the Mari texts, may, indeed must, be more precisely characterized, and in two ways. One way is in the ascertainment of whether it is a social or a political situation that is in evidence; the other is to determine whether it is a matter of ideology or practice that is at stake. In the case of the dual terminology of king and clan borne by Amorrite rulers of the Old Babylonian period discussed earlier in this chapter, it is a matter of both. Or, rather, of all of the above.

Here is the point of departure between my own understanding of the situation at Mari, and those of Fleming, Charpin, and Durand, who have explicated the complexity and significance of the Mari materials in ways to which I could never aspire. When Durand (2004) argues that as the Amorrites settled they abandoned the clanic identities employed by pastoralists for urban affiliations, save for those situations where the title of the kings represents "a souvenir of the ancient way of life" (as in the case of Sin-kashid, called the King of Uruk and of the Amnanum),[61] he is trying to reconcile what remain to him essentially contradictory entities. The King of Uruk is the epitome of the urban sedentary world; he is the state, and yet, as king of the Amnanum, a Yaminite group (Charpin 2004a: 108), he must be leader of another kind of entity altogether, something that sits apart from the state. To read Amnanum or even Amurru as an ethnicon (e.g., Kamp and Yoffee 1980) is one way of solving the problem, but the evidence simply does not support it (Marchesi 2006).

I would understand this practice of employing a double title a little differently. It does not represent two different worlds, the world of the sedentary state and that of the tribal polity, and where one identity gives way to the other, but rather different locations within the same world, locations shared by everybody. It is the recognition of two overlapping networks of interaction that are configured in different arenas and yet are not at all mutually exclusive, that can indeed from time to time completely coincide: those of polity and ancestral group identities. One is political, one social, and both represent identities that are current and ubiquitous, not only in the Old Babylonian period but throughout the fourth and third millennia as well. Their dual deployment in the manner of titulary of this kind is, however, entirely political, and indeed ideological.

61 And perhaps the King of Larsa and Father of Yamutbal, although these are considered two separate titles. For a discussion of the very complicated nature of the Larsa titulary see Chapter 4.

I use the term "ancestral group" here in a very specific sense: it approaches what many people mean by tribe without using any of the language associated with that concept, for words such as "tribe" and "clan" are so abused and misused, they carry so much inappropriate baggage (Mafeje 1971), that, while describing something essential, they have come to completely misrepresent what that essential something is: no more or less than one aspect or another, one level or another, of the kin-group. The term "ancestral group" has multiple associative levels. Those levels start with the extended family and/or household; while households comprise members unrelated by blood, the positions and functions of the unrelated people within it were nevertheless expressed in familial terms (Gelb 1979), and they end with the largest possible umbrella – common descent from an apical ancestor. The fact that descriptions of both tribe and ethnic group, and even to some extent the nation-state, have long been defined by the same elements – a name, a common ancestor, common history and memory (Smith 1991) – demonstrates this very issue: that forms of social interaction have no necessary political outcome, but may be subsumed by, deployed in, give rise to, a number of different political situations.

What does it mean, then, to be both leader of a polity and leader of an ancestral group? This does not represent two political entities brought together under one leader, nor is the leadership of the one, the polity, to be formulated in terms of the other, the ancestral group, in the manner of the patrimonial household as proposed by David Schloen (2001). A polity may incorporate many ancestral groups, although equally it may be synonymous with one. An ancestral group may encompass members who practice diverse subsistence practices, and who are dispersed over diverse locations and/or multiple polities, for there is no rule that says a family named together must stay together.

Perhaps a better question is this: what does it mean when one *identifies* oneself as both leader of a polity and leader of an ancestral group? Because identities can only be understood as contextualized: by the situation in which they are invoked and by those in light of whom they are presented. We should understand this assertion of identity on behalf of rulers such as Sin-kashid, King of Uruk and the Amnanum, and Zimri-Lim, King of Mari and the land of the Hana, as the product of a situation where identity is in question. It is possible that this may mean little more than a dynastic shift, an internal struggle for power; perhaps names and their history are not known, or not thought to be known. These kings as individuals are newcomers to the scene, and not because they are pastoralists, nor because they are Amorrites (who have been in evidence for quite some time by now), but because they are challengers, usurpers (or in some cases are themselves challenged). That Zimri-Lim was not the military commander who gained his own throne, but was installed there by a general as rightful heir, and that Sin-kashid was the founder of a new dynasty and his origins unknown (Charpin 2004a: 108 and see n. 435), suggest that each had his own concerns about legitimacy.

And yet it is more than that. What we see in the Mari texts is a situation where the very prominence of the ancestral group, mobile or sedentary, Yaminite, Numha, Simalite or Yamutbal, is an attestation to the inefficacy of the usual ties between members of a community, however that community may be defined by its members. Usually linkages between members of the group do not need explicit invocation; usually they are not tested as much as they seem to be in the Mari letters; when they are, it is often because the group concerned is at risk of fragmentation. Fragmentation might be assumed to have been the result of the continual warfare attested in the historical records of the early second millennium, but in fact this was probably no more intense than usual. In the third millennium, Mari was party to incessant conflicts involving Ebla, Nagar, and Kish (Archi and Biga 2003), not to mention whatever battles the ambition of Akkadian kings brought down upon it. Rather, I would suggest, this state of war was itself a product of the pressure under which various communities – some sedentary, some mobile, but especially when sedentary *and* mobile – were placed in a time of unusual fracture and fluidity. As groups experienced disruption through separation from their kin, from their home territories or resource base, and as groups came increasingly in contact with unknown others as competition grew, retraction and consolidation of group membership, boundaries, and identity might be expected, leading in turn to greater potential for conflict. In traditional reconstructions the Amorrites wreaked chaos and destruction in their movements across the "fertile crescent"; in more recent times they have been seen as themselves created by the dissolution of settlements impelled by factors beyond human control (Weiss and Courty 1993; Sallaberger 2007); in fact, to anticipate the conclusions of Chapter 4, it was the deliberate creation of fracture and fluidity within ancestral groups by human agency that gave rise to the entity we have come to define as the Amorrites.

The prominence of the ancestral group goes beyond the Mari archives however. In the land of the four riverbanks, in the prime period of "state formation" (from the Uruk period/Late Chalolithic until at least the end of the Old Babylonian period/Middle Bronze Age), structures and practices that have in the past been considered either tribal or statelike are found together within the same polity, in every polity that is closely examined. Kinship co-occurs with class and "king"; authority is equally engendered by and embedded in jurisprudence and tradition; bureaucracy exists, but serves specific and limited functions; sovereign territories and boundaries are no more defined in one form than another. It is for this reason that such classificatory difficulties, whether classification is appropriate or not, have always plagued discussions of the emergence of the state. I would therefore modify Yoffee's (2005: 41) rule, "if you can argue whether a society is a state or isn't, then it isn't," to the following: if a polity is in some lights a state, while in others it seems to be a tribe, then the entire concept should be revisited. If a complex society is one where interpersonal relations and sociopolitical structure are no longer grounded in horizontal and vertical ties of kinship, whether in practice or in ideology, but is based only on class divisions and institutional affiliations, then the evidence does not in fact indicate that ancient Near Eastern societies were structured in this way to the degree commonly assumed. What we have in the past interpreted as self-perpetuating and independent institutions are simply concretized versions of previously abstract social principles now operating in public domains. But those abstract social principles are still there. They still work, at both public and domestic levels.

There is, I would argue, a reason for this. And that is mobility. Not because pastoralists are tribal, but because the practices of kinship, among other things, facilitate the extension of both time and space so that those who are physically apart may remain conceptually together. No doubt the preexistence of kinship allowed for the practice of mobility, but mobility reproduced kinship in certain ways – primarily in the increased significance of genealogy and descent, variously constructed and deployed.

Ethnography, when treated properly, helps remove the blinkers that have long obscured evidence of such factors. Because as prevalent, but perhaps less obvious, as the examples of pastoralist raiding and extortion to be found in the ethnographic literature are the examples of the operation of deeply embedded, as well as temporally contingent, social structures and practices that allow for the maintenance of social ties over time and space (Galvin 2008).[62] The structures concerned are not particularly obscure – marriage rules and genealogies constitute two of the most powerful – but that they operate in this way becomes evident only when the situation arises that calls them into play.[63] The very essence of genealogy is the fact that it is entirely malleable – at least until it is written down (Shryock 1997; Eickelman 1998). It allows for the construction and deconstruction of social relationships whenever required. Marriage similarly allows for the creation and continuation of connections, and especially for the extension of social relationships across space. Rules of marriage and descent are not as reified as the codification of them in ethnography sometimes lures us into thinking. They are highly responsive to contingent circumstances and may be both consciously and unconsciously manipulated.

Together or separately, such structures and practices preserve relationships between groups that may have little or no contract throughout that time; they accommodate strangers within a descent and/or coresidence system (Irons 1974); they maintain social cohesion in groups split over subsistence practices

---

62   And see Galvin 2009 for further bibliography.
63   Kinship, for example, has become more important in post-Soviet Mongolia as a way of facilitating access to resources as centralized responses to pasture and crisis management have collapsed (Galvin 2008: 374–6).

(Humphrey 1979) or space (Marfoe 1979). They also have outcomes that shape both environment and landscape, so that these are not always determinative but are themselves subject to social process (Humphrey et al. 1999; Frachetti 2008). These examples do not provide any sort of rules as to ancient behavior. I would not want simply to replace one set of ethnographic analogies with another. But they should serve to sensitize the modern scholar to the hints in the evidence that these kinds of structures and practices might have been in place in the past.[64] The point is this: social relationships do not necessarily break under adverse circumstances but rather may stretch and adapt, shift and retract – frequently in order to include unrelated groups rather than exclude them – and any number of structures, practices, and ideologies exist that may accomplish this. In the ancient Near East inclusion/exclusion is wrought, among other things, by the powers of the divine or, rather, the other worlds, for the dead are equally engaged in manipulating these relationships, and in countering as well as construing the reality of actual blood relations.

64　See Wossink 2009 for just such a study.

CHAPTER TWO

WOOL, WRITING, AND RELIGION

The intersection between the dead, the divine, mobility, sociopolitical structure, and indeed, intellectual history, is nowhere clearer than in discussions of a site called Arlsantepe, located in the Malatya plain just west of the Euphrates River in southern Turkey (Frangipane 2001, 2002; Fig. 1). Occupied from the mid-fifth through third millennia, it is the latter part of this period that provides the starting point for my discussion of mobile pastoralism and its significance in the emerging sociopolitical constructions that characterize later millennia. It is here that complexities of both the situation on the ground and the templates of the mind are most apparent, and they are encapsulated particularly in the discourse about a single tomb.

Commonly called "royal" (Frangipane et al. 2001), this tomb lies alone at the edge of the site (Fig. 3) as it was at the beginning of the third millennium (Arslantepe level VIB2; Table 3), a thriving village consisting of houses and their related productive activities according to the excavator, Marcella Frangipane (Frangipane 2007/8: 174-6). Frangipane suspects that the tomb was built in, or even slightly before, an earlier phase of this village (VIB2a) when it consisted only of a fortified hilltop (as created by the preceding levels of occupation), constructed slightly ahead of the expansion of settlement outside the walls (Fig. 3) and over the rest of the mound (VIB2b; cf. Palumbi 2008: 149, 153 who prefers to see the tomb as built before the wall).

The village of this level, level VIB2, is considered a devolution of the urban heights reached in preceding phases of the site, especially, in terms of population density, that of level VII, dating to the early to mid-fourth millennium, while the so-called Palatial Period, level VIA, dating to the late fourth millennium, is claimed as the apex of sociopolitical complexity. It was in this latter period that Arslantepe was clearly in contact with southern Mesopotamia in some way. Level VIA was destroyed by fire and replaced by an ephemeral camp-site (level VIB1) considered characteristic of Transcaucasian mobile pastoralists

Table 3. Arslantepe Stratigraphy

Date	Level	Description
3800–3500	VII	Most extensive occupation, contains "elite" building and "ceremonial" building
3500–3000	VIA	"Palatial" period, with Temples A, B, and "residential shrine"
3000–2900	VIB1	Two phases of wattle and daub structures, postholes, and possibly the "royal tomb" (my scheme)
2900–2800	VIB2a	"Fortified hilltop" Construction of "royal tomb" (Frangipane's scheme)
	VIB2b	Village of domestic structures

(Palumbi 2007/8) before the fortification walls of VIB2a were built. In this transition from palace to village, architectural features characterized as public and urban gave way to ones labeled domestic, and burials, previously found under the floors of buildings, disappeared altogether with the exception of the stone-built "royal tomb."

The richness of this tomb, then, might seem all the more surprising given that this period of occupation is characterized as neither "complex" in contrast to the preceding fourth millennium levels nor even urban. The single inhumation inside the stone-lined cist grave (Fig. 4),[1] a primary, articulated male thirty-five to forty-five years of age, was accompanied by only fifteen pots but by considerable quantities of metals in copper, silver, and copper-silver alloy, including pins, bracelets, beads, a belt, and weapons. Remaining traces of organic materials indicate that the body had been wrapped in a cloth and placed on a wooden board, and there was also some sort of beaded garment over the head and torso (Frangipane et al. 2001). But the most remarkable attribute of this burial was not what was *in*side the tomb, but what was *out*side: the bodies of four adolescents graced its roof, and depositional history as well as palaeo-pathological evidence indicate they may have been sacrificed (Porter n.d.).

These four individuals were represented by two full and two partial skeletons placed in pairs at each end of the tomb. Lying on top of the tomb lid itself is a complete female and a partial body that the palaeo-pathologists (Schultz and Schmidt-Schultz in Frangipane et al. 2001) suggest is male.[2] On a slightly higher earthen ledge around the lid is a parallel pair, although both bodies here are female. Skeletal analysis shows that all bodies had suffered some degree of trauma, but whether that trauma was cause of death is not entirely clear. However, the Arslantepe team was persuaded that these individuals were the victims of sacrifice by the position of the bodies: all gave some indication that

---

1 A cist grave is a small pit dug into the earth that is lined with, and capped by, stone slabs.
2 Given the lack of any substantial evidence to confirm this suspicion, and in light of certain patterns presented by these bodies, to be discussed in detail shortly, I think it is quite likely the individual identified as male was in fact female.

Arslantepe

Level VIB2

Fortified
Hilltop

"Royal" Tomb T1
Level VIB1? VIB2?

Village

3. Plan of Level VIB2 Arslantepe with village, fortified hilltop, and "royal" tomb. Redrawn with the kind permission of authors, from Frangipane et al. 2001: fig. 2, and Frangipane et al. 2009: fig. 2.

0   10 m

they may possibly have been standing or kneeling before being pushed down, with varying degrees of force, face forward onto the tomb (Frangipane et al. 2001: 111, 129). Reinforcing this image is the fact that the hands of three of the figures are very close together and in front of the face, perhaps indicating that they had been bound.[3]

But there are further levels of intrigue to unfold here. The male/female pair on the lid of the tomb were wearing diadems in copper-silver alloy, an unusual amalgamation, while the male inhumation inside the tomb was equipped with a belt (or perhaps another diadem) in this metal and both were decorated in the same manner. The male/female pair wore veils, traces of which still remained,

3   Although it should be noted that hands in front of the nose is also the attitude of prayer.

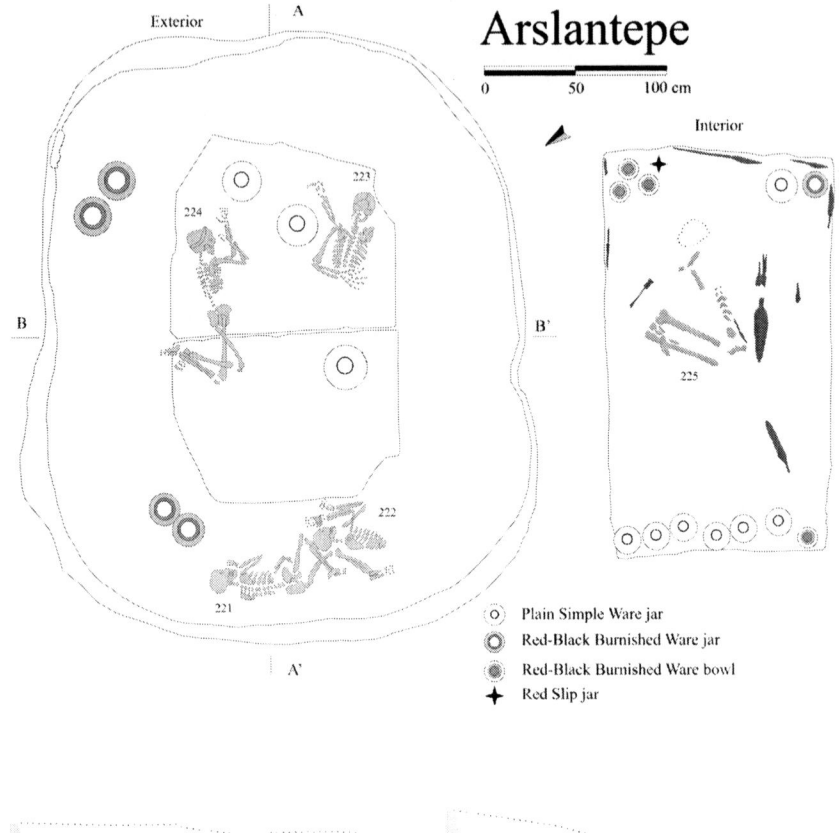

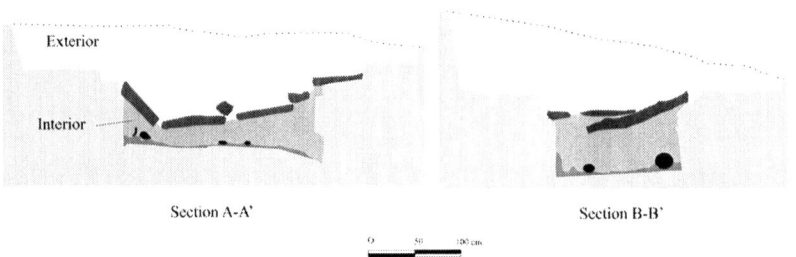

4. The "royal" tomb at Arslantepe, with exterior deposition, interior deposition, and sections. Redrawn, with the kind permission of authors, from Frangipane et al. 2001.

and cloth was also found on the two pins that each of them was wearing. The high concentration of limestone beads in the vicinity suggested that, like the paramount inhumation, these two individuals were also wearing beaded garments of some sort (Frangipane et al. 2001: 109).

The female bodies on the ledge around the tomb's lid were unadorned. But they were associated with a distinctive type of pottery, Red-Black Burnished Ware, a handmade ware that has been the object of much attention (Sagona 1984; Marro 2007; Palumbi 2007/8, 2008). Four pots of this material were placed on the ledge in two pairs (Fig. 4), one near the head of the intact female, the other on the ledge above the intact female on the roof (Frangipane et al. 2001: 112). Next to the bodies lying directly on the roof of the tomb were three

wheel-made vessels belonging to the "Late Reserved Slip" assemblage characteristic of the Euphrates from southern Turkey to northern Syria.[4]

This distinction in pottery wares has been attributed great interpretative significance, and – along with other elements of the mortuary material
including the metals, the tomb type, and, as well, the human remains – is considered to represent the intersection of two quite separate cultures: one "local
Mesopotamian-type culture" and the other "Eastern Anatolian/Transcaucasian
culture" (Frangipane et al. 2001: 113; Frangipane 2007/8: 181), with the latter originating in, or related to, the Kura-Araxes culture (Palumbi 2007/8). The
former is associated with the "original," urban, complex polity of the late fourth
millennium, the "Palatial period," when contacts with southern Mesopotamia
were at their apogee, the latter, with the indigenous, mobile populations
of the mountains who are assumed to have succeeded, if not destroyed, the
settlement of the former. In some way or another, these two groups, then, are
present in the tomb in the following goods: spearheads, the abovementioned
Late Reserved Slip as well as Plain Simple Wares are "Mesopotamian"; allocated to the Transcaucasian/Kura-Araxan sphere are the double-spiral pins,
spiral hair rings, copper-silver alloy belt and diadems (that is, the very clothes
that three of the five members wear), metal vessels, axes, chisels, gouges, and,
last but by no means least, the stone-lined cist itself (Frangipane et al. 2001;
Palumbi 2007/8: 152).

Two basic scenarios, with all the required caveats (such as Frangipane et al.
2001: 112, n. 5), have been proposed to explain this conjunction. In scenario
one, the tomb represents the last vestige of the urban elite from the Palatial
period (Frangipane et al. 2001). As is the nature of nomads, their presence at
the site after the destruction of the palace was transitory, with the subsequent
inhabitants resuming the pottery traditions and other cultural attributes of
their world before it was interrupted, although not, apparently, the centralized
institutions that characterized the urban period. The body inside the tomb is a
king,[5] and two of the bodies outside the tomb are closely related to him, probably blood kin, certainly of high status, as they wear the same kind of costume.
The other two bodies, then, are the servants of the adolescents laid out on top
of the tomb (Frangipane 2007/8: 176), maybe even captured Transcaucasian
slaves, for they are seen as placed at the feet of the other two and are lacking
material signs of status.

In this case, the quantitative dominance of material attributes considered
Transcaucasian (and therefore as belonging to a mobile population) is subsumed under a set of deeply ingrained, but little interrogated, associations that
equate levels of material substantiality with levels of sociopolitical complexity,

---

4   And which seems to come to an end around the vicinity of Qara Quzak (Porter 2007b).
5   Although in the 2007/8 publication Frangipane is more inclined to refer to "chiefs."

which allows Frangipane (2007/8: 184) to state that this very important personage "mainly used the symbols referring to the traditional cultural world of
Uruk origin." The solidity of construction of the tomb, which is itself acknowledged to be alien to the Euphrates valley in its basic design, the high status
that a wealth of grave goods automatically infers, the presence of anything
"Mesopotamian," even if it is only a dozen or so pots in Reserved Slip Ware,
seem to require a sedentary urban background for their conceptualization if
not production. At the same time, the presence of features thought indicative of
pastoralists, such as the Red-Black Burnished Wares and metallurgic tradition,
are found at least as early as the last phases of level VII (Frangipane 2002: 127;
Frangipane et al. 2001: 135). There was, ergo, an economic interaction between
pastoralists and town dwellers throughout that time, that "must therefore have
been, at least partly, a peaceful phenomenon, perhaps breaking out into conflict
at times, as always occurs in relations between nomadic and sedentary peoples
living in and exploiting the same territory" (Frangipane et al. 2001: 136). Just
as Frangipane describes the relations between mobile and sedentary groups as
an oscillating power struggle (Frangipane 2007/8: 186–91), so she herself oscil-
lates between seeing the paramount burial as that of a Mesopotamian king or
a Transcaucasian chief in origin. In either case, the materiality of this tomb
represents two distinct cultural, ethnic, and subsistence groups.

In scenario two, the question of sacrifice is disregarded.[6] In this reconstruction the paramount burial is still local to Arslantepe (Palumbi 2008: 152),
but here the elite of the site have incorporated the material attributes of an
expanding culture with which they have increasing contact. As Uruk waned,
Kura-Araxes waxed, and those who chose allegiance to one or the other were
in contest. The essence of the problem for Palumbi, who espouses this second
view,[7] is also the question of material wealth and sociopolitical hierarchy, for
the Arslantepe tomb, always called a "royal" tomb, is "clearly a prestige and rank
burial" (Palumbi 2007/8: 152; Palumbi 2008: 148).[8] The Kura-Araxes burial
tradition, as fitting a mobile, kin-based society, does not manifest distinctions
in individual status and power, but rather exemplifies a family-based ethos, and
so there is a problem attributing the inhabitants of the tomb to this culture.
At the same time, since power in the Mesopotamian tradition was vested in
"religious, administrative and maybe even peaceful traits," and the Arslantepe
tomb includes weapons, its occupant must be (a) a warrior (also Frangipane
et al. 2001) and (b) a member of the ruling elite of local pastoralists. In which
case, it must be an elite that adopted the mortuary practices of what was now

6   Although cf. Palumbi 2008: 153, where it is evidence of a coup – an intriguing idea but not
     warranted by the stratigraphy of the tomb deposition itself – as will be discussed in detail
     in Chapter 3.
7   And substantially followed by Frangipane in the conclusion to her 2007/8 article.
8   Although in this latter publication the paramount burial is a chief rather than a king.

the more powerful tradition to differentiate themselves from the residual urban power groups, while at the same time employing imagery of the previous era. The use of Mesopotamian pot styles and the placement of the tomb on top of the mound were both means to claiming legitimate power.

However, this explanation still begs as many questions as it answers about material culture and identity, mortuary practices, and mobility, not to mention the extraordinary (Porter n.d.) act of sacrifice apparently in evidence. I suggest that the choice is in fact "none of the above." Such dualities not only obscure what is really going on, but are not necessitated by the material culture of the tomb in any way. Part of the problem is that material culture is treated only as a direct representation of an actual social and cultural situation. It is not understood as available to be manipulated in the accomplishment of ideas and goals, or deployed in the production of identity in ways that have nothing to do with status. The other part of the problem is that the anthropological model, especially where materiality implicitly means hierarchy, is so powerful in Near Eastern studies that many anomalies are subsumed by it. In this model, grave goods are indicative of social status, while solidity equals stability and ephemerality equals mobility. In fact, the two ceramic types, Reserved Slip Ware and Red-Black Burnished Ware, are commonly found together in cemeteries and settlements near Arslantepe and beyond (Palumbi 2007/8), and equally significantly, *both* are associated with the occupation levels of the so-called Palatial period; and yet at the same time the presence of Red-Black Burnished Ware in this tomb is considered to represent a new condition. A similar situation is also apparent for the metal work. There are clear connections with the metal production of the Transcaucasian culture, but some of these pieces are "practically identical" to those found in Building III of the earlier level VIA (Frangipane and Palmieri 1983: Fig. 4, 403; Frangipane et al. 2001: 113; Frangipane 2007/8). Two avenues of theoretical concern emerge here: the way we think about the evolution/development of pottery assemblages in particular and cultural assemblages in general, and the way we think about the relationship between those assemblages and their producers.

Another is an understanding of burial practices that privileges the political over the cosmological. At the same time, the careful, even patterned, placement of certain items in, on, and around the tomb is acknowledged, as is the fact that the burial was accompanied by a ritual of complex dimensions. This placement includes not only the four adolescents, but also the metals set in the corners and along the walls of the chamber, and pots, grouped according to ware in discrete positions in relation to the body. That the practices resulting in such deposition may be associated with fundamental conceptions of life, death, and the nature of the universe – that is, religion – rather than ethnic identity or social status is unconsidered, as is the possibility that such ritual practices, because they embody and enact cosmological conceptions, are both deeply entrenched in tradition and integrally related to personal and group identity. This has major implications for the intent and meaning implicit in the act of sacrificing the four individuals that comprise part of the burial. Palumbi (2007/8: 152–6, 160), though, is quite comfortable suggesting that a group of people living at Arslantepe, heirs of the fourth millennium tradition, suddenly abandoned their own religious beliefs and practices for the sake of political power, without recognizing that religion completely imbricates with politics and power, whatever the nature of one's culture.

An additional twist lies in this notion of "Mesopotamianism." It is in the Palatial period that contact with the south is manifest in some imported goods – not in fact more than the supposedly Transcaucasian materials present in this level – and one of the very distinctive features of this phase is argued to be the evidence for indigenous complexity (Frangipane 2001, 2002). Unlike the case at other northern settlements that manifest contact with the south at this time, Arslantepe was not particularly influenced by southern culture nor was its "urban" nature generated by it, as it was already in existence, and with comparable large-scale buildings, in the previous level; so the main competing assemblages here are both local, or at least northern, in origin. Reserved Slip Ware seems increasingly to have been indigenous to this Upper Euphrates region (Dessine 2008: 21; Porter 2007b).

The problems disappear, though, if instead of understanding the tomb and its constituents as two separate bodies of material culture representing two separate cultural and ethnic groups either successive to each other or coterminous, we approach it from another direction altogether, one where the data, and not the established model, form the basis of interpretation (and cf. Bernbeck and Pollock 2002). There are two ways one might follow this path to understanding the burial at Arslantepe: one is in the disposition of the burial itself, the other is in its temporal context, the context not just of Arslantepe, but of the situation in the fourth millennium as a whole. It is during this period that several significant transformations are thought to take place, transformations that result in the very situation that is the theme of this book.

Because many of the issues here have a long history, both in terms of academic tradition and in terms of sociopolitical relationships established at least seven hundred years before the tomb is built, it makes some sense to start at the beginning of this history, in order to arrive at a nuanced understanding of the final manifestation of those relationships within the burial, the discussion of which will not now resume until the beginning of Chapter 3. Despite being the object of concentrated research for some decades, the fourth millennium BCE (the so-called Uruk period[9] of the Mesopotamian past) remains a time of both

---

9   And see Butterlin 2003 for a critique both of the label and the definition of an Urukean cultural assemblage.

obscurity and mystique. And yet to it are now attributed the defining moments of human history (Pollock 1992: 297) – the emergence of the city (Adams 1981), the advent of the state (Wright and Johnson 1975), and the introduction of the first forms of writing (Nissen et al. 1993), seen as an integral part of the development of a highly structured and systematized economy (Algaze 2001, 2008). Although common sense would indicate that these events all in some way relate to the apparently explosive growth of the ancient city of Uruk at this time (Finkbeiner 1991) and the reason this period bears its name, the fact remains that we have little direct archaeological evidence for much that is claimed for the site (Nissen 2001) and little understanding of how the events themselves came about.

One thing has always seemed clear. All these innovations are, like the growth of Uruk itself, somehow rooted in the landscape of Mesopotamia and therefore its economy – that is, in the intensive cultivation of cereals through irrigation. This fundamental premise is the traditional inheritance of the field of Near Eastern archaeology, and one that remains largely unchallenged. It underpins explanations of what is actually the best attested – and most distinctive – of the Uruk phenomena: the apparent expansion of the people of Uruk into realms far from southern Mesopotamia.

Identification of the "Uruk expansion" is in the first place based on the widespread distribution throughout Syria, Iran, and Turkey (Fig. 8) – and even as far as Middle Egypt, the shores of the Caspian Sea, and Pakistan – of the many distinctive features of material culture that archaeologists believe to have originated in the south (although this is now, pot by pot, under challenge). Perhaps the best known and most distinctive, and certainly most ubiquitous, object, is the beveled-rim bowl, the function of which is still disputed. In addition, the transported Uruk assemblage contains many elements, ranging from specialized ceramics such as vessels with drooping spouts (Fig. 5) to architectural features such as the use of offset buttressing and wall cones for decoration. The complexity and extent of this assemblage, not to mention its geographic range, defies explanations based simply on trade, diffusion, or even imitation. Moreover, its distribution is not uniform, and that has made it difficult to develop a coherent theory of expansion that successfully accounts for all variation. While we speak of this assemblage and the expansion as Urukean, we simply do not yet know if Uruk was the sole center contributing to this situation, or if other southern cities were involved.[10]

---

10   Schwartz 1988, 2001: 235; see Pollock 2001 for the complexity of this issue. Consensus seems to be forming around the idea that there were multiple southern settlements involved (such as Forest 1999; Stein 2001a: 302). While I would prefer therefore to use "south" to encompass the possibility of multiple sources of the expansion, but which should by no means be taken as indicating a unified process, the use of "Uruk" to define the southern material assemblage found in the north and east is so ubiquitous as to be unavoidable.

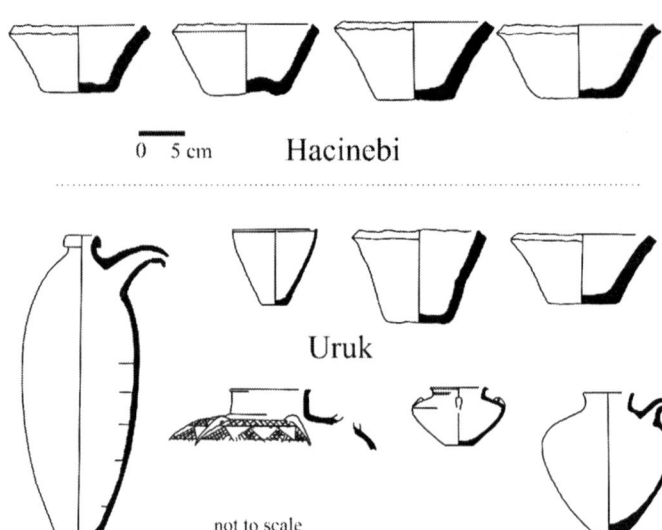

0   5 cm   Hacinebi

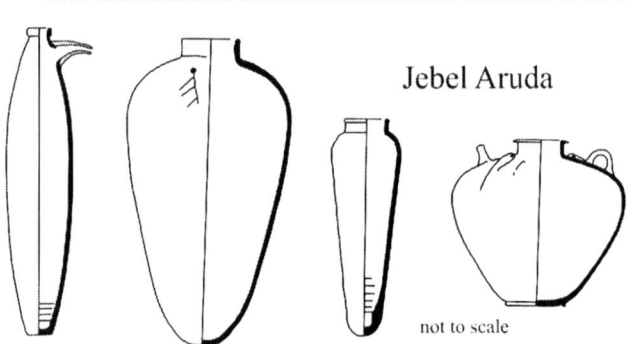

5. Ceramic elements of the Uruk assemblage. Hacinebi, redrawn from Stein 2002; Uruk, redrawn from Nissen 2001; Jebel Aruda, redrawn from van Driel 2002.

Uruk material culture is found embedded in these regions in what Guillermo Algaze (2001) has classified as essentially three ways (with variations):

Type 1: as a more or less complete, free-standing cultural assemblage, including architecture, artifacts, administrative technology, and artistic motifs;

Type 2: as a discrete assemblage of major elements of Uruk material culture – primarily pottery – found within or near local settlements;

Type 3: the presence of some elements of Uruk material culture – again primarily pottery – found distributed either randomly or uniformly through local settlements.

It is the first type, found at the site of Habuba Kabira South in the Middle Euphrates region and at Susa in Iran, that has occasioned so much interest. Habuba Kabira comprised a complete walled city, with an associated religious complex located high on the top of the nearby mountain, Jebel Aruda. From the first, Habuba was interpreted by Eva Strommenger (1980) and Dietrich Sürenhagen (1978, 1986) as a colony – a group of actual Urukeans who established a duplicate of their home city far from their point of origin. It is Algaze's explanation of this situation, however, and its relationship to the subsequent development of the state, that is best known. Basing his argument on the world systems model of Immanuel Wallerstein (Algaze 2005 [first published in 1993]), Algaze proposed that the more developed south had an insatiable need for resources not contained in its homelands, especially metals. These resources were required to maintain the power and position of burgeoning elites as much as for the satisfaction of more basic needs. The south – Uruk – moved out to obtain them, encountering little resistance in the less developed north. By adding value to raw resources, which were then channeled back as finished goods to the cooperating groups in the north, the impetus for state formation in the hinterlands of Mesopotamia was initiated. Emerging elites were thus created and supported by access to the finished goods; at the same time further development was stifled by dependence on the southerners (cf. Peregrine 1996: 3; Rothman 2002: 58), so northern states could not attain the true complexity of the south.

In this scenario, specific sites had specific relationships to the resources at stake – some were for direct control, some were for extraction, others shipping entrepôts – but all were tied to the control of exchange, either by indigenous communities or by intrusive ones. Not only that, but most sites with Uruk materials were nodes within the same system. For example, Hacinebi, excavated by Gil Stein (1999a, 1999b) and located east of the Euphrates in Turkey, was considered by Algaze to be the home of middlemen who lived in a separate quarter from the locals, and since the site was set away from resources it must have served as an entrepôt. Arslantepe, where southern imports are found side by side with locally made copies, served for the indigenous control of metal extraction. The presence in the Middle Euphrates of Habuba Kabira South and earlier in the same region Sheikh Hassan, because they were walled colonies, are argued to have a coercive function in persuading local communities to give up their goods in an unequal exchange. As a correction to the various criticisms leveled at the world systems model, Algaze subsequently proposed (Algaze 2001: 49)[11] that variations in distribution of Uruk materials correlate with the nature of the indigenous communities the colonists encountered, ranging from mobile pastoralists to incipient states. The particular nature of observed settlement patterns is, he argues, a classic example of control structures that inhibit the range of choices open to indigenous communities and that are typical of colonialist exploitation of subordinate groups.

If colonialism was the basis of our understanding of the Uruk expansion in the 1980s, where the polity of Uruk dominated this far-flung region in order to fulfill its needs, then postcolonialism, or rather one small aspect of the diverse body of theory that word now covers (Patterson 2008; Featherstone

11   See also Stephen and Peltenburg 2002; Algaze 2008.

2005; Ahluwalia 2001; Dirlik 1994), provided the basis for the challenge to it in the nineties.[12] The focus then was on the need for a better understanding of the colonized. Archaeological attention was directed to the sites in the so-called periphery and energetic arguments have been made, not for relations of dependence in the hinterland, but for autonomy and power in the north (such as McMahon and Oates 2007) – that several if not all of the sites with which Uruk engaged were sufficiently developed that they could encounter the south on their own terms. Mitchell Rothman, for example (2002: 58), argues that the north was almost as highly developed as the south, that the Uruk expansion is simply an increase in long-standing systems of exchange (also Frangipane 2001; Oates et al. 2007; cf. Butterlin 2003), and that north and south benefited alike – or at least those seeking to establish and hold power in each area benefited. The most sustained critique of Algaze's interpretation of the Uruk expansion, however, has come from Gil Stein, worked through the results of his excavations at Hacinebi. Stein (1999a, 1999b, 2001a, 2005a, 2005b) argues that southern cities could not possibly have sustained a position of dominance so far from any effective means to enforce it, and so the sequestered enclaves of Uruk materials seen at sites such as Godin Tepe and, apparently, Hacinebi itself do not represent colonial overlords, but trade diasporas that were permitted by local authorities to establish small outposts at these sites because the benefits of such a situation reinforced the status of local elites (and cf. Lupton 1996).

Such positions seem to me in the long run simply defensive, and the shift from asymmetric to symmetric exchange as the foundation of the relationship between north and south merely perpetuates the same one-dimensional construct of power as previously pertained. The essential interest lies not in who dominated whom, but in how interaction changed the nature of existence for people living in both areas[13] in whatever domain we may access such experience: economy, religion, society. Postcolonialism, in breaking down traditional, binary categorizations – us/them,[14] south/north, public/private, center/periphery, dominant/subaltern, civilized/uncivilized – allows us to move toward an understanding of the multiple outcomes of contact (Dirlik 1994) between peoples defined on both sides by a concatenation of interests, including (but by no means limited to) class, gender, ethnicity, and culture. If postcolonialism is

---

12 See Butterlin 2003 for a comprehensive summary of the divergent positions and Ur 2010 for the most recent overview.

13 A central problem for which, whatever its eventual acceptance, Algaze 2005 [1993] did provide an explanation.

14 With the "us" most often referring to the modern West, the inheritors of all that the advent of civilization brought. Indeed, it might be argued that the entire debate on the Uruk period perpetuates modern-world colonial (and materialist) relationships by focusing on issues of concern to academics embedded in Western capitalism (Spivak 1988; Bahrani 2003), to whom economics and assymetrical power relations are central.

to enrich the discussion as fully as it might, many issues other than the agency and autonomy of the indigenous should be considered.

Simon Featherstone (2005: 7) summarizes the key concerns of postcolonialism today as "nationhood, cultural identity and hybridity; the effects of and responses to diaspora, a questioning of inherited, colonial-influenced historical narratives and essentialist descriptions of race." Substitute "state formation" for "nationhood," and "ethnicity" for "race," and these are, or should be, the central problems of the Uruk period. For the sake of this discussion, however, the inherited colonial narratives are not those of the Mesopotamians themselves,[15] but rather a more contemporary form of colonialism, where "the heartland" (Adams 1981) of civilization, southern Mesopotamia, is appropriated as the very origin of Western civilization (Bahrani 2003: 35) and where archaeologists of the north, Syria, and Anatolia have long felt themselves the subaltern,[16] ignored by the hegemonic discourse.

Although the focus in postcolonialism was initially on this discourse (Said 1978) and centered on the analysis of text – that is, what colonizer and colonized say about themselves and each other, how writing constructs difference – more recent postcolonial studies have turned to concepts of practice and materiality (Parry 2002; Featherstone 2005) in a particularly serendipitous turn for archaeology. Practice theory (Bourdieu 1990 [1980]; Giddens 1979), where action produces and reproduces the social structures and interactions that shape agency, is increasingly the basis of understanding the production of archaeological remains, the construction of identity, and the process of change (Dietler and Herbich 1998; Dobres and Robb 2000; Porter 2010b). Materiality, variously defined as the physicality of matter (Boivin 2008) or the social relations between things and people (Tilley 2007) has become for a small group of practitioners the means of understanding both the complexity of objects themselves and the complexity of the social and political relationships embodied in the things we make (and which make us, in ways that transcend the economic relationships these things were once thought merely to represent). Just as text, therefore, so too material culture may be a conscious and unconscious articulation of identity, offering an advantage that text, the traditional locus of postcolonial studies, does not. It provides evidence of "the material realities" (Patterson 2008) of life. This is in fact the basis of one critique of postcolonialism – that there

15 Or at least not in this particular instance. As will become evident in Chapter 4, however, there is a part of the problem that does involve an ancient indigenous Mesopotamian narrative that can be construed as essentially colonialist.

16 Although not entirely accurately. As with postcolonialism in general, there is now a wide range of usages attached to this word, but I mean it as Spivak (1988) does, to denote those situated outside hegemonic power structures, rather than those at the bottom of them, who are nevertheless still able to negotiate within them. Archaeologists working in Syria and Turkey certainly labor within the hegemonic discourse as they endeavor to turn it their way.

is a wide gap between the voice of a writer and his or her actual situation in life. Literature can resist at the same time as the writer is oppressed, but studies of material culture allow for the possibility of seeing both states of being at the same time.[17] Such studies reveal material culture to be both a source of, and a locus in which, discrimination, differentiation, and hybridity are engaged through discursive practices (Webster 1997). And it is the twinned concepts of differentiation and hybridity that form the basis of most archaeological appropriations of postcolonialism.

Too often, though, Homi Bhabha's initial intention in delineating these concepts is lost in archaeological treatments. Based on the understanding that culture is neither "primordial" nor "homogenous" but is continually interpreted, appropriated, and contested by multiple entities within any given society (a perspective I share), Bhabha (1994) argues that, in order to exert control, the colonial authority maps out and reinforces discriminatory patterns of difference. Colonialism "requires the production ... of identity effects through which discriminatory practices can map out subject populations that are tarred with the visible ... mark of power" (Bhabha 1994: 111). Rather than resulting in a simple domination and thereby repression of the colonized, the practices and processes of discrimination result in hybridity, where the intersection of different ways of reading what would be the materials of authority both perverts the colonialist intent and empowers the colonized. And so the subaltern gaze frames the colonizer even as the colonizer would pin the subaltern to a board like a butterfly: captured, categorized, and thereby controlled.[18]

Bhabha (1994) exemplifies this by describing the British ploy of distributing free bibles in Hindi, with the aim of converting the natives to Christianity so that they would then reject their own culture and accept their place in the empire. Indians would perceive that the British and God were, if not synonymous, at least hand in hand, and would thus embrace the rightness of British ways. But instead the "natives" brought their own understanding to their engagement with the Hindi bibles; for in accepting that they were indeed a gift from God, the very possibility of their association with the British was rejected. The British contravened the laws of God by eating meat and could not therefore be in any way party to His gift. And so the intent of the British was appropriated and subverted.

A rather different example may be drawn from a context somewhat closer in time and space to this discussion. The discovery many years ago of a monumental building at Tell Brak (Mallowan 1947) bearing bricks stamped with the "divine" name of Naram-Sin – that is, ^{d}*na-ra-am*-^{d}**en.zu**, where ^{d} stands for **dingir**, the sign

---

17 Although there is no question, this is a matter easier said than done, as will be seen below.
18 Not coincidentally, the very mission of much archaeology is to capture, categorize, and control.

indicating the bearer belongs in the other world[19] – presents just such a moment of hybridity. Naram-Sin appears to have been the first king we know of to be deified within his own lifetime. But **dingir** as a determinative was applied to human names in the north before the advent of Akkad (Archi 2001), as an indicator of ancestral status. Although the chronology of events is not yet secure enough to know whether Naram-Sin was already considered divine when this building was constructed, or whether in seeking to dominate the north he appropriated a symbol that situated him within a local historical discourse, never intending to represent himself as a god, it is clear that this symbol of authority had different meanings to different constituencies both past and present (Porter 2010b), transforming not only relations of power, but also culture, in each. The notion of the divine king, although never naturalized as it was in Egypt, becomes part of the discourse of rule in Mesopotamia (Bernbeck 2008b; Michalowski 2008).

Hybridity, then, is not the mere melding of technical influences, differentiation, delineating differences in style, but where "the structure of meaning and reference [is an] ambivalent process" (Bhabha 1994: 37) and where resistance is always implicit.[20] The cultural constructs thus reached in the intersection of multiple meanings in a single sign – or as Bhabha puts it, the revaluing of symbols – constitute a third space: something that is neither one thing nor the other, but that draws on both to become something else again, something new. The third space is, to many scholars, now one of the defining hallmarks of colonialism, but one recent writer on the topic, Chris Gosden, argues that hybridization "implies the meeting and then changing of *fixed* identities" (Gosden 2004: 69; my italics), and it is therefore an inappropriate concept prior to the sixth century BCE because identities were very fluid until then. Many postcolonial theorists would question, though, whether such identities have been construed as more fixed than they actually were (Young 1995), and Bhabha himself certainly would not require identities to be fixed as much as differentiated, a subtly different condition. In the case of the Uruk period, we should not confuse the notion of "fixed," or even "differentiated," with "defined." Northern communities had definable indigenous identities partly produced by previous experiences of culture contact such as in the Ubaid (Henrickson and Thuessen 1989; Frangipane 1997, 2001; Butterlin 2003; Stein and Özbal 2007). So did southern communities. These were never fixed, as no identity is, but were constantly in the process of production.

To Gosden (2004: 41–81), then (and cf. Butterlin 2003), this means that northern and southern identities were much the same thing, for this is "a point

---

19   Traditionally known as the "divine determinative" necessitating that the bearer was a god, more nuanced understandings now acknowledge that this sign may be applied to a range of other worldly beings, such as demons, ancestors, and so on (Pongratz-Leisten 2011).

20   Of course, the meaning of hybridity is a prominent topic of debate within postcolonial studies. Compare, for example, Young 1995 and Kapchan and Turner Strong 1999.

in time where a shared cultural milieu united essentially similar peoples over a broad area." Yet the only way we can know if people across the ancient Near East were similar at this time or not is through material culture. And since the appearance of shared cultural milieu was arguably the product of the Uruk expansion (especially if the expansion is viewed as the exercise of economic and political dominance), we are left with something of a dilemma. Moreover, diverse sociopolitical identities may well be subsumed within an apparent material unity; rather than creating *social* unity, shared culture may itself constitute repression, while differentiation is resistance. But for most archaeologists grappling with this problem, the fact is that the recognition of a phenomenon that might be labeled "Uruk" is no more or less than the recognition of a set of material attributes that had a point of origination and a sphere of distribution in space *rendered visible against a backdrop of difference*. That is, the whole Uruk expansion is only knowable because its materials are unlike those of the northern Late Chalcolithic cultures (Stein 2005b: 162),[21] and those differences remained evident in some places over extraordinarily long periods of time.[22]

Yet it is not as simple as this, as the viewing of Uruk material culture through the lens of hybridity will show. For one thing, the question of the material manifestations of identity is a vexed one, as every archaeologist will acknowledge (S. Smith 2003). Just how do people make, use, and deploy material culture in terms of identity and how does the experience of making, using, and deploying material culture shape identity? There is no one-to-one relationship between artifact and sociopolitical organization, or between artifact and identity, let alone artifact and culture; people can adopt a new material repertoire while remaining ideologically or politically the same, just as people may maintain their traditional material repertoire while profoundly altering the way they think and behave. The entire discussion of the Uruk period remains at best mechanical, at worst meaningless, without significant theorizing as to some of these issues. Stein's (1999b, 2001a, 2005b)[23] description of the deployment of material culture in the expression of identity broaches such theorizing, in that it details his understanding of how colonists and locals would be expected to behave, but it does not interrogate that relationship in ways that the essential issues of postcolonial theory demand. It does not allow for the alternatives that the history of the ancient Near East, let alone the subsequent myriad examples of culture contact, tells us are possible.

---

21   And even if there are regional variations in the precise distribution of the Uruk assemblage (as Butterlin 2003).

22   Notwithstanding the possibilities that some materials traditionally identified as southern may actually have originated in the north first. This has been proposed for Reserved Slip Ware, for example (Dessine 2008), band-rim bowls (Pollock and Coursey 1995: 114), and coarse conical bowls (Frangipane 1993b).

23   Also Pearce 1999; Helwing 2000; Stephen and Peltenburg 2002.

Citing parallels with Mesoamerican situations, Stein (2001a: 283) suggests that foreigners express their identity on a public and domestic level with practices that "should differ from local patterns in the host community while resembling the cultural practices of the homeland." Yet at Kültepe, the famous second-millennium example of an Assyrian trading post located in far distant Anatolia, there were *no* outward manifestations of Assyrian material culture or identity, with the exception of the cuneiform records of that colony's doings. Nevertheless, the Kültepe traders, many of whom married local women (Veenhof 1982), lived within a cultural framework that included the social and judicial mores of the homeland. A similar situation might be noted with the supposed Akkadian overlordship at Tell Brak, where there is little evidence of southern material culture,[24] and only inscriptions suggest the presence of foreign domination (idem in Oates et al. 2001: 338; although cf. Porter 2010b).

Stein (2005b:168) claims that the differences between the Uruk and the Assyrian trading system are "superficial," suggesting that the Kültepe traders were attempting to minimize conflict by adopting the outward material trappings of their place of residence, but this submerges the significance of choice and the centrality of identity to matters of economics, when instead all three are integrally intertwined. The materiality of identity should be taken seriously, and this question of difference, and the lack thereof, should be probed more deeply. Although Stein interprets both as trade diasporas, it may be that Kültepe and Hacinebi are the locations of completely different kinds of culture contact. While we have direct evidence for trade as the basis of Assyrian presence in Anatolia (in the documentation of those exchanges), that the Urukeans abroad had a similar mission is still only an academic construct, in varying degrees drawn from/imposed upon the material remains – remains, despite the dominance of this interpretation, that are still susceptible to alternative reconstructions. In either case, we should not expect uniformity. Foreigners in a strange land face a series of choices as to how they will exist in, and engage with, that land. Many factors determine that choice. Receptivity of the local populations is one, but there are others: the nature and duration of the foreigners' purpose and the nature of their experience in the new land; the nature of conceptions of identity, and the personal as well as institutional significance of that identity; the circumstances under which that identity becomes threatened; the ways in which identity is an internal template rather than external expression. And then there is the question of what happens to the second and third generation of colonists, those born in the "new" land, whose birthplace constitutes part of their congenital identity.

On the other hand, our contemporary experience of globalization, which converges with and emerges from the postcolonial condition at many points (Dirlik 1994), raises several possible issues regarding the spread of "Urukness" across

---

24 The so-called temple of Naram-Sin notwithstanding.

the geographic arc traditionally called the Fertile Crescent. For one thing, it provides a demonstration of the intricate networks between, and multiple layers of, economic structures, trade, population movements, and "culture-creep," as well as the array of contingent responses and outcomes that such networks bring in diverse situations. For another, it demonstrates that one way identity often crystallizes is through contact itself, because it is not until faced with strangers that the need to invoke identity arises (Porter 2002a, similarly Helwing 1999). Differentiation may be engendered, not by a superior power seeking to perpetuate its control, but by an indigenous population as a form of resistance. Identity is also mobilized in the face of competition and conflict. There are many situations where a blurring of boundaries between the intrusive and the intruded-upon occurs as they intersect, followed by a strong – indeed sometimes violent – reaction against the sense that one identity is subsumed within or replaced by another. This reaction plays out in a reassertion, if not reification, of local identity (Lionnet 1993: 105) sometimes manufactured to meet the new crisis[25] as a tool of political opposition – opposition to the dominant group, to unseen economic forces. Globalization, when it results in the apparent spread of a single culture,[26] can solidify traditional identities just as much as it mobilizes new ones. Yet in so doing traditional identities are themselves in some way transformed.

It may be seen, then, that identities are contingent. They are rarely fixed or unchanging (Tilley 2006: 8–10) at any point in time, and if they are, it is because specific situations give rise to this outcome. Fixed identities, where the meaning of symbols and social values are reified and distinct, are an *alternative* to hybridity and may also be an outcome of it, but they are not its necessary precondition. And if "identity is neither essentialist nor foundational, but strategic and positional" (Meskell 2002: 293), then this requires the reexamination of every supposed example of culture contact in the Uruk period – on its own terms – if the nature of that experience and its outcomes is to be understood. Because if "colonialism created new worlds through the meeting, clash and sometimes merger of varying values" as Gosden (2004: 23) states, then this should be evident archaeologically. And when these individual episodes of contact are reexamined (especially interrogating the evidence for differentiation and hybridity), the "Uruk expansion" is revealed not as a unified multitiered system with different kinds of sites acting as different nodes, but as largely system-less: diffuse, diverse, situational, and, over time, highly fluid.

A basic reconstruction of the geographic and chronological processes of the expansion is indicative of the shifting, and sometimes even transitory, character of contact. Improved calibration systems of radiocarbon dating allow a

---

25 Indeed, this is at least in part what "the invention of tradition" (Hobsbawm and Ranger 1983) is about.
26 And it usually *is* only apparent, as in fact hybridity is often in effect.

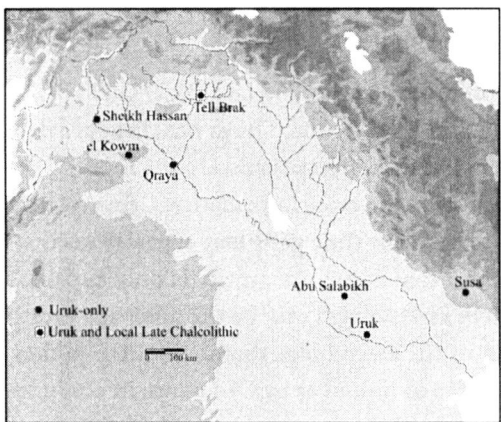

Early phase, 3700–3400 BCE

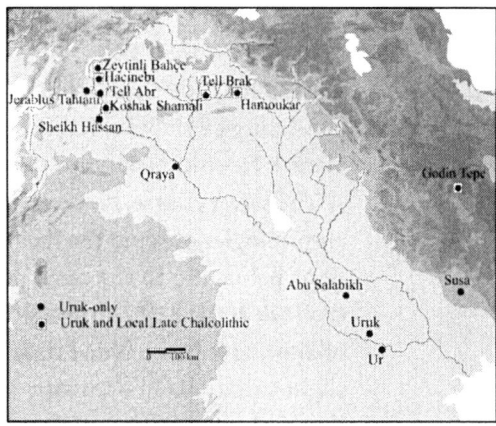

Middle phase, 3400–3250 BCE

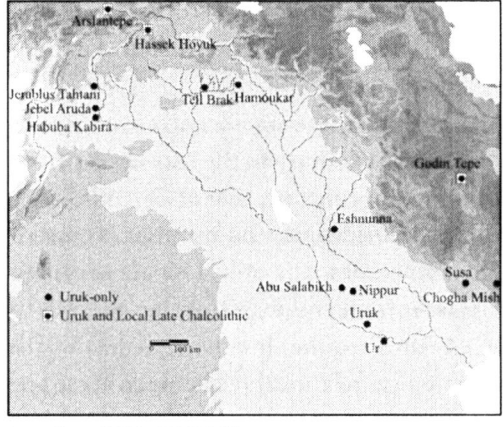

6. Early, middle, and late phases of the Uruk expansion.

Late phase, 3250–3000 BCE

more precise plotting of the time periods in which relevant sites were occupied (Wright and Rupley 2001). Although this process is by no means complete, it now seems clear that the expansion took place over a very long period – minimally 500 years, maximally 700 – in a series of movements, and in various directions. In the past it had been understood as a unitary phenomenon compressed within the short time of the Late Uruk period, about 150 years. The chronology is complicated, and there are various ways of dealing with its inexactitude. The safest course is to lump together sites that fit within a certain time span on the basis of the grossest measurement. In this case, the history of Uruk and Uruk-related settlement (ignoring its precise nature) may be divided into three basic groups (Fig. 6): early (3700/3600–3400 BCE),[27] consisting of Susa, Abu Salabikh,[28] Qraya, Tell Brak, and Sheikh Hassan; middle

27 And see Rothman 2001 for the chronological chart as agreed upon at the Santa Fe conference by scholars working in this period.

28 Apart from the complexity of the stratigraphy and chronology, for which see the comprehensive treatment by Butterlin 2003, there is the question of the precise relationship

(3400–3300/3250 BCE), in which Hacinebi, Zeytinli Bahçe, Kosak Shamali, and Godin Tepe[29] are added to the preceding group; and late (3250–3000 BCE), consisting of Habuba Kabira South and Jebel Aruda (Qraya has disappeared), Hassek Höyük, Arslantepe (Hacinebi has disappeared) and Godin Tepe.[30]

The safest course, however, is not always the most informative. Gross relative chronologies obscure the fact that significant time gaps may separate occupations belonging to the same period, so that contemporaneity is only apparent (Pollock 2001: 210). Although pottery assemblages may be the same at a group of sites, as it is the broad definition of the assemblage that defines the period, slight variations in occupation histories as hinted at by C14 dates, in conjunction with the location of sites, reveal what I think is a telling series of shifts. If one hundred – or even fifty – years separate the Uruk manifestation at one site from another (that is, two or three generations) then any sense of cohesion that *we* see today in archaeological terms is in fact highly attenuated in terms of individual human experience.

In addition, the nature of occupation shifts quite significantly over time at several sites, and not necessarily in the same direction – in the Late Uruk period contact at Tell Brak reaches its floruit and, in contrast, that at Zeytinli Bahçe devolves (Frangipane 2007a). Finally, attributions depend on what is considered necessarily evidence of contact. Sometimes it is only a single southern characteristic that is present; sometimes it is an entire assemblage. Subject to the usual caveats that any use of C14 dates require, it is nevertheless worth parsing as finely as possible the chronological relationships between these settlements. While it is well recognized that kinds of Uruk occupation correlate with three main geographic and cultural ranges, it is less clear that the expansion took no obvious spatial path in chronological terms, and that this lack is itself meaningful.

The geographic distribution of Uruk-only sites (Fig. 7), as distinct from sites where Uruk material is co-located with indigenous materials, is restricted to three – or perhaps two – distinct locales: southern Mesopotamia proper; the Middle Euphrates where indigenous occupation seems sparse to nonexistent;[31]

of Susa and the Susiana plain to Mesopotamia. Should it be considered a single cultural entity, or two different spheres that from time to time merged? In either case Susa is evidently closely tied with Mesopotamia, and it would seem specifically with Uruk, from the Early Uruk period on (Butterlin 2003: 310–13), well preceding any other exterior attestation of southern cultural materials.

29 This is represented by Godin VI (Badler 2002).

30 There are, of course, other sites not included here, and a very large number of sites recognized in surface survey and attributed to the Uruk period because of the presence of beveled-rim bowls in particular. For the problems with such attributions, see following. But without being able to attribute these sites to a reworked chronology, or to a kind of occupancy, i.e., local or intrusive, they contribute only to the geographic picture.

31 A large section of the river between Abu Salabikh and Qraya lacks much evidence for any type of site at this time. Geyer and Monchambert (1987) found Uruk materials at Ramadi

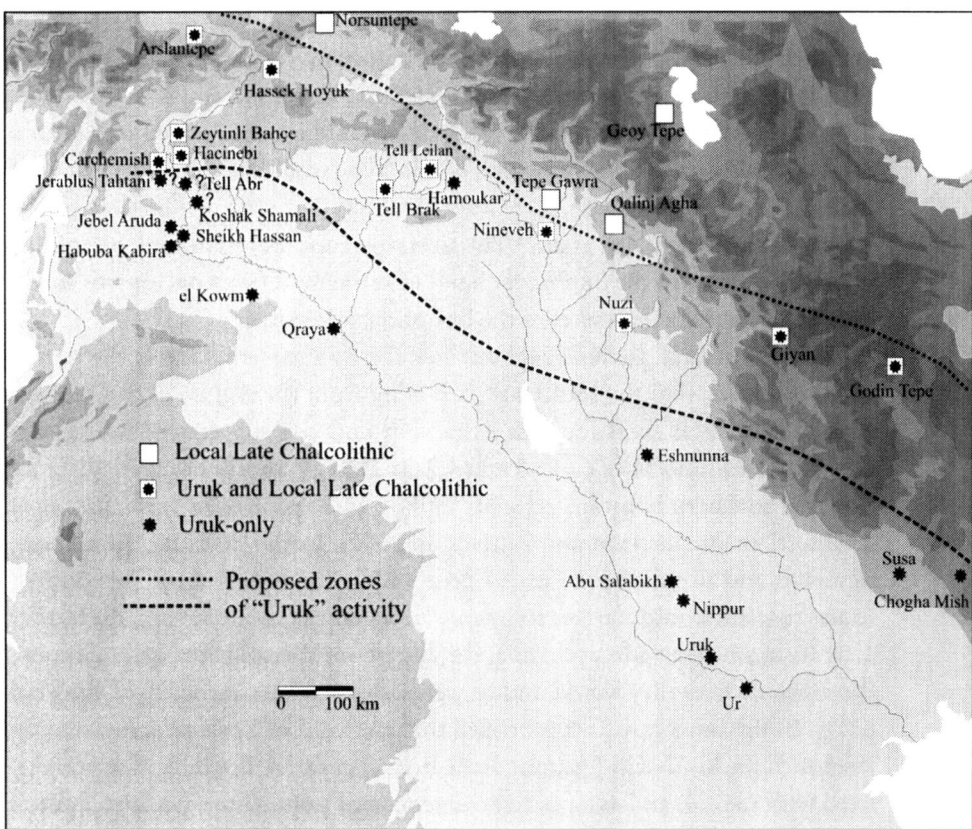

7. Map of Uruk-only, Local Late Chalcolithic, and co-located sites.

and the inner Iranian plain to the foothills. It is possible to see this last region as essentially one and the same as Mesopotamia at this time, I think, especially as there are fifty-four sites that manifest Middle and Late Uruk occupation in the Susiana plain (Potts 2009: 16).[32] I include el-Kowm with the Middle Euphrates: given its ephemeral nature and the fact that animal remains indicate that the herding of sheep and goat and the hunting of gazelle were prime activities at this time, as well as its triangulated location between Qraya and Sheikh Hassan, it seems likely to be an activity station within the orbit of those sites.[33] Then there is a band of sites containing co-located southern Uruk and Late Chalcolithic

near Mari, however. There is also a seeming absence of sites in the area between Qraya and Sheikh Hassan, but five sites with "Uruk" materials on the surface have been recorded in surveys in that space.

32 This fact is in itself telling, and in two different ways – (1) it is likely that many of these sites are not contemporaneous, but, as was the case in the rest of southern Mesopotamia, there was a high rate of abandonment and foundation (Pollock 2001: 211); (2) this fluctuating settlement pattern in the south corresponds, in general terms, with shifting settlement in the areas of the expansion.

33 I do not include Jerablus Tahtani, because while Uruk occupation seems to replace indigenous occupation there, the relationship between the two is problematic in both chronological and organizational terms.

materials that sweeps the inside arc of the mountain ranges from the Taurus to the Zagros, almost as a protective barrier (cf. Helwing 1999 and Schwartz 2001: 255). A very few sites with both types of assemblage are located well within the mountains themselves, of which Godin Tepe would be the prime example. Indeed, for obvious reasons there are only a very few sites of this time period known in the mountains at all.[34] The sites that contain local Late Chalcolithic materials only form the outermost band of settlement (with one or two exceptions), marking the perimeter of the line of the joint sites.[35]

There are several possible explanations for this pattern. One is the nature of the materials that the south was extracting from the region, in conjunction with the methods used for that extraction and the subsequent transportation of the commodities concerned (Algaze 2001);[36] another is sheer distance from the southern homelands (Stein 1999b); while yet a third is the nature of local settlement (Stephen and Peltenburg 2002). In the first case, goods such as metals and obsidian are located deep within the mountains,[37] key trading routes to them would traverse steppe and river valleys; in the second, the farther away from southern Mesopotamia, the less power the colonists had to impose themselves where they would and so were subject to the authority of the local polity. In the third case, it is proposed that the kind of Uruk settlement correlated with the kind of indigenous settlement encountered, which in turn correlated with rainfall and associated environmental possibilities (see also Pollock and Coursey 1995). Thus, the Middle Euphrates was dry, largely unsettled, and suitable only for mobile pastoralism;[38] the Upper Euphrates, in a higher rainfall zone, had a stronger agricultural base and consequently a quite dense network of settlements. In an area dominated by mobile pastoralists rather than settled communities – from Carchemish to Mari, for example – Urukeans were free to establish their own major centers. Or, rather, they were constrained to establish their own settlements. If they wanted to live in this area in any permanent and substantial way, they had little choice but to start from scratch. In the north, though, the presence of a well-established settlement network widened their range of options and reduced the need to be self-sustaining.

This explanation raises a further possibility: that mobile pastoralism itself was a key orientation of Uruk and Uruk-related sites. With their location in

---

34 The sites in the upper regions of the Euphrates such Samsat and Norsuntepe line the passageway through the mountains.

35 Although there are frequently reported in surveys scatters of very small sites in the vicinity of major Uruk/Late Chalcolithic centers – or, perhaps better, excavated settlements – that are said to be Uruk only, as Stephen and Peltenburg (2002: 174) note.

36 See Algaze 2008: 68–92 for the most succinct expression of his understanding of the Uruk expansion.

37 See Stein 2005b: 146 for a useful map of potential resources.

38 Although of course there were significant settlements in this area at various points in time!

the piedmont and/or proximity to the mountains, the Upper Euphrates sites are just as embedded within a pastoralist zone as are the sites of the Middle Euphrates. In fact, all three bands of contact clearly intersect with the two basic pastoralist landscapes of the Near East – the steppe and the mountains. Such a statement is a little disingenuous, however, because steppe and mountains dominate the geography of the Near East; the pastoralist component of these environments remains an afterthought in most discussions. I have remarked elsewhere that the Euphrates and Tigris are thin strips of green in a vast brown landscape. Nevertheless, it bears reiterating that, although we have a tendency to see the settlements and fields of the river valleys as embedded in an essentially hostile landscape, the more arid lands around them are no less significant in subsistence, demographic, or cultural terms. Despite our usual assumption that farming is inherently more important, there is no reason to assume that farming has primacy over any other function, or that cereal cultivation was the object of the colonial enterprise along the Euphrates and thus the reason for settlement. Cereal cultivation merely *enables* settlement. It is not a necessary precondition for it.

Further, we too frequently fail to recognize that the river valleys have multiple constituencies exploiting it for multiple uses – farming, herding, trading, and traveling – and that all these functions coexist and are interdependent. Indeed, most of the locations where Uruk materials are found are susceptible to multiple explanations – such as the Anatolian mountains, where pastoralism or mining are both feasible, or Godin Tepe, which is located in an area with potential for relatively easy transit, but is not necessarily established there because of it. In proposing mobile pastoralism as a fundamental component of the movement of southern populations outwards, I do not mean to extract other factors from the equation, only to invert the relationship between them. The exploitation of metals and other raw materials may well have been part of the resulting interactions between indigenous and intrusive populations, but they are certainly not the only potentials implicit in the geography of the expansion. First, we discover more sites that are accessible as opposed to sites that are inaccessible. Second, whatever the economic foundation of the settlements and unless prohibited by other considerations, people will tend to locate in an area that allows easy access to other places. Third, and most important for this discussion, pastoralists may use the same routes of passage that traders (and any other travelers) do. Therefore settlements that are closely connected to pastoralism either as service centers, marketplaces, or points of residence will be located in places convenient to pastoralist passage. Those same settlements will also need areas suitable for agricultural production, again for their own needs and for the needs of the communities they support.

While others have certainly discussed pastoralism as a factor in the expansion (Adams 1981; Wright 1989; McCorriston 1997; Kouchoukos 1998; Algaze

2001, 2008),[39] few have systematically explored the evidence for, the processes by which, or the implications of this situation for the various changes that transpired in the fourth millennium. This is in large part because the nature of mobile pastoralism is considered antithetical to those changes – urbanism and associated administrative technologies, especially writing – and therefore pastoralists and pastoralism could provide no kind of dynamic in their engendering. It is also a product of the fact that evidence for pastoralism is purely circumstantial. But such evidence, indirect though it may be, is to be found in every kind of source at our disposal, and since the evidence for current reconstructions is equally circumstantial,[40] this should not preclude examination of alternatives.

The chronology of the expansion is just such a source of circumstantial evidence. Movement out from the south is demonstrably piecemeal and slow (Fig. 8). The earliest Uruk materials found outside the immediate zone of Uruk itself is at Susa, to the east. Sometime later, contact is evident at Qraya on the Euphrates at its junction with the Habur. It is close to, but perhaps followed by, the material far closer to home (home being Uruk) at Abu Salabikh. Uruk materials at both Qraya and Abu Salabikh first date to before 3800 BCE, according to Wright and Rupley (2001: 120). Both Susa and Abu Salabikh might be considered part of the heartland of the culture that characterizes Uruk, but I would not so consider Qraya.[41]

Interestingly, perhaps the first evidence of contact between the south and true north is at Tell Brak, where in level 16 a few beveled-rim bowls were found. Dates for this level vary. David and Joan Oates (1997: 287) placed it around 3500 BCE, with which Wright and Rupley concur (2001: 101–2). Subsequent work at the site, however, seems to have pushed the date back to before 3600 BCE (it is considered Late Chalcolithic 3; see, for example, Rothman 2002: 52, table 2) and perhaps as early as 3700 BCE (Akkermans and Schwartz 2003: fig. 6.3; Oates 2005: 18–21). This would correspond to the establishment of Sheikh Hassan around 3680/3600 BCE.[42] A walled site of approximately one hectare, Sheikh Hassan is the first so-called Uruk colony, with the possible exception of Tell 'Abr.[43] It contains a cell building similar to that of Zeytinli

---

39   Algaze (2001: 49), for example, acknowledges a connection but nevertheless maintains the role of Uruk sites as "mediators of exchange."

40   One of the criticisms of Algaze's explanation has been that there is no material demonstration of the commodities Mesopotamians supposedly extracted from their hinterlands as present in any greater quantity in the south than before or after (Weiss 1989).

41   Several installations for fire were found, and Buccellati (1990b) has interpreted this as a salt-processing center.

42   However, this is labeled Late Chalcolithic 4 in Akkermans and Schwartz 2003: fig. 6.3.

43   While the colony status of Sheikh Hassan, Habuba Kabira, and Jebel Aruda is well known, Schwartz (2001) also includes Tell el Hajj, Hadidi, Mureybit, and Tannira in this category, although I doubt that there is enough exposure at these latter sites on which to base this

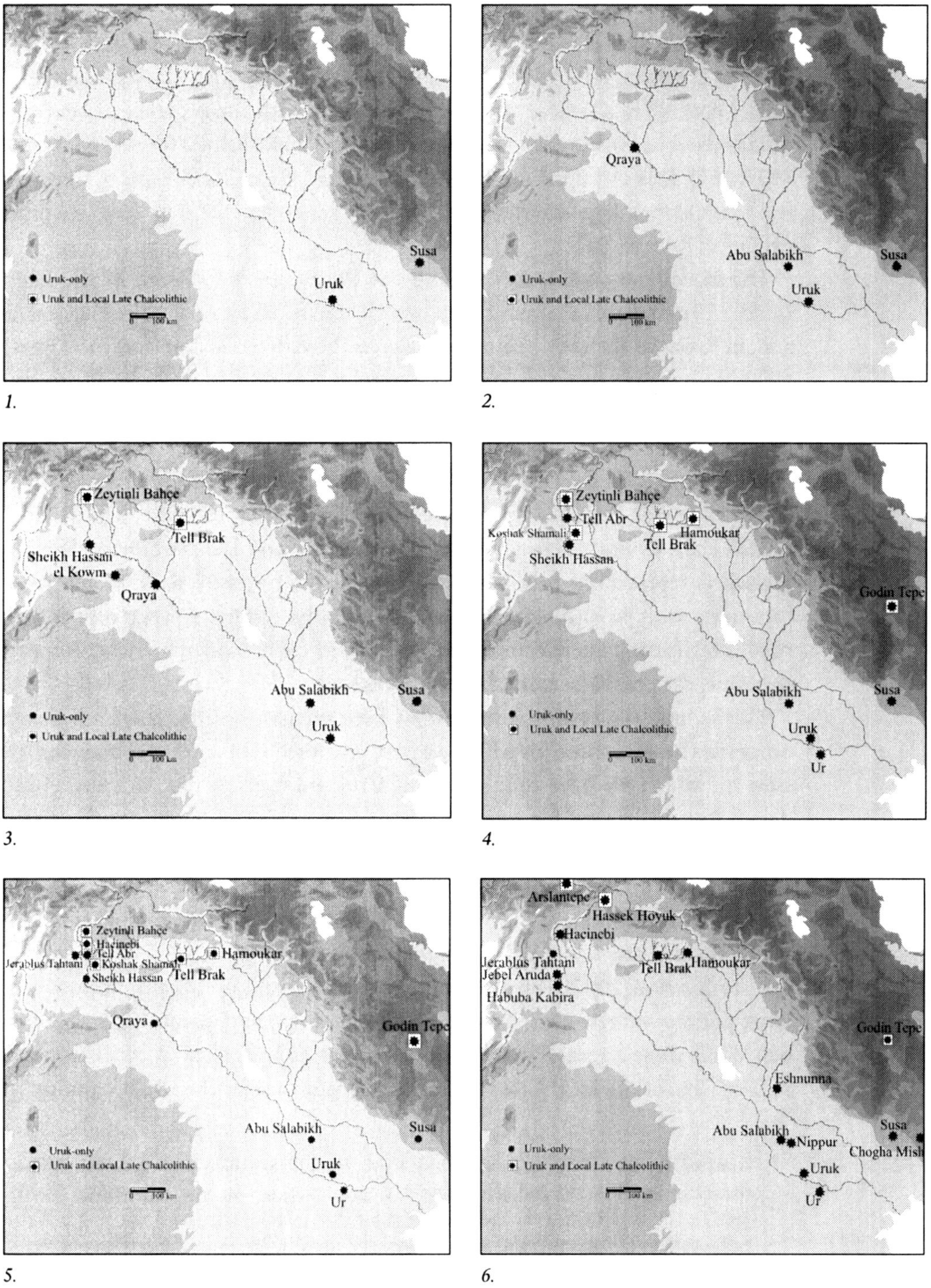

1.

2.

3.

4.

5.

6.

8. An alternative mapping of the Uruk expansion, from early (1) to late (6).

Bahçe, with which it is contemporary (Frangipane 2007a). In the mix at this point is el Kowm, a hunting station in the desert, and then Hacinebi demonstrates contact in a similar manner to Tell Brak, with the presence of beveled-rim bowls – but nothing else – at the end of Late Chalcolithic 3 (Stein and Edens 1999: 167). It is not until the subsequent period, Late Chalcolithic 4, that the full Uruk assemblage emerges and Hacinebi seems to take over from its near neighbor, Zeytinli Bahçe.

The initial movement north along the Euphrates is followed in the later Middle Uruk by a dual spread even farther north to the Anatolian Euphrates and, in Syria, to the east, primarily between the Eastern Habur and the Tigris. Notable sites that demonstrate occupation at this time (c. 3500 BCE) are, on the Euphrates, Jerablus Tahtani (Stephen and Peltenburg 2002) and Tell 'Abr (Hammade and Yamazake 2006) and, in the east, Hamoukar (Reichel 2002, 2009).[44] Expansion into the Iranian foothills is evident at Godin Tepe (Badler 2002). Later still, there is a significant change in the location of Uruk and Uruk-related sites. Contact is established at Arslantepe and Hassek Höyük. Sheikh Hassan is replaced by new implantations on the opposite bank of the river beginning with Jebel Aruda, followed by Habuba Kabira. A large number of small sites, mostly unexcavated, seem to show traces of Uruk material culture at this time, the precise nature of which is unclear.

This is, unquestionably, a somewhat false picture, because there are many other sites besides those for which we have reworked C14 dates and many other sites for which we have indications of Uruk interaction but no substantial data.[45] But this is true for every reconstruction of the path and nature of the Uruk expansion. The exposure at some of the sites argued to be one kind of settlement or another is simply too small to be in any way definitive. This is the case with Tell Brak for example, where the thirty-odd square meters about which there is any detail pales in comparison to the postulated 55 ha size of the site (Ur et al. 2007); this is also the case with Jerablus Tahtani, from which Uruk pottery was retrieved in a two-by-six-meter trench (Peltenburg et al. 2000: 68). While there appears in the excavated areas at both sites to be a complete replacement of the local Late Chalcolithic assemblage by the Uruk – gradually

conclusion, and so I will not account for them. Hadidi's so-called Uruk material dates to the transition from the end of the fourth to beginning of the third millennium (Porter 2007a). The criterion for the inclusion of these sites by Schwartz seems not so much the completeness of the repertoire as the absence of contemporaneous indigenous materials. More convincing are the materials from Tell 'Abr (Hammade and Yamazaki 2006), which on the basis of ceramic parallels may be attributed at least to the Middle Uruk phase if not definitively as early as Sheikh Hassan.

44 Both sites seem to be lacking a preliminary phase of contact in which beveled-rim bowls only are found. However, since contact in this phase seems to have been very small-scale, it is possible that it simply has not been found as yet.

45 See, for instance, Potts's (2009) notation of eastern sites with beveled-rim bowls.

in the case of Brak and suddenly at Jerablus Tahtani – it is perfectly possible that excavators hit upon a small enclave within the indigenous settlement of each site. That Uruk materials are found in areas TW and CH at Brak does not in any way indicate a complete occupation of the site by an Uruk population. TW is located on the northern slope of the high mound and therefore was possibly external to the main settlement (and indeed, a monumental gate lay beneath this area in the late Ubaid period [McMahon and Oates 2007]); CH, toward the southern edge of the mound, may likewise be peripheral. Trenches opened recently in areas TX and UA are also on the sloped sides of the mound, north and south respectively (Emberling and McDonald 2003: 2, fig. 1). In fact this situation raises some interesting possibilities – it may be that two separate southern enclaves, or *karum*s, are located at Brak, which given its regional significance would hardly be surprising. It is certainly possible that different Mesopotamian settlements maintained different connections with settlements to the north and east. Algaze (2008: 113) proposes a "political balkanization" for the southern Uruk, and although I would question the idea that we can readily draw political boundaries around sites on the basis of site sizes and levels of settlement hierarchy,[46] nevertheless, for reasons which will become clear later, I too do not think the expansion is sustained by a single center.

Any interpretation therefore has to remain speculative until these details are fully fleshed. The point, though, is this: the first pattern to emerge is that there *is* no obvious pattern – no concerted movement in one direction that might indicate a material goal toward which the expansion was directed. If, for example, Qraya is the first site at any distance from the homeland, and its pyrotechnic facilities were for the processing of salt (Buccellati 1990b), an interpretation by no means the consensus,[47] salt is certainly not the apparent target of subsequent contact with sites in the far north.

But what is? I would suggest that while the overall pattern of expansion seems like a gradual rise, retraction, and collapse, the small shifts within this mapping should be given due consideration, for they break down the picture of systematic and monolithic movement and reveal it to be, in essence, a series of stops and starts. What happens at each point is in part a product of the previous point and in part a product of the new situations in place at that moment in time. The relocation of a colony presence in the Late Uruk period from the left bank of the Euphrates at Sheikh Hassan, to Habuba Kabira and Jebel Aruda

---

46   The situation at Tell Brak, ancient Nagar, should provide sufficient warning about the limitations of this approach (see also Ristvet 2008). The discovery of cuneiform tablets from the site of Tell Beydar, ancient Nabada, revealed that site to be a subsidiary settlement of the polity of ancient Nagar, for which Nabada seems to have been regional coordinator of agricultural and pastoral production from a number of smaller sites.

47   Although as will be seen, large-scale ovens are a feature of more than one location of contact materials.

on the right bank of the river, while at the same time southern presence expands in the Habur and especially at Tell Brak, suggests that for some reason there was a reorientation in focus from the Jazireh to the west and far northeast. And yet farther north, as Hacinebi ceases, a group of settlements including Arslantepe and Hassek Höyük start to show evidence of interaction with southern populations. There is no explanation that readily accounts for the ebb and flow of contact across the landscape, the consistency with which settlement changes yet the inconsistency of those changes – no explanation except one. Access to regions of pastures fluctuated because of changes in one or more of the following elements: rainfall (affecting both grass growth and water source); intergroup political relationships; expanding and contracting sedentary settlement. While each of these factors might impinge upon the operation of a trading network, it is unlikely to be so recurrent, and so seemingly random a feature, over this time and space. And although this scenario might be implicit only in geography, it is certainly possible to offer a more substantive argument for it. Close attention to small patterns within larger ones reveals a process – and indeed a performance – of contact that is ultimately oriented to mobile populations.

So now it is the postcolonial approach to the nature of contact itself, not just the when and where of it, that is at stake. I do not intend to substitute one model imposed upon the data, that of hybridity, for another, that of world systems (Algaze 2005 [1993]) or distance parity (Stein 1999b). Rather, I wish only to ask of the archaeological data the questions that postcolonialism warrants. Space precludes a comprehensive treatment of all the relevant sites, but a survey of some of the more prominent materials suffices to demonstrate the possibilities of reinterpretation – and the possible depths of that reinterpretation – that such questions raise.

Arguing that distance from the homeland inhibited the Uruk inhabitants of Hacinebi from asserting their original military and organizational dominance (and thus maintaining the innate superiority of the south), Stein understands the phase of occupation there labeled B2 and dated 3600–3300 BCE (Stein and Edens 1999: 168)[48] as bearing witness to the segregated coexistence of a population derived from Southern Mesopotamia inserted in the midst of a northern polity (Stein 1999a: 16). This southern population is identified by the confined distribution of ceramics, wall cones (but no extant architecture),[49] bitumen, clay sickles, pins, cylinder seals, and other forms of administrative technology (Stein et al. 1997) within a local, Late Chalcolithic assemblage. Stone tools and botanical and faunal remains indicate that the southerners remained self-sufficient

---

48　But cf. Stein 2001a: 301, where the beginning of Uruk occupation at Hacinebi is dated to 3700 BCE.

49　Whether dated to Phase A (Butterlin 1999) or Phase B1 (Stein and Edens 1999), the terraces on which this occupation was located were built by the local inhabitants of the site.

and did not participate in the economic system of the local population, a population that itself remained uninflected by proximity to the southerners.

I am not as sanguine as Stein (1999a, 1999b, 2001a; Stein and Edens 1999, and cf. Butterlin 2003), however, that the Uruk assemblages and Late Chalcolithic assemblages dated to phase B2 represent coterminous but sequestered occupations. Almost all the artifacts found for this phase at Hacinebi, including pottery, were retrieved from ash, trash, or wash – from middens inside rooms, from slope erosion, or from pits. When artifactual material is in situ or associated with floor levels of architectural units, it consists of local Late Chalcolithic items with or without beveled-rim bowls (but very often with).[50] The deposition pattern of this refuse does not really allow for a clear understanding of the relationship between the people who made and used the Uruk materials and the people who made and used the local Late Chalcolithic, because it is difficult to explain just how it got where it did. Pits, for example, are complicated, because even when one can detect the surface from which they were dug, it is hard to know if that activity was part of the original use of the surface or whether it postdated it. It is also difficult to know just how the contents of the pit got there – by people disposing of their own mess, or by people disposing of rubbish others had left behind.

At first, though, the Uruk materials seemed to be confined to the eastern side of a wall (Fig. 9) that ran along the northeastern edge of the mound, through operations 1 and 6, while the local Late Chalcolithic is confined to the west. This material was chronologically mixed, containing Middle and Late Uruk forms in the same deposits (Pollock and Coursey 1995).[51] But subsequent excavations turned up "mostly Uruk" deposits alongside local Late Chalcolithic deposits in operations 14 and 15, so that it seems the wall was no longer separating the two populations. According to the segregation scenario, even if the wall ran through both 14 and 15, thereby describing a rather small arc, only one community should have been recognizable within that arc – the local Late Chalcolithic. Why, then, would the Uruk occupants of the site be disposing of their rubbish inside the houses of the local inhabitants while those inhabitants were still there? Although I generally think it a fool's game to predict what

50   Beveled-rim bowls occur with Late Chalcolithic materials in a number of contexts: for example, the southeast room of the yellowish brick building in operation 12 (Stein et al. 1997: 118); the house in operation 15 where there is a "high concentration of Mesopotamian Uruk ceramics in the ash and midden that fill the rooms, and … two complete bevel rim bowls in the floor deposit of the southern room" (Stein et al. 1997: 114–15); and in operation 4, where perhaps the most extensive architecture for phase B2 contains local Late Chalcolithic materials with beveled-rim bowls (Stein et al. 1996: 217). Operation 7 is in the area characterized as entirely local Late Chalcolithic, and it too contained pits full of Uruk materials, mostly beveled-rim bowls, with some local wares.

51   Although some forms may have proved to have had a longer lifespan than previously recognized so that this occupation dated to only one period.

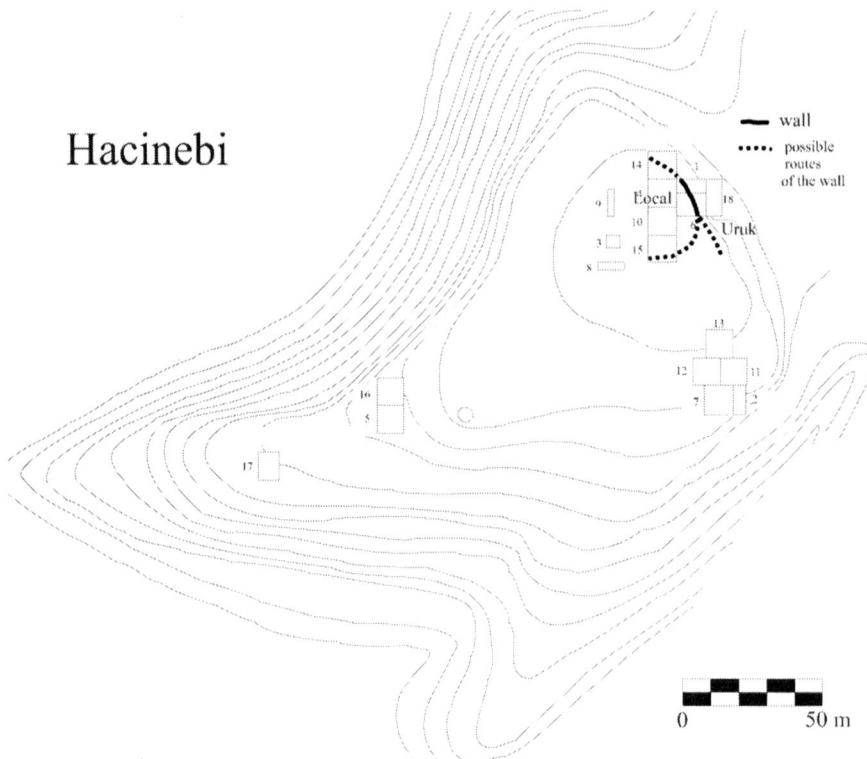

9. The location of the wall dividing local and intrusive populations at Hacinebi. Redrawn from Stein 2002.

people would or would not do, in this particular instance it really is difficult to imagine any scenario where this might be the case.

There are two issues that confuse things further. One, it is not clear whether the excavators think that the midden and trash deposits inside the rooms were debris from the activities of the people who built and used these houses, piling up on floors as they lived there, whether it was dumped subsequent to that, after the rooms were no longer in use, or even whether it was later fill. If either of the latter two alternatives proves to be the case, then the possibility arises that the Uruk occupation was subsequent to the local Late Chalcolithic, not contemporaneous with it. The Uruk inhabitants would therefore have tossed their trash over the walls and on to the steep slope of the mound and used abandoned houses as refuse containers. Or they may have moved into empty houses abandoned by their original occupants and reused them. The buildup of rubbish deposits inside rooms, which is rare in permanent sedentary occupations, *is* characteristic of "planned abandonment and/or anticipated mobility" (Berelov 2006: 136). In this case Uruk deposits could easily end up side by side with Late Chalcolithic remains left in these contexts, appearing to be "interstratified" (Stein and Edens 1999: 169). The consistent presence of *some* local Late Chalcolithic ceramics and the occasional sealed basket in deposits characterized as "mostly Uruk" would be explained by exchange with local Late Chalcolithic peoples elsewhere.

Two, even though a wide range of Uruk pottery types and other components of material culture are present at Hacinebi, much of the material in these "Uruk" deposits may have consisted almost exclusively of beveled-rim bowls (Fig. 5), the most common vessel type belonging to the Uruk repertoire at the site by a dramatic percentage (Pollock and Coursey 1995; Pearce 1999). From time to time contexts considered Uruk are noted as consisting of beveled-rim bowls, such as the pits in operation 7,[52] but it is not clear if this is *always* noted when it is the case, or only occasionally. It is now increasingly evident, though, that beveled-rim bowls appear at Hacinebi *before* the rest of the Uruk repertoire (Stein and Edens 1999: 168). Indeed, through detailed stratigraphic analysis and reanalysis of sites containing evidence for Uruk presence in some way, Pascal Butterlin (2003) has determined that, no matter the nature of interaction, be it colony, enclave, or outpost, contact is often first presaged by a phase in which beveled-rim bowls alone appear (see also Stephen and Peltenburg 2002: 175; Badler 2002: 84; Helwing 2005) within a local assemblage[53] – although it is important to note that this does not necessarily occur at the same time everywhere. Crucial therefore to understanding the nature of contact – or if indeed there was any – at Hacinebi is the function and origin of these distinctive vessels.

The consensus for some time has been that the beveled-rim bowls are ration bowls (Nissen 1970; Zagarell 1986; Johnson 1987; Butterlin 2003; cf. Oates et al. 2007: 596), standardized containers in which allotments of unprocessed cereals were doled out to institutional dependents – primarily, at this time, of the temple – or performers of corvée labor. Quite apart from the reservations that accompany this theory – the actual lack of standardization in the bowl sizes (Beale 1978), what indeed constitutes standardization, and the questionable evidence for any such system in the fourth millennium (Chazan and Lehner 1990 and see below) – it is hard to imagine why ration bowls would appear across the countryside prior to any evidence for the institutions/population they rationed, thus undermining two essential components of the original colonial hypothesis: (1) that it is a system exported whole and intact, and therefore with the complicity of one or more centralized and controlling authorities; (2) that it represents a wholesale movement of people. This is a conundrum of the chicken-and-egg variety however, for the function of the bowls has in part been determined by their distribution. These bowls are simply ubiquitous.

---

52   See note 49 above.
53   Lupton (1996: 41) also notes this phenomenon as a shared feature of Grai Resh, Tell Leilan, and Tell Brak. Susa should also be included in this group (Butterlin 2003: 310). Jerablus Tahtani may prove an exception, as this phase is absent there, meaning either there is a hiatus, or that for some reason this site does not fit into the pattern established by the majority of contact sites (Stephen and Peltenburg 2002: 175).

They are found everywhere, from the vicinity of the Caspian Sea to Pakistan (Potts 2009) to Egypt (Joffe 2000; T. A. Wilkinson 2002) and, as seen from the numbers at Hacinebi (indeed from Uruk itself), they comprise as much as seventy to ninety percent of the assemblage at several sites (Chazan and Lehner 1990: 26), although at others they constitute but a few sherds. Two hundred and fifty thousand such bowls were found at Chogha Mish (Delougaz et al. 1996). In the past, the recovery of a beveled-rim bowl in surface collection has been thought enough in and of itself to indicate some form of contact with southern Mesopotamia.

Beveled-rim bowls are coarse and, because of their frequency, thought to have been mass-produced[54] – even though they are also thought to be hand- (Badler 2002: 84) or mold-made (Nicholas 1987; Goulder 2010). They are found in every kind of spatial context – public and domestic buildings, interior or exterior space – and were very often made locally (Berman 1989; Stein 1999a: 16; Potts 2009). They have been variously interpreted as salt containers, as tentatively proposed by Potts (1984) and more strenuously argued by Buccellati (1990b); yogurt containers, where the porosity of the fabric allows the whey to drip through (Delougaz 1952: 127–8); bread molds (Millard 1988; Chazan and Lehner 1990 and now Potts 2009; Goulder 2010); votive containers, whether as offerings for the gods (as Beale 1978) or as taxation (per Nicholas 1990); and they certainly sometimes held bitumen, although probably as a secondary use (Stephen and Peltenburg 2002: 176; cf. Stein 1999b: 150). Not all of these possible functions are mutually exclusive – bread, for example, might be an offering, as indeed may salt (Potts 1984). Salt might also have been a commodity controlled and doled out by institutions. One could no doubt collect one's portion of grain and then bake one's bread in the same vessel, thereby emphasizing dependency on the powers that provided this basic necessity.

But whatever the bowls prove to be, each of the explanations clearly shows that they were not just a form, one that might be adopted by anyone because of its utility or technical advantages, but rather were deeply embedded in a cultural locus, so that it seems it must have been the locus itself that was in place wherever there are beveled-rim bowls. Technologically sophisticated they are not. This is their very point – they are easily made, easily broken (although remarkable numbers of intact vessels are recovered) domestic objects so frequently found that everyone probably had or used one or more of them; therefore they must have been part of something that everyone did all the time. This pertains

---

54 This issue of mass production is complicated. Although the term seems often enough used as denoting simply a commodity made in large volume, it should be adduced on the grounds both of frequency and standardization and implies the consistent output of a specialist. This would seem inapplicable to the beveled-rim bowls, for all the signs, such as an actual *lack* of standardization and the varieties of finished product, point to these as objects that may equally be made in a domestic context.

whether or not the bowls were imported or locally made, a determination that does not simplify the matter one way or the other. Imported bowls might have been used by southerners who had emigrated, or by locals who wished to associate themselves with whatever the bowls represented. Émigrés might have used local materials to make their bowls; locals might have used local materials to copy others' ceramic vernaculars.

If votive containers, the beveled-rim bowls were part of a religious system where the contents – the offerings – were as significant as the medium through which they were offered. If ration bowls, then they are emblematic of a highly structured and very specific kind of sociopolitical organization, and indeed this is one reason why the idea of Uruk colonialism has proved very powerful: the system was so specific that it can be recognized (through the bowls) as functioning far from its point of origin. If bread molds, then the bowls speak to daily practices that are an intrinsic part of social identity. Bread is the most basic form of sustenance; shared sustenance creates and maintains social relationships from the familial, where it is at least as instrumental as blood (Carsten 1995; Ferraro 2008), to the international (Williams 2005).

The fact that beveled-rim bowls appear before the rest of the Uruk assemblage raises another question: that of origin. Are they originally local to the north, part of the chaff-tempered, handmade Late Chalcolithic repertoire, with which they would seem to fit? Or are they a southern phenomenon (Stein and Edens 1999: 168; Butterlin 2003: 320, but cf. Helwing 2005 and Oates et al. 2007: 596; Potts 2009: 12)? Certainly they have always been taken as the latter, and the earliest recorded beveled-rim bowl at Warka is found in Level XII of the Eana precinct (Nissen 2002: 5), well before any of the other sites that manifest the southern pottery repertoire, according to the Santa Fe chronology (Rothman 2001: 7). The first beveled-rim bowl at Susa comes from level 22 there, which may be at least as early as Eana XII, depending on the length of the hiatus after the preceding occupation (Butterlin 2003: 310–11 and plate 12).

But bread mold or ration container, we now have to explain why these vessels spread so far so fast if they are not (yet) accompanying a residential population/ work gang/administrative structure. The fact that, while some were imported, many were made at the dispersed sites in which they are found would seem to invalidate the suggestion that they are a trade-good container or disposable packing (as proposed by Abdi 1999, cited in Potts 2009), as would the impracticality of the shape for any sort of long-distance shipping.[55]

---

55 Buccellati's suggestion that they were salt containers has not been borne out by residue analysis. Even if they were, they were more likely for localized salt extraction and drying than shipment vessels for long-distance trade. Potts (1984) suggests that the tall conical cup of the subsequent period may be an *auget* for collecting salt, but this is subject to the same reservation. Bitumen drips on the bowls are not uncommon, but this is sufficiently infrequent as to represent only an isolated practice of secondary use (Goulder 2010).

Butterlin (2003) argues that the Uruk phenomenon is essentially an expansion of ideas, not people, where newly emerging polities adopt those technological innovations of the south[56] which facilitate that emergence, as all are part of a proto-urban "culture world." The same conditions, although appearing slightly later in the north, give rise to the ready adoption of the new technologies of urbanism developing in the south in a process of acculturation brought about by long-term, continual contact between different parts of the urbanizing world. Beveled-rim bowls spread because they are easy and cheap to make (Butterlin 2003: 344). Potts (2009: 12) makes a similar point (also Goulder 2010), noting in a consideration of the precise distribution of these vessels in Iran and Pakistan that it "is inconceivable that Sumerian or Susian enclaves lurk beneath the surface of every site on which BRBS have been found." The frequency of beveled-rim bowls in the east ranges from but a few sherds to tens, if not hundreds of thousands of vessels, and they seem to have been locally produced, as is often the case in the north (as has been noted). Potts suggests that, while the bowls may have a single function, that of bread mold, they are unlikely to have a single context of use. At those sites where they are thick on the ground they may represent bread produced as rations for a Mesopotamian-style labor system by centralized, industrial-sized bakeries, while at those sites where only a few are recovered they are more likely to represent the transmission of taste – a taste for the kind of bread, a new kind, that Mesopotamians used (cf. Goulder 2010: 359).

Potts, however, does not delineate the mechanisms of this transmission, which begs as many questions as it answers. Presumably, in this reconstruction, key centers in the east – identifiable because they contain masses of beveled-rim bowls – were incorporated into the Mesopotamian system, or at least borrowed its basic sociopolitical structure of indentured or corvée labor drawn from the surrounding hinterlands. That labor was paid with bread. Those who experienced this bread would immediately prefer it to the bread they had eaten all their lives and so would choose to make it at home (cf. Badler 2002: 84); their neighbors, once having had access to it, would also make the switch.

As widespread as the bowls are, there are still Late Chalcolithic sites contemporaneous with and well within the core zones of their use that do not have them. Any explanation for the function and distribution of beveled-rim bowls must take into account not only how many are found, but also where they are found and, in equal measure, where they are *not* found. It must account for their extraordinary consistency in form, fabric, and manufacture across a vast geographic *and* time range, especially as they are locally produced and might therefore vary in at least nuanced ways. In fact, since everyone was making their own, and often in places where there was already an indigenous tradition of mass-produced bowls and plates, it would not be unreasonable to expect

---

56   Which to all intents and purposes includes the Susiana plain.

regional distinctions in style and/or fabric while maintaining a general similarity of form. For example, no one would ever confuse an Egyptian bread mold, from which this explanation derives (Chazan and Lehner 1990; Potts 2009), with a Mesopotamian one; despite manifesting the same basic idea, they are quite disparate in shape and fabric. The differences might be explained as a result of independent traditions (Joffe 2000: 118), even though various Mesopotamian artifacts have been found in Egypt (for details, see T. A. Wilkinson 2002). The nature of the connection and its impact on the transmission of influences remains to be established (Butterlin 2003: 151–7).

Indeed, if everyone was making their own beveled-rim bowl, it would be well to inquire as to why there is absolutely no indication of identity manifest in these bowls – no differentiation, by the merest hint of a potter's mark, between the centralized industrialized production of the bakery and the household that was also employing the form – or did everyone get the bowl with their bread from the bakery, keeping it thereafter at home? In which case, one might imagine hundreds, perhaps even thousands, of these accruing in the lifetime of a single house. But if everyone was making their own bowls at home in all these different regions, why is there no micro-styling evident (Dietler and Herbich 1998),[57] nothing that says in some way, "this bowl belongs to family X" or that denotes other social relationships?

Postcolonial theory prompts these and other questions, questions based in the relationship between food and identity. For example: if this is about a better-tasting bread, why do some Late Chalcolithic communities choose *not* to adopt the new bread? And why would only a *few* people, within those sites where limited numbers of bowls are found, take to the new bread and not everyone? There is now a considerable literature on food and eating (see Mintz and DuBois 2002 for a survey), but the upshot is that there are no rules, nor are there permissible assumptions other, perhaps, than that taste is not innate but culturally constructed,[58] and any number of factors may contribute to that construction. Food preferences may be conservative, but they may, equally, change readily and rapidly (contra Pearce 1999: 36). Patterns today in the use of thick and flat breads in Syria are quite distinctive for example. "Syrian-style bread," or "two-layer flat bread," comprises eighty percent of all bread consumption. Single-layer flat bread, now confined to rural domestic production, and Western breads available

---

57 It is in fact possible that such microstyling exists – no one to my knowledge has yet taken a systematic, detailed approach to an analysis of precise measurements of hundreds of thousands of bowls from across such a broad geography that might reveal, if not consistency of size for rationing, consistent groupings of attributes. Goulder (2010) argues that one bowl served as a mold for another bowl, which should be evident in such a study, and which would presumably reveal regional patterning.

58 I am not referring here to genetically determined tastes, for example, where some people taste the bitterness in grapefruit and others do not.

in the cities and larger market towns comprise ten percent of total consumption respectively (El-Haramein and Adleh 1994). In my own observations, many villagers often profess a preference for town bread, the two-layer bread, stating that only cost and availability prevent them from eating it every day. Sometimes this choice is a matter of signaling sophistication and sometimes it is a product of more mundane concerns, especially when expressed by women, who seek release from the daily task of breadmaking. Others reject the notion that town bread is better, and in doing so, often associate their preference for village bread with the superiority of a traditional way of life and/or rejection of the city and, sometimes, of the idea of government control. There is no question, however, that town bread is more expensive, and that individual responses to it can be dictated by consideration of cost. On the other hand, Western-style breads are unpopular in Syria. They are a "blended" product, a Western idea made locally on Western machines with local materials,[59] and satisfy no one. Yet it is nearer to the taste of home and so consumed by many, but by no means all, of the expatriate community. Finally, in much of Syria the thick bread often thought of as "Turkish" or "Turkish-style" is unavailable, although not always unknown. It is consumed primarily in areas where there are populations who identify themselves as non-Arab and/or non-Muslim, even though "Turkish-style" breads are consumed in Turkey by a predominantly Muslim population.

All these responses to different kinds of bread would suggest a clear if implicit relationship to identity embedded in a mix of geographic, ethnic/national, political, economic, personal, and even religious factors, although they would not suggest that the relationship works in any one way. Anthropological archaeologists also now see food as an integral component of and venue through which identity is expressed, especially in the modes of practice theory. If so, bread, something one eats many times every day from infancy, is surely a key, and beveled-rim bowls an equally key, symbol of that identity – so much so that the subsequent cuneiform sign for bread looks very much like a beveled-rim bowl, as proponents of the bread-mold function are quick to note.[60] While this is not to say that identities cannot be consciously or unconsciously re-formed, rejected, and/or adopted, it would seem to indicate that a shift in consumption of such a staple is unlikely to be only a simple matter of fad or fancy, or indeed its opposite, sheer conservatism. If we invoke Bourdieu's notion of habitus as the basis of the relationship between quotidian practice, such as breadmaking, and identity, where the performance of daily tasks deeply engrained in bodily

---

59 The quality of the flour was often blamed in frequent conversations about the difficulties of getting good bread.

60 At the same time, proponents of the ration-bowl theory note that the cuneiform sign meaning "to eat" also employs a bowl (with a human head) that looks like our beveled-rim bowl (Nissen 1988: 84–5). But of course what food would be more symbolic of eating than bread?

motion reproduces within the individual the social structures and skills that create that individual's links to society, then those things associated with such tasks, such as bread molds, are indicative of one's conception of self: in other words, I use this bread mold because I am a member of this social group at the same time as I am a member of this social group because I use this bread mold.

As with any situation in which ethnographic examples are invoked, however, a brief survey of studies of changing consumption patterns will not only provide examples of shifting food preferences that take place in tandem with culture contact, it will also offer an equal number of examples that occur without such contact. In situations of colonialism either outcome, at least in part, is a product of the nature of the colonial encounter itself (Goody 1982), just as it is a product of preexisting ideas about food production and consumption. In colonial attempts to domesticate Africans by inculcating the arts of domestic service, for example, hybridity comes into play. African cooks were trained to reproduce the culinary experience of the colonist's original home, using local and imported goods; this was supposed to translate into the adoption of European ways in African domestic contexts. But whereas cooks and other domestic servants in white households were men, men did not cook in their own homes because that was women's work. And women continued to prepare the traditional meals as they always had because this fulfilled notions of what a good wife did. At the same time, there are very clear notions, notions that transcend class divisions, of what constitutes a proper, satisfying traditional meal, and this has remained unvaried from pre- to postcolonial times (Hansen 1999).

The question of shifting food preferences and the relationship of identity to food consumption is worthy of some detail because much is made of this issue in the discussion of the Uruk expansion. Emulation, an explanatory approach that itself might be argued as a profoundly colonialist view of the interaction between cultures – and, what is more, a direct outcome of hierarchies of development to which models of complex society are inextricably linked – is increasingly gaining ground as an explanation of the distribution of the Uruk repertoire and variation in its patterning.[61] It has been suggested (Lupton 1996) that this is a form of peer-polity interaction (Renfrew and Cherry 1986), where some groups use intrusive or "novel" resources to differentiate themselves from others of their own kind (Gosden 2004: 33). The group thus distinguished is universally claimed to be elite, or incipiently so. But the idea that Uruk materials within northern and eastern sites represent local elites emulating a superior culture requires considerable thinking. There are several questions: Is this actually an emulation of behavior, ideologies, or ways of life far more profound than the copying of a bowl? Would local elites, in order to further their status,

---

61   Wattenmaker 1990: 68; Lupton 1996: 68; Schwartz 2001; see Stein 1999a for a cogent discussion.

utilize mundane artifacts such as bread molds? Or eat products viewed as foreign? Stein (2001a: 282–3) suggests they would not, that emulation would be confined to moments of public display, where nonelites would be most likely to see such signs of their betters' status; whereas the presence of an intrusive repertoire in a domestic or private context must surely indicate the presence of actual colonists. Stephen and Peltenburg (2002) also suggest that the presence of different groups of people might be recognized in the archaeological record on the basis of the way they do fundamental things, rather than in exceptional items that may be deployed as a means of ascriptive status. At Hacinebi, Stein (2001a) has argued that stable relations with the host community may have been maintained through intermarriage, which raises more questions. If the two groups intermarried, does this mean the material culture of the male dominated that of the female? This seems unlikely, in terms of domestic tasks. It has been proposed at Hacinebi that local women were spinning fibers even in the contexts that appear to belong to the intrusive population, suggesting that southern women did not live there (Keith, in Stein et al. 1997: 139), but other explanations are equally possible: spinning may be a task organized according to social position or it may be a specialized skill not yet available to other population groups. As for cooking, would women cook in an unfamiliar way with unfamiliar implements to please their husbands? Would men know how to make a hearth as in their homeland? They well might, especially if they are ritual specialists and the fireplace is part of ritual practice. Simplistic correlations between hearth style, food production/consumption practices, and ethnic identity are simply not tenable when the distribution of variations in fireplace style is carefully considered. Moreover, it is not uncommon for colonists to employ local servants, who then attempt to produce the incoming group's original food preferences – using their own implements and locally available ingredients to create dishes that subsequently become integral to the national cuisine of the colonizers (if the British experience is anything to go by).

While I incline to the bread-mold function for beveled-rim bowls, I suggest a different way of understanding their distribution and interpretative significance. Their introduction constitutes at some sites a sharp demarcation when juxtaposed with local Late Chalcolithic traditions, a distinction that becomes even more marked when the full Uruk repertoire arrives. At the same time, other local Late Chalcolithic settlements – Arslantepe, Tell Brak, and Susa – have their own parallel and precedent version of this form in play at the time of the beveled-rim bowl encounter. Brak, like the Euphrates site of Arslantepe, represents a strong northern indigenous power that in some way accommodates Urukeans,[62] and, just as at Arslantepe, southern material attributes intervene

62 The question at Brak is whether Urukeans took over the settlement and established a colony there, as the local repertoire is ultimately replaced by the intrusive one in the limited

in what is certainly a ritual, if not religious, context. While Arslantepe does not ever manifest a beveled-rim bowl horizon, the appearance of the first bowls at Brak intersect with a ceramic sequence dominated by an earlier mold-made and "mass-produced" bowl form, as well as platter (Emberling and McDonald 2003: 2; Oates et al. 2007: 591, 596),[63] and the same is the case at Arslantepe. This suggests that the function of the mass-produced bowl, in whichever form it takes, has ritual connotations; that this function transcends individual cultural constructs or is engendered by earlier contact; and that it is ripe with possibilities of hybridity if northern and southern mass-produced forms appear much the same, are used in the same contexts, but are construed differently in their original locations. The fact that beveled-rim bowls do not subsequently become merged one way or another with local ceramic vernaculars, although they are made with local materials and continue largely unchanged over hundreds of years at sites scattered apparently randomly across the landscape, also raises questions of differentiation, where some people seek to make clear the distinction between themselves and others. But whether differentiation was externally generated by an intrusive population in order to control or indigenously so in order to resist, or both – or even neither – can only be recognized within settlements by the kinds of places in which the bowls appear.

It has already been established that the first beveled-rim bowls were recovered from Hacinebi on floors of local buildings (see note 49 above). And while the "full range" of Uruk ceramics is present at Hacinebi, even in so-called Uruk deposits beveled-rim bowls constitute approximately ninety percent of the sherdage (Stein 1999b: 148–9). "Tens of thousands" of beveled-rim bowls have also been found at Tell Brak (Oates 2002: 120) in the two small excavated areas that reached Uruk/local Late Chalcolithic period levels that lay eleven meters below the surface of the mound. Tell Brak, ancient Nagar, has proved to be a major regional center, probably since its inception (Oates et al. 2007). The discovery of several beveled-rim bowls stacked in two ovens dating to the Late Uruk period has been adduced as possible support for the salt hypothesis (although it seems more likely to me to support the bread-mold argument), but the earliest attestation of the bowl comes from level 16, where five sherds – thought to be extruding from disintegrating brick and therefore even earlier – were found with a

units excavated, or whether the local elite maintained its authority and simply adopted southern styles in emulation of what they viewed as a superior culture if not power. There is little question that the discussion (Lupton 1996; McMahon and Oates 2007; Oates et al. 2007) is driven by the issues of colonialism mentioned at the outset of this chapter. At Arlsantepe the situation is a little different. Materials southern in origin are side by side with what are apparently local copies (Frangipane 1997, 2002).

63   This local Late Chalcolithic bowl/cup form is understood as provisioning a centrally controlled labor force – that is, as a unit of rationing by Oates (Oates et al. 2007: 596 and Frangipane 2002), but this is surely on the basis of the dominant interpretation of the beveled-rim bowl.

local Late Chalcolithic assemblage corresponding in time to the Middle Uruk period (Oates and Oates 1993: 181).

The context at Brak in which the Uruk encounter is first evident, no matter how tenuous that evidence might be, is a tripartite structure first built in level 18 (dated to c. 3800 BCE) and termed a secular "feasting hall" (Oates et al. 2007: 594) because of the large domed ovens and open grill-style hearths[64] found in the attached courtyard, and the associated faunal remains (and plates) attesting to the preparation of large-scale meals based on meat (Emberling and McDonald 2001). The hall continued in use through levels 17–15 (Oates and Oates 2006b; Oates 2005: 20–1)[65] when it was adjacent to a succession of other tripartite structures that are labeled elite houses (Fig. 10).

Determining the difference between sacred and secular functions through architectural form is problematic, however, as such separation of domains is really a contemporary practice, our habit, rather than one that necessarily pertained in the past. It is especially so in this early period, when the kind of formalized form, function, and practice of the cult is not yet established.[66] Although the excavators interpret the building as a *secular* feasting hall, it is likely that such distinctions were simply nonexistent: political acts were overseen by religious specialists and could take place within a religious context; feasting may be a religious practice in celebration or commemoration of sacred figures and events, but those participating can certainly, indeed on many occasions should, include more than only a priesthood. Moments of feasting may be religious or profane or both at the same time; they may also be small-scale events and private, or large public occasions that involve many members of the community. They are a means of creating social relationships (Helwing 2003; Pollock 2003) that often involve extending those relationships over multiple planes of existence. That feasting maintained the connection between this world and the netherworld in the ancient Near East is well known. That it created and stretched social relationships, especially political relationships, between this world and the divine world is not quite as well delineated yet, but is becoming increasingly so. Our understandings of the separation of authority into sacred and secular structures competing with one another has a lengthy and still largely unexamined intellectual history that is very much tied up with the discussion of the Uruk period and the Uruk expansion. The origin of the state in the south has long been thought to lie in, if not an actual theocracy, then certainly the rise of the temple institution from its fifth millennium precursors, as seen in the remarkable sequence of tripartite structures at Eridu – although the assumption of a religious function

---

64 A feature already characteristic of both indoor and outdoor locations in level 19 (McMahon et al. 2007: 150).

65 In McMahon and Oates (2007: 149) it is level 14.

66 Level 18, where this building was found, is itself over an earlier industrial building, already indicating that there has been a substantial change.

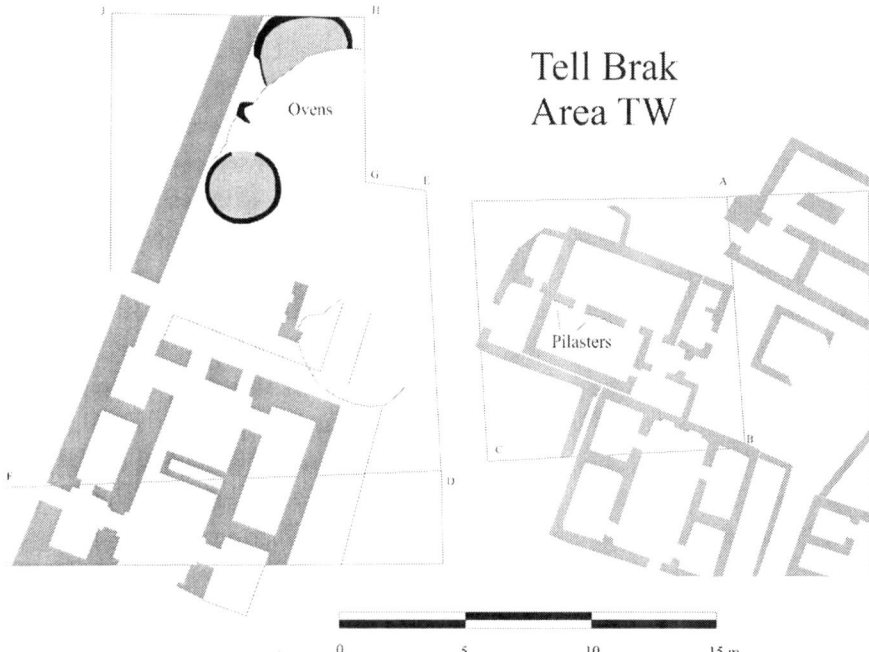

Tell Brak
Area TW

10. The level 18 Local Late Chalcolithic "feasting hall" at Tell Brak TW with associated level 16 structures. Level 18 reproduced with the kind permission of authors from Oates et al. 2007; Level 16 redrawn from Oates 2005.

of the tripartite buildings has been seriously questioned (Forest 1987), with alternative reconstructions identifying them as domestic residences (Roaf 1984), perhaps of "big men" or extended families. In the north, in contrast, state formation is largely accepted as deriving from a transition in power from "chiefs" to "kings," reflecting as much as anything the dominant academic disciplines in each area: the south, because of the early discovery of cuneiform tablets, has been viewed through the lens of Assyriological practices and paradigms; the north, which has only recently come into its own as a focus of research, remains primarily the purview of anthropological archaeology, particularly in this period.[67]

The determination of function, therefore, is so closely allied with regional theoretical perspectives and developmental histories that we must be quite cautious in such attributions, looking closely at any detail that might be informative. It is further complicated by the fact that tripartite architecture became so widespread in the fifth millennium that it may now, in the Uruk period, be considered local to the north, and therefore, like any local adaptation, cannot be assumed to have maintained the function (whatever that was) of its original manifestation in the southern Ubaid culture. In fact there is only one proper tripartite building in Level 16, and if it is an ordinary domestic house then some unusual social practices would appear to be in evidence. This structure

---

67   See Helwing 2003 for a useful summary of the situation.

is certainly smaller than the feasting hall (which itself is argued by Emberling and McDonald [2001: 24] to be too small for living quarters), and it has slightly different architectural embellishments. It abuts a second structure characterized by elaborated architectural features, but it is quite self-contained, unlike the feasting hall, which is integrally connected to the cooking area. Frangipane (1997: 49, n. 16) has suggested that tripartite temples and residences may be differentiated according to the size of the ancillary rooms, while Oates (2007: 162, n. 5, 163) veers between suggesting that storerooms indicate a non-ritual function and noting that they are a common feature of religious institutions. But is size difference enough to assume a domestic rather than public or even specialized ritual function? While Oates (2005: 18; also Frangipane 1997: 49, n. 16) does note that there is no reason why the house of the gods and the houses of people may not be much the same, there are nevertheless some fundamental differences that are significant, not just in general theoretical terms, but in terms of fathoming what is going on in this area and how it relates to contact.

This second structure of level 16 contains one long room, marked by niches in the short walls at either end, behind a slightly shorter room (due to the bent-axis form of the entrance) that was decorated with a pilastered façade (Oates and Oates 1993: 174–5). A number of "high status" goods were retrieved from this area, and it is here that the first beveled-rim bowls appear (Oates and Oates 1993: 181). As well as sealings thought to be from cylinder, not stamp, seals and bearing designs not dissimilar to ones found at Susa (Oates and Oates 1993: 178; Felli 2000, 2003), excavators found eye idols and, buried in the courtyard to the east, a cache of beads in multiple materials including silver (Oates 2005: 22). This has been interpreted as elite control of the burgeoning wealth of Tell Brak at this time. But if these buildings were secular and residential, the lack of hearths in either structure at Brak is a puzzle. It is possible that the occupants had a function closely associated with the feasting hall and received their meals from there, but its ovens are unlikely to have been in use every day, if only because they would have required large amounts of fuel. I think it doubtful that these buildings belonged to individuals or individual families in the manner to which we are accustomed, with the materials found there constituting personal wealth,[68] but rather that they were used to gather and store materials that belonged to, or were to be used in, whatever concept or situation the feasting

68 Despite the fact that a mainstay of "complex society" models is the notion of a social hierarchy created and maintained by accumulation of, and control over, material goods, there is little actual evidence in the fourth and third millennia of a concept of personal wealth. Extracted from assumptions derived from the model, there are two main locations of accumulations of materials that might be thought to represent wealth: burials, and here it is well established by now that many factors other than, or in addition to, representation of social status engenders grave goods; and public contexts such as "palaces." This pattern in and of itself indicates that such accumulations should be thought of as the property of the establishment, or on some occasions the community, and not the individual.

hall enacted. This would seem to be substantiated by the fact that hulled barley and flax seed were stored in jars in the courtyards of the feasting hall and
the tripartite "house" and associated buildings in similar proportions but in
different relationships. In the courtyard around the ovens, the jars with their
various contents were placed in separate areas; in the smaller buildings, jars of
different contents seemed to have been side-by-side. Wheat chaff was also kept
in a jar in both courtyard and the side room of the smaller tripartite structure,
which would seem an unusual practice and perhaps had some sort of symbolic,
rather than practical, significance. A jar of flax seed was found in the side room
of the pilastered building of the level 16 complex (Hald and Charles 2008: S38).
The bone and chipped stone remains from this complex would suggest that
food was actually prepared here (Emberling and McDonald 2003: 8), food that
may have been used in the feasting hall. In addition, the other objects from this
structure may have constituted a ritual assemblage – a large wooden platter and
wooden paneling or screen,[69] a stone fruitbowl, an alabaster bowl, and some eye
idols, while in the courtyard of the feasting hall, in level 16, several mace heads
were found (Emberling and McDonald 2003: 13, fig. 15).

That concept which the operations of the feasting hall enacted is tantaliz-
ingly glimpsed in two small details. One is a partially revealed structure, dated
to level 18b (McMahon and Oates 2007: 150; Oates et al. 2007: 590, fig. 4) and
not yet discussed in publication, with an intricate stepped end to an interior
room that I suspect will prove to be a temple; the other is the location of these
structures, the feasting hall of level 18 through 15 and associated buildings,
over the monumental structures of level 20 in the vicinity of the north gateway.
While the buildings of level 20 and 19 are attributed an industrial function
by the excavators (Oates et al. 2007),[70] it is possible that this was, or became, a
reception area for important visitors and foreign dignitaries, with whom cor-
dial relations, trading engagements, or even military treaties were cemented by
feasting (and cf. Oates et al. 2007: 596). This might be further inferred from the
fact that by level 11 this area is dominated by the full repertoire of Uruk characteristics, including two keyhole ovens (Oates 2005: 27).

A similar duality – or better, ambiguity – of function is evident in contact
period architecture at Arslantepe level VIA (Fig. 11), dating to the late Uruk
period/ Late Chalcolithic 5 (c. 3350–3000 BCE) and which the excavator terms
a "temple-palace complex" (Frangipane 1997: 52, 2002)[71] – "temple" because

---

69 And see the discussion of Ebla in Chapter 3 for a similar situation: a room with specialized
    equipment, screen, and possible association with feasting.
70 I suspect the implication, then, for the excavators was that those who were involved in this
    function became the elite occupying the later level 16 houses.
71 Although by 2007 Frangipane refers more often to the Level VIA structures as "a 'palatial'
    complex." See, for example, the title of Frangipane 2007b. The religious function of the
    cellae is now subordinate to the economic in the redistributive potential of the stores.

Arslantepe

11. The level VIA temple complex with "residential" sector and level VII Building XXIX at Arslantepe. Redrawn, with kind permission of authors, from Frangipane 2002: figs. 2 and 4 and Frangipane et al. 2009: fig. 10.

of the style and fittings of two main rooms, "palace" because of the presence of unusual quantities of sealings in storerooms adjacent to the temple units. There is no reason to presume a palatial function for this complex, nor even an administrative one, if "administrative" here is to be understood as the overall organization and control of the polity in which the site of Arslantepe is situated. The two thousand sealings recovered (Frangipane 2007b: 29), and the commodities and their sources that they represent, are intrinsic to the activities within, and function of, the core elements of the complex: the temple *cellae*. The variety of sealings only indicates the variety of people who were supporters of the temple, contributing materials for its sustenance – whether voluntarily or involuntarily we cannot know.

This complex is in fact two separate constructs divided by an alley or corridor gated at the southwestern end of the street (Frangipane 2007b: 49, fig. I.16), each construct based around a temple with associated stores, workrooms, and no doubt residences for its attendant personnel. Even if one might justifiably quibble about the "temple" label, preferring to see the *cellae* as "shrines," each complex is organized around a differentiated, specialized space that has installations for the performance of limited and specialized acts. This is clear both in the shape and organization of the rooms, and the contents found in situ within them. The intrinsic unity of each construct, however, and their connection to each other, may be inferred from the repetition of architectural plan and, as well, the decorative elements found on walls outside the core temple units themselves. These decorations included geometric designs, some made with a stamp, and wall paintings of figurative content (see Frangipane and Palmieri 1983: fig. 5; Frangipane 1997: 65, fig. 14; 2001: 338, fig. 9.9).

It is particularly interesting that these decorated walls are not found in the temples themselves, but in spaces that segue to them: in the alley and in the small rooms behind Temple B and the front rooms of Temple A, including the latter's entranceway. One figurative painting actually adorns a storeroom (A364) on the other side of the street and associated with Temple B. Although the storerooms A365, A364, and A340 (illustrated in beautiful detail in Frangipane 2007b) do not link directly to Temple B and were built subsequent to it (Frangipane 1997), the fact that the ancillary rooms within the Temple A unit contained exactly the same functions as the storerooms behind Temple B renders it likely that the latter also constituted a unified complex.

It is the contents of all these rooms, however, that provide a vivid, if ambiguous, glimpse of a moment in the life of the temples,[72] where vessels containing certain commodities are brought into the building by a wide variety of people, opened, the contents disbursed, the vessels then resealed and stored, and the contents deployed in a number of possible ways. It is here that ambiguity arises. Frangipane (1997; 2007b) suggests that the commodities were redistributed. There are several reasons for this supposition; one of them (graphically indicated in Fiandra and Frangipane 2007: 418–19) is the fact that the storerooms open not to the temple, but to the courtyard. In contrast, I suspect that the

---

72 Although the action is not as immediate in Temple A, where the bulk of the vessels were in ancillary rooms accessed through high doors/low windows.

goods in these rooms were all consumed by the temples – notwithstanding the lack of direct connection between store and *cella* – in ceremonies or for the daily support of the institution(s). And if it is permissible to posit rooms not yet attested (as would be the case for the domicile of the royal residents, for example), then one might equally suggest a feasting space as part of the complex. Certainly the courtyard onto which the storerooms face could have been the location of large-scale rituals, although this proposition is not necessary, as a coherent interpretation can be provided for the extant materials as they stand, no matter the nature of the larger context into which they fitted.

The supplies in the stores would not in the end have provisioned many people for very long, and Frangipane herself suggests that they constitute a recent collection of materials, some of which are clearly disbursed in the *cella* judging from the presence not only of vessels but also *cretulae* in Temple B. The understanding that goods were opened at least, if not used, immediately after they arrived comes from the fact that the sealings were not broken but concertinaed, implying that the mud on which the image was impressed was not yet dry, since it was pushed aside on opening instead of shattered. It seems possible that, rather than disbursed, the contents of the vessels were checked on arrival, perhaps to ensure that they were what they were supposed to be, or perhaps to keep track of who had sent what – as it may not have been apparent at the outset just what each vessel contained. The contents of the vessels may have been doled out in small units for daily rituals and for consumption by the temple attendants, rather than distributed to a large-scale dependent personnel or corvée labor (contra Guarino 2008), with the vessels closed and resealed each time. The three fenestrated long-stemmed bowls found near the altar seem to have contained substances in use at that moment, taken from the jars nearby. The remainder of the pots were found in the northwest corner of the *cella* (Frangipane 2007b: 42, fig. I.12) and appear to represent past and/or future use.

Ultimately, though, it is the presence of mass-produced bowls that is considered cogent evidence for the redistributive aspect of the VIA complex and that gives rise to its label "palace." Over a hundred specimens of a local conical bowl form were found in storeroom A340 (Frangipane 1997: 66) behind Temple B, while more were found in the storerooms, on window ledges, and on the floor of Temple A, where they are interpreted as having contained meals for distribution (Frangipane 1997: 69). There is a long-term precedent for this situation. Found in the earlier monumental structure of level VII and dated to c. 3800 BCE (Frangipane 2002: 124) was a large deposit of local mass-produced bowls scattered on the floor of the central room in what also seems to be a temple (Fig. 12), so designated because it contained a large, raised, rectangular structure, a platform or dais, and a hearth (Frangipane 2002: 124). Frangipane calls this building (Building XXIX) "ceremonial," however (also Guarino 2008), a further indication of ambivalence based on the putative redistributive function

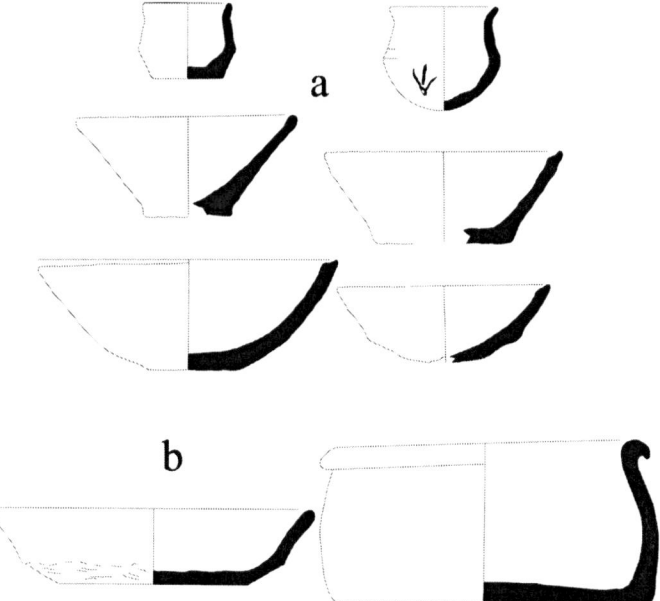

12. Mass-produced pots from Arslantepe and Tell Brak. Group A from Arslantepe level VII, redrawn from Frangipane 2002: fig. 10b. Group B "pie plate" and "casserole" from level 16 at Tell Brak, redrawn from Oates and Oates 1993: fig. 54.

of the bowls, more of which were found in a small side room of the structure where they were presumably stored, as they were stacked in upside-down piles. Sealings were also found in this room.

Here too, however, the evidence suggests not that materials are being disbursed outside of the temple *through* a ceremonial context, rather, the bowls strewn on the floor indicate that whatever they contained is being used *in* a ceremonial context. The distinction may be subtle, but it is important, not least because of the implications of the "foreign materials" involved. Of those vessels in the vicinity of the altar of Temple B, level VIA, is a Red-Black Burnished Ware *pithos*; two long jars identical in shape to southern Uruk vessels, but made of a paste that seems to be characteristically local, are among the northwestern group. One small, sharply carinated and red-slipped jar is typical of "Uruk" contexts at Hassek Höyük, Tell Brak, and also Habuba Kabira South, and is of a paste unknown in the local Late Chalcolithic materials at Arslantepe (Frangipane 1997: 56). The assemblage of this room also included Reserved Slip Ware (illustrated in Frangipane 1997: figs. 8–9).

It is time now to bring back to mind the discussion of the later Arslantepe tomb with which this chapter started. One of the issues mentioned then was the separation of exactly these two ware groups into ethnic/cultural markers of, on the one hand, a nomadic, Transcaucasian (and beyond) population and, on the other, an elite (and obviously sedentary) Mesopotamian population. In level VIA both kinds of wares are present, and present together not only in structures with religious connotations but also in the very same ritual activity. That wares so thoroughly identified with outside groups are found here raises many questions, not least about the redistributive function of this complex. Would outsiders contribute to a system to which they did not belong and from which they gained nothing? The question can be resolved in several ways – either these two groups were not outsiders, this was not a redistributive system, or the situation in which they participated transcends simple dichotomies of "us" and "them." Proving which alternative is applicable is not easy, and the result is often a product of one's theoretical persuasion rather than any convincing evidence.

I propose that the mass-produced bowls, much as at Tell Brak, fulfill a ritual function, and although excavations at Arslantepe have not yet revealed a "feasting hall," the temples themselves may serve as such in both levels VII and VIA – where obeisance before other worldly beings, oaths, and similar acts are cemented by, if not feasting, then consumption of specially designated items. In level VII this seems quite clear; the interior features of Building XXIX consist of a central large platform with a hearth along with the mass of bowls on the floor (Frangipane 2002: 127). It is also possible in the buildings of VIA, where there are several movable "tables" that might have served food prepared elsewhere. Any temple calendar is full of different levels of performance: daily, small-scale actions and periodic, usually larger-scale, occurrences. The numbers and kinds of people involved, as well as the materials employed, also vary according to the nature of the performance. The bowls located in the stores cannot tell us how many people participated – in which kind of ritual, on how many occasions – without our knowing exactly what the functions of the bowls were. Even the bowls in the *cellae* themselves may not relate to the number of people present, but to the number of contributions that were placed before the gods – either at the requirement of the temple or at the petition of the individuals involved.

If the bowls are bread molds, as are the beveled-rim bowls, then they are not used to receive unprocessed goods from the jars in the stores. If they are not bread molds, as seems most likely, then they are used in a different way than the beveled-rim bowls. As I have suggested for Tell Brak, feasting at Arslantepe was a regularized but not necessarily frequent activity that took place in specialized contexts, and it is in these contexts that Urukeans, or at least their pottery, intersects. Three beveled-rim bowls were found in fill materials of this area (Frangipane 1997: 70, n. 39), and although their rarity is unusual given their general prolixity, their presence should not be discounted. It is not remarkable that there are so few beveled-rim bowls at the site if it is initial contact that is represented; it *is* extraordinary that they never *become* a feature of the Arslantepe repertoire, at least in the excavated areas, when there are actual southern vessels in use in level VIA. Yet it should be remembered that at Arslantepe contact was later than at Brak, and it may be that the pattern of events has changed – either because of the nature of Arslantepe itself – its own complexity inhibiting Uruk takeover as is usually argued, or because the general practices of contact, their organization, maybe even their raison d'être were changing. In fact, I doubt

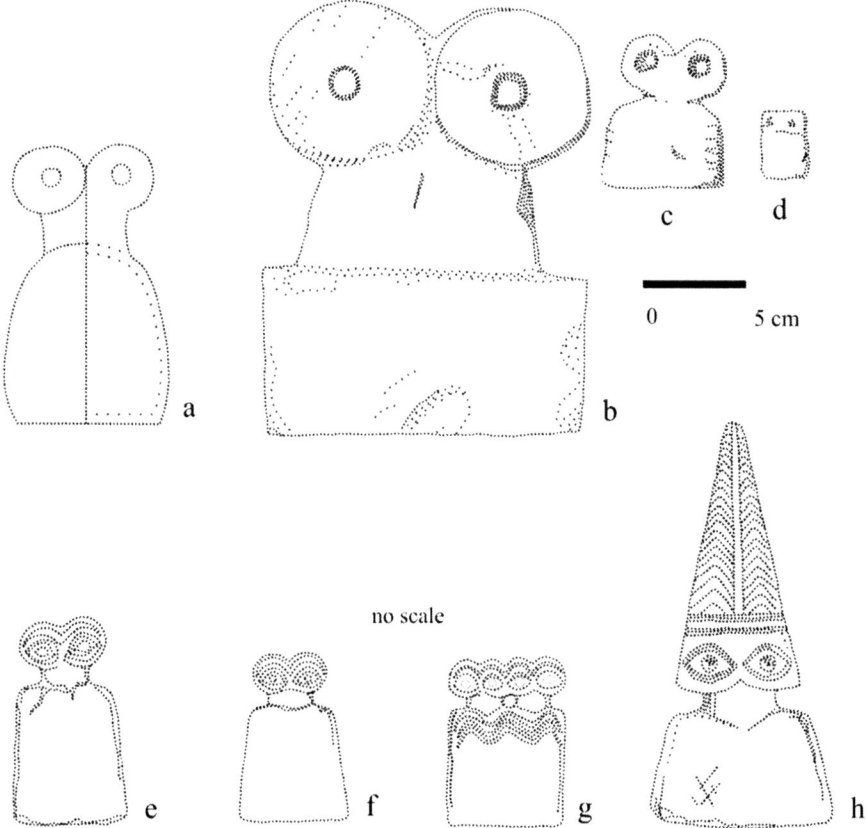

13. "Hut symbols/spectacle idols," *a* (redrawn from Breniquet 1996), *b–d* from Hacinebi (redrawn from Stein et al. 1997); "eye idols" *e-h* from Tell Brak (redrawn from Oates 2005).

that the fundamental reason for contact was changing. Despite the distance in time between the first evidence of it at Brak and later at Arslantepe, both sites contain some very significant clues as to what that reason may be, and at both places the clues point to the same thing: wool.

That the introduction of woolen textiles and a wholesale shift from flax took place in the Uruk period, if not before, now seems clear (McCorriston 1997; Kouchoukos 1998; Sudo 2010), the sociopolitical ramifications of which were discussed in Chapter 1. Further evidence places that transition even earlier in the fourth millennium than previously recognized. Already in level 20 there are indications that woolen textile production was a major part of the economy of Brak. These include a number of spindle whorls in the tool assemblage, and although weights are not provided – which would indicate whether they were used for wool or flax (Keith in Stein et al. 1997: 137; Sudo 2010) – they seem to be of the kind appropriate to wool. A "spectacle idol" (Fig. 13) reused in a wall was also found in level 20 (McMahon and Oates 2007: 153–4). Often equated with eye idols, it has been suggested that these objects, considerably larger and more rudimentary than the eyes, were used in textile production (Breniquet 1996;

Emberling 2002), perhaps for dipping yarns in dye, perhaps for twining threads into two-ply yarn; similarly with the closely related "hut symbol" that precedes them chronologically.[73] The resemblance in form is, I think, no coincidence. It suggests an integral relationship, without implying primacy of one or the other, between the two items, one functional, one representing abstracted notions of being – whether human or otherworldly is unascertainable. Although to date the specimen reused in level 20 (and therefore even earlier in origin) is the first example of this kind of artifact, it is possible that spinners transformed some kind of ontological/anthropomorphizing statement, or their adherence to a divine entity, into an object that lay at the heart of their work.

A transitional form between spectacle/hut symbol and eye idol is noted at Arslantepe and in Mallowan's collection from Brak (Trufelli 2000). Most eye idols come from the early fourth-millennium foundations of the so-called Eye Temple in the only other area to reach this period at Tell Brak, area CH (Oates et al. 2007: 596). Some, though, were found in the pilastered house of TH level 16 (Oates 2005: 21). In level 19, large numbers of spindle whorls are found in the building adjacent to the heavily walled structure with basalt threshold (McMahon and Oates 2007: 151). In this same period spindle whorls were cut from cattle bones, which would not only render them very light, as appropriate for spinning wool, but would also carry symbolic value (Weber in McMahon and Oates 2007: 167–70; however, cf. Frangipane et al. 2009: 6). At Hacinebi it has been determined that the weights of spindle whorls in both pre-contact and first contact levels (where the majority were found) are suitable for spinning and plying sheep/goat fibers (Stein et al. 1997: 138).

While spindle whorls and spectacle idols suggest woolen textile manufacture, it is the animal bones that prove most persuasive. Sheep and goat remains overwhelmingly dominate the faunal assemblage here, and they continue to do so in level 18–16 (indeed, throughout the fourth millennium), with an increasing proportion of sheep over goat – as might be expected if wool production was intensified (Weber in McMahon and Oates 2007: 168). But the faunal remains found in area TW are being ceremonially consumed in the feasting hall[74] and so this shift might have more to do with food preferences than with general patterns of animal husbandry, although I think it highly likely that the two were symbolically synonymous. At the same time, the morphology of the sheep remains from this area indicates that they were wool-bearing

73 All three kinds were found at Hacinebi (Stein et al. 1997), although the "hut symbol" is more likely to be an andiron there.
74 A correlation between the dominance of sheep/goat bones and "larger" (read public?) buildings at Abu Salabikh is also noted, while "lower status" residences are characterized by a preponderance of cattle at that site and elsewhere (Pollock 1999: 112). Rather than understand this as a reflection only of status, symbolic meanings associated with caprids in a time of economic and social change wrought by the new textile industry should also be considered.

and/or the product of long-distance pastoralism; they were large, with evidence of big muscle mass developed perhaps through supporting the weight of fleece, high mobility, and/or pasture in rough terrain (Weber in Oates et al. 2001: 346). It has been argued that at Umm Qseir, on the Habur, large-boned sheep were southern in origin (Zeder 1994: 116), because they stand out within the caprine assemblage as a whole and have been detected at Middle Euphrates colony sites (but cf. McCorriston 1997), where it has been assumed that settlers brought everything, including animals, with them. But if large-boned sheep occur in pre-contact and first contact levels at Tell Brak, then they are as likely to be local as imported. We should not expect, though, a single pattern reflecting a single behavior; rather, wherever the first wool-bearing sheep originated, they, and/or their product, would quickly become sought after, and in a variety of ways. Thereafter, who owned what sheep and where they grazed them might be impossible to detect.

At Arslantepe, a dramatic reduction in pig and a growing emphasis on sheep (and to a lesser extent goat), which now comprise eighty-two percent of the collected faunal remains (Frangipane 1997: 68), is quite clear and takes place over the change from level VII to VIA, dominating thereafter (Frangipane et al. 2009: 17, 27). But as important as this shift is, it is the wall paintings (Fig. 14) adorning the temple complexes that are particularly suggestive as to its potential significance. Both figurative paintings are about animals – human–animal connections, no less (contra Frangipane 1997: 65–7). On the one that decorates the street, behind which is Temple B, the dominant image is of two opposing horned animals flanking the traditional stalk of wheat.[75] A miniature human figure holds ties that loop the left horn of the left animal. Left of the human figure are two objects that I suggest also represent animals or, given the one/two legs, perhaps birds, but here in an increasingly abstracted form.[76] This second motif, where the animals do not oppose but follow each other, may be compared to images from the sealings recovered from Arslantepe (Fig. 14). While the animals portrayed on most of the sealings usually have sufficiently defined (although not always differentiated) heads, tails, and legs that they are

---

75   For an interesting albeit late parallel, see the lower registers of the Ninizaza stele from Mari (Margueron 2004: 56).

76   The comparison with the royal threshing scene proposed by Frangipane (1997; also Baltali 2007) is derived predominantly from traces of an element located beneath the human figure holding the animals by a thread attached to the horns. This element could, in fact, be anything, and as drawn in the reconstruction (Frangipane 2001: 338) seems unlikely to turn to the left to form the sled. It is not evident in the published photograph (Frangipane 1997: 66), which to my eye differs from the artist's reconstruction in a number of small but potentially significant ways. Moreover, the objects interpreted as canopies do not in any way resemble the structure that surmounts the seated figure on Mesopotamian sledges, and the figure itself, which sits behind the driver, is not in evidence in the Arslantepe picture. Finally, the photograph of the painting contains hints of an animal surmounting the scene in the same way as the picture from Room A364.

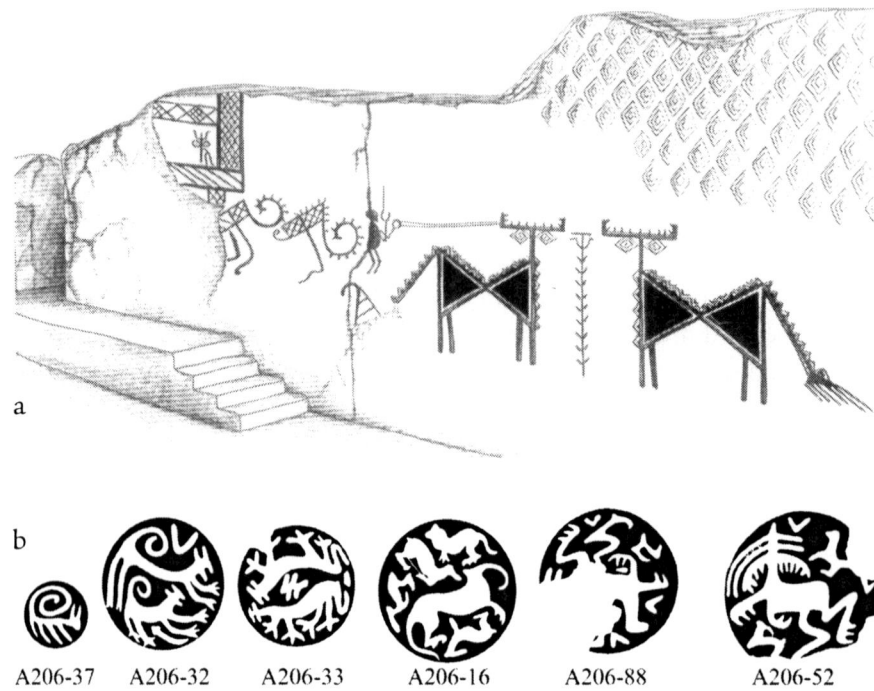

a

b

A206-37 A206-32 A206-33 A206-16 A206-88 A206-52

c

14. Seals and wall paintings from Arslantepe VIA: (a) from corridor in front of Temple B, reproduced with the kind permission of the School of American Research and Marcella Frangipane; (b) seals redrawn from Pittman 2007; (c) painting from storeroom A364 (south of Temple B), illustration courtesy of Marcella Frangipane.

recognizable, not all do. For example, see A206-016 and A206-052 (Pittman 2007: 187, 200 respectively) in Fig. 14b below. It is easy to see the development of the abstraction in some of the highly schematized renderings of certain animals (for example, A206-032 to A206-033), but it may also be suggested that the abstraction has particular meaning – that the animals have crossed from a realistic/worldly depiction to the representation of otherworldly or "fantastical" (Pittman 2007) beings. The animal basis for these two figures on the alley wall - one of which has only the most residual demarcation of a head and would seem to be missing a leg - is supported by the presence of a curled tail, which is very similar to the portrayals of dogs[77] on sealings such as A206-037 (Pittman 2007: 195). The fact that several of the creatures on the seals have rectangular bodies (A206-052, A206-088; Pittman 2007: 200, 212) suggests that the transition from the image on the seal to the one on the wall is possible.

That the animals in these wall paintings assume mythical dimensions is entirely in keeping with their locations in the temple complexes. The painting in the storeroom A364 behind Temple B must be seen in a similar vein. Here too it is an animal–human relationship that is depicted, for surmounting the humanlike figure is the body of a four-legged furred or hairy creature and, contra Frangipane (1997: 64), certainly not a canopy.[78] The curled appendage on the left is the tail of the animal, depicted in the same manner as the tails of the two box shapes on the corridor painting and the canine/feline beasts on the seals. The "fringe" is a common device for depicting hair on human or otherworldly beings, as seen at Halawa (Luth in Orthmann 1989: 104, pl. 67) and in depictions of furred or haired animals on pottery (e.g., Sconzo 2010: pl. 132, nos. 1527 and 1528). The chest rises to the right, where the neck and head is worn away. The humanlike figure is fringed in the same manner as the animal, suggesting that he is wearing a cap of animal fur/hair.[79] The figure stands behind a bench of some kind and,[80] interestingly, is represented by a series of triangles just like the animals on the alley painting. A line connects the figure to the beast that surmounts him, resembling the way in which the figure is connected to the animals in the other painting. This image is repeated throughout

---

77   Although I think they are felines!
78   Frangipane and I could both be accused of seeing what we want to see here, what fits in with our respective predispositions, but that is entirely the point. The data do not stand beyond interpretation, pure and clear, especially data such as artistic representation. It is often murky, open to a variety of readings and reconstructions. And even when it does seem clear, that clarity comes rather from the degree of naturalization that the model has undergone than from any inherent quality of the material.
79   I am reminded of the much later pot from third-millennium Tell Banat decorated with human figures holding kites and goats. The clothes of the figures and the goats are depicted in the same way, suggesting that the figures are wearing goatskin cloaks.
80   For the clearest example of this painting see the Arslantepe website at http://w3.uniroma1.it/arslantepe/dipinti.htm.

the room (Frangipane 1997: 64), and in one iteration a second figure, possibly female, is evident (Frangipane 1992).

I do not claim to understand what these paintings mean, whether the figures are superhuman/divine and the animals mythical, or whether this is a depiction of a realistic, mundane scene. But I do think that they help to explain the presence of "southern," "local," and "Transcaucasian" wares in the same ritual space. They also explain why these apparently separate cultural traditions are evident in the Arslantepe "royal" tomb of the next phase of occupation.

These wall paintings are not cultic objects but signifiers of identity, positioned in spaces where people unfamiliar with the complexes, but not outsiders, might be expected to need signposts to find their way – people bringing stores to Complex B, where it is room A364 that opens onto the courtyard; people passing through the alley looking for their destination; or entering Temple A. The figures represent the constituency of the temple establishments, and the human–animal connection that is the theme of the paintings suggests a constituency invested in mobile pastoralism.[81] This contituency is not necessarily culturally or ethnically separate from the population of Arslantepe. That there are two *cellae* in this complex, divided by an alley but unified by both design and practices,[82] is suggestive of two groups that are essentially the same but that differentiate themselves one from the other. The basis of this cleavage might be social – perhaps defined by ancestral or lineage group or other forms of sodality – or it might be religious, twinned temples being far from uncommon, with each dedicated to a different member of the pantheon, or perhaps to a spousal pair. I doubt that this is the case here, however, for the reasons delineated below. There are many kinds of associations in which groups are founded and many reasons for their differentiation. In this instance, two temples are not defined by ceramic affiliations with one culture or another, one ethnic group or another, one subsistence method or another – and especially not one level of civilization or another – because Red-Black Burnished Ware, Uruk vessels, Uruk-style vessels, and a local Late Chalcolithic repertoire are present side-by-side in each temple *cella* (Frangipani and Palmieri 1983: fig. 19).

Red-Black Burnished Ware has long been identified with mobile pastoralists if only because of its wide distribution from the Caucasus to the Levant – two Red-Black Burnished Ware vessels were found in a mid-third-millennium tomb at my own site of Tell Banat on the Middle Euphrates (Porter 1995). But this does not mean that the ware belonged only to mobile groups, or, if the ware is the product of mobile groups, that those groups were external to Arslantepe. The presence of Red-Black Burnished Ware in the building immediately before

---

81 Whether of cattle, sheep, or goat and whether the horned animal images represent one or the other of those animals.

82 And in use at the same time, although Temple A was built subsequently to Temple B (Frangipane 1997: 49).

the temples of level VIA, Building XXIX, is evidence of this, and there is clearly a tradition of people using it in rituals in both levels VII and VIA. In Temple A, small vessels and fruit stands in Red-Black Burnished Ware are found in both the stores and the *cella* (Frangipani and Palmieri 1983: fig. 19). In fact, Frangipane (2002: 125) notes that Red-Black Burnished Ware becomes "typical of period VIA" and constitutes eleven percent of the assemblage (Frangipane and Palmieri 1983: 354), at least in the vicinity of Temple A and Building III. Red-Black Burnished Ware is present in the Late Uruk period in the Uruk enclave at Godin Tepe (Badler 2002: 83), and at Hassek Höyük and Habuba Kabira South it comprises around ten percent of the assemblage (Helwing 1999: 95, fig.1; see also Sürenhagen 1986: 22).[83] Habuba Kabira South is the one site that all analysts agree is a Mesopotamian settlement. Mesopotamian materials are also known in the Transcaucasian region during the fourth millennium, and perhaps earlier (Kohl 1989; pers. comm. B. Lyonnet).

The southern vessels, and their locally made counterparts, become part of this same admixture at Arslantepe. For a long time it was thought that all vessels that looked like southern Uruk pots *were* southern Uruk pots. Then it was ascertained that some of those vessels were locally made products that looked exactly the same as southern vessels; others were obvious, and inexact, "copies." These vessels were called Uruk-style or Uruk-related and were seen at some sites as evidence of emulation or – as at Hassek Höyük and in a more nuanced interpretation – hybridity (Helwing 1999). Although Hassek Höyük has been typecast as an Uruk enclave/outpost site, true Uruk pottery is actually rare there and is confined to a specific location (Helwing 1999: 97).[84] Instead, the assemblage is characterized by a combination of local wares and what Helwing considers a hybrid repertoire.[85] This hybrid group consists of local forms produced by southern technology – the fast wheel and mineral-tempered fabric – and southern shapes made in a local chaff-tempered ware. Hybridity here is interpreted as evidence of, on the one hand, an obvious desire by local potters to use better technology and, on the other, their somewhat inadequate attempts to reproduce Uruk materials, either as a gesture of affiliation or in order to serve a southern clientele (Helwing 1999: 96–7).

Several questions present themselves at this juncture, starting with whether the entire ceramic requirements of a single Uruk community *could*, let alone *would*, be provided by imported goods alone. Does the desire to maintain cultural integrity outweigh the impracticalities of shipping fragile pottery vessels over the kind of distances involved? There are no behavioral expectations to be

---

83   It is possible this commensality in percentages of Red-Black Burnished Ware at different sites is not coincidence, but points to a regularized context, use, or function of this material.

84   The significance of which will be discussed below.

85   Also noted at a site that bears many similarities to Hassek Höyük, and that is Godin Tepe (Badler 2002).

met here, no permissible assumptions as to what colonists would or would not do. When away from home many of us have a desire at some point for the products of our origin, products that do more than satisfy taste buds – they remind us of our identity. These items become luxuries even when modern transportation is available. There are those people who want, and are able because of the sponsorship of state or nongovernmental organizations,[86] to duplicate as far as possible all the attributes of their culture of origin, from foodstuffs to furniture. For the rest, some expatriates choose (or are obliged) to make do with substitutions and approximations, while others readily immerse themselves in the culture of their host country. Since we know that people may integrate, assimilate, acculturate, borrow, creolize, and hybridize (see Lionnet 1993, Kapchan and Turner Strong 1999, and Palmié 2006 for the complexity of these terms) in a variety of situations, and, equally, that they may not, the fundamental question of interest is surely: why does one or the other occur?

If it is truly a merging of separate cultural traditions – and given the understanding of hybridity outlined earlier in this chapter, the presence of local and "blended" wares in the Hassek Höyük buildings would be better called creolization – it would be impossible to tell if this was a product of acculturation of foreigners or local emulation of intruders. I doubt, however, that this phenomenon represents the changing identities of people living at the site. At third-millennium Tell Banat, the same process is observed. Two distinct bodies of ceramics in one occupation phase borrow from one another in the next phase. These are Euphrates Banded Ware and Plain Simple Ware, and while they were for some time considered the products of different social groups (Carter and Parker 1995), work done at Banat clearly proved that the two wares were not only made in the same pottery workshops (McClellan and Porter 1998) and fired in the same kilns, but were used in the same ritual contexts. One group of pottery, Plain Simple Ware, was used in every kind of context – domestic, public, ritual and so on. Euphrates Banded Ware was used *only* in ritual contexts, and primarily mortuary ones at that. What is more, Euphrates Banded Ware was consistently deployed in the mortuary practices of different sectors of society, a society crosscut not by class so much as by differing views of what society should be (Porter 2002a, 2002b). Subsequently, certain characteristics of each repertoire – forms from one, ware from the other – crossed over to become new categories that were less restricted than the previous ones (Porter 1995, 1999, 2007b; McClellan 1998).[87]

---

86 U.S. Diplomats and soldiers abroad have access to the PX; organizations such as ICARDA provide furniture and make arrangements for the non-tariffed importation of food items and cars.

87 This example serves to raise another point: the larger significance or meaning of an object is not immutable (Joyce 2008). Something that has a specific role in one period may accrue multiple meanings in another; something that is sacred in one period may become quite prosaic in the next.

There are many reasons why potters choose to modify and adapt their technological and stylistic traditions, because "technologies are meaningful acts of social engagement with the material world that express and contest social values and judgments … and that can be put to political and practical ends simultaneously" (Dobres 2000: 129). So the task is to identify what those political and practical ends may be, and here the key lies in the fact that change is far more usual than the converse – *not* adapting new methods and styles, *not* developing new forms, whether through the subtle changes wrought by repetition over time or by encounters with other ways of doing things. The extreme longevity not just of Uruk forms, but of assemblages defined as local Late Chalcolithic as well – despite subtle shifts in shape and relative quantities of form – is remarkable, for if change is "the intentionless invention of regulated improvisation," like a "train laying its own rails" (Bourdieu 1990 [1980]: 57), then not changing takes considerable effort.

In fact what we see in these assemblages is not even so much the *absence* of change as it is concerted efforts *not* to change (see also Collins 2000: 65), and these efforts appear to be driven not by the producer, but by the consumer. In terms of the Uruk and Uruk-related ceramics, the so-called copies, including even the more rudimentary versions of Uruk pots, should be understood as just as Urukean as the southern imports. Perhaps some were made by professional potters sent from Uruk who were part of the movement of southern peoples through the north (Wright 2001: 135); perhaps some were made by nonspecialists seeking to replace familiar forms. But whatever the case – and even if made by locals and not émigrés – there is another consideration that overrides the issue of who made them, and that is: why *continue* to make them? Uruk specialists are right, then, to focus on why copies were produced, but they have located the question in the wrong domain, driven as they are by the complexity model. In contrast to the situation at Banat, where the role of specialized wares clearly shifted from their mortuary use to more mundane contexts, the Uruk replications should be seen as preserving the idea of what the original pot should be, because *change* was the very thing these pots were deployed to deny.

Part of the problem lies in the division of materials into "southern" and "northern" assemblages, in which one of the main points of differentiation has long been the issue of temper and technology. Chaff-tempered and hand-made wares are northern, while grit-tempered and wheel-made wares are southern. This has had at the least an unconscious (although often enough it is quite conscious) effect on characterizations of the societies associated with these two assemblages. Chaff tempering generally leads to coarse-grained and less durable fabrics, so is less technologically advanced than grit. Ergo, the societies that used it were perceived as not as developed as those which used mineral temper – even though there is no situation where mineral temper is not known in association with vegetal-tempered wares, it is just used in smaller quantities. Therefore, the use of chaff tempering was not from ignorance of a superior technology but an active choice, for reasons we simply have not thought about sufficiently. Nevertheless, the common consensus is that if northern potters do not subsequently adopt grit tempering and a fast wheel after those features become available, they are "conservative" (as Helwing 1999: 98).

Yet the archetypal Uruk pot, the beveled-rim bowl, is chaff-tempered and hand/mold made, that is, shaped by hand over a mold (Goulder 2010). In contrast, one of the characteristic Mesopotamian diagnostics, certainly in Frangipane's understanding, is the Reserved Slip material – wheel-made, grit-tempered, and now probably local Late Chalcolithic in origin (Dessine 2008), so local in fact that it is largely confined to the Upper Euphrates region in both the fourth and third millennia[88] (Porter 1999; 2007b; see n.4 this chapter). While the northern origins of Reserved Slip Ware have only recently been proposed, the fabric of the beveled-rim bowl is as much a defining feature of this vessel as its shape. The beveled-rim bowl is not the only chaff-tempered vessel known as Urukean. The coarse tray and conical cup are also made in this fabric.

This fact alone must indicate there is something amiss with some of the basic conceptual frameworks that archaeologists bring to the interpretation of this pottery. But an added element confirms it: it is repeatedly argued that the fast wheel was introduced because it answered the demands of a centralizing state (e.g., Nissen 2002: 9), as it enabled greater quantities of more standardized items to be produced. Why, then, was it not employed for the one vessel produced in simply astonishing numbers, evidence of, according to the ration-bowl theory, state demand – the beveled-rim bowl?[89] The different ways in which different vessels are produced cannot be reduced to a secondary outcome of processes of sociopolitical complexity. There is another way of thinking about this issue that focuses not on levels of technological accomplishment – of which each pot is simply a by-product – but on the nature of the vessels themselves, a way of thinking that also pertains to recent views of Red-Black Burnished Ware as the product of dynamics of movement (Rothman 2003). Since not all elements of an assemblage transfer from one area to another uniformly, one has to ask: why are some forms, some techniques, some attributes selected and others not? There are reasons why each vessel takes the shape it does, in the ware it does, and is transmitted where it goes, reasons that I suspect could be consciously articulated by the vessels' makers – and they lie as much with how, where, and

---

88 A fact that Frangipane herself notes.
89 Although Goulder 2010 argues that making this vessel on the wheel would not in fact be more efficient.

why people use a pot (Porter 1999; Pearce 1999: 36; Forest 1999: 147; S. Smith 2003: 33) as in the how, where, and why of its production.

At this point, though, we have to confront some of the fundamental conundrums still facing any discussion of the relationship between southern Mesopotamia and the north, the most critical of which is the fact that what is labeled "southern" has largely been defined by northern discoveries. This is well known among archaeologists working in the period; it is accepted as unfortunate then promptly ignored; subsequent interpretations are erected entirely on the basis that we already know what southern material culture looks like and what it was used for. Even if the specifics escape us, that it was in some way a product of and in service to – or even productive of – an embryonic state is almost universally accepted.[90]

This comes about because of the nature of excavation at Uruk itself. The problems are thoroughly delineated by Hans Nissen (2001, 2002), who points out the most salient facts for this discussion: the pottery assemblage from Uruk is defined by only partial and decidedly biased reporting, and all the material from the deep sounding – the prime chronological reference point – comes from rubbish deposits within a specialized, public context. While the key concerns of this situation are considered by most scholars to be chronological, for me the contextual limitations are equally critical. Most of what is known from Uruk in the fourth millennium derives from around or beneath the massive (and empty) monumental complexes at the heart of the site, the Anu terrace and the Eana precinct (Nissen 2002: 6) – religious and/or ceremonial structures. At Susa, too, which was the earliest place to manifest a duplicate of Uruk material culture (Nissen 2001: 162; Butterlin 2003: 298), excavations focused on monumental public contexts.

Then the middle Euphrates sites of Habuba Kabira and Jebel Aruda were found, and pottery identical to that of Uruk was recognized, to general excitement. Other revelations included a city wall, an extensive complex of domestic houses of middle-room/tripartite type, and evidence of town planning. But there was also a small body of material *not* like what had been found at Uruk, and which was, ergo, local. At the same time, however, some cultural elements not then – or subsequently – recovered from Uruk itself were also categorized as Urukean. Two things happened as a result of this: (1) what was at Habuba Kabira South was extrapolated as typical of the southern repertoire, even when actual parallels were lacking, and (2) those elements which did not fit anyone's idea of what southern material culture should be like (at least in part because of its assumed superiority) were relegated to the local sphere. But there are major contextual differences between the materials

90 Although for an important, and insightful, divergence of opinion, see Frangipane 2001, 2002.

derived from Uruk and Habuba, and these have never been paid sufficient attention.

The potential significance of contextualizing ceramic assemblages has been made clear over and over again. From studies of pottery from the Middle Euphrates in the third millennium it has become apparent that despite a superficial regionalism in ceramic forms, wares, and technologies, there is in fact a very basic, underlying assemblage, Plain Simple Ware, that extends over a vast area, on top of which is superimposed geographically restricted assemblages such as Euphrates Banded Ware, Metallic Ware, Reserved Slip Ware, and Scarlet Ware (see also Nissen 2001: 175). When examined in detail, one of these assemblages – Euphrates Banded Ware – turned out to be a highly specialized repertoire used in public, and often performative, contexts; I suspect the same will prove to be true of some of the other categories. In contrast, Plain Simple Ware vessels were used everywhere for more mundane purposes such as storage and daily meals, as well as in specialized contexts, where their purpose may still have been essentially related to the routines of everyday life. I am certainly not arguing that what is true of the third millennium is true of the fourth. What I am claiming is that when determining whether there are, or are not, patterns in the precise distribution of forms in Chaff-Faced, Red-Slipped, and other wares *within* sites, and not just *at* sites, it is necessary to resolve some of these problems. Instead we have drawn simplistic correlations of ware types with ethnic groups and ethnic groups with subsistence activities, and, in the circularity that bedevils analyses of this period, *vice versa*. Investigating a second aspect of this patterning is also essential: the precise location of what type of specialized materials are found where, within which settlements, and how regularly they appear. These are questions too often subsumed within a gross analysis of settlement patterns.

For example, the Chaff-Faced vessels found at Habuba Kabira South were assumed alien to the Uruk assemblage and were therefore considered evidence of the colonists' dependence on indigenous farmers for agricultural products (Sürenhagen 1986: 21–2). Chaff-Faced Ware was defined as local to the north first in phase F of the Amuq sequence proposed by the Braidwoods (1960), with true Uruk materials appearing at the end of the phase, and both being replaced by Plain Simple Ware in phase G. But chaff temper, while dominant, is not the totality of northern assemblages, and it is also used across a very wide geography (it is found as far from the Amuq as Lake Van) and in considerable quantities (Marro 2007; Sagona and Zimansky 2009: 166). Even in the material characterized as indigenous to the north there are certain vessels, such as the hemispherical and conical bowls, that are sand-tempered, thin-walled, and possibly wheel-made (e.g., Pollock and Coursey 1995: 105–6). Obvious correlations between ware, form, and function in the indigenous corpus suggest that the analytical focus should be shifted from chronological issues to spatial ones. Vegetal tempering is applied to forms most likely used in food storage and preparation (such as cooking pots and storage jars), while grit- and sand- tempered vessels are in forms used for food/drink presentation and consumption (such as small bowls). In addition, chaff-tempered vessels typical of what is called the local Late Chalcolithic are certainly known in the south, from the Hamrin to Susa to Abu Salabikh, and even at the site of Uruk itself (Pollock and Coursey 1995: 115). Given that, still, the actual development of the sequence at Uruk and its full ceramic constituents are unknown, and given that grit-tempered wares are certainly present in Amuq F (which in any case is attributed far greater authority than is now warranted), the focus on chronological issues has unduly skewed our ideas about the relationship between different kinds of pottery wares and forms in this period. While a detailed examination is beyond the scope of this work, even a rudimentary consideration of form and function throws some basic assumptions about the Uruk expansion into doubt.

That doubt starts with the very nature of the settlement of Habuba Kabira itself. The archetypal colony site, it is understood as an essentially domestic settlement with a full complement of functions (Kohlmeyer 1996), albeit a settlement with a mission: the control of interregional trade (Sürenhagen 1986; Algaze 2005 [1993]). The large structures located in the south of the site – in Tell Qannas (Finet 1980) – constitute the public sector that administered the community on behalf of its parent polity and served some of its religious needs, supplemented by temples found at the nearby mountaintop site of Jebel Aruda (Fig. 15). Alternatively, Jebel Aruda provided the administrative function for Habuba Kabira (Schwartz 2001: 248). Smaller settlements nearby supplied the town with its subsistence needs. The overall picture of settlement, then, is that Habuba Kabira, as the southern offshoot in the area, was the focus of all activity around the region, including that of the Aruda complex.

But was it? Reexamination of the C14 dates (Wright and Rupley 2001) suggests that it is possible Jebel Aruda was established earlier than Habuba and that, rather than secondary to it, the relationship may have been reversed, with Habuba Kabira instigated in order to support or expand the functions of the mountaintop complex. In this scenario Habuba Kabira would serve as a collecting point for goods destined for the temples, provide additional service personnel and congregation for the temples, as well as fulfilling other functions. But given that there are eight kilometers between the two sites, it is also entirely possible that they were to all intents and purposes unconnected.

Consisting of a central precinct comprised of two temples, with contemporaneous residential areas on either side (Van Driel 2002), Aruda is generally thought of as an elite settlement and therefore a regional administrative center (Sürenhagen 1986; Kohlmeyer 1996), as much as anything because of its defensible position (Algaze 2005 [1993]: 25; however, cf. van Driel 2002: 191). In this

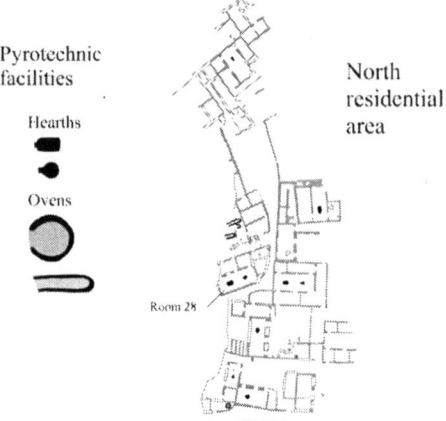

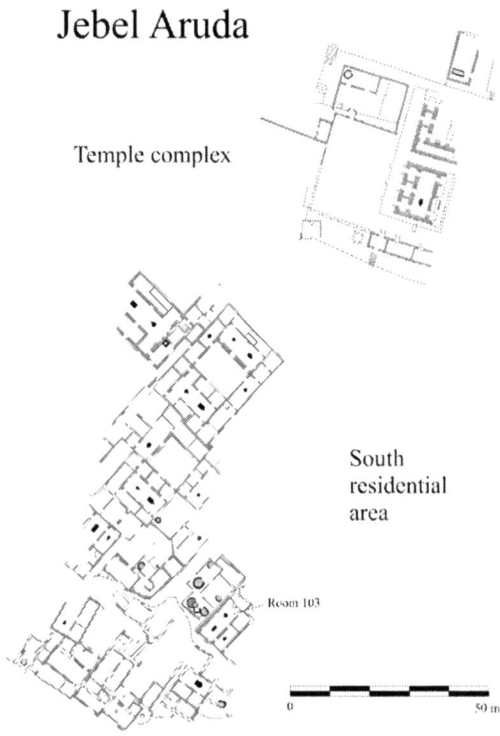

Pyrotechnic facilities

Hearths

Ovens

North residential area

Jebel Aruda

Temple complex

South residential area

Room 28

Room 103

0　　　　　　　　50 m

15. Plan of Jebel Aruda showing the distribution of pyrotechnic facilities. Redrawn from van Driel and van Driel Murray 1979, 1983.

view, the secular structures housed the ruling "elite," and the temples were the basis of their ideological power. The traditional focus on trade, defense, and administration as dynamics determining the location of settlement is firmly rooted in certain kinds of functionalist thought, and although Near Eastern archaeologists are sometimes reluctant to embrace other approaches, different ways of thinking about human relationships to landscape (such as Tilley 1997, 2004; Bradley 2000) should at least give us pause. The mountain is extremely visible, its top dramatically shaped, and it is an unmistakable landmark by which to navigate from either west or east. It possesses a numinous presence of its own (cf. van Driel 2002: 191), especially when viewed from across the river at certain times of day. The Uruk complex in a saddle near the top of the mountain is somewhat sequestered and difficult to access, and while this certainly may have provided an element of protection, when considered in the context of the religious function of the site it is also a powerful force for instilling certain mind-sets. It is possible to imagine that the arduous climb to the top gave one the sense of a goal struggled for, a privilege earned, or was symbolic of an ascent to the heavens – perhaps even the duplication of a cosmic journey. This component of my understanding of the Aruda complex is speculative – we are limited in our ability to know what people in the fourth millennium thought. Yet it is no more speculative than the argument that defense or trade is a prime determinative in the siting of this, and too often every, settlement. Nor should defense be assumed as the "commonsense" explanation, because what is commonsensical is entirely culturally constructed. If one lives in a world where the power of the supernatural imbues everything one knows, it makes perfect sense for the otherworldly significance of the physical landscape to be important in deciding where to erect a temple, especially if the landscape is an essential concern in the first place. By landscape I mean the larger expanse in which Jebel Aruda is situated and from which it is viewed: the confluence of river valley and steppe. If landscape were *not* an essential concern, then there is no reason why the regional administrative center of the Uruk colony system might not have been located within the fortified settlements of Sheikh Hassan or, later, Habuba – or, if independent of those communities, in a new place just like theirs.

The mountain is a potent symbol throughout Mesopotamian history, where it is the primal landscape of human origins, the place of the gods, and at the same time the netherworld (Katz 2007: 173, n. 29; Porter 2007/8; and see Chapter 4). It is worth noting here that in the archaic tablets from Uruk one of the avatars of Inana is "Inana of the Kur," **kur** meaning mountain (Szarzynska 1993: 8–9). At Uruk itself, the White Temple of the Anu sector was raised high over the surrounding complex by an eleven-meter-tall platform (Nissen 2002: 8; Algaze 2008: fig. 2) and would have been not only a beacon for the eyes of all those living in the city, but also a constant reminder of the origins of the cosmos, as well as its organization and structure. It has been argued that the city of Uruk's prime significance in the fourth millennium, the very reason for its growth, lay in its role as the religious center for all of Sumer (Steinkeller 1999b). Given that, of all the structures said to parallel those of the south, the temples of Jebel Aruda compare most closely to those of the public precinct of Uruk itself, a particularly close relation between the two centers may be proposed. As an outgrowth of Uruk, the key to Aruda is surely its religious rather than administrative function. I acknowledge that religious and administrative functions are not mutually exclusive, especially not in Mesopotamia, but this is not about an original theocratic state. It is about another set of issues altogether. It is about the way we interpret material assemblages.

If the temples are the raison d'être of this site, then the houses that flank them in two separate enclaves to the north and south (Fig. 15) are home to the personnel of various levels and duties that run them, and for whom social status is subordinated to professional status. The contents of those houses may be understood in part as in service to the domestic requirements of those functionaries, and in part as in service to the requirements of the temples themselves. In a suggestive but preliminary study of the residential areas (van Driel 2002), differential distributions of pottery and other objects indicate differential function of architectural units. For example, elongated, round-based jars (Cat. 33 in van Driel's typology), which most likely contained oil, are not found in any quantity in the northern complex where there was strong evidence for food preparation, but were much more common in the southern area, where a group of forty such vessels were found in one room. If these jars were indeed oil containers, the oil's primary use may not have been for domestic purposes. In contrast, at least one kind of Chaff-Faced vessel – the long-necked rimless jar or cooking pot (Cat. 19) – was found only in the northern complex. A short-necked, round-bodied Chaff-Faced jar (Cat. 29) was found evenly dispersed across both complexes. At the same time, scrapers were retrieved only from the buildings of the southernmost section of the south and not at all in the north, and in each area spindle whorls were particularly associated with a tripartite structure, although they were not exclusive to it. Imported and locally made Uruk red wares are concentrated in the south; drinking sets (one of which was found in the Red Temple's terrace) are recorded in diverse (and generally unspecified) places.

Because this was not a complete examination of all artifact types found at Jebel Aruda, firm conclusions are premature. Nevertheless a picture does start to emerge from this process. The central tripartite structure of the southern complex was a key gathering point of resources and equipment, including some numbers of a vessel type thought to have been used in beer-making (Cat. 35). In contrast, the southernmost sector of the southern complex and the center of the western side of the northern complex were perhaps the loci of processing/manufacturing and cooking or other specialized activities, because particularly prominent among their installations are a variety of pyrotechnic facilities – hearths and fireplaces. This patterning would suggest that contents and/or function – not the kind of pottery – determines where a vessel type is deployed, and contents can no more be associated with an ethnicity than can ware types. There are several possible interpretations of these patterns in addition to the standard reasoning that they are the result of tribute collected from the surrounding Urukean communities, part of which was gained by trade with indigenous farmers. Perhaps religious specialists had local domestic help, or it may be that a wide constituency (not just people of Uruk descent) contributed to the upkeep of the temple. Perhaps Chaff-Faced Ware, as well as some grit-tempered and Red-Slipped wares, were different components of the same repertoire, fulfilling different kinds of function. The former may have been used in manufacturing and domestic, or earthly, contexts; the latter in ritual, or otherworldly, ones.

There is another element of the "Uruk" assemblages that remains to be brought to the fore – its intrinsic materiality. These forms are so visible to archaeologists, so distinct, because they have very particular characteristics that contribute to very particular experiences with them, including strange shapes, three-dimensional decorations, and a highly tactile nature. Both visual and tactile experience of Uruk vessels may be described with the following words: "sharp" (carination), "knobbed" (nose- and other lugs), "bent" (drooping spouts), and "smooth" (slipped and burnished surfaces). Red-Black Burnished Ware is especially glossy, almost slick. Beveled-rim bowls are coarse and scratchy to the touch, and while this might not be part of the conscious articulation of the reasons for making these objects, it is certain that on some level it is understood that people should feel their roughness, that roughness was considered an acceptable, if not outright desirable, property. These kinds of attributes are not arbitrary. *Feeling* the bowl, holding the nose-lugs, running one's hands over an exaggerated shape, are physical reminders of what it is the vessel is in service to, and although we might not know what roughness or smoothness symbolized, that roughness or smoothness accrued symbolic meaning is beyond doubt, because these are very pronounced characteristics of the fourth-millennium materials. We should also consider the fact that these vessels, and especially beveled-rim bowls, are used in certain contexts so regularly that they should be synonymous with them, so that even *making* the bowl is inculcating the thing that the bowl is for, whatever that may be. This, I think, is a significant component of both the context of their use and the fact that they are likely to be handmade. Yet because of their coarseness the beveled-rim bowls are usually considered valueless, and thus obviously disposable, fit only for the lower levels of social hierarchy – another way in which implicit notions of development derived from anthropological archaeology, in conjunction with notions of aesthetics from art history, attach to assumptions of function. These vessels are denied any concept of "specialness" in their relationship to their users, and the same is also true of the more elaborate vessels. And yet it is their very specialness that defines them, even to us.

I would argue that the "entire set of Uruk cultural innovations" (Nissen 2001: 162) as seen at Uruk and as duplicated at sites such as Habuba Kabira and Hassek Höyük – especially the ceramic assemblage – is actually not that at all. It is not the quotidian repertoire of domestic life or even the mundane materials of a powerful secular elite, a state (incipient or otherwise) that can afford luxury vessels for ordinary purposes – nor is it mutually exclusive to either of those contexts. The ceramic assemblage consists of specialized vessels with very particular characteristics, and the contexts in which they are found – locally derived or intrusive – are specialized contexts. The attributes identified as "Uruk," the Red-Slipped, wheel-made, grit-tempered, and materially distinct ceramics, the wall cones and rosettes, even the seals and sealings, are, in one way or another, the material culture of religious practice. The attributes identified as "local," especially Chaff-Faced Wares, may be just that; they may also be Urukean at the very same time, because this pottery is part of a widespread ceramic vernacular that comprises a cultural *koiné* across much of the Fertile Crescent in this period, a *koiné* that would be far more visible if broader contexts had been excavated at more sites and more detailed analyses of those contexts undertaken. From here on in, then, rather than northern and southern, local Late Chalcolithic and Uruk, I shall call the materials traditionally labeled Uruk and Uruk-related "specialized wares," and those traditionally labeled Late Chalcolithic "daily wares," with the proviso that I am well aware that these categories are by no means clearly bounded. The question then remains: if the geographic and cultural discreteness of these assemblages is removed, is there still evidence of an Uruk expansion differentiated from local inhabitation given the already blurred inheritance of architectural forms descending from the fifth millennium? The answer is yes, because the concentrated distributions of the specialized and daily assemblages still point to different practices and distinct processes.

Such functional differentiation between ceramic assemblages might seem to be belied, though, by the distribution of these materials across architectural units at Habuba Kabira, a site largely understood as residential. Yet if Habuba Kabira existed to support the temple complex at Jebel Aruda and its constituency (who have not yet quite entered the picture, but will do so soon), it is possible that, rather than fulfilling all the requirements of daily life, much of the activities of these houses was directed toward supplying the temples, their gods, and their attendants. Again, detailed analyses may reveal specific functional differences within the various architectural styles at Habuba, which include the standard tripartite/middle-room houses and variations of single-halled structures (Kohlmeyer 1996: 95–7). There is one element already evident. Not coincidentally, one version of the single-halled structure classified as the "single longitudinally flanked hall building without transverse extension" (Kohlmeyer 1996: 94, fig. 5 e–f, 96, fig. 6a–c; see also Sürenhagen 1978: 47) is identical to the two temples of Arslantepe Level VIA and contemporaneous with them (Fig. 16). There is also a structure from this level at Arslantepe that conforms to the same plan and is determined on the grounds of ceramic assemblage to be a residential building, in which one room functioned as a shrine (Frangipane

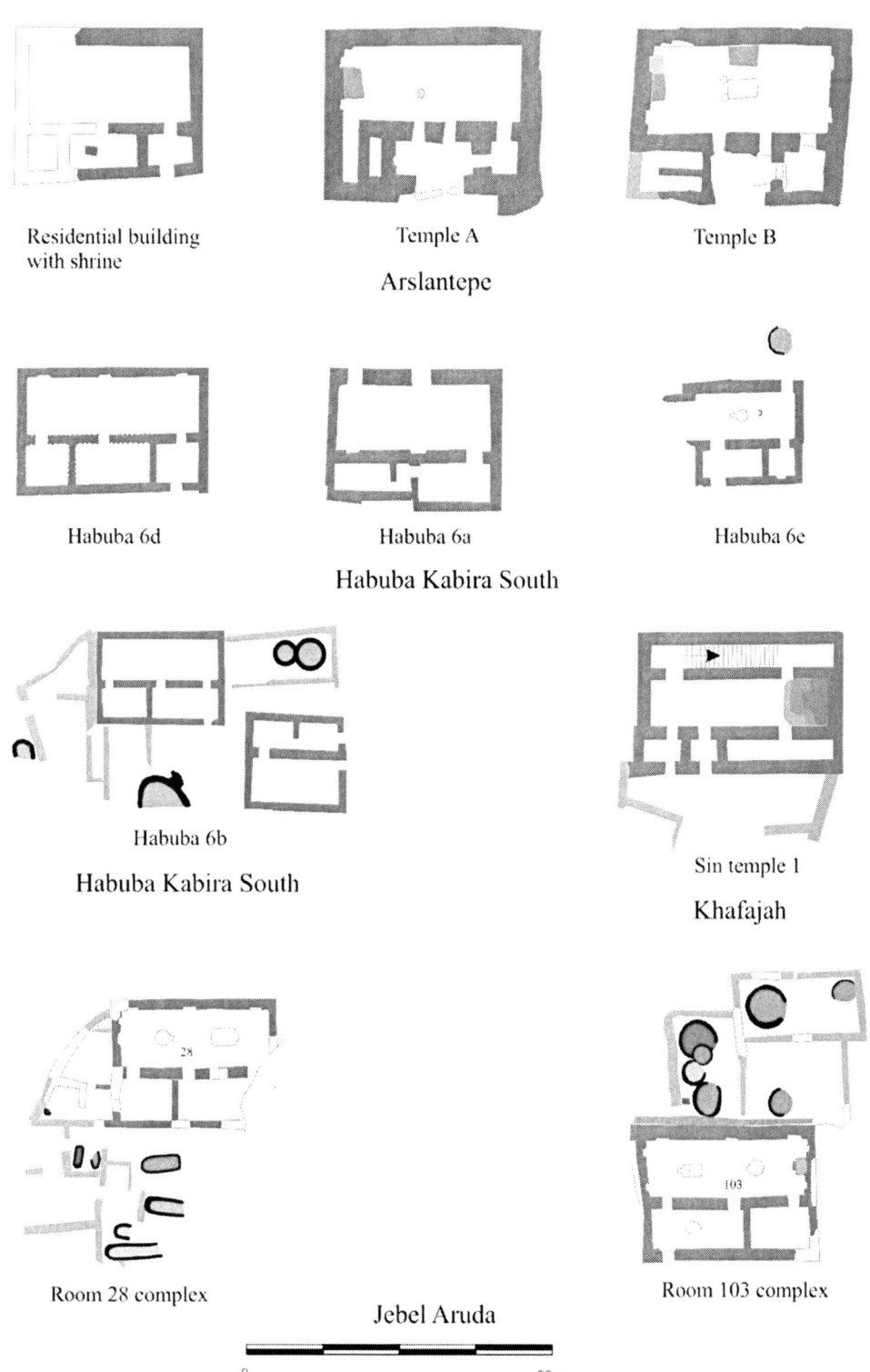

Residential building with shrine

Temple A

Temple B

Arslantepe

Habuba 6d

Habuba 6a

Habuba 6e

Habuba Kabira South

Habuba 6b

Habuba Kabira South

Sin temple 1

Khafajah

Room 28 complex

Jebel Aruda

Room 103 complex

0   20 m

16. Single-halled buildings from Late Uruk period sites. For Arslantepe, redrawn from Frangipane 2002; for Habuba Kabira South, redrawn from Kohlmeyer 1996; for Khafajah, redrawn from Delougaz and Lloyd 1942; for Aruda, redrawn from van Driel and van Driel Murray 1983.

1993: 215). This building lies over an earlier "monumental" house of level VII. There is one single-halled structure in each of the residential complexes at Jebel Aruda (van Driel 2002). Rather than implying that the function of the Arslantepe structures is in dispute, an implication that the interior furniture of these *cellae* (Frangipane 1997, 2007) categorically refutes, to my mind at least, this correspondence necessitates a reconsideration of the role of the structures at Habuba and Aruda.

There is a conflation between religious and domestic architecture already in evidence for both the fifth and fourth millennia, and it is difficult to ascertain whether this is a slippage that occurs only in modern archaeological analyses or is emic.[91] Both are probably the case. But in this instance – in conjunction with the clear evidence of ritual activity in the Arslantepe structures and the regularly spaced distribution of this form within residential complexes at both Habuba and Aruda – it is the association of the single-halled, flanked form with living spaces, physically and morphologically, that points to a specific kind of function, a religious function, one that is by no means excluded by the temple architecture of Jebel Aruda and Tell Qannas but is complementary to it. Indeed, at Aruda, in the southern example of this kind of building, the interior fittings of one room, Room 103 (Figs. 15, 16), warrant the label "shrine" (van Driel and van Driel Murray 1983: map 3). Two hearths, one rectangular and one keyhole-shaped, line up with a podium set in a niched wall, in front of which were scatters of beads and seashells. In fact both short walls are niched. There is also a keyhole oven in the southeastern room, while to the northwest of Room 103 there is another room with three large circular brick ovens, perhaps of beehive shape, with stoking holes (the fourth is smaller and built later [van Driel and van Driel Murray 1983: 22–3]). There is a parallel structure in the north residential complex, Room 28, although there is no podium on the equivalent wall. However, its opposite wall is destroyed so it is not certain that this single-halled structure did not have a podium, too (Figs. 15, 16). Interestingly, this structure is also flanked by an open area containing a series of fire installations,[92] in this case of the long oblong kind. One may suppose, then, that regular and large-scale food preparation was associated with both these structures and that, similarly to Tell Brak, the beehive oven baked, among other things, bread. It is unfortunate that in neither example is the surrounding space fully delineable so that we might know if such events took place only inside the building, in which case the participants would be limited, or outside, when larger groups could be included. It is also noteworthy that pits in these complexes contained masses of destroyed beveled-rim bowls and flowerpots.

91   For a salient discussion of this issue see Baltali 2006.
92   In fact the frequency of pyrotechnic facilities and the organization of the tripartite structures at Aruda are such that one questions whether these complexes were primarily residential at all.

I suggest that these smaller, single-halled units are "domestic" temples that serve another component of the otherworld in addition to that of the public cult manifest at the large central and ornate structures so emblematic of the city of Uruk itself: they are the "houses" of ancestors, and they originate in the ancestral practices of households, as manifest in the residential structure of Arslantepe level VIA (Frangipane 1993a: 215–16). The interior fittings of the rooms, in this single longitudinally flanked hall building similar to the temples, simultaneously differentiate it from and connect it to them (Fig. 11). The large room that in the temple complexes comprises the *cella* here contains wall paintings and a central platform (Frangipane 1993b: 138), while a much smaller room, accessible only from the larger space, contains the same furnishings as the *cellae*. These include fenestrated bowls, tables for offerings, and Red-Black Burnished Ware vessels "generally associated ... at Arslantepe with places of worship" (Frangipane 1993a: 215), as well as a spouted "Uruk bottle." One Red-Black Burnished Ware vessel was embellished with a relief of a goat.

The domestic nature of the "residential structure" as a whole is not in fact clearly represented by the architecture or fittings of the building, but is argued by the excavator on the absence of administrative features, as well as on the grounds of continuity with the residential buildings from level VII that lie directly beneath it. The area is too damaged by later pits to allow us to be sure that domestic functions were, or were not, practiced here. However, the absence of one attribute certainly differentiates it from the other "monumental buildings" of both VII and VIA, and that is the large quantities of mass-produced bowls, in situ and in storage, which presuppose the involvement, in one capacity or another, of a number of people. These people may have made votive offerings or partaken in a feast. They may have moved through the temple *cellae* individually or in groups. They may never have entered the structures at all. But that they existed is attested in the more than two hundred different seals delineated from discarded sealings (Frangipane 2002: 127; Pittman 2007), a number too great to represent only the administrative personnel of the settlement.

In contrast, the small room of the "residential structure" is clearly the location of religious practices, yet there is no indication of the feasting or offering activities that took place in the temple complexes. Even if not residential, and a case can certainly be made for this, the religious function of the building seems confined to one small component of it, the diminutive dimensions of which indicate that ritual participation was restricted to one or two people, conceivably the head of the household or enterprise that occupied the structure. This is commensurate with the practices of small-scale ancestor traditions where the next in line is responsible for the commemoration of family forebears. And it is different from the other structures at Arslantepe, Habuba Kabira South, and Jebel Aruda, which, while based on the exact same architectural principles and manifesting some shared ritual practices, embrace a larger constituency.

Rather than the individual family or household, participants in these latter contexts comprise, I would suggest, the ancestral group. Although the wall paintings in Arslantepe's temple complexes are argued to hybridize Uruk elements – the threshing scene – within indigenous traditions because of the presence of wall paintings in level VII (Baltali 2007) – which might seem to indicate that these were essentially local ancestral groups – the distribution at intrusive sites of the single-halled longitudinally flanked architectural form necessitates that this is not the case. Indeed, I read no southern scenes in these pictures,[93] but would still argue that the presence of an entirely local symbolic expression in these temples does not preclude a southern usage of them.

Now the constituency of the so-called outposts, enclaves, and colonies starts to come into focus, because there is a twinned delineation of public cult and ancestral group that is the product of a very specific situation. It could be argued that both serve only the Uruk populations visible at each of these sites, but the reality is that, with the exception of Habuba Kabira itself (the most sizeable of Uruk settlements) and earlier Sheikh Hassan, that population is very small indeed. Hassek Höyük, and similarly Godin Tepe, consists of limited facilities, many of which are of specialized function. It is not known quite what comprised the architecture at Hacinebi, only that it was located in an area that had monumental platforms in the previous period. That the decorative elements of Uruk public architecture were found in various trash deposits suggests that there was probably a religious complex here too, and the excavators certainly claim a public one. Even at Abu Salabikh much of the architecture revealed was public/monumental and/or specialized. The area characterized there as industrial consisted of fire installations, one of which was full of beveled-rim bowls and conical cups (Pollock 1990; Pollock et al. 1996); whether a kiln or an oven, one may wonder if this was not to provision a feasting space, perhaps related to the nearby platform. In area TW at Tell Brak in the Late Uruk period, a very large building, only partially preserved, is flanked by a series of rooms containing the classic Uruk-shaped keyhole hearths (Oates 2005). Hearths do not have only a domestic purpose; cooked food does not have only a domestic destination. Offerings to the gods and other observances are prepared through fire, and this is obvious at Jebel Aruda (van Driel and van Driel Murray 1979), where the temples of the central complex are flanked by equally large structures with massive fireplaces, one in the *temenos* (with a large keyhole-shaped oven) and one next to it (with a long oblong fireplace).

The "Uruk" section of Hassek Höyük (Fig. 17) consists of large single-celled spaces, a grill-based structure commonly called a granary, a middle-room "house," and most likely a monumental building, also probably of tripartite

---

93   See note 76 above.

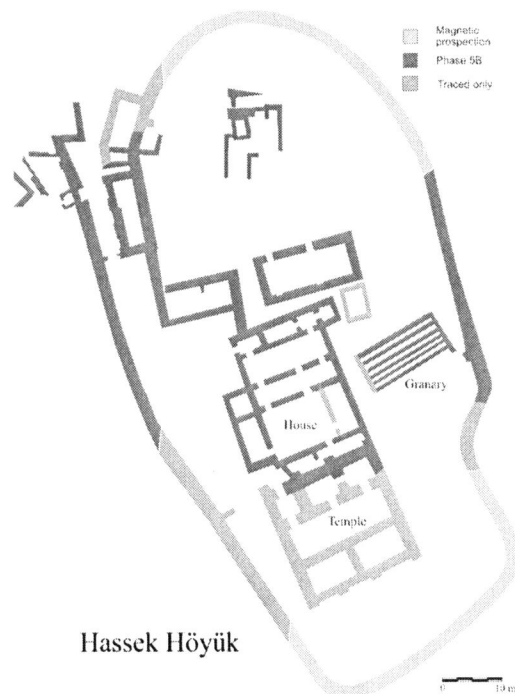

Magnetic
prospection
Phase 5B
Traced only

Granary

House

Temple

Hassek Höyük

17. Hassek Höyük. Redrawn from Lupton 1996.

plan, all within a walled oval.[94] Although the house is approximately the same size as the monumental building there are some differences between them. The northern component of the middle-room house has "domestic" features such as a fireplace and storage facilities, although the fireplace is said to be local rather than southern in design (Lupton 1996: 60). Nevertheless, in domestic structures at Jebel Aruda, too, there is a regularized pattern of keyhole installations in the central hall of tripartite units, placed in front of rectangular ones, while small and large, round, oval, horseshoe, and indeed keyhole fire facilities are located throughout the entire settlement (van Driel and van Driel Murray 1979, 1983). There is a patterning, though, to this distribution that is important: the repeated use of the keyhole and rectangular hearths together indicates a separation of functions in some way, but whether this was based on substances prepared, bread and meat for example, or on the destination of those substances, such as food for humans versus food for otherworldy beings, remains to be seen. That only the rectangular hearth is found inside the temples at Aruda perhaps indicates the latter. Obviously hearth shapes have practical and symbolic confluences, exactly as pottery does, in ways quite in evidence in the earlier feasting halls of Tell Brak.

---

94 This building is very largely reconstructed through magnetic prospection and subject therefore to debate. Sagona and Zimansky (2009: 155–6) do not include it in either their reconstruction or their discussion. I think there is sufficient indication to accept the placement of a substantial building here.

Although almost entirely reconstructed through wall tracing, the monumental building at Hassek Höyük was perhaps in basic tripartite style, with thicker walls than the house. Decorative aspects typical of Uruk public structures were found out of context (Lupton 1996: 60; Helwing 1999) but are presumed to have come from it. Rather than the public building (which may have essentially had another constituency altogether) serving a residential Uruk population whose focus lay in trading activities taking place elsewhere, it is possible that here too the occupants of the houses lived there in order to serve the monumental structure, the temple. Attendant personnel for whatever public function such buildings served needed housing and there is rarely any evidence that such personnel lived in the structure itself. The location, then, at Hassek Höyük of the one concentration of southern pottery in a corridor between the house and the temple fits with other patterns in the distribution of the specialized assemblage. This ceramic repertoire was the equipment of religious enterprise, and there were times when "the real thing" was required as well as times when locally made versions were acceptable; the distinction lies, I think, in the *materials* used in the performance of religious observances. And I do not mean here the pots themselves, or rather *only* the pots themselves, the nose-lugged jars and bottles with drooping spouts and so on, but their contents, which I suggest have to do with the particular and distinctive attributes of these vessels. Those contents – wine, resins, oils, unguents, and animal fats – are entirely appropriate to ritual use (Algaze 2001: 53–4; Katz 2007: 170). It is not hard to imagine that substances used for certain tasks – such as the anointing of the cultic statue, for example – should be authentic and from the homeland. It is not hard to imagine that such substances, because of their religious role, were signified in precise ways and that those ways carried over to the vessels that contained them. In those instances where specific liquids and unguents were not required in the performance of particular rituals, the locally made substances in the locally made goods were sufficient for the task.

In this reconstruction too, as in current interpretations, the focus of southern presence is turned outwards, away from the settlements in which the southerners themselves are situated. It is directed not so much toward an activity such as trade, however (although the ultimate motive is still economic), as it is to a population, one much larger than the merchants and entrepreneurs posited in other scenarios. This population is not directly visible in the settlements we have recovered nor indeed is it actually there, except on certain occasions. I am reminded of Potts's (2009) observation that there could not possibly have been southern residents, and (contra Goulder 2010) certainly not administrators, at every place where beveled-rim bowls are found, and he is right. But there *is* one kind of southerner that could certainly, at one time or another, have been making and using beveled-rim bowls everywhere that traces of Uruk materials are recovered: mobile pastoralists.

Mobile pastoralism accounts for the particular nature of Uruk materials and especially for the volume of beveled-rim bowls, which has never been proportional to the limited architectural remains that can be attributed to resident southern populations. It is the one general dynamic that accommodates all the various strands of this very complicated story: where most instances of southern presence are located in or adjacent to the steppes of the Middle Euphrates and Susiana plain, the mountains of Iran and the Upper Euphrates; where in most cases those settlements have (or consist of) public installations, often explicitly religious ones in which a central temple is flanked by residential structures that house the support personnel; where some of those southern religious structures are found in long-established northern (and eastern) settlements, and are not focused on those settlements but are rather sequestered from them; where pottery assemblages are remarkably unchanged over a long period of time, long even in usual archaeological terms; where southern imported goods are found side by side with locally made versions and indigenous materials, but where attribution to different ethnic identities does not successfully accommodate all variations; where beveled-rim bowls in small or large quantities are found in places where no other Uruk attributes occur or where southern populations are not yet in evidence. Mobile pastoralism is the one dynamic that accommodates all the activities and relationships that shift over time and space.

This is how I think it worked. Since the starting point is at Uruk itself, evidence for the impetus behind movement outwards remains circumstantial, as it is in any version of the story, but it seems highly likely that it was related to the changing settlement patterns in southern Mesopotamia in the early fourth millennium, and especially to the physical growth of the city of Uruk with its rapidly expanding economy. Part of that economy was the burgeoning of a formalized textile industry that was increasingly focused on wool, giving rise in turn to the expansion of pastoralism (Kouchoukos 1998; Kouchoukos and Wilkinson 2007). Two phenomena therefore occurred at once – the city expanded, incorporating a considerable amount of space, and more land had to be put under cultivation to feed the growing population. This reduced local areas available for grazing the flocks kept by city dwellers, as was argued in 1974 by Lees and Bates (and cf. Nissen 1980).

That the growth of Uruk outpaced its available sustaining area as early as the Early Uruk period has been demonstrated by Susan Pollock (2001: 192–5), who proposes that this therefore required the extraction of tribute from rural areas around it, which contributed to a centralizing administration that comprised the basis of state formation. There is an alternative to tribute however, one that does not require or result in centralized administration: commodity exchange. Textiles, the raw materials for which could be gleaned from animals herded far away, could be exchanged for food products, especially grains and vegetables produced in nearby areas, and this exchange could be entirely familial in basis. Issues of shipment costs and spoilage suggest that this kind of exchange would have been localized in the south, however: other settlements in the vicinity of Uruk would also have expanded their land under cultivation whether their population expanded or declined at this time, thus further pushing animal husbandry beyond the confines of southern Mesopotamia. Herd numbers would increase as the manufacture of woolen textiles increased. Expanded herds would require both more pasture to support the flocks and more people to manage them, so that, in addition to the small-scale, domestic, and localized herding that doubtless always existed as a subsidiary agricultural practice, a broader-scale form of pastoralism came into being, one with larger herds and longer movements. While the expansion of pasturage around settlements in the Uruk period (because of wetter conditions, described by Wright [2001: 128]) might have benefited localized husbandry, this would not have accommodated the volume required for the increased manufacture of textiles (Pollock 1999: 103–10).

Such expansion did not then bring about centralized control but was, as I think subsequent patterns of expansion indicate, familial (in its largest sense) in operation while at the same time supported by the public sector, and hence the dual set of religious practices in evidence in the colony system – those of public cult and ancestor traditions (and cf. Buccellati 2008: 148–9). The public sector was probably quite limited in its function at this point, however, maintaining relationships with the gods being one of its prime duties, and was not yet autonomous from the community of households that supported it. Although it is not ideal, I use the term "household" here, conflating it with "family" quite deliberately, and for two reasons. One reason is because Mesopotamians themselves used the word "house" to describe their social formations, whether secular or sacred, domestic or public. In some essential way it was the structure that defined the unit.[95] The other reason is because family was not just the basis of the social relations that constituted the house, but how those relations were described (Gelb 1979), whether or not based in blood. I suspect, however, that there were ways that nonbiologically related members of the household became socially incorporated into the group even if the relationship was only one of service.

But the term "household" should not be taken as synonymous with the *oikos* structures postulated for the third millennium of Mesopotamia (Pollock 1999: 118), and the risk of this is why "household" is not an ideal term.

---

95   Glassner (2003: 164) puts forward a controversial suggestion that the **é** sign probably originally represented a weaving loom. He notes that **é** can designate "'temple,' 'house,' the people that belong to a social group under the same roof; kid, 'reed mat,' or **líl**, 'breath' or 'spirit.'" It is tempting to speculate that there is a connection between **é** as house and **líl** as spirit, since the spirit or shade – ancestor – is essentially constitutive of the house over time.

Fourth-millennium households are far from the massive temple estates argued to have arisen then and were unlikely to be centralized in the same way. Domestic (again, not an ideal term, but nor is "private") households are rarely attested in the official texts (or are rarely thought attested), but are increasingly determined in all periods to be the basis of the socioeconomic organization (e.g., Adams 2007) of the city, in addition to whatever role public institutions (sacred or secular) play at given points in time. McCorriston's understanding that the new woolen textile industry was family based, as was most of the economy, is, I think, correct,[96] and others have also argued that people in the fourth millennium were providing a significant proportion, if not all, of their subsistence for themselves rather than receiving it from a public institution (Frangipane 2001: 310–12; Bernbeck and Pollock 2002), and that the expansion of pastoralism necessary to feed the textile industry was controlled by the communities from which pastoralists derived (Pollock 2001).

For many, however, the concept of administrative technology – that is, cylinder seals and mass-produced bowls – cannot fit into a model of household production, despite the fact that the bowls at least are recovered from houses as often as they are from obviously public contexts (Frangipane 2001: 311–12). To maintain this position is to imagine two things: that the flow of goods is bidirectional only – in to the public sector, out to the private; and that households are autonomous units – not just free from larger oversight but unconnected to other members of society, other groupings, other institutions. On the contrary, households may contribute to the commonweal; they will certainly contribute to religious institutions and they will exchange with both like and unlike entities for different commodities. They have as much need to control their own production in these networked social and economic relationships as any public institution and are therefore likely to use seals to do so. Certainly in the Neolithic period, when stamp seals were already in use, there was no state involved, and the technological advances represented by the cutting of cylinder seal designs did not require state sponsorship.

There were a number of forces pushing pastoralism into zones well outside Uruk's immediate ambit. It is still not quite clear when the Susiana plain became in essence part of Mesopotamia, but it is likely this was the first direction toward which expanding herds would turn (cf. Kouchoukas 1998). The Susiana plain was not empty, of course, but it is unlikely that its textile production and consequent herd size had expanded much beyond the village scale by this time, so pasturage was available there. But not for long. As this region became increasingly incorporated into the Uruk world, changes in its own subsistence and industrial practices added pressure to the carrying capacity of this landscape too, and so pastoralist groups from Mesopotamia and from Susiana moved farther outwards.

96 See also Frangipane 2001: 310–12.

The expansion of mobile pastoralism did not happen all at once. Instead it can be seen from the chronology of contact, the directions of contact, and the context of contact that it was aggregative and multimodal. I suspect that initially households from the south went north in search of wool/woollen textiles[97] rather than to practice animal husbandry, which was as yet still more local in basis, for it is increasingly evident that it was the north that pioneered this industry. Small groups of people ventured forth to establish exchange relationships with northern centers that were already well enmeshed in wool production, in addition to exploring the steppes west of the Euphrates, as evidenced by the early presence of Uruk materials at Qraya. Then other southern sites were no doubt drawn into the Uruk economy – as at Abu Salabikh, the next site to attest to subscription to the material culture we characterize as Urukean. We do not know much about the nature of contact at Qraya, whether this was a wholesale implantation of settlement or a point of interaction with a local population. But given the nature of the evidence at other sites, especially Tell Brak, I propose the latter, because there seems to have been a particular process by which contact was first engendered, and it was to have a significant outcome for subsequent movement.

That process was feasting. It has already been demonstrated at Tell Brak that interaction with Uruk is first seen in feasting contexts, and the same may have been the case at Hacinebi, where the manufacture of woolen textiles at this time is well established (Stein et al. 1999) and where first contact appears, from the little that remains, to have been in public areas and consists of large quantities of beveled-rim bowls. It is tempting to interpret the pyrotechnic facilities at Qraya as feasting installations too. As noted earlier, social relationships are established by food, deals ratified with feasting, and it is often the case that an exchange cannot take place unless it is situated within social connections which must therefore be created (Porter 2009a; see Parker Pearson 1997 for a cogent example). So outsiders seeking wool would be accepted into these new worlds through social contracts, perhaps fictional kinships, brought into being over food. The locals hold the feast, in their traditional manner, to engage with the newcomers who, like every good guest at a feast, bring their own contributions – contributions that speak of their intrinsic identities and/or their perception of the identities of their hosts. In this case it would have been traditional southern bread, baked in beveled-rim bowls. Hence the repeated patterns of Uruk contact, which is represented initially by beveled-rim bowls, usually only a very few at first, found in association with specialized, ritualized spaces characterized by indigenous versions of mass-produced crockery.

It is Tell Brak that allows us to reconstruct with some degree of reliability the process of this feasting. Two very different kinds of cooking facilities were

---

97 Wool itself, while light, is very bulky and not as cost-effective to ship as the finished product.

found in area TW, along with large quantities of cereal grains, large quantities of rough platters, and the carcasses of whole animals, large and small. The domed oven has been proposed as the locus of breadbaking and the roasting of small animals and birds, while the series of parallel brick fire-pits were used for barbequing sheep/goat and cattle (Weber, in Emberling and McDonald 2003). Several separate feasting events have been reconstructed for the various levels of occupation in this complex, which accommodated anywhere from more than a hundred to, in the first contact level, fifty people (Weber 2008). So feasting was a well-established local practice, one, what is more, with its own material repertoire. At Brak key dishes were served/prepared on the platters, recovered in such quantities that they are anachronistically likened to today's paper plates (Oates 2005). It is not their lack of value or ease of production that makes them disposable, however. To the contrary, it is what they signify in these kinds of contexts that is the very reason there are so many of them.

Elsewhere, as Frangipane (2002: 126) notes, "mass-produced bowls are one of the most significant features of Late Chalcolithic production in the northern Mesopotamian environment and each of the main cultural regions there had their own way of making these products." And in each of these instances the mass-produced bowls occur, en masse, in public contexts. At Arslantepe, Brak, and Susa the deployment of coarsely made vessels, left in situ in ritual moments, provides the point of intersection with the same kind of vessel from the south – the beveled-rim bowl. Its use as a feasting object, most probably for bread, best explains its frequency, its style of manufacture, its disposability, and its diverse but recurring contexts. It is found in domestic rubbish deposits, public buildings, and private houses (as at Hacinebi). It is frequently associated with ovens (Goulder 2010: table 3).

Feasting is not just a state event, or even a cultic one; it is practiced just as often by communities and families on both secular and sacred occasions, and the bowls are certainly found in these different kinds of locations. The "enormous quantities of bowls" repeatedly cited can be broken down into different kinds of frameworks: a monthly feast for a hundred people would yield 1,200 vessels in a year; a daily feast for ten people produces 3,650 over the same time period. If every kin-group within a modestly sized community consisting, say, of ten such groups, had a monthly feast, then twelve thousand bowls would be used annually, and vast numbers of them would rapidly accumulate.

The bowl's deployment on special occasions explains one of its most puzzling aspects, especially in terms of the ration theory: the evident discard of perfectly functional vessels in such quantities as to suggest that they might have been used only once. This fact, in and of itself, would further suggest that practicality does not determine the bowl's disposition, but that its significance in a particular situation does – after having been used in a feast or religious observance it was not to be used again, for it was dedicated to that occasion.

Moreover, conformity in its style, size, shape, and methods of manufacture was engendered not by technological advantages but by its function as a marker of identity deployed in the kind of ritual contexts – sacred and secular, public and familial – that reproduced that identity.

But northern and southern mass-produced vessels, even if used in the same kinds of contexts, did not provide their users with exactly the same kind of experience. And here for the first time the real postcolonial meaning of hybridity is evident, and evident as a powerful dynamic for subsequent history. I want to remind the reader that hybridity is not indicated by the mere transference of goods, symbols, and ideas from one group to another but by the *transformation* of those goods, symbols, and ideas through the intersection of different understandings of them.

For the people of Tell Brak at least (as it is not yet known what was the case at other northern sites), one component of feasting, one meaning materialized in the vessels with which the feast was performed – a meaning quite different from that materialized in the southern vessels – was death. At a satellite site of Brak, Tell Majnuna, a large-scale feasting event (dating to the same general period as contact) was conducted in conjunction with a mass secondary deposit of at least sixty-six individuals, including male and female juveniles and adults (although no infants), all of whom had been buried, or in some cases perhaps excarnated, elsewhere (Weber 2008). It is not known why these bodies came to be deposited where they were, although theories abound, but the picture of the feast itself is pretty clear, and it is exactly the same as that found in Area TW in Brak itself: whole animals were roasted and their bones smashed for the marrow (Weber, in McMahon and Oates 2007). Other kinds of provisions for the event were supplied by a number of people, judging from the variety of sealings recovered. It is impossible as yet to tell whether those provisions were from a central authority or from a broader community, but it is more than likely that the exclusive association of the state with sealing practices has been vastly overestimated, as already discussed, especially since that quintessential diagnostic of southern presence, the cylinder seal, is now argued to have appeared first in the north (Felli 2003; Matthews and Fazeli 2004).

Moreover, as Frangipane notes (2001: 322), in earlier periods stamp seals were clearly employed by households. In small- and large-scale events, in ones that celebrated the community, as well as ones that were more exclusionary in nature, it was important that contributions and participation were recognized; the goods provided would have been sealed and their sealings duly noted. This, then, would be exactly parallel to the quantities of *cretulae* and their disposition at Arslantepe in the slightly later period if the temples there are, as I propose, ancestor houses. The contents of the vessels in place in the temple *cellae*, clearly in use in the performance of rituals, and in the storerooms, which are insufficient for any sort of redistributive system, were provided for specific occasions by the members of the community who supported those particular institutions, and we are lucky enough to have one of those occasions preserved in situ.

It is starting to appear as if feasting over mass burials might be a northern tradition, for at Domuztepe in the Halafian period a similar "death pit" has been found, in which there are strong indications that the human components were not just sacrificed but also cannibalized (Carter n.d.). While there is no evidence for these kind of practices at Majnuna, Jill Weber (2008) puts forward a provocative argument that the members of the Majnuna death pit were essentially "decommissioned," removed from society just as each feasting event in area TW seemed to signal the end of that phase of occupation there. Certainly bodies are manipulated in the construction or perpetuation of kinship by movement and disarticulation in the north during the third millennium (Porter 2002a), and it is more than possible to imagine that groups could be removed from the social system in the same ways. Although who and why will probably forever remain a mystery, a group of war dead seems unlikely to encompass both genders and the age-range incorporated in the Majnuna death pit, whereas an extended family or lineage group would constitute just such a mixture of individuals. Infants who do not yet have social personae might be precluded from this kind of ritual.

While feasting can have multiple contexts, most of which are well known, in the north it seems to have had threatening as well as positive undertones, terminating kinship as well as creating it. This differs greatly from what (little) evidence we have for the south, and certainly at Uruk, where the pottery came from trash deposits that may have derived from a number of places, but where much of what was excavated was associated with public cults. If beveled-rim bowls were involved in the provisioning and worship of the gods and wide-scale public events taking place before them, and some of the buildings in the Eana precinct at Uruk can hold from three hundred people upwards, then not only are the mortuary connotations of the mass-produced vessels absent (at least as yet), but different connective structures that integrate the various components of society are in place in each area. To date there is little evidence of public cult – the temples of the gods in the manner known so well in Mesopotamia – in local Late Chalcolithic sites before the late Uruk period. Rather, in the north, the focus is on communal ritual.

It is not just the coarse, mass-produced bowls that are latent with hybridity – it is architectural form, in the tripartite structures that have similar but diverging roles in north and south, and it is sealing practices as well. But similarity in form masks difference in function – these materials house, even hide, different ways of thinking about the social organization and interactions of the people who made them, just as shared concepts – marking the source and ownership of goods, for example – can take the different forms of stamp and cylinder seals.

This, then, is hybridity in action, and its result is not what most people would presume. Instead of creolization only (which undoubtedly occurred but to a much lesser extent than presumed), the outcome is simultaneous strategies of differentiation and integration – differentiation between northerners and southerners, integration between mobile and sedentary components of the same populations. I can reconstruct two possible paths to these outcomes, each of which might have been in play in the differing circumstances encountered at one place or another and depending on who, exactly, is making contact.

On one path, divergent understandings brought to things that seem to be the same would lead not to a consummation of mutually beneficial trading agreements, but to rejection – such as, for example, might happen when people who believe that the gods must sanction trade arrangements find out that for their potential trading partners it is the dead who have the last say. Such a situation might result in mere disdain coupled with distrust, or it might result in outright conflict. Or perhaps the newcomers failed to recognize that indigenous practice varied from their own; if exchange outside of kinship networks was prohibited, for example, marriage to local women would be required for trade to ensue. Such was the case with European interaction with southern Madagascar in the eighteenth century AD, which resulted in a century of extremely violent interaction (Parker Pearson 1997: 408). There are many possibilities that might be found once such questions are in play, but to date such questions simply have not been asked.

On the other path, evident similarities in outward form might lead to social convergence; the incoming group not only adopting local lifeways but also forming actual social connections, a situation that was also potentially catastrophic for the south. If a rapidly expanding economy based on textiles is dependent on a steady supply of wool, then the loosening of the loyalties of the people who ensure wool's availability as they are subsumed within another society becomes a significant problem. And textiles, as soon as records become intelligible, are revealed to have been far and away the largest component of the Mesopotamian economy other than subsistence production of cereals, far exceeding metals and semiprecious stones, which were always in very limited distribution (Frangipane 2001: 215).

Whether via one path or the other, the destination was the same: differentiation. Strategies clearly shifted from small-scale contact in indigenous contexts to the wholesale establishment of southern facilities sequestered from indigenous occupation by a variety of means – a shift that reflects change in (or the major escalation of) procurement strategies. Extensive, broad-scale, mobile pastoralism was to be the basis of the Mesopotamian textile industry, and it was to remain so for millennia. However, this no more removed southerners from contact with indigenous northern groups than had previous strategies, for two reasons: southern pastoralists were not the only practitioners of animal husbandry in play in these areas, and southern pastoralists were not independent of the needs usually provided by settled communities. With regard to the first point, northern centers had their own mobile pastoralists, although these groups were perhaps more locally based, as the resources around the settlements of which they were part were not so circumscribed. Regarding the second point, sources of the additional subsistence needs that almost every pastoralist group requires would have been obtained where possible from local communities.

If "theoretical models of discrete bounded cultures ... seem strangely inappropriate today" (Tilley 2006: 17), then the appearance of such bounded cultures as Uruk and local Late Chalcolithic communities become after first contact requires explication and explanation. This boundedness lies in the determined preservation of material culture forms over several centuries, by importation and replication, and it also lies in the repeated demarcation of Uruk complexes from local ones, as at Hassek Höyük and Godin Tepe, and outright fortification, as at Sheikh Hassan and Habuba Kabira. Walls may be understood as evidence of an isolationist posture rather than of the forcible implantation of colonies (Algaze 2001: 59) or another similarly aggressive stance. The people of Uruk kept themselves consciously and deliberately separate from the other groups with which they were in contact. Such separation speaks not of control but of the complete opposite: of aliens in a strange land determined to keep their community and identity intact. And they did this, I would argue, to preserve social relationships threatened with fragmentation and dispersal as a consequence of mobility and distance. The scattering of segments of the population over much larger distances than before – a population that was intended to remain part of the core settlement in a social sense – certainly raised the risk of the incipient separation of those who managed the sheep from their original communities. With separation came the potential for two serious outcomes: the city's loss of control over the raw materials that comprised the new economy, and the disintegration (or at the least dislocation) of its society, especially its families, which would be split in two. But whereas both Bates and Lees (1977; Lees and Bates 1974) and McCorriston (1997) understand this process as leading to the marginalization of pastoralists in all senses, the evidence shows that this did not happen. Countermeasures were introduced, strategies to allow sedentary and mobile parts of the population to remain connected, to stretch over time and space the ties that bind.

These countermeasures started with the establishment of service nodes, hubs in a shifting network of pastoralist movements – north, south, east, west – that intersected in particular with the river valleys which provided water, the agricultural needs that all pastoralists have, and especially as central locations for the performance of various activities crucial to creating social and political integration even in fully sedentary societies. Service sites were located progressively northward and eastward as movements spread farther outwards, and they shifted as circumstances warranted the reorientation of routes and pasture. By the Late Uruk period they were well entrenched. But their role was far more significant than merely serving as transshipment points or areas where such subsidiary activities as the collection of metals or the exchange of products between pastoralists and farmers could take place. They were locations where individual communities and individual households from the southern alluvium could reconstruct the twofold practices that engendered a structural integration between sedentary and mobile components of the family: ancestor traditions and the cults of the gods.

The gods provided a buffer that inhibited the subsuming of southern identity to northern culture as time and distance attenuated attachment to home. I do not mean to suggest that religion is in any way at this stage coercive or supervisory, or even a manipulation of ideology in order to fool the participants into surrendering the products of their hard labor, as is often suggested for antiquity (e.g., Liverani 2006). Instead, for a group of people who are attenuated, due to mobility and distance, from the normal attributes and accoutrements of their identity, sending out religious specialists was a crucial way of keeping pastoralists active participants in the system, which was in turn crucial to the growth and success of the south. The temple's close association with mobile populations gave it a unique tie to pastoralist production oriented to wool, a situation we see reflected in subsequent millennia. Given that this was the case, the need for the appropriate, indeed authentic, ritual materials was strong, for they were central in maintaining the ties between those dispersed far from home and their familial and institutional allegiances. They were the essence of maintaining Uruk-ness, for using local materials is the beginning of slippage to local systems of belief, of the syncretism that was the very thing to be avoided – but which nevertheless occurred from time to time. It was also a matter of efficacy, for imitations lack the power of the original.

Note that I have not used the word "state" throughout this discussion. If the Uruk expansion was far more dispersed than we had previously understood, if the movements involved were more domestic than previously thought, then we need not adduce the necessary presence of a full-blown state as the expansion's progenitor. My reconstruction does not require a highly centralized and coordinated polity with the resources to accomplish territorial or economic expansion, and I do not understand the religious sector to have been a de facto state, although it was a suprafamilial institution. At this juncture political concerns were still largely in the hands of the community.

Which leads us to one of the most significant issues of the Uruk expansion: its role in the emergence of writing toward the end of the fourth millennium. Explanations of the process through which writing came into being, and what it signifies, fundamentally change within the dynamic of pastoralism.

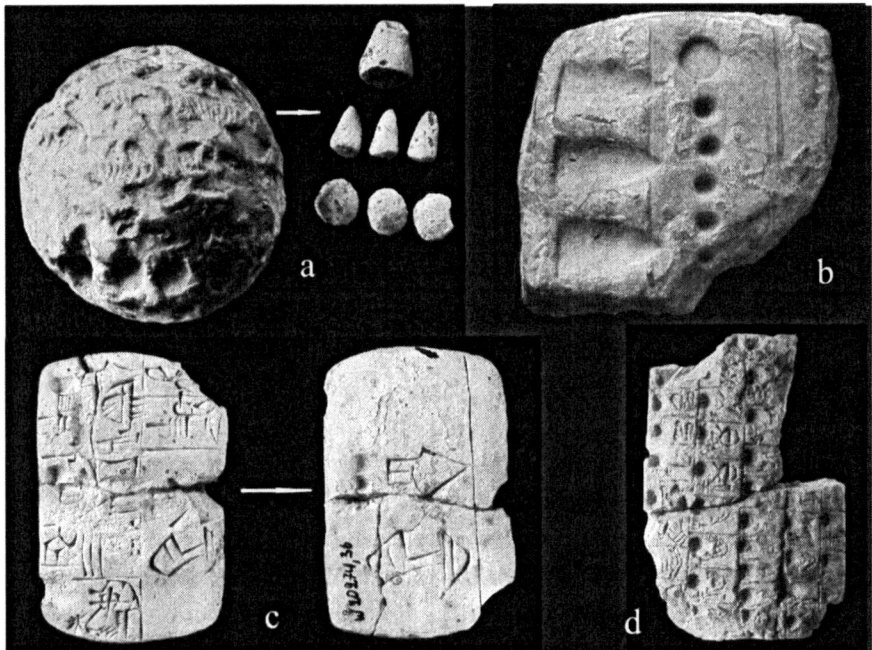

18. Bulla, tokens, and tablets. Reproduced with the kind permission of the University of Chicago Press, from Nissen et al. 1993: figs. 8, 25, 87, 111.

In the prevailing view of writing's emergence, almost every element of current understandings of state formation is vested in this most important innovation: the economic basis of its evolution; its function as a tool of power; the assumptions of its necessarily sedentary origins; and its essential equation with civilization (and "it" here may be read as referring equally to writing and to state formation).

Because this view of writing is so deeply entrenched, it is necessary to go into some detail as to how the theory is currently constructed and how it is subject to deconstruction – which makes this discursus, or perhaps excursus, longer than ideal.

It was around c. 3400/3300 BCE that the first clay tablets, with the first notations generally counted as true writing, were produced in the ancient Near East. The dominant explanation (Nissen et al. 1993; Trigger 2004) for this innovation sees writing as the logical, if not inevitable, outcome of evolving administrative and economic technologies, technologies that started some four thousand years earlier in the Neolithic period when small, plain stone or clay objects in a variety of shapes were used to denote a range of commodities and their quantities (Fig. 18). Around the beginning of the fourth millennium this system was modified by the addition of more complicated objects. Shortly thereafter, tokens were kept on strings, the ends of which were sealed with lumps of mud or encased in clay balls or envelopes.

In these instances the clay was impressed with a seal, the scene on which (we suppose) indicates either the person responsible for the transaction or the person recording it – and sometimes, when there are two sealings, both. But because the tokens were invisible once they were encased, or so the argument goes, the contents were subsequently marked on the outside of the envelope (Schmandt-Besserat 1992).

Writing, then, seems the obvious next step. If one can tell what's inside by looking at the outside, then an actual object to represent the goods and their quantities is no longer needed. All that is necessary is a drawing of the object. The tokens themselves disappeared, leaving only their markings, and as the tokens were no longer used the clay bullae no longer needed to be hollow; thus the solid clay tablet was born. This is the "revolutionary" evolutionary moment when writing was truly born, for many proponents of this school, and it is now that the impressions on clay may be called "signs," a stage often referred to as "proto-writing." At first, two signs seem to dominate – circles and bullets (Fig. 18b). These are numbers, but they are numbers in which certain *kinds* of commodities are implicit, although not the actual commodity itself, for it turns out that there are over a dozen ways of counting and each is associated with particular categories of goods. For example, one counting system pertains to dead animals from sheep/goat herds and some kinds of jars containing liquids (Nissen et al. 1993: 28). One system seems to relate only to the germinated barley used in beer brewing, while another counts grains, cheese, and fish. It is not always clear what the different items have in common, although in the last instance it is proposed that they are all rations. However, much of this is reconstructed not from tablets of the time period, but from later materials where the relationships are clearer, so it is by no means certain that this was initially the case.

Because the first notations recorded very specific things, though, especially animals and cereals, their purpose is understood as the tracking of commodities – whereby small objects controlled the flow of larger ones (but cf. Ross 2010). And so the story goes that it is in the service of an increasingly complex economy that writing emerged, when face-to-face interaction was no longer sufficient to keep track of exchange; writing was a way of controlling the wealth that the new governing elite used to create, and then reinforce, its power (J. Cooper 2006: 87).

The materialist basis to this evolutionary view leads to an undue emphasis on one kind of tablet over another and one kind of generative context over another, revealed in frequently iterated statements such as, "in the beginning writing developed more or less exclusively within the limits of bookkeeping" (Nissen et al. 1993: 30) or "writing began as a system of demarcating things, with property and its accounting and not, therefore, with language and its representation" (Sanders 2006: 8); and ubiquitously expressed, one way or another, "writing developed as a direct consequence of the compelling demands of an expanding economy" (Nissen et al. 1993: 116).[98]

However, immediately after the tablets that contain numerical impressions only, *two* kinds of tablet appear: tablets that record things and numbers (I am deliberately refraining from using the words "commodities" and "quantities"), and tablets that record lists of things. There are tablets listing kinds of fish, birds, and cattle; metals; pots, or rather their contents; cheeses; and textiles. There are lists of kinds of sheep, pigs, trees, and wooden objects; place names; textiles; grain; and occupations. Different categories are combined in lists in ways that are not immediately sensible to us. Apart from the occupations, these lists are too often dismissed as of no real conceptual or ideological significance, and it is hard to find any systematic treatment of them, although Veldhuis (2004) understands the list to be the basis of intellectual endeavor. The list of occupations receives so much attention because it is assumed to reflect and establish the social hierarchy on which the first state is predicated (Nissen 2002: 13).

These texts are thought to be word lists, and to go hand in hand with the accounts only as teaching tools for a newly emerging group of professionals, the scribes. Many copies of some of the lists have been retrieved, especially the occupations list, which has 165 versions dating to this archaic phase of writing alone, a fact that in itself is assumed to support the standard interpretation of the occupations list as setting the sociopolitical status quo. It seems that there was only one version at first, though, copied continually over a hundred-year period. So we should not imagine vast schools of copyists churning out these new texts, but only a few versions every couple of years. The lists continued to be copied throughout the third millennium.

Glassner (2003) considers the lists not lexical so much as thematic, the main concern of which is not the things listed but the signs that represent them. He understands them as ways to work out what signs for things should be. And they in fact often include signs that are never attested in use. At the same time, however, the endeavor is, as he suggests, a kind of proto-Wikipedia, a way of putting the world in order. One such list even starts with the line "when the advice and divine orders were offered, at that time the secret knowledge of the experts was delivered," according to Glassner's translation (2003: 193).

This is deeply significant. Whether or not the writers of these tablets set out to determine the foundational aspects of the universe as they knew it, they created objects that did just that, objects the materiality of which reproduced in the very making and especially the copying of them, an understanding of how

---

98 Although Damerow (2006: 7) does remind us that "Writing is not just a technique developed to serve a universal human need, but rather it is a social process of knowledge representation based on human interaction and historical continuity."

things should be, what they should look like, and where they should be. Because ideas on clay become enduring, they can be consulted and confirmed, but they cannot be changed. The lists indicate that there was thought to be a proper order to things – although we can't quite see what that order is – and this would imply that certain things needed to be done in the properly sanctioned way, with the proper implements and the proper tools. These things tend to be ritual things. The materiality of the tablets, organizing a cosmic order, goes hand in hand with the materiality of objects organizing and ordering cultic practices. And, because the universe was created by the gods, it is then ultimately a divine order that these tablets represent.

That there is a perceived relationship between things which serves to constitute a proper cosmological order, a relationship that precedes writing, is evident right at the outset when the relationship is first materialized in tokens, when the shape of the token denoted both item and quantity. It is maintained in numbering, where things are to be counted by thing-specific systems. It is perpetuated in the use of determinatives, which are signs that precede a sign and indicate to what realm that sign belongs. Establishing the relationships of things – and in particular apportioning them to different planes of existence, different kinds of materials and positions – is fundamental not just to writing but to how the world should properly work. The best-known determinative is the **dingir** sign that precedes the writing of any divine being's name. Determinatives are usually considered to indicate which reading a sign should have, as many signs have multiple readings, but determinatives are more than that. The determinative tells the reader what kind of being a person is, or substance a thing is, and thus implicitly maintains order in the world – an order established in these lists.

Failure to recognize this has in the past led to a limited understanding of Mesopotamian cosmological constructs. For example, it has long been thought that when the **dingir** sign is present it must mean that this was a name of the god, but it has become increasingly evident that the dead, especially when they are ancestors, and various supernatural animals and human–animal hybrids are also so designated. This makes perfect sense because they are all not properly human. They are otherworldly.[99] However, they are certainly not worshipped. So when Gilgamesh's name appears with a **dingir**, this does not necessarily mean that he is a deity and is worshipped as such, but perhaps that his particular nature as son of the wild cow Ninsun, a goddess, and a human father places him outside the purely earthly sphere. Alternatively, if mentioned in an historical rather than literary text, the **dingir** might indicate that Gilgamesh is dead, or an ancestor.

99   A state of being that Pongratz-Leisten (2011) designates with the word "divine," but that, for me, is too closely associated with deities to register the difference; hence I prefer "otherworldly."

Moreover, the list of metals is constructed in pairs. The first of the pair gives a metal object, then this object is repeated, preceded by the sign **an**-, which is the sign for god or sky, or the divine determinative (Ross 2010; Pongratz-Leisten 2011). Its use in this way suggests to me that the contents of the earthly world were imagined in this list with their counterparts in the world of the gods. Because almost a thousand years later another version of the metals list specifies that the pair is copper, it is thought that **an** must indicate some sort of copper alloy (Ross 2010), but this I think is not the case. **An** is not attested with this meaning anywhere else, and it is hardly inconceivable that the significance of the metal list changed over a thousand years, because meaning is an historically and culturally contingent construction. This possibility then raises questions about the idea that every single thing in human existence was thought to have a divinity in charge of it – for example, rather than a god of bricks, or a god of the pickaxe, perhaps what is represented in the writing "**dingir** pickaxe" is the pickaxe that belongs in the world of the gods. That is, there is a whole set of otherworldly counterparts of human things.[100]

Indeed, many of the so-called "accounts" – the materials that are assumed to demonstrate the economic nature of Mesopotamian reality – are marked with notations indicating that the goods on them are to be associated in some way with various divinities or their temples or with some other construction we are unable to identify, but which does not seem to become an institution of a secular state. That the relationship of signs on these accounts is purely one of credit and debit in the service of a state-dominated extractive economy should perhaps be reassessed; many of these first tablets may record offerings directly to the gods, or to the temple to be used in the upkeep of its personnel (Szarzynska 1993), or they are things that already belong to the gods, things that exist in their world.

Glassner's argument that writing was an invention, "a new science of analogy," developed by priests well-versed in the construction and reading of signs in the entrails of sheep or the flight formation of a flock of birds, is in keeping with my understanding of the events and processes of the Uruk expansion. And it answers the one question that evolutionary explanations fail to address – why now? Why after thousands of years of the token system did a qualitative, not just quantitative, change take place in recording systems?

What *was* different now were the three interrelated concerns of dispersal, order, and change brought into being by the Uruk expansion. The shift from tokens to tablets and the subsequent development of cuneiform is related to a greater degree of absence in economic and social relations than ever before. It may be understood as a strategy of integration in response to the absence

---

100 Pongratz-Leisten (2011) notes that the objects of cultic performance also have a divine nature.

not only of merchants, but also of whole sections of the population. It is easy to maintain accounts between those present in communities, based on face-to-face interaction, even as population densities increase. The merchant knows with whom he has done business and where to find these people through the crowded streets of newly emergent cities, which after all never attain great size in the fourth and third millennia, the site of Uruk notwithstanding. It is not so easy, though, when one's debtors are mobile and their presence is sporadic. But it is more than just the elaboration of business transactions that is the critical variable here – there is something else. It is the dispersal across the landscape of religious specialists and the world they needed to control. It is the concomitant dynamics of differentiation and integration.

What does it do, ordering the universe in a certain way and teaching this to a group of people who then carry it to places faraway when they take up their posts as scribes or priests? Not, I venture to suggest, what we might first think, which is that culture may now be shared and the far corners of the world drawn together. At first the introduction of writing and the classification of all aspects of existence were highly exclusionary and, I would suggest, intended to be so. It drew together those who shared the same language, a "collectively shared cognitive order" (Kopytoff 1986), as it rendered it impenetrable to those who did not. And it put that cognitive order in the control of a very few people. The first writing was simply not accessible to anyone not trained in it, especially if we understand it not as a pictorial representation of a material world, but as the rendition of both abstract constructs and parts of language. Only a handful of people, and we know some of them by name, had the opportunity to learn to read and write, and this remained the case for over fifteen hundred years. If writing was indeed language-based – and this is still hotly debated (Glassner 2003; Rubio 2006a; Michalowski 2006a) – it was a language only one group of people spoke, Sumerian, and it was a language with a very limited geographical range. If writing was not language-based, it still had to be a recognizable system in order to have any effect on the wider world into which it might reach, and this it quickly was not as signs became further abstracted. In the best of worlds, only a few people could read.

So while writing is certainly one means of stretching time and space, it may also operate as a strategy to counter the effects of change, for it has the potential to reify knowledge, culture, and identity. Writing, then, goes hand in hand with religion as a means of integration and differentiation. This is not to suggest that the expansion was centralized, sponsored by the temple, or indeed, that the temple constituted the state although it did comprise the public arm of southern corporate identities – that is to say, the city, and the city was composed both of groups of households and of multiple ancestral groups. The interrelationship of these elements in southern cities is not yet archaeologically – nor for that matter, textually – very clear, but is a matter of theory because we still know little about the actual working of fourth-millennium societies there. However, that temples comprise the one institution that cross-cuts ancestral/household connections at this time – the locus of what is in essence civic ties (Crawford 2002) – is manifest both in their design and in their spatial relationship to the rest of the community.[101] This is how we may understand their central location and position on acropoleis at Uruk and other sites – not as an expression of dominance and exclusivity, looking down on the lower echelons of society, but as rising above the mundane allegiances of ancestral groups and family networks, as linking people from any part of the city to the beings beyond, visually and conceptually. As for secular leadership at this juncture, whether in the form of a group of elders, a ruling family, or a powerful individual, it was likely vested in the maintenance of those same household and ancestral groupings.[102]

If the economy of the city is predicated on the production of textiles, and that production is accomplished through mobile pastoralism in one form or another and practiced by households, then the city will not only maintain a number of different mechanisms to ensure control of mobile pastoralism and those who practice it, but will also actively support it. The outcome of this support will be highly integrative, tying pastoralists to their community of origin by creating conditions of dependence – in this case, on the gods – and it will have an impact upon the nature of the city itself as it creates the structures and practices that allow it to offer that support. The power of the temple evident in southern Mesopotamia in the early third millennium, its dependence on textile production and coteries of attached personnel, all may be seen as a result of its role in maintaining the rootedness of mobile groups in their original communities.

Yet there is a parallel but ultimately opposing force in operation, and that is the maintenance of cohesion within fragmented households through ancestor practices. It is the function of integration that is parallel to the role the temple plays in the expansion, but in this locus it emphasizes the part – the household – rather than the whole – the city (cf. Crawford 2002: 47). The outcome of this will be discussed in Chapter 3. For now, and at long last, the journey returns, and ends, at Arslantepe where this chapter began (although not yet with its tomb).

Visually claiming affiliation with animal husbandry, architecturally claiming affiliation with both physical and social structures located in the domestic domain, the single-halled structures of the Arslantepe temples are representative

---

101 I concur with Bracci (2009) that there is a relationship between spatial organization and society, although I do not necessarily share her understanding of that relationship.

102 In the third millennium, households remain a crucial economic unit and kinship a significant means of networking households and institutions together (Stone 2007).

of the second means by which mobile pastoralists were integrated within their society of origin: kinship. "Temple" is a problematic label, for it risks conflation with the buildings of the gods discussed above. And yet not to call these structures temples risks reducing the significance, and especially the religious significance, of these practices. Even though I do not think the dead were worshipped in the same way as the gods (Porter 2002a), ancestors were as central to cosmological constructs as any otherworldly being. The only resolution I can suggest is to follow indigenous practice and label the structures of each set of practices in terms of the house: the house of the gods and the house of the ancestors.

Despite the confusing affiliations in material repertoire here, I understand the Arslantepe structures as truly hybrid entities that are yet ultimately "southern" in orientation. Although the reality of the ethnic identities of those participating in these complexes is undoubtedly far more multifarious than this, it is not that reality with which we should be concerned, for it is in the end unknowable and essentially immaterial. What *should* concern us is indigenous self-conception, and *that* depends on the locus and occasion in which identity is invoked. In this context it is the ancestor from whom the members of the house of the ancestor claim descent or with whom they desire affiliation (an ancestor that one might suggest is directly represented in the wall paintings). This determination requires careful delineation of conflicting material elements, and one category of material culture should not be privileged over another as expression of identity. Different relationships are forged with different things, in different ways. But we can think about the nature of those relationships and what it is that each of these categories – pots, paintings, and plans – does, the different things they symbolize; and we can think about how what those things do reflects the one identity that *is* truly significant here: that of the ancestor or ancestors.

On the one hand, the tradition of wall painting is already established at Arslantepe in the previous level, and its use here would seem to imply continuity within a local population. Colors and geometric motifs are the same in levels VII and VIA (Baltali 2007). However, the iconographic elements are obviously different from one level to the next, whether or not one invokes the threshing scene, and the prominence of human–animal interaction in level VIA is itself quite new. It cannot be presumed that wall painting is a northern attribute only.

The sealings, locally styled and given most weight in analyses of Arslantepe VIA, might in fact be the least relevant indicator of what is going on. A current southern presence is not necessary for the subscribers to these ancestor houses to claim a southern identity – by which I mean that the eponymous ancestor that defined the group may have lain sufficiently far in the past that the personal, as opposed to historical, identity represented in seals had shifted. There is still a chance, too, that the goods that the seals mark might have been collected through exchange – in order to provision the rituals, especially if they contained staples such as grain – so that their point of origin has nothing to do with their point of use, although I doubt this was actually the case.

On the other hand is the architecture of the houses of the ancestors, which is deeply embedded in southern colony sites and which, given this context, is difficult to conceive of as local. While there may be continuity in function in the residential area near the temple complexes, there is no continuity in plan (Frangipane 2002: fig. 1, cf. fig. 2); the structures of level VII are quite different from those of level VIA, so that there is something new occurring here also. In addition, the Arslantepe ancestor houses are situated vis-à-vis the main, and presumably indigenous, occupation of Arslantepe in much the same way as at other enclaves – at its fringes, in this instance on the southwest perimeter of the site.

Southern ceramics, however, and I include in this category both materials made in the south and those made locally, while present, are few. Since it is becoming increasingly evident that Uruk pots are rarer than first assumed at several enclaves (e.g., Helwing 1999), this fact alone does not make the case for local origin. I have already argued that ceramics do not break down quite so neatly into southern and local repertoires, nor does the way in which those repertoires were deployed. A careful study of exactly which forms in all kinds of fabric continue from the preceding period, which forms are new, and precisely where they are distributed, not just at Arslantepe but also throughout the region of contact, is still needed.

What does continue from level VII into VIA, and beyond, is Red-Black Burnished Ware, which has been given a certain prominence in the discussion of ethnicity at Arslantepe since it is thought to indicate specific ties to the Transcaucasian world of the northeast. Pot styles in and of themselves do not equate with ethnic or even cultural identity, and the cultural complex defined by Red-Black Burnished Ware may in the end consist of nothing more than a ceramic technique (Smith 2005: 258). Bounded regional distribution might seem to provide the linkage with identity at its grossest level, in that this material was first developed in, and was confined to, a certain area, but in this instance that distribution is transcended by two factors. The first of those factors is mobility, the second, function. Red-Black Burnished Ware spreads across a wide geography within a system of intense contact wrought through mobility not only of pastoralists but also the small migrations of sedentary farmers and traders (Marro 1997; Frangipane 2001, 2002; Rothman 2003; Palumbi 2007/8; Sagona and Zimansky 2009: 166). It is also likely that Arslantepian pastoralists traversed the Caucasus in their own movements (contra Palumbi 2008: 152, and see below), just as there was a long history of contact between this region and Mesopotamia, despite the distances involved; Halaf and Ubaid complexes are found there (Smith 2005: 254) as well as southern materials in the Uruk period (pers. comm. B. Lyonnet). But the selection of Red-Black Burnished Ware that appears in the temples and, later, the tomb, at Arslantepe is not a product of a generalized diffusion or the presence of specific population groups but of the specific attributes of the pots as used in specific ritual contexts. Ceramics have functional and symbolic meaning; they are used in certain regions but are not necessarily restricted to certain groups; they appear in certain situations in which many different groups in the same region may participate. And that is the case here.

These ancestor houses are clearly incorporating mobile pastoralists into the social realm and doing so through ritual practices that are especially dependent on the sharing of substance, food. More than this, the sharing of food is no doubt creating socially constructed kinship that links not only mobile and sedentary populations together, but also groups that may belong biologically to different ethnicities or descent lines but now claim membership in the descent groups embodied by the Arslantepe ancestor houses. That lineages of different ethnicity and speakers of different languages may belong to the same tribe and understand themselves as intrinsic, even biological, members of it was amply demonstrated by Barth (1961); that descent structures are malleable enough to allow for the integration of all sorts of biologically unconnected parties needs no further argument.

Stein (2005a, 2005b) and Rothman (2003) both assert that distinct ethnicities "will" or "should" maintain distinct cultures, especially in the fundamentals of food production, preparation and consumption, and other subsistence practices. And so they may; and when they do, it is for specific and contingent reasons. But equally they may not. Divergent groups may assimilate readily, adopting the lifeways of others in a short space of time. Often only residual hints of original, or other, identities remain, and there are no rules as to which group's culture will dominate or how creolization will occur. If we were to accept for the moment that distinct ceramic assemblages exist, and that those assemblages are in some way equatable to distinct regional if not ethnic groups, then the picture presented by the material remains of the Arslantepe ancestor houses is one of three separate communities participating in the commemoration of the same ancestor. This is certainly possible and would suggest that over time, and especially over movement, different entities became incorporated within the one group.

So how to define whose/which identity is paramount? Relative quantities of ceramic types do not clarify the matter, because these ancestral groups were clearly not entirely separate from the settlement in which at least some of them were resident, even if separation was the aim. Again, it is contextual. Since the context here is the house of the ancestor and the identity is of the descent group, it might be argued that the elements of material culture most closely associated with the perpetuation of the ancestral persona will be most closely tied to original identity (notwithstanding some slippage), because the practices of perpetuation are where habitus, indeed a discursive consciousness of habitus, truly lies. Because maintaining linkage with the community defined by the ancestor is the essence of ancestor practices, and the ancestor himself embodies the past, while it is longevity that authenticates the claims attached to ancestral identity, it may be proposed that people will consciously engage in commemoration with materials that invoke both past and identity as best they know and understand them, whether they are conscious of the point of origin of the ancestor or not. Those materials are: the house, because the relationship between ancestor and house is most fundamental and most intimate; any actual representation of the ancestor, therefore iconographic elements; and the ritual paraphernalia employed in his (or her) commemoration.

Therefore we should turn to the pottery that is most likely to function in that capacity, rather than the storage containers for mundane goods such as grain for bread-making, which relate more to the point of production than to the locus of consumption. Containers for sacred oils and unguents, however, are a different matter. The drooping spout and nose-lugged pots most regularly appear in cultic contexts of one kind or another and are argued to contain specialized substances for the performance of ritual. The fenestrated bowls on which offerings were obviously presented are another such form. These are as yet neither definably local nor southern, in my estimation, and they also occur in Red-Black Burnished Ware (Frangipane and Palmieri 1983: 357). They certainly become a local tradition subsequently, lasting well into the third millennium along the Euphrates.

The most problematic issue, though, is that the mass-produced bowls in use in the level VIA ancestor houses are not the beveled-rim vessels of the south, but the bowls of the north. It seems to me that the bowls speak to the identity of the living rather than the dead, in that they appear to have been used by the members of the ancestral group in performance of an aspect of ritual not directed toward the ancestor him/herself but in cementing relations with each other: feasting. This would seem to be substantiated by the fact that all the above ceramics occur in the shrine of the residential structure of this level but the mass-produced bowl does not (Frangipane 1993a: 215).

Arslantepe, perhaps more than any other contact site, is a nexus of intersection for the four major geographical regions that come together in the far north (Rothman 2003) – Transcaucasia, central Anatolia, Mesopotamia, and, I would add, northern Syria – in large part because of its location and its complexity, the latter itself in large part engendered by these very intersections. It is very probable that Arslantepe always served as a hub in the movements of the populations of the northeast, whether one-directional or seasonal, offering goods and services that few other sites could provide. It would therefore be particularly prone to this kind of social syncretism. I do not imagine that attempts at differentiation in evidence in the second half of the fourth millennium actually prevented such shifts, especially at the edges of any group, from occurring, and occurring in multiple directions. Some southern mobile pastoralists undoubtedly merged with Transcaucasian and/or Anatolian ones and vice versa, especially since the dual religious practices that served to maintain the cohesion of the southern groups were, at least as far as we can tell, in place at one end of the system only. Distance is no necessary obstacle to this reconstruction (cf. Palumbi 2008: 152), because these movements may be quite long-term, taking place over years, even decades, rather than only annually. The extent, duration, and direction of pastoralist movement are always contingent on prevailing circumstances, and the longer the time away from the community of origin, the greater the potential for incorporation with other ancestral groups. But there is an even simpler explanation. If people divide their life between two or more places, then those places are equally significant to their identity.

The people who used these ancestor houses were unified and distinguished by factors not directly reflected in material culture assemblages but in practices in which the material assemblage was deployed, some of which could be locally provided, some of which had to come from the homeland in order for proper practices to be maintained, some of which came from other places in which that group was present. Two groups converged in this part of Arslantepe, but they were not two cultures competing with each other, one to be submerged by the other – one sedentary, one nomadic; one highly developed, one less developed – rather they were two ancestral groups that claimed a southern ancestral identity and were each defined by sedentary and nomadic components that were joined through descent. This is visible right at the point where those components intersect: in the structures and institutions that kept them integrated.

Why, then, is it not until toward the end of the fourth millennium in the south that we see specific spaces that might be interpretable as the loci of the ancestor practices that are a foundation of kinship systems, and that are certainly known from textual attestations once texts become fully intelligible? It is not coincidental that at Khafajah, north of Abu Salabikh and located near the confluence of the Tigris and the Diyala rivers, the history of the misnamed Sin Temple[103] at the end of the fourth millennium and beginning of the third, bears witness to a shifting – and intensifying – relationship between household and temple (Fig. 19) that can be understood as an outcome of the experiences of expansion, parallel to that emerging elsewhere. The earliest structure recovered[104] and embedded in a rapidly expanding area of domestic houses, this

---

103　So-named because of the discovery, in robbers' pits in the latest levels of the structure, of an inscription on a statue initially translated by Jacobsen as belonging to a priest of Sin. Jacobsen subsequently revised his reading, but it was decided to maintain the temple's label for the sake of clarity (Delougaz and Lloyd 1942: 6–7).

104　Cf. Bracci (2009: 10), who claims that the Sin Temple and Nintu Temple were the first structures built. In fact, Delougaz et al. (1967: 2) state that "the lowest levels reached at Khafaje immediately above ground water, were tapped only in soundings in squares N 43–44, O 43,

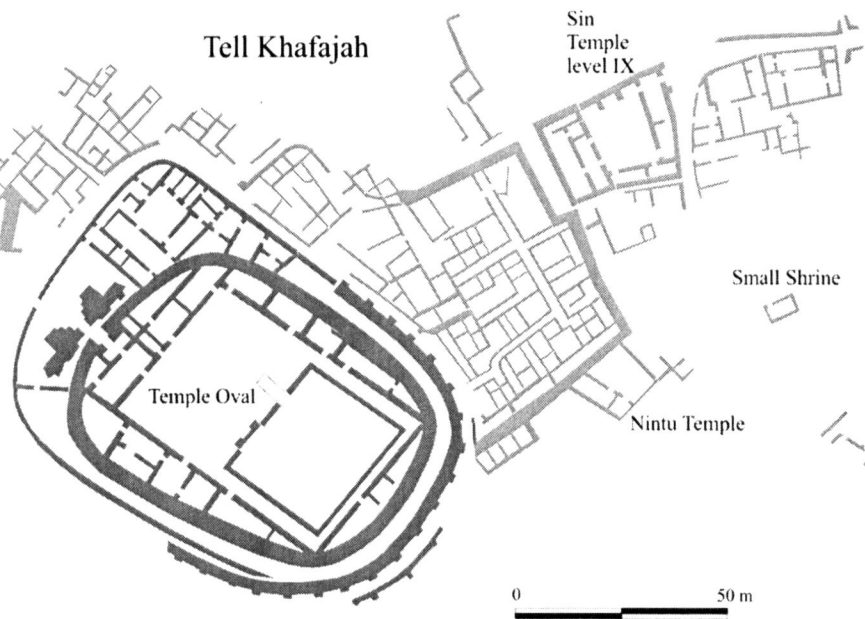

Tell Khafajah

Sin
Temple
level IX

Small Shrine

Temple Oval

Nintu Temple

0   50 m

19. The Sin Temple and environs at Khafajah, with Temple Oval. Redrawn with kind permission of Oriental Institute Publications, from Delougaz et al. 1967.

temple contains an architectural element that qualifies as a "single longitudinally flanked hall building *with* transverse extension"[105] (Kohlmeyer 1996: 94, fig. 5a–d; my italics). (See Fig. 16 for details.) Here the transverse extension is the long narrow space to the west filled with brick that served as the basis for a stairway. The court that later developed to the east was, in the first levels, simply an open space between the temple and surrounding houses (Delougaz and Lloyd 1942: 14, pl. 2).

When the massive third-millennium Temple Oval was constructed, the Sin Temple was not replaced by the new building but continued in use, subsumed within, and barely differentiated from, the residential quarter that lay outside the Oval's walls. It seems likely that the Sin Temple as well as other, smaller religious structures[106] dating to the earliest levels housed a parallel set of practices

and P42–43. Consequently the building remains at these levels were too fragmentary to reveal any coherent architectural units. …in squares O43 and P42, no connection between these early remains and the lowest of the *uninterrupted* sequence of house levels for they were separated by a layer of unstratified rubbish" (my italics). Certain objects are designated as deriving from materials below the Sin Temple as well. These squares are all in the area of the Sin Temple, and, in short, it is not known of what the lowest levels of occupation in this area consisted. What is clear is that there was a change, signaled by the trash layer, and a new building level of houses corresponding with Sin Temple level IV was constructed.

105 In contrast to the Arslantepe structures which are *without* transverse extension.

106 Another very small, single-roomed temple was built in the midst of the houses of Level 11 and corresponding to Sin Temple V (Delougaz and Lloyd 1942: 104–12).

observed by familial groups that, given the style of the structure, were likely based on ancestor traditions. Unfortunately, the lowest levels of residential occupation concurrent with the first building of the Sin Temple were not excavated as they lay below the modern water table and were separated by a thick layer of trash from the first "coherent" level of architecture investigated (Delougaz et al. 1967: 2). That coherent layer, House Layer 12, accompanied the rebuilding of the Sin Temple in level IV, which itself represented a marked differentiation from the earlier material. The previous structure was carefully filled in and the new structure effectively raised on an artificial terrace. The long narrow stair at the west end was abandoned, and added to the basic plan is another court containing two domed ovens, interpreted as kilns by Delougaz and Lloyd (1942: 22-3) but displaying no typical features of kilns such as stacking floor, firing chamber, and flues. It is noteworthy that the many objects found in the temple *cella* included a female statuette no more than 11 cm tall with carved, and not inlaid, eyes, and a number of spectacle idols (Delougaz and Lloyd 1942: 26-8).

These ancestor houses are themselves the third space (Lionnet 1993) of postcolonial theory. They are an innovation, an outcome of contact, shaped by the clash of similar yet ultimately divergent understandings of religious and social organization, for as far as I can see they are not in evidence in the south prior to this time, and they are not an indigenous feature of local Late Chalcolithic architecture, although they incorporate elements of northern tradition. They are newly derived from previous (and continuing) ancestral practices, emerging predominantly in the late Uruk phase. When southerners met the inhabitants of northern sites in feasting contexts, the first step on this path was generated by one or more of several possible ways of interaction. Either feasting successfully established meaningful social connections through shared substance, and perhaps also through the manipulation of genealogies, or divergent understandings of this process led to the establishment of clearly differentiated identities. It is the latter case that seems most frequently borne out by subsequent events, but that is only, perhaps, because it is the most archaeologically evident. The remains at Arlsantepe demonstrate the potential complexity of this issue, which may have played out similarly in other instances, while those of Hamoukar would seem, at this early stage in its excavation, to manifest an alternative outcome - conquest (Reichel 2009). It should not be thought by any means that there was an homogenous process or outcome to an initial situation - or even that the initial situation was the same in all cases.

In tandem with this differentiation in northern and southern identities was the coming together in colonies of different households. With different familial allegiances, probably even from different cities, coresidence brought into being a further step in the consolidation of identity - this time not between north and south but in distinctions between households originating within southern cultural traditions. This process also served to render visible individual sets of kin relations, inhibiting the gradual absorption of the mobile components of those households by another household. Kinship forms past and present linkages between people so fundamental that they are rarely expressed but always practiced, linkages that serve to keep those who move *far* from home from *leaving* home altogether. Kinship also facilitates resolution of the practical and social difficulties inherent in a multiresource economy,[107] such as integrating summer grazing in the agricultural lands along river courses and canals, a situation often cited as a locus of conflict. These kinds of activities do not require a centralized institution to coordinate (contra Van de Mieroop 1993a) but are readily accomplished on the kin-group level in ways that obviate that "uneasy relationship" and "incipient conflict" that is almost always mentioned when pastoralists are invoked. Ancestor practices, the definition of social units through descent, which had presumably taken place previously only within households, were now externalized into separate spaces around which related families aggregated. Different ancestral groups therefore constitute the community of Habuba Kabira South, are part of the personnel at Jebel Aruda, and are in evidence at Arslantepe. It is no coincidence that the shrine of the Arslantepe level VIA residential structure also contains some pottery designated as southern (Frangipane 1993a: 215).

At the same time, the temple institutions of fourth-millennium Mesopotamia did not operate alone, nor were they autonomous, even in the south (Pollock 1999: 101). Rather, they accompanied the households that established branches of themselves in the colonies of the Middle Euphrates and elsewhere. The term "colony" remains appropriate whereas "colonialism" does not, because these centers remained attached to the home city – that was their very purpose. And it is evidenced by the inescapable fact that, over a period of several centuries, styles in material culture did not diverge between the various points in the system (Stein 1999a: 21); changes over time tracked between south, north, and east. This would suggest not just continued interaction but continued identification of one community with another, southern bases and northern offshoots, maintained by conscious effort. The flow of contact was not merely bidirectional, however, and relationships of power were not analogous to parent/child. Both constituted a complex network that enmeshed members of the extended family located in residences in the south, in the north, in the east, and in whatever pasture the concatenation of current conditions rendered available.

Although it is increasingly recognized that fourth-millennium Mesopotamian society was organized through multiple, coexisting bodies (Rothman 2007: 238-9), the understanding that Mesopotamian cities were constituted by networks of households with little centralized authority is controversial for those

---

107 For a contemporary example of such a situation and how and why it works as it does, see Lancaster and Lancaster 1998.

scholars who see class as supplanting kin as the basis of social organization and the specialization of task as supplanting a domestic mode of production – both of which phenomena are thought to be not only manifest in the events of the fourth millennium but generated by them. In this new economy, workshops, usually controlled by a centralized authority, were responsible for the production of all but agricultural surplus. The standard professions list, which is read as a hierarchically organized rendering of key positions in the city's administration, would seem to confirm this scenario (Nissen 2002: 13–14). Yet the fact is we do not know the meaning of the term that starts off this list nor the relationships between the entries. We only know what people thought these meant some two thousand years later, when an Akkadian translation of the list was made. There are no theoretical grounds for thinking that the original meaning of the text was maintained over this time, for readings are not immutable and are shaped by situations in existence at the moment of the reading – in this case, when there was a clear-cut organization topped by a king. And indeed, writing itself was not the purview only of the temple, for archaic tablets have been found in a variety of places, both at Uruk itself and elsewhere (Collins 2000: 56). The other context often adduced as evidence of a specialized economy in the late fourth millennium is the area of the Sin Temple at Khafajah (Delougaz and Lloyd 1942: 6–7, and see Chapter 3 here), where surrounding residential structures contain little indication of manufacturing activities (Pollock 1999: 98–100). As yet, however, there is no material indication that temples were self-contained units that managed specialized production and dependent personnel. Rather, as Pollock argues, they were supported by a system of tribute, although (contra Pollock) this did not constitute a significant or dynamic component of economic practice. It was not demand for and control of tribute that gave rise to the temple's wealth and power in the third millennium; it was its fundamental role as a force of integration.

The current reconstruction of an emerging state in the fourth millennium, whether by advocates of the north or of the south and however the state is defined, is predicated on understandings of the material culture of the expansion as reflections of phenomena that can only be generated by a state. The extent of distribution and consistency of form in those vessels found across vast geographies must have been accomplished by some form of coordination organized by or in the service of a centralized, redistributive authority; cylinder seals showing designs read as elite expressions of power and technologically as well as artistically demanding, must have been produced by a skilled craftsman in the employ of a centralized authority, for only in this context would craftsmen have had the freedom from labor to produce such "works of art"; administrative technologies such as writing and sealing had to have been generated by a state. These connections, however, are based on one theoretical paradigm brought to the evidence, a paradigm that while naturalized is not itself evidence. Archaeologists, and for that matter historians, are in the business of weaving whole cloth from random fragments of found thread. It should be clear by now that the same archaeological materials are open to very divergent interpretations depending on, first, the theoretical premises from which one proceeds and, second, the questions one asks of the data. The second is in turn a product of the first.

CHAPTER THREE

FROM TEMPLE TO TOMB

If the temples of Arslantepe level VIA materialize the practices of differentiation and integration arising from the desire to maintain connections between the sedentary and mobile members of the social group, and if the distribution of objects within those temples is not in their first meaning a direct statement of separate ethnic identities but the remains of practices that end up producing at least the idea of a single identity, then that identity is manifest, if not accomplished (because identity is never realized but always in construction), in the tomb of the next period: level VIB. Here, the combination of material elements, many of which demonstrate direct continuity with the assemblage of level VIA, are so thoroughly fused that there is nothing that can be considered Transcaucasian, local Anatolian, or Mesopotamian, only "Arslantepian."

This becomes clear through the application of basic archaeological method: consideration of context. The precise placement in time and space of the burial itself, and more particularly of every item that goes to comprise that burial, inside and out, reveals that it was not composed to demonstrate the power of one group over another – whether in terms of ethnicity or social or political status and despite the common characterization of this burial as an example of retainer sacrifice – but was composed in, and simultaneously resulted from, the performance of a ritual aimed at another audience altogether. And this was indeed a performance, and quite a dramatic one at that. The deposition of all its elements was patterned, deliberate, and meaningful. Some aspects of that meaning we shall never be able to reconstruct, but others become obvious from consideration of the patterns themselves.

The patterns begin, for us at least, with the last part of the performance, the deposition of the four adolescent bodies on the outside of the tomb (Fig. 4). Although Frangipane et al. (2001: 121) state that the lower half of the male skeleton had fallen into the tomb when the roof collapsed, the absence of the lower portion of one body, from pelvis to toes, in both pairs can hardly be a mere coincidence. The presentation of the four bodies is far too deliberate for that.[1] These individuals are all young, but within this age bracket a very clear opposition was set up in the positioning of the bodies – each pair contains the two ages, and each age is diagonally placed opposite each other (Fig. 20). Another aspect worthy of note is that none of the violence evident in the remains of these adolescents was necessarily the cause of death, or occurred at the time of death; rather, it occurred long enough *before* death for healing to have commenced (Schultz and Schmidt-Schultz in Frangipane et al. 2001; Palumbi 2008: 109), and indeed, some of the hemorrhaging evident might have been caused by disease rather than blunt force. The third thing to observe is that although the male skeleton (if indeed it is male) contributes to some patterns, it does not contribute to all of them – indeed it stands out as being remarkably healthy, at least as far as skull and torso go.

The sequence of events giving rise to this picture may have been more prolonged and certainly more complicated than a single funereal episode. Analysis of the tomb's soil layers shows a distinct difference between the soil inside the tomb and the soil among and over the bones on top of the tomb (Fig. 4). The interior material is "clean," consisting of a 10–15 cm layer of dirt over the burial, on top of which was a sandy layer 2–3 cm deep (Frangipane et al. 2001: 120). The exterior material contains the kind of detritus associated with remains of living contexts – bits of sherd, charcoal, stone, and clay. The paleopathologists working on the bones (Schmidt and Schmidt-Schulz in Frangipane et al. 2001: 129) suggest this means that the people on top of the tomb were "not regularly buried" and that earth covering them accumulated gradually as debris from the adjacent settlement, but in fact the first thing it suggests is that the sealing of the tomb and the deposition of the bodies on top of it were not a single event, but a series of events – perhaps two, perhaps three – that took place over an extended period of time.

If it was a single deposit, covered over by natural processes such as wind blowing or rain washing materials off the slope behind the tomb, this same material would have filtered down into the tomb below, before and after the lid was broken. In my experience, a lid does not act as a sieve for small fragments of debris, but the material that finds its way in through cracks or settling is the same as that which is on top. It is possible that the interior of the tomb had been lightly backfilled, but if so, this clean material would have had to have come from some distance, as the tomb itself was dug into earlier habitation layers covered by fill layers (Frangipane et al. 2001: 106); the material taken out of the original pit, and thereby the adjacent spill convenient for backfilling, would have

---

1　Moreover, it seems highly unlikely, although not of course impossible, that the small bones of the hand lying behind his back, over the lower spine and pelvis, would remain in place while the lower bones slid down the slab and into the space below.

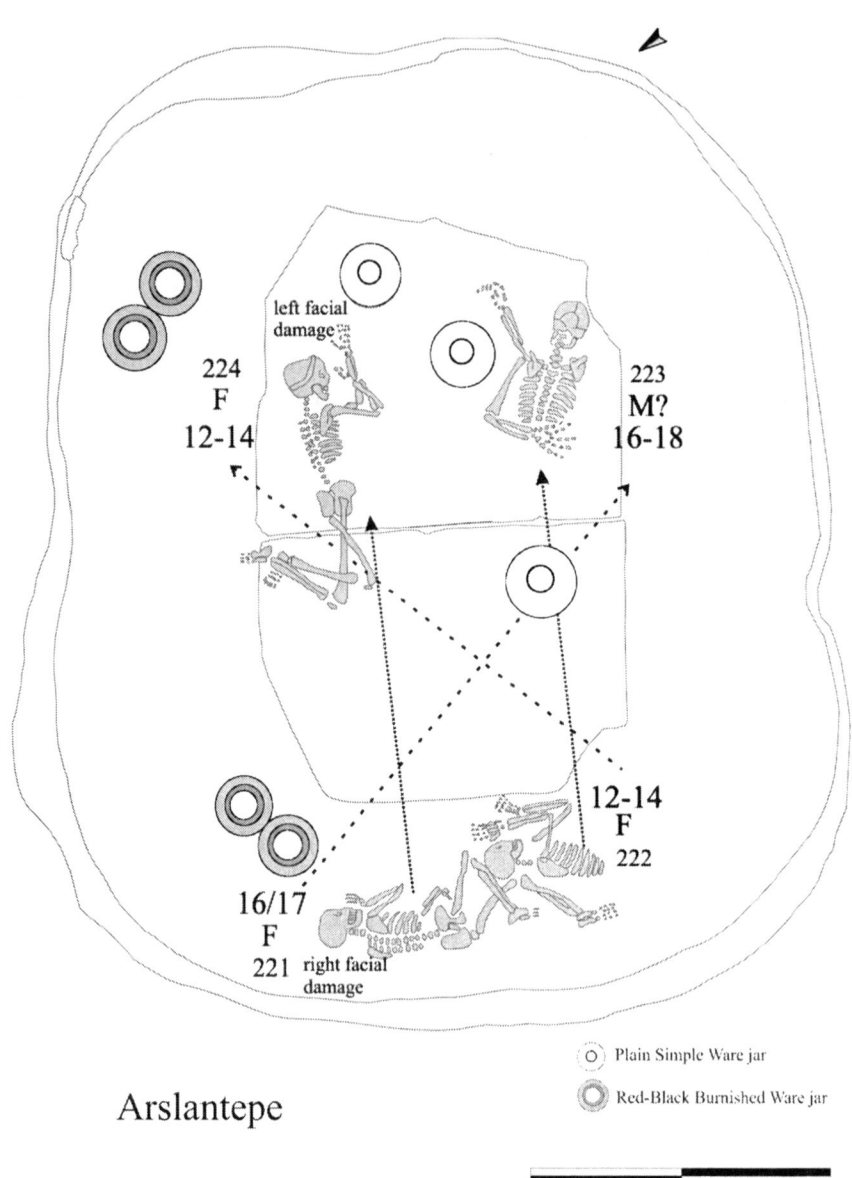

left facial
damage

224
F
12-14

223
M?
16-18

12-14
F
222

16/17
F
221   right facial
damage

Arslantepe

○ Plain Simple Ware jar

◎ Red-Black Burnished Ware jar

0   50   100 cm

20. Mirrored features of the Arslantepe sacrifices. Adapted from Frangipane et al. 2001.

contained just such detritus. But the tomb contained lighter, cleaner material, which typically is silt-blown or, more rarely (and quite detectably), washed in to the empty space inside the tomb; this suggests that the tomb, while closed by the limestone slabs, was left uncovered by dirt backfill. Although it might seem counterintuitive to us, in the later third millennium aboveground tombs become common, as do tombs with lids forming part of the surface and semi-subterranean tombs (Porter 2007/8). Subsequently – and just how much subsequently could perhaps be ascertained by precise analysis of the depth and deposition history of the soil inside the tomb – a ritual was enacted on top of it. The amount of dirt filling the tomb would suggest to me that it was exposed for more than a few weeks and less than a decade, but this is only a guess.

So the tomb was constructed, the body and goods placed in it, the lid closed, and then it was left.[2] Sometime later, another event took place on the tomb, and from here at least three scenarios are possible. In the first scenario, three ill or injured women and one healthy (?) man (?) were brought to the outside of the tomb. They were costumed appropriately for the performance of a ritual which they enacted, and then they were bound, placed on and around the tomb and left to die of starvation, which in their debilitated state would have been quite rapid. The people who put them there returned at a later date when they extracted the lower halves of two of the individuals and filled in the pit on top of them. In the second scenario, two of the individuals were cut in half and their lower portions removed, while the two complete bodies were pushed into the pit, and all were buried immediately, perhaps while still alive, since there is no obvious cause of death. The collapse of the tomb's roof without significant wash through into the tomb below, as well as the undisturbed nature of the two complete skeletons, which while broken up by the weight of soil do not seem to have been disturbed by carrion-eating animals, all suggest to me that the tableau on top of the tomb was indeed backfilled soon afterwards, although not necessarily immediately – perhaps as the bodies started to decompose – but they were not left exposed to fill in through wash and wind over a lengthy period of time. That the tomb's lid was smashed by the weight of soil also implies a heavy deposit at one time and not a gradual accumulation over years, which settles over, and often actually preserves, skeletal material, so that even though the weight might ultimately crack the stones of the tomb's lid, the burials would not be quite so badly damaged.

The third scenario, although I think it ultimately somewhat less likely, is that the four bodies were deposited in two *separate* events, with the second replicating, although perhaps poorly, the first. This scenario is suggested by the location of the female pair, not on the lid itself, but on the ledge slightly above the lid. It is also suggested by a possible chronological difference in the pots associated with the various stages of inhumation (iterated by Frangipane et al. 2001; Frangipane 2007; Palumbi 2008), itself a complex matter. It would explain both the duplication and the disparity between the two pairs of bodies,

---

2   Palumbi (2008: 153) suggests that the two individuals lying on top of the tomb itself, those attributed high status because of costuming, were victims of a coup, killed and tossed onto the tomb on their way home from the burial now that their protector was dead. Appealing as this scenario might be, it would seem to be obviated by the sequence outlined here; if they were the product of a coup that took place some time later, one might ask why the tomb was exposed, for in other instances where this was the case, commemorative rituals were in evidence.

because ritual is rarely enacted in exactly the same way from one time to the next for a number of reasons, some of which have to do with changing circumstances, some of which with the passage of time. So if, for example, the lower half of the male skeleton did indeed fall into the crack between the two stones when the lid broke, replication of this situation might explain the partial body in the second pair, but it would also suggest that the lid was broken and that this was visible at the time of the second ritual. In which case, the tomb might have been susceptible to plundering, and questions would also be raised about the lack of significant disturbance to the complete body if it had been exposed for a while.

The exact mirroring of the bodies themselves, so that the two pairs, if facing each other, would be almost identical, matching torso with torso, facial damage with facial damage, does imply (to me at least) that the first scenario is the most likely, and that all four bodies were players in the same scene, because there is nothing lost through memory here or through varying contingent circumstances. Nor is there any real chronological difference between the pottery types included in and on the tomb; the various ceramic elements in this tomb have been in place, in the same general contexts, for some hundreds of years by now. Finally, given that there is little enough evidence on which to attribute gender to the two partial skeletons, especially the one identified as possibly male, I am inclined to think that they were probably of the same sex. The differences in costuming then, and in grave goods, would have other interpretations. Perhaps, as the excavators assume, they are a function of status. Perhaps they are a function of role. That the bodies are arranged in so careful a manner certainly suggests they have a tale to tell.

One possibility is that these bodies are enacting a myth or story, and that each body constitutes a particular persona in that story. Costuming, for obvious reasons, is perhaps not discussed as much as it should be. Distinctions in garb may be allocated not on the basis of who the body *is*, but who the body *becomes* in the ritual itself. Some figures have lead roles; some are only supporting players. I am not suggesting the practice of substitution here, where the king is ritually killed in the person of a surrogate, but rather that the playing out of myth (Brown 2003, Laneri 2002) or the re-creation/representation of certain groupings of people means that the *role*, not the actual person, is uppermost.

This is further signified by the fact that these four players were most likely sacrificed – not to demonstrate the ability of a ruler to dispose of people as he pleased, a show of his absolute power over life and death, but to provide the bodies necessary to play out this scene. Hints as to just why this was done lie in the stratigraphic sequence of events and the patterning of its composition, which in all its detail accomplishes one very specific scenario: mirroring.

Table 4 shows that detail. The two groups of two bodies duplicate each other in almost every respect – indeed, if all four are female as I suspect, in

Table 4. Patterning in Arslantepe sacrifice.

Skel no	Sex	Age	Diadem	Clothing	Trauma	Peri-mortem injury	Disease	Childhood illness @ age
221 full	F	16/17			Left face Blunt Force broken foot	weeks 2 years	Meningeal	2,3,4,6
222 part	F	12–15			Back of head broken ribs	weeks weeks		4
223 Part	M	16–18	Yes	Yes				None
224 full	F	12–14	Yes	Yes	Right face Blunt Force? lesion on arm	weeks 1 year		3,4,5

all respects. Mirroring is, I would argue, a very explicit expression of views of cosmological organization, and especially of the relationship between the world of the dead and the world of the living, where they are the same but opposite. It is reproduced in few burials (Porter n.d.), and it might therefore be suggested that its enactment, in bringing those worlds closer together and rendering the connection between them visually explicit, is warranted only by extraordinary circumstances.

Mirroring also highlights another issue not often considered when the sacrificed are thought of as at the disposal of the powerful: the fact that victims are in some way selected. In this instance it suggests that the biography of the individual was a crucial part of the reason they were chosen for sacrifice, given that both full-bodied skeletons manifest a series of childhood illnesses. Perhaps they were considered special because they had survived, blessed by the gods; perhaps they were considered pitiful, calculated to appeal to divine sentiments (although the portrayal of the gods in much later texts certainly does not reveal a warm and fuzzy side to them). Alternatively, the choice of people already injured or ill might have been a way of minimizing the social cost of producing this tableau, which might in turn imply that it was not something willingly done, but something that *had* to be done.[3] In mirroring a cosmological understanding and freezing a ritual performance through the use of sacrificial victims, this deposition was ultimately transcending time in a way that the actions of living beings simply could not. And those who live in time-lessness are only the denizens of other worlds, not this one. Therefore this burial speaks to members of those other worlds – the divine or the dead – as much as to members of this world.

---

3   The male (?) figure duplicates but breaks the pattern at the same time, standing out because of his health, so there is something significant about him, perhaps to do with gender; or it may simply be that there were no other ill people available at that time.

We can also be sure that all the materials inside the tomb, as well as those surrounding the bodies outside it, are just as meaningful as the bodies themselves. They have been carefully placed. But they do not reproduce some innate character of the primary inhumation. The metals may have symbolic meaning far more complex than denoting an individual's warrior status, desired or real. For one thing daggers, spears, and arrowheads are included with female burials as well as male, just as jewelry is included with male burials as well as female. Gender, then, is not the qualifier of these types of burial goods, nor is biography be it in terms of the life events of the interred or their social status; a concatenation of features, such as construction, placement, and body treatment, all have something to say and must be taken into account (Porter 2007/8). What is more, status may accrue for a variety of reasons that have nothing to do with wealth and power but speak to some other kind of distinction, such as an ability to communicate with otherworldly beings. For another, objects classified as weapons are often used in religious rituals, as attested by the group of projectile points found in the *Riemchengebäude*, possibly a storage structure for materials used in rituals taking place in one of the temples of the Eana precinct at Uruk (Pollock 1999: 101; Wright 2002). At Arslantepe itself, two caches of spears and daggers, some with marked resemblance to the items in the tomb (Frangipane et al. 2001: 113), were found stratigraphically superimposed in level VIA Building III (Frangipane and Palmiere 1983: figs. 17–18, 62), the part of the complex adjacent to Temple A (Frangipane 2007b).

The east and south corners of the tomb were delineated with spearheads standing more or less upright and so seem to have been spaces of some significance – all the Red-Black Burnished Ware vessels inside the tomb were located there (Fig. 21). Three bowls were found in the east corner with a unique example of a Red-Slipped jar, while two small jars, one in Red-Black Burnished Ware, the other in Plain Simple Ware, were located in the south one. Spearheads were also arranged around the head of the body, while the rest of the weapons were in a pile associated with the back. Such placement might suggest that the weapons had a protective significance as much as it might suggest that the interred was a warrior. Also in the east corner was a collection of jewelry – bracelets and rings in silver and copper-silver alloy. The remaining jewelry seems to have originally adorned the body itself.

The vessels lining the northwestern wall of the tomb, in contrast, were wheel-made Plain Simple Ware storage jars, some in Reserved Slip, with one Red-Black Burnished Ware bowl. Frangipane (Frangipane et al. 2001: 109) makes a clear distinction between the function of the differently placed vessels, one that corresponds closely, but not identically, with ware types: the small vessels in the corners and around the body, mostly Red-Black Burnished Ware, are for presentation/consumption; the larger vessels against the wall, mostly Plain Simple Ware, are for storage. So why then would Red-Black Burnished Ware and Plain

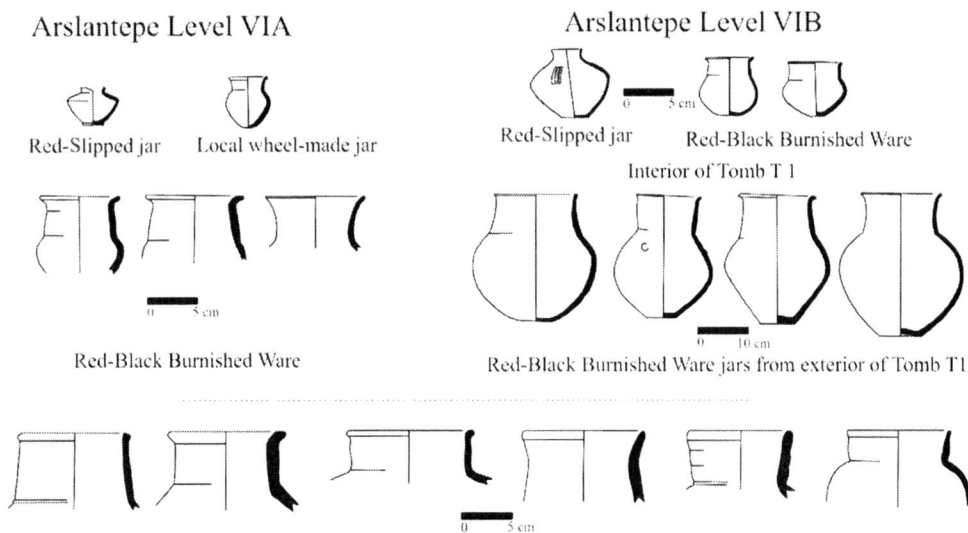

21. The pottery from Arslantepe VIB Tomb T1 (redrawn from Frangipane et al. 2001) with comparative material from Arslantepe level VIA (redrawn from Frangipane and Palmieri 1983) and Uruk jars (Type E) from Habuba Kabira (redrawn from Surenhagen 1978).

Simple Ware denote different social statuses or different ethnicities when placed outside the tomb? It is claimed that "The 'royal' tomb of Arslantepe perhaps exhibits two aspects: on the one hand it contains elements of both cultures symbolically placed side by side, on the other, there is a different positioning of the pottery in the local VIA tradition associated with high-ranking personages (decorated with jewels and diadems) and the Transcaucasian pottery placed around the edges of the pit, perhaps associated with the two girls who were without funerary gifts" (Frangipane et al. 2001: 113).

It is clear that the vessels incorporated on the outside, just as on the inside, of the tomb, as well as belonging simply to different ware groups, have some kind of functional differentiation, one set from the other, even though it is not as obvious as the differences between storage jars and cups and bowls. I suspect the Red-Black Burnished Ware pots are vessels for pouring liquid, facilitated by the burnished exterior which reduces porosity and by the cylindrical necks (which themselves bear striking resemblance to the cylindrical necks on some of the earlier Uruk vessels) and open mouths (Fig. 21). Here too we should not dismiss the significance of the materiality of these vessels, their multiple relationships to the senses: the vivid colors and smooth surfaces that invite both eye and touch, the shape and size of the body (with its slight carination) that fits satisfyingly into two hands and leaves the long necks free to pour without contamination from human contact. It might be imagined that this group of vessels was used for libations accompanying, even closing, the deposition of the four adolescents. Hence their placement, as the final act of the ritual, on the outer ledge of the tomb in two pairs of two – echoing again the grouping of the bodies, but not necessarily (and contra Frangipane et al. 2001: 112; Palumbi 2008: 112) distinguishing them.

As for the differing forms of Red-Black Burnished Ware, changes in style in a type within an assemblage are only normal, and the ones evident in the assemblage here are not very pronounced. There is, to my mind, an entirely continuous Red-Black Burnished Ware tradition between levels VIA and VIB2 (Fig. 21). But the difference between earlier and later corpuses is equally to be explained by the fact that there were no contexts excavated in the previous period in which a libation ritual, or another activity concerning the contents of these vessels, took place. This very distinctive kind of production and its specific manufacturing techniques were not new to level VIB inhabitants of Arslantepe, and no element of it has to be understood as imported at this time. The small bowls and jars are already known from the VIA repertoire (Frangipane 2001: 119), and it is to be noted that a very similar vessel to the cylindrical necked Red-Black Burnished jar is to be found in Arslantepe VIA in Building III (Fig. 21), the only significant differences between them being overall size and the proportions of neck to body. This form also occurs in the early stages of the Kura-Araxes ceramic repertoire, the "proto-Kura-Araxes," which is equivalent to Arslantepe level VII (Sagona and Zimansky 2009: 166 and fig. 5.10;[4] see also Palumbi 2008: fig. 3.7). However, the shape of the body and the cylindrical necks of this later group of Red-Black Burnished Ware vessels might each be seen to derive from different components, in different wares, from the VIA assemblage. As already noted, some of the Uruk jars have cylindrical necks. The appearance of newness may be a result of blending of ceramic traditions.

There are many small material indications of direct continuity from the temple complexes of the previous period only some twenty meters way, albeit by this stage buried. The Red-Slipped jar in the corner (though I have not seen either piece in person) appears very similar to the Red-Slipped jar found in the *cella* (room A450) of Temple B (Fig. 21); and there, too, the ceramic collection may be divided into storage containers and presentation/consumption vessels, the latter category including the mass-produced coarse bowls. In that instance, though, the one Red-Black Burnished Ware vessel, also from the *cella*, is for storage and not eating or drinking. Nevertheless, it is to be observed that whereas the "fruit stands" or "high-stemmed bowls" of the *cella* in Temple B are wheel-made and grit-tempered, several of those in Temple A are in Red-Black Burnished Ware (Frangipane and Palmieri 1983: fig. 19). Metalwork is another category in which there are close affinities with the techniques and styles of the earlier period at Arslantepe, as already noted. At the least, the particular metals and ceramics present in the tomb complex now comprise a single cultural and

---

4   The second example of group 5.

sociopolitical entity, whatever may have been the case previously. But I think we can go further than that. Continuity in some larger, and immaterial, ways is evident between VIA and VIB2, between the temple complex and the tomb; the same structural elements of sociopolitical interaction and integration – kinship, especially descent, and the invocation of otherworldly powers as the object of commonality – are all in evidence at once here, although in different manifestations.

Because of the intervening levels associated with mobile pastoralists on the grounds of the sporadic, sparse, and scanty nature of occupation (Palumbi 2008), and seen as "radically new" by some (Matthews 2003: 130), the location of the tomb in the region of the VIA temples and the even earlier monumental constructions is seen as an appropriated affiliation of the earlier culture, if the Transcaucasian/Kura-Araxan elements dominate, or as a relict but legitimate affiliation, if Mesopotamian ones do. But by now there is no specified Mesopotamian identity left, for reasons that I will explicate below – although neither should the material and sociopolitical culture of this tomb be seen as external to the settlement, originating from far to the northeast. It is all local. It is in this moment of visibility predominantly defined by its mobility. And it is a continuous, inherited culture.

It is simply not known why the Uruk expansion came to an end. All that is known is that at around 3100 BCE materials characteristic of southern Mesopotamia are no longer in evidence outside of southern Mesopotamia itself, the colonies of the Middle Euphrates disappear, and several local Late Chalcolithic sites come to an end or give way to new kinds of settlement, as is the case at Arslantepe. Thereafter, there is thought to have been a five-to-seven-hundred-year gap before anything of a complexity equal to that accomplished in the fourth millennium reemerges with the sudden rise and rapid spread of "secondary urbanism" (Mazzoni 1991). It is in this context that the occupation of Arslantepe VIB1/2 is located.

Given the reconstruction put forward in the previous chapter, it should be no surprise that I see things somewhat differently. The broad outlines of the situation are as follows: the processes of differentiation and integration described in Chapter 2 were effective – so effective that there were wide, and unintended, consequences. The increased definition of the ancestral group in the late fourth millennium wrought the very fragmentation it initially combatted. Rather than the social group splitting between mobile pastoralists and sedentary farmers, however, individual ancestral groups split from the larger communities of which they were part, many moving away from the centers with which they had been affiliated before and forming their own, smaller-scale communities. This is manifest in the particular nature of occupation and its attributes that define the first centuries of the third millennium in the north. As was stated in the previous chapter, the expansion of mobile pastoralism for the production of wool, following both localized and broad-range[5] strategies, was not the pursuit of southern Mesopotamians alone but was a strategy probably developed first in the north, and certainly practiced extensively there. But the creation of self-differentiation was very much a southern process, evident in the presence of intrusive settlements. Differentiating oneself to some degree does have the result of defining the other, even if the other does not actively seek a countering discrimination of itself; but those who broke away were, I propose, by and large the southern constituency of these sites because local settlement in the Upper Euphrates (especially in the Carchemish region [Falsone and Sconzo 2007; Frangipane 2007; Quenet 2007]) continued, as it may have (although the connections are less well-exposed) at some key sites in the east (Fig. 22). The fragmentation of these southern groups led to a rearrangement of both local and intrusive practices of animal husbandry (cf. Palumbi 2007/8: 159), with some groups no doubt returning far south while some local groups no doubt expanded downstream and to the east. The fragmentation of the dense network of economic interactions that resulted from this breakup had an effect on those local settlements (Porter 2002a) no matter their participation in mobile pastoralism, and led to the diminution of some sites and to the end of others, but the nature of culture for those that survived did not change. We do, though, now see a different component of it.

Confining the discussion for the moment specifically to Arslantepe, several simultaneous outcomes seem likely. Tying the two groups of Mesopotamian pastoralists to places that were associated with their ancestors in the form of the two temple complexes, no matter how contrived that might have been, led to an increasing identification of those groups with that place and an increasing attenuation of both sedentary and mobile components of those two groups[6] from the communities of their southern Mesopotamian origins. The degree to which the settlement of Arslantepe collapsed can only be ascertained by the expansion of excavation of the relevant levels, but it should be no surprise if those same pastoralists were to continue to return to a place that had become ancestrally sanctioned, even if the structures in which that sanctioning took place are no longer visible. The absence, then, of the small temples in which the solidarity of the kin-group was grounded in the practice of ancestral traditions, made way for alternative practices that were blended, and ultimately local, in both style and conception.

---

5   The term "broad-range" pastoralism is to be preferred to "long-distance" pastoralism because it implies nothing about the nature of movement, its direction, or its length, nor does it imply a continuum into which any given example must fit at a precise point. It implies only that the scope of movement is not immediately local and that a variety of types of movement and strategies are possible within this rubric.

6   And, of course, potentially other such groups. It is because only two ancestral temples at Arslantepe are exposed that I limit the discussion to two seceding groups.

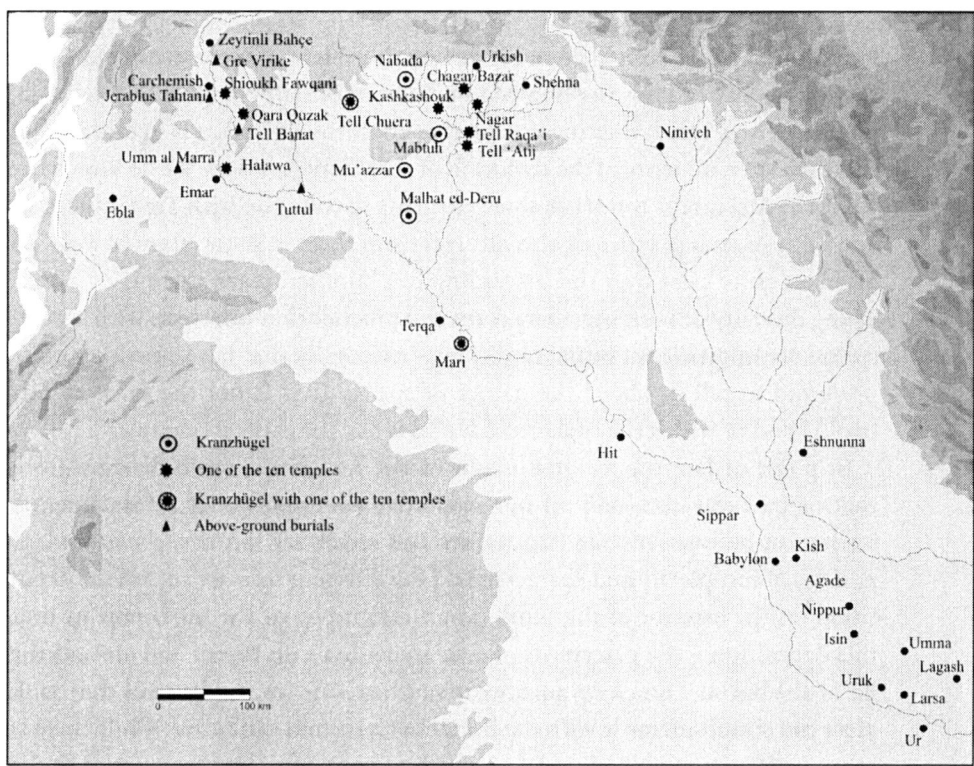

22. Map of the third millennium indicating the location of the ten temples, key *Kranzhügeln*, and above-ground mortuary remains.

Nor should it be surprising that pastoralists from Arslantepe or from southern Mesopotamia who pastured at some point in the realm of the Caucasus or the Kuru-Araxes in the fourth millennium adopted materials local to those regions. The degree to which differentiation from, or affiliation with, the material worlds of these regions occurs is no doubt a result of many factors, such as the degree to which pasture is freely available or the kind of political control local groups have over which territories – factors that may be summed up by what strategies are deemed most likely to gain access to the resources any given group is seeking. A more problematic issue, though, is the adoption of materials that should overtly signify ideological/cosmological conceptions, such as the structural form of a tomb would represent. The degree to which form relates to practice and belief is a complex theoretical matter, as is the degree to which people borrow form and ignore practice, or the degree to which people abandon their own traditions and adopt others and under what circumstances, but in this particular instance the issue may be addressed on a more practical level.

Some hundreds of years elapsed between the temple and the tomb, a period during which many societies changed dramatically and yet remained the same in key fundamentals. These ancestral groups, once Mesopotamian, are now thoroughly local, the processes of transformation already evident in Arslantepe level VIA. Since we simply do not have fourth-millennium mortuary materials, there is no way of knowing how Mesopotamian burials compare to this tomb, no idea of how much they diverge from or conform with what is in evidence all this time later, no sense of the evolution of mortuary practices. We do know that while the Arslantepe tomb has some elements in common with Transcaucasian and Kura-Araxan practices it also diverges from them in some essential ways. As becomes quite clear over the succeeding five hundred years, there is an astonishing diversity of both mortuary form and practice that intersects with a widespread commonality of burial traditions – a diversity that has something quite profound to tell us about the nature of society (but is not the topic of this book),[7] and of which the Arslantepe burial is but the earliest example.

In point of fact my reconstruction of the Arslantepe tomb diverges from that of its excavators only in our respective assumptions of a fundamental separation between mobile pastoralists and sedentary farmers, the attendant notions of complexity and character, and the different roles we accord the deposition on the exterior of the tomb. The stratigraphy of the tomb tells us that this deposition – the placement of four individuals on top of and around the lid of the burial – was a commemorative event, one (or maybe two) that took place not simultaneously with the burial but a certain time after. While there is as yet little comparable material in which to contextualize this practice at the beginning of the third millennium, the wealth of material in the next phase, the mid-third millennium, indicates that commemoration at this time, too, was the enactment of kinship, and specifically, descent. To narrow the focus of this confluence of data even further, the nature of the fourth-millennium remains and the nature of the early and mid-third-millennium remains would suggest that it was descent as deployed in the definition of territorial extent (Porter 2002a). Religion is as inextricably bound up with practical concerns now as it was previously, indeed, as it always is in a world where otherworldly beings are vital, immanent forces. But the location of religious practices has shifted somewhat, from the temple to the tomb.

Both the Upper and Middle Euphrates of the mid-third millennium are now notable for the wealth of burial data retrieved, and this is at least in part because much of it is peculiarly visible. It is also because many of these inhumations, or inhumation fields, have distinctive and localized characteristics. From the platforms and chambers at Gre Virike (Ökse 2005), to the aboveground burial mounds at Tell Banat (Porter 2002a, 2007/8), the in-house tombs at Titris Höyük (Honça and Algaze 1998; Laneri 2002), the burial enclosure at Umm al Marra (Schwartz 2007), and the mortuary houses of Tell Bi'a (Bösze 2009), there is a reason that at this time so many settlements had their own, very particular

---

7   See Schwartz 2007; Peltenburg 2007/8; Porter 2002b, 2007/8, n.d. for preliminary discussions of the significance of these various burials.

ways of burying certain members of society. Indeed, the Transcaucasian kur-gans, large earthen mounds superimposed over a stone burial chamber, to which the Arslantepe tomb is compared, are exactly this – territorial definition through rendering visible the dead. The Arslantepe tomb differs from many of these later burials in its lack of visibility – its subterranean status does not demarcate territory,[8] whether of the polity or the individual household, in the same way that the aboveground structures do. But the conjunction of sacrifice here with a distinctive mortuary structure has its own kind of visibility, espe-cially if the act was left open to the gaze for even a short time. Human sacrifice was simply not a common practice. It is discernible in only four places over a seven-hundred-year period, places distributed from one end of the Euphrates to another (Porter n.d.). Given its rarity and the element of display manifest in the stratigraphy of this event (and in the others), it seems likely that knowledge of the sacrifice alone made this an enduring monument, serving in memory the same function performed by the visibility of the later structures.

So the Arslantepe tomb is symptomatic of a process that becomes very pro-nounced in the Middle to Upper Euphrates (and elsewhere) late in the second quarter of the third millennium – the demarcation of territory through par-ticularized burials – and it may be proposed that at least some of the variation manifest in these burials is correlative with variation in details of sociopolit-ical organization and/or land tenure practices (Porter 2000). This is an out-come of the breakdown of the southern system of interconnection at the end of the fourth millennium and was probably, at least in part, even its cause – not because ever-incipient conflict between nomad and farmer at last burst forth, so that states declined and tribes now reappeared to take their place, but because ancestral groups became so defined that the system fragmented in a very par-ticular way. The different communities created through this process, commu-nities still consisting of sedentary and mobile components, claimed their own sociopolitical space and territorial definition.

The result of this process is manifest in the mid-third millennium with the florescence of individual polities characterized by individual sociopolitical constructs that seem to have emerged along individual trajectories (Porter 2007/8; 2010a). The process itself is evident in the archaeology of the interven-ing phase, between the burial of Arslantepe and the burials of the mid-third millennium – that is, in the first century and a half of the third millennium.

Although there is a consensus that certain features characterize occupation at this time, that what little settlement there is tends to limited complexity (Akkermans and Schwartz 2003: 231) and is concentrated in the river valleys (Hempelmann 2008: 155), this period is still poorly understood. I suspect we

---

8   Although there has been some speculation as to whether this structure was covered with a mound, it seems unlikely.

have rather a skewed picture of just what the nature of the post-Uruk settlement was like. For one thing, with the exception of those large sites under excavation for decades, much of this material has come from salvage projects resulting from the construction of new dams, where work in Syria and Turkey has largely been concentrated since the 1970s. For another, the series of extremely large round sites called *Kranzhügeln* that are located in the steppe regions may have originated at the beginning of the third millennium also.[9] If so, this would radically change our understanding of settlement patterns in this period.

Another attribute that is thought to characterize this period is a high degree of regionalization (Morandi Bonacossi 2000: 1105;[10] Akkermans and Schwartz 2003: 231–2; Frangipane 2007: 139; Palumbi 2007/8: 159), with little economic interaction or cultural continuity from one small ecological zone to another. This is now to be challenged as long-term projects reach earlier levels and results from salvage programs become increasingly available. Occupation in the early third millennium is attested at more and more sites, whatever their relationship with the previous period. Within these settlement shifts certain features emerge that can be found in both the Euphrates (Upper and Middle) and Habur settlement systems, previously considered quite distinct. The nature of these features, their chronology, and their ubiquity are telling.

One such feature is a series of small single-roomed structures (Fig. 23) felicitously called "the seven shrines of Subartu" by Roger Matthews (2002), although they in fact number at least nine (and possibly ten) if one dispenses with the traditional focus on the Habur and the Euphrates riverine systems as separate and unrelated that has inhibited understanding of the archaeological record in Syria to date. Containing installations indicative of ritual function, these buildings are usually square (two are actually quite rectangular) and freestanding; they do not form a room within a larger complex, although some are part of agglutinative architecture. They accommodate few people and are accessed through a solitary entrance. Those listed by Matthews have doors located on either the north or the east wall, and when the latter, the doors are toward the north. Most of them are associated with various forms of human representation (Matthews 2002), an unusual attribute at this time, and they contain similar interior furnishings such as benches and podia.

These structures themselves are evidence of a commonality that extends across the north, because to the temples Matthews recognizes at Tell Brak, Tell Chuera, Tell Raqa'i, Tell Kashkashouk, Tell 'Atij, Chagar Bazaar, and Mari, I would add three more. The first, although not the earliest, comes from Qara

---

9   A superficial examination of surface sherds at several of these sites conducted by myself, Thomas McClellan, and Paola Sconzo in 2007 showed sufficient indication of earlier material to suggest this possibility; also Lyonnet 2009: 181; Meyer 2010b.
10   And see this reference for additional bibliography.

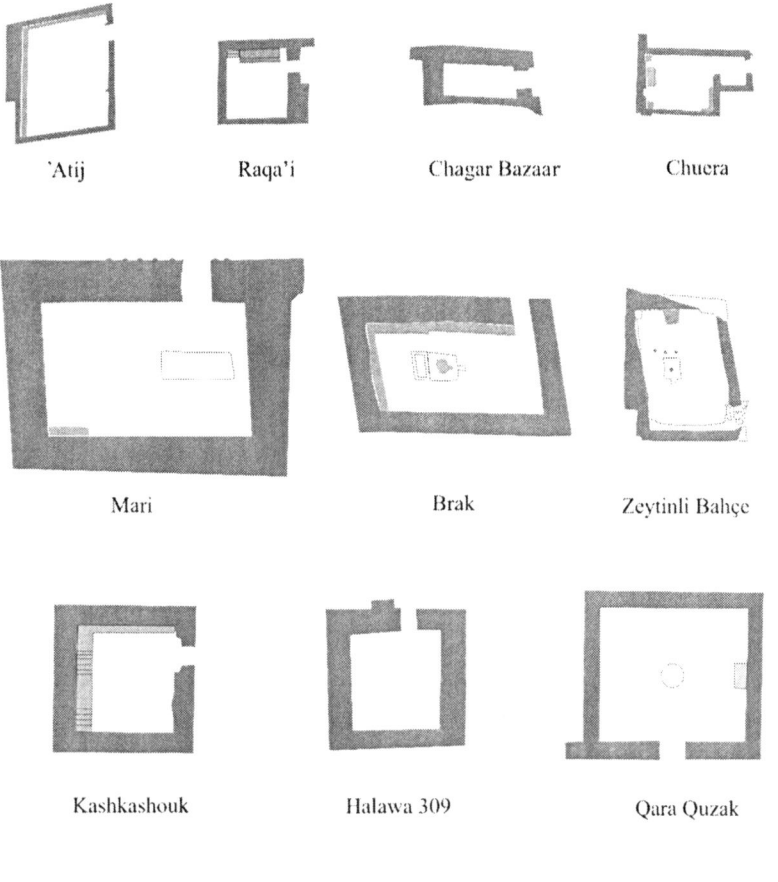

'Atij   Raqa'i   Chagar Bazaar   Chuera

Mari   Brak   Zeytinli Bahçe

Kashkashouk   Halawa 309   Qara Quzak

0   5   10 m

23. The ten temples of the Trans-Euphrates. The temples from 'Atij, Raqa'i, Chagar Bazaar, Chuera, Mari, Brak, and Kashkashouk are redrawn from Matthews 2002; Zeytinli Bahçe is redrawnfromFrangipane 2007a; Halawa from Orthmann 1989; Qara Quzak from Olávarri and Valdés 1996.

Quzak, a very small site that lies on the edge of the cultural zone that constitutes the Upper Euphrates. Dated to the period between 2900 and 2600 BCE, and most likely belonging to the earlier end of it, this 8.2 by 8.4 meter building differs from the others only in that it has a doorway midway in the south wall (not the north), immediately opposite a circular depression in the floor that had been burnt. On either side of this circle (but some distance from it) were two aurochs horns, while against the east wall was a plastered mud-brick plinth (Olávarri and Valdés 1996). An object made of stone, labeled a "massebah" by the excavators, and a large jar in the vicinity of the plinth - altar - completed the furnishings of this structure.

Although freestanding, the Qara Quzaq temple did not, however, stand alone. It was abutted on the west by a walled trapezoidal space with its own entrance, also opening to the south, from which one could access three smaller rooms. The trapezoidal room was decorated with wall paintings, although these were badly decayed and no figurative components were recovered. The excavators interpret these rooms as the residence of the temple personnel. Opposite the

24. The White Monument at Tell Banat North. Photo by author.

temple is a two-chambered, vaulted and semi-subterranean structure that is thought to have been a burial structure because there was little trace of domestic activity and because installations for ritual offerings were present (Olávarri and Valdés 1996). Although this has been viewed as "tentative" on the grounds that no human remains were found (L. Cooper 2006: 149), the potential import of an earlier infant jar-burial, itself contained in a small stone cist located under the earliest wall of this vaulted structure (Olávarri and Valdés 1996: fig. 2), should not be discounted. Nor does it obviate the potential for a close conceptual connection between the two structures. Infant burials are little considered unless through extraordinary grave goods they provide evidence of inherited status; social consequence, however, is not dependent only on position within a hierarchy and may be accrued for a variety of reasons. Obviously an infant is not an ancestor in any biological sense, but a child may nevertheless have lineage significance even, or perhaps especially, if its early death indicates the end of the line. Alternatively, a medical condition may give rise to a magical or otherworldly importance. A mortuary meaning to this space would certainly seem perpetuated in the next construction in this area, a large two-room, above-ground building, each room containing a primary inhumation, one a woman, one a child. It is worth noting here that in one of the seven shrines – that of Tell Raqa'i – two burials, one of a child, were found in the temple precinct (Schwartz 2000: 170).

Particularly interesting, however, is the situation of this complex, which is set on an artificial platform over two meters tall and made of mud-brick – located, what is more, on a high terrace on the central part of the site (Olávarri and Valdés Pereiro 2001). Qara Quzaq itself is a small, conical mound that stands high in the floodplain of this narrow point in the Euphrates River. It is a local landmark, visible from every direction as one comes across the various passes from the steppe and descends into the valley. It is very similar in overall appearance to the White Monument of Tell Banat North (Fig. 24) and in its visuality within the landscape, albeit on a minor scale, to Jebel Aruda.

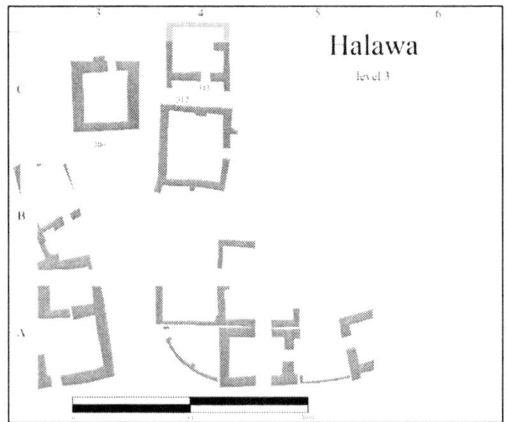

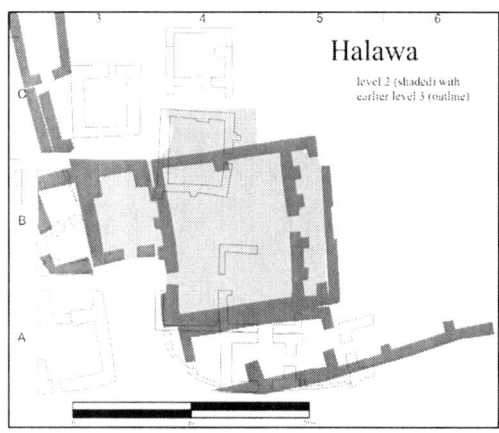

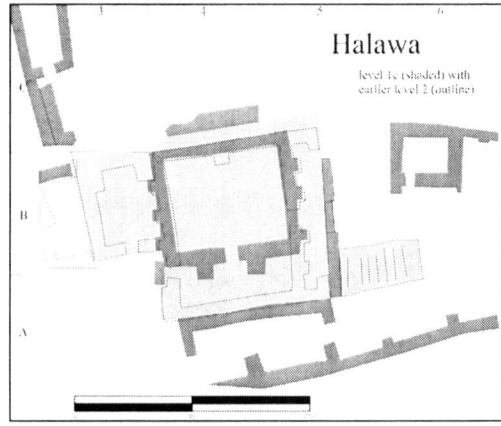

25. The sequence of temples at Halawa Tell B, from earliest (level 3) to latest (level 1c). Redrawn from Orthmann 1989.

At Halawa, farther south on the Euphrates, a series of superimposed single-roomed square structures begin with three such buildings arranged in a tight grouping (Fig. 25). One of these (309) had an off-center opening on the north, flanked by a buttress. Another (313) was entered from the south, while the third (312) was accessed from either the west or east (Orthmann 1989: 91). There was no coordination between entrances here that might indicate they were conceptualized as a single unit, and indeed the construction of 312 seems to have narrowed access to 313. Interior fittings such as plinths against the wall (much like all the other buildings in this category) indicate specialized function, while the three spatially separate structures might indicate separate constituencies. It is separateness that I think visually and conceptually distinguishes these three buildings from the surrounding similarly styled but agglutinative architecture characterized as domestic (Orthmann 1989). Despite the fact that these structures are similar in plan to houses, the presence of a series of wall paintings in these buildings might also set them apart from ordinary domestic structures, and the content of those paintings even more so (Orthmann 1989). From room 312 comes a painting of a large oval face, ringed by a band of geometric

26. Two wall paintings from Halawa: *top*, from room 312; *bottom*, from room 101. Illustrations courtesy of Winfried Orthmann and Jan-Waalke Meyer.

design and surrounded by full figures of what are generally taken to be humans (Akkermans and Schwartz 2003: 227), all associated with different objects or activities, most of which are not very clear (Fig. 26a). But there is one being in each of the northwest and northeast quadrants whose round face and strongly delineated nose echoes the main element of the painting, and in the southwest quadrant one figure at least has a long pointed proboscis that can only be a beak. It is interesting, then, that the northwest round face seems to be surmounted by a shape that looks suspiciously like a bird (and note the deliberately tentative language), while the figure with round face in the northeast quadrant is flanked by appendages that surely blur the distinction between arms and wings. Other elements of the painting include more traditional renditions of human figures, vegetation – perhaps the standard wheat sheaf – and at least one quadruped that seems to be directly linked to the round-faced figure with the bird head-dress. This painting has been interpreted as depicting the worship of a cultic image (Akkermans and Schwartz 2003: 227), but it might be proposed that it is also a representation of the essential elements of the cosmos, with the core components of the human world surrounding, and surrounded by, the various inhabitants of the superhuman world.

Wall paintings, however, are not confined to these three structures, but were also recovered in two other rooms (304 and 314) from this level, rooms assumed to be houses, although it might be proposed here too that the presence of wall paintings renders them something else. Both are to the south of the three temples, and 314 in particular is comparatively large, a square and plastered room with an internal buttress or plinth. A painting from the third phase of the early third-millennium occupation, from a four-roomed building located outside the temenos wall of the temple of that period, stands out. It is very difficult to interpret because of poor preservation (Fig. 26b) and possibilities range from a depiction of a sacred tree flanked by boats carrying people (Dunham 1993) to an anthropomorphic cult image with large eyes holding the same kind of vegetation as the figure on the northwest quadrant of the earlier painting just discussed (L. Cooper 2006: 93–4). The central element is a thick, solidly colored cylinder, and it is indeed surmounted by two circles. It looks very much like a spectacle idol (see Chapter 2); the tree branches, palm fronds, or wheat sheaves are not just arms, though, because there are three on either side of the trunk so that it is not unlike the winged figure in the northeast quadrant of the painting from room 312.

The second phase of early third-millennium occupation at Halawa contained a structure that bore some similarity to the contemporaneous temple at Qara Quzaq. A mud-brick platform was built to a height of one meter over the leveled remains of the three small buildings, on top of which was placed a single square structure, at 12 by 10 meters a little more than double the size of the earlier ones and slightly more elaborated (Orthmann 1989: 89). Flanked by two smaller rooms to the west, both west and east walls were buttressed on the exterior four times, and both gave access into the interior, although the eastern entrance appears to have been the primary doorway. The eastern ends of the west/east walls were also buttressed, this construction forming a narrow, crenellated forecourt. Inside the *cella* were benches lining the walls.

The plinth in this instance was against the north wall, so that, as at Qara Quzaq, the acolyte turned right to face it on entering. While these plinths are often called altars, they in fact may have been stands for statues or other cult objects (Orthmann 1989: 92). Like Qara Quzaq, the adjacent room contained a place for fire (although little else), and both temple precincts were distinguished from the surrounding settlement by an enclosure wall. A second externally buttressed and niched building, also interpreted as a temple (Orthmann 1989: 95–6), was found in the precinct of this level. The main temple was then elevated again in a subsequent rebuilding phase so that it now sat atop a series of platforms, overlooking the surrounding community. In this phase the entrance was moved to the south, and another small square temple, also with a southern doorway, was added to the precinct to the east.

A possible addition to this group, and one that would then prove to be the earliest in the sequence, is found at Shioukh Fawqani at the very beginning of the third millennium. This square structure, labeled Building 3 (Morandi Bonacossi 2000), is entered on the east end of the south wall through a foyer that also gives access to a single square room to the south, which is, ergo, entered from the north. There were no benches lining the walls of this structure, and no evidence of a plinth, although the western end of Building 3 was no longer extant and something might have been located there. Instead, the eastern wall of the Shioukh Fawqani structure is buttressed, and in the middle of the east wall, halfway between each buttress, is a niche near which was a crucible for copper making. The foyer through which Shioukh Fawqani Building 3 is entered appears similar to the forecourt that differentiates the level 5 "sanctuary"[11] of Tell Chuera from the rest of this group (Fig. 23), but at the latter site the interior fittings are quite clear.

The niche and buttressing of Building 3 are more than reminiscent of the architecture of the Uruk period, although not as refined. This is not surprising given that Shioukh Fawqani attests some kind of continuity with that period in its ceramic assemblage, and that there was no break between the late fourth-millennium and early third-millennium layers (Morandi Bonacossi 2000: 1106–7). It is not, I think, coincidental that north of, and adjacent to, Building 3 was a structure, Building 2, containing a domed oven that consumed almost all the interior space. In light of the discussion in the previous chapter, it seems quite possible that these two rooms are functionally related, as indeed is the third in the series, Building 1.[12] In this room the presence of facilities for food preparation, as well as fireplaces, have led the excavators to read it as a domestic structure – a house. But here too the activities that took place in the room may have been related to the third structure of the sequence. Food was prepared in Building 1 and some of it cooked there, while other substances – bread? – were baked in the domed oven in Building 2, subsequently to be consumed in

11   Moortgat and Moortgat Correns's (1976) "Heiligtum."
12   The numbering of the buildings here reflects the sequence of construction (Morandi Bonacossi 2000: 1108).

Building 3. One wonders whether the three freestanding, single-room structures in the earliest phase of Halawa may not also be functionally related. While not denying a religious use, Morandi Bonacossi (2000: 1109) suggests that Building 3 was not restricted to such, but rather had multiple functions, comparing it to the reception hall of today's villages.

If the Shioukh Fawqani complex represents a transition between the Uruk materials of the late fourth millennium and the early third-millennium "shrines of Subartu," then the relationship is quite clear at Zeytinli Bahçe (Frangipane 2007a: 131). Not only does Room A133 of the first post-Uruk levels there contain a bench and podium in the opposing wall, but the center is dominated by a rectangular hearth (Fig. 23) typical of the Uruk period, especially as seen at Jebel Aruda (Fig. 15), and as also found in the later temple from Tell Brak.

In addition to the Qara Quzaq and Halawa structures, the chronology and geography of these putative temples at the more northern sites indicate that the tradition is to be recognized first (as early as the very beginning of the third millennium) in the Euphrates, subsequently spreading eastward to the Habur, where the temples of Tell Raqa'i, Tell 'Atij, Kashkashouk, Chagar Bazaar, and the Ishtar temple at Mari are all attributed to Early Jazireh II (EJ II) - that is, 2600-2500 BCE.

In between, however, are the adjacent sites of Kharab Sayyar (Meyer et al. 2003; Hempelmann 2008) and Tell Chuera, which now show clear evidence of foundation at the beginning of the millennium (Meyer 2010b). Little enough has yet been exposed at any of these sites, so that we cannot say what is not there, only what is. Although no temples have been identified within the first phases of occupation at either Tell Chuera (its square structure dates to EJ II) or at Kharab Sayyar (where only a small step-trench has reached these levels), close contact with the Euphrates region is manifest in the material culture of the first occupations at the latter site. The architecture at Kharab Sayyar conforms to the square pattern known from the Euphrates, with occasional buttresses and especially buttressed doorways that open on the southeast (Hempelmann 2008: 161). The ceramic assemblage of this small site contains in its first levels Reserved Slip Ware and, in the next levels, the cyma recta pots that are so characteristic of the Upper Euphrates region starting at, and north of, Qara Quzaq (Porter 2007b). Kharab Sayyar and Shioukh Fawqani both have big domed ovens placed in confined spaces, although that of Kharab Sayyar is in the open. Hempelmann (2008: 155-6) notes that all the elements of the early repertoire at Kharab Sayyar can be found in the Euphrates, leading him to posit that the site was founded by immigrants from that region, and I have argued elsewhere (Porter 2009a) that various material relationships between the Balikh sites and some Euphrates sites not only continue into the early mid-third millennium, but are strong enough to propose that they are a product of a specific kind of interaction.

The temple at Brak is dated to 2700 BCE (Matthews 2000: 1008) and falls midway chronologically, as Kharab Sayyar does geographically, between the shrines of the Euphrates and the Habur. This building seems to combine many features of all the temples. Similar in size to the second temple phase at Halawa, it has benches around two of its walls as at Kashkashouk (Suleiman and Tarakji 1995), a strange installation in the middle of the room that seems to serve multiple functions, and most notably the same kind of rectangular fireplace – "the sunken area of plaster floor with traces of heavy burning" (Matthews 2002: 186) – that is found at Jebel Aruda, where it is juxtaposed with the keyhole fireplaces (Fig. 15; van Driel and van Driel Murray 1983: map 3), and also at Sheikh Hassan, as Matthews (2003: 110-1) notes. It is the installation, however, that is most intriguing. Called an altar and consisting of a plastered container made of mud-brick, it seems to have been a kind of cupboard for materials associated with the practices of the temple. It contained a number of sealings (immediately evoking the temples of Arslantepe and Jebel Aruda), a large blade, a model wheel, and an unbaked object that looks remarkably like a mason's trowel and has been associated with portable hearths[13] (Matthews 2003: 109-10).

Of the fact that the series of buildings discussed here are all the loci of specialized, ritual practices of a religious nature there can be little doubt. They are, in one way or another, distinguished, indeed often segregated, from everyday function, no matter how much like those everyday structures they may look. This is accomplished in practices such as the careful preparation for their foundation by the construction of a sterile layer, for example, or brick platform. Some of them are raised high, and when they are rebuilt or come to an end many are carefully cleaned out and filled in. They are in some way separated spatially from other components of the settlement in a *temenos* or enclosure, or, as at Kashkashouk, simply by isolation. Wall paintings, while perhaps not exclusive to religious structures, are certainly associated with them, and niches, podia, and plastering are common features.

The presence of sealings in the Brak building might indicate to some, as they have for Arslantepe, a primarily secular function, but as argued in Chapter 2, in this kind of architectural context these are just as likely from sealed offerings made to the temple, offerings that are obviously monitored by temple functionaries (Matthews 2003: 113). Those offerings come from the constituency of the temple as well as its priests, and just who that constituency might be is discussed below. That there are only nine seals attested at Brak does not diminish

---

13 However, a similar object found at Tell Banat proved to be one of three legs for a triple-bowled cultic vessel that was of very coarse, crumbly, and barely baked fabric not dissimilar to cooking-pot ware. The wheel, although called a "wagon" wheel, may equally well have supported an anthropomorphic vessel or model chariot.

this likelihood, because it is not to be presumed that this, or any, of the square shrines houses religious observances attended by the entire settlement.

Cylinder seals were also found in the *cella* of the Sin Temple at Khafajah (Delougaz and Lloyd 1942: 16), and there are parallels between the Khafajah temples and the northern ones in several small details that indicate a common heritage rather than necessarily direct interaction. The altar/box of the Brak shrine is similar to one found in the roughly contemporaneous fourth phase of the Nintu temple at Khafajah (Delougaz and Lloyd 1942: 97) and, even more provocatively, may be related to similar features in Temple A at Arslantepe (Fig. 11). The first, A47, is located behind the podium/bench/table set against the east end of the anteroom, A46, to the temple *cella* (Frangipane and Palmieri 1983: fig 23A). It seems to have been accessed from the roof, but at its base was a fireplace. Behind it is a long single space, A77, where the majority of *cretulae* from this building were found and that forms part of the temple *cella* itself, adjoining the second such feature, A84. This was a brick box against the east wall of the *cella* and flanked to the south by a plastered bench. It was presumably the focal point of whatever activities took place in this room. In addition, the stepped altar of the Raqa'i temple is known in all three of the small Khafajah structures (Schwartz 2000: 177). The bird jars found in both the Small and Sin Temples (Delougaz and Lloyd 1942: 105 and 18 respectively), with their thickened heads, immediately evoke the figures on the wall painting from Building 312 at Halawa, while the painting variously interpreted as a sacred tree or spectacle idol is echoed not only by actual spectacle idols found in the earliest levels of the Sin Temple (Delougaz and Lloyd 1942: 28-9) but also by the image on a stone vessel in the Small Temple (Delougaz and Lloyd 1942: 104), so that, really, one may take one's pick as to what the Halawa painting represents. The construction of a brick platform by which a rebuilt temple was raised is known at Halawa, Raqa'i, and the Khafajah Sin Temple (Delougaz and Lloyd 1942: 21–3). Finally, a mid-third millennium cultic addition to the domestic houses at Khafajah is a more rectangular version of the square temple (Delougaz and Lloyd 1942: 114), paralleling those at Brak and Chagar Bazaar. Similar comparisons could no doubt be made with other Mesopotamian sites (e.g., Schwartz 2000), but these are sufficient to make the point.

The question, then, is: just what role did these small, and rather simple, structures play in the settlements that housed them? A first consideration is the surviving evidence for the nature of practices that took place within them. It has been suggested for the Euphrates that these are "communal places of worship," (L. Cooper 2006: 143), while for the Habur it is argued that they are, in at least one instance, the extension of elite authority (Schwartz 2000: 178). Neither interpretation takes adequate account of the form of these structures or the conceptual frameworks they embody. Temple designs are not just practical; nor are they merely imitations of human residences because their builders cannot imagine anything else. There are reasons why some temples conform to one kind of design, while a nearby one follows another. There are reasons why some temples stand alone and others are embedded in dense networks of rooms, why some are deliberately set high above their surrounds and others are not. The implications of all these attributes need therefore to be further investigated. The very nature of these distinctive structures – their design, their size, their situation, and their location – cannot be divorced from the kind of religious practices that take place within them, and in conjunction tell us about the context of those practices.

Can a temple be a communal place of worship if it is so small that only five or six people can effectively function within it, or if its rituals are a mystery hidden from all but specialized officiants? Such is the case with the buildings at Tell Raqa'i, Tell Chuera, and the first structures at Halawa Tell B. Even the largest of them, those of Halawa Tell B (which in phase 2 is 12 x 10 meters [Orthmann 1989]), Qara Quzaq, Tell Brak, and Mari, could not accommodate more than a small group of people to be counted at most in the tens – unlike, for example, the niched and buttressed structures at Uruk in the late fourth millennium, some of which could contain at least three hundred individuals. In some essential way, then, the practices in these small temples are exclusionary, which does not in and of itself clarify the matter much, although it should immediately obviate any idea that these structures are a direct reflection of an egalitarian "tribal" society. Certainly attendance to deities seems generally exclusionary – few buildings known as temples to the gods are large enough to incorporate any sizeable congregation, although many of them do have extensive outside spaces in which the public, precluded from the mysteries of the cult, may still partake in associated rites. And this is an essential part of any religious system where ideology is implicated in the perpetuation of political power.

Those who hold power, however it may be organized, are sanctioned by their particular association with divine authority, but equally essential is the participation of the public in supporting and maintaining that power, as neither intimidation nor manipulation is successful over the long term. In order for religion to effect public complicity in the system of rule, that public must, on the one hand, be directly involved in religious practice and, on the other, not quite attain full access to it. It must be kept at a distance yet also beguiled and intrigued. If, on the other hand, the public is completely removed from such religious practice, it has little sense of the power of the gods, little desire to be part of that power, and no awareness of the specialness of the people who are. This pertains whether the temple is in service to a secular authority or is itself the authority. The dependent personnel who form the economic basis of the temple in the *oikos* construct (Pollock 1999) are also more likely to comply willingly if they experience some sense of attachment to the religious mysteries in whose service they are bound.

It is in this framework that the temple oval at Khafajah – which is, conceptually and materially, markedly different to the Sin and other small temples that preceded it in the residential sector – may be understood. The Oval itself, and the temple that surmounted it, is highly visible (Delougaz 1940), has considerable exterior space for large-scale participation, and yet is strongly demarcated, even sequestered, from its place within the community by both its elevation and its walls. This is not to say that completely exclusionary structures dedicated to the gods cannot exist, but that when they do, they are not working as an extension of elite power over a subordinate public. Rather, they are more likely to reproduce explicit connections between their constituents and their gods that have little to do, at least directly, with external politics. And since these wholly exclusionary structures are often embedded in the seat of secular power, in monumental building complexes commonly called "palaces," those constituents would seem to be rulers.

Our temples, however, are not located in monumental secular complexes. They are located within residential areas in every case, even the Ishtar temple at Mari (Margueron 2004: 247), although this one is distinguished from the others in the group by a large porticoed forecourt. And, moreover, the temples actually take a common house form – the house form in place at the time of the earlier structures on the Euphrates. So one has to ask: why are some temples like domestic structures while others are not? Or, because we do not always know in which direction the connection passes, why are some domestic structures built as versions of temples and others not? If considerations of agency form part of the theoretical ground on which analysis proceeds – as indeed it does for me – it should become apparent that a particularly close relationship in architectural style is likely to signify some kind of conceptual relationship as well. Which is to say: there are no accidents. Whether or not people are able to articulate the reasons for certain situations, and whether any articulated reasons are adequate to express all that is going on in those situations (Porter 2010b), the similarity of the "ten temples of the Transeuphrates" to house layouts[14] (especially the earliest of them) is, I would argue, a material manifestation of a probably explicitly understood relationship between the constituent population of the temple and its object of attention – that is, the ancestor. The ancestor is the house; he and/or she is the basis of its origins, the degree and nature of its social interconnections, its history.[15] The house of the ancestor is the place where the

---

14 I suspect that further excavation will warrant the addition of Tell Ghanim al-Ali to this list. Indications are that this site was established at the beginning of the third millennium, and it is argued to have cultural connections to prime areas of pastoralist use in the steppe behind it (Hasegawa 2010; Nishiaki 2010).

15 Many of the recent contributions in the 2010 special edition of al-Rafidan, such as Cooper 2010, Meyer 2010b, and Lönnqvist 2010, seem to assume an exclusive, even causative, relationship between the practice of ancestor traditions and pastoralism that is far from

family commemorates its past, even if at the same time the house houses a house society. Definition by shared substance, definition by lineage, and definition by marriage are not mutually exclusive forms of kinship, only different ones; they integrate each family into such dense networks of interconnections that anthropologists struggle to find the limits of any social group, to reconcile diverging practices and ideologies, and to figure out why some people belong to a group and some do not.

But in case one would then expect ancestor temples to accommodate a large constituency, it should be pointed out that ancestor practices may be exclusionary as well, for while ancestors define[16] the family, writ small or writ large, this does not mean that all members of that family necessarily participate in the maintenance of ancestor traditions. Descent is the basis of both inclusionary and exclusionary social relationships, and whether responsibility for ancestor traditions is the province of the current lineage head (or heads), the eldest son or direct offspring, whether the group constitutes the extended family, the lineage, or even a tribe, and whether it comes together to commemorate the ancestors as a whole or only through selected members, will depend on the situation in which ancestors are invoked, the role they have in the internal sociopolitical organization of the group, and the external relationship of the group to a larger society. And ancestors may have a public and/or a private place. The *kispu* of the Old Babylonian period, for example, the regularly performed commemorative ritual at which the living and the ancestors partake of a feast, reproduces the lineages and histories of the polity as well as having a place in family life that has nothing to do with public concerns. Whether in defining the ruling family or the private family, or interconnecting both, it is the family that is the essence of ancestor practices.

It is entirely feasible that the houses of the gods and the houses of humans are also conceptually, and thus physically, related, and I admit some evidence is difficult to adduce for either case – statuary, for example, could equally represent ancestors or deities. Any mortuary association surely tips the scales on the side of the ancestors, and there are two places in the sites under consideration here where the connection is explicit. The first, and earliest, is at Qara Quzak. The temple is part of a complex that includes a structure that probably initially was a tomb but subsequently became a house. It is preceded by an infant-jar burial, distinguished from normal infant burial practices by being placed in a stone cist grave. Adjacent to this and also part of the complex is Tomb 12, a building comprised of two square rooms (Valdés Pereiro 1999: 120) that housed, in one

the case. Very different kinds of societies practicing a wide range of subsistence patterns and lifeways are ethnographically attested as paying attention in various ways to their ancestors.

16 I use the word "define" not in terms of establishing the boundaries of the group but in terms of constituting the basis of its identity in certain contexts.

room, an infant, and in the other, an adult female. Like several later funerary structures of the Euphrates region, it was above ground. But what is particularly significant is that the bones of both bodies show blackening, most likely the result not of burning the body (as Olávarri 1995) but of cooking/heating it in some way – either through smoking, boiling, or perhaps roasting. Such treatments are becoming increasingly attested in the mortuary practices of both the south and north, and are evident in the transformation of collagen in bone (Baadsgaard Monge and Zettler n.d.; Pfälzner 2007; Porter 1995). The practice seems to be associated with the preservation of the bodies for display. It does not last long and is in no way equivalent to mummification, and so is suggestive of short-term, special ceremonies where those so treated were paraded or visited for a period after death or the funeral, but not much beyond – at least as far as human interaction went. It is not by any means a ubiquitous practice. Only some of the deceased warranted it; only some of the deceased were so distinguished. If the practice was to suggest, as I argue that the sacrificed adolescents on top of the Arslantepe tomb do, the conferment of some kind of eternality upon these particular dead beyond what was normal for everyone else, then it is more than plausible there is a connection, in some way, with ancestorhood. In fact, in each instance where some kind of heating of the body is determinable, be it the human sacrifices of the so-called Royal Cemetery of Ur or the burials beneath the Late Bronze palace of Qatna, the act is closely associated with commemoration. That it is a woman and child who may be so treated at Qara Quzak, and that the child seems to have an identity separate from its mother in having its own mortuary space, is certainly unusual.

I do not think it a coincidence that the Ishtar temple of Mari also overlies two of the three corbelled stone tombs (Jean-Marie 1990) constructed at the end of Mari Ville I, just after the site was abandoned (Margueron 2004: 90–92) around 2700 BCE. The excavator considers these tombs as marking the abandonment of Ville I and the construction of the temple of Ishtar as instigating a completely new phase of occupation because of the nature of change in the signification of the space – that is, from a tomb to a temple. But I suspect that they go together, conceptually at least, and that the construction of the tombs in fact marks the moment of reoccupation. Indeed, I would go further and question whether the phase directly beneath the tombs was not also integrally related to this sequence, at least in terms of memory, for in the remaining vestiges of this level and in addition to the housing into which the tombs are inserted, there is a 5-meter-square room with a doorway to the south. The issue of the length of time between the end of Ville I and Ville II remains unascertainable, although Margueron (2004: 126–7) does not rule out the possibility in fact of continuous, albeit much reduced, occupation. In any case it does not matter. For the place of the ancestor to be translated from the actual burial to a site of commemoration probably takes some time.

The process of transformation from house to tomb to temple is clear at Tell Chuera, although in this case it is not a square building that is at issue. Rather, it is the temple *in-antis* – a simple rectangular structure with a forecourt created by the extension of the long walls past the short one in which the entrance is placed (Fig. 27) – a temple type that succeeds the square form at Qara Quzak and Halawa but precedes it at Raqa'i. Interestingly, a structure of *in-antis* type is found in the third-millennium levels at Hassek Höyük, in conjunction with some single-roomed buildings (Sagona and Zimansky 2009: fig 5.4). Ralph Hempelmann (2010) has demonstrated that the Kleiner Antentempel, famous as the locus of one of the few examples of statuary (as opposed to clay figurines) found in the north, developed out of a much earlier house that contained a rare, intramural burial cut beneath the floor at the end of that phase of its existence. Hempelmann proposes that the burial is that of the founder of the house,[17] and that in subsequent levels his heirs commemorated their ancestor(s) with appropriate rituals that included statues. Eventually the significance of these figures to the social group inhabiting this part of the site was such that they warranted a temple of their own, and the statues that had been passed down from generation to generation took their place within it.[18] It is possible, then, that the two lots of two anthropomorphic figurines found in association with the temples at Kashkashouk (Suleiman and Tarakji 1995: 179) and Raqa'i (Schwartz and Curvers 1992) may perhaps have fulfilled a similar role (Matthews 2000: 1008). There is, however, a significant difference between the small temples and the temple *in-antis* form, and one that perhaps explains the evolution of the structure in the first place. The latter is open and inclusionary and generally has space for much larger numbers of people. It would seem that no longer is a system of limited participation in ancestor traditions appropriate. Now the larger kin-grouping was involved in some way and, apparently, in the task of defining itself in contradistinction to others (Porter 2009a).[19] A similar change may be manifest at many of these sites, and not only in this shift of temple types.

A direct connection with an original burial is not essential for these temples to be ancestral spaces, however. Although we are used to thinking about ancestors in terms of their burial places, a tomb is not necessary for the practice of ancestor traditions (Porter 2002a: 4). At different times and places, different locations for different rituals associated with ancestors are attested. In the later second millennium responsibility for the ancestors seems to have been passed down to the oldest son along with statues or figurines of those

---

17   See Hodder and Değerlendirmesi (n.d.) for the concept of the "history house."
18   Thus is resolved a thorny problem in Syrian chronology, for the so-called Meselim statues have on art historical grounds been seen as much earlier than their find-spot, dated on archaeological grounds.
19   Porter 2009a expands on this in detail. For the latest on the history of occupation at Tell Chuera, see Meyer 2007, 2010a.

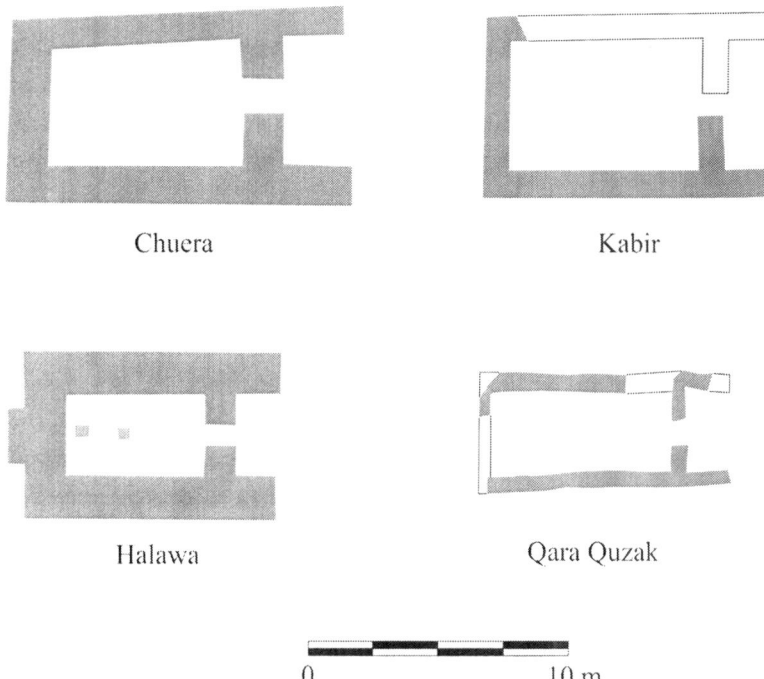

Chuera

Kabir

Halawa

Qara Quzak

0   10 m

27. The temple *in-antis* plan. Chuera, Kabir and Halawa are redrawn from McClellan 1999; Qara Quzak is redrawn from Valdés Pereiro 1999.

ancestors (van der Toorn 1994, 1996). It is not clear where the Old Babylonian *kipsu* took place but it does not seem to have been the tomb itself. In this same period though, at Ur and Nippur, there are installations within houses, pedestals or offering tables, which may have been the focus of ancestor-related ritual and where perhaps their representations were placed (van der Toorn 1996: 70). While a family may be divided over many houses, and a house may contain people who are not members of the family, nevertheless there is inevitably a close connection between family identity and the physical structures in which the family lives. If the founding ancestor is interred in one place but the group moves to another, this does not mean that the ancestor is no longer relevant but, on the contrary, is possibly even more important in constituting the identity of the group and even in establishing its relationship to a new place. Of necessity, commemoration takes place in a different context. In such a situation the connection between ancestors and the family may be replicated by employing the house shape for the building in which the ancestor is commemorated and placing it in or adjacent to the residential areas in which the descent group lives. Here, then, the precise spatial relationship between temple and town is important. Whether it is freestanding or enclosed, one of a number of such structures or singular, or maintained over centuries or subject to change have the potential to tell us about the nature of social organization at that place and how it developed over time.

Too little of the relevant period is excavated at either Shioukh Fawqani or Qara Quzak for us to have much understanding of the relationship between these structures and the residential population, although it is quite possible that since the temple/burial at Qara Quzak was partially enclosed, it was of limited access. It is also possible, since the phase beneath it is so little attested, that the relationship of this structure to the residents of the site changed over time. This certainly seems to be the case with the history of the sanctuary at Tell Halawa B. In the first phase of occupation the three separate buildings were not surrounded by an enclosure wall and were free of access. That there are three would seem to imply three different descent lines – whether small-scale such as a family, or larger-scale, such as a lineage. The settlement at this stage was small however, and it seems unlikely that three separate lineages, as opposed to extended families, would have been in place. At Tell Raq'ai, for example, the total constituent population is estimated at about thirty people (Schwartz and Klucas 1998) – a size so small that it barely constitutes an extended family. Its single temple could readily serve one kin-group. At Tell Brak, a considerably larger settlement at this time by all indications, we might expect several such temples in several residential neighborhoods.

At Halawa, on the other hand, three gave way to one, and the temple became increasingly segregated from the surrounding tell. It is hard to know which of the several possibilities explain this transition. Perhaps three families merged into one over time through marriage; perhaps competition among lineages ended with only one emerging as dominant (Peltenburg 1999, 2007/8). Perhaps as the social conditions of the city changed as it grew and, as different kin-groups joined it, the relationship of the temple to the community changed so that it was no longer synonymous with the social constituency of the group living there. It is noteworthy that after Halawa Tell B was abandoned, occupation at the adjacent Halawa Tell A was founded in a tomb in the dolman tradition, H-600, which lay on virgin soil (pers.comm. R. Hempelmann). It has been proposed that an artificial mound covered the tomb (pers. comm. P. Sconzo).

There is another option to consider. Lisa Cooper (2006: 160) suggests that the mortuary connection of the Qara Quzak temple and the platformed structure of Halawa Tell B in its second and third phase require two essentially different kinds of religion. Yet that both structures have in common the fact that they not only reflect, but also utilize, the house form characterizing the local residential repertoire would seem to render them in critical respects the same. The definition of "temple" in ancient times was "house" – the é (Sumerian) or *bitum* (Akkadian) – of the gods, but it is also clear that public cult and domestic ritual are differentiated at Mari in Ville II and at Khafajah, to provide just two examples. I do not wish to imply that the cult of the gods and ancestor practices are mutually exclusive. They are complementary parts of a single cosmological construct, and no doubt intersect far more often than we realize; indeed, families are often associated with particular divinities as well as ancestors and it is perfectly possible that these become conflated over time.[20] I do wish to argue, though, that the particular organization, not to mention centrality, of the one part – ancestor traditions – is especially significant at certain points in time.

The combination of all these factors suggests to me that the ten temples are either houses of the ancestors or originated in the same, becoming over time houses of the gods. Each of them defines a descent group in its new relationship to space, and their chronological and geographical distribution reflect the ebb and flow of these recently emergent, self-contained communities that calved from earlier settlements, as they traversed the landscape in smaller-scale movements and more restricted territories than characterized the previous era. Some are still in the same general places they were before, such as at Arslantepe; some moved away, and it seems that one direction in which some of these groups were migrating was eastward from the Euphrates. At Arslantepe, the severing of the ancestral group from the temple gave rise not just to a redefinition of the group through a burial, but also to what was in effect a reclamation of place. At other sites, tombs gave way to temples, especially house-temples, directly or indirectly. Directly, as at Qara Quzak, where the temple and tomb are co-located; indirectly, as at Halawa, where the ancestral burial is unknown but its role in descent structures is reproduced in the practices of an ancestral house. This tradition, derived from the practices associated with the single-halled structures of the late fourth millennium, was maintained as various groups reconstituted themselves in other places, even as the basic house form became more elaborated in residential complexes at those sites.

Inclusionary practices such as feasting – evident in the mass-produced bowls on the floors of the Arslantepe VIA structures and the multiple sources of provisioning for the temples – were no longer in play, however. Perhaps societies were now structurally bounded because of the practices of integration and differentiation of the previous period; perhaps they were simply redundant, as the group constituted a single ancestral entity. At the later sites of the ten temples, internal differentiation, initially at least, was not a factor, although external definition, the establishment of a physical boundary to the settlement thus delineating those inside from those without, was important; several settlements at this time are surrounded by thick walls. It is noteworthy that the earliest example of a very small yet fortified settlement is that of Arslantepe VIB2a, which overlays the first reoccupation, VIB1, after the abandonment of the temple complex of VIA; the architectural remains of VIB2, both within the wall *and* without, are characterized by square (4 x 4 meters; 5 x 5 meters) and also rectangular (ranging from 4 x 5 meters to 4 x 6 meters) structures with openings to the north and east (Frangipane and Palmieri 1983: fig. 5; Frangipane 2007/8: figs. 4a, 12a, and 13d).

---

20   For example, in the Ur III period, the statue of Ur-Nammu's commemorative mortuary
     rituals is placed in the temple of Enlil at Nippur (Katz 2007: 169).

It is also important to understand that the stratigraphic position of the tomb is insecure. Frangipane makes a case that it was built after the wall of the fortified village (of which very little as yet is known; Frangipane 2007/8: 188) and so belongs to level VIB2b,[21] while Palumbi (2007/8: 150) places it between level VIB1 and VIB2 – in which case the tomb would essentially signal the founding of the village. Equally possible however (for the conceptual barrier to this situation is, I hope, by now removed) is the fact that the tomb went with VIB1 – the wattle-and-daub structures of the seasonal pastoralist encampment. There is no "old and new tradition in dialogue" (Palumbi 2007/8: 152) but a cultural continuity, only now in a new context.

The sequence at Arslantepe is indicative of another factor that makes itself felt at this time. In Chapter 1 I discussed the conditions that may give rise to raiding, the overly deterministic activity considered endemic among mobile pastoralists. One such condition was the breakdown of opportunities for pastoralists to both gain and shed products necessary for subsistence. Another was the closing of social boundaries as an outcome of any number of possible situations. Both would seem to be in evidence at the end of the fourth millennium and in the early third millennium. In addition to the retraction of social boundaries as a result of differentiation discussed above and economic isolation resulting from the breakup of the Uruk system in the north, territorial instability arising from the widespread reorganization now obvious in settlement patterns must have contributed to instability in intergroup relations, leading to the construction of massive enclosure walls around a number of small – some little more than a hectare – sites. Note the term "breakup" rather than "breakdown"; I do not see this phase as a collapse or a dark age. Rather, it is a period in which there was considerable jostling for new positions in space, brought into being by the existence of new, autonomous ancestral groups (constituting, still, mobile and sedentary members) now detached from their original connections and therefore seeking to establish themselves elsewhere. That process was facilitated by the establishment of ancestor houses in the center of these small communities as an overt expression of social identity.

There is no particular diminution of cultural complexity, only a diminution of scale, as large groups fragment into smaller ones to begin the process of regrowth. These ancestral groups were smaller-scale because they were no longer connected to a world with high demand for wool, although textiles were still doubtless essential. From contemporaneous records in the south and from Ebla somewhat later, we know that textiles were used for gifts to the gods, in payment for services rendered, and as diplomatic gifts between polities, functions

21 I suspect that the association of the tomb with the village within the wall is a product of Frangipane's understanding of monumental construction as essentially complex and therefore to be associated with a relic southern, or southern-influenced, population.

that would still have pertained even in this smaller environment – although it is less and less likely to be as small as we currently think it, because there were at the very minimum three major settlements in place at this time: Mari, Tell Chuera, and Tell Brak.

In the Euphrates region at least – thus far there is no indication of this phenomenon in the Balikh and Habur, although I have argued that a connection is formed between the two regions by the temple *in-antis* form (Porter 2009a) – there is a continued emphasis on ancestor practices over time, and the form they take now suggests that the relationship of individual ancestral groups to space, and to each other, is still very much in play. Distinct, monumental aboveground and semi-subterranean tombs mark the interior of settlements as well as the land around them, starting not long after the first phase of the house temples, at around 2700 to 2600 BCE (Porter 2002a, 2007a) at Gre Virike, Jerablus Tahtani, Tell Ahmar, Tell Banat, Tell Bi'a, and Halawa Tell A. I have also suggested (Porter 2009a) that the distinctive attributes of the first phases of occupation at Tell Banat, especially the aboveground mortuary monuments (McClellan 1998), indicate that it was the ancestral site for a polity located elsewhere – in a manner analogous to the situation revealed by the Ebla ritual, where kings and queens celebrate their wedding by visiting the tombs of significant ancestors located outside the city of Ebla itself (Fronzaroli 1992; Biga 2007/8; Porter 2007/8, and see below). I proposed that Tell Chuera was the center of that polity, although I would by no means argue that this is the only possibility, just the one that seems most likely in light of the current evidence. But the larger process that I think is revealed by the emergence of these monumental burials is the reexpansion of the territory over which mobile pastoralists moved. From the broad range of the late fourth millennium to a restricted and localized range in the early third millennium, we once more witness an extension of territorial range one hundred or so years later. In the south at this time there is evidence of closer contacts with the Persian Gulf (Potts 1993; Peyronel 2006), usually attributed to the development of sea trade, but it is also feasible to posit an increasing southeastern orientation to the movements of Mesopotamian pastoralists.

In sum, there is no overall or fundamental change in the significance of textile production, the relationship between sedentary and mobile members of the community, or even the number of pastoralists, taking place over this five-hundred-year period, just shifts in their organization and relationship to place as well as somewhat different ways of maintaining integration (because not every site at this time in the north manifests an ancestor house and not every site is the result of new social groups relocating). This has significant implications for understandings of what is usually termed "secondary" urbanism/state formation in the north, manifest in the cities of the mid-third millennium – secondary because the growth of Uruk and expansion of southern culture into the north is primary. It has always seemed as though there should be a direct relationship between these two phenomena, but as yet it has been difficult to bridge the very long gap between them, if only because few of these small sites dating to the early third millennium grow progressively into the major settlements of the mid-third millennium. Moreover, in the measurements of anthropological archaeology they apparently show no evidence of the hallmarks of complexity, the institutions and organization that characterize both the polities of the late fourth millennium in the south and those of the period of urban florescence in the north, the mid- to late third millennium. I would make the case, however, that they do.

Or rather, I would make the case that the structures and practices of social and political interaction evident in the small settlements of the early third millennium and, as well, in the larger ones that are now being revealed (Meyer and Hempelmann 2006; Margueron 2004) both derived from the Uruk period *and* are still in practice in the larger-scale polities of the mid- to late third millennium. The mysteries of the Uruk expansion, its rise, demise, and especially its connection to the subsequent spread of both urbanism and the state, exist in part because of the assumption that the primary, if not solitary, considerations are a set of dynamics that can only be generated within a sedentary world. In this view, mobile pastoralism is increasingly acknowledged as part of a larger economic system, but that it should be generative of anything, let alone the hallmarks of civilization, is still too often considered inconceivable. Textile production is certainly important in this model but mobile pastoralists are not, except inasmuch as they interrupt the stability of sedentary existence. In the reconstruction presented here, certain other consequences are now evident, and they have major implications for understanding the nature of the city and polity in both north and south.

The first consequence is that, rather than as a reflection of an actual sociopolitical situation, the material record should be read as the result of practices intimately related to contesting ideas, actual situations, and desired situations – in all domains of life. A surprising proportion of those practices are constituted by ritual, religious and otherwise. As delineated above, it was the practices of differentiation and integration that, while maintaining connections between households spread over differing subsistence practices in the fourth millennium, led to the definition of sociopolitical entities based in individual and self-contained ancestral groups in the early third millennium. Ancestors and temples structured sociopolitical relations between members of the polity then, and continued to stretch those relations across various forms of spatial dispersal in the later third and early second millennium.

The second consequence is that, rather than diverging trajectories resulting not only in unlike organization but in differential levels of complexity, the subsequent histories of north and south arise from the same set of processes, deploying the same building blocks of society and polity in slightly varying ways because of varying contingent circumstances – circumstances that include among others geography, topography, and climate but are by no means determined by those factors.[22] There are, in turn, further outcomes of this: the same processes are likely to give rise to underlying similarities in these different areas, which are as significant as the overt differences, so that differentiation between north and south is more apparent and morphological than real. The association of certain kinds of practices with political form or levels of complexity – kinship with tribes and civic ties with state – are obviated; there is no single explanation for, or way in which, the polity comes into being, nor the shape it takes.

Take, for example, Ebla. Ebla is considered the paradigmatic Syrian example of a highly stratified and centralized state where all material wealth, and consequently power, was vested in the royal family based on the discovery of a monumental building called Palace G and the 17,000-odd tablets it contained (Astour 1992; e.g., Steinkeller 1999a: 300; Schloen 2001: 268; Akkermans and Schwartz 2003: 235–44). A detailed reexamination of these materials, however, provides evidence of multiple kinds of relationships between people, and between people and otherworldly beings, that alters our picture of the organization and operation of power there, as well as other aspects of ancient life. These relationships, brought into being by practice, are entirely in keeping, although not surprisingly not unchanged, with those evident in the preceding period.

It is not yet known exactly when Ebla was founded, nor what constituted that first settlement, for the earliest phase of occupation there has not yet been revealed archaeologically, and since writing itself may not have been introduced at Ebla until the time of its third last king (Archi 2006: 101), any intimation of its origins can only be inferred from much later texts. King lists (Archi 2001), which comprise genealogies and are perhaps to be associated with invocation of the dead in post-funerary mortuary practices, are one source; another are ritual texts that provide instructions for three episodes of one such practice – the pilgrimage to the tombs of some of these dead kings on the occasion of the simultaneous marriage and accession of new kings. I will discuss this ritual in much greater detail below, for it is one of the most significant sources we have from northern Mesopotamia in the information it gives us about social, cosmological, and political relations and their interdigitation. But the starting point is the current focus of discussions of third-millennium Ebla: Palace G (Fig. 28).

Built on the western side of the upper mound of Tell Mardikh, the site of ancient Ebla, the central element of Palace G as it has survived to this day is a large, open space, a "city square" (Matthiae 1981: 68) at least fifty meters long and flanked on two sides by a sprawling agglomeration of rooms. Porticoes

---

22 Adams (1974, 1981) argues for localized developments congruent with individual environmental conditions.

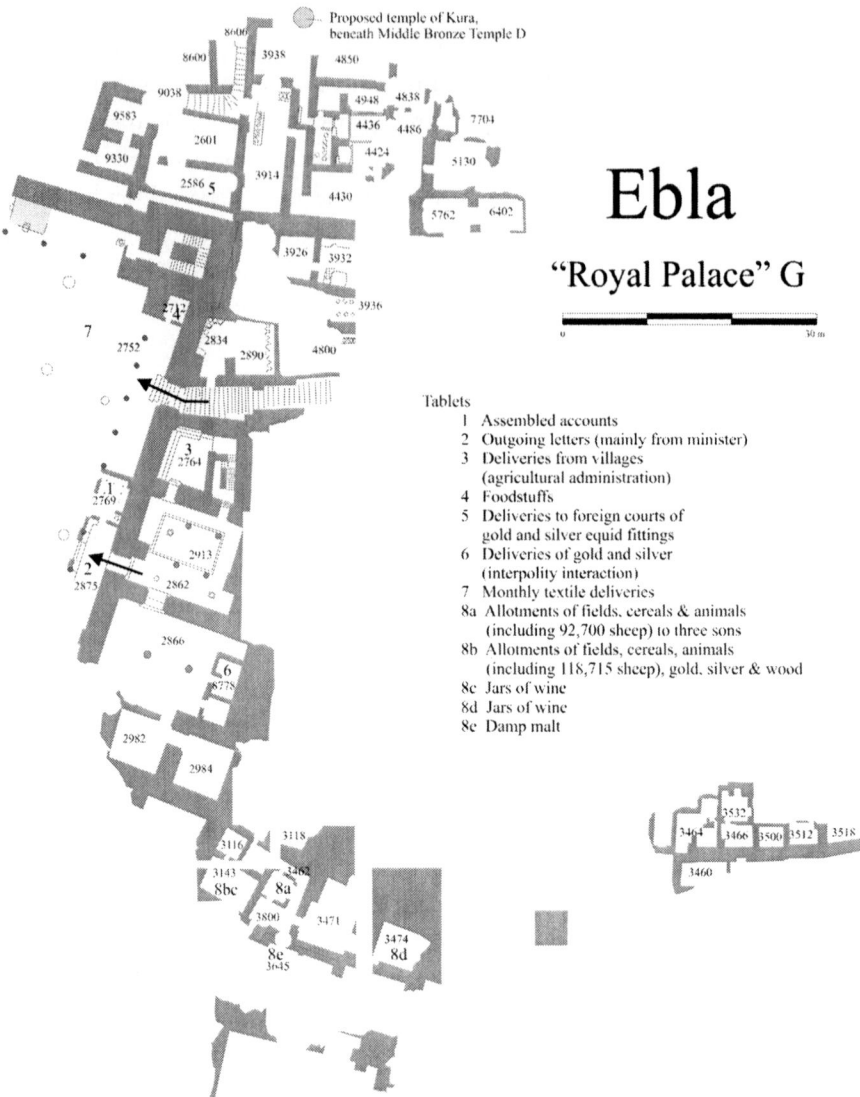

28. The extant plan of Ebla Palace G, with find-spots for tablets. Redrawn from Archi 2005 and Matthiae 2008: figs. 3.2, 3.6, 3.8.

formed by regularly spaced columns mark the transition from closed to open space on the eastern and northern edges of the square. I choose that order – from closed to open – quite deliberately, because directionality, and what it represents of the relationships between the inhabitants of the building and other populations, is very complex at Ebla.

I suggest that, in essence, it is here the inhabitants of Palace G come *out*, rather than the inhabitants of Ebla go *in* to the building. Foreshadowing the outcome of the following description, this is not because the reigning family is sequestered from the masses due to its superior wealth, status, and power, but because inhabiting the building is the performance of the multiple sets of relationships

Ebla
"Royal Palace" G

0   20 m

▲ Wooden inlaid objects

■ Pieces of lifesize statuary

✱ Gold inlay

● Water feature
    cistern/well

29. Enlargement of the main section of Ebla Palace G, with find-spots for selected objects.

that this family enacts in its incumbency of the building, relationships between beings on different planes of existence and in different social (and physical) situations in life, all of whom constitute the totality of the polity. Coming *out* of the building into the plaza is a key part of rituals that affirm the essential unity of the polity in the person of the "king."

To see this, it will be necessary to go into some considerable detail as to the layout of Palace G (and see Fig. 29), but first a word about language. The term for the leader of Ebla is usually given as the Sumerian **en**, corresponding to

Semitic *malikum* (this last is rarely written, however) and translated as "king." The female equivalent, more commonly written in the Semitic form, *maliktum*, Sumerian **dam-en**, is translated as "queen" (Archi 1982: 201–2). However, this rendering inevitably conjures up models of monarchy that are simply inapplicable, in my view (although not in the view of others), to the nature of the position at Ebla and other (but not necessarily all) third-millennium polities.

It is commonly held that the power of the king is absolute, that he in essence owns or controls most or all property within the state, and certainly labor if not life. Steinkeller (1993: 124, n. 48), for example, in summarizing the groups supported by what seems to be a large quantity of land, states that "one can confidently surmise that all these holdings formed part of the royal domain" (also Schloen 2001: 268), while Archi (1992: 25) understands political and religious power to be concentrated in the king. The increasingly unavoidable recognition that others share this power, however, even if in ways as yet poorly understood, has given rise to token acknowledgments of oligarchy; nevertheless, discussions remain firmly focused on the king. No caveat or avowal to the contrary can negate these unfortunate associations. This is a case where the use of the word has driven the interpretation of the role and its place in the larger society, and in order to escape this another label is necessary – but "leader" or "ruler" also perpetuate the underlying sense of autocracy *and* aristocracy that so thoroughly imbue both historical and anthropological reconstructions that alternatives are still insufficiently examined.

My reading of the evidence suggests that the family that occupies Palace G at any one time is to be conceived of as the core of the polity – a first family among families, not as the top of a hierarchical chain of families in the fashion of the patrimonial household model (Schloen 2001), but instead, the center of a network of families (Porter 2000). The key here is "at any one time," because at Ebla until the last years of the archive period, succession does not appear to have been transmitted in traditional dynastic fashion – that is, passed from father to son – or, at least, it is not known if it was (Archi 2001: 11).[23] This renders traditional lineage terminologies inapplicable too until we know what qualified any given **en** to assume his position and how succession was established. So I will simply refer to the inhabitants of Palace G as the incumbent family, the male of which is Sumerian en, the female, maliktum, adopting into English terminology the ancient names (and not therefore continuing the tradition of bolding and italicizing them). This I hope conveys incumbency of *a*, if not *the*, key position in the social and political life of Ebla, without the monarchical connotations of even the word "reigning." Although the reasons for alternating languages in referring to the en and maliktum are not clearly understood, that there *were* reasons should at least be recognized by maintaining this distinction.

---

23   See Dahl 2003 for a study of transmission at Ur III Umma.

I am afraid we are stuck with the label "Palace G," though, because it would be just too confusing in terms of the literature on the subject to change; but since almost every building uncovered at Ebla is termed a palace by the excavators, this word may be read as simply synonymous with "public."

Behind the open square that occupies such a large part of this structure and adjoining the eastern portico is the "administrative quarter" of the palace, where most of the tablets and many of the artifacts for which Ebla is famous were found. This is the ground floor; in addition, there was an upper level that may have included the residential quarters of the incumbent family,[24] accessed from the square by several stairways in different parts of the complex. Two stairways are of central concern to this discussion, however, for they are clearly more than just utilitarian in function: one is monumental with basalt steps,[25] located in the center of the eastern portico and leading from the associated structures on top of the acropolis, and the other is narrow and dark, located in the corner of the two colonnaded façades and enclosed by thick walls. Thought to be a tower by some (Matthiae 1981: 68; Akkermans and Schwartz 2003: 235) but probably just a stairwell, the eastern and southern sides of this structure were marked by two very small vestibules. Room 2712, one of the vestibules, opened onto the eastern portico and contained a group of texts recording food allotments for the court and other personnel such as weavers and messengers (Archi 1982); the other vestibule led directly to the northern portico, in which, situated toward the western end as excavated,[26] was a mud-brick platform, interpreted as the dais for a throne (Matthiae 1981: 69).

Paolo Matthiae, the director of the Ebla excavations, calls the external stairway "the Monumental Gateway," while he labels the internal staircase the

24 Dolce (2006: 176 and nn. 16–17) certainly understands the two western rooms to the north of the store behind the plaza, rooms 2601 and 2586, as private apartments because of the carved wooden furniture they contained, implying that the raised elevation of these rooms puts them on a second story. But these rooms are equivalent in level to the upper part of the alimentary area, to be discussed in detail further, under which were the levels of the earlier building, so that this is a terracing and not a second story; and, too, the discovery of a group of tablets in room 2586 (Biga 1988) might perhaps obviate the suggestion that these were private apartments. Numbers 2601 and 2586 do seem to be an integral part of the northern group of rooms, but there is no communicating door between this section and the alimentary area, and, as Dolce notes, a difference of 3.5 meters in height between them and storerooms behind the audience court. It seems possible that these rooms were part of an original administrative/storage unit prior to the addition of the plaza and the rooms to the east of it and were still used as such up until the end of the palace.

25 In reconstructions this monumental stairway is presented as emerging through a unified façade on the western face of the building, but it is perfectly possible that the stairway simply bifurcated two separate quarters – the earlier food storage and preparation areas and the later administrative section – and was itself unroofed. For more on the relationship between sectors of the palace, see below.

26 Matthiae (1981: 71) argues that this dais would have been centrally located, so that the east/west length of the square was probably about forty meters in length.

"ceremonial stairway" since one could access the portico with the dais from there. Both staircases may have been involved in various rituals, either independently or together. A processional would have been made to the square from the uppermost levels of the building via the monumental staircase, and it seems just as likely in the absence of any direct evidence that the dais held something other than the en's throne. For one thing, this rectangular platform has steps leading to its top from the front, the south, and on the west side next to a door to a storeroom, but not on its east side facing the door from the stairwell,[27] which, if this was the pathway of the en's progress to his seat, might be expected. Rather, I propose that the square – "plaza" is a better name as this open space is not, as far as we can tell, square – was set up in this way for regular performance of rituals where the key figure(s) emerged from the center of the building via the monumental stairway to the center of the plaza, turning north to face the dais on which, I further propose, was a statue, or more probably a pair of statues, of what might be termed the palace's patron deity/deities. The steps to the dais were located where they were in order to tend the statue/s from the storeroom behind it, as well as by the participant(s) in front, while the internal staircase allowed servitors to spirit away offerings, especially food offerings, to the upstairs apartments on completion of the ceremony.

This interpretation is based on several small pieces of evidence, textual and archaeological. For one thing, part of the stone hairdo belonging to a large statue and cut to carry the headdress of a god rather than an en, was found on the bottom step of the monumental staircase, suggesting that it was removed from place at the time of the destruction of the building – perhaps in an attempt to preserve it. Since such statues were clad in gold and silver it is also possible that those who destroyed Palace G ripped the figure apart to take its valuable metals (Archi 2005: 83). For another, lists of food apportioned to the en's table include the same stuffs, in smaller quantities, given to the god Kura, followed by "the gods of the region" (Archi 1982: 210, 2005: 83–4) and, as will be seen below, Kura has a very particular association with en-ship. That this food comes from the palace stores, and not those of the temple, suggests that it is the en's responsibility to feed the god; it also suggests that this was a daily occurrence. It is thought that this activity took place in the upper level of the public sector, on the acropolis (either in a temple or in the private quarters of the palace), and that the piece of the statue found on the bottom of the stairs was dragged down to the plaza from the top (Archi 2005; cf. Dolce 2006: 182, n. 46). There is some reason, though, to think that this might have been a public ritual, held in the open space of the plaza.

27 Although a pit does interrupt this side of the dais, judging from the photograph (in Biga 1995: 145) traces of steps would seem to have been evident here if they had ever existed.

It is also interesting that there is no access to the administrative sector on the south side from this stairway, although there is access to the alimentary sector. A small door from the monumental stair leads to a room on the north that Matthiae (1981: 74–5) initially understood as a guardhouse but that subsequent excavations clearly showed to be a "kitchen," which on its west side contained storage jars set into a counter and on its east side contained eight hearths set in a row (Mazzoni 1993). These rooms were therefore an integral part of the food storage, processing, and preparation complex located on this side of the building and situated on a series of terraces rising to the north that accommodate the slope of the mound here. The kitchen next to the monumental stair was on the lowest of three levels, rising to the series of rooms on the middle level used in the preparation of cereals, and up to the room for making olive oil and associated features, next to the religious complex on the northernmost and highest level. One may readily imagine the en and entourage proceeding down the staircase, handed through this door freshly cooked food prepared in the adjacent rooms and continuing through to the plaza to place the offering before the god. Servitors (perhaps priests, perhaps regular palace servants) waiting in the vestibule from the internal staircase, shielded from view by the buttress that flanks it (Matthiae 1981: 69), may have facilitated the feeding of the god, particularly by discretely removing the meal and returning it to the en's family upstairs. The three water features noted in the plaza are each located at appropriate places for acts of lustration that might mark stages of this ritual: before presentation at the transition from inside space to out, before the dais at the point of consumption and on completion of the meal, and again at the transition from outer to inner space.

Modern-day viewers of these sorts of rites often have difficulty with the difference between appearance, which is understood as reality, and belief, contributing, I think, to the sense that such rituals are about elite manipulation and subjugation of an uneducated, unthinking, general population and not really part of a real, active, way people understand their worlds to be. If the god is a wooden and metal-clad statue, surely on-lookers were aware that it could not eat? If those same people can see that the food is untouched, how can they believe it to have been consumed by a god? Is there some sort of sleight of hand that deceives the eye – the food is there and then it is gone? Strange as it may seem, there is little question that statues of the god were understood to *be* gods, not just mere representations of them (Berlejung 1997; Hurowitz 2006). Something like the Hindu concept of *prasad* is an appropriate route to understanding this practice – that the god takes, blesses and returns/reciprocates the gift enhanced, and the viewer would not expect to see this process take place because it happens in otherworldly time and space. Such blessing would render the food particularly appropriate to subsequent consumption by the en and family, especially if the god concerned was one intimately connected not only to the en's incumbency but also the identity of the polity.

Ebla is frequently cited as the example of a secular authority independent of theistic control in contrast to the city-states of the south that are "owned" by the god, but the history of the palace itself suggests this is not entirely the case (Mazzoni 1993: 403). Palace G did not have its origin in what many understand as its prime feature, the administrative sector – viewed as housing an essentially materialist enterprise, the control of Ebla's wealth in order to cement the prestige and power of its elite (e.g., Mazzoni 1999: 611; Dolce 2008: 66, n.14) – but rather in its ritual/religious associations. The administrative sector, along with the plaza and the two major stairways, are later and much more monumental additions located at the periphery of the older complex. The oldest section of the palace excavated to date (as opposed to the oldest excavated levels in this area [Mazzoni 2003]) is the area of alimentary materials that directly connects the plaza to a religious structure on the acropolis beneath the second millennium temple, Temple D (Mazzoni 1993, see fig. 29). The alimentary complex contains installations of its own, implying particularistic activities.

We cannot know if those activities, the ones taking place in the alimentary sector, were secular or sacred, but it is highly unlikely there was any indigenous concept of a separation between these domains; it is equally unlikely that these rituals would be purely personal, for the key thing to understand about the incumbent family is that they did indeed embody the polity – not because they dominated or owned it, but because they were its public face, and it was their task to ensure its perpetuity and stability which could only be done by maintaining proper relationships with the gods, with Ebla's constituents, and with its counterparts. There is no manifesto that tells us this, but it is implicit in material and textual records of what the incumbent family does, where they do it, and who they do it with – starting with the kitchen next to the monumental stair. This part of Palace G might well have served the inhabitants of the palace their daily meals, but it also provides for other functions. The rooms onto which the olive press opened housed specialized pottery equipment and some sort of installation in the floor (Mazzoni 1993: 400), the purpose of which is unknown – perhaps intended for libations of the oil prepared next door? Here surely are some of the components of drinking or feasting rituals, that, given their location, most likely served the religious structure under the second millennium structure, Temple D (Matthiae 2008: 46); if this is the temple to Kura (as will be argued shortly), it is the temple where foreign dignitaries came to swear treaties (Archi 2005: 84). Mazzoni (1993: 400) notes the rarity of this pottery at Ebla, which suggests there was a specific assemblage for cultic use, just as there was a specific assemblage for aspects of mortuary ritual on the Euphrates (Porter 2002a). If it is simply luxury ware for general palace use, however, fragments of this pottery would be found, I should think, at least occasionally in other contexts where the inhabitants of Palace G might be thought to eat or drink.

The discovery in this area of a plaque depicting women in a ritual, one of whom is holding a cup (found next to an actual cup), in the intervening level between an earlier structure and the floors of Palace G itself (Dolce 2008) would almost seem to be beyond mere coincidence, and is suggestive of a long history of ritual practice for this section of the building that perhaps originated in the "pre-palatial" structures of earlier rulers (Mazzoni 1999: 612–3).[28] And it was on the last floor level of Palace G in Room 4436, the floor prior to destruction, that limestone inlays of mythological and human scenes were found that had originally formed part of a twelve register picture on wood (Matthiae 2008: pl. 15). This piece, commonly but erroneously called the "Ebla Standard," was assumed to have originated in some other context (Matthiae 1989; Dolce 2008),[29] but one might also wonder if it was stored here, to be produced only on specific ritual occasions, or was even perhaps a permanent installation. Matthiae's (1989) reconstruction of the archaeological remains posits a large panel made of vertical planks, dismembered and carted to different parts of Palace G for reuse in prosaic contexts, with two single planks inserted face-down into "furrows" on the floor in this room. What becomes clear on studying the photographs, but is not so explicit in most descriptions (such as Dolce 2008 and including Matthiae 1989), is that these are not some casual irregularities made by wear and tear, but very regular excavations in the floor (Fig. 29, Room 4436) that were clearly created to hold some sort of feature that defined, perhaps decorated, this room. There were three such (and possibly four or five, see Matthiae 1989: pl. 1) grooves that limned a rectangular space (Room 4436), adjacent to the room containing the enigmatic installation in its floor (Room 4448). Inlays were also found in the east-west groove to the south, although not in order, and were scattered on the floor of other rooms in this complex. Dolce (2008: 67, 72), following Matthiae, claims that the events celebrated in its panels were long past, and that the standard originated in the earlier structure of G5, became obsolete and was therefore discarded, ending up reused as a floor board. The history of this piece therefore reflects the history of Ebla as visible in this area: an early development toward complexity and growth of power beginning in the first half of the third millennium, followed by some sort of retraction due to either internal instability or external threats, that was somehow overcome as witnessed in the emergence of the state in the period of Palace G and the archive which is, as often noted, the floruit of Ebla's power.

---

28 Dolce (2008: 67) claims these earlier levels must be a palace too, but it is simply not possible to be sure as yet.

29 See the bibliography and photographs in Aruz 2003: 175; Dolce 2008; Matthiae et al. 1995.

But the archaeological evidence is difficult no matter which scenario proposed, and Matthiae's preferred explanation, that individual planks were placed face-down to cover the grooves, does not really explain why there would be inlay all over the floors of this and other rooms, nor why there would be grooves in the first place. I see no reason why the inlay may not actually have been set in some sort of structure that encompassed three or four sides of this space, placed upright in the furrows that the boards were supposedly used to cover (cf. Matthiae 1989) and were therefore "properly" used in the context it was found. The one difficulty being the peculiar fact that, whereas in the south groove the pieces lay as if they fell from an upright face, the pieces of inlay found in the west groove lay, it would seem, exactly as they had been originally placed on the wood, with each of the successive registers moving south to north represented by a figure. They were not, however, intact.

This inlaid work was undoubtedly ideologically and historiographically highly important, at least at one point in its life and, I propose, at exactly this point – at the end of Palace G. If so, it is certainly possible that on the threat of destruction of the palace, efforts would be made to ensure its safety. If the wooden panels had been in place for some time it is likely that both wood and adhesive would be dried out and brittle, hasty removal resulting in loss of integrity, even breakage. I envisage a fragment left upright in the western end of the northern groove that fell, or more likely was pushed, into the western groove left by evacuation of its panel, other pieces falling apart as they were carted off. The fact that several fragments of inlay, identical to the ones found in the northern part of the palace, were also found in various parts of the administrative sector (Matthiae 1989: 38–9), including in front of the plaza, suggests other possibilities to that Matthiae proposes – that there were other objects of a piece with this one, similarly decorated, located in the storerooms here; or even that this was where the panels from 4436 were carried for safekeeping. This reconstruction of events does not in any way deny an older making of the panels themselves, which would have been curated from generation to generation.

In the end, whether or not the inlaid work was erected in these grooves as an intact series of panels or as a broken object used as filler, there are two things to note: one, as Matthiae (1989: 42) observes, the depictions of mythological beast and human warriors, itself an uncommon combination, may be read as the alignment of supernatural and earthly spheres; and two, these grooves were designed to take some sort of unusual and large-scale installation, such as a wooden screen, which further brings this area of the building out of the purely utilitarian and into the representational.

Since the inlaid panel appears to be earlier in style than the time of the destruction of Palace G, and since the alimentary unit is one of two places where earlier third millennium material is attested in the vicinity of Palace G, it is not unreasonable to posit a perpetuation in use of the work and, perhaps, function of this particular area.[30] The question is, was the relationship between this earlier material and Palace G essentially continual, a palace evolving and expanding over time as the wealth and power of the elite grew (as Archi 2006: 98–99), or was there a break between the earlier materials and the level that represents Palace G of the archive period? Mazzoni (2003: 180) conceives of the earlier space in the northern section of Palace G as radically transformed in the later ones, since stone tool production took place in a room of the structure below the rooms of the olive press and reused standard. However, there is simply as yet insufficient evidence to begin to discuss the relationship between tool production and governance. Certainly there were changes, just as there were changes within Palace G itself. The concatenation of the addition of the plaza and the lower administrative rooms, followed by the filling in of part of the eastern portico on the southern end to house, in Room 2769, the main archive, and in the room next to it, 2875, a scribal office, might be thought to accompany the growing power of the elite based on its privileged relationship to the gods, a power which would allow it to take more and more from the people who are ideologically bound to submit. This spatial arrangement has also given rise to reconstructions where the king seated on his dais receives tribute from his people as well as foreign visitors, which was then handed over for registration by the scribes, while some of the visitors would have passed from the forecourt into the palace to do business (Matthiae 1981: 78; Archi 2005: 94).

But I cannot see these changes as an increasing expansion, and especially not secularization, of political authority (Mazzoni 1991; Dolce 1998). This is because, in the first instance, there is at least a history of en-ship maintained over many generations in the two "king lists" recovered from the archives (Archi 2001) and in the performance of ancestral rites involving those kings that, even if it does not extend as far back as the 28th century BCE (Archi 2006: 98), nevertheless is indicative of a longevity to the polity of Ebla that will, I am sure, eventually be exposed archaeologically. These traditions come together in a group of texts that document a major ritual to do with en-ship as performed by the last kings of Ebla. In the second instance, as these ritual texts show, the primal relationship between en and various other inhabitants of the cosmos remains unabated whether or not the administrative activities of the palace expand – which it certainly seems they did, continually. This however may be as much a product of time as any qualitative, or even dramatically quantitative, change in the nature of the polity. It is easy to imagine that large numbers of documents accrue in the life of the palace and eventually warrant new storage space, just as

---

30　The second being the unit beneath the most southern and eastern series of rooms illustrated in plans of Palace G, rooms 3464 and 3466, characterized as storage facilities (Mazzoni 1991, 1993, 1999). Earlier third-millennium material was also reached in Area CC (Matthiae 2000).

it is easy to imagine the number of family members and dependents increasing over time and requiring expanded quarters. This is why the archive only covered the last fifty years of so of the palace's life. Either earlier documents were destroyed as no longer relevant or they were stored in an inner/upper room of the building, not yet uncovered or no longer extant. The consequent discovery of small numbers of "living tablets" (that is, ones in use and not put away) at the time of destruction of the building in most rooms of the administrative quarter renders this increasingly likely. It also renders the conceptualization of spatial organization a very interesting mix of functionality and ideology, as the distribution of these tablets is segregated by subject and type. I will propose below that this is representative of the polity itself.

Moreover, the plaza – or rather something approximating this open space – may well have been in existence prior to the construction of the inner staircase, the eastern façade, and the administrative quarter, which were all clearly added as a single unit, because the monumental stairway takes a turn at its western end and the last three steps are in limestone rather than basalt. Whereas Matthiae (1981: 74) views this stair as constructed from the audience court up to the acropolis because of his understanding of the plaza's function, I view it from the opposite direction, and consider it to have been the main passageway from the palace to the lower city when the palace was confined to the upper slopes of the acropolis at the beginning of its history, reoriented toward the bottom when the new rooms were added. The stairway aligns reasonably well with the alimentary sector adjacent to it, until the thick wall of the plaza; it is the administrative side, to which there is no passage, that is disjunctive. The two rooms to the northwest, rooms 2601 and 2586, may have been part of a similar unit to those behind the eastern façade, with the carved wooden furniture in one part of a reception room (or simply stored) and the tablets in the other, just as any other grouping of documents (although they are stylistically as old as any in the archive [Dolce 2006]). These rooms are equivalent in level to the upper part of the alimentary area, so that this might form part of a coherent complex, an earlier phase of Palace G that contained all the functions of the later phase, but distributed differently. There is, however, no extant door between this section and the alimentary area.

That the plaza is not so much a city square where commoners awaited sight of their king or a receiving yard for the goods and tribute that sustained the palace, as much as it is a ritual space, is suggested by the several large limestone eyes found scattered on the ground there, especially in front of the eastern portico (Matthiae 1981: 72). These eyes were most probably from statues (Matthiae 1995: 316, 320), their number[31] indicating that several such objects were distributed in this space. Here I would return to the question of directionality in

31   As yet unspecified.

consideration of whether the square is really a public space, completely open of access, and whether the only extant entrance into the administrative quarters from the plaza, via the scribe's "writing room" 2875, is truly functional on a daily basis. Dealing with the last issue first, an unusual, and rather overlooked, feature of this room is the rounded and decorated threshold of two steps that rises up from the writing room, Room 2875, to the level of the plaza, the aesthetic pleasures and prestige of which would have been appreciated when viewed from the inside, from the east toward the west (as indeed it is photographed in Matthiae 2008: fig 4.9), rather than from the public side, the plaza. While the fragility of the inlay itself is not enough to argue for only occasional use at best (for it could have been regularly replaced and the steps of the internal staircase were embellished in an even more delicate way, with inlaid wood [Matthiae 2008: fig. 3.11]), the dimensions of the "steps," which are rounded and not flat-topped, add to the sense that these inlaid bands were not particularly functional. From personal experience with the rounded bands of the exterior of Banat's White Monument (McClellan 1998; Porter 2002a), such surfaces are very easily damaged by careless foot traffic, and the distance from the floor of the plaza to the floor of the writing room seems too high and too wide to think that people simply stepped over them. Stepping *down* from the plaza would put body weight on the heel of the foot, grinding down on the top of the band as one lifts to continue to the next step; stepping up transfers less weight to the ball of the foot. It is difficult to tell precise details from the plans, and from the photographs (Matthaie 1981, see also 1995, where the step seems less obtrusive, and 2008: fig. 4.9), but the transition from writing room to plaza is certainly not an uncomplicated one. And so I suspect that the portico rooms are auxiliary to this interior space, rather than liminal space mediating the transition from the plaza to the palace. I wonder whether the administrative quarter was ever really meant to be publicly accessible from this plaza except under extraordinary circumstances, and was not first and foremost purely internal working space. Or at least that is how it ended up. The doorway through the façade, echoed by the door of the writing room, may have been intended as a main entryway at the outset, one that could be carefully controlled, but need soon overcame intent. There is a staircase, however, off room 2764 and it is possible that the original administrative complex and main reception space was above, subsequently expanded below.

The plaza was not the only room where significant statues were found. As one entered hall 2862 from 2866 inside the administrative sector, one was apparently met by life-size representations (Archi 2005) of the figures embodying, literally, the polity of Ebla. Whether these figures represent the divine pair or en and maliktum (and there is a point at which there is not in fact much substantive difference), the situation of these statues and other adornments is not coincidental. Progressing from hall to inner court, the presence of inlay pieces here has been claimed as evidence that one was surrounded by decorated walls featuring images of the king, along with wild animals and divinities (Archi 2005: 94). The concatenation suggests that it is here that the iconography of the state was represented. That state was, however, conceptualized as consisting of multiple components, not just its ruling couple.[32]

This, I think, is the significance of the distribution of the tablets according to topic – such as the contributions of the villages of the Ebla polity, the rations for the palace staff, or the property holdings of the first family (Archi 1993) – indicating not only that work space in the palace was conceptualized as segregated/dedicated according to function (Archi 1982), but also that the palace materialized the entire sociopolitical entity that is Ebla. There was a room for recording the produce of the villages contained within the territory of Ebla, there was a room in the southern-most (as currently excavated) section of the building where the gifts of the king to his sons were recorded, and one where deliveries of wine and malt to various people, from inside and outside the city, were noted (Archi 1993).

This is not to argue intent, that the palace was *designed* as a representation of the body politic, but it is to argue practice. Since Palace G *functioned* as such, it came to embody such. And although it is sometimes claimed that the palace essentially "owned" the whole of the kingdom, these tablets contain evidence of complex and multidimensional relationships in the circulation of goods offered in tribute, local and translocal prestation, and exchange. The flow of goods was certainly not all one-way. The palace, while it should not be conceived of as "paying" (in the sense of money) for goods, certainly often reciprocated for the commodities it received. Mazzoni (2003: 197) notes that "high-value prestige goods were manufactured in, and owned by, the state and their use was restricted to the sphere of the palace and its personnel." This may be so, but they were not, I would argue, intended to enhance the person of the en so much as the polity the person embodied.

And those goods were not all destined for humans. Considerable quantities of materials went to feed and clothe – in fact, to make – the gods (Archi 1999, 2005). And the gods did not just pertain to the palace, even if the palace was charged with certain aspects of their upkeep. The gods of the city belonged to everyone.

This brings the discussion back to the question of the approximately life-sized statues kept in the palace, especially those in 2862 and the ones (most likely a divine pair) that I propose sat on the dais in the plaza. To understand

---

32 Of course this inner court was not the only room that was richly decorated or furnished. Inlaid wooden objects were found in a small room north of the portico, room 2601 (Aruz 2003: 174, no. 114), and from room 4436 (see above). Other rooms, undoubtedly storerooms and workrooms, also contained considerable quantities of precious objects and decorative elements.

the relationship of these figures to Ebla and to the concept of rule, it is necessary to delve into the ritual texts housed in the archive to which I have repeatedly referred.[33] It is one of the single-most important set of texts from Ebla
in what it tells us about indigenous conceptualizations of existence, as well as
social and political relationships. It is, however, extremely difficult to interpret and opinions vary as to the meaning of some key words (cf. Fronzaroli
1992; Archi 2002a; Porter 2007/8; Biga 2007/8). It has variously been called
the "pilgrimage ritual," the "funerary ritual," the "accession ritual," and now,
most commonly, the "wedding ritual." It is, apparently, all of the above. The
funeral for a deceased en, the accession of the new en, and the marriage of en
and maliktum are all intimately bound in a journey taken by the incumbent
couple through the countryside to visit the burial places of some of their predecessors – and, in a new twist, it needs now to be investigated as to whether it may
be that the couple who take this trip are those both dead and alive, given the
recent discovery that an aspect of third millennium (and later) funerary practice could involve the corporeal remains of the dead who have been preserved
by some form of heating/cooking as discussed previously (Baadsgaard, Monge,
and Zettler n.d.). The progress of this ritual to tombs/funerary places may be
as much about translating the deceased en to ancestor status as it is about
invoking dynastic succession and, since this concept is as yet still in question, is
perhaps better thought of as *creating* the kinship necessary for succession.

There are three extant records of the ritual (there are some indications of yet
an earlier version [Fronzaroli 1992: 180]). Texts A and B represent two separate versions, because the minister and the officiating priests are named in both
texts and different people fulfill those functions in each. As no names are registered in text C it is difficult to establish the occasion of its recording, but it
is generally considered a shortened version of B (Fronzaroli [1992: 180]; pers.
comm. M. Bonechi).[34] The performers of the ritual in each version are referred
to by title – "en" and "maliktum" – never by name, as is also generally the cus-
tom in administrative texts (Fronzaroli 1992: 166, n. 5). However, it is generally
accepted now that one version is for Irkab-Damu, the other for his son and successor Ishar-Damu (Archi 2001: 4).

As much as a description of a particular act by particular personages, these
texts delineate how, where, when, and by whom the ritual is to be performed.
Dates for the occurrence of events are clearly specified, as are the gifts and

---

33 (ARET XI (TM.75.G.1823 [text A] + Tm.75.G.1939 [text B] + TM.75.G.1672 [text C];
Fronzaroli 1993; see Fronzaroli 1992 for discussion).

34 My deepest thanks to Marco Bonechi for discussing this text with me in all its particulars,
and especially to the Arrison Family Foundation for affording us the opportunity to work
on it together for two months. An English publication of the text by Bonechi, with contextualization by Porter, is in the works. Any mistakes made in describing and interpreting
ARET XI here are entirely my own, however.

offerings to be made. Fronzaroli (1992: 183–5) notes certain formal characteristics, substantiating the idea that it is a set of instructions, while the naming
of some of the participants in the rites also grounds them in historical reality
(Fronzaroli 1992: 184), whether or not there are three documents composed for
three specific marriages, or two variants of the same document.

To summarize the narrative of the ritual briefly (and bearing in mind that
some details are subject to revisions not yet published), the en takes the maliktum in marriage, in the house of his/her father.[35] Offerings are made to the sun
goddess[36] and to Ibbini-Lim,[37] a deceased en, as part of the ceremonies, and
then the en pours oil upon the maliktum's head. Subsequently the maliktum
goes to the temple of Kura. Here she makes offerings to Ishara, Kura, and his
wife Barama, and sacrifices to Kura, Barama, Ishru, and Aniru. The next day the
couple begin a journey that takes them to several places outside the city of Ebla.
On the second day of the journey they sit on "the thrones of their fathers" at
a place near the Waters of Mashad. The stay at Mashad would appear to take
several days. The text at this point describes the preparation of a caravan, after
which it returns to the itinerary of the journey.[38] One wagon[39] contains the
statues of the divine pair Kura and Barama and other statues of deities, four
oxen, and attendant priests. The members of the caravan are richly provided
with textiles, jewelry, precious metals, and oils for ritual acts. The entourage
continues toward Nenash, on the road to Lub.[40] Before reaching Lub however,
they turn toward the town of Irad.[41] At Irad a sacrifice is made to Abur-Li'm,[42]
a deceased en. The next stop is Uduhudu[43] where offerings are made to the
deceased en 'À-ma-na.[44] Then, on the road to Niap, the caravan pauses to make

---

35   The difference in possessive pronoun is important here, for it is thought to indicate much
     about royal relationships. Fronzaroli (1992: 173) accepts that it is the house of the father
     of the en, but this is by no means certain. If it is the house of the father of the maliktum,
     does this imply it lay outside Ebla? Or did maliktums come from the city itself?
36   This itself is an unusual feature, although the sun goddess is not unknown in the northern
     region (Archi 2006).
37   The 10th en.
38   However, the caravan is prepared on the fifth day of the ritual, and the itinerary would
     appear to resume at the fourth day (Fronzaroli 1992: 175).
39   Fronzaroli (1992: 177): chariot.
40   Lub was a well-known town within the territory of Ebla, and also known for the temple of
     Hadda, to which kings made journeys in order to present offerings there. Irak-Damu pos-
     sessed landholdings at Lub.
41   Irad is not otherwise known as yet from published texts (Fronzaroli 1992: 177).
42   The 16th en. Also listed in TM.74.G.120, 1: obv.II: 5, 11th en from Ishar-Damu; and last en
     listed in TM.75.G.2628, 1a: obv.III: 5.
43   The location of a sanctuary of the God of the Underworld and part of the official cult.
     The person to whom an offering is made here is also a deceased en, the 22nd, as registered
     in TM.74.G.120, obv.III: 9, and the same entity that TM.75.G.10167 records as ^{d}En-ma-nu
     and to whom Ir'ak-Damu makes offerings (Fronzaroli 1992: 176, n. 51).
44   The 5th en.

offerings at Bir, not to a deceased en, but to the God of the Underworld. This is repeated at Niap.[45] From there the caravan departs to the key location of the performance of the ritual, Nenash/Binash.[46] The following acts take place in a structure that Fronzaroli (1992: 173; accepted by Archi 2001: 5; rejected by Viganò 1995: 218) has identified as the mausoleum.[47] This is the **é** *ma-tim*, or **é** *ma-dím*. This structure at Nenash is also attested in ARET III 858 rev. X: 1-2 (Archi and Biga 1982) as noted in Bonechi (n.d: n. 154), and is translated as "temple" by Pettinato (1992: 256), who equates it with a structure called the **é** *mah*, thought to be a temple in the acropolis at Tell Mardikh (also Viganò 1995: 218 n. 20). Bonechi (1993: 36) identifies an **é** *ma-tim* at Ebla itself, in ARET VII 93 obv. I: 1-III 1 (Archi 1988b). If this structure is indeed a funerary building or **é** *ma-tim*, then its identification with the so-called royal hypogeum at Ebla, dated to c. 2300 BC (Mazzoni 1995: 101; Matthiae 1997a) is not out of the question. But there is also a funerary structure denoted by the term **é** x **pap**, and which may be more properly identified with the hypogeum (Fronzaroli 1997: 16–17), although Archi (1996a: 17) reads this as a term for a funerary ceremony (also Archi 2002a and cf. Biga 2007/8; Porter 2007/8: 206–7, n.34). There are certainly several examples of monumental tombs of one style or another associated with public buildings in Syria (Porter 2007/8; Peltenburg 2007/8) and, too, evidence of repeated ritual performance occurring inside them, Tomb 7 at Tell Banat being only one example (Porter 2002a). Building 7 at Banat, with which Tomb 7 is associated, is now understood as enclosing a mortuary mound much like the White Monument in concept, and may perhaps function as a mortuary structure related both to the earlier mounds and to Tomb 7. This interpretation raises the possibility that Building 7 is an **é** *ma-tim*, while Tomb 7 is an **é** x **pap**.[48]

45 Also the location of the practice of the official cult involving the God of the Underworld. The ens of Ebla went there for this purpose, as well as the en and maliktum of Emar (Fronzaroli 1992: 176).

46 This town is known as the place where a particular fabric was manufactured – *maš-da-bù* (Fronzaroli 1992: 176). For the reading Binash, see Milano 1990a: 373 and Bonechi n.d., identifying then Nenash with modern Binash, nine kilometers northeast of Ebla. On the basis of the journey as described in ARET XI it is difficult to assess the distances covered, as the route seems very roundabout. It is possible that Nenash, at the end of the trip, was actually on the return journey and back toward Ebla. In ARET II 6 (Edzard 1981) this town is the seat of Rashap, Eblaite God of the Underworld (Bonechi 1993: 79). Bonechi (n.d.) reads the element **pú** of this geographic name as having to do with cisterns (cf. Matthiae and Pettinato 1976, where Pettinato reads **gigir**[ki], an administrative quarter within Ebla; and contra Pettinato, Archi 1995: 269) and notes that this place is nearby the town of Bir, also meaning "well" or "cistern." A number of other terms for water are associated with the God of the Underworld, suggesting that there is a particular relationship between them (and see Bonechi 1999, 2001 for a fuller discussion of the lexicon relating to hydrology at Ebla).

47 See below for further discussion.

48 It should be noted that the gifting of textiles or metals to an **é** x **pap**, whether tomb or funeral, does not require death to have occurred, but may be provided well in advance

Returning to the pilgrimage, the **é** *ma-tim* is purified and then a ritual is performed. Offerings are made for the god Agu, the statues of Kura and Barama enter, and the en and his consort move into separate chambers, seemingly within the **é** *ma-tim*. Offerings are made to the deceased ens Ibbini-Lim,[49] Shagishu,[50] and Ishrut-Damu.[51] The couple leave the **é** *ma-tim* to sit on the thrones of the fathers until dawn. On the next day a lamentation is recited and a ritual involving "the new Kura and the new Barama" and the "new en and new maliktum" is performed.

There are three seven-day cycles of rites performed in the **é** *ma-tim* as recorded in each of the three recensions, texts A, B, and C (Fronzaroli 1992: 180). The en and maliktum seem to sleep in their respective chambers inside the **é** *ma-tim* on each of these nights and then come out to their thrones. On each day the maliktum's face and hands are covered by a veil by "the woman of Nenash," and as the sun moves across the door of the "chamber of Kura,"[52] the maliktum sits at the left of the en. At specified times, a priest offers seven sacrificial animals, seven small cakes, seven pure tablets, seven special vessels, and seven jugs for Kura and Barama and deceased ens Ibbini-Lim, Shagishu, and Ishrut-Damu, as before. Finally, in text A, the last ritual act is the washing of the head of the en and head of the maliktum, and wedding gifts (equids and sheep) are listed. However there are some key differences between A and B as far as details of the rituals go. In B, four garments are woven for Kura, Barama, en, and maliktum during the stay in the **é** *ma-tim* and it is also recorded here that they return to **sa.za$_x$**^{ki}.[53] Fronzaroli (1992: 180) suggests that two of the seven-day ritual sessions take place in the temple of Kura there, and it is Shagishu, Amana, and Igrish-Halab[54] to whom sacrifices are made. The en and maliktum go then to the temple of the gods to

(cf. Biga 2007/8: 251). It is attested throughout the land of the four riverbanks, at various points in time (such as Gelb, Steinkeller, and Whiting 1991; Foxvog 1980; Stone and Owen 1991), that compensation for certain transactions, especially the transferral of land to a new owner, consisted at least in part of a promise to maintain the ancestor rituals of the previous owner and to provide for their mortuary endowment. It is clear that such provisions were for the future event, and not, or not only, in the case of the Bilalla text (Foxvog 1980), a current one.

49 Also known from TM.74.G.120, 1: obv. III: 4 (ARES I, Archi et al. 1988), where he is 17th en on this list. Note that Ibbini-Lim was also part of the actual marriage ceremony at the beginning of the ritual.

50 TM.74.G.120, 1: obv. III: 6, 8th en.

51 TM.74.G.120, 1: obv. III: 3, 11th en.

52 Evidence perhaps to suggest that Kura is to be identified with the God of the Underworld rather than Hadda (Bonechi 1997 discusses the possibilities of both attributions), for it is unlikely that this passage refers to actions taking place in the temple of Kura mentioned at the beginning of the pilgrimage.

53 It seems odd that the caravan would return to Ebla in the middle of the ritual, although this is no doubt possible if Binash, the location of the **é** *ma-tim*, was indeed very near.

54 The king before Irkab-Damu (Archi 2001: 5) TM.74.G.120, 1: obv. I: 3, 3rd king; TM.75.G.2628, 1a: obv. I: 5, 2nd king.

eat the offerings of **sa.za$_x$^{ki}**, lie on sheets of linen and their heads are adorned in a particular way.

Just where, or what, the **sa.za$_x$^{ki}** might be is another mystery. Consensus amongst Ebla's epigraphers and others (Archi 1982: 209, 212; Milano 1990a, 1990b: 10; Fronzaroli 1998: 110; Matthiae 2008: 34) currently identify it as the palace, but certain factors mitigate against this as an easy answer (pers. comm. M. Bonechi). The action of the ritual texts seems to imply that it is something apart from, and outside of, the city. This is also apparent in a journey undertaken by certain people from Ebla in a "confraternity," a religious brotherhood (Fronzaroli 1997; Archi 2002b) that performs special duties for the god 'Adabal of Luban, where **sa.za$_x$^{ki}** is the eleventh of thirty-nine stops around the countryside (Archi 2002b). Ens depart from Ebla travelling via **sa.za$_x$^{ki}** to Armi (ARET IX Bonechi 1997: 509). It seems rather redundant to note that the king leaves Ebla (that is, his palace) to go to **sa.za$_x$^{ki}** (that is, his palace) or note that food for palace consumption comes from **sa.za$_x$^{ki}** (Archi 1982: 209), unless these two names are placed in apposition to each other for poetic purposes, which, in administrative texts, seems unlikely.

On the other hand, Text B of the accession ritual (for such, in my opinion, is the key act here)[55] notes that the en and maliktum travel to **sa.za$_x$^{ki}** in the middle of the ritual, and once there, reside in the temple of Kura for two periods of seven-day rites (Fronzaroli 1992: 180). Since there is thought to be a temple of Kura on the acropolis, this would support the idea that **sa.za$_x$^{ki}** is the acropolis/palace of Ebla. It may be that Ebla is organized similarly to Mesopotamian cities such as Uruk, which in the Early Dynastic period carries two Sumerian names, Kulab and Kulag, which may refer to sacred and secular components of the city, respectively, or, as thought in the context of Ebla, upper and lower towns. On the other hand, Kura is clearly tended to at other places during the ritual and, in another offering list, receives gifts at Uduhudu (Archi 2001: 5), a small and otherwise insignificant town. Since Kura is so closely identified with en-ship it is not unreasonable to suppose that there are sanctuaries devoted to him associated with the resting places of Ebla's deceased ens, even if his primary role is confined to the precincts of Ebla.

The actions described in these texts without doubt indicate that Eblaite conceptions of, and actions toward, prior ens extend far beyond that of simple care or provisioning of the dead in the afterlife, or even just their commemoration. These are neither perfunctory acknowledgement of dead relations, nor propitiatory responses toward ghosts. They demonstrate instead a complex ideological interplay between deities, ancestors, and the concept of rule that we are only

---

55   Made explicit in TM.75.G.1730 (Fronzaroli 1992: 184; cf. Viganò 1995: 218). "For the enthroning of the en," and "the en's attaining to sovereignty" are connected in TM.75.G.1730 to the purification of the **é** *ma-tim* and the consigning of furnishings to the caravan.

now beginning to grasp. That the ultimate destination of the journey, and the place where the greater part of the action takes place, is a funerary structure and not a temple of a god[56] is pivotal, and whether or not the physical remains of an en were actually interred in the é *ma-tim* is irrelevant. The dead ens are certainly part of the same ritual process, the same set of carefully defined acts that are directed to the gods and also to the living. Indeed, in one of the most symbolic acts recorded in this document, the gods themselves, Kura and Barama, are taken into the é *ma-tim* and are transformed by their sojourn there, as are the royal couple. In an as yet unknown way, they become "new."[57] It also suggests that Kura and Barama, en and consort, are intimately connected in terms of the legitimation of the new couple as incumbents of the throne. Pomponio and Xella (1997: 245) argue that Kura and Barama are the superhuman archetypes of en and maliktum, and the marriage ritual signifies the divine apotheosis of the royal couple. Kura and Barama are certainly equated with the en and malik-tum in other instances. Each is given a special garment woven by the woman of Nenash. A ritual is performed on all four, although the nature of the ritual is unclear.[58] But I do not think that the en and his consort become divine exactly. Rather, they merge with their "tutelary gods" (Archi 1988a, 2005; Pomponio and Xella 1997: 245), perhaps to become their embodiment on the earthly plane or perhaps only to become divinely sanctioned. Or perhaps, since succession is not necessarily directly inherited, such a ritual is necessary to *make* Kura and Barama the tutelary deities of this new incumbent pair, who may have had other divine affiliations prior to attaining this position. But whatever else is the case, that the merging takes place in a mortuary context seems to indicate that the apotheosis is from a simple, living person to a being, if not already an ancestor, now at least in the right social and cosmological condition to become one (Porter 2007/8: 207).

These rituals also show that sacred and secular space are hardly to be so divided – that rituals involving the divine in a very active way will take place in "palatial" structures and mundane locations, inside and outside space; in short, that there is nowhere the divine is not implicit. But spatial segregation does relate to different ways in which the gods are present and active. On the one hand, the temple is the locus of public cult and it is the place where people are suppliants before the gods. On the other hand, it is not to be

---

56   See Bonechi n.d. for a detailed discussion of the relationship between é *mah* and é *ma-tim*, and the likelihood that either represents a temple.

57   Archi (2005) associates this with the renewal of the metals that clad the statue of Kura on an annual basis.

58   Fronzaroli has translated it as "to make shine"; Bonechi (pers. comm.) suggests an act of lustration or purification (see also Viganò 1995: 216–19 on the ritual bath), and Pettinato has proposed that it is simply the making of offerings.

conceived that the gods are confined to the temple or may only be addressed there. When the very existence of the en is so thoroughly embedded in his relationship with the divine, it is likely that the god is present in the places where the en is, and not just in a shrine where the en may make personal obeisance. Since it is the en's position, his job as embodiment of the polity that is at stake, by very definition meaning those who constitute that polity, then the god will be present in the places where representatives of this other part of the equation at least, the people of Ebla, may bear witness to this relationship - in the plaza.

Therefore the prospect of a roughly life-size statue of Kura (and most probably Barama, although she is little mentioned in the records [Archi 2005]), as attested in annual accounts of metals (in which it appears that the statue is reclad with gold and silver each year [Archi 1996b, 2005]) located on the dais of the plaza, is not surprising - a statue of Kura who is the en just as the en is Kura (and Ebla), a relationship that is public in its essence. We need not postulate an origin in the apartments above for the statue whose remains were found on the bottom of the monumental stairway at the time of the destruction of Palace G, when another location is nearer at hand - the dais. This might perhaps be confirmed by a tablet (TM.75.G.118+152) found in the writing room that, according to Archi (2005: 91), mentions: "two gold statues from Mari presumably representing the two gods: standing respectively on a bull and on a human-faced bull and placed '(at) the gate of the house.'" The location of the gate is a matter of conjecture, but until another monumental entranceway on the order of the basalt stairway in the center of the plaza's eastern facade is revealed, this locus of transition from inside to outside has to be considered the most likely point. And how interesting it is that much of Ebla's statuary was made at Mari, or by Mari craftsmen, including those objects that are most closely identified with the very essence of the polity - not to mention the fact that considerable portions of the precious materials involved came via Mari (Archi 1999, 2005) - Mari, who as often as not was at war with Ebla.

The identification of Kura, a name unknown outside of the Ebla texts, is therefore of some importance in understanding the nature of en-ship at Ebla and the ideology of the incumbent family, as well as ancestors and their cosmological implications for rule. However, this identification is still unclear. Bonechi (1997: 499–501) suggests that Kura is an hypostasis or avatar of the storm god Hadda of Aleppo, and the fact that royal names frequently include three words that are epithets for this god, *da-mu*, *kam₄*, and *li-im* (Fronzaroli 1998 cf. Bonechi 1997) - all of which, interestingly, are kinship terms - might support this association. But since weapons are never dedicated to Kura whereas they are to Hadda of Aleppo, who has a decidedly militaristic function (Fronzaroli 1997; Archi 2005: 85), this perhaps is to be rejected.

Also a contender for the statue in the plaza is 'Adabal.[59] 'Adabal is a key god of the region west of Ebla, with major cult centers in at least three places, the primary one being Luban. He was also the recipient of the largest number of sacrifices offered at Ebla itself (Archi 2005: 98). A special community of followers of 'Adabal, the **šeš-II-ib**, is comprised of members of the polity, including ens, ministers, and their families (Archi 2002b). Their responsibilities include making pilgrimages from 'Adabal's cult in Luban around the countryside. 'Adabal is also attested at Darib and Ibal (Pomponio and Xella 1997: 270–1), two locations with considerable, although quite different, import for Ebla – Darib, as will be seen below, is the home of some of Ebla's regnal ancestors and Ibal is apparently related to mobile pastoralists. Perhaps Kura *is* an hypostasis or avatar of 'Adabal, for thus would be accomplished the unity and integration of the polity of Ebla. The connection with Darib and the fact that pilgrimage is a critical part of the rituals concerning 'Adabal both suggest it. Since 'Adabal is given weapons, however, several of which are "**Mardu**-daggers" (Pomponio and Xella 1997: 264), the objection to the identification with Hadda of Aleppo would apply here, too. Mardu, written **mar-tu** or **mar-dú**, is the Sumerian word for Amorrite, and it occurs comparatively frequently in the Ebla texts.[60] 'Adabal has been characterized as a lunar deity (Lambert 1985) and as an hypostasis of the storm god (Pomponio and Zella 1997: 287–8), although little is known about this god either. What *is* known is that if Kura is the god of Ebla, 'Adabal is the god of the lands around Ebla, particularly (if the historical geography is correctly understood) to the west.

All these limitations and unknowns notwithstanding, two main gods, Kura and 'Adabal, in association with their spouses, occupy a significant position in terms of Ebla's materiality, cultic observances, and political ideology and identity. Archi (2005) identifies the statues in the interior "throne room" with 'Adabal and his consort because tablets relating to the deliveries from the larger region around Ebla are located there, but if this is a throne room (which I doubt), it would seem an appropriate location for Kura and Barama. However, I would propose that rituals associated with en-ship should be in a public place, a place not about business but about display. Therefore Kura and Barama are the most likely contenders for placement on the dais in the plaza.

With the exception of the incantations, all the attestations of ritual practice at Ebla serve to interconnect the various constituencies of the polity through pilgrimage – attendance to the cult of 'Adabal, for example, takes the polity of Ebla as represented by the **šeš-II-ib** brotherhood to the countryside (Archi

---

59   Or, in earlier literature, **Ni-***dakul* (Archi 1985), or **Ni-***dabal* (Pomponio and Xella 1997: 286–8).

60   There will be considerable discussion of the Amorrites in Chapter 4, where the currently preferred spelling, Mardu, and not Martu, will be employed.

2006: 98), to the small towns where this deity had his main cultic presence, even implying Ebla's subservience to this god. Daughters of the ens were priestesses of 'Adabal in Luban; as already noted, 'Adabal himself was resident in the palace (Archi 1996b). At the same time this ties into the fact that the accession pilgrimage through the countryside in all its pomp and circumstance brings to the fore very specific sociopolitical ideologies that are incorporative of the living world beyond the palace. The model here is the right of the king to rule – validated through divine sanction, historical reference, and the repetition of tradition – but it would be a mistake to suppose that political legitimation or affirmation of lineage links was all that was involved. For one thing, the first-person plural is repeatedly used in the ritual (Fronzaroli 1992: 183), which effects the assimilation of other participants, such as priest and minister, Woman of Nenaš and Man of Harugu, with king and maliktum, thereby de-signifying the image of royal couple as isolated at the apex of the social hierarchy, and also effecting the incorporation into this process of the larger social grouping – the people of Ebla as a whole.

The successive performances of this ritual are enough to show that, contrary to widely held opinion, divine participation is as integral to the conception, perpetuation, and rule of the city of Ebla (and from what we know of Hadda of Aleppo, we might add that city too) as it is in any city-state of southern Mesopotamia. It is simply manifest and accomplished differently. Ebla is also considered different from southern polities because there is no manifestation *in* Ebla itself of the vast independent temple estates that characterize the south; all the evidence (primarily textual, as there is not much archaeological data on third-millennium temples at Ebla) shows that temples there are subordinate to the en. Indirect information from institutions such as the **šeš-II-ib**, however, intimates that this might not be a matter of variance in institutional structure as much as a question of spatial distribution. Cultic centers and their households may not be located in the administrative centers that constitute the capital cities of northern polities but (like the loci of 'Adabal's cult, which number some forty-odd [Archi 1992: 26]) are situated in towns that otherwise have little political profile (cf. Matthiae 2008: 102). As Archi (2006) notes, Aleppo did not bring fame to Hadda, Hadda brought fame to Aleppo.

The problem is that what is known about the institutional organization of religion and the organization of temple economies comes only from the records of those limited parts of it that intersect with the interests of the administration of the polity as housed in the palace. In contrast, many of the archives from southern Mesopotamia come from temples – the famous Bau archive is one such (Foster 1981) – and this situation has long been argued to have unduly slanted conceptions of the institutional organization of public and private, secular and sacred authority in Mesopotamia itself. Variation in types of sources does explain the discrepancy to some limited extent. More important to my mind is the nature of the intersection between religion and polity in the locus in which it is encountered: what is visible is the en's gods, the polity's gods, as they work to structure and perpetuate the operation of both. But this is in no way the sum total of those gods. It is only one end of a duality that in one way or another seems to stretch across vast tracts of the countryside. There are records of some of the goods the palace gave to the hypostases of those gods when in Ebla, but we have no idea of the totality of materials coming into the temple of 'Adabal at Luban, for instance, from all over the region, no knowledge of the extent of that temple's control or wealth – only that the en of Ebla pays obeisance to it as a member of the **šeš-II-ib**. And yet there is a very intimate relationship between this god and the polity of Ebla, so that we cannot think of this as Ebla's subordination to the greater power of the gods of another polity. It should also be noted that this duality is by no means to be considered as exclusive to Ebla – other polities may have had exactly the same kind of relationship with their own gods and indeed with 'Adabal himself.

It is possible that temple estates located outside the main cities of the north were independent of secular control, but whether or not this is the case, there is an additional import to such a situation. Cultic centers located in the countryside are vital hinges in complex networks of integration that draw together administration and populace, city and countryside, mobile populations and their sedentary kin in ways that transcend the centrifugal forces of fragmentation and dispersal.

Although there is no clear archaeological evidence of any such temple estate located outside an urban center, I can think of one archaeological setting susceptible to reading in this way. Along the Habur River (south of the Habur triangle) are a series of small, apparently agriculturally specialized sites (Fig. 30) that have long proved a puzzle, although not all of the many small sites that cluster along the banks of the river here should be considered specialized. Occupied from the early to mid-third millennium, and therefore much earlier than Palace G at Ebla (and I am in no way suggesting a connection), one site in particular stands out.

This is Tell Raqa'i, home of one of the small square temples discussed earlier in the chapter. In its middle phase of occupation, c. 2700/2600 BCE (Schwartz and Curvers 1992), it consisted at its center of a large round building divided into numerous small spaces, surrounded by three architecturally differentiated sectors (Fig. 31). Moving clockwise from the west around the building, these are: small, detached two-roomed houses; a triangular temple precinct flanked by two mirrored structures sharing the attributes of the houses; large multi-roomed housing; work areas. The site is estimated to have been home to very small numbers of people – somewhere between twenty and thirty-five individuals (Schwartz and Klucas 1998). The number and kind of installations in all parts of the site, including silos and ovens, contribute to the overall understanding

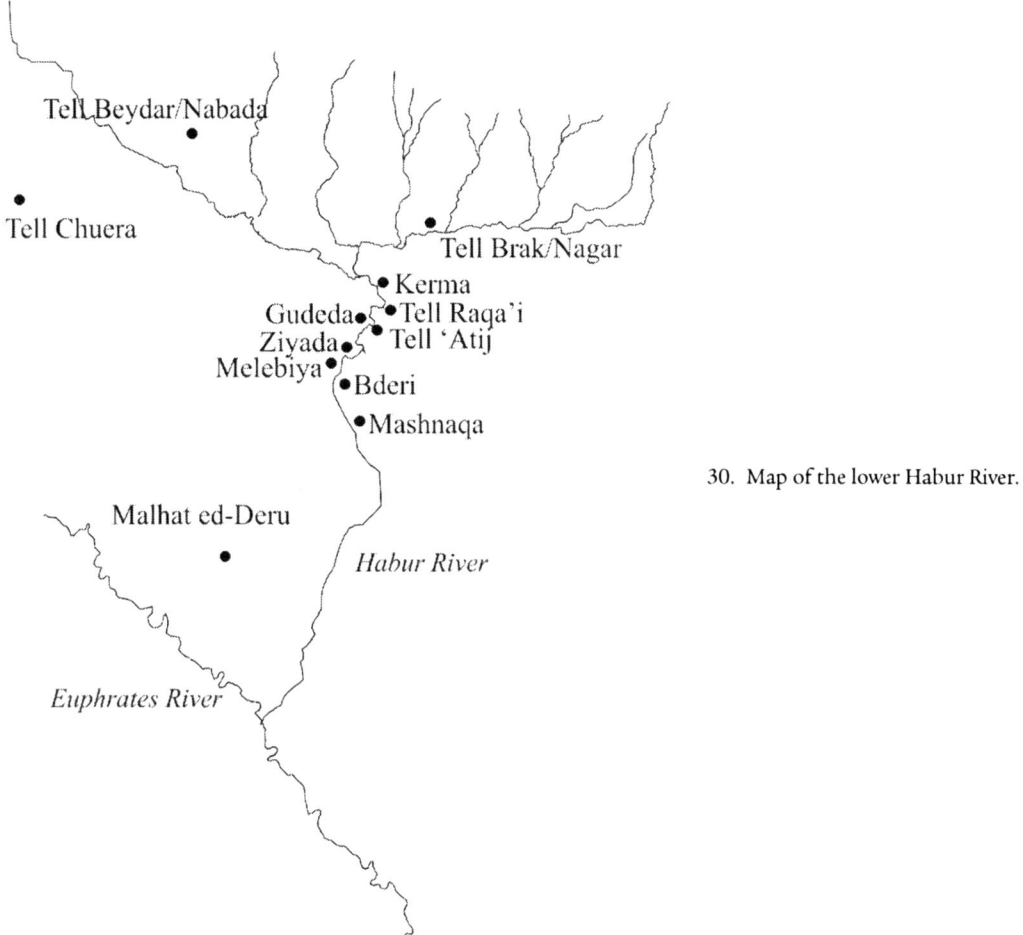

Tell Beydar/Nabada

Tell Chuera

Tell Brak/Nagar

Kerma

Gudeda Tell Raqa'i

Ziyada Tell 'Atij

Melebiya

Bderi

Mashnaqa

Malhat ed-Deru

Habur River

Euphrates River

30. Map of the lower Habur River.

that its primary raison d'être was as a grain collection and processing center. The buildings of differentiated function seem quite extraordinary for a site this small, and they are taken as a correlate both of social differentiation and of political hierarchy. There are thought to have been class differences among the inhabitants of the site pursuant to the site's function within a larger polity (Schwartz and Klucas 1998), for such complexity would seem unsustainable in an autonomous polity of this size.

The two most favored explanations for the existence and function of these sites, including Tell Kerma, Tell 'Atij, and Tell Gudeda (Fortin 1998a) are that they were all part of an integrated system (Schwartz and Curvers 1992) that served a larger center such as Mari (McClellan and Porter 1995; Fortin 1998a, 1998b) or Tell Brak; or that they were part of a mobile pastoralist subsistence system, a source of cereal products, granaries for the lean months (Hole 1991; Zeder 1995, 1998; cf. McCorriston 1998). There is no conclusive evidence that supports one scenario over the other, only a theoretical position, an overall view of how things worked in the third millennium of Syria in which one explanation

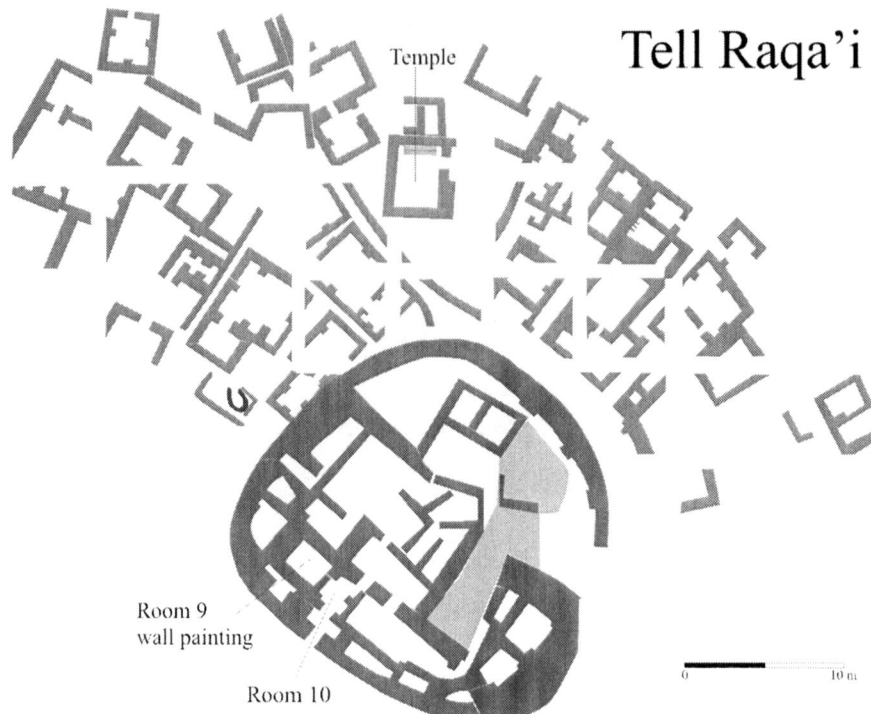

31. Plan of Tell Raqa'i showing the round building of level 4 adjacent to the plan of level 3. Redrawn with kind permission of the authors, from Schwartz and Curvers 1992: figs 8, 10.

fits better than another. Even the concept of agricultural specialization is a theoretical construct; all that is empirically established is that agricultural products were present and processed at these sites. The function of the architectural units and the degree to which agricultural activities might be thought beyond normal levels for sites of this time has certainly been challenged (e.g., Pfälzner 2001).

There is another possibility to consider: that Tell Raqa'i fulfilled all of the above functions and more – that just as significant to the raison d'être of the site as the silos and storage facilities, and entirely intertwined with them, are the nonstorage spaces of the round building and the subsequent temple precinct to its north.

Although the site may have had its initial genesis in the grill buildings at the base of the various occupation levels, which are widely accepted as grain storage facilities, the subsequent round building was not purely agricultural or utilitarian in function. The excavators, Glenn Schwartz and Hans Curvers (1992: 407), note that the eastern part of the structure consists of silos and platforms, but that the western part consisted, at least initially, of rooms with other functions – one had a number of sealings, another (Room 9) had at least one wall decorated with a painted scene. The fragment that remained depicted a figure turned to the left and holding some sort of object. It is impossible to predict the nature of this scene, but a cultic context for the painting certainly seems possible (Dunham 1993). Wall painting, as seen above, is not unusual in specialized structures and may indicate that this room had a specialized function. Alternatively, since rooms outside the temple *cella* at Halawa and, earlier, at Arslantepe were decorated in this manner, this room may have provided a foyer to another space. I am increasingly of the opinion that ritual practice takes place over much larger and more diverse spaces than we currently define. Scholarship tends to see the temple as the only locus of religious activity, yet even streets leading up to it are often essential parts of the performance, and rooms that mark the transition from "profane" to "sacred" or, better, mundane to trans-mundane loci are employed in any number of ritual contexts. Nor are rituals confined to one condition or the other – religious or secular – but very often bridge or encompass both.

Room 9 is by no means the largest of the spaces in this part of the building and would seem inadequate for ritual/religious purposes, although that is to presume that more than one or two people need take part in a ritual for it to have widespread significance. Its shape, especially in conjunction with room 10, is suggestive of a temple *in-antis*. Beyond these hints of a religious function to this room it is impossible to go. The western part of the building was subsequently blocked off, however, creating additional storage space, and one wonders if this was either a cause or an effect of the construction of the temple built outside it.

The entranceway to this later temple precinct was on the north, past the two mirrored buildings that flanked the open space in which it was set (Fig. 31). The precinct as a whole was oriented to the exterior of the site, not the interior – not to the round building. The temple itself was approached from the east side, but access to the north was later restricted by the extension of the already protruding west/east wall.[61] The two northern rooms were also added later, but installations were found in place beneath them (Schwartz 2000: 167). Following Moortgat (1967), Schwartz (2000: 171) suggests that such restrictions are part of a marked separation of the sacred from the profane that seems to come into being at about this time, at least in southern Mesopotamia. I would suggest that it is not domains of being that are at stake here, or even institutional competition, but rather simple control of access, a very different thing. Restricting access or controlling the numbers of people present implies changing ritual practice, and this may be as much secularly as religiously generated.

We do not know how any of these sites along the Habur articulate with each other; together they may make a fully autonomous system in the absence of any external participants, integral to the sustenance of towns such as Bderi and

---

61   Schwartz notes that it was blocked, but passage seems possible on the west side, while whether the east was fully closed or controlled through a gate is obscured by the balk.

Melebiya. Yet while 'Atij, Gudeda, Kerma, and Raqa'i have attributes that are specific to themselves, they seem to duplicate several functions, suggesting they may each provide for a different constituency – various pastoral groups, for example, who claim a section of the river banks as their territory. And while the discussion in general focuses on what these sites may disburse, and to whom they disburse it, equally important is the fact that they are collection points for some kind of sustaining area or hinterland. The sites are spaced fairly regularly at two kilometers apart. Is this sustaining area only the immediate catchment for each site, or are materials delivered from farther afield? And who does the temple service – the inhabitants of Raqa'i only? All settlements in this area? Or beyond? The fact that after initial occupation the faunal assemblage undergoes the same transition seen in fourth-millennium sites on the Euphrates – to a specialization in sheep/goat at Raqa'i, 'Atij, and Gudeda (Akkermans and Schwartz 2003: 219) – is provocative. I have already argued that this temple, and the others like it, were the focus of ancestral groups and I will elaborate further on that proposal.

It is possible to see the whole site as essentially a temple complex duplicating the functions one might see contained, for example, within the Khafajah oval (Fig. 19), a location of religious rituals that included feast and sacrifice and that wrought ties to its constituents by collecting and redistributing grain. The temple itself is very small, providing no grounds for argument one way or the other; the central *cellae* of many temples are small (Schwartz 2000). Size relates more to the kind of practice conducted within or around the structure than to the nature of the institution. If the entire site is a pilgrimage site, for example, the mysteries at the heart of its significance may be open to only a few – the **šeš-II-ib** brotherhood at Ebla was comprised of pairs of representatives at any one time (Archi 2002b). Large numbers of people may still take part in the journey and the larger cultic occasion, witnessing the key moments at a distance, while the brotherhood might enter the *cella* to perform their obligations alone.

In this light, the storage and cooking facilities at the site may have supported the preparation of foods, especially bread, for the festivals; the two-room houses may have operated essentially as guesthouses, for in later times we know that senior personnel, even the en, participated in the **šeš-II-ib** pilgrimage, and they had to have been housed somewhere. Again, I am not in any way suggesting that there is a direct connection here, only that the Ebla ritual serves as an illustration of the kind of practices that might be considered for other contexts.

The larger buildings on the east side of the temple housed the families that served the facility. At the same time, the accumulation of grain at this site and the others had purposes – and meaning – beyond the immediate; just as wool was converted into textiles that were utilized to accomplish the needs of the institution in the south – as compensation for services, as gifts to gain allegiance, and so on – so too grain, with its finite life, was functional as the wealth of the establishment only if it was used in these kinds of ways. But none of the possibilities currently in play are mutually exclusive. The location of a religious center in this region of the Habur might be understood as a way of maintaining the ties between mobile and sedentary components, as discussed in the previous chapter, and indeed could have been an outcome of them. The distribution of grain, whether to urban centers or mobile groups, or more likely to both as equal constituents of the same entity, was just one more thread in a web of linkages that sustained the integrity of the community. The lack of any wealth evident in these sites, such as we are used to judge wealth in materials like precious metals and artworks, is no particular inhibition to this proposal. In the first place, what counts as wealth is purely contextual; in the second, items such as cultic statues are rarely found at any site. The level 3 temple at Raqa'i had been cleaned out and filled with bricks for the subsequent building level (Schwartz and Curvers 1992), so it seems reasonable that anything of this order would have been removed.[62]

If perchance Raqa'i were to prove an example of this kind of system, then it raises another whole set of issues about how archaeologists conceptualize the spatial components of political, social, and even religious organization. The fact that northern sites do not compare in size and density to southern sites is argued to be a simple product of the limitations of agricultural possibilities there, where the irrigation practices known in the south, which allowed for maximal growth (Archi 1992: 24), were not practicable (Wilkinson 1994). This construct is entirely predicated on the understanding that size and density are desirable, that bigger is better. The reasons for this are obvious – southern cities are more like our cities; linkages between the ancient world and our own, on which is based the heritage of Western civilization, are most evident here.

There is another way to think about the population densities of the south – they are themselves constrained by the restricted availability of productive land and the irrigation systems that service it. These factors promote the concentration of large numbers of people in confined spaces, a situation not in and of itself desirable. That at least one writer thought it positively *un*desirable is evident in the story of *Atrahasis*, which presents the noise and squalor of overcrowded cities as the essential ills of humankind (Lambert and Millard 1999).[63] In the north, however, space is vast, yet few places seem devoid of human activity in the third millennium, and it is becoming increasingly clear that those activities are interconnected in a multitude of complex ways, one of which is

62 The silos at 'Atij were also – apparently – swept out, so that few traces of their putative contents remained (Fortin 1998a). This seems extraordinary lengths to which to go (and one has to wonder whether they were in fact ever actually used?). Such an action would seem to demonstrate a concern for the nature of cessation beyond an orderly reorganization of the activities at these sites, or even abandonment.

63 Although that is by no means all there is to this story, to be discussed in detail elsewhere.

the stretching of political relationships over this space through multiple kinds of exchanges with other worldly beings. The spatially dispersed practice of religious ritual can be thought of as experiential integration.

Ancestors, discussed previously, are another way in which the spatial dispersal of fundamental components of conceptual, structural, and even actual sociopolitical operation is evident. For reasons we do not yet fully understand, ancestors at Ebla are certainly not conceptualized as confined to, even if they were physically housed in, the city, and those associated with certain places were most likely buried in those places. Because if a tradition of dynastic burials was in place at Ebla, given the prevalence and monumentality of burials from this period found at other sites, many of which are conspicuously aboveground, it seems likely that more tombs would have been recovered than the empty hypogeum – a hypogeum that was never used, rather than robbed.[64] I mentioned above that Tell Banat presents just one such site, a ritual commemorative place housing some of the ancestors of a polity with its administrative center elsewhere, proposing Tell Chuera for that purpose and characterizing this arrangement as a bifurcated polity (Porter 2009a). This term indicates that different components of the polity were not spatially contiguous; it also should be taken to mean that there are dual places of deep and abiding significance to the conceptualization and perpetuation of the polity, a division that is not necessarily religious and secular, but may be, or that does not necessarily constitute a double administration but, equally likely, may.

There is considerable evidence in the documentation that a similar situation pertained at Ebla, although rather than a bifurcated polity, I would propose that Ebla is better characterized as a dispersed polity (Porter 2010a), for the following reasons: multiple elements constitute the structure of power at Ebla; these elements are spatially distributed – they are not all housed in the mound of Tell Mardikh itself – but they are all contained within a spatially contiguous polity. Two other towns emerge as prominent locations of ancestor traditions, and ancestor traditions in association with gods. Such, for example, are the offerings listed in ARET VII 150, where the text specifically states "**dingir-dingir-dingir en-en al$_6$-tuš** in *da-rí-íb*^{ki}" – that is, "gods of the dead ens when they reside/rest/remain[65] in Darib." **Dingir-dingir** is the plural of "gods," and the third **dingir** is the denotation of ancestral, that is otherwise worldly, status.[66] Darib is thought

---

64   Robbing, or sanctioned removal, of the contents of a tomb leaves some traces behind. Of the several tombs that had been reopened and emptied of their contents at Banat, none were completely devoid of any signs of use: either fragments of bone remained; or, more often in the case of Banat, objects, the supposed quarry of robbers, were left behind. In one instance these consisted of a silver neck torque and bracelets (Porter 2002b).

65   And see Fronzaroli 1992: 173–4, n. 37.

66   I diverge from Archi and other Ebla scholars markedly here in my understanding of the nature of ancestor traditions, and how therefore I read passages such as this. See for example Archi 2001, Biga 2007/8.

(Archi 1986, 1988a: 106) to be modern Atarib, thirty kilometers north of Ebla, an identification argued as confirmed by the discovery there of a limestone head of a statue – that of an en, according to Matthiae (1980). Some of the deceased ens attested in these documents are invoked at more than one place, however. Igrish-Halab is found at Nenash and Darib; Ishar-Malik at Ebla and Darib; Ibbini-Lim at Ebla and Nenash; 'Àmana at Uduhudu and Nenash, and so on (Archi 1996a: 14–15). If there are practices directed toward these ancestors in both these places, as seems to be the case, and as only one location can house the actual body of the en, then some other kind of structure – a cenotaph or an ancestral house – must have been the locus of the second set of practices. The plurality of terms (**é** *ma-tim*, **é** *mah*, and **é** x **pap**) evident in the text for ancestor-related structures would seem to confirm this. It is difficult to know whether this reflects a shift over time in the prominence of one location over another in the performance of ancestor practices, but if the essence of ancestor practice is itself the preservation of tradition over time, then this explanation seems unlikely, and in the accession ritual some ens just seem to be equally important in two places at the same time. Ancestor traditions are without doubt flexible, change with changing circumstances, and can be consciously manipulated for political ends, but the time period concerned, some fifty years in terms of the actual writing of the texts, is very short. Perhaps each place embodies a different concept within the larger ritual and ideological complex. This too is paralleled by the situation of the gods.

But the Ebla accession ritual is more than just an outing, a royal progress to commune with, and impress, the population located in outlying villages – more even than a statement of the essential unity of the kingdom and its perpetuation over time. It is the transcendence of boundaries between life, death and divinity, or perhaps better, the merging of these states of being, which were in any case never conceptualized as being quite as separate as we would make them today. The old king becomes an ancestor, the new king gains the possibility of becoming an ancestor, and the king and the god are in crucial ways rendered inseparable. The fact that statues of the en and maliktum are made to be left at various points on the pilgrimage, in the **é** *ma-tim* of a deceased en, and for various gods (Archi 2005: 91, n. 34), suggests the conscious transcendence of time and space on two simultaneous planes of existence. Again, the en and maliktum are in two places at once, just as gods and ancestors are.

This relationship is more subtle and in some ways more profound than simple deification, for the en and maliktum, either living or dead, do not become gods.[67] The use of **dingir** before the names of the dead is simply an indication

---

67   The assumption by Ebla scholars (Archi 2001; Dolce 2008) that this is in fact exactly what happens does not capture the complexity and subtlety of ancestor traditions, not just as attested ethnographically or interpreted anthropologically, but as attested by the third-millennium sources of the land of the four riverbanks. Ancestors are just not treated as

that they have otherworldly status (and cf. Glassner 2003: 201). They are not worshipped, or even venerated, for this last word does not quite capture the nature of practices and concepts associated with ancestor traditions, my preferred term (Porter 2000). Ancestors are maintained: they are tended, curated and invoked for their powers both benign and dangerous. They are very real beings with very real presence in the daily lives of the living, but they exist outside the bounds of the human realm.

This then places in somewhat different light the recent discovery of two female statuettes from new excavations in Palace G. Presented as the material avatar of a cult of dead queens (Dolce 2008), one figure, seated, is clothed in a dress made of gold (Matthiae 2008: pl. 29). She holds a cup. The other, made of wood and stone, is standing with her hand before her face in a traditional gesture of prayer or obeisance (Matthiae 2008: pl. 31). Matthiae states that this pair represents the living maliktum at worship of one of her dead and subsequently divinized predecessors (Matthiae 2008: pl. 30), arguing that dead queens were turned into goddesses in a private royal cult. There is no guarantee that these two figures functioned as a pair, but if they did, then the very public nature of the accession ritual, notwithstanding the mysteries that took place inside the é-ma-tim and é x **pap**, throws into question the "private" nature of this practice. There is a way in which ancestral traditions may be thought private as they involve an individual's dead progenitors, but in general this is not the case in antiquity, where ancestors are the web that connects society. In particular, it was certainly not the case for the rulers of Ebla, to whose position ancestors were critical, with a power in the system all their own.

This combination of data – the ritual and the female statuettes – in addition to attestations in accounts of palace expenditures of the gifts given to the dead "ladies of Ebla" (Archi 2002a) indicate that the maliktum herself is more than a mere appendage to the king, given in exchange for a special relationship with the state, but is crucial to rule, that she has her own genealogical tradition that plays into dynastic legitimacy. It is the maliktum herself, and not just marriage as proper for a person in high position, as completing some sort of essential dyad, or as providing an heir, but the actual woman, who is necessary to accession. The marriage that instigates the journey takes place long before the king is, apparently, actually married! According to Alfonso Archi (2006: 102), the epigrapher for Ebla, Ishar-Dammu married in the fourteenth year of his reign, Irkab-Dammu perhaps around the fifth year. Marriage to the maliktum of the ritual, therefore, was perhaps not the defining marriage of the en's

the gods are treated. The use of "dingir" attached to the name of a deceased individual, whether en or not, simply indicates that they are "alive" but not present on the earthly, human plane. This situation is also represented visually by treatment of eyes in statuary and images, to be discussed in detail elsewhere.

familial life, and certainly secondary wives are attested. And yet it *is* the one that defines accession.

Since, with the exception of this last pair, it is possible that there was no blood relation between successive kings, it may have been that accession was transmitted through the female. This does not mean that the maliktum ruled and the king was merely her consort – rather that the concept of rule and its origins or legitimacy was far more complexly derived than from a simple transmission by birth. Is this some form of sacred marriage, as attested in the Ur III period of the south (see Chapter 4)? An aspect of sacred marriage is perhaps embedded in the synchronization of king and maliktum with god and goddess, because both the accession ritual and sacred marriage are ways of tying leadership to the divine world through idioms and practices of kinship (cf. Bahrani 2002, and see below); but I think that is not what is really at stake. The ritual is ultimately about accession to the throne, and for this to happen, the disparate elements that comprise the kingdom of Ebla, its power and it populations, must be in accord. One of those elements is the connection to the kingdom garnered through a certain woman. It is especially interesting, then, that one of the first acts of the ritual – in the context of what is thought to be the wedding ceremony itself – is an offering, not to the sun god but to the sun *goddess*. It is also interesting that the word for the female member of the incumbent pair is usually written *maliktum*, while the king is far more often referred to by the Sumerogram **en** – at the same time, *malik* forms a frequent component of personal names (Archi 1982: 201–2). While this may reflect scribal practice, since scribes were trained in a southern tradition (perhaps at Mari), it does not explain why the female is referred to in the indigenous language, which perhaps suggests some particularity about her position deriving from local practice. That the portrayal of a woman seated before a standing female in the plaque found beneath the alimentary sector of Palace G parallels the two female statues found in the same area but not at the same time, neither of whom seems to be a divinity (Dolce 2008; Matthiae 2008: fig. 9.5), indicates an established understanding of a ritual perhaps to do with a hitherto unknown aspect of the maliktum.

Already, then, it can be seen that frameworks of power at Ebla were understood by Eblaites themselves as involving many more elements than only an autocratic king. As well as divine – or more broadly since we are to include ancestors, otherworldly – input into Ebla's governance, the en and maliktum share the political and administrative stage with other human actors. One is the minister referred to occasionally above but not yet discussed. This figure is as present in the records of the palace as en and maliktum. Unlike the incumbent pair, however, the ministers are usually named – so many times in fact that in the early years of work on these texts theirs were thought to be the personal names of the various ens to whom the texts referred. The power and wealth of the minister, both of which seem almost equal to that of the en, are evident. This immediately raises questions about the basis and organization of power at Ebla. Might this be interpreted as power sharing? Is it family based, the minister belonging to a subsidiary branch of the house/lineage/family, while the en is the head of that body? Another possibility is the idea of a corporate dynasty, where rule is in some way passed across a plurality of royals (Michalowski 1988: 271) or collateral lines (Biga and Pomponio 1987: 61). The crown is common property within this extended family, even though held by only one member at a time.

One concern is the fact that the minister has so much power[68] and wealth that he could surely challenge – even usurp – the position of the en, so that family ties might be understood as the mechanism that inhibits this from happening. These interpretations, however, are working within the dominant theory of rule: that it is highly restricted, kept within a single family at the top of society. There is no evidence for the minister's membership in this family, only that he is part of the en's household, that is, a member of the palace, which is obviously because he is administrative-assistant-in-chief. There is no reason to think that the minister does not come from another family at Ebla altogether, one for which perhaps this position is reserved.

The idea that extended family units or households, kin-groupings of some kind, might be the founding social framework for Ebla organization has not been much discussed, in part because of its tribal overtones, in part because there is little direct evidence for it in the archive of this one family. The "aristocracy" or "elite" often mentioned by commentators but little attested are thought to comprise only the offspring of king and minister as well as a few high officials (Archi 1992: 26), and this in itself is telling: all those who are considered to comprise the elite of Ebla are functionaries, defined entirely by their jobs. Meanwhile, archaeologically invisible but hovering in the background of the court is a group of people called **ab** x **áš**. Archi (1982) translates this as "elders," although Marchesi (2006: 14) claims that the term **ab** x **áš** indicates not elders, but a class of officials. Nevertheless, the **ab** x **áš** are often present at moments of decision making, albeit their views are not actually represented in the palace sources.

Just who constitute the elders, or how one became a member of this group is completely unknown, although I would speculate that this too is family based, with the elders being heads of households within the polity but located outside the palace, probably, given the lack of domestic architecture as yet exposed for this period, outside of the city altogether. There are, however, references to the representatives of houses in the same texts that list elders as recipients of goods (Archi 1982: 215), and so **ab** x **áš** might well have consisted of the

---

68   See, for example, Tonietti 2010, where the minister wages war on behalf of Ebla, occupying conquered cities.

leaders of different pastoral groups belonging to the polity of Ebla. Houses do not always seem to be constituted by family groups, though; sometimes they are professional in composition, sometimes units of production (Archi 1982, 1992; cf. Milano 1990b). Such suggestions are of course just that – suggestions. But the point is this: unless we approach the evidence with a broad selection of possibilities we are simply not going to ask adequate questions of it, and so will continue to perpetuate a reconstruction built on as equally shaky ground as any alternative reconstruction.

The term **ab** x **áš** in any case implies a population represented in distinction to the palace, but that are nevertheless implicit in the palace's administrative function. This in no way requires a tribal origin for such a political system. This might suggest the **ab** x **áš** have their own authority, if in a different sphere, but it need not necessitate that such authority is "dialectically against the king" (Archi 1982: 207). Two parallel structures of power and/or authority may exist side-by-side, in congruence or in competition, at different times (Stein 1998). In another scenario, the organization of power at Ebla may be a function of dispersed spatial morphology, intimately related moreover to the spatial configurations of cult and tradition discussed above. In this reconstruction, **ab** x **áš** could constitute part of the administration in locations at a remove from Ebla itself, and who are present in the city when issues concerning the polity as a whole are at stake.

Wherever the location of the **ab** x **áš**, it is certain that the polity of Ebla was composed of multiple institutional units and multiple social groups, dispersed across the landscape in a variety of ways. It is also certain that the polity of Ebla was geographically vast. How then was any sort of sociopolitical coherence and integrity maintained? As should be clear by now, I consider certain cosmological conceptions and practices key;[69] integrally connected to them, indeed essentially filaments of the same thread, are social frameworks (more commonly investigated as structural) and both may be grouped together under the rubric "the geography of kinship." This geography not only interconnects those within the polity, it extends the limits of the polity itself.

Kinship as a network that links people over time and space is difficult to detect at Ebla because such connections between people are so basic, so foundational, that they require no explication. But they may be glimpsed in operation from time to time, as has been seen already with ancestors in this chapter. They are also evident in the use of kinship terms, especially in Eblaite onomastics (Bonechi 1997; Fronzaroli 1998). Thus far this evidence attests primarily

---

69   These would usually be termed "ideological," but I find this word problematic for the following reasons: it implies a separate domain of practice that, as I have already made clear, does not represent the situation in the land of the four riverbanks; in the discourse of anthropological archaeology in the Near East it is too closely associated with the idea that ideology is controlled by an elite that manipulate it for their own materialist purposes.

to kinship as an operative factor within the public sector, but it also attests indirectly to kinship as a prevailing conceptual framework of the broader community, in two ways. First, ancestor traditions, which comprise the practice aspect of descent systems, work to establish en-ship only because everyone understands the system and recognizes its authority; everyone understands the system because this is the way everyone configures their own existence in terms of the dimension of time. Second, the spatial dimension of kinship, the living relationships that spread across society in ever-widening ripples, seems to be physically reproduced at Ebla in multiple ways, institutionally and individually, an example of which are the *kam$_4$-mu*. A term meaning family, the *kam$_4$-mu* are clearly some sort of institutional group (they are known also at Armi, for example), and they are understood as the family of the incumbents of the palace, but family who were not located there, not even in the city of Ebla (Fronzaroli 1998). Instead they were to be found in various parts of the polity, or, at the least, the actions with which they are connected in the documents that record them took place at a variety of locations.

This situation is paralleled by the relationship of the sons of en and minister with the countryside of Ebla, where their names are connected with land, houses, and sometimes households as well as whole villages distributed around the landscape. Commentors on land tenure issues at Ebla take the idea that these "princes" own landed estates and villages very literally (Steinkeller 1999a; Schloen 2001), in keeping with the general gestalt of the autocratic or, in Schloen's case, the patriarchal, king. Without becoming embroiled in the continual debate over communal versus private ownership and royal versus nonroyal sectors, this literalness is, I think, unnecessary. For one thing, many of the relevant texts are telegraphic, and the exact relationship between name, item (whether field, house, or village), and place, is rarely established. Instead it is interpolated, the nature of that interpolation depending on one's understanding of the larger sociopolitical system and, beyond that, one's theoretical position on ownership in the ancient world.

For another thing, this view fails to capture the essential tenor of many of the economic transactions recorded in the texts, which document the multidirectional circulation of a variety of goods and services among a wide variety of beings in a wide variety of places – places located not only beyond the confines of the palace, but beyond the polity of Ebla itself. As noted previously, this constitutes prestation[70] – one gives and one gets (not necessarily at the same time),

---

70 This term has very divergent meanings, depending on the academic field in which it is used. Dictionary definitions are confined to payment or services rendered. In British history it is rather specific in denoting certain church tithings; in sociology it tends to refer to government allowances, not unlike the payment of rations! In anthropology it refers to the practice of gift giving in building relationships of mutuality, especially as explicated by Mauss (1990 [1922]), in which the ideological component of gift giving is as significant, if not more so, than the material aspect.

and each act binds the giver and getter together in intricate relationships of obligation and esteem (Mauss 1990 [first published 1922]; Heim 2004). The assumption that this is a one-way situation, that the giver is obliged to contribute because the palace dominates, or because a prince owns at the very least the production of the village, is belied by the fact that kingdoms such as Emar made "deliveries" to the palace just as did local millers and weavers. On other occasions those kingdoms received palace goods – including, in the case of the maliktum of Emar, land and settlements (Fronzaroli 1984).

Deliveries, therefore, were not necessarily the obligation of the subordinate, but the practice of a relationship. It is in this way, too, that the deliveries of materials and work from those who are compensated by food allotments should be approached. I say "compensated" because the understanding that the grain, bread, or textiles people such as weavers, messengers, and millers receive are rations demands the understanding that they are dependent personnel, and the same arguments as above hold here too. These people do not belong to a fundamentally separate class, distinct from the rest of the population located in villages and towns scattered across the landscape that comprised the Ebla polity (Schloen 2001: 267), and who also make deliveries to the palace; they simply have specific tasks.

This argument has another archaeological dimension as well. The repeated notation at various sites (such as Mazzoni 2003: 185, Wattenmaker 1994: 199–203) that nonelite households use the same materials as elite ones – or rather that there seems no distinction to be made between households on the basis of portable artifacts alone (and I would add in many instances, architecture) – surely warrants rethinking issues of status, hierarchy, and class in more complex ways. Rather than assuming that lower echelons of society imitate their betters and so use the same material culture, we should recognize that other situations are equally likely: hierarchy is not manifest through mundane goods such as pottery; or, since few sites manifest architectural distinction beyond that which separates public from private housing, and those that do may be explained in multiple ways as suggested for Tell Raqa'i,[71] it seems likely that hierarchy is not always operable as the governing principle of social organization. While there may be divisions or differences between groups of people on various bases, some of which are socio-economic, some of which are not, those differences do not qualify all aspects of life. Some members of family groups may be richer than

71 It is in fact very interesting that Tell Raqa'i is one of the few sites for the third millennium in the north that does show marked differentiation in the architecture of its housing, for models of complexity based on site-size hierarchies predict that sites as small as Raqa'i should show no such stratification, being composed of lower-order producers either independent of, or in service to, the higher-order sites. At the same time, large sites, which these models predict should be the home of elites, rarely show more than a basic separation between public buildings and domestic habitations.

others, but this says nothing about social distance between relatives. In fact, at Banat, distribution of pottery repertoires follows function rather than status – certain classes of ware that might be qualified as luxury wares, although I would call them specialized wares, are found, not in elite versus nonelite contexts, or even in public versus private contexts, but in ritual versus mundane contexts (Porter 1999, 2007b). Separations between groups of people within polities in the north are much overdrawn, for they are neither materially nor socially so distinguished. Instead, as often as not, distinctions are made on the basis of what people do and the location they do it in.

Whatever the actual nature of the relationship between the en's family member and rural village, the gift of land from the palace to a person called Ingar suggests that geography is a very meaningful component of it, for the fact that Ingar will be expected to make his residence outside the city at least sometimes is made explicit – twice (see Schloen 2001: 270, for a rendition in English). The precise nature of "outside the city" depends on understanding of the term **uru.bar** however. While **uru.bar** is thought by Archi (1982) to designate the "suburbs" of Ebla in which some of the "dependent personnel live" and therefore located within its immediate orbit, this is a situation that should be archaeologically readily evident, with small sites scattered around the main mound. Until such sites are recognized and excavated, it seems more prudent to understand **uru. bar** as in some way referring simply to that part of the polity that is *not* the city.

What is important here, however, is the idea that distributing personnel, and especially kin, throughout the countryside effectively extends the en's presence in a particular way; that the en expects those kin to actually be there, and not just siphon off the commodities of the region apportioned to them, suggests that presence is not just domination, but is in turn the establishment of a relationship – as is kinship – based in mutual responsibilities and obligations. It is in this light that we might perhaps understand the **sa.za$_x$^{ki}**. I have already discussed issues concerning the relationship of the **sa.a$_x$^{ki}** to Ebla itself: while Archi considers the name to designate the palace, I am inclined to read it as intimately connected to it but not synonymous with it, proposing that it is located outside the mound of Tell Mardikh itself and constitutes the private properties, in distinction to the public or palatial properties, of the incumbent family. If my reading that the maliktum has a significance of her own in the transmission of position at Ebla proves valid, then perhaps the **sa.za$_x$^{ki}** might even be the household of her family.

Certain features of the organization, structures, and practices described here are not unique to Ebla. The *kam$_4$-mu* and **en.en** of the polity of Armi are also recorded in the Ebla archives.[72] That Ebla and Armi share these institutions

---

72 **En.en** are known at a number of sites (Astour 1992), but it is not always clear whether they are living or dead. In the case of Armi it seems clear to me that these **en.en** are ancestors.

does not immediately suggest, however, that they were common throughout the north, for other indications suggest Armi is very intimately connected to Ebla – perhaps even in the kind of ways I have postulated with Banat and Chuera (Porter 2009a),[73] where Banat is the ancestral site for pastoralists centered at Chuera who utilize the riverbanks in their territorial range.

Armi "seems to have been a privileged destination for short-haul journeys made by the ruler of Ebla," according to Milano (1990a: 335; Bonechi 1997: 509), on one of which the representatives of Ebla met with those of Kish and Nagar in what is taken to have been some kind of political summit (Biga 1998: 18–19). That it was held at Armi suggests a ritual/cultic aspect to this site, as such meetings often took place in these kinds of locations. Armi also has a privileged position within the court of Ebla itself. Allotments of cereals for one month include "of Tubuh-Hadda, of the ma-lik-tum (of Ebla), of Ar-mi^{ki} and of Kura" (Bonechi 1997: 512). Included in the list of foods for the en's table for one day are himself, the maliktum, the **en.en** (i.e., ancestors),[74] various (some of whom are named) sons and daughters of the en, elders, and fellows of the **en. en** of Armi (Archi 1982: 205–6). Archi (1982) argues that the **en.en** in the first instance must be kings of foreign cities visiting the court, but living en from outside Ebla would surely be denoted by the place they came from, especially since the **en.en** from Armi are so recorded. Maintaining the reading of ancestors here is entirely appropriate to the familial context of this text, however, for giving food to the ancestors may, when within the household as opposed to publicly celebrated occasions, be daily. On the other hand, the foods consumed at the en's table are not recorded every day, so it is possible that this is a particular day. This reading would then imply that the **en.en** of Armi are also ancestors, the "fellows" perhaps being their caretakers in the manner of priests, or even their lineage descendents. Whether living or dead, that Armi has a presence at the familial table as opposed to a state occasion suggests a special relationship – literally. The connection of Armi with Kura in the preceding quote furthers the likelihood that some form of kinship existed between the two polities – but it is unlikely to have been one of descent, as Armi is not listed as a place in which ancestor practices are performed. One possibility would be that this is where the maliktum came from. This relationship though is fluid, certainly historically contingent, and no guarantee that Ebla and Armi might not find themselves in conflict with one another; the existence of a treaty with Armi would surely confirm that at one point they did!

The details suggest that Armi and Ebla are involved beyond simple vassalage, because the many other polities that occupied such a position do not duplicate

---

73   In fact Otto (2006) has proposed that Banat is Armi/Armanum, but in my opinion there are some chronological issues that need to be resolved before this can be accepted.

74   See Astour 1992: 23, n. 134.

the same kinds of connections; Kura in particular seems to be confined as an object of worship to the Ebla polity. A son of Ibrium is named Yenhar-Armi (Bonechi 1997: 508), a god of Armi is erected in the palace of Ebla (Bonechi 1997: 516), and an unpublished text indicates that Kura (and a god called Ada) is to be found at Armi (Bonechi 1997: 508). Finally, Armi/Armanum is also closely associated with Ebla in the inscriptions of Naram-Sin. Yet there is no indication that Armi is to be found *within* the territory of Ebla even as it may well be part of the polity. Bonechi (1991) suggests a location in the vicinity of the Amanus, which raises the possibility that this is the summer range for Ebla pastoralists.

Which itself raises another question: is this network of gods, ancestors, elders, family members, and other kin dispersed across the polity and beyond in the extension of sociopolitical relationships over time and space - and in direct continuity from the ways the social group were framed and maintained in the earlier third millennium - merely residual? Or is it still working to keep a "multi-sited community" (Bernbeck 2008a) and mixed constituency of urban, suburban, rural, and pastoralist members of the polity intact, as I would argue is indeed the case? The relationship of pastoralism to the urban polities of the mid- to late third millennium is controversial indeed. For example, it is frequently iterated that all pastoralism in the third millennium, even in the north around Ebla and in the Habur catchment, must be state-controlled and therefore localized, and that this is something quite other than the pastoralism apparent in the Old Babylonian period, since there was no room for independent nomadic tribes around polities such as Beydar and Ebla (Sallaberger 2007: 418; Ristvet and Weiss 2005: 11). Population densities and the power of the state preclude the "free space" that nomads occupy. In this view, long-distance mobility not only equates with tribal organization and independence, it demands them. This position is especially evident in the following statement by Archi (2006: 99):

> It is increasingly clear that we must abandon the idea that nomadism, in one of its several manifestations, represented an inevitable form of society for all of those who spoke a Semitic language. The environment in which they lived has always favoured pastoralism. Urban and sedentary societies could, however, have been directly involved in the transhumance of their flocks, without leaving much space for tribes with a dimorphic way of life, such as those known from the texts of Mari in the Middle Bronze period. The palace administration of Ebla, for example, controlled through its officials approximately 100,000 to 130,000 sheep and goats and more than 10,000 heads of cattle. This did not, however, mean that pastoralism was the dominant element in the economy of those states.

Archi, in countering the position of scholars such as Steinkeller (1993) and Renger (1995: 283), who argue that the Semitic population of the north (especially in the area of Kish) had nomadic roots (also Zarins 1990), in fact presents a picture somewhat akin to my own understanding of how things worked – namely, that pastoralism was embedded within the sedentary social and political system as well as economy – and he is right to argue that there are absolutely no grounds to assume a relationship between ethnicity and subsistence. Where we diverge is in the implicit understanding that pastoralism and sedentary herding are mutually exclusive, that nomadism is exterior to the world of the urban state, and that pastoralists are perforce different in their sociopolitical organization to farmers, so that "pastoralism" and "tribe" are interchangeable. Therefore, pastoralism and the government of Ebla are also mutually exclusive because the government of Ebla is in no way tribal.

Other scholars see evidence of pastoralist connections to Ebla (Bonechi 2001), particularly in traces of kin structures detected in vocabulary, personal names (Bonechi 1991, 1997), and categories of people. Of this last are the kam_4-mu, interpreted by Fronzaroli (1998) as closely related to the $damu$-$damu$, which is itself a technical social term derived from pluralizing "$damu$," or "blood" (Bonechi 1997). The administration of Ebla may deploy the $damu$-$damu$ and kam_4-mu as they will, suggesting to Fronzaroli (1998: 112) that since the baseline meaning is blood, this social grouping must be kinsmen with particular connections to the royal family (à la Mari), and since the kam_4-mu are often found in apposition to $damu$-$damu$ in the administrative texts, then kam_4-mu in some way qualifies $damu$-$damu$ – probably as the families that sent the kinsmen to do the bidding of the palace. But Fronzaroli then makes a leap, one that is difficult to support as it stands: the kin are seminomads with "preferential relations to the royal family." This link can only be presumed on the grounds that kinship equals tribalism, and tribalism equals pastoralism.

Despite the fact that there is as yet insufficient detail to make a valid comparison, there are ways in which the Eblaite kam_4-mu parallel the Mari Hana. The kam_4-mu are very closely associated with movement in all the references to them listed by Fronzaroli (1998) and, in conjunction with that movement, they are given certain tasks, such as receiving and transporting goods, especially flour; inspecting and maintaining water systems; performing military functions; and, when they are in or near the city, they receive rations. They are, as Fronzaroli notes (1998: 111) always the kam_4-mu *of* someone or somewhere, and everyone seems to have them – Ebla itself and various of its functionaries, including the king, but also other political entities such as, already noted, Armi. Similarly, everyone seems to have *hana*, and among the myriad activities in which they are involved, Zimri-Lim's *hana* collect delicacies for his gastronomical delectation, kill a troublesome lion for local farmers when soldiers fail in the attempt, work as guards in the palace, fulfill military duty, help allies, and receive grain rations when they are working in the employ of the crown (see Heimpel 2003: 582–3 for a partial list).

If the kings of Ebla belong to a kin system, however, this does not mean they are tribal, nor does it mean they are seminomadic in origin – but nor does it mean they are not. In neither view of Ebla's relationship to pastoralism is the question established as a matter of evidence rather than prejudice. That if *mobile* – that is, according to all these scholars, *independent* – pastoralism were to prove central to the economy Ebla would somehow be diminished has long been the subtext in this debate. The urban and the mobile are assumed to be mutually exclusive as are tribe and state, while equally nomadism and tribe are synonymous. Indeed, most mentions of pastoralism or nomadism are accompanied by the word "tribe."[75] This is to some extent the Assyriological field's inheritance from Rowton – politics are conflated with subsistence practices and movement is assumed to determine sociopolitical functioning. There is a fundamental flaw in Rowton's logic though, for he (1967b: 114, and repeatedly thereafter, such as 1976a, 1976b) characterizes tribe and town as "two very different social morphemes." Although most anthropological archaeologists would consider tribe a political rather than social morpheme, a town is neither, nor is nomadism a form of society. One may live in a town no matter how one is organized and with whom one has social connections. If the social basis of the tribe is kinship, there were also millennia in which kin-based societies lived in towns – even cities. What Rowton should have contrasted here, in terms of his own dualisms, were tribe and state – and neither form of social/political organization requires a type of habitat. Neither form of social/political organization as delineated in contemporary scholarship, however, adequately represents the empirical complexity and diversity of sociopolitical organization in the ancient Near East.

There are several different issues involved in the view of third-millennium pastoralism as state-controlled in contrast to the Old Babylonian world of independent nomads free of state oversight. As should be clear from Chapter 1, this is a misreading of the Mari tablets, a large part of the content of which consists of the very fact that pastoralist groups were utterly bound up in the polities, and politics, of the day. They were simply not physically located in the city of Mari and its various counterparts, and they were not the passive, subordinate subjects we assume those under political control must be – the peasant farmers (we think) we know so well. A new set of issues is evident here: the nature of the physical attributes and organization of the state in the north, in actuality and in academic ideology; animal husbandry practices; and how these

75　I give a random sampling in the following references to indicate just how ubiquitous this conflation is: Rowton 1965–82; Gilbert 1975: 66; Adams 1978: 334; Charpin and Durand 1986; Sumner 1986: 207, 1994; Maisels 1990: 186; Dever 1992: 85, 89, 1995: 294–5; Postgate 1992: 85; van der Steen and Saidel 2007. Many of these are not recent, but they are foundational, their positions the basis of much subsequent work and rarely reexamined.

two factors relate to ancient/modern concepts of distance and its role in social cohesion/cleavage.

With the exception of the second-millennium Hurrian horse-training manual written for the Hittites, called the Kikuli texts, there is little *direct* information about the details of animal husbandry in the ancient Near East. And since private archives are rare at any point of time,[76] we have little firsthand knowledge of what nonofficial actors did with regard to such practices. What information we do have is indirect, from the south, and largely from the administrative records of various public institutions (Liverani and Heimpel 1995), especially temples, whose concern is not the details of husbandry but only the details of its output (Waetzoldt 1972; Adams 2006a). Nonetheless, it is possible to build some slight platform of understanding from these sources, a platform from which reconstruction may proceed.[77]

One such body of data comes from a temple in the city of Ur during the Ur III (2100–2000 BCE) and the Old Babylonian periods (Van de Mieroop 1993a). While it is impossible to adduce specific counts of this temple's holdings there is enough information to suggest considerable numbers. In one month, some seven thousand sheep (and one hundred goats) are brought to the temple by twelve "shepherds" for wool collection. In one year, ninety-one "shepherds" are attested. Shepherds are known to take care, according to Postgate (1975), of anywhere from four to 270 animals, or, according to the texts used by Van de Mieroop, a hundred to a thousand animals.[78] As will be discussed, I think it rather likely that there was no *herd* that consisted of only four sheep, unless it was a rather poor family's domestic holdings, but rather, that only four sheep were contracted out to that particular herder who had the care of additional animals – his own or those of others – as Van de Mieroop (1993a) has pointed out (and cf. Dahl 2003: 205).

At the opposite end of the scale, Algaze (2008: 87, n. 18; cf. Adams 2006a: 151) questions whether a thousand animals per shepherd is feasible, and while I agree that other people were involved in the care of these herds, in fact the ratio of animals per caregiver would depend directly on the circumstances of the care – whether penned, grazed locally as in fallow fields, or pastured in the open steppe. The more stationary the care, the more intensive the caregiving, and hence the greater the labor requirements. Animals that are penned need

---

76 Although according to Jason Ur (2004) the third-millennium collection of texts recovered from Tell Beydar may belong to a household rather than the state.

77 Despite the fact that, as Liverani (Liverani and Heimpel 1995) points out, figures to do with the growth of herds are formulaic as a response to lack of real information when herds are managed by someone else.

78 Adams (2006a: 151) notes that such divergences in numbers of animals per shepherd raise questions as to the reliability of the textual tabulations.

fodder continually provided, which involves comparatively large numbers of people; animals that are grazed locally need watchers to ensure they do not cross boundaries of cultivated fields and to move them between those fields to water. As well, additional foddering may be needed for some months of the year, as is the case today in the vicinity of Umma (Ochsenschlager 2004). Another factor determining herder/herd ratios is the constituency of the herd as created by kill-practices. Maximizing the number of lactating females at the expense of young males and older animals results in leaderless flocks, which therefore require more human input. In modern studies the periods of intensive labor – lambing and shearing – require several people, often an entire family with supplemental hired (and professional) labor for two hundred sheep (Marx 2006: 83). But even calculating from a modest number of one hundred animals per herder, no less than 9,100 sheep (with some goat) may be assumed, and averaging out the numbers given in the monthly figures (Van de Mieroop 1993a: 165–6), which would yield 583 per shepherd,[79] we may expect the total flock of this temple at any one time to have far exceeded nine thousand.

Wool deliveries to various cities in the Ur III system, however, tell another story. These are so immense (Waetzoldt 1972) that if even approximately accurate (cf. Liverani and Heimpel 1995) some millions of animals must be postulated on the basis of yield per animal ratios. Half a million sheep are attributed to Ur alone (Algaze 2008: 82). Because of the particularities of the Ur III economic and political system (see Chapter 4), though, it is difficult to assess how this relates to the size, nature, and organization of animal husbandry in other regions or in earlier times. I will argue that the Ur III kings radically transformed the organization of pastoralism by bringing it from essentially private to largely state control. Yet this should not affect dramatically the quantity of wool consumed in textile production, which was always a fundamental part of the economy, especially the temple economy, and even if there was also a fair amount of domestic production for internal household use.

Interestingly, the herds of the temple of Nanna discussed by Van de Mieroop were managed not by temple personnel, but were contracted privately, assigned to "shepherds" who may also have had care of their own or other people's animals (Van de Mieroop 1993a; Adams 2006a: 149), and who, in this period at least, were tied to different households (Dahl 2003: 205). I have registered the term "shepherd" here in quotation marks because a number of different strategies may be designated by this term. It does not necessarily imply professional herders employed by the temple, but rather denotes anyone entrusted with the care of the temple's herds, and may range from flocks kept within the confines of the domestic household to those grazed in the steppe by pastoralist families.

79 Cf. Adams (2006a: 151–2), who gives a median of 400 per shepherd at Umma, a number he considers beyond the care of a single individual.

It may be proposed, I think, that in fact these shepherds were only the designated recipients of temple property on behalf of a family, families, or pastoralist group, wherein more than one member would be involved in some aspect of care, and were not the responsibility always of a single person (and cf. Algaze 2008: 87, n. 18).

Note that even if the number of sheep postulated for Ur on the basis of Waetzoldt's (1972) figures were to be reduced by half, this still results in unsustainable numbers of animals if they were not to be grazed far afield, and this is just one city among many that produced woolen fabrics. The sheep/goat holdings of the Nanna temple (which also owned considerable numbers of cattle) alone are sufficient to raise the question of local sustainability, and this is one temple in one city in a region that had many, many cities with many, many temples, of which many again relied on textile production as their economic foundation. While these quantities may seem unrealistically high in light of modern-day figures, it must be remembered that yields would have been considerably lower in antiquity both because of techniques of fleece removal (plucking predominated) and the genetic makeup of animals. Breeding for fleece would not have equaled modern productivity.

It is inconceivable that even a significant portion of the numbers of animals implied here would be herded as locally as the perimeters of the irrigated lands that constitute the locale of these city-states, for several reasons. Contested land usage and issues of carrying capacity are but two. Documents from the archives of the Third Dynasty of Ur, at the end of the third millennium, suggest that localized husbandry was a resource-intensive as well as labor-intensive affair, for fodder was (had to be?) provided by hand for these animals.

> -360 fattened sheep. Their grass carriers, 24. Grass-carriers stationed at ....
> (wages of) 6 PI, 4 ban. Their shepherds for fattened sheep are 2 in number. Their assistants are 2 in number.
> -40 fattened oxen. R. III. Their shepherds for fattened oxen are 1 in number. (Those) stationed at ... and hay-carriers are 7 in number. (Sharlach 2004: 32)

It is possible that these were special animals destined for sacrifice and so were treated with unusual, ritualized, care, but this seems unlikely given the quantities of animals so dispatched in this period. It is more likely that animals kept in, or immediately adjacent to, the city required significant input to keep them fed. Four people are assigned to the care of 360 sheep, with twenty-four more needed to provide fodder. Imagine the number of personnel needed for, say, 9,000 locally kept animals; extrapolating from the above figures, it comes out to 600.

Instead, we must understand the majority of animals, that were used for wool rather than meat, as having been variably dispersed across all available ranges, including upstream of the Tigris and Euphrates, in the Transtigridian lowlands and the Zagros mountains, down the coast of the Persian Gulf and even across to the Levantine coast – wherever, in short, there was available pasturage not in use by, or that could be successfully wrested from, others. There is, I think, very direct evidence of this in the Mari texts. Political interactions and trading relations certainly extended across these distances, witness the various contacts with Hazor, for example (Horowitz and Wasserman 2004). Message carrying, a task that pastoralists were known to undertake (see Chapter 4), was a significant part of that international contact (for Hazor, see Durand 1997: 583, letter 390; 1998: 669, letter 851; for the general situation, see Lafont 2001; Bonechi 1992). Mesopotamian pottery dating to the early second millennium has been found in the settlement of Tell Abraq in the Emirates, and Omani stone has been found at Ur (Potts 1993: 431–2).

More to the point, the Mari texts and documents such as these from the temple in the city of Ur, although not contemporaneous, bracket animal husbandry, wool production, and the textile industry. From Mari, on the one hand, there is copious evidence about the sociopolitical interactions of pastoralists who care for sheep and goats, but little information about their herds, and less about the products of those herds and their destination. It certainly cannot be imagined that herds and their products were irrelevant, that animal husbandry was just a means to an end, a way of being mobile. From Ur, on the other hand, there is information about the animals and how they fit into the urban end of the spectrum, but not about the people who care for them, or where they do so. When juxtaposed in this way these two sets of documents highlight just how much it is the immediate concerns of writers that condition the ideas we have of the nature of the ancient world (Adams 2008). These texts also reflect fundamental issues of organization. As noted previously, Ur III kings were to change earlier practices from attenuated management, where mobile components of kin-groups cared for the animals in the steppes and highlands outside the irrigated zones of the south at a substate level, to a highly controlled situation, where large-scale animal husbandry was brought under state oversight. It is the former practice that characterizes the north throughout the third millennium, leaving therefore far fewer records of its traces.

But if the Ur III scribes did not see fit to include details of animal husbandry in their records this may not have been only because of the state's sheer lack of interest in the menial classes that undertook this labor (Adams 2006a). Liverani and Heimpel (1995) have argued that the greatest concern in record keeping seems to have been with maintaining regularized herd numbers rather than producing any real account of what actually happened, because the animals were beyond direct control of the recordkeepers, and this I suggest is further evidence of distances involved in the pasturing of these herds. It would be easy enough to send out an inspection team if the animals belonging to the Nanna temple were kept in the vicinity of Ur, similarly for the animals of

Umma.[80] That this was not done – that dead animals were accepted only if their hides could be produced, and live births were an ideal but modest and sustainable total – suggests that this was because herding was by and large practiced beyond Mesopotamia, and therefore beyond oversight.

This distribution of animals beyond the confines of Mesopotamia itself has several implications. The first, in the context of this discussion, is that the risk of loss to the temple was high if shepherds could escape to the steppe and mountains where temple dominion held no sway. What, then, inhibited caretakers of temple herds from simply absconding with their charges, charges that would provide the basis of considerable wealth in a new life somewhere else? The power of the god might be one factor, but not, I think, the only one. As important, if not more so, is the fact that these people, no matter how far they traveled, were firmly ensconced in Mesopotamian sociopolitical and ideological systems because they were deeply rooted in families and communities there, families and communities that comprised farmers, potters, metalworkers, fishermen – in short, all the productive tasks that contributed to Mesopotamian economy and society, including local and broad-range pastoralism. This is hinted at in these particular texts about the temple herds of Ur, where shepherding is a family business involving brothers, fathers, and sons, and where "subsistence fields," fields that provide the livelihood of their incumbents, are assigned to shepherds and cattle herders (Waetzoldt 1987: 128-9; Van de Mieroop 1993a: 169). Situations where those managing animals are associated with fields (Sallaberger 2004), or where people somehow labeled pastoralists undertake "sedentary" activities such as weaving (Buccellati 1966), often seem puzzling, as they are, according to most frameworks, mutually exclusive. Sometimes rather contorted explanations are derived to account for such incongruence. But they make perfect sense if contextualized within family-based economic practices, where some members are sedentary, some mobile. While Van de Mieroop, Adams, and Algaze all make mention of difficulties imputed to distance and separation, whether social or geographic, in the practice of pastoralism that suggest to each of these writers an immediate localization of the herds noted in some way in these texts, all of these problems may easily be resolved by contextualizing pastoralism in kin-based social relationships. Reciprocal rights to labor and resources such as pasturage, water, fallow fields, and stubble, even communication and transport of goods, may be engineered sometimes through immediate and horizontal family ties, such as one's living kin, sometimes through more distant, vertical linkages – linkages of descent, beyond the span of the living individual.

---

80 Dahl (2003: 75, n. 198) does in fact note an inspection tablet from Umma for shepherds, cowherds, and the staff of the palace, and we may expect this to refer to animals that *are* kept locally.

Adams (2006a: 153–4), for example, suggests that the requirement to bring to the temple the hides of its animals who died in a shepherd's care, as well as the practice of frequent small deliveries to it, demands local pasturage, but there are many possible constructs to do with the movement of goods and labor between members of kin-groups that obviate this as a problem. The designated "shepherd" does not even need to be with those who care for the sheep if such an undertaking is structured within a family enterprise, as so much of Mesopotamian labor was (Steinkeller 1987a). Algaze (2008: 88) notes the increased labor needed at certain times of year, such as breeding. This additional labor requirement may be met by a number of different strategies – one (noted in Porter 2002a) is the reciprocal exchange of work with relatives engaged in cultivation – members of the family engaged in pastoralism help with harvest, members of the family engaged in cultivation help with breeding and plucking.

It is within family-based economic practices, which themselves give rise to the lack of direct evidence, that we must understand a good deal of the animal husbandry that took place in the north, where foddering also seems to have been practiced even though the spatial constraints are nothing like those of the south. At Tell Brak, ancient Nagar, seed remains (Charles and Bogaard in Oates et al. 2001: 319) and the morphology of animal bones (Weber in Oates et al. 2001: 346) indicate that sheep/goat as well as cattle were foddered, and the texts from Tell Beydar, ancient Nabada, which was at this time subsumed into the polity of Nagar, also provide evidence of foddering – at least for equids and occasionally oxen. The high quantities disbursed for state visits from Nabada's Nagarian overlord indicate just how much animals could consume – 180 equids over ten days were allotted some 6,000 liters of grain (Sallaberger 1996; Oates in Oates et al. 2001: 292) or approximately 8,000 pounds – which in turn implies just how much land had to be under cereal cultivation in addition to the amount needed for subsistence, let alone surplus, in order to fodder or graze animals locally. At the same time, since increasing aridity and increasing population nucleation would have acted as a drag on the productive potential of these centers (Wilkinson et al. 2007: 53), it is simply not feasible that all the animals involved in this system, no matter who controlled them, were housed within or immediately adjacent to the city and foddered. They would therefore have been taken farther afield.

Just how much farther afield is the question. But any reconstruction of pastoral production and its relationship to settlement is fraught with problems because it is predicated on preconceptions of what is likely. For example, a recent modeling of the Beydar settlement and resource system that seeks to move away from static and mechanical reproductions of ancient subsistence (Wilkinson et al. 2007) incorporates a number of critical variables including the idea of human agency, but in terms of animal husbandry considers only small-scale domestic herding as practiced at Beydar, allowing twenty-five animals as the optimal holdings of a household (Wilkinson et al. 2007: 60–61). This model does not, therefore, allow for animal husbandry as part of a surplus system of either households or the state that might be based in wool and textile production.

However, wool, usually but not always in the form of textiles, was an essential element of payment (Waetzoldt 1987; Potts 1993: 424–5), gift giving, ritual performance in sacred and secular contexts such as commemorative mortuary practices (Archi 2002a) and the dressing of deities (Wright 1996, 1998), and is attested almost everywhere, north and south, as a major element of the economy (as Stein 2004 above). This is in marked distinction to the very small-scale consumption evidenced in the use of penned herds, of twenty or so animals each, kept within the settlement, and grazed in local fallow fields. Used mainly for secondary products such as milk, this practice is observable in any Middle Eastern village today. Wool from these animals is also occasionally used for domestic purposes such as the stuffing of pillows, and more rarely, for the weaving of mats on looms made by placing four pegs in the ground set for the desired length and width. Wool from small-scale domestic herds does not amount to quantities sufficient for large-scale production of textiles.

But even twenty-five animals per household, if the population of Beydar is to be estimated at 1,700 (Wilkinson et al. 2007: 66), which might divide into a minimum of 150 households, allows 3,750 animals, a number that would stress the grazing land available in the vicinity of Beydar, which itself was limited by the fact that Beydar controlled a number of subordinate villages (Sallaberger and Ur 2004; Wilkinson et al. 2007) that would also have had their own domestic herds with access to the same spaces. The whole region of the Habur was densely occupied in the third millennium (Lyonnet 1998, 2000; McClellan et al. 2000), which raises issues of available space, assumed by Sallaberger (2007) and Ristvet and Weiss (2005). Nor does this figure of 3,750 sheep/goat allow for any publicly held herds as are evident at Ebla, where estimates of the king's own herds are currently at 11,401 head of cattle and 118,715 sheep (Steinkeller 1999a: 300; see Archi 1993: 12–14, 2006: 99) based on a single text. The same ruler also gave three of his sons some 93,000 sheep and 2,400 cattle and calves, which Archi seems to understand as deriving from the first set of figures. It seems unlikely to me that the king would give the bulk of his property away, and I think we can accept that this text is not a complete accounting of all royal properties, and certainly not of all holdings for the polity. Adducing another line of argument, the monthly numbers of sheep consumed in sacrifice, at the royal tables, and for the support of messengers often total several thousand, and can be as high as 4,500; many of these seem to come from the palace holdings (Archi 1982), which at such rates of slaughter would soon be exhausted.

While the spatial configuration of the polity of Ebla is quite different from that of Brak/Beydar it too consisted of multiple layers of resource catchment that contributed to the sustenance of the kingdom as a whole. To exclude pastoralists – or, rather, mobility – from consideration in the management of a minimum of 200,000 sheep/goat in the vicinity of Ebla, and to assume that their care was essentially sedentary, is problematic from a purely practical perspective and unnecessary from a theoretical one. Some 67,000 sheep/goat, apportioned to shepherds from twenty-two villages, are recorded (Archi 1993: 15, n. 30). This is more than 3,000 sheep per village, a large number to manage and feed. Even cattle at Ebla were to be located in the steppe, as tablet TM 82.G.266 listing 760 calves from there (Archi 1993; Steinkeller 1999a: 316) indicates. It is unlikely that such numbers could be housed in the immediate vicinity of Ebla, or even within its territory alone for very long, without, at best, running out of pasture rapidly and, at worst, risking serious degradation of the local environment – even with optimal climatic conditions. This volume of animals suggests that several strategies, much as described by Stein (2004), and including broad-range pastoralism, were in use at Ebla, none of which fell beyond the polity – by which I mean "royal" and other households, "high" and "low" (cf. Biga 1995: 297). This is further substantiated by the provision in the treaty with Abarsal for pasturing Ebla's sheep there, which states that if the en of Abarsal does not allow them water in his territory then he is breaking his treaty oath (Archi 1993: 7). There is little consensus, though, as to just where Abarsal is to be located.

However, neither localized nor broad-range pastoralism need be performed under a particular form of sociopolitical organization or a particular degree of mobility. If documentation of the precise management of these vast numbers of animals is lacking, then management was not the concern of the central administration of Palace G but rather was in the hands of families within the state, as is increasingly clear at Brak/Beydar (Ur 2004; Porter 2007a), and is exemplified in the temple texts from Ur.

I am sure some will think that my concerns here are mere quibbles, that what I am trying to describe in an integrated socioeconomic and political system where broad-range pastoralism is as significant a component as cereal cultivation is just "seminomadism" or, in the case of a situation with major urban centers involved, "semisedentarism," but the differences between these kind of labels, which lack any analytical utility, and what I am attempting to explicate, are considerable. In the most important ways of thinking about the subject, distinctions between "sedentaries, half-sedentaries, half-nomads or nomads" (van Driel 2000: 266) simply do not matter. What matters is the way people perceive, and produce, their relationships with each other in situations where members of the group do different things; what matters are the outcomes contingent on those ways.

We will only see those ways, however, if we bring a different perspective to the sources. Most writers readily acknowledge that the ancient record is only partial. The monumental buildings of urban centers and the archives of various administrative institutions that form the bulk of current information do not tell the whole story, and there have been various attempts to redress this. In the late 1980s and early 1990s a small but enthusiastic movement toward the archaeology of villages and rural landscapes sought to bring the "people without history" (Wolf 1982) into the narrative (Schwartz and Falconer 1994; Stein and Rothman 1994), and although this seems to have made too little headway, it gave rise to an investment in landscape archaeology that widens the archaeological perspective to include the interstices between cities where so much critical activity happens (Wilkinson 2003). Nevertheless, not only is there not yet incorporated into this landscape any theoretically rigorous way of reaching that activity, or a nuanced understanding of its residents, we are still extremely reliant on the materials derived from major urban centers for the kind of detailed pattern in material culture over time and space necessary, and for chronological control (Porter 2007a). Since the sources are largely unchanged, then, it is incumbent upon archaeologists to find better ways of thinking about how those sources reflect the undocumented populations that make up the polities of which we see mostly the public part (Porter 2010a, 2010b).

We do not see in texts the fact that mobile pastoralists and other peripatetic groups are as central to the polity as the farmers toiling in the barley because most of our archives are from palaces and temples and concern the administration of a limited range of situations, while this arrangement is usually domestic rather than political. It occurs within families and is not therefore a state concern. We do not see it in archaeology because as yet we have no theoretical way of truly coming to grips with the materiality of mobile pastoralists if and when they are at home, whether home is in the steppe or the city – when they are indistinguishable from their sedentary siblings.[81] It is only when they are in places *we* think no one else could or would live that we think we might see them because any trace of activity there could only be the remains of pastoralist presence, but recent work such as that of Michael Frachetti (2008) in Eurasia, long seen as the epitome of nomadic territory, shows that perhaps we have not got that quite right either. There the term "pastoralist settlement" is not oxymoronic, as Marx (2005) and Frachetti and Mar'yashev (2007) have shown. The main reasons we do not see mobile pastoralists in text or trench is because we are blinded by our own views on who they should be and what they should do.

Anthropologists, whatever the theoretical persuasion and actual interpretation, describe multiple ways in which mobile pastoralists and sedentary farmers may be the same sociopolitical unit and the multiple social-political identities that may be held within the same person. Salzman (2000) describes multiresource pastoralists in Baluchistan; Lancaster and Lancaster (1992) do

---

81 This is a different understanding to that of van der Steen and Saidel (2007: 1), who see nomads as "acquiring material culture through exchange with the sedentary societies."

similarly for the Arabian Peninsula. Marx (2006: 90) records pastoralists in the Sinai who belong to two tribal groups: one membership affords rights to the trappings of a sedentary existence – house and farmland; the other allows grazing rights anywhere in the region. This is not to argue that because there are modern examples of this situation, it must have pertained in the past, only to give some slight indication of the variety of constructs that may have been possible. Marx (2006: 90) goes on to say that "in no sense is either kind of tribe a total society or a focus of solidarity; it is merely one of a variety of organizations in which the nomad participates. The nomad's social round unfolds in numerous organizations which are neither hierarchically articulated, nor centrally controlled. Every person belongs at each moment to a large number of corporate groups, such as trading and herding partnerships and descent groups, maintains networks of kinsmen and friends." The same is equally true of sedentary – just as much as mobile – members of the ancient polity.

CHAPTER FOUR

TAX AND TRIBULATION, OR WHO WERE THE AMORRITES?

For most students of the ancient Near East, the archetypal nomads and paradigmatic outsiders in the prebiblical world are unquestionably one and the same people, the Amorrites[1] – a group about whom, in fact, we have remarkably little information. We know that the Amorrites are nomads only because the Mesopotamians tell us so and, apparently, in no uncertain terms. But we do not know who they were or from whence, exactly, they came. Invading, infiltrating, or simply migrating into Mesopotamia in hordes, waves, or dribs and drabs (the evidence is sparse and confusing), somehow, someway, the Amorrites took control of Mesopotamia in the nineteenth century BCE. This occurred after a period of political upheaval that saw the collapse of history's first great but short-lived empire,[2] the Third Dynasty of Ur[3] (c. 2100–2000 BCE),[4] and the subsequent rise to a more localized hegemony of the cities of Isin and Larsa (c. 2000 BCE). Later, under the most famous Amorrite of them all, Hammurabi (c. 1790–1750 BCE), Mesopotamia as far as Mari on the Euphrates was reincorporated into a single political entity centered at

---

1 See, for example, Schwartz 1995.
2 In the past, history's first empire was thought to have been that of Sargon of Akkad and his heirs in the third quarter of the third millennium, but there is a growing consensus that this was largely a product of historiography rather than actuality; see the collected papers in Liverani 1993. It should be noted that there is also some debate as to whether the Ur III polity can be properly called an empire.
3 When referring to the rulers of the time, the term "Third Dynasty of Ur" will be used. When referring to the chronological phase to which this dynasty gives its name, I will use Ur III. For the chronological scheme see Table 1.
4 In general dates given are approximate, even when historically as opposed to archaeologically derived, as there is still considerable variance in dating schemes even among those who subscribe to the same chronological system. This work follows the Middle Chronology.

Babylon. Hence the era of Amorrite political dominance is called the Old Babylonian period.[*]

Once in power there is little to distinguish Amorrites from Mesopotamians – no evident separation of one group from the other, no difference in material culture, no texts written in Amorrite. But there *is* an astonishing number of historical, economic, ritual, and especially literary texts recovered from this period – in both Akkadian and Sumerian. And many of these texts, especially the literary ones, seemingly put forward excoriating descriptions of the Amorrites and of mobile life. Others actively lay claim to a nomadic inheritance, and still others give us glimpses into the daily lives of mobile pastoralists, how they were organized, what they did, and where they went. Dual, and diametrically opposed, worlds are thereby understood to have existed in antiquity: one of agricultural wealth, stability, and civilizational pursuits, the sphere of Mesopotamian cities; the other rootless, wild, and materially poor – the domain of the steppe, where nomads roamed untrammeled.

This kind of duality is also clearly represented in one of the first, and certainly most famous, stories in ancient literature, the story of Gilgamesh.[5] Taken purely on its literary merits at this point and not as reflecting the exploits of an historical personage,[6] this story, at least in its most widely distributed version today,[7] describes the way Gilgamesh, king of the city of Uruk, comes to find a best friend with whom he embarks on various ill-conceived misadventures, loses that friend because of them, and consequently experiences one of the most profoundly disturbing moments of the human condition – the realization of his own mortality. It is this last that is usually understood as the raison d'être of the epic. Gilgamesh, as king of one of Mesopotamia's most historically and ideologically important cities, is commonly recognized as emblematic of the

5   In Sumerian, the Babylonian name Gilgamesh is rendered Bilgames, according to George 2003 (also Veldhuis 2001), although not everyone subscribes to this position (Fleming and Milstein 2010: 8, n. 21). For the sake of clarity I will keep to a single spelling.

6   It is a long-held tradition in Near Eastern studies, but one with little foundation (George 2003: 101–6), that Gilgamesh was an actual king of the Early Dynastic Period (c. 3000–2400 BCE), although the figure who in much later tradition is known as his father, Lugalbanda, *is* attested in an Early Dynastic literary text from Abu Salabikh (George 2003: 5). The name preceded by the **dingir** sign is found in an Early Dynastic list from ancient Shuruppak (George 2003: 119), and this is its earliest attestation.

7   That is, the Standard Babylonian version, compiled in the first millennium BCE (George 2003: 381).

---

*   This chapter is based on texts. I am deeply grateful to Lance Allred, for his advice on the Sumerian materials, and to Dan Fleming, not only for his advice on issues of Akkadian, but for conversations over the last decade or so about all the topics with which this book is concerned. The fact that I might sometimes ignore the better judgments of my advisers should not be held against them! The research for this chapter was undertaken while I was a Visiting Fellow at the Institute for the Study of the Ancient World, New York University in 2007/8.

very heart of "civilization"; his new companion, Enkidu, being from the country in its various guises, is the representative of all that is opposite. The story took many forms, in different languages, before its final version was accomplished in the first millennium BCE, and so did the nature and relationship of these two characters.

The history of the Gilgamesh tale begins with four[8] separate stories written in Sumerian,[9] of which only a fragment of one story was recovered from an Ur III context;[10] the others are known only from Old Babylonian contexts. Each of these stories is a separate, self-contained adventure. In the most commonly attested story, *Gilgamesh and Huwawa* A (George 2003: 8),[11] Gilgamesh seeks to establish a reputation that will transcend even the limits of death, and it is the cedar mountains that offer an ideal opportunity for a suitable escapade. Enkidu, a slave, advises his master to tell Utu the sun god of his plans, for this is Utu's territory, and Utu will help him in his endeavor. Gilgamesh makes a sacrifice and conveys his message, to which Utu responds by asking why he needs bother

---

8   A second *Gilgamesh and Huwawa* story may be counted as a fifth, but for the sake of this discussion the differences between them are not important.

9   And each of these stories has multiple versions deriving from different places. Sometimes there is considerable divergence between them, so it is difficult to discuss any given story in detail because those details vary. Sumerological tradition has always chosen one text, usually the most complete, as the basic, or original, or correct version, with all the others considered not just variants but deviants. However, John Lynch (2010) has demonstrated that each version of a story must be treated as an entity unto itself and dealt with on its own terms. Some are thereby revealed to be pretty exact copies, others to tell a significantly different story. This of course complicates attempts to have a general discussion as to the meaning of a text, as does the fact that there is often considerable discrepancy in translations of the Sumerian. I have chosen here to follow the versions published by Oxford University's invaluable Electronic Text Corpus of Sumerian Literature at http://www-etcsl.orient.ox.ac.uk/ (Black et al. 1998–2006), for several reasons. It renders this material accessible to everyone, and the reader of this book can easily follow the discussion along with the texts from this website; not only that, but the lines click back to the transliteration, and as the cursor passes over each word in transliteration, the root and definition of that word is given so that the reader can access the basic argumentation behind a translation; in so doing, it fulfills the best aim of the scholarly endeavor in accomplishing such outreach. In addition, as a joint undertaking that was for some time revised and adjusted (the project is now closed), engagement with the community of Sumerologists has rendered some degree of consensus in translation notwithstanding criticism of individual readings. There is also a published version of these translations to be found in Black et al. 2006.

10 Gonzalez Rubio's forthcoming work *Sumerian Literary Texts from the Ur III Period* is cited in a number of sources (such as Fleming and Milstein 2010: 9, n. 24; George 2003: 7) as providing evidence of at least one exemplar from Ur III sources, but I have not had access to this work. In addition see Cavigneaux and al-Rawi 1993 for an Ur III fragment of the *Bull of Heaven*. Not altogether clear as yet is any indication that these are the same texts as those Sumerian stories recorded in the Old Babylonian period.

11 There is a second version of this story recovered from a different city. It varies in some details, and we have far fewer copies of it.

as he is already noble. Gilgamesh explains that only renown[12] will last beyond death, describing a scene of bodies floating in the river that suggests the city is in the grips of famine or disease. Utu then tells him about the seven impediments to his passage through the cedar mountains – the impediments are the powers of the guardian of the forest, Huwawa (different versions of the story describe them as "warriors," "terrors," or "auras") – and how to disarm them. Utu presumably thinks Gilgamesh plans to harvest the massive cedar trees that grow in this area, but Gilgamesh perhaps already has other plans, for what could bring him more renown than destroying the supernatural being Huwawa?

Huwawa is portrayed as a monster by Gilgamesh – and also in various images recovered from the ancient world – yet he is understood by the gods as a divinely appointed otherworldly being who should not be harmed. But harmed he is. Gilgamesh calls for a bevy of young men to accompany him on this journey, those with no personal attachments to be left in distress if anything should happen to the menfolk – bachelors like Gilgamesh himself – and they all set off, eventually to arrive at their destination. Gilgamesh and Enkidu start chopping down the cedars, thereby disturbing Huwawa who comes out of his lair and looses his powers upon the interlopers. Gilgamesh and Enkidu both lose consciousness. Enkidu comes to first, prodding Gilgamesh to wake up. When he does, he is furious, refusing to turn toward home until he has taken his vengeance. Enkidu tries to persuade him from such a plan, but Gilgamesh is not to be deterred, arguing that together they will be invincible. Enkidu is still afraid, but Gilgamesh confronts Huwawa and, although shaking in his boots, begs to become Huwawa's kinsman, which presumably would then establish the rules, rights, and obligations of their future interaction. The way kinship is to be accomplished here is through two gifts: Gilgamesh's sisters and special foods.

It is all a trick, of course. After seducing Huwawa into handing over his powers one by one, each in the form of a cedar tree, Gilgamesh attacks him and ties him up. Huwawa reveals himself as pitiable, for he has no family, and when he calls upon Utu to help him, his main complaint is that family is just what Gilgamesh promised, and then denied, him. Gilgamesh is overcome with compassion and decides to set Huwawa free. But now Enkidu steps in, pointing out that a vanquished enemy is not to be trusted, and when Gilgamesh doesn't listen to him, he steps forward and dispatches Huwawa with a swift blow to the throat.

Huwawa is not the only supernatural being destroyed by these two characters, however. In another story, Gilgamesh takes on the Bull of Heaven. Again, Gilgamesh turns his eyes to the mountains, from whence he will bring all the goods that will enrich Sumer – cattle and sheep, metals and jewels – and that will make him famous. But the story actually starts, after a prologue that situates

---

12 Fleming and Milstein (2010: 183–4) translate this as "I will set up my name," which has provocative overtones of the practice of establishing commemorative stelae.

it within the performative context of a song about the great Gilgamesh, with Inana, the goddess of war and sex, with whom Gilgamesh has more than one run-in. It is unclear, due to the condition of the tablet, what her problem may be, but she waylays Gilgamesh[13] on his way to the temple – her temple – where he will act as judge. There is some sense of competition in the exchange that follows, with Gilgamesh promising not to exceed his bounds, but, speaking "with a snort,"[14] Inana does not seem to believe him. The implication appears to be that Gilgamesh has become so great that he threatens the power of Inana herself, for Uruk is her city. She asks An, her father, to give her the Bull of Heaven so that she may use it to kill Gilgamesh. An does not want to concede, as the bull will leave giant cowpats everywhere and besides he will die from hunger as he cannot graze on earth. Inana then behaves like a spoilt child, screaming with anger, and An gives in. She takes the bull to Uruk, Gilgamesh's home, where it wreaks havoc. Gilgamesh threatens to kill the bull, humiliate it, and feed it to the widow's sons, which he then proceeds to do. He butchers the beast and with utter disrespect throws a haunch at Inana; then he strikes her, and she flees. No wonder she hates him. At the same time though, the horns of the Bull of Heaven are dedicated to Inana in her temple. Perhaps this is a statement of Gilgamesh's power: he is so great that he can dispose of Inana's own property as he likes, and in offering it back to her is further insulting her. But it seems more likely that in resuming his attentions to Inana in the temple and making her a gift of the emblem of his might, he is reconciled with her.

In *Gilgamesh, Enkidu and the Netherworld*, in contrast, Gilgamesh helps Inana when she has problems with a tree – a very special tree. In this story, the action is not presented as a song in the manner of a praise poem, but is set long, long ago, in original times, when the correct and proper order of the world was established. This story, too, is about power, for the tree that Inana saves from a primordial storm is the **halub** tree[15] – the *axis mundi*, the tree that connects all planes of

---

13   George (2003:11) notes that an unpublished tablet makes it clear this is to bring him to bed, as is indeed the case in the later version. And as in the later version, he refuses her advances, to his cost.

14   Black et al. 1998–2008, line 19, http://etcsl.orinst.ox.ac.uk/cgibin/etcsl.cgi?text=t.1.8.1.2&charenc=j#.

15   See Gadotti 2005 for a comprehensive discussion of the various approaches to this tree. She (2005: 78–80) notes that in the third millennium the **halub** tree was associated with a place called Gubin, and that Gubin seems to have been mountainous, located somewhere south of Mesopotamia, and that the wood from there was used to make divine statues. As will be seen below, this relationship with mountains is quite important. In the Ur III period, however, at the end of the third millennium, it was not uncommon for **halub** wood to be made into parts of furniture in conjunction with precious metals (Gadotti 2005: 82–4), which suggests that **halub** items were not for the everyday, notwithstanding that leftover pieces were used to make smaller objects such as trays and cups (because, of course, ritual activities use special vessels). The fruit of the **halub** tree was used in offerings before the **du₆-kù**. **Du₆** has a number of religious significances in its various combinations. It is the

existence. Inana replants the tree in her garden, a clear appropriation of the fundamental elements that constitute the cosmos, but she cannot bend it to her will. She cannot cut it down and fashion it as she likes into furniture that she makes, owns, and controls,[16] because denizens of the otherworlds (the snake, the ghost of a young woman, and the Anzud bird) become embedded in the very structure of the tree as it grows. She asks Utu to help her, but he refuses. She turns to Gilgamesh, here called her brother, and he obliges. He kills the snake, drives out the girl and the bird, and, much as with the cedars, cuts down the tree and strips its branches, this time giving them to Inana for her furniture. But the roots Gilgamesh kept for himself, making a pair of objects, the **pukku** and **mekkû**, terms that no one has ever quite been able to interpret.[17] Whatever they may be, they seem to have been used in a game, one that Gilgamesh carries to extremes and for which he seems to be punished when one of the objects falls down into the netherworld. Of course, the object is made from the roots of the tree which themselves were entwined with the netherworld. For most readers it is from this point on that the significance of the story starts, with the focus now turned to the netherworld and Gilgamesh's supposed encounter with his own mortality, for he sends his servant Enkidu down to retrieve the object. Enkidu fails to follow the advice given him to extricate himself and appears to be stuck there.

But I do not think it is quite that simple. It is Gilgamesh's assistance of Inana's grab for power, his own appropriation of some of that power, and the particular nature of its locus that are the start of the problem. Indeed, the passage where Gilgamesh is described as playing with the objects made from the **halub** tree seem to indicate that he is mad with power:

> He played with the ball (?) in the broad square, never wanting to stop playing it, and he praised himself in the broad square, never wanting to stop praising himself.... . For (?) him who made the team of the widows' children —, they lamented: "O my neck! O my hips!" ... But early in the morning as he —, the place marked, the widows' accusation and the young girls' complaint caused his

holy mound, an altar (Gadotti 2005: 95), and a burial mound (Richardson 2007). Finally, **halub** wood is deployed in incantations. All these attestations of the use of the wood confirm, I think, its function, whether oak or cherry tree, as a religious symbol, as indeed does its mention in a mortuary ritual dating to the Ur III period (Katz 2007: 176).

16   Because there are attestations in administrative texts that **halub** wood is used for certain kinds of furniture, it should not be thought that that means Inana's desire for a chair and a bed here is purely practical. Mesopotamian literature, in both Sumerian and Akkadian, is riddled with symbolism and full of references that, while completely opaque to us, obviously had meaning to its audience, something we too often forget. So the reader or listener to this story knew exactly what kind of furniture was made from **halub** wood, what it was used for, and what its significance was, which added additional layers to the tale and to Inana's actions.

17   They are now usually described as a ball and mallet, although there seem to be unquestionable phallic overtones to these terms (Cooper 2002; Walls 2001).

ball (?) and his mallet (?) to fall down to the bottom of the nether world. (Black et al. 1998–2006: t.1.8.1.4, lines 151–165)

As is usually the case, Gilgamesh petitions one god to help him, who ignores him, so he asks another, Enki, who agrees to help. Enkidu is brought back to the world of the living, and Gilgamesh, full of curiosity, asks him about the nature of the netherworld, as anybody would. Enkidu does not want to tell him at first, supposedly because it is so hideous, but as he describes the situation of various people it becomes clear that, if one dies in the proper circumstances, one's lot in the next life is actually quite fine. The essential condition for a proper death is to have enough offspring to guarantee that the commemorative mortuary rites will always be performed. While it is generally assumed that this is to ensure that the dead will always be provisioned with the necessary sustenance, the fact that renown is an adequate substitute for children, which is why Gilgamesh seeks it in other stories, indicates that it is memory that is essential. One exists in perpetuity in memory. The greater the deeds, the longer the memory.

Gilgamesh, Enkidu and the Netherworld is a complicated text for many reasons, not least of which is the number of versions and degree of variance between versions (and see Gadotti 2005; Lynch 2010 for details). It has been interpreted as portraying a significantly different approach to death than is seen in the other text on this topic, *The Death of Gilgamesh*, but in fact it does not. In this latter story Gilgamesh dreams he is dying and despairs. Even though he is powerful like a god and his mother is a god, he nevertheless is destined for the netherworld. But his advisers point out that, on the one hand, he knows that death is the outcome of being born and, on the other, there is a well-established way of dealing with it – the practice of ancestor traditions. I should note that Enkidu in this story is presented as a "comrade" rather than as a servant, and the advisers mention him as a kind of enticement to Gilgamesh – when Gilgamesh is in the netherworld he will be reunited with Enkidu. This is the first intimation of a relationship between the two that transcends master and servant.

All three texts, including *Gilgamesh and Huwawa*, portray commemoration as the basis of the afterlife, and confirm that if one has no children then fame is another route to it. In one ending of *Gilgamesh, Enkidu and the Netherworld*, a clear link is made to *Gilgamesh and Huwawa*. In another version of the ending, Gilgamesh apparently realizes that he has neglected his own ancestors and they are suffering in the netherworld, so he makes statues of them before which the proper ancestor practices can be performed (George 2003: 14). In one version of *The Death of Gilgamesh*, the fact that existence after death is a function of memory is made explicit, and again statues of the ancestors are mentioned. The story of Huwawa is connected to the story of Enkidu in the netherworld and that of Gilgamesh's death in another way, too. The mountains to which

Gilgamesh ventures are not just territory beyond the ken of Sumer, because **kur** is the place of the netherworld and this is of ongoing significance in all the Sumerian literature, as will be seen below. There is a level on which the whole story of Huwawa evokes at the least undertones of dealing with the demons of death, if it is not an actual allegory for it. Huwawa, of course, is not the god of the netherworld, but that these kinds of parallels would be raised in the mind of the reader/listener is obvious.

The underlying meanings, heavy symbolism, and allegorical nature of much of this material are often understated, but it must be remembered that these are but pieces of a larger cultural whole in which the original recipients of this material were deeply embedded. All three texts also share another and somewhat more mundane feature: power. In *Gilgamesh and Huwawa* and in *Gilgamesh, Enkidu and the Netherworld*, it is the jostling for power, wresting it even from the gods, that is the center of the narrative; in *The Death of Gilgamesh* that contest proves all for naught. Gilgamesh might have become powerful like the gods, he may be part god, yet he lacks the one thing they have – immortality. Nevertheless, it is not a fear of death that is portrayed in this text so much as it is the realization that Gilgamesh's quest to be one of the gods, to possess the one thing that separates them from a very talented humanity, has ultimately failed, so at the same time this text also deals with the problem of why, since he is part divine, he nevertheless dies, and as such is an ontological problem, not a humanistic one. Even in death, though, Gilgamesh occupies a unique place at the head of all the dead, becoming judge of the underworld.

If death and the afterlife are viewed as the connecting theme to these tales – as the basis of a Gilgamesh "cycle" (Gadotti 2005) – the exception is *Gilgamesh and Aga*. Aga, king of Kish, sends to Uruk envoys whose task it is to tell that city to submit to the hegemony of its northern neighbor. Gilgamesh meets with the assembly of the city, the city's elders, and argues that they should reject such demands and attack Kish. The assembly takes some persuading, but eventually they give in. Aga then besieges Uruk. One of Gilgamesh's soldiers volunteers to fight Aga in man-to-man combat, but before he can challenge Aga, the soldier is captured and beaten. He still has the strength to tell Aga of Gilgamesh's beauty and might, which is so great that just the sight of him is enough to cast down armies of thousands. Such is the case when Aga does indeed lay eyes on him (although, presumably given the rest of the story, he has in fact seen him before). Aga is captured, but instead of killing him Gilgamesh shows mercy and releases him because Aga had in the past given Gilgamesh refuge when he was a fugitive. Thus, as well as physically powerful, Gilgamesh is a man who honors his debts. Although *Gilgamesh and Aga* differs from the other three stories in a number of ways – it is the only tale in which there is no mention of Enkidu, and the story is not about a heroic exploit (there is no mention of Gilgamesh's military action, for example) – it shares with *Gilgamesh and Huwawa* the idea of clemency. And it shares with all stories this foundational issue of power. In this case it is the power of Gilgamesh's own person: his beauty, his strength, and his justice.[18]

Several of these themes – and exploits – are taken up in the next major version of the Gilgamesh story at our disposal, the one compiled in the Old Babylonian period, written in Akkadian, and called the "epic" of Gilgamesh.[19] This is an altogether more complicated story. It takes some aspects of the accounts outlined above but not others, and it combines them with completely different portrayals not only of Gilgamesh, but also of Enkidu, who now becomes Gilgamesh's equal and opposite. Now they are partners in adventure, if not crime (although given some of their acts against the cosmic order this is not inappropriate), and the nature of their relationship is something of a "bromance" (in current parlance) whether or not there is any homoerotic subtext (Cooper 2002; Walls 2001).

The story as it is generally accessed is put together from fragments of a number of recensions. It is also often supplemented with materials from the version assembled, and canonized, in twelve tablets in the next millennium (see, for example, Dalley 1998) on the grounds that the original basis of the first-millennium epic was actually the second-millennium version. George (2003) puts forward all the extant Old Babylonian pieces, while Fleming and Milstein (2010), in examining two of those pieces, the one known as the Yale tablet and the one known as the Penn(sylvania) tablet, reveal that between the Sumerian-language stories and the epic there is an intermediary phase, constituted by a stand-alone Akkadian version of the Huwawa story. That phase, however, is attested only as it was adopted into the larger narrative. Although the Yale tablet, which gives the story of Huwawa, follows on from the Penn tablet, which describes the meeting between Gilgamesh and Enkidu, and appears even to have been written down by the same hand (George 2003: 159), the language describing Enkidu is considerably different (Fleming and Milstein 2010). One tablet uses terminology that describes wild animals; the other, domesticated herds. According to Fleming and Milstein (2010: 11), Enkidu is wild, raised among the beasts in the Penn tablet, while in the Yale tablet he is a shepherd; in Penn, he is transformed by sex with the woman Shamhat so as to bring him into the human world; in Yale, since he has never been apart from it, no such rite of passage is necessary. In Penn, and as so aptly put by Fleming and Milstein, Enkidu is Gilgamesh's passion; in Yale he is only his partner.

---

18 It also ties in with the Sumerian King List in its ideas about regional primacy and the competition for kingship.

19 Although I do not think "epic" an appropriate label, I will maintain it as a means of distinguishing the compilation of the larger story from its component pieces, especially since all extant versions of the Gilgamesh stories other than the Standard Babylonian, whether in Akkadian or Sumerian, were written down in this period, so to refer to it as the Old Babylonian version is both confusing and erroneous in that they are *all* Old Babylonian in date.

However, if the Yale tablet was merely the reconstitution in Akkadian of the earlier Sumerian tale of the defeat of Huwawa, it would not be of concern to my discussion, which would then focus only on the Penn account. But although there is a sense that the Old Babylonian epic is in some essential ways the compilation and framing of the Sumerian stories (considered by many the originals [Tigay 1982]), even though it is not a translation of them, there are some fundamental differences between the Babylonian and Sumerian stories that warrant a slightly different perspective. And these differences lie in the nature of Enkidu. In addition to Penn calling him wild and Yale calling him steppic is the fact that in both tablets Enkidu is no longer Gilgamesh's servant but a being from a world outside Uruk, however that world is defined. In both tablets he is a fully drawn character, a counterpart to Gilgamesh and not just a subordinate. Therefore the epic has to be treated as its own, independent story, with its own meaning and intent, even if the writer drew on an earlier story at certain points for details. It is for this reason that I diverge slightly from Fleming and Milstein (2010: 5) in seeing not the portrayal of the Huwawa story as the main focus of the epic, but the redefinition of the characters of Gilgamesh and Enkidu as the raison d'être behind this new story – for new I think it is. Rather than a recasting of the Huwawa story by the addition of a new prologue, it is the narrative of the Penn tablet that is the starting point for this scribe, and the Huwawa story that is added in by drawing on the Akaddian, rather than Sumerian, prototype.

The following summary of the story is based on the Fleming and Milstein (2010) translation but with my own interpretative inflection. What is left to us of the Old Babylonian epic starts with Gilgamesh awaking from a dream in which something fell from the skies, a dream that he relates to his mother. His mother, Ninsun, tells Gilgamesh that the something is a someone – someone just like him but who is born in the steppe and raised in the highlands (the two ends of a transhumant pastoralist cycle, and one entirely appropriate to the Mesopotamian landscape). Gilgamesh has a second dream, this time of an axe that, when he saw it, gave him great joy; he loved it like a wife and set it by his side. His mother presumably informs him as to the meaning of this dream too, but since the tablet is broken at this point, all we know is that this someone will be Gilgamesh's rival.[20] Meanwhile, Enkidu is immersed in seven days of sexual activity with Shamhat, who brings him to the shepherd's hut as a kind of halfway house, where he learns human habits. While Enkidu is there (and still with Shamhat, although now presumably purely for fun and not for any transformative potential), a man passes by on his way to a wedding. He explains to Enkidu the city's practice of droit de seigneur, which upsets Enkidu

---

20 George (2003: 175, col. II, line 43) reads here "equal," although in Column V, line 195 the respective translations are reversed, with Fleming and Milstein using "equal" and George, "rival."

and prompts him to go to Uruk. When he arrives there he draws a crowd, which compares him to Gilgamesh, and once more their parity is established. Enkidu confronts Gilgamesh as he would enter the bride's bedchamber, and the two wrestle. Interestingly, Gilgamesh cedes. He takes a knee and then turns away. Enkidu speaks to him, praising him (one would assume, profusely!). It is from here that the Yale tablet picks up, but its beginning is damaged. It does seem, however, as if Gilgamesh and Enkidu are making plans. The next thing that is sure is Enkidu's fear, and it is probably in response to Gilgamesh's outline of the plan to attack Huwawa, which he then repeats. Enkidu remembers Huwawa from his time in the highlands and knows how terrible he is. Gilgamesh, however, is irritated by his friend's concern, and Enkidu gives in. They have weapons forged and they tell the elders of Uruk what they plan. The elders also think it a foolhardy undertaking and advise against it. Gilgamesh has his way.

Other tablets now provide the narrative of the actual encounter, which, although not written by this same scribe, is most likely to represent, in its broadest details at least, a facsimile of what the "epic" would have contained. Schøyen tablet 2 conveys a series of dreams and begins with the peerless pair asleep on their way to meet Huwawa. This time it is Gilgamesh's turn to be afraid, and Enkidu's to urge him on. Three times this happens; three times Enkidu reveals to Gilgamesh that one of the gods is with them on this venture. Then Enkidu himself succumbs to fear and it is Gilgamesh who no longer hangs back. Finally, the tablet from Ishchali describes the deed. Somehow Huwawa's auras are negated and together Gilgamesh and Enkidu slay him.

The multiplicity of stories about Gilgamesh and Enkidu is an important starting point for understanding the Amorrites. A more traditional approach would no doubt begin with what are considered historical texts, such as the royal inscriptions or onomastic patterns (such as Buccellati 1966 or Streck 2000) where names with Amorrite linguistic elements are traced over time and space. And these are certainly central to reconstructing the story, as will be seen later. But the literary materials are equally important for two reasons. One, particular passages from them have been powerfully influential in shaping our picture of the Amorrites, their relationship to pastoralism, their external origins, and the views of others toward them; two, when taken as a whole, certain features become evident in the literary production of the Ur III/Old Babylonian periods that are not seen when isolated literary texts are here and there inserted into an historical reconstruction.

This is not to say that my task here is to extract history from literature, as used to be a common practice in Assyriology but is now, rightly, criticized (Liverani 1993; Veldhuis 2004). Rather, the task is to treat these stories as literature, recognizing that the production of literature has an historical dimension. Literary theory today allows for many analytical approaches to text, all of which, by focusing on different aspects of writing, storytelling, and reading, offer valuable insight (cf. Black 1998: 42–9). One may read a story written at any time, in any place, with no knowledge of its context, and still understand it, or at least one layer of it. Context, however, brings another dimension to text because no writing is ever produced in isolation. Writers are themselves products of their environment, so the views of the world they present, the ideas they convey, intentionally or otherwise, are influenced by that environment, just as readers are shaped by their own time, situation, and experience in ways that inflect how they receive the text. At this distance we have to work hard to glimpse double meanings, cultural referents, symbols, and puns, and assuredly miss most,[21] whereas they would be immediately clear to a contemporaneous audience.

Moreover, when the production of texts is so tightly contained in very specific and limited settings, those settings perforce shape the text. Much has been revealed in this regard by understanding the schoolroom contexts of most of the earlier copies of Mesopotamian literature that survive (Veldhuis 2006; Tinney 1999a; Delnero 2006), but those contexts were themselves situated within larger contexts – the politics of the administrative system that trained and employed scribes. While I certainly do not wish to argue that context is the only consideration in approaching literature, I do claim that it is an important one, a source of some information that has bearing on the meaning of the text for the audience of the text's time, whatever the meaning of the text for the audience of *this* time, and that therefore context should not be ignored. The line between drawing historical information from a text and reading a text in light of historical information is fine, but it is one that can be satisfactorily navigated.

Furthermore, since texts are certainly susceptible to multiple readings (and contingent meanings at that), at least one of those multiple readings is provided by understanding the author's intent; another is provided by understanding the factors that shape the author's intent and that shape the text beyond intent – factors that include context, especially the dialogic relationship between texts. If one reads the story of Gilgamesh standing alone, the portrayal of a dual Mesopotamian world, one divided between steppe and city, is clear enough in the separate and contrasted origins of the two characters and in the situations in which the interdependence of the one with the other is asserted, although the meaning of that division is certainly less clear. If one considers this story in the context of its supposedly earlier precursors, namely the five Sumerian stories of Gilgamesh, the nature of the Old Babylonian characters is startling, in that they become exactly that – characters, with emotions, histories, and aspirations.

I am hardly the first to remark upon the dramatic differences in Gilgamesh and Enkidu from one set of stories to the next, or on the difference in the nature

---

21 See Noegel 1996: 170, n.s. 6, 7 for a bibliography of work on wordplay; also Alster 2002 and Vanstiphout 1996. More generally, see Michalowski 1996 for the nature of Sumerian poetry; also Black 1998.

of the texts themselves, or even on the relationship between historical events – the emergence of the Amorrites – and these changes. But those differences pose some serious questions in light of the understanding of the relationship between pastoralism and polity proposed in this work. If, as I have argued, pastoralists were not separate and external entities to the urbanized world of the Near East in the fourth to second millennia BCE, with a fundamentally different form of social organization, and if the Amorrites were pastoralists, why is it that one aspect of the Old Babylonian story is the iteration of the essential and necessary unity of the steppe and city? It clearly speaks to a situation where there is, in some way, at least a *perceived* division between these two arenas, established by the very efforts to present a case for the opposite. The worlds of the city and the steppe are contrasted, and by no means only in favor of the city. Indeed, the dual nature of Gilgamesh himself – part human, mostly god – can be seen as "ambiguation," the (re)creation of an earlier ideal (Bernbeck 2008b: 158).[22] So the distinctions are in fact perpetuated at the same time as they would be negated, and it appears they are perpetuated by the very people one might think would not see themselves in this way – the Amorrites. Again, we arrive at this idea that the Amorrites are somehow different and apart and, what is more, that they so positioned themselves.[23]

How and why do we end up with this picture? There are two ways to develop the answer to this question. The first is through the contextualization of the neo-Sumerian stories;[24] the second, through discussion of the Old Babylonian versions of Gilgamesh in Akkadian. These two different ways of seeing, and telling, the stories of Gilgamesh and Enkidu constitute a debate with one another. The stories do not simply belong to the inhabitants of separate cultural spheres who view the world so differently that they inevitably, and unthinkingly, produce different versions of a well-known tale. There is no Gilgamesh norm[25] from which all other versions are deviations. Each story is a specific act of composition or compilation with specific reasons for its production.

---

22 It is not quite clear to me in this passage whether Bernbeck attributes the origins of the story to an actual early, sociopolitical egalitarian period in Mesopotamian history, when he says the story is "a typical tale from an era 'before difference,' before the appearance of difference in the world," or whether it is to a mythical one.

23 For an informative study of the relationship between mobile identity and literary narratives, see Bettini 2006.

24 The term "neo-Sumerian" is used to indicate that, while the Third Dynasty of Ur represents a resurgence of Sumerian culture, this is not because this was an original Sumerian-speaking population reclaiming their throne, but rather an adoption of an earlier culture and language. Good arguments have been presented (e.g., Rubio 2006b) to the effect that Sumerian had died out by the late third millennium. Shulgi, for one, did not speak Sumerian as his native tongue but as a second language if we are to take the praise-hymns that extol his mastery of foreign languages (Klein 1981) at face value.

25 Contra George 2003: 4, n. 3, where he states it is "clear that the second millennium [Gilgamesh] was characterized by a profusion of deviant texts."

The question is: what do the differences between one version and another tell us about those reasons?[26]

At the least, the Old Babylonian production is an appropriation of an established literary trope used as a vehicle through which to tell a story of consequence to its writers. This is a common habit for Mesopotamian writers: characters, themes, tropes, even direct quotations appear and reappear in various stories (see Katz 2007: 171, n. 20). Sometimes this might serve as a kind of shorthand: the audience – reader or listener – knows exactly what they are supposed to think when they receive these set pieces, so the writer does not have to say much else on the topic. Sometimes it might be to prime the audience, as it were, to render them receptive to what comes next, a way to sneak in something new and provocative. Sometimes it may shake them out of their conditioning. In any of these cases, the literary practice of appropriation is a manipulation of the recipient to further a calculated end. Gilgamesh and Enkidu, then, are known characters through whom multiple stories may be told, characters – even when not characterized – who are not subordinate to the specific narrative of their exploits, but stand on their own, somewhat akin to the English figures of Punch and Judy. Certain basic story lines are expected, certain dynamics are in play, but the details and outcomes vary with each telling or performance, just as over the four-hundred-year history of this puppetry the characters of Punch and Judy themselves, and their social role, have undergone significant changes.

But the Old Babylonian "epic" of Gilgamesh is also a direct answer to the view of the world presented in the neo-Sumerian stories, and understanding the origins of either worldview places us in a difficult, and unusual, methodological and theoretical fix, because we cannot simply turn to the history of the respective periods to find the answer. Both the Sumerian and the Babylonian materials come to us from the same place in time, and sometimes from the same space. They were recovered from scribal schools of the Old Babylonian period and are now interpreted as teaching materials. It is usually assumed that the Sumerian stories are all older than the context in which they were found, dating at the very latest to the Third Dynasty of Ur, and were simply preserved by the practice of copying. If it were not for the one or two Sumerian fragments from Ur III contexts that concern Gilgamesh[27] we would have no direct evidence of this, and we cannot know if the stories as written then were the same as those "copied" in the Old Babylonian period. As Fleming and Milstein (2010) have demonstrated, the Old Babylonian versions themselves share small but very significant differences in terminology that render both new contexts and new meaning to the separate sources. Furthermore, the Sumerian texts were long believed to be relics of the

---

26 Therefore, the diachronic dimension to interpretation that Cooper 1996: 52 argues is necessary if we are to understand what each version of a text means is indeed crucial to my task in this chapter.

27 See note 10 above.

original Sumerian culture of the Early Dynastic period[28] rather than the production of the neo-Sumerian world of the Third Dynasty of Ur, which would also accord them vastly different content, meaning, and purpose. While there may be indications that Gilgamesh was known in the Early Dynastic period as a mythical or literary character (if almost certainly not an historical one[29]), it bears repeating that we know nothing of any story itself, and so can only understand the stories we actually have, in the time and place we find them.

Take the tales of Enmerkar, for example, also written in Sumerian and recovered from the same find-spots as the other Sumerian texts. Forming a coherent story cycle, four narratives relate the exploits of this king known from the Sumerian King List (Vanstiphout 2004). The two Lugalbanda stories – *Lugalbanda in the Mountain Cave* and *Lugalbanda and the Anzud Bird* – are but halves of the same tale. The story of Lugalbanda takes place within the framing device of Enmerkar's war with Aratta, which is the subject of the tale of *Enmerkar and the Lord of Aratta*. The relationship of both Enmerkar and Aratta with Inana forms part of the driving narrative, but although this seems incongruous in the Lugalbanda stories, it is fully explicated in the Enmerkar ones. Both kings thought themselves chosen by the goddess – which can only be interpreted as a claim to Sumerian-ness, because through the texts of Sumer Inana is known to us as *the* Sumerian goddess. It is obvious that the messenger in the Enmerkar stories becomes Lugalbanda himself, although he is not named at that point, and it is in *Enmerkar and the Lord of Aratta* that the significance of the **mesh** tree and Anzud bird is established.

But while the two Lugalbanda tales follow in narrative sequence, and the two Aratta tales follow in narrative sequence (although the perspective shifts from Uruk to Aratta),[30] the Aratta and Lugalbanda tales do not, although the listener/reader gains more from Lugalbanda if he or she knows Aratta. Whether or not Enmerkar was an historic king, and whether or not Early Dynastic tales concerning his conflict with Aratta once existed (and I sincerely doubt it, for reasons that will become clear below), these tales as we now have them are clearly a product of later times (Cooper 1993b). This is established alone by the anachronistic mention of Mardu in two of them, so that they cannot therefore be faithful copies of an Early Dynastic original. In the absence of any

---

28 See, for example, Cooper 1993b.

29 The Sumerian King List was originally taken as an historical document, but see now Michalowski (1983) and Steinkeller (2003), who demonstrate that it is at best history manipulated to an end. See also Michalowski 2006b for a discussion of the Tumal text, in which the name Gilgamesh is written, where it too is recognized as a school text associated with Ur III materials.

30 Although Vanstiphout (2004) places *Enmerkar and En-Suhgir-ana* first, this story is clearly a continuation of *Enmerkar and the Lord of Aratta*, for after Aratta is saved from defeat at the end of it by the breaking of the drought, En-Suhgir-ana gets carried away by his own ego, taking the war back to Enmerkar and thus prompting his own defeat.

earlier versions we do best to start with the premise, until demonstrated other-wise, that the *whole* story cycle was made up at that time.[31] When these stories are considered as a product of the later period rather than the earlier one, a whole range of new meanings come to light and various anomalies (that are otherwise confounding) dissolve.

One approach, therefore, would be to consider the debate between the Sumerian and Old Babylonian versions of Gilgamesh as contemporaneous – as between two bodies of work in different languages produced at the same time – on the grounds that each version is not merely a copy of an earlier text but understood to be produced at the time we have their extant versions. While there may well be earlier versions of the neo-Sumerian stories dating to the Ur III or Early Dynastic period, and earlier versions of the Old Babylonian story dat-ing to the Akkadian period (or whenever), in certain ways of approaching text this is irrelevant in the absence of those versions. At the very least, as Veldhuis (2002: 128) observes,[32] we cannot be sure that the Old Babylonian versions of earlier works are exact copies uninflected by the concerns of the copyists, and, as Delnero (2007: 110) points out, neither preservation nor reproduction was in fact the purpose of these texts. They constituted a way of teaching Sumerian language and cuneiform writing, so faithful rendition of an original was not their goal. It is certainly clear that in some circumstances at least, scribes felt free to change aspects of the stories for their own purposes or, perhaps, at the behest of a higher authority. Divergent versions of a number of texts, recov-ered from two different places but presumably dating to the same time, from the tale of *Gilgamesh and Huwawa* to the literary letters of Shulgi, show signifi-cant differences in meaning (Tinney 1999b: 45; Lynch 2010),[33] and when ver-sions of stories *are* found from different points in time, it becomes clear that "Mesopotamian literature was not static, but continued to develop and change" (Michalowski 1976: 8). Perhaps composition was also part of the curriculum. Perhaps various genres of literary endeavor had a store of stock templates that were then taken and adapted to specific circumstances. The texts as we have them should therefore stand on their own terms and not on the basis of some supposed situation.

If one were to take this position, the Sumerian stories and the Akkadian stories might perhaps each represent a specific section of Mesopotamian soci-ety at that time with its own worldview. The juxtaposition of text and language might represent exactly what it appears to – a contest between Sumerians and Akkadians – if the Third Dynasty of Ur was actually a resurgence of a Sumerian

---

31   In fact, as will be seen later in my own story, Aratta itself is part and parcel of a set of polit-ical issues that are of prime significance in a specific time period.

32   Brisch (2007: 20) also observes that scribes were perfectly able to change original versions of royal texts.

33   See below for the Puzur-Shulgi correspondence.

population repressed by the Akkadians, an idea few subscribe to now. In fact, this use of Sumerian is argued to represent an appropriation of an older cultural complex by usurpers as a way of denying the validity of those overthrown and distancing their memory (but cf. Woods 2006). Ishbi-Erra, the first ruler of the Isin dynasty that emerged out of the collapsing Ur III empire and once a functionary of the last Ur III ruler, immediately adopted Akkadian rather than Sumerian for his building inscriptions (Michalowski 2005a: 200),[34] postulated as a sure way of distinguishing himself from his predecessors. But Ishbi-Erra may have been an Amorrite, and his literary reputation, at least, accords him a Mari origin (Michalowski 1995), although this is highly problematic due to the nature of the source. Descriptions of Ishbi-Erra appear in the Sumerian so-called literary letters, which contain so many anomalies that it is hard to know how to contextualize them properly. It is not at all clear at this point whether Ishbi-Erra is situated as an outsider by himself/his supporters, by his opposition, or quite arbitrarily. This, in conjunction with the introduction of the new elements to the Gilgamesh story outlined above – especially the presence of Enkidu in the steppe, a place supposedly equally outside the traditional Sumerian landscape – broadens the dimensions of the problem so that the factions under consideration would seem most likely to be Sumerians and Amorrites.

But what of the Akkadians? If the Sumerians are overthrown at the end of the Third Dynasty of Ur, surely the Akkadians are in contention for their own resurgence? In this scenario, the Akkadians would write in Sumerian, while the Amorrites would write in Akkadian, and in either case the use of language would be an associative, and perhaps political, act: for the former a grasp on the past against a threat to the present, for the latter – well, there's the rub. There is just something profoundly problematic with any answer that implies Amorrites were denying wholesale their own identity and claiming someone else's through the appropriation of Akkadian language (Sanders 2006: 6), or through the reconveyance of Akkadian stories, or through any other such cultural or political process (such as Van de Mieroop 2004: 85), because such answers are based on the understanding that Amorrites, as nomads, were in some way conscious of their own inferiority. Moreover, Hallo's (2006: 88–9) suggestion that Old Babylonian scribes were preoccupied with the coming of their rulers' Amorrite ancestors hardly explains why they would insert such recognizably derogatory descriptions of them into earlier texts – and get away with it – and in addition assumes that the scribes themselves could not be Amorrite, an assumption for which there is absolutely no basis other than traditional prejudice.

---

34 Although other texts attributed to his reign are in Sumerian; see below for further discussion.

This question of language and identity is complex; the fact that there is not a single text written in Amorrite raises the question of whether such a language even existed, as the sole source for it is the delineation of a very few non-Akkadian elements in personal names (Whiting 1995: 1233; Michalowski 2006a: 162) that constitute variant spellings rather than divergences in linguistic structure. Whether this is sufficient to represent something as distinct as a language, dialect, or even colloquial variance is itself controversial, and is ultimately a theoretical rather than evidentiary problem. Views range from what has been labeled the "maximalist" position (O'Connor 2004: 462) – that these linguistic elements demonstrate the existence of an entire, independent language (Buccellati 1966, but cf. 2008: 143; Gelb 1980), the position that still dominates – through the view that those elements give evidence of dialectic variance only. In my view, the relationship between Akkadian and elements recognized as Amorrite may reflect a situation somewhat akin to the relationship between modern standard Arabic and colloquial Arabic: one is the educated language of public discourse derived from classical Arabic and used primarily for writing or formal occasions of speech; the other is the parlance of everyday life, rarely written, in which grammatical accuracy and perfect pronunciation are irrelevant, while regionalism, group identification, and fashion are not (Ingham 2006). But despite the fact that sometimes these forms may be mutually incomprehensible, they are, in the end, the same language. Huehnergard (1992: 159, 1995: 2122) argues that, given the geographical and temporal range of names incorporated under the Amorrite rubric, as well as the range of linguistic variation in the elements that identify them, it is most likely that a number of different languages are represented under this rubric. This turns out to be the case in attestations of Mardu in other regards as well, to be discussed below. Rather than different languages though, dialectical variants of Akkadian from across time and space are no doubt conflated as this thing called "Amorrite," as are references to various people and places.

Whatever one's view concerning the existence of an Amorrite language, its written absence is certainly not because people from the desert were conscious of their own inferiority and desperate to claim civilization, as traditional views have too long had it (such as Forest and Gallois 2007: 19). Nor is it sufficient to understand this as an attempt by the Amorrites to hide their external origins, to pretend they were always there, although usurpation is a particularly disturbing idea to Mesopotamian consciousness of order, despite – or perhaps because of – its frequency.

Three texts complicate things further. One, related to one of the first successfully expansionist Amorrite kings, Samsi-Addu, invokes the two great kings of Akkad, Sargon and Naram-Sin, in a list essentially understood to be a genealogy (Archi 2001: 10), although a "fake" one. The other two documents are also genealogies that claim Amorrite origins even though their subjects are, as individuals, far removed from any life as mobile pastoralists. These are the Assyrian King List[35] (hereafter AKL; Landsberger 1954: 33; Lambert 1968: 2) and the genealogy of Ammi-Saduqa, otherwise known as the Genealogy of the Hammurabi Dynasty (hereafter GHD; Charpin and Durand 1986; Charpin 2004a: 235–6). The GHD consists of a list of nineteen names followed by a list of nine more names of those known to have been previous rulers of Babylon, the city Hammurabi ruled. Seventeen of the first nineteen names are also found in the AKL and labeled as "kings who lived in tents."[36] The names are thought to be those of "tribes" – which no doubt derived from their eponymous ancestors, as is common practice today. And, as the names of tribes, these genealogies are as much geographies as anything else. They tell us about the groups that made the land of the four riverbanks their home.

This common list of kings who lived in tents is considered the "real" genealogy of Samsi-Addu subsequently deployed, strangely, in both AKL and GHD. The interspersal of tribe- and city-based legacies in these texts has caused much confusion in the decades since they were found, and attempts to reconcile what seems a rather profound duality have ranged from suggestions that it reflects the underlying sedentarization of nomadic Amorrites (Van de Mieroop 2004: 84; similarly Durand 1998: 108, for Samsi-Addu himself) to the very valid realization that ways of life – mobile pastoralism – and tribal identity are hardly synonymous and that other considerations obtain. The deployment of Samsi-Addu's genealogy in that of the descendants of Hammurabi would indicate a conception of a common ancestral origin for these kings (Charpin 2004a: 151); the deployment of the previous rulers of Babylon would indicate the legitimacy of Ammi-Saduqa's succession within the city's own historical tradition (Charpin 2004a: 235).

But there is something more. Ammi-Saduqa's genealogy precedes an invitation to *kispu*, the mortuary ritual that commemorates dead ancestors through regular feasting (Porter 2002a); a text documenting Samsi-Addu's *kispu*, found at Mari, is preceded by the allusion to genealogy in the invocation, not of the ancestors listed in the AKL but of Naram-Sin and Sargon (Charpin and Durand 1986; Durand 1992: 118–19; Durand and Guichard 1997: 64) – thus leading modern scholars to see Samsi-Addu as something of a pastoralist parvenu, an ancient social climber who casts himself as the heir to Akkad by this and other means. At the same time, his (debated)[37] origins in the city of Ekallatum, his titulary, and the particular organization of his rule have led many to see him as fundamentally more "Mesopotamian"[38] – or at the least more distant

---

35   Known in two versions, one from Khorsabad (Poebel 1942; Gelb 1954).
36   Bonechi (2001: 58) argues a similar situation for Ebla text TM.74.G.120, characterizing the distant dynastic past of Ebla kings as mobile.
37   See Chapter 1 for some of this discussion, and Charpin 2004a: 148 for more details.
38   On this topic see more below.

from his tribal origins – than that other famous Amorrite king, Zimri-Lim (Durand 1998: 107–9; Fleming 2004: 123–4). However, as argued in Chapter 1, we should understand both Samsi-Addu and Zimri-Lim as no more or less "Mesopotamian," "tribal," or "civilized" than any other king of the land of the four riverbanks.

If it was the legitimacy of the urbanized Mesopotamian world that was desired in this association, though, then the recent empire of Ur might have served this purpose as well as the more distant Akkadians. Additionally, unlike the other genealogies that provide successive lists of rulers, this document ignores the rest of Sargon's heirs, including Naram-Sin only. But the *kispu* of Samsi-Addu found at Mari (Durand and Guichard 1997: 63–70) is not in fact a genealogy as are the other texts discussed here. It is a proscription for a ritual, and as such the listing of names takes on a very different character. It is, first, conducted in the throne room of the palace. This in itself sets the ritual apart from other *kispu* that we know to be domestic/familial and conducted in houses. This one is a state ritual, conducted in a state context, not for people whom Samsi-Addu claimed as his own forebears, but for the forebears of the state, that is, *for the dead of the throne room*. Naram-Sin controlled Mari; it is not surprising, then, that his presence and that of his ancestor Sargon (who may or may not have controlled Mari [Porter 2007a] but certainly claims to have done so) is to be found in the throne room from the time of Akkadian domination (along with other significant leaders of the city), most probably in the form of a statue. Naram-Sin certainly established his continued presence in the far-flung parts of his domain by sending out statues and stelae of himself (Porter 2009b), and Durand and Guichard (1997: 43) suggested that the surprising presence at Mari of the text of *The Rebellion against Naram-Sin* might be because it formed part of a suite of materials recited in the *kispu* – in this case before effigies of Naram-Sin and Sargon. They also note that along with power in a new place comes responsibility for the cult of the preceding rulers. This, as will be seen below, is not a coincidence. I disagree, however, with Durand and Guichard's conclusion that these texts are only copies of the ritual that would have been performed at Ekallatum. As Samsi-Addu's *kispu*, which elevated it to a political and not only familial rite, it would have been performed by his sons, Isme-Dagan and Yasmah-Addu, at both Mari and Ekallatum shortly after their father's death, notwithstanding the threat of imminent attack by the forces that established Zimri-Lim on the throne soon after. Charpin (2004a: 150) notes that Yasmah-Addu in particular tied his dynastic origins to this "Akkadian" tradition.

It is, though, the juxtaposition of Naram-Sin with the Hana Yaradum (see Durand 1992: 119; Charpin 2004a) and with the Numha, another "tribal" group, that has always seemed so incongruous as to be susceptible to no other interpretation than Samsi-Addu's desire to be seen as the heir of the Akkadians – and not just politically, although one wonders, then, just why the "tribal" element was ever mentioned at all. Durand and Guichard (1997: 64) interpret this as a standard practice of placing in apposition the *political* line of descent, whatever blood relations involved, with the familial/ethnic context that one actually comes from. But there is another way of thinking about this juxtaposition: Samsi-Addu took Mari from Zimri-Lim's predecessors,[39] Yahdun-Lim and his son, the patricide Sumu-Yamam, and perhaps from his father's father, Yaggid-Lim. Yaggid-Lim is mentioned in texts found in the *shakkanaku* archive at Mari, suggesting he might have ruled there, but it has been pointed out that those tablets might have been moved to Mari when Yahdun-Lim took control (Charpin 2004a: 134). Although we know little about him, Yahdun-Lim's kingdom was quite expansive, ranging from the area of Eshnunna's control of the Euphrates to Tuttul at the confluence of the Balikh, and in competition with Samsi-Addu's kingdom at Ekallatum (Fleming 2004: 9). Numha and Hana Yaradum may represent the mobile populations of both kingdoms, united in the throne room of Mari under Samsi-Addu.[40]

It seems clear that the Numha are Samsi-Addu's people (Heimpel 2003: 18). It is not clear what the term Hana Yaradum means. Durand interprets it as those who were not indigenous to the Euphrates but migrated there, but I wonder if it does not somehow designate a larger conceptualization of Mariote pastoralists, larger even than Simalite and Yaminite. If Hana are Zimri-Lim's people (Fleming 2004: 79) then they are surely Yahdun-Lim's, and if the different generations of this family are likely to share conceptions of identity and nature of rule, then the collective nature of that rule (Fleming 2004) is such that Hana are very likely part of the ideology, if not iconography, of the throne room in some form or another – one might even propose that Hana here is the founding ancestor of the Lim family. As to why Samsi-Addu (or his son) would think it appropriate to perform a *kispu* for his enemies, people he conquered, this is in keeping with an ethos of rule that accommodates and incorporates conquered polities with a somewhat benign hand. Samsi-Addu made rulers his vassals rather than deposing them altogether (Van de Mieroop 2004: 101), tying them to him by investing in temple construction and by acknowledging local deities (Charpin 2004a: 151–2), sometimes by linking them with his own preferred divinity (van Koppen 2006: 103).

Rather than having anything to do with a spurious cultural identity, or even only political manipulation, we should think of these genealogies in a quite different way – in terms of what they do. There is a profound, and complex, multiplicity of both function and meaning here that in scholarship is divided

---

39 See Chapter 1 for a discussion of Zimri-Lim's parentage.
40 Another connection between Numha and Mari is to be seen in the fact that one of Zimri-Lim's aides was a chief of pasture over Numha and Yamutbal groups as well as Simalites (Fleming 2009: 229, nn. 12, 23).

into separate domains of study but that most certainly would not have been experienced as such by Mesopotamians themselves. In one domain, the historical, on one layer, the material, these genealogies are the attribution of a past that serves political purpose – be it to create historicity, establish alliances, obscure origins, or embed their subjects in time and space. In another domain, the anthropological, genealogies are tools of kinship – and kinship, as seen in the previous chapter, is the essence of social and political interaction. It is not that both Samsi-Addu and Ammi-Saduqa mix genealogy with *kispu*, but that *kispu* and genealogy are one and the same thing. Moreover, every change of rule is like death, a moment of great peril when boundaries are permeable and the perpetuation of the social body is threatened. Just as with death, *kispu* and other mortuary rituals are a means to repair the fabric of society, at least in part, by the creation of new relationships between all beings in the cosmos; the creation of an historical past serves to paste over the vulnerability of transition. Lambert's (1968) comment that the GDH is not an historical ancestry but a prayer to the dead used in the *kispu* misunderstands the relationship between ancestry, the dead, and history – they are inseparable (Porter 2002a). They are certainly directed toward the same ends. And they are inseparable from politics, whether as the production of identity or as legitimation (Seri 2005: 37–8; Archi 2001); historical *reality* is never the issue. *Kispu* is another means of creating kinship: it produces as it reproduces descent through action, and not just with living people via descent constructs or with the past via the dead, but with the gods and via ancestors who straddle both planes of existence.

Kings, too, mediate between human and divine worlds (Glassner 2003: 203; Michalowski 2008: 34); this is a critical part of their function and they are selected by the gods to do just that, according to many oracular and prophetic texts (Heimpel 1992: 4–21; Steinkeller 1999b: 113, n. 34; Westenholz 2007: 308; see also Charpin 2004a: 236). But their contractual obligations in this regard are not established through legal means. They are established through the same means as the obligations of the human world – by kinship – and in exactly the same way as earthly political relationships – by marriage (Cooper 1993b; Steinkeller 1999b).

Traditionally understood as ensuring fertility (Jacobsen 1975; Klein 1992, but cf. Bahrani 2002), the attestation of sacred marriage (the union of king with goddess) in a number of literary texts indicates that royal–divine relationships, especially of the Ur III period, were often expressed in what is essentially a kinship metaphor (Jones 2003), whether or not such a marriage was ever enacted (Sweet 1994). It is in the literature of this time period that Enmerkar, for example, is presented as a sexual partner of Ishtar (Cooper 1993b: 83). Royal inscriptions and hymns name various Ur III and Isin kings as "husbands of Inana" (Steinkeller 1999b: 106, n. 4), and it is only for rulers of this period that there is any evidence that the rite may have actually been performed (Steinkeller 1999b: 130). This is not coincidence. Moreover, rampant sexual imagery in hymns such as *Ur-Nammu the Canal Digger* (Tinney 1999b) and other royal literature also perpetuates this connection between kinship (in its horizontal form and in which reproduction is implicit), order and rule (Cooper 1993b: 86). Although Cooper (1993b: 89) rejects Hallo's suggestion (1987: 45–52), derived from Jacobsen, that the purpose of sacred marriage is to produce an heir and establish that heir's divine descent, his own suggestion (1993b: 90; cf. Bahrani 2002: 19–20) – that sacred marriage is about the regulation of proper relations between people and between people and the gods – is not actually mutually exclusive to these other ideas but the result of them, because there is an unquestionable interconnection between kinship ties created through marriage and the kinship of descent. In the end it is not that the *heir* is divine that is important, but that *descent* is. Just as sacrifice creates an idiom of blood enacted to create and cement newly formed kin relations (Durand and Guichard 1997; Porter n.d.), so too is sacred marriage the enactment of kinship. All these rituals have to be properly executed and appropriately established for right order to exist: "the sacred marriage functions to re-establish annually a whole set of mutual obligations between the people and the gods who have become in-laws as a result of the marriage" (Cooper 1993b: 91).

In any case, Ur III descriptions of sacred marriage are surely also about harnessing the power of Inana, one more link to otherworldly status.[41] If the king fulfills his obligations, the gods not only allow him to rule but give him the support without which he could not be successful in human terms. The onus is on humans, not on the gods, to maintain their place in, and therefore the right working of, the cosmos. The gods are under no obligation at all.[42] Here we enter the domain of the religious/philosophical (and at the same time we are back firmly in the material), with politics at the forefront and without, I hope, the cynicism that a focus on power at the expense of the philosophical so often produces. Religion, when considered in terms of power, is too often understood as the self-conscious manipulation of ideology in order to advance individual material ends; I think this is not the case here. Successful earthly rule and right cosmological order are inseparable simply because there is no separation between domains in Mesopotamian ontology and practice (also Veldhuis 2004). And what breaks right cosmological order? Usurpation.

41 Jones (2003) suggests that the sacred marriage put the king into a feminized role that showed him in a poor light because Ishtar (Inana) behaved in a masculine fashion. However, this is to ascribe a set of culturally specific gender norms to ancient Mesopotamians that I do not think is appropriate. The blurring, even shifting, nature of so-called feminine and masculine attributes is sufficiently frequent and sufficiently irreducible to positive or negative context that we may understand indigenous conceptions of gender, especially in sacred contexts, to be quite complex.

42 Although there are intimations in works such as *Atrahasis* that when the gods break contractual relationships the results are just as dire.

Cosmological order was established with the very first texts, the lists that comprise part of the archaic corpus produced at the beginnings of writing (see Chapter 2). When stories are set in the far-distant past, it is because it was at the beginning that right order was established, and that order is always reviewed (whether briefly or at length) in the introduction to such stories. It might be posited that the more egregious the transgression of order, the lengthier the prologue that invokes it. Usurpation is an affront because someone essentially severs and then steals the divine contract (Charpin 2004a: 235–7). The emphasis in titulary formulae on appellations such as "true" and "faithful," from the Early Dynastic until the Old Babylonian periods implies as much (Westenholz 2007), and the link between usurpation, such titulary, and sacred marriage is rendered quite explicit in at least one text. The reign of a nameless but "true" king commences when he crosses the threshold to the Eana of Uruk – when he goes into Inana's temple. Candidates for this king are Sin-Kashid (King of Uruk and king of the Amnanum), a usurper, and Hammurabi, a conqueror (Westenholz 2007: 309).

Much, then, must be done to restore the contract with the gods and at the same time negate the very act that broke it. From the genealogies of Samsi-Addu and Ammi-Saduqa to the Sumerian King List in both its Ur III (Steinkeller 2003) and Isin-Larsa versions (Michalowski 1983; Seri 2005: 34), as well as to (I propose) the literary compositions of the Ur III and Isin dynasties (Flückiger-Hawker 1999; cf. Berlin 1983; Veldhuis 2002; Brisch 2007: 19–22), statements of where people come from, who they are, and what the past was, are all designed[43] (and I use that word advisedly) to establish legitimacy certainly but, more than this, to make and maintain a deep embeddedness in socio-cosmological linkages formed through kinship. These linkages are understood to be the foundations of the way the world works on every plane of existence. It may be observed that almost every such episode of history-making, as these texts are, is closely related to an episode of usurpation or conquest, which is itself a form of usurpation. Any moment when the natural, established, or anticipated order is abruptly curtailed, or even visibly under threat, is a form of usurpation.

Many of these pieces are in fact competing sets of kin linkages and may be promulgated by both usurper and usurped, and it is in this light that the debate between the Sumerian and the Old Babylonian "epic" of Gilgamesh stories assumes new dimensions. Certain elements appear over and over again when the neo-Sumerian literary production of the period is considered as a whole, and it becomes clear with every iteration of those elements that there is an intended message. The key to understanding this message, to understanding

---

43 Prosopographic considerations therefore become problematic. Archaizing, and indeed modernizing (Hallo 2006: 87), were, to the scribes who knew their craft, an essential part of the task (Rubio 2006a).

why so many texts are concerned with these issues, lies in one particular story: *Lugalbanda in the Mountain Cave.*

In this story, Lugalbanda, along with his seven older brothers, leaves Uruk with the armies of Enmerkar to lay siege to Aratta. Shortly after they depart, while traveling through the mountains, Lugalbanda falls violently ill. No one can help him. So his comrades prepare him for death, leaving him in a cave in the mountains with all the appropriate accoutrements, and go on their way. Lugalbanda beseeches the gods to aid him, and they do. He emerges from the mountain cave, creates water, and hunts for food. He takes the provisions left for him, and with the animals he captures, he makes the feast for the gods that they requested of him in a dream. They join him at the wondrously elaborate banquet he has prepared. There follows a long and fragmented description of some of the denizens of the supernatural world accompanied by various incantations. Then, in *Lugalbanda and the Anzud Bird*, our hero encounters the bird that gives its name to this part of the tale and resolves to make a banquet for Anzud's family so that the bird will help him find his brothers and rejoin the troops. Again, Lugalbanda prepares a fabulous feast, and when Anzud returns he finds his baby fêted and sated. Lugalbanda and Anzud establish a warm relationship – partly because of Lugalbanda's care of the baby bird, partly because of his flattery of Anzud himself. Anzud offers Lugalbanda his choice of rewards. Lugalbanda asks for and is awarded the power of running and he is given some advice: not to reveal the fate that has been fixed for him. Lugalbanda finds his friends, appearing among them as if by a miracle. They are astonished and ashamed because they had left him for dead. Lugalbanda and the army of Enmerkar then proceed to Aratta, where they establish the siege. But it does not progress well and Enmerkar wants to send a message to his goddess, Inana, whom he fears has abandoned him in favor of Aratta; this could be the only explanation of his failure to prevail and his enemy's ability to resist. Lugalbanda volunteers, knowing that he can reach Uruk in a matter of moments. He crosses seven mountains to reach Inana. He conveys Enmerkar's message. Inana tells Lugalbanda how to conquer Aratta.

Such are the bare bones of the story. But the tale is about more, much more. It is about the past and its role in the present and the future. It is about life and death. Indeed, from the moment Lugalbanda falls ill in the mountains to the moment he rejoins his brothers in the camp of Enmerkar, the story operates as a metaphor for death in the classic tripartite formula of a "rite de passage" as outlined by van Gennep (1960 [first published 1909]) and as noted by Vanstiphout (2002: 264): "separation, transition and (re)integration, or if you prefer, the preliminary, liminary and postliminary moments." Each stage is marked by a feast, either before or after completion. The sojourn in the mountain cave is clearly the moment, the process, of separation. The transitional stage is represented by the journey through the mountains, and the rather feverish description of

Lugalbanda's companions here, the spirits and demons, surely denotes denizens of a dark and shadowy liminal place. The arrival at the tree of the Anzud bird – which (as in the tale of *Gilgamesh, Enkidu and the Netherworld*[44]) itself is the *axis mundi* of this story (Falkowitz 1983: 105), the structure that links and orders the levels of the cosmos – marks the beginning of reintegration. It is the Anzud bird that gives Lugalbanda the means to find his place in the cosmic scheme, and to return to the world of human beings – but not exactly to life. Through this gift, Lugalbanda has now become something more than human.

This metaphor of death is employed for a single, very specific purpose: to accomplish the apotheosis of Lugalbanda. He is transformed from the insignificant eighth brother to a powerful being. He is translated from a mere mortal to a supernatural – or as I prefer, otherworldly – being. He becomes the apical ancestor of a new order. This work, like all the others, has multiple levels of meaning, but whatever the origins of the Lugalbanda stories, in this version it is a wonderful piece of political propaganda. And it is but one of a number of texts that constitute a concerted literary production that establishes a whole backstory, including worldly and otherworldly kin relations, of a certain figure: the first king of the third dynasty of Ur, Ur-Nammu.[45]

Each of the five Sumerian stories about Gilgamesh (including Huwawa B) is concerned with, as well as power, order, and in intersecting ways. Gilgamesh challenges divine order in *Gilgamesh and Huwawa* but is reconciled with it when he chooses not to kill Huwawa, even though this is not a practical solution militarily and is necessarily resolved by having Enkidu commit the act. In *Gilgamesh and The Bull of Heaven* it is in fact Inana who challenges order by preventing Gilgamesh from undertaking his duties, but they too are presumably reconciled, after some rather vicious behavior on the part of both, when Gilgamesh returns to Inana's service in her temple. In *The Death of Gilgamesh* death itself is the natural order, and in *Gilgamesh, Enkidu and the Netherworld* it is clear that Gilgamesh, in appropriating for himself some of the cosmic power inherent in the **halub** tree, is changing a very particular order: the relationship between the divine and the earthly worlds in the body of the king. There are intimations of divine kingship in these stories and they are not entirely unambivalent.

Gilgamesh himself though, while portrayed as a great, and at times good, king, lacks the sort of characterization we see in the Old Babylonian version.

44　Although it seems to be a different tree. I suspect that it is the signification to Mesopotamians of the individual trees – the **halub** versus the **mesh** tree – that lies behind the distinction, not that only one tree can represent the *axis mundi*. The **halub**, especially if it is a cherry (Gadotti 2005), may say something to the reader about Inana; the **mesh**, about the mountains or about Lugalbanda himself.

45　Two spellings of this name are commonly found in the literature: Ur-Nammu and Ur-Namma (Frayne 1997). Both spellings are attested in various ancient documents, but there is some evidence to suggest that Ur-Nammu is the older, and therefore probably original, version (Allred 2006: 9, n. 15).

He is in fact a cipher, a means of conveying messages about the nature of king-ship and a model for its righteous execution. When he disagrees with the elders in the story of Aga it is because he has placed his trust in Inana. He shows justice to Aga because Aga has once done him a kindness; it is done now to him. While he might be thought to bemoan his ultimate fate in *The Death of Gilgamesh*, the message is obvious that it is Gilgamesh's good actions – leading the right kind of life, fulfilling the right social processes, undergoing the right rituals – that transcend mortality. In the story of Huwawa he shows compassion, and seeks and gains renown. With great deeds and a statue, Gilgamesh endures forever through commemoration and invocation,[46] because through commemoration and invocation one becomes an ancestor, and it is as an ancestor that one lives forever. Since Gilgamesh is apparently a bachelor here, as in the Old Babylonian version, renown must perforce take the place of offspring.

Enkidu, a subservient companion to Gilgamesh at best, is also a cipher in the neo-Sumerian stories. His role seems to be, in *Gilgamesh and The Bull of Heaven* at least, sycophant-in-chief. And it is not Gilgamesh who kills Huwawa – in fact Gilgamesh wishes to spare him – it is the hireling Enkidu who in this regard at least appears to be something like a nursemaid, along to protect Gilgamesh from his own better nature. Presumably the audience was as famil-iar with Enkidu as they were with Gilgamesh, because he has no contextualiza-tion and yet is named. But his origins have no role to play here as they do in the Old Babylonian version, where they are invoked as the vehicle for a whole other story.

We should be suspicious (at least) of the coincidence of five stories that pre-sent a Gilgamesh who is strong, powerful, often pious, and also an agent of change in the same general chronological framework as a king who claims to be his brother, and of stories that focus so much on posterity. We should be equally suspicious of a narrative that transforms Gilgamesh's – and therefore that same king's – father from minor figure into a magical, even otherworldly one, thereby creating a very special apical ancestor for a new dynasty. Whether constructed in the time of Ur-Nammu himself or one of his descendants, the Enmerkar and Lugalbanda cycle, the Sumerian Gilgamesh stories, the concerns with sacred marriage, and I would suggest perhaps also *The Death of Ur-Nammu*, all constitute a powerful ideology designed to accom-plish the same ends – the glorification, legitimation, and, particularly, divine associations of that king and his successors (Klein 1976; cf. Vanstiphout 2004: 11; Michalowski 2006a: 172). Similar concerns are found in the royal praise lit-erature of Ur-Nammu and Shulgi (Flückiger-Hawker 1999; Klein 1981), where

---

46 This is in fact the message of any number of texts, from diverse periods, that make refer-ence to the afterlife and must be understood as an inculcation of the desired order rather than as a societal expression of religious belief (Veldhuis 2004).

two themes predominate: the virtues of the king and the essential unity of the urban triad of Uruk (whose rule was usurped by the new leaders of Ur), Nippur, and Ur (Brisch 2007: 22).

Ur-Nammu is indeed commonly seen as a usurper, and a particularly egregious one at that since he may have overthrown his brother,[47] and as such his position must be justified. While chronological attribution of individual components of the Sumerian literary compendia is highly problematic, the completeness of this story set, as well as its elaborateness and doggedness of message, suggest that it is not random, nor the simple product of a whimsical scribal manipulation (contra Tinney 1999b: 45), but was composed in response to some very specific circumstances. At the very least, if it were the product of scribal rather than royal will, the consistency of intent over time indicates that scribes must have been dealing with real philosophical problems presented by historical circumstances at the same time as they were consciously or unconsciously reproducing the dogma of the age. In regard to the first, Gilgamesh is not Ur-Nammu himself; he is his brother, a telling substitution for the brother that Ur-Nammu overthrew. Gilgamesh is emblematic of the duality of kingship, the power to do right and the incipient ability to transgress, although he ends up on the right side of the line – establishing a different order but order nevertheless. However, the immortality of divinity is not his. Instead an earthly substitute, one that is still otherworldly in its associations, is claimed: commemoration through renown.

And along with the presence of Ur-Nammu, inserted in a variety of ways in these texts, is the presence of another body: the Mardu. The Sumerian name for Amorrite, Mardu figures large in the discourse of the Third Dynasty of Ur. When in *Lugalbanda* Enmerkar tells Inana of all the things he has done, he says: "For fifty years I built, for fifty years I was successful. Then the Mardu peoples, who know no agriculture, arose in all Sumer and Akkad. But the wall of Unug extended out across the desert like a bird net" (Black et al. 1998–2006: t.1.8.2.2, lines 290–321). This reference, actually one of the more neutral toward the Mardu, is anachronistic in a number of ways – if Enmerkar is an Early Dynastic ruler, there is no reference to a wall in any source until Shulgi, and there it is a wall of Ur rather than Uruk. While Mardu are perhaps attested as early as Early Dynastic I and certainly by Early Dynastic III, they are not associated with

---

47 Ur-Nammu is thought to have been a member of the royal family and a senior officer in the army of Uruk, although this is problematic, as the only text providing any such evidence is severely damaged and the relevant words entirely reconstructed (as Allred 2006: 9, n. 16 shows). Nevertheless, a familial relationship between Utu-Hegal and Ur-Nammu is widely accepted, be they portrayed as brothers, father and son, or merely in-laws (Sigrist 1992; Dahl 2003: 97, n. 235). Whether or not he proves to have been a member of the Uruk polity, the change that takes place at this time is itself a radical usurpation of previous order in its "return" to an older one.

trouble in any way until the Akkadian period at the earliest, and even then it is not the Mardu who are the problem, but rebellious southern kings (see below). There are similar references, some more and some less expansive, in a number of different texts written in Sumerian.[48] Some are highly derogatory, others adulatory, some merely neutral; and some seem highly incongruous in their context, thus rendering the situation difficult of interpretation and explanation. One thing can be said for certain: these references do not reflect an historical reality; nor is it exactly a straightforward matter of the ordered creation of an historical fiction, because there is no easy pattern to be detected in the references to Mardu scattered across the various neo-Sumerian texts.

Figuring out what the diverse references to the Mardu mean and what they can tell us about these enigmatic people is complicated by the fact that very different kinds of sources from very different time periods have been conflated into a single problem – and even the texts that seem to belong together, such as certain Sumerian documents, are actually quite different genres (cf. Cooper 1983: 30–33), perhaps even from different times. Royal inscriptions, for example, are not to be considered the same as literary texts, but even the literary texts are not commensurable (Michalowski 1976: 5–8). Although the fit is not always comfortable and indeed sometimes counterproductive (Michalowski 2006b: 145), Sumerologists have divided this material into various categories (as Black et al. 2004 and Cunningham 2007), which include laments, debates, dialogues, praise poems or hymns, and, in particular, certain letters that seem to constitute something other than an actual correspondence (contra Jacobsen 1953: 40, n. 45 and Michalowski 1993: 4; but cf. Michalowski 2005a: 200), unlike, for example, the Mari letters. These are the so-called Royal Correspondence of Ur. Understanding these letters, their chronology, and their relationships to other kinds of texts is critical for sorting out what exactly is going on with the Mardu, because it is in them that the bulk of the references to the Mardu occur and, whatever the current views within confined Sumerological circles, these references are widely taken as historical fact (at worst) or (at best) as evidence of what all Sumerians believed.

The historical value of these letters has been the subject of some debate (Huber 2001; Michalowski 2005a; Hallo 2006, among others), but now it seems increasingly accepted that they in fact have none, at least not as far as their subject matter is concerned. Fabienne Huber (2001) has tabulated the many correspondences between letters and made a convincing, although controversial (e.g., Hallo 2006), argument that these letters were not only student exercises composed on a set theme – with certain lexical and grammatical requirements evident, while at the same time the composers were allowed freedom of expression – but also that they all originated in the Old Babylonian period. They are

---

48   See Buccellati 1966: 89–95 for a summary of literary texts mentioning Mardu.

not therefore copies of earlier materials. On these grounds, she identifies three fundamental groupings of texts, in which letters purportedly by Shulgi and letters purportedly by his grandson, Shu-Sin, are considered coterminous.

While the duplication of grammatical particularities and phraseology tells one story, the content of the letters themselves tells another; and *this* story should not be underrated. It may not establish the precise date of the literary letters, but it certainly establishes important relationships between them. I will here reproduce the sense of the narrative these letters contain rather than render any sort of precise retelling of the translation. (The Electronic Text Corpus of Sumerian Literature provides easy access to this material.[49])

The story begins with the much put-upon official Aradmu, who seems to receive a constant barrage of instructions from his ruler, Shulgi, the second king of the Third Dynasty of Ur and Ur-Nammu's son. Shulgi tells Aradmu to go to Subir to see what is happening in that land in consultation with Apillasha, the "Sage of the Assembly." On the way Aradmu is to check on the provinces and see that everything is in order there. Now we do not actually have this letter, but we do have Aradmu's reiteration of Shulgi's instructions at the beginning of his response to it (t.3.1.01/RCU 14). Aradmu complains bitterly about his treatment at the hands of Apillasha, claiming that he, and therefore Shulgi, were not treated with due respect; that Apillasha tried to intimidate him by a show of strength and rough treatment; and that Apillasha was so covered with jewelry that he was surely suggesting his status was equal to the supreme lord Shulgi himself!

Shulgi sends a sharp response (t.3.1.02/RCU 2) telling Aradmu that it sounds like *he* is the one getting an inflated sense of his own importance, that Apillasha is entitled to a certain display of status, both because of his own accomplishments and because it is a strategically useful thing to allow. Apillasha needs the outward appearance of authority in order to do his job (which is to keep his territory secure) and, on a personal level, because if he does not feel important he will start to make trouble. Shulgi then upbraids Aradmu for not following his instructions to the letter, and reminds him that there are some actual elements causing trouble that still need to be dealt with – the XX (name missing from the text) and brigands. Aradmu is instructed to send the first to the desert and the second to the fields, presumably to perform required labor for the crown.

49   In general, the literature on this material numbers the letters according to the system established by Piotr Michalowski in his dissertation on the "Royal Correspondence of Ur" (Michalowski 1976). However this work is not readily available to the general reader, while the ETCSL is, and moreover the translations of the latter supersede the former in terms of recent developments in the field. Michalowski's final treatment of these letters is awaited with eager anticipation but is unfortunately not available before this work goes to press. There is, as in any translation of an ancient text, often divergence among scholars on the meaning of key words and sentences. At some point the choice of translation becomes an individual judgment call – and the judgments I make are not so much on the grounds of linguistics as on the basis of larger theoretical and historical contextualizations that themselves often shape the linguistic outcome, in the past as well as the present.

These two letters at least are so precise in their content and in the problems they are addressing that it is not unreasonable to propose that they are perhaps modeled on an original set of documents, if they themselves do not comprise an actual copy of the original correspondence. The same is not quite the case for the associated documents, however, which are on the one hand rather generic and, on the other, somewhat muddled. But they connect in terms of their content so thoroughly that they cannot be separated out from the first lot. At about the same time, in narrative terms, as Shulgi sends the letter about Apillasha, he also sends one instructing Aradmu to fix a breach in the irrigation system (t.3.1.10) – although this letter about the waterways is not actually addressed to Aradmu but to Puzur-Shulgi, who is the subject of another, associated group of letters concerning the fortress Igi-Hursaga, of which he is commander. I will return to him later. The fact is, Aradmu actually answers this letter in two separate missives of his own, stating that he has drained the flooded lands and started work on the watercourses, which means we can be reasonably confident either that he was the proper addressee and that the scribe made a mistake and put in Puzur-Shulgi's name for Aradmu, or that at one point more or less the same letter addressed to Aradmu existed. Aradmu also has some involvement with the fortress (t.3.1.08/RCU 10) as Shulgi's general factotum, so it is not surprising, perhaps, that this substitution was made. This kind of thing seems to have happened a lot, due to the teaching methods of scribal schools. Scribes apparently learned their craft through memorizing a text and then writing it down (Delnero 2006) – one explanation (but I doubt the only one) for why there are often many versions of a text, with only slight differences between them, recovered from different cities.

In any case, Aradmu sends Shulgi a rather formal letter in answer to this one (t.3.1.03), with a somewhat indignant attitude manifest in the comment "my Lord, you have given me instructions about every matter from the salt waters and the borders of the land of Mardu" (Black et al. 1998–2006: t.3.1.03, lines 3–6). There are a number of variants[50] of this geography in the duplicates of the letter, one citing Dilmun in the place of Mardu, another Subir. The sense is clearly the whole extent of Shulgi's remit, and the message is that

50   One of the very difficult aspects of the Sumerian literary production, especially the letters, is the existence of multiple versions of them – some more, some less faithful in their duplication. As already noted, there has long been a sense that an authentic original exists from which all others derive, and that variation therefore is deviance. Delnero (2006) seeks to find a systematic way of determining which was the original by studying the variations as errors of memory. However, it seems to me that, given the origin of these variants in different places, it is not quite so simple. The fact that different names and places are found in letters from different scribal schools points to local traditions and versions of history, as will become clearer below. Similarly with variants in texts of the Gilgamesh stories. What is equally interesting, however, is the fact that there was clearly a centralized syllabus for scribal education so that all cities followed the same training schedule, using the same materials – even Susa (Steinkeller 1987: 21).

Aradmu has everything under control. This letter is of note for this discussion because it is the first mention (in this reconstruction of the narrative of the letters) of the Mardu, who come to figure more prominently in subsequent communications.

Meanwhile, Aradmu also sends a more detailed and more discursive letter (t.3.1.11/RCU 3), specifying what he has done in regard to each of Shulgi's instructions. The incipit is missing, but he informs Shulgi (again) that work has started on the waterways, that the "bandits and brigands" are working in the desert. He then goes on to describe what might seem to be their waywardness in keeping with their status as brigands, although he is actually specifying their labor. The men work with animals and in the fields; the women, carrying spindles, are weavers.[51] This passage is not as anomalous as perhaps it first sounds: it describes a common seasonal pastoralist practice of seeding a marginal area not worth cultivating under normal sedentary cereal regimes, abandoning it while traveling with flocks, to come back to it only when it is bearing grain and may be used for pasturage. Indeed, it is a description I might have written myself after observing the summer routines of pastoralists in the vicinity of Tell Banat. This passage is worth quoting in full here:

(Version 1)

As for their men and their women, the man among them goes wherever he pleases, the woman among them holding a spindle and hair clasp in her hand goes the way of her choice. In the vastness of the desert they set up animal pens and after setting up their tents and camps, their workers and agricultural labourers spend the day together on the fields.

(Version 2)

As for their men and their women the man among them goes wherever he pleases, the woman, holding spindle and hair clasp in her hand, going the way of her choice. In the vastness of the desert they knock up animal pens and they lie in green[52] meadows in their tents and camps, their workers and agricultural labourers spend the day together on the fields. (Black et al. 1998–2006: t.3.1.11, lines 1–7, from Aradmu to Shulgi)[53]

Aradmu then goes on to grovel a bit about the matter of Apillasha, swearing that he has done everything he has been told to do, is a loyal subject and great friend of Apillasha, and is indeed securing the foundations of the province.[54]

---

51 The only suggestion I have to offer as to the hair clasp is that it constitutes a symbol of portable wealth.

52 The word "green" is not actually in the original as far as I can see.

53 That is, RCU 3.

54 Another letter is associated with this group, but only at a distance. It is from the merchant Ur-DUN to Shulgi (t.3.1.11.1/RCU 1) complaining of poor treatment by Apishalla.

This selection of letters, then, constitutes a connected, if not entirely coherent, sequence of events and so may be labeled Group A (see Appendix). Notice that a particular phrase is used in the above quote (Version 2) that associates two other texts with this one, clarifying exactly who these "brigands" are in the process. It is the phrase, "they lie in green meadows in their tents," which is also found in Version B from Susa of the letter from Shulgi to Puzur-Shulgi (and addressed here to Puzur-Numushda) about the fortress: "and the people of the widespread Land lay in green meadows. I made them rest in spacious habitations, in peaceful dwelling places. As for their men and women: the man among them goes wherever he pleases and the woman with spindle and hair clasp goes wherever she pleases. After they had set up stock pens in the vastness of the desert, and established their tents and camps, the workmen and the laborers spend the days in the fields" (Black et al. 1998–2006: t.3.1.08, Version B from Susa, lines 8–13).[55]

This text is the one that seems more than any other to undermine the historicity of the literary letters, being seen at best as a very poorly executed exercise (Huber 2001: 184). In fact, version B from Susa takes half of the letter from Aradmu to Shulgi about bandits and Apillasha (t.3.1.11/RCU 3), and half of the letter from Shulgi to Puzur-Shulgi, Version A, about the fortress Igi-hursaga (t.3.1.08/RCU 10) and puts them together; this, while perhaps an error (although I would not assume it), is not coincidental. It is because the subject matter of these two texts is so closely related. The letter to Puzur-Shulgi to hurry up work on the fortification is the result of the problems caused by pastoralists, and although this is not stated explicitly, the writer clearly knows it.

Since the above quote is a description of pastoralists, it makes some sense to insert it here. But the connections between these two letters may be even more direct. That the subject in both t.3.1.11/RCU 3 and t.3.1.08/RCU 10 are Mardu,[56] and it is therefore the "bandits" of t.3.1.11 who cause the work on the fortification, is evidenced by the third use of the phrase "to lie in the meadow," found in *Enmerkar and the Lord of Aratta*. The Sumerian "**kur mar-tu u$_2$-sal-la nu$_2$-a**" (Black et al. 1998–2006: t.1.8.2.3, line 144) is not usually translated as "the mountain Mardu, lying in the meadow" in the English rendering of this story. Vanstiphout (2004: 65) gives this line as "and even the land Mardu, resting in green pastures"). In Black et al. (1998–2006) it is rendered as "the Mardu land, resting in security." I suspect this was the translator's way of reconciling what must have seemed quite contradictory concepts, given the traditional

It echoes the first letter from Aradmu in stating that when he arrived at the palace gate no one inquired after his business and mentions Aradmu himself, who has gone from Zimudar to Simurram. It is possible that this is the first in the series, prompting Aradmu's trip, but I doubt it because Shulgi's instructions are so clear in Aradmu's own letter.

55 That is, RCU 10.

56 In fact, not only are they Mardu, used here generically, they are none other than the Tidnu, who I will argue shortly were the focus of Ur concerns with mobile pastoralists.

frameworks by which the Mardu in general and this particular historical conjunction are understood – that Mardu should be found within the kingdom
of Ur. Moreover, as the third in a sequence in *Enmerkar and the Lord of Aratta*,
this phrase is descriptive of the Mardu's particular nature, just as Akkad is the
"land possessing all that is befitting" and Sumer is the "great mountain of the
magnificent *me*."[57]

Such an image might seem to some as of an unimaginable day when the
Mardu would be at peace, bucolic rather than brutish. However, several things
emerge in these letters (and the parallel reference in *Enmerkar and the Lord of
Aratta*) that suggest this is not a utopian, and impossible, vision but something
that, if not already in existence, soon will be. This is the earliest example in
existence of governmentally enforced sedentarization of mobile groups. To see
this, we need to tell the full story of this group of letters too.[58] And, contrary to
general opinion, the starting point is t.3.1.08/RCU 10, Version B, cited above.
This is not just a variant of Version A, but one of two separate letters about
the same topic, between which Puzur-Shulgi's (or Puzur-Marduk's or Puzur-
Numushda's) reply intervenes.

In Version B, Shulgi begins by describing the peace that he had brought to
the country, a peace he seeks to maintain by repairing and/or expanding the
fortification under direction of Puzur-Shulgi. It seems that omens warned
Shulgi that trouble was coming, and he sends Aradmu to Puzur-Shulgi to help
with this work and directs the governor of the province of Zimudar, Lu-Nanna,
to join his troops in readiness. The project is urgent and they are to work at it
day and night, a phrase also found in Aradmu's letter to Shulgi (t.3.1.11/RCU
3). But it seems it is too late. Puzur-Shulgi answers his king, telling him that he
knows the omens and, what is more, a recaptured prisoner has told him that the
enemy is nearby, but he cannot finish the fortress or guard the cities from attack
with the resources at hand. Puzur-Shulgi then goes on to describe in detail the
various problems with the fortifications and informs the king that the enemy is
camped in the hills. He requests 7,200 soldiers to work as basket men bringing
in the necessary materials for construction.

---

57 Vanstiphout 2004: 65, lines 142–3 has "twin-tongued Sumer – great mound of the power
    of lordship – together with Akkad – the mound that has all that is befitting."

58 There is a third group of letters that do not really concern the discussion of the Mardu, being
    a self-contained treatment of relations between Shulgi and a captain in his army, Aba-indasa,
    as mediated by Aradmu. The letters are, in this order: t.3.1.05, where Aradmu reports that
    Aba-indasa is missing a significant number of troops; presumably Shulgi's answer, t.3.1.13.1,
    but it is so fragmentary that it is impossible to know; Shulgi to Aradmu (t.3.1.06.1) about a
    letter from Aba-Indasa, where it is clear that Aba-Indasa's explanation is not sufficient and
    he is in considerable trouble; and Aba-Indasa's poetic plea to Shulgi to be restored to his
    love (and to his mother) in t.3.1.21. Although I think these letters do fit into the sequence I
    am outlining here, referring to an action within the conflict within the Mardu, there is little
    enough specific detail to form a precise connection. I therefore label them Group A.1.

Then comes an extremely important statement, one that unfortunately has several variants: the enemy has devised their plans concerning this: "I will resettle them." This is a comment that harkens back to the beginning of Shulgi to Puzur-Shulgi Version B: "over all the foreign lands and the widespread people, each of their towns and all their provinces, and the people of the widespread Land lay in green meadows. I made them rest (?) in spacious habitations, in peaceful dwelling places" (Black et al. 1998–2006: t.3.1.08, Version B from Susa, lines 3–7). This strongly suggests that Shulgi was trying to trammel the movement and activities of the Mardu, and that they were resisting. The alternates variously have the enemy deciding to resettle their own people or Puzur-Shulgi resettling them.

That the Mardu in this instance are specifically the Tidnu is made clear in the next letter, Shulgi to Puzur-Shulgi, t.3.1.08/RCU 10, Version A. Here the framework of Version B is used, and the beginning and end are cited directly because it is after all about the same topic, with a clarification inserted. The matter is urgent because the Tidnu have come down from the mountains – perhaps this is the enemy who was in the mountains previously – and, the main import of the letter, Lu-Nanna and his troops are redirected to join Puzur-Shulgi and Aradmu (who is clearly already there). There is some thought that maybe Lu-Nanna won't show up; Zimudar, after all, probably has stronger allegiances to the east than to Sumer, given that it lay in the tax-paying provinces between Mesopotamia and the Zagros and was therefore appropriated territory (Steinkeller 1987b: 36–37, esp. n. 56). Meanwhile, Aradmu also replies to Shulgi (t.3.1.06/RCU 6), one of those shorter, more formal, and formulaic missives in which the king is assured of his greatness and informed that the "rebellious Mardu" have turned back. This seems to bring the matter to a close, thereby constituting a second, connected collection of letters, Group B.[59]

Except ... there are three other letters seemingly associated with these two letter groups. The first, from Shulgi to Ishbi Erra about buying grain (t.3.1.13.2), reproduces an extensive quote from Shulgi's letter about Apillasha (t.3.1.02); the second, from Sharrumbani, another "Sage of the Assembly" to Shu-Sin (t.3.1.15), reprises the issue of the fortification and the Tidnu and is partnered with the third, a letter from Shu-Sin to Sharrumbani (t.3.1.16) that shares some features with both groups of letters.

The letter from Sharrumbani (t.3.1.15) parallels in many respects that of Puzur-Shulgi (t.3.1.07). Both are responding to their king's orders to work on the fortifications, because both are faced with impending doom – for Puzur-Shulgi it is a nameless enemy, for Sharrumbani it is the Mardu, and in this

---

59 Although one more letter from Aradmu to Shulgi (t.3.1.04) employing the phrase "the widespread people," which seems to be characteristic of this group, may also fit here. This letter assures Shulgi that all the people adore him.

last letter the wall itself is named for the enemy. Sharrumbani has a "can-do" attitude, however, and is far more positive than Puzur-Shulgi, whose letter is really one of complaint. Perhaps this is because of their respective positions. Sharrumbani after all is "Sage of the Assembly" and so presumably has more ability to marshal the necessary resources, along with more military responsibility under normal circumstances, and thus has more experience in dealing with a crisis. Both men mention 7,200 workers – Puzur-Shulgi needs them to assist in carrying baskets, Sharrumbani has them but wants soldiers. Both mention, although in quite different contexts, their inability to guard all the cities, and in both letters the enemy is camping in the mountains. However, Shu-Sin's response (t.3.1.16/RCU 18) – connected to Sharrumbani's letter by the former's denial (lines 39–42) of the latter's request to free the workers from their labors on the wall so they could join military action – bears little connection to any of Shulgi's letters, although it does reference that king and his fortress.

These two letters constitute an isolated pair that clearly relate to the Puzur-Shulgi letter as, perhaps, a prototype, or as a paired exercise where the scribe was first to write a letter in the name of Shulgi, then one in the name of Shu-Sin. The letter from Shulgi to Ishbi-Erra (t.3.1.13.2) can be safely removed from any of these groups. Its quotation of t.3.1.02 in the delineation of the subject's ability to choose personnel and to execute his own punishments, as the rights and responsibilities of high position, is simply a matter of formula rather than copying. Using prescribed wording for certain situations accounts, I think, for a number of parallels between texts.[60]

Shulgi to Ishbi-Erra (t.3.1.13.2) does, however, connect to the last group of letters under consideration here. These all concern the story of Ishbi-Erra, the successor to Ibbi-Sin and the founder of the Isin dynasty. This group of texts is conceived as following immediately on from the previous two groups; it continues the same narrative history, following directly from the Mardu's initial uprising. One pair of letters is between Puzur-Shulgi (here governor of Kazallu) and Ibbi-Sin about Ishbi-Erra; the other is between Ibbi-Sin and Ishbi-Erra himself, with Puzur-Numushda (a.k.a. Puzur-Shulgi) mentioned in one of this last pair of letters as commander of the fortress Igi-hursaga.

In this story Ishbi-Erra goes from hero to villain, from inside man to out. He starts as the favored "son" (undoubtedly an anachronism) of Shulgi (t.3.1.13.2), who gives him "the cities of the province, the land of Mardu and Elam" and proclaims him his equal. He instructs him to buy grain. This letter is in essential ways apocryphal, and not just because Shulgi's name is imposed where Ibbi-Sin's should be. It is to explain how Ishbi-Erra could be in such a position of power as to be entrusted with so much, and his mention as a house-born slave perhaps echoes Sargon's myth of origins. It seems, indeed, more of a literary

---

60   See Huber (2001) for a comprehensive collection of parallels, with variant interpretations.

device than an epistolary project. It is so excessive in its praise that it could well have been concocted at Ishbi-Erra's own behest or at the behest of his supporters (although excess and praise are integrally related in the production of the "hymn" genre). Equally, it could be seen as a necessary backdrop to his subsequent fall from grace/rise to power, because it seems he takes the silver given to him to buy grain and in some way engineers Ibbi-Sin's political demise (t.3.1.18). Ishbi-Erra engages in price gouging over the grain, which cripples Ibbi-Sin in one way, and is accused of allowing the Mardu to come into the land by not helping Puzur-Numushda battle against them, thereby crippling him in another way. The gods have turned against Ibbi-Sin and he is in dire straits.

Ishbi-Erra responds (t.3.1.17). He tells Ibbi-Sin that it is all part of a master plan – he has heard that the Mardu have invaded and so he has bought up all the grain – 72,000 gur (the price had gone up because of the war) – and brought it inside Isin for protection. But his exact relationship to the Mardu is a unclear in this letter. In one sentence it sounds as if he is using the Mardu to seize control; in the next he is complaining that they are too strong for him, and it is because of them that he is unable to take the grain for threshing. I suspect that the contradiction is intended to show Ishbi-Erra as playing a double game. In any case, he tells Ibbi-Sin that if he can come and get the grain, it is all his, and it is enough to keep him going for years, so he should not fear the Elamites, who apparently have been causing Ibbi-Sin as much distress as the Mardu. Indeed, the first (in terms of narrative sequence and the development of the story) really pejorative language in all these letters so far is used of Elam – it is "the raging dog," "the destroyer." Mardu is simply "the enemy" and "hostile."

This final episode in the sequence, labeled Group C, explains just how Ur fell and Isin rose. In the next set of letters, Ishbi-Erra's double-dealing becomes clear. Puzur-Shulgi writes to Ibbi-Sin because Ishbi-Erra is now threatening him, having taken several cities, and claiming divine approbation for Isin's elevation over all the land. He wants to take refuge with Ibbi-Sin in Ur if Ishbi-Erra should get any closer. Ibbi-Sin is not impressed (t.3.1.20). He turns on Puzur-Shulgi/Numushda, accusing him of not taking action that might have forestalled Sumer's abandonment by the gods. And then he lets fly with a searing attack on the traitor Ishbi-Erra. He is an ape, a dog, dishonest, he stinks like a garlic salesman, is a criminal, and worst of all, not of Sumerian origin!! Twice he is called a man from Mari. It should be remembered that Mari at this time is not known to have been an Amorrite polity, although Ishbi-Erra's name is Amorrite in construction (Michalowski 1995: 185; cf. Michalowski 1983: 33), but was under the dominion of the *shakkanaku* and firmly intertwined with the Third Dynasty of Ur itself through marriage – to the extent that the Mari king, Apil Kin, became part of Ur III royal ancestor traditions (Boese and Sallaberger 1996; Michalowski 2005a: 204–5, cf. 2005b). Yet Ishbi-Erra's outside status is what is brought to the fore, and his externality is highlighted not only in the discourse apparently of the vanquished (who might then set out to vilify their conqueror), but in what is purported to be his own acknowledgment of his triumph (Michalowski 2005a). Just as in the days before "political correctness," every society had its characterizations of certain populations or places as less than desirable, expressed very often as jokes; here, Mesopotamians may have cast Mari and Mariotes as the epitome of bumpkinness.

So what, exactly, are these letters and when were they written? In a way neither of these questions really quite matters to what is of interest in this discussion. Whenever they were composed and/or executed[61] – and I really do think they are a product of the Old Babylonian scribal schools, dating no earlier than the end of the twentieth or beginning of the nineteenth centuries (Huber 2001; cf. Hallo 2006), and not copies of earlier materials – they were written around histories of a relationship between the Third Dynasty of Ur and Mardu. They appear upon first examination to be presented from Ur's perspective; if they are, they would seem to have been written from a very different position than that of the other Ur contrivance, the Gilgamesh and Lugalbanda stories. But I do not, in fact, think they are. And here is the crux of the matter. In none of these groups of letters are negative sentiments about the Mardu, Tidnu, or pastoralists expressed. The letters are merely descriptive. Indeed, at the end of the very last letter it is made clear that the Mardu rising up from their mountain lands is not entirely a bad thing. The Mardu will defeat Elam and capture Ishbi-Erra and all will be well. The pejorative remarks so ubiquitously associated with Sumerian views of the Mardu are all confined to other genres.

The history of Ur and Mardu is ultimately peripheral to the outcome of the story, which is the advent of Isin and the fall of Ur. Even so, it is difficult to see the letters purely as Isin's self-laudatory propaganda, given the descriptions of Ishbi-Erra's actions and character, nor does an attribution to Ur fit very well. They may perhaps constitute a kind of "fall" story, akin in intent to *The Curse of Agade* (Cooper 1983; Glassner 1986) and *The Lament over Sumer and Ur* (Michalowski 1989), but there seems too little of the hyperbole usually associated with that sort of situation. Rather, I suggest, the letters reflect an "impartial" understanding of events based on whatever sources were available to the scribes of the Old Babylonian period, whether they were documents, traditions, or experiences and observations, or a combination of these. This is not history as we understand the word. These letters are not factual accounts of what went on in the time of Ur. They were not intended as such. Whatever underlay them, the letters as we now have them were intended first and foremost as pedagogical exercises (Huber 2001) and may have been generated in a variety of ways: as translations (from Akkadian to Sumerian), dictations, copies, and/or memorizations. Or they may be the result of exercises in original composition. Woods

---

61 The word "copy" in the context of these scribal exercises is problematic, as it assumes preexisting, and implies authentic, documents that are simply reproduced.

(2006: 97) notes that letters require a "higher degree of productive proficiency with a language" than do other kinds of administrative texts. Variations within versions of the same letter may also represent essentially the same exercise given to successive scribal classes and classes in different places.

It is a mistake, I think, to assume a global explanation for any problematic aspect of the entire corpus because it is clear that there were multiple skills required and multiple techniques employed in conveying those skills. There seems little doubt, for example, that scribal students were expected to study, as well as epistolary form, the poetic techniques that appear in the letters and that for some scholars give them the aspect of literature (Steinkeller 1996: 148–9). In both groups A and B there are two types of letter connected by topic – detailed, directed missives (t.3.1.01/RCU 14; t.3.1.07/RCU 11) and formulaic general ones (t.3.1.03; t.3.1.06/RCU 6) in which the glory of Shulgi is the real subject of discussion. Letters of this last type seem primarily to be exercises in the art of "buttering-up the boss" (cf. Hallo 2006: 88). Scribes as well need to be versed in styles of argumentation, presenting both positions in a debate (positive and negative cases), because opposition is a fundamental precept of Sumerian literature, as can be seen in the prevalence of debates and dialogues (Alster 1990). Hence most of these documents are paired. Whatever form they take, they are all about the business of the state.

If documents produced in the time of Shulgi or Shu-Sin were used by successive classes of trainee scribes to write these letters, all well and good. But they need not have been. It is not as *actual* history that we should see the letters, but history as understood by the writers of the letters – vague and confused perhaps, embellished if not often fabricated, and futile as sources of fact or social attitude. And as such, they are not entirely fictive. They give us a view of how the Mardu came to be (and where they came from) that is not inflected with the kind of vitriol, even simple negativity, that modern scholarship has all too long attributed to the entire sedentary population of Mesopotamia. Those kinds of descriptions come from a specific kind of text; and those texts are not as straightforward as we like to think.

The picture of Mardu that emerges from the literary letters is this: while the Mardu have different sets of social norms, allowing a greater independence of action than Mesopotamians might be used to, they are otherwise rather familiar. They are threatening as any contender for regional hegemony is threatening, whether rival Sumerian king, Elamite, or Eshnunnan. Mardu are located in the mountains nearby to Sumer, but also make use of the immediately adjacent steppe. What has long seemed strange to us – yet seems unremarkable here within the context of the letters – is that they are both perfectly accustomed to agricultural work and at home with cities. It is possible to see this as reflecting the current situation of Mardu at the time of the Old Babylonian scribal schools, a conflation of who they are now with who they once were, but in the next set of texts to be considered, the Mardu very explicitly do *not* know any of these things.

References to Mardu also occur in literary genres other than letters. This group of texts comprises one praise poem, *Ishme-Dagan A-V*,[62] the Lugalbanda cycle, the Enmerkar cycle, *Gilgamesh, Enkidu and the Netherworld, Enki and the World Order*, and the *Curse of Agade*. I will return later to a discussion of the relationship between the praise literature and the year names and royal inscriptions of Shulgi and Shu-Sin, which are traditionally adduced as mutually supportive materials, although there are serious chronological issues that raise doubts about such connections. In this discussion I wish to track the deployment of very specific phrases that qualify the term "Mardu" as pastoralists versus those that qualify the term as anathema, and the various contexts in which they occur.

The phrases are:

1) A: **mar-tu lu₂ še nu-zu** [63]
   the Mardu, people who know no barley (*Lugalbanda and the Anzud Bird*)
   B: **mar-tu kur-ra lu₂ ce nu-zu**[64]
   the mountain Mardu, people who know no barley (*The Curse of Akkad*)
2) A: **iri nu-tuku-ra e₂ nu-tuku-ra [mar]-/tu**[65]
   to those who have no towns, to those who have no houses, Mardu (*Enki and the World Order*)
   B: **mar-tu e₂ nu-zu iriᵏⁱ nu-zu lu₂ lil₂-la₂ hur-saj-ja₂ tuc-a**[66]
   The Mardu know no houses, know no towns, ghosts who sit in the hills (*I-D/A-V*).[67]

The last phase, which I have rendered as "ghosts who sit in the hills," is translated by Black et al. (1998–2006: c.2.5.4.01: lines 266–7) as "primitives who live in the hills." Again, this is a matter of interpretation filtered through preconception: since the Mardu are despised, the phrase must refer to their subhuman and therefore uncivilized status (Cooper 1983: 30) – of the possible meanings wind/ghost/spirit/fool given to **lil₂**,[68] it is the last that is chosen. However, the context in which the Mardu appear in *Gilgamesh, Enkidu and the Netherworld* (Ur version) should not be forgotten:

> "Did you see the citizen of Girsu who refused (?) water to his father and his mother?" "I saw him." "How does he fare?" "In front of each of them are a

62 Two praise poems of Shulgi (B and C) also contain the word "Mardu," but these citations are unqualified by any descriptors and refer to Shulgi's mastery of multiple languages.
63 Black et al. 1998–2006: c.1.8.2.2., line 304. This phrase is also found in an inscription of Shu-Sin.
64 Ibid.: c.2.1.5, line 36.
65 Ibid.: c.1.1.3. lines 131–2.
66 Ibid.: c.2.5.4.01: lines 266–7.
67 Lieberman (1969: 58) has "may the **mar-du**, who does not know a house, who does not know a city, the man of the wind." Buccellati (1966: 93) translates the phrase as "the awkward man living in the mountains."
68 Allred pers. comm.; see http://psd.museum.upenn.edu/epsd/nepsd-frame.html.

thousand Mardu, and his spirit can neither … nor … The Mardu at the libation place at the entrance (?) to the nether world…." (Black et al. 1998–2006: c.1.8.1.4, lines 20–28)

As the Mardu are located in the mountains and as the mountain is the netherworld, it makes a good deal of sense that they would guard the way to the afterlife for this man who has committed a terrible sin. The reference, therefore, in the *Ishme-Dagan Hymn (A-V)* is to the synonymous function of **kur** with the netherworld (Wiggermann 1996), and so the use of the term "ghosts" is obviously a pun, but perhaps also expressive of some much more profound conceptualization about human relationships with the other world. The liminal cosmological status of the Mardu as guardians of the netherworld may be implicit in their liminal geographic status as, at this time, ranged on the plains and foothills between Mesopotamia and the Highlands.

There is another, and very important, dimension to this discussion. One of the traditional views of Sumerian culture and society holds that Sumerians viewed the landscape beyond the city as uncivilized and dangerous and the inhabitants of that landscape as less than human (Cooper 1983; Black 2002). A particular association is drawn with mountains (such as Wiggermann 1996: 215) that derives both from the word **kúr** (Akkadian *nakru*), meaning "strange, foreign," and the Sumerian habit of using two different words for land, **kalam** and **kur** – "our land" and "their land" (Fleming 2004). **Kur** also designates a single mountain (Steinkeller 2007b: 223), and as there are no mountains in Sumer itself, **kur** must, it would seem, of necessity indicate foreignness, which by further extension means hostile. Hence the identification with the netherworld, which is, ipso facto, strange and hostile (Steinkeller 2007b: 231).[69] Mardu are only designated in Sumerian texts with **kur**, taken by most scholars as indicating not only that they come from a foreign land but that they are strange, alien in more senses than one. What further complicates this imagery, however, is the portrayal of Sumer as a mountain; Enlil, a prominent god in literary texts, is designated as **kur-gal**, "great mountain," and rules from the **Ekur**, or "mountain house" (Wiggermann 1996: 209), as does Shulgi (Frayne 1997: 98–9). Moreover, Steinkeller (2007b: 227) argues that if **hursag**, "mountain range," was a simile for a temple in poetry, as it often was, then strength and beauty must be implied in the image of mountains. This suggests that "fear" and "hostility" are not embedded in either **kur** or **hursag**, but rather, perhaps, "power" and "awe." It also suggests that "foreignness" is not quite the key association of the word, but instead, "otherworldliness" (see the examples of Steinkeller 2007b: 230).

On the earthly plane, the larger context of all but one of the above-listed phrases regarding Mardu may be understood as a general overview of the

---

69 Rendering the use of **kur** as alienation at the demise of various kingships in the Sumerian King List (Cooper 1983: 29) perhaps a double entendre.

geopolitical situation where Mardu is but one of a number of other entities with which Sumer interacts, while the immediate context is always related to animals. In *Enki and the World Order*, the Mardu's role as pastoralists is established in the cosmic scheme of things, and they come up in an interesting position: listed after Meluha, Magan, and Dilmun, all of whom bring Enki things as is only befitting. In contrast, Mardu actually receive something from the god, the animals that constitute their livelihood. This line then refers back to the earlier sections of the piece where Enki is establishing all that is good about Sumer, and so the Mardu would seem to be understood as an intrinsic part of that world. And yet it also places them within the orbit of the Arabian peninsula, reflecting, I would suggest, the traversing of conceptual space as well as the physical distance that mobile pastoralists might be expected to cover. As noted in Chapter 3, the northern focus of southern-based pastoralists collapsed at the end of the fourth millennium, when much increased contact with the Arabian peninsula is attested (Peyronel 2006). That this conceptual/physical space was not confined to the mountains is evident in this and many other texts, especially *The Curse of Akkad*. Here Mardu bring animals for Inana and are juxtaposed between Sumer and Meluha, Elam and Subir. Unlike the case with the letters, there is actually an Ur III version of this story, but it is not sufficiently preserved for us to know whether the Mardu were originally included in this list. Mardu, then, occupy a unique place in Sumerian geography – they are an intrinsic part of the Sumerian world, utterly embedded within it rather than just known to it, and yet are associated with other places.

The text in which Mardu seem most extraneous is the story of *Lugalbanda and the Anzud Bird*. Enmerkar complains to Inana about her diminished regard for him after he has done so much for Uruk, the only fly in the ointment being the Mardu who rose up over Sumer and Akkad – but even then he protected his country by building the wall that (presumably, for it is not actually specified) kept them out. As already mentioned, this is entirely anachronistic but at the same time not pointless. It is the prevailing view of the conflict between Ur and its enemies at the time the document was written. The very different inclusions of Mardu in the Enmerkar and Lugalbanda texts (in the first, Mardu are part of the view of the world; in the second, they are accorded the rote description) tend to confirm my suspicion about the relationship of these four texts – that the Lugalbanda cycle was hooked onto the Enmerkar cycle sometime after the initial composition of the latter, but not too much later, for they are both part of the Ur III canonization of its kings. It is possible that the Lugalbanda Mardu were simply inserted into later copies of this text. But these two story cycles reflect, at least, the beginnings of a change in attitude toward the Mardu that takes place within that dynasty, and it starts with Shulgi and culminates with Shu-Sin.

Before we can deal with the "historical" documents (and I use quotation marks to indicate my skepticism that the factuality traditionally extracted from them is especially sound) of these two kings, their inscriptions, two more stories have to be explained. This is because the invocations of the name Mardu in the stories just discussed are not in and of themselves particularly derogatory, unless one believes that not knowing grain, houses, or cities is in itself truly barbaric – as scholars of this material have been convinced that Mesopotamians themselves thought. But to "know no barley" is simply to say "is not a farmer." All these references have taken on the connotations they carry because of only two texts, one of which is *The Marriage of Mardu* (e.g., Cooper 1983: 30–33), a story that seems to express absolute contempt for these people. It is a text that has become, like the Nuer for anthropology, axiomatic of nomads and, in this case, of how the ancient world felt about them.

> Now listen, their hands are destructive and their features are those of monkeys; he is one who eats what Nanna forbids and does not show reverence. They never stop roaming about …, they are an abomination to the gods' dwellings. Their ideas are confused; they cause only disturbance. He is clothed in sack-leather …, lives in a tent, exposed to wind and rain, and cannot properly recite prayers. He lives in the mountains and ignores the places of gods, digs up truffles in the foothills, does not know how to bend the knee, and eats raw flesh. He has no house during his life, and when he dies he will not be carried to a burial-place. (*The Marriage of Mardu.* Black et al. 1998–2006: t.1.7.1, lines 126–41)[70]

This passage, especially the last section, has long been accepted as an accurate reflection of Sumerian/urban views of the Amorrites, as containing some essential historicity (Cooper 1983; Postgate 1992: 83–4; Van de Mieroop 2004: 78), and as tantamount "to an ethnography" (Whiting 1995). But this citation reveals more about contemporary Western scholarship than it does about ancient identities. It goes unchallenged because it confirms our own prejudices about nomads. This passage is taken out of context, egregiously so, for when we see it quoted time and time again the rest of the story is missing. It is presented alone, as an example of how people in the urban world felt about Amorrites. Yet it is part of a much larger story – a story where Mardu is presented as affluent

---

70 Buccellati (1966: 331) translates the last line cited here as "on the day of their death they are not buried." He notes (Buccellati 2008:155) that this Sumerian view is at odds with my suggestion (Porter 2000, 2002a) that pastoralists bury their dead, which would certainly be the outcome of the Black et al. translation and if this passage were a legitimate reflection of actual Mardu social practice. However, the idea that Mardu are not buried on *the day* of their death merely implies that they are buried some time after, a practice often observed among mobile groups who keep their dead to inter in the traditional burial grounds to which they will return in the course of their migrations. An alternative translation has it (Van de Mieroop 2004: 78) that "he is not buried according to proper rituals."

and certainly associated with the urban world. The basic representation of the character of Mardu and his situation in life is neither hostile nor negative.

Mardu, the subject of this story, is prosperous and strong. He and his people live in houses around a city – in a suburban rather than rural (let alone wild) milieu. He lacks only a wife. When a festival is announced in the city, he and his friends decide to go and have a few drinks and compete in a tournament of strength. Mardu is so successful that he draws the eye of the god Numushda, in whose honor the festival is being held. Numushda offers his champion various prizes, but Mardu claims his daughter, Adgar-kidug, instead. The god agrees, but his daughter seems less alacritous in accepting Mardu's proposal. Her friend advises against it in no uncertain terms – indeed, the friend's words on the subject constitute this famous quotation. But her advice goes unheeded, and on the contrary seems to be just the prod that Adgar-kidug needs to announce her intent to marry Mardu.

If this story constitutes the elevation of Mardu to the realm of the gods (Klein 1997), it has a political context as much as any other of these texts. The question, however, is this: does the text constitute a rejection of such an event or the explanation and promotion of it? I incline to the latter interpretation, on the grounds that the girl accepts Mardu, and, because the context of this negative statement about Mardu is the prospect of loss of a member of the group – a daughter, a friend – to another group that will take her away; it is the thought of going outside the group that is repugnant, not the nature of the group itself. The friend's sentiments would seem, indeed, to be a commentary on exogenous marriage practices. It would not matter who Mardu was – the king of Eshnunna for example – the description would also be virulent, not in these specifics perhaps, but virulent nevertheless.

In either case, the story expresses dual and contradictory sentiments that are equally integral to the dramatic action, so the one cannot be dismissed in favour of the other. If we were to think that a disaffected scribal class inserted, as a deliberate and subversive act (such as Hallo 2006: 88), the negative stereotype of their overlords into stories perpetuated as a connection between dynasties, then we would have to imagine one of two scenarios – either *all* these texts in Sumerian were only for use in the schoolhouse, never to be read to the ruling elite, or a conspiracy of silence reigned. Even if, as is often remarked, most kings could not read (Shulgi, however, is credited with this and many other skills), those who read these texts aloud in any context would have had to skip over such references in the hearing of their Amorrite masters. The material as we have it is late, but not, I can only conclude, so late that it is the fiction of Old Babylonian scribes; Ur III remnants of some of these stories attest to their existence at that time. We cannot know how much any of the stories were altered over time, however, resulting in the copies retrieved from Old Babylonian contexts.

A positive view of Mardu is not in itself an anomaly. There exists a "**shir-gida**"[71] and a hymn to the god Mardu, for whose temple materials are drawn from the Drehem storehouses in Ur III times (Buccellatti 1966; Sharlach 2004: 110). As other nonliterary references (to be discussed below) indicate, various people labeled Mardu are deeply embedded in the state system; there is, therefore, no need to reason this material away as a product of the new age when Amorrites ruled, their attempt to explain the elevation of their god to the pantheon, or, if from an earlier period, as a reflection/representation of the gradual assimilation of a foreign element into the Sumerian community. There is nonetheless the possibility that *The Marriage of Mardu* was not authored or conveyed by an Amorrite source, but is of a piece with the other Sumerian stories (and distinct from the letters) under discussion here, because all of them *do* attribute an identity, a function, and a location to Mardu – that of an outsider. The text might be read as establishing a history of Mardu in which his transition from insider to outsider is plotted, just as was the case with Ishbi-Erra. Mardu is derogated similarly to Ishbi-Erra, too, when as a man from Mari he is likened to a "monkey from the mountains" with the "mind of a dog" (Cooper 1983: 33; Michalowski 2005a: 203). The creation of the "outsider" in this way is a standard rhetorical technique, a way of dialectic, the relationship of which to actual social practice of the period can only be established by other sources.

There are two strands, then, to the neo-Sumerian literary production (excluding the letters) with which this chapter began. On the one hand are the relationships with Gilgamesh, Lugalbanda, and Ninsun; the reclamation of great historical authority in their Sumerian-ness; and the portrayal of kingship, not just as good, but as part of the right and proper cosmic order. On the other is the reiteration of Mardu identity, not as subhuman barbarians (contra Cooper 1983), but simply as belonging outside the bounds of the empire. Both strands end in the same knot, a knot fashioned by usurpation. In this case, it is Shulgi's usurpation. While the Sumerian stories of Gilgamesh, Enmerkar, and Lugalbanda establish Ur-Nammu as a legitimate king, divinely sanctioned and as entitled to rule as his predecessor, Utu-Hegal (Hallo 1966: 137; Brisch 2007: 20), a broader view of Sumerian literature reveals a far more comprehensive program of indoctrination than just a new history of one king.

I do not mean to suggest that Shulgi overthrew his predecessor and is laying claim to a place in Ur-Nammu's dynasty, to which he is not entitled. Shulgi's is a legitimate succession in the Ur III dynasty. Yet he usurped the known, predicted, "natural" order – and violently so – when, in consolidating the Ur III empire, he rearranged the fundamental economic, political, and religious structures of Sumer, primarily via the institution of a new taxation and redistribution

---

71 That this word is not translated is because it is not known what it means. It denotes a literary form, however, in the same way as does the word "hymn."

system. This served to rupture both the political autonomy and the economic self-sufficiency of the cities of the south, in a way that was never before accomplished. Other far-reaching consequences included severing the networks of social relationships maintained through the extension of families across different livelihoods and geographies – especially, but not only, between farmers and pastoralists located in southern Mesopotamia and the east, respectively.

That Shulgi's militaristic intentions were to bring under his domain the territories between the Tigris and the Zagros, in order to extract taxes from them, has long been well established (Steinkeller 1987b). His year names record a progressive incorporation of the area east of the Tigris and Persian Gulf (Fig. 32) into his realm (Frayne 1997; Sallaberger and Westenholz 1999: 141–3; Van de Mieroop 2004: 70, 73), especially the foothills and mountains; while it has been argued that this was in response to the troublesome nature of the area (perhaps because it was home to a significant nomadic population? [e.g., Steinkeller 2007a: 225]), and that everywhere else in the kingdom was peaceful (Sallaberger 2007: 433),[72] we should not take Ur's word for it – especially not the word as it is presented in literary sources. There is another way to look at the year-name data: Ur was the aggressor, targeting the eastern lands and mountains because they contained something it wanted – something that heretofore had not been under the control of the state on such a massive scale: pastoralism.

The eastern lands were, and still are, prime pastoralist territory. They were used for grazing the animals, not only of private households and state and temple estates within the Third Dynasty of Ur (and before), but also of the other polities in the area, such as Elam and Anshan, Eshnunna and Susa. Control of these lands would have meant that private households could no longer operate independently in regions beyond the state and would also expand the herds the state could command – or at the least on which it could levy taxes, as it appropriated those previously belonging to other states, bringing them under the control of the regional administrators who were responsible for sending them into the coffers of the realm (Steinkeller 1987b; Sigrist 1992; Dahl 2003; Allred 2006). Two concentrated periods of conquest[73] are centered around two major undertakings that, rather than mere constructions, constitute major events – the building of "the wall of the land" in Shulgi Year 37 and the building of the stockyards at Puzrish-Dagan in Shulgi Year 39 (Frayne 1997: 106–7; similarly Sallaberger and Westenholz 1999: 143).[74] It is no coincidence that these events were very close in time. The one required the other. Both were essential steps in

---

72 Although according to Group A of the literary letters, Subir was unstable (Michalowski 1989: 53).

73 At least conquest as represented by Ur, for we only have the official rendition that they were successful.

74 Although Puzrish-Dagan, also known as Esagdana, was in existence long before this (Sharlach 2004: 13).

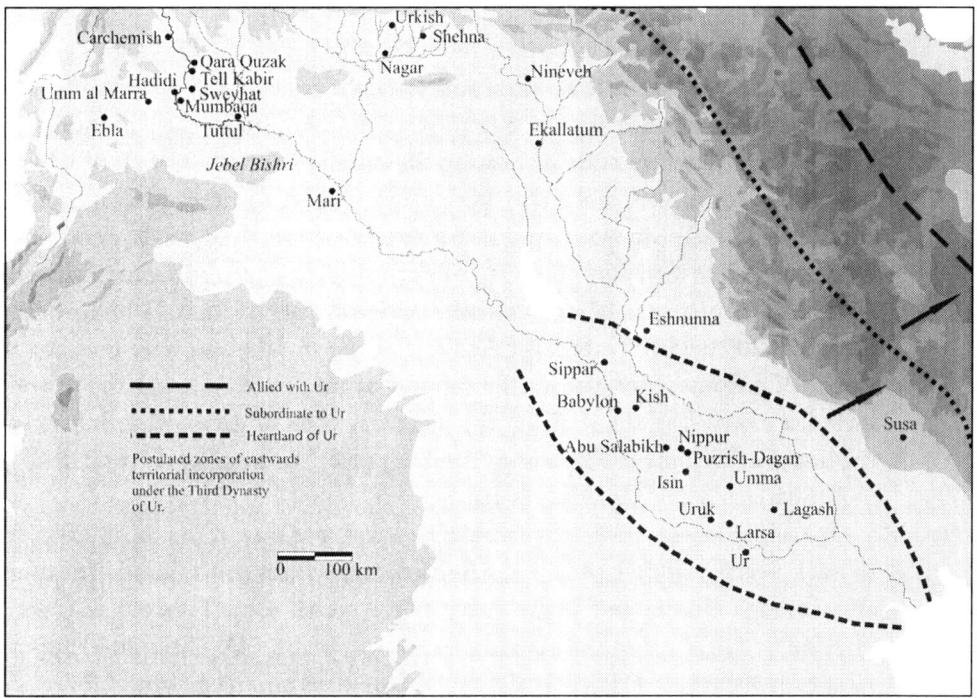

32. Map of the Ur III expansion.

further subordinating Sumer as much as the east. I would attribute to Shulgi an ultimate goal in all this maneuvering: to so negate the centrifugal impulse of the city-states as to prevent even the possibility of a revolt similar to the one suffered by Naram-Sin. Conflict between the kings of Ur and "local aristocratic families" (Maekawa 1996: 154; also Steinkeller 1987b) was frequent, exacerbated by the increasing abrogation of the power of those families.

Shulgi sought to accomplish Sumer's subjugation through, among other means, the continued elaboration of something called the **bala**, just one of several forms of taxation and extraction extended across the empire (Steinkeller 1987b). One element of the two basic components of the **bala** seems to have been a rotating responsibility for the upkeep of the state's main cultic centers by the core and is argued to have been the continuation of an earlier form of religious amphictyony (Hallo 1960; Maeda 1994; Sharlach 2004). Shulgi's radical innovation, however, was the engineering of a system of redistribution under the purview of the crown that was so complicated and multidirectional (Sharlach 2004) it created a structural interdependence between contributors, not unlike that in evidence in the global economy at the time of writing this chapter (2009) – and probably with similar catastrophic outcomes. Umma, for example, sent considerable quantities of grain, animal fodder, reeds, wood, and workers to Ur; reeds and wood to Uruk; grain, wood, and reeds (as many as 65,000 bundles in one year) to Nippur; and to Puzrish-Dagan, barley, reeds, and timber. Other commodities, in smaller quantities, such as beer, bitumen, and leather, are also recorded (Sharlach 2004: 35–40). Umma *received* various goods that it then passed up to the central authority, the crown, while certain officials there received supplies for the administrative tasks under their authority – such as local funerary cults or hosting diplomatic visitors – not all of which was locally consumed, since they were often sent on to other places. Lagash contributed nearly fifty percent of its barley production, flour, reeds, wood, and fodder, as well as men and women to work the mill in Puzrish-Dagan (Sharlach 2004: 95); Umma sent laborers to other cities as part of its **bala** obligations (Sharlach 2004: 160). Materials taken out of the storehouses were used for a variety of purposes, not just for the support of the provinces and Nippur, and included crown festivals such as "the mortuary cults of deceased members of the house of Ur," for the **ki-a-nag** "drinking place" or **nag lugal** "royal drinking" (Sharlach 2004: 52; Lynch 2010).

One of the key elements of the **bala**, however, and one of the most difficult to track, was livestock, to which the Sumerian provinces contributed little over all (although Umma and Lagash gave to the crown some livestock that was physically transferred to the key cities in Shulgi's realm – Ur, Uruk, and Nippur [Sharlach 2004: 111–12]). Animals were also used within the provinces for royal expenses, especially if the king came to visit, and governors "paid for" livestock to be sacrificed in the central shrines of Nippur. At the same time, animals were sent from crown herds to the provinces on a regular basis – often involving large numbers (Sharlach 2004: 123) – so that the net appearance of livestock transactions by the core provinces seems to have been withdrawal rather than contribution. The focal point of these various movements of livestock (primarily cattle, sheep, and goats; also some equids) were the stockyards of Puzrish-Dagan, built for the purpose near Drehem. Puzrish-Dagan was the eastern depot for redistribution in the province of Nippur and processed other commodities as well as livestock. It also housed a treasury (Sharlach 2004: 14). Puzrish-Dagan supplied the animal needs of state cults, especially those at Nippur and at Ur, but also at Uruk (Sharlach 2004: 110). While numbers fluctuate from place to place and according to month, the figures can be vast. In one instance about 375 sheep were apportioned for one month's sacrifices in the central shrines, as were 40–120 oxen (Sharlach 2004: 107). Annual totals on occasion amounted to 350,000 sheep and goats alone (Robertson 1995: 446). However, sacrifices in the Nippur temples, which were called the **bala** of a given province, came not from that province but from the royal herds – although the animals that constituted the **bala** of a province were fed and maintained by that province, and it is not entirely clear from the records where exactly the animals actually were: they may have been herded outside the province (Sharlach 2004: 109), and vast quantities of fodder were shipped to them, along with the personnel to care for them.

This is where the Mardu come in. Mardu feature regularly in the Drehem archive and in administrative texts from other cities (Buccellati 1966). This kind of attestation indeed constitutes the bulk of references to them. Mardu are contributing to, *and* withdrawing from, the **bala** system from Puzrish-Dagan (e.g., Goetze 1953: 103; Buccellati 1966), bringing in fat-tail sheep, and taking out other kinds of animals. One name in particular stands out as the recipient of frequent withdrawals from the **bala** – Naplanum. Head of the Emutbal, founder of the first Amorrite dynasty of Larsa (although at this time he was associated with the city of Kisig [Steinkeller 2004: 39; Michalowski 2006c: 59, but cf. Buccellati 1966: 319]), Naplanum occurs in the Drehem texts at least seventy-five times.[75] Whereas most of the livestock transactions at Drehem do not record the actual movement of animals so much as which province bore the cost of supporting them and in which province's name they were sacrificed, animals were physically moved to Naplanum (or at least to Naplanum's holdings) and on one occasion are recorded as having been shipped upstream. Yet because it has always been assumed that Mardu equates with nomads – which equates with outsiders, which essentially means enemies – the transactions involving Naplanum have been interpreted as gifts, and the significance of the fact that he also contributed to the system is largely overlooked. Although his name occurs from time to time in the same lists as men labeled foreigners, Naplanum was not placated or bought off because he was an enemy ("booty" is registered only three times in the texts, unusual for a group of people supposedly constantly at war with Ur) or paid because he was a mercenary, but because he was a regular participant in the system.

The animals sent to Naplanum are very often designated by a specific term: **kin a-al-la-nu-um mar-tu-še₃**, or, "to the place of Naplanum Mardu" (pers. comm. L. Allred). **Ki**, meaning "place," is never used with Mardu in Sumerian texts, only **kur**, and the association of **ki** with Naplanum's personal name indicates not a land, a fixed place in either geographic or political terms, but the place where Naplanum happens to be. This, it is clear in the texts, may change, for goods are directed to Napalanum in/at **kur** Mardu, Kisig, and then **kur** Mardu again (Steinkeller 2004: 39). Not only does Naplanum seem to move, he moves between different kinds of places – town and country. This juxtaposition of what is understood as mountain/steppe and city has long confounded interpretation – was Naplanum a nomad or not?

The question need not puzzle us. Moving between town and country is precisely the way some mobile pastoralists live. Naplanum himself did not have to be present in either place in order to receive the deliveries, but as a pastoralist he certainly may have moved back and forth between them with ease.[76] That

---

75 And three times at Girsu; my thanks to Lance Allred for collating the mentions of Naplanum.
76 It should be noted here that leaders were usually not performing the daily work of caring for sheep, so their movements, presence or absence, among those who were, and their residence in the city, were conditioned by other factors.

he maintained a residence in town does *not* mean that Naplanum has sedentarized, or is trying to become civilized, giving up his Amorrite/mobile roots.[77] Leaders and elites of mobile groups are well known in contemporary situations to maintain urban residences for a variety of reasons (Porter 2004; Shryock 1997) – to enjoy the fleshpots no doubt, but equally to have a place where they can conduct economic and political interactions with their sedentary contacts. More to the point is the fact that this is also attested in antiquity, in the Old Babylonian period no less, where the giving of houses – sometimes even entire towns – located in one polity to members of another polity was standard diplomatic practice among urban leaders (Eidem 2000: 258-9). It was a sign of political recognition, if not honor, to be awarded such a property, for this does not seem to have been a situation where one simply bought a house somewhere as a second residence, but one where a house was given, or petitioned for, as a mechanism of political alliance. As Eidem (2000: 258) notes, these houses had a symbolic, as well as economic and diplomatic, function.

On the other hand, dual urban/rural residence is hardly uncommon (see Schloen 2001: 270 for an example from Ebla and Wiggermann 2000: 173 for the Middle Assyrian period). There is no reason to assume that Naplanum is not from the heartland of the Ur III kingdom[78] and, like many of the names regularly attested in the Drehem archive (Sharlach 2004: 109), is appearing here in an official function, perhaps as owner of extensive herds. The text TRU 320 where Naplanum has contributed animals in excess of the requirement (Buccellati 1966: 80; Lambert 1962, for original), and other instances where his accounts are balanced, suggest this. This is not to say that an either/or choice must be made here, that Naplanum is either a Mesopotamian or a pastoralist – it is perfectly possible to be both.

Only forty percent of all the personal names qualified by Mardu are linguistically "Amorrite" in construction (Buccellati 1966: 100); twenty percent are Sumerian; and the rest are Akkadian or unknown. This has major implications, for it is the understanding that Amorrite is a foreign language, and that the Sumerian word **mar-dú/mar-tu** is synonymous with it – in conjunction with the literary letters – that has provided the substructure of our reconstructions of their origins and history. Buccellati (1966: 255) interprets this phenomenon as a product of progressive sedentarization, where the origins of the person are maintained, at least by the bureaucracy, despite his changed circumstances and attempts at assimilation in adopting a local name, especially

---

77 Anthropological approaches to mobile pastoralists in the 1970s and early 1980s were preoccupied with this issue (e.g., Salzman 1980), and this work was highly influential on understandings of pastoralism in the ancient world.

78 Shumi-hinni, "father of the Yamuti," also received animals from Drehem and is listed with ensis of Ur. On these grounds Buccellati (1966: 337) suggests he was a nomad whose territory was entirely within the confines of Sumer.

since this linguistic division in Mardu names is associated with the archives of specific places – approximately sixty percent of Mardu names at Drehem, Isin, and Ur are Amorrite, while a similar proportion of Mardu names at Lagash are Sumerian, while Umma shows a somewhat more balanced mixture.

But the patterns do not quite support this view. For one thing, whatever the linguistic origin of the name, the materials or situations connected with Mardu all involve animals or their by-products. In the case of Drehem, it is livestock; in the Isin archive, leather; in Lagash, weaving. For another, the situation of Mardu in relation to these commodities is such that they are intrinsic to the system and not external to it.

At Isin, the leather to be expended is for the making of commodities, primarily containers and sometimes also shoes given to various people designated Mardu. It is not the commodity that is at stake (although the commodity is what is distributed), but the material – the leather itself. If these Mardu were foreign mobile pastoralists, with their own means of producing leather goods, they would surely have no need of expenditures from the Isin storehouses. If the commodities were merely gifts or rewards, then (like coals to Newcastle), containers and shoes were not particularly thoughtful. Contra Buccellati (1966), whether or not these Mardu are mentioned with Mari or Dilmun (and association with people from these places is not surprising, as both may be thought of as anchors of pastoralist landscapes and might be utilized by anyone at a given point in time), they are at the least imbricated in the system, taking part in an exchange where their traditional material is transformed, on their account, into something else.

The Mardu attested at Lagash (and Umma) are more than engaged in exchange with the Ur III system, they are deeply embedded in it. All the records in which the word **mar-du** occurs are exactly the same kinds of receipts in which any Sumerian living in Lagash might be found – legal texts, ration allowances (the bulk of references), expenditure of foods for offerings, records of fields, and work assignments (Buccellati 1966: 310–11). The majority of those receiving rations are women (see also Sigrist 1992), four of whom are mentioned together six times. Some of the women in these texts are labeled **arua**. This is a specific category of gift to the temple, for its support, and it could consist of animals and/or people – primarily women and children, and far less often men (Gelb 1972). **Arua** personnel were sometimes slaves, sometimes free, always dependent on the institution to which they were given, and were often those who could no longer be supported by their family due to economic distress. Sometimes, however, they were prisoners of war donated by the king (Gelb 1972), and it is possible that it is in this capacity that the Mardu **arua** are found here. But in at least one instance a Mardu, rather than an offering, was the offerer, donating a donkey to the temple (Gelb 1972). This would indicate both that this fellow was potentially a member of the society served by the temple and that Mardu **arua** women were not necessarily only booty.

We do not know what these women did at Lagash. The 5 **sila** barley allotments given to each of them is far below the monthly rations for even the most poorly paid dependent women (millers and weavers) in the Ur III period, who receive a minimum of 30 **sila** monthly. Even immature children are given at least 10 **sila** each (Maekawa 1980: 96). While this might suggest that these women were not reliant on an institution for their total subsistence, and that the 5 **sila** in these texts was a supplement to some other form of income, **arua** women are by definition temple dependents *without* other support. Their inclusion in this category demands that this ration should be seen as something above their usual upkeep.

Because as many as six thousand weavers were employed in Girsu[79]/Lagash, a city also notable for the vast quantities of animals it supported (Maekawa 1987: 53), it seems not unlikely that the Mardu women were weavers. Although not all women were weavers, weavers were almost always women and their children, with **arua** women in particular fulfilling this task. Athough wool was also disbursed to workers independently of the workshops and privately produced cloth was brought to temple and palace (Wright 1996: 99), most weavers attested in the texts belonged to temple households and it is argued they were largely indentured servants or essentially slaves. Such women are generally considered to have been outsiders, prisoners of war, or foreigners (Wright 1998: 65-6) - particularly since, unlike other (male) workers who operated in kin-groups (Steinkeller 1987a), they seem detached from any larger social or familial context in the documentation (and hence McCorriston 1997). It is also possible that this attests only to the alienability of women - that the critical definition of a kin system was a male not a female domain - or that this particular job (and thereby the women who performed it) was socially debased.

Whatever the case of the Mardu women receiving rations at Lagash proves to be, textile production does not seem to be related to the animals in the **bala** texts, despite both the number of sheep (and goats and cattle) cycling through the system and the cultic value of cloth (Wright 1996). Texts from Ur and Umma do, however, document the extent of this industry as based on locally obtained wool (Waetzoldt 1972; Van de Mieroop 1993a: 161; Algaze 2008: 77-92). We can only assume, I think, that textile production, too, was absorbed by the crown, for Shulgi's "reforms" (see Yoffee 1995: 295; Allred 2006: 6-8 for a summary) spared no one, from the most menial to the most sublime. In this view, the Ur economy can perhaps be likened to a draconian program of nationalization, where every opportunity was taken to appropriate resources to the state (Wright 1998).[80] Appropriation also included the vast holdings of the temple estates

---

79   Girsu is a town within the city-state of Lagash, at one point becoming its capital.
80   Nevertheless, the state's control of labor was not total - it took from family organizations but did not control all their labor/production. For part of the year at least, the workers'

(Dahl 2003: 100), which now became crown estates in practice if not in appearance (Steinkeller 1987b). Since these temples had huge resources devoted to textile production, this too became the king's. It is not clear to me if such action was for the personal aggrandizement of the king, the power of the state (Adams 2006a), or the better redistribution of resources to the members of the polity – or, perhaps more likely, that all three were considered one and the same thing.

But none of Shulgi's reforms could have been possible without the wars against the highlands, which would have served to shut down independent herds of the provinces pastured to the east and also prohibited alternative supply systems that would allow the provinces to bypass the crown. It started, significantly, with Der in Year 21 (Frayne 1997: 103) – significantly, because (as I argue elsewhere [Porter 2009a]) the place-name Der is to become in the Old Babylonian period the basis of sociopolitical identity for Simalite groups, to whom Zimri-Lim, one of the most famous of Amorrites and the king of Mari, belongs, and it derives from this Transtigridian Der. It is this first move – in what turns out to be an elaborate game of subjugation, competition, and resistance – that puts it all in play, culminating in the "Amorrite" dominance of the land of the four riverbanks some hundreds of years later.

Moreover, it is around this time that the transformation in the operation and recording of the state-controlled economy comes into existence, as seen in the "flood of documents" beginning after Shulgi Year 20 (Englund 1991: 258). Campaigns thereafter are very focused on the eastern and northeastern lands. Years 24–27[81] record the destruction of Karahar, Simurrum, and Harsi, repeated in years 31–32, when Karahar and Simurrum are again destroyed, along with Anshan in years 33 (according to a Puzrish-Dagan tablet) and/or 34 (Steinkeller 2007a: 226). Perhaps these campaigns proved costly – or perhaps simply unsatisfactory, for shortly thereafter construction of the wall commences: (Year 37), "the year the wall of the land was built" (Frayne 1997: 106).

This is the **bàd-ma-da**, "the wall of the land." Because of the extensive discussion of the work on a "wall" in the literary letters, the two are thought connected, so that the "wall of the land" is the wall "facing the highland" (the wall of Black et al. 1998–2006: t.3.1.08; Michalowski 1989: 53; 1976: 84), that is, the Zagros; and the wall facing the highland is against the inimitable enemy, the Tidnu (cf. Allred 2006: 12–13). Whatever one's position on the basis of the letters – whether or not they are derived from original and authentic Ur III documents – such connections are methodologically problematic because of the insecurities of their chronological attribution. We simply cannot be sure that the letters, or any documents from which they might be

---

time seems to have been their own and they could dispose of it as they wished (Wright 1996: 90).

81 Hereafter all year names are according to Frayne 1997, with which Sallaberger and Westernholz 1999 is largely in concordance.

derived, are historically accurate or actually date to the time of the rulers who purportedly sent them.

I will assume, for the time being, that the story told in the literary letters constitutes a fair representation of how things usually were or could often be. Delays in the construction of the wall in letter t.3.1.08 are mentioned in association with the Tidnu having "come down[82] from the mountains" (Michalowski 1976: 199). Frayne (1997: 106) understands the Tidnu coming down from the mountains as a hostile act on their part, but it is entirely possible that it was simply a regular, annual movement out of the highland pastures to the lowlands; it might have been referenced as an indicator of season, and hence of rapidly passing time. This is in keeping with the beginning of the passage, where the builders are given one month to finish the wall. The recent translation of this letter by Black et al. (1998-2006) certainly does not connect the urgent need to complete the wall with any sense of ferocity or threat from the Tidnu; if it were to be taken literally, one might wonder if there was an agricultural crisis of some kind, where the regular pastoralist movement to riverine pastures would render catastrophic an already tenuous situation – a late crop not yet harvested, for example.[83]

However, as I have argued above, the literary letters do not bear much relation to the historical inscriptions and year names of Ur III kings (where the focus of Shulgi's eastern interests are well-known entities such as Der and Anshan), and if this is so, then to my knowledge the only mention of Tidnu that could perhaps be attributable to Shulgi comes in Shulgi U. A prayer poem to Nergal, Shulgi U states: "Wherever you stride, all their troops suffer.... Anshan and Tidnu, Nergal, wherever you stride, all their troops suffer" (Black et al. 1998-2006: t.2.4.2.21, lines 24-26). Unfortunately, the argumentation connecting the hymns with year names and inscriptions is always so circular that little faith can be placed in it. Otherwise, a careful sorting of the references shows that it is only the Mardu who are mentioned, in a neutral manner, in sources authoritatively dated to Shulgi. It is not until the reign of Shu-Sin that real hostility toward the Mardu erupts, when a specific group of Mardu, the Tidnu, become the subject of a very targeted campaign – a campaign waged by both militarily and propagandistic means.

Although all Tidnu are Mardu, not all Mardu are Tidnu, and it is important to keep them separate. The name Tidnu occurs in apposition to Mardu so frequently, including in the genealogy of Ammi-Saduqa[84] (GDH, Finkelstein

---

82 Cf. Black et al. 1998-2006 below: "returned."
83 In which case, Sallaberger's (2007: 445) suggestion that this might simply be a structure to keep sheep out is tenable. However, unless the structure was rather substantial, the sheep's caretakers, rather than the sheep themselves, could readily knock down any impediment to their movement. Indeed, this might be seen in Shulgi's letter cited above.
84 Where it is spelled **Di-ta-nu**.

1966) and the genealogy of Samsi-Addu[85] (AKL, Gelb 1954), that some scholars have assumed it is simply another word for the Amorrites (Whiting 1995:
1232), contributing to the general idea that Mesopotamians felt great hostility
toward these people who were fundamentally outsiders. But detailed consideration of the two names (as Marchesi 2006) shows that **mar-dú** constitutes the
name of a general category, while Tidnu is a specific group within that category
(Marchesi 2006: 12). What is more, it should be clear by now that I do not consider the designation Mardu to be an ethnicon (contra Kamp and Yoffee 1980,
cf. Marchesi 2006), nor **kur** Mardu a "kingdom" or any other form of geopolitical reality rooted in place. The term has a far more generic, and at the same
time far more layered, meaning, as proposed above. Tidnu, however, while also
not an ethnicon, is more specific. Attributes associated with Mardu are therefore not necessarily to be associated with Tidnu. Such is particularly the case
with the question of location and origins (contra Marchesi 2006: 17); whereas
Mardu are attested within many Mesopotamian cities, Tidnu (with the possible exception of Steinkeller's [1992: 260-65] problematic reading of **éren + x** as
Tidnu [but cf. Marchesi 2006: 22-3]) are not.

The first such mention of the Tidnu is in a *Sammeltafel* (a collection of inscriptions copied onto a single tablet) recording events of Shu-Sin, Year Three.
Adduced by Gelb (1980) and Frayne (1997: 290) as evidence for a western location of the Amorrites because it lists Shu-Sin's wars against Tidnu and what is
spelled Yahmad, but taken to be Yamhad (Owen 1993), this is the only time the
name Tidnu – as opposed to the term Mardu – is not directly associated with
the east, nor with the polities of Anshan and Elam. At the same time, given
that this passage follows an inscription referring to Year Three's destruction of
Shimamum (the location of which is most likely in the region of Diyarbakir,
certainly Transtigridian [Sallaberger 2007: 442, cf. Marchesi 2006: 13–14]),
there is still a mountainous connection, one within a likely pastoralist range, if
based in the Diyala or Jebel Hamrin (Michalowski 1976: 104–11).

The first unequivocally attributable mention of Tidnu is found in Shu-Sin
Year Four, the year in which Shu-Sin "built the Amorrite wall called 'it keeps
Tidnum at a distance'" (Frayne 1997: 290). While most writers seem to accept
that this was indeed a second wall (Sallaberger 2007), Michalowski (2005a: 200;
1983) suggests that Shu-Sin simply renamed the original wall built by Shulgi,
although he understands that the original wall was not a wall per se, but a line
of fortifications much like the Roman *limes*. If indeed a wall ever existed, it is
possible that Shu-Sin copied an accomplishment of his predecessor (a common
habit of Mesopotamian rulers). However, the fact that a specific people are
cited – in contrast to the more generic statement of Shulgi – renders it, I think,
most likely that Shu-Sin rebuilt and extended an earlier construction in the

85 Where it is spelled **Di-da-nu**.

face of a real conflict. That the conflict was with the Tidnu, the central issue of importance, is made explicit in two additional inscriptions: one (purportedly on a major cult statue [Frayne 1997: 293]), echoes events in years Three and Four, describing the rebellion of Simanum and Habura followed by a mention of Mardu and Tidnu. Here, several lines later, is the second of only two calumnious descriptions of the Amorrites (the first, of course, being that contained in *The Marriage of Mardu*): "Since that time, Mardu, a ravaging people, with the instincts of a beast, like wolves ... the stalls" (Frayne 1997: 299; also Buccellati 1966: 94). The final inscription, E3/2.1.4.17, is a little more restrained, referring to the time (Year Four) Shu-Sin built the wall and returned the Mardu to their land: "The year Shu-Sin, King of Ur, built the Amorite wall (called) 'It keeps Tidnum at a distance' and returned the 'foot' of the Amorites to their land" (Frayne 1997: 290).

The picture, then, of Mardu in the inscriptions and archival texts is different than the history reconstructed from the letters. It is a picture of a group of people who are just like anyone else, except for the fact that they are not farmers; just like anyone else, they are woven through the Mesopotamian world in most of the aspects evident to us in the texts – starting with (as the table below shows) the Early Dynastic period, when people labeled Mardu receive rations at Shurrupak. They have various jobs (e.g., Buccellati 1966: 17, 43, 340–44), ranging from the menial to the official, from the military to the cultic (e.g., the position of lamenter, for which more than one Mardu received rations). They receive food allotments and work assignments (e.g., Buccellati 1966: 35). They even own fields (e.g., Buccellati 1966: 45).

Is this a case of progressive sedentarizaton, as is often suggested? Of nomads gradually infiltrating the civilized lands? I do not think so. Buccellati's (1966) categories of resident and nonresident Mardu do not necessarily represent two separate entities, people leaving their origins behind and changing the very nature of their being, but simply parts of the same entity, occupied in different aspects of subsistence. Indeed, they may up until this point be parts of the same family (certainly the same ancestral group), with regular interchange between them, as discussed in previous chapters. Although we have little direct evidence of this in the Ur III materials, Naplanum – whose story to date has been told in light of standard preconceptions, already thoroughly delineated, about nomads in general and Amorrites in particular – proves an apt illustration. Naplanum's purview encompasses the city and the steppe (he has people in both) – the core components of the economy, even the state – and this is not extraordinary. Rather, it is quite ordinary.

Then things changed. While Mardu continue to be attested as embedded within Mesopotamia throughout the Ur III period, the Tidnu emerge as an enemy early in the reign of Shu-Sin. The proximate cause of this conflict was

Shulgi's construction of the wall and of Puzrish-Dagan, steps in the progressive appropriation of all aspects of the economy that began halfway through his reign and changed the situation of mobile pastoralists in the eastern lands in general – and, in particular, of the Tidnu whose primary range, at this time at least (despite earlier references at Ebla, discussed below), is between the Tigris and the foothills of the Zagros.

The response to Shulgi's construction was not immediate, however, because it would have been some time before its punitive costs, both economic and social, would be felt. Not only would mobile pastoralists lose much of their autonomy, grazing lands, and market under this new economic regime, when the expansion of the **bala** system brought their traditional pasturage under military control (Steinkeller 1987b), but they would also lose their inherent connection to the Mesopotamian world as key components of extended households/ancestral groups spread across diverse subsistence practices. The wall, in whatever form it took, actual or symbolic, was meant to keep them out. The usual practices that sustained the integrity of the family when stretched over time and space were, at minimum, impeded. That the consequences were not quite those anticipated by the state is evident in the state's reaction to them: vilification through a variety of textual means. It hardly needs documentary evidence to demonstrate that the wall was ultimately ineffectual for a number of practical reasons, and that those it was meant to control sought to escape that control.

I would suggest that resistance came not only from those left on the outside of the wall; it also would have come from those within it, because the Tidnu were no more alien to Mesopotamia than other Mardu, despite common acceptance (based on the Ebla texts) of a western origin for Tidnu and Mardu alike (Buccellati 1966; Sallaberger 2007). I will explain this in detail shortly, but for now I wish to return once more, briefly, to the stories with which this chapter started. The conflict between crown and country constitutes the subtext of the entire cycle of the Enmerkar and Lugalbanda stories, which are ultimately about Inana's divine – and antecedent – approval of Uruk's (that is, Ur's) subjugation of the east. I mentioned above that the role of Aratta as the antagonist in this cycle was no coincidence. Scholars have long thought that Aratta, whether mythical or real, was located in the east because the passage where the teeming hordes of the eastern mountains are to grovel in the dust for the goddess mentions Susa and Anshan. The riches of the mountain are for the wealth of the **gipar** – the goddess's holy house. For Inana, read the rulers of Ur; for the **gipar**, read their royal palace.

This discourse is constructed in the face of a far more complex reality than the dualistic interpretations to which Mesopotamian studies are too often given, where Sumer is good/safe/deservedly triumphant and anywhere else is bad/dangerous/deservedly subjugated. Whereas Vanstiphout (2004: 9) claims the subject matter is the supremacy of Uruk over Aratta as representative of "uncivilized" regions – synonymous with all foreign countries – the tale instead is situated in a contest between fairly equal claimants who are but reflections of each other, especially in that both the king of Uruk and the lord of Aratta are loved by Inana. Indeed, *Enmerkar and the Lord of Aratta* is presented from the perspective of Enmerkar, while *Enmerkar and En-Suhgir-ana* (which would perhaps be better named En-Suhgir-ana and the Lord of Uruk) presents the perspective of the Lord of Aratta – even though it is in this story that he eventually gives way. Aratta may be at a distance from Uruk, but it is far from alien to it, nor is Aratta the antithesis of Uruk. Aratta is not (contra Vanstiphout 2004: 6) "non-Sumer"; it is Sumer's matching counterpart. This is evident in a number of ways, not least of which is the contrast between the metaphoric/symbolic mountain – the mountain of Sumer – and an actual one – the mountain of Aratta (Steinkeller 2007b), because, as discussed above, the mountain is deeply significant on many levels. Both kings claim to be nurtured by the soil of the other; it is also clear that both places are dependent on the riches of the other, and that barring the way between them has dire consequences. Aratta is at risk when its crops fail, crops that Enmerkar has in abundance, and Uruk is at risk when the magician renders its livestock unproductive. That Uruk prevails is not to destroy Aratta, but, in subsuming it, to render such ties even more inviolable.

At least that is the plan. This text, like the others of neo-Sumerian production, is metaphor and propaganda at the same time. It is not a literal description of the people who live in the mountains because, for its didactic purpose to be successful (the acceptance of the new order, the order designed by Shulgi where the mountains are subject to his rule), the objects of the propaganda (those who must be persuaded of the appropriateness of a new situation) must not see themselves as subjugated but feel only a gentle familiarity, a sense of proper outcome that shifts them to a different way of viewing the world and their place in it. Whether the riches of the mountains lie in its metals rather than its fleece, whether the subject is the kingdom of Anshan or the mobile Tidnu, does not really matter. The message is really for those within the realm of Ur, those whose livelihood and family relationships are split apart by the creation, now, of a bifurcated world.

The message would appear, however, to have failed. Before it is possible to discuss further an ancient insurgence, though, it is necessary to preempt a little academic resistance. The proposal that the Amorrites are not the antithesis of the Mesopotamians in all things, and are not even foreigners, is radical, especially in light of the long scholarly tradition that has accepted the Mesopotamian sources at face value and sought to identify a homeland for the Amorrites in them. Opening the way for an uncritical acceptance of the Mesopotamian view on this topic is the modern understanding that pastoralists are fundamentally separate from the sedentary world, a view bolstered by literary descriptions that confirm our stereotypes. Extract that understanding from the equation and it is evident, from the earliest attestations of the word "Mardu" until the Ur III period, that there is no imperative to externality – nor is there any necessary direction from which the Mardu came.

And this is where things grow really quite complicated. Not only are kinds of sources conflated, and from different periods and places, but issues are also collapsed into a single problem. The story of the Mardu as extracted from an indiscriminate mingling of historical and literary text is bound up with a search for their original location and the meaning of their name (as, for example, Lönnqvist 2008) – a very modern – and Western – need to locate, fix in place, and thereby control, everything in our purview. Three geographies seem to be in evidence in these sources, and the endeavor for the most part is to determine which provides the real origin of the Amorrites. Consensus seems to have it that they were originally from the west, even more precisely, that they came from the area between the Middle Euphrates and Jebel Bishri (Buccellati 1966; Whiting 1995; Streck 2000: 26; but cf. Durand 2010: 261–2). Jebel abd al-Aziz and Tur Abdin have also been proposed, and the recent discovery of the site of al-Rawda (Castel and Peltenburg 2007), a large circular settlement in a steppic zone in the region of Homs, has prompted the proposal that they came from farther west still (Sallaberger 2007; Lyonnet 2009; cf. Porter 2007a; 2009a). Attestations of an eastern location, such as found in the literary letters, have been resolved as evidence of their progressive movement eastwards and then south, finally arriving in Mesopotamia proper (Weiss and Courty 1993; Charpin 2003; cf. Porter 2009a).

Yet, although statements such as "the Amorite land was always situated near Jebel Bishri" (Sallaberger 2007: 445) are common, this is not quite the case. This orientation comes from two sources, the Ebla texts and two Akkadian inscriptions, one each from Naram-Sin and Sharkalisharri. Taking them in chronological order – and chronological precision is very necessary in this discussion – the situation becomes a little clearer.

There are over thirty references to Mardu in the Ebla texts, quite extraordinary in comparison to the numbers found in Akkadian or even Ur III administrative sources, and they present in a very different way. One of the most notable distinctions is that Mardu is written at Ebla with **ki**, in contrast to the Sumerian sources. **Ki**, meaning land, may have multiple uses at Ebla. Usually written following a toponym, although there are rare occurrences where it stands alone, **ki** may refer to a city (most often the case) but also to the polity of which that city is a part, as well as the territory – the general land – encompassed by that polity (Bonechi 1991). Mari[ki] may mean the *city* of Mari (located at Tell Hariri); the kingdom of Mari (its political identity) or the *land* of Mari (the territory that comes under that polity's purview). These distinctions may be subtle, but they are important; they allow for the use of **ki** as denoting a broad concept of the entity referenced – one, what is more, that is not necessarily *fixed* in place.

Attestations of the word "Mardu" in the Ebla texts are spelled variously Mardum[ki] or Mardu[ki] / Martu[ki] (Archi 1985) – that is, Amurrum as opposed to Amurru – and Pettinato (1995) has determined that these terms in fact refer to two separate entities, arguing that the first, Mardum[ki], was a small, unimportant settlement not far from Ebla. Mardu[ki] is mentioned in conjunction with its **en** and its elders (**ab x áš-sù**)[86] in four out of twenty references, while only three texts mention the **en** of Mardu without elders, suggesting that they were perceived of as critical components of political identity. Mardum[ki] has a **lugal** rather than an **en**. Both Mardum and Mardu[87] had overseers (Archi 1985: 12, attestation 10 and 12). The overseers of Mardu swore an oath, assumed to be part of a treaty, to Kura, the city god of Ebla, while Mardum participated in the cult of 'Adabal (see Chapter 3), another very important deity at Ebla (Archi 1985: 9, attestation 16), but a deity integral to the larger region as well (Archi 2002b). Archi (2005: 84) notes that it is at the temple of Kura that allied cities came to swear their oaths, so one wonders if the respective associations of these names with Kura or 'Adabal is telling of the nature of the relationship of each group. The references seem, on the face of it, to indicate that Mardu[ki] designates a polity rather than an ethnicity, and one fixed in place. This in itself might be enough to support the widely held belief not only that Mardu was the word that meant west[88] but that the Amorrites were western in origin, refugees perhaps from a collapsed state, as Weiss and Courty (1993) have proposed in reference to the Habur. Just where that place might have been, however, is not so clear. Geographic indicators for Mardu[ki] in the Ebla texts seem to reference anywhere from the Mediterranean to Jebel Bishri (Bonechi 1993, 1998) and beyond.

None of the evidence, however, demands a territorially fixed or distinct political entity for this name. Listed in conjunction with Ditanu and Ibal, all these groups with their **en** and elders, not only Mardu, are associated with pastoralism and mobility. **Da-da-nu[ki]** is thought an archaic spelling of Ditanu and therefore equivalent to Tidnu (Marchesi 2006: 11–14, n. 33), while Ibal is described by a gloss as "of the steppe."[89] Discussions of these names proceed on

---

86 Translated alternatively by Marchesi (2006: 14) as a class of officials. See Chapter 3.
87 Only one of these references, no. 7 in Archi's (1985) list, spells Mardu with a *d*.
88 Whether secondary to the existence of a place-name or not: cf. Liverani (1973: 103), who argues that there was a place called Mardu west of Mesopotamia and hence the cardinal point gained its name, with Archi (1985: 8), "its original meaning indicated a cardinal point ('west') and secondarily a people living to the northwest."
89 In contradistinction to "of the canal" (Astour 1992: 34; Bonechi 2001: 60–62). This distinction in associations of Ibal may well parallel the bifurcated geography typical of mobile pastoralists in the second millennium (Porter 2009a), and for similar reasons.

the understanding that all three groups are external to Ebla on the grounds that they receive textiles. Those places that receive textiles are independent of Ebla; those places that do not receive textiles and other gifts are part of Ebla. It is also assumed that places listed together are located near each other, so that the Mardu **en**, the Tidnu **en**, and the Ibal **en** follow each other as recipients of fabric from Ebla because they are not only in close proximity to each other, but also to Ebla. Therefore the argument that the Amorrites originated in Syria in general and in the region of Jebel Bishri in particular would seem to be supported.[90]

This is an unnecessarily restrictive understanding of the practice of prestation on the one hand and, on the other, hardly does justice to the complexities of interactions between Ebla and those with which the polity had dealings, complexities which were far-reaching indeed (Archi and Biga 2003). No geographical constraint is implicit in this practice, nor does the duality between internality and externality replicate the multiple kinds of relationships that existed between Ebla, its neighbors, allies, and even constituents – few of whom were actually present in the city. The role of overseers, for example, was often to mediate between the administration and its dispersed components – who as primary producers were critical to its well-being, such as is evident at Umma in the Ur III period (Dahl 2003; Adams 2006a). The oath to Kura may in fact indicate, rather than a treaty between unrelated entities, a reinforcement of ordinary obligations to the polity. And, as argued in the previous chapter, I propose that the recognition of **en** and elders of Mardu, Ditanu, and Ibal is evidence of a certain kind of political organization utterly unrelated to whether these groups are mobile or sedentary – a political organization parallel to that of Ebla itself. That Ebla and Mardu here both have their own **ens** does not necessitate political distinctions between these two groups. The urban **en** may simply have a mobile counterpart, yet another arm in the complex structure of rule for that polity.

As also argued in the previous chapter, Ebla has its own mobile pastoralist component. Again, Mari in the Old Babylonian period offers a model for

---

90 At least two research projects, one Finnish (Lönnqvist 2008, 2010), one Japanese (Ohnuma and al-Khabour 2010), are currently investigating this question. However, findings of these projects do not quite support the contention that Amorrites came from Jebel Bishri. While it has been demonstrated that there was significantly increased activity in the Middle Bronze Age in the Bishri area (Nishiaki 2010: 45; Fuji and Adachi 2010: 73), this does not of course mean that there was increased *Amorrite* activity. Unfortunately, these projects seem to take it as already proven that Amorrites had their home at Jebel Bishri and therefore accept that the archaeological remains found there are Amorrite (such as Lönnqvist 2010: 170). This situation is of course hotly debated within Asyriological circles still. If the builders of the cairn fields around Jebel Bishri *were* Amorrites, however, it seems their exploitation of the area would have occurred after Amorrites were present elsewhere. Nevertheless, these projects offer major archaeological investigations of mobile pastoralist groups in one key area of pastoralist activity.

understanding these names and their relationship to the Ebla polity. Mardu, Ditanu, and Ibal are similar to the terms Hana, Numha, and Yaminite,[91] with similar differences in degrees of closeness and kinds of interaction with the polity from whose perspective we see these groups. Indeed, the two Ibals – that "of the steppe" and that "of the canal" may well parallel the bifurcated geography typical of mobile pastoralists in the second millennium (Porter 2009a), an example of which is the group who came to dominate Larsa toward the very end of the Third Dynasty of Ur, the same group led by our old friend Naplanum. Naplanum the Amorrite, who interacted with Ur III authorities on a regular basis, is now to be identified with Naplanum the (apocryphal?) founder of the Larsa dynasty (Steinkeller 2004: 36–40)[92] that emerged, along with Isin, as a leading power after the collapse of Ur.

It is not at all coincidental that the evidence as to Naplanum's relation to place in the Ur documentation, prior to his takeover of Larsa, alternates between the heartland of Mesopotamia and upstream Euphrates, because this is later evidenced as the territorial range of the Yamutbal. A particular phenomenon gives tantalizing evidence of the relationships at stake in this book: between town and country, mobility and sedentism, north and south. As discussed previously, two areas are associated in this post-Ur period with Yamutbal: the region of the Jebel Sinjar *and* the heartland of southern Mesopotamia around Larsa – and not just around Larsa, but also around Mashkan-shapir, much farther to the north. Moreover, there are six town names that are duplicated within these two regions of Yamutbal, the northern and the southern: Harusanum, Kaspanum, Lakusir, Rasum, Razama, and Tilla (Charpin 2003: 14). A multitude of implications stem from this duplication, a duplication that is clearly not an accident. One of those implications is that towns may be associated with – no, more than that, actually *belong* – to pastoralists (cf. Fleming 2004), because that is who the Yamutbal (a Simalite group) are, according to the several sources at our disposal: pastoralists. Another implication concerns the nature and meaning of the word "Mardu."

---

91 Another intriguing possibility is found in the name of the king of Mardu[ki], whose name is Yamuti/um (Archi 1985: 10). This name is found in the Genealogy of the Dynasty of Hammurabi and the Assyrian King List as one of the common ancestors of Samsi-Addu, and is taken as the name of a tribe (although it is better termed "ancestral group" for the reasons outlined in the previous chapters). It has also been associated with Naplanum himself (Buccellati 1966: 320; cf. Steinkeller 2004: 40) as well as the Yamutbal.

92 Although cf. Charpin (2004a: 69), who supports Edzard's proposal that this is something of a fabricated king list by Larsa compiled in order to demonstrate a prior claim to hegemony when in conflict with Isin. Steinkeller's (2004: 40) argumentation here may sometimes seem a stretch, but the association is nevertheless tenable given (1) the continued connection between the Yamutbal and the leaders of Larsa and evidence that the latter derived from the former, as well as the relationship between the Yamutbal, Larsa, and Mashkan-shapir, and (2) the arguments to be outlined below.

It is now necessary for another, hopefully short, excursus. It has been argued that the phenomenon of "mirrored toponyms" (Durand 1992; Joannès 1996; Charpin 2003),[93] especially of Yamutbal names, is evidence of the migration of Amorrites from the west and their eventual sedentarization in the south. On the contrary, these towns are not simply settlements belonging to another system that pastoralists become involved with, or adopt, as they move about the country. Neither is the practice of duplicate naming a case of a simple nostalgia for a homeland nor is it indicative of broad-scale diffusion of a group.

First, there is no clear evidence of directionality or temporal distinction in these duplications (Charpin 2003: 19). Southern names, for all we know, may precede northern ones; the doubling of place-names is not attested before the beginning of the second millennium or indeed before the Old Babylonian period, after the Amorrites are present throughout the southern region. Some of the names are not known at all until this period.[94] Nevertheless, Charpin (2003: 18) argues that mirrored toponymy may be linked with collapse of settlement in the Habur at the end of the third millennium that surveys "have clearly established" (see also Weiss and Courty 1993), stating that, with the exception of Nagar, none of the thirty names referring to sites in the Habur found in the pre-Sargonic Beydar texts are attested in the Old Babylonian tablets. Conversely, none of the settlement names of this same region known in the Old Babylonian sources are present earlier, with the exception again of Nagar.

This linkage is problematic. The Beydar texts (Ismail et al. 1996; Milano et al. 2004) are referring to the world that is important to Tell Beydar, ancient Nabada – a confined perspective, because Nabada's role is not political so much as it is administrative, supervising components of the agricultural regime[95] of ancient Nagar/Tell Brak (Sallaberger and Ur 2004; Archi 1998). There is no reason for the toponymics there to represent a comprehensive geography of the Habur region, and, as I have argued (Porter 2007a), evidence for collapse in the Habur and elsewhere is much less secure than previously assumed. While there are certainly connections to be made between mirrored toponyms and the third-millennium north, these are not such that a point of origin for the Amorrites can be argued (contra Porter 2007a), nor an explanation for population movements proposed; rather, they serve to show the cultural context in which this

93   Also Durand 1998: 111, where the meanings of some names refer to features of places the Amorrites encountered on their way, such as "bridge," "place of the tombs," and so on (but see Porter 2009a).

94   I thank Brendon Benz for compiling and analyzing the published references to the toponyms that manifest two locations. There may, of course, be unpublished attestations of some names of which I am unaware.

95   Meant in the broadest possible sense, so including animal husbandry of which broad sheep/goat pastoralism and more locally adjacent donkey breeding would both be components.

Table 5. Attestations of the label "Mardu" outside literary sources.

Time	Text	Place	Publication
EDI c. 2800	Ugula Tidnu (if **éren + x** = Tidnu)[d] "chief" or "overseer" of the Tidnu	Ur	Steinkeller 1992
ED IIIA c. 2600/2500	1. 900 liters of barley for PN / **Mar-dú** 2. 45 men receiving 1 loaf of bread; 28 women receiving 1 loaf of bread/**Mar-dú** 3. Utu[b] returned to **kur** (land) **Mar-dú**… from the **kur Mar-dú** he took a bull[c]	Sh'pak Sh'pak Sh'pak	1. Pomponio and Visicato 1994[d] 2. Jestin 1937 3. Diemel 1923
Ur-Nanshe	"erected the embankments of the **Dasal** (canal) **Mar-dú** Bridge of the Amorites? Duru$_x$ (Ù)-Mar-dú(-ne)	Lagash Lagash	Marchesi 2006: 23–24
"Pre-Sargonic"[e]	the Amorite shepherd (**sipa mar.dú**)	Mari (deriving from Lagash?)	Bonechi and Durand 1992[f]
EBIVA c.2350 (c. 30 refs. to Mardu in all)	1. king of Amurrum (**en mar.dú**[ki]) with his *šaybum* officials,[g] king of Tidnu (**en da-da-nu**[ki]) with his *šaybum* officials and Ibal of the Steppe 2. TM75.G.1317; TM.76.G.533 (See Archi 1985)	Ebla (list of fabric recipients)	Archi 1985 Marchesi 2006: 14, n. Streck 2000: 31
Akkadian Naram-Sin Sharkalisharri	Defeats Sumerian coalition at Basar, the mountain range of the Mardu. Defeats great revolt Defeats **mar-dú** at **Basar**	Jebel Bishri	Frayne 1993: E2.1.4.2[b] E2.1.4.6 Thureau-Dangin 1903
Ur III Gudea....... Shulgi..... Shu-Sin	**hur-sag** (mountain) **Mar-dú-ta** Year 37, builds wall of the land (**bàd-ma-da ba-dù**), called elsewhere "the wall facing the highland" and perhaps related to the Tidnu; Year 40, record of "Amorrite booty." **mar.tu** […] the Tidnu, the Yamadium came forth together with [them] (ie Shimanum and Khabura) and the[ir] rulers … him"[i] *and a few lines further on….* "since that day **mar.tu**, destructive people of dog-like mind, like wolves, the stalls…"	Jebel Bishri	Statue B Edzard 1997: 34 Frayne 1997: 106.[j] E3/2.1.2 Frayne 1997: 297–299. E3/2.1.4.1

[a] Steinkeller 1992: 260–65. Cf. Marchesi 2006: 22–3.

[b] Utu is the sun-god.

[c] Translation by Marchesi (2006: 23).

[d] Discussed in Whiting 1995: 1234; Marchesi 2006: 23.

[e] Bonechi and Durand (1992: 158) suggest this text is earlier than the Eblaitic literary texts.

[f] Cf. Marchesi 2006: 24, n. 99.

[g] This term is usually translated as "elder," although Marchesi 2006 disputes this reading. See Chapter 3.

[b] Frayne 1993: 91 has "Basar, the Amorite Mountain"; Marchesi 2006: 16, n. 56 has "Basar, the mountain range of Amurrum."

[i] This inscription is known to us in an Old Babylonian copy.

[j] See also Sallaberger 2007: 443.

feature is embedded – and its very long history (cf. Porter 2009a). Once a connection with the putative northern collapse is removed, the directionality of the toponyms is open, and the priority of southern attestations of Amorrite presence (as seen in Table 5 above) takes on new significance. The first we know of anyone called Mardu is in the south, present in ways that are internal to the life of Mesopotamian cities. It follows that, notwithstanding whether it was the cardinal point or a way of designating people that came first, if the association between them is made at this time, then a large part of the land of the four riverbanks falls west of Shurrapak and Lagash. And it may be proposed that in the early third millennium this was a prime grazing area for Mesopotamian pastoralists, especially after the retraction from the north that occurred at the end of the fourth millennium.

Some of Naplanum's successors at Larsa (see Table 2) bear titles employing the word "Amorrite"[96] (Steinkeller 2004), indicating a continued relationship between pastoralist and polity. It is accepted that this is a relict of earlier times, maintaining a now irrelevant identity – or the last vestiges of a pastoralist lifestyle – as it is progressively abandoned. Zabaya and Abi-sare are called *rabian Amurrum* (rendered by Seri [2005: 95] as a royal title, Amorrite king); Kudur-mabuk is called *abu Amurrim* (father of the Amorrites [Frayne 1990: 206; Seri 2005: 67]) by his son, Warad-Sin, in years 1–6 of his reign, and later *abu Emutbala* (years 1–12 [Frayne 1990: 202]).[97] The fact that not all kings of Larsa (especially Warad-Sin, Kudur-mabuk's son) attest Amorrite connections, however, has contributed to the idea that in this dynasty we see the transition from tribal nomad to urban king in process (Fleming 2004: 124, 160), a transition that involves a wholesale adoption of Akkadian culture (Van de Mieroop 2004: 85; Jahn 2007), with the goal of becoming true members of the urban/civilized world ([Oates 1986: 55–6] synonymous in such discourse). Not too much can be made of this, it seems to me. For the particular case of Kudur-mabuk and his sons, the shifting history of relations between Emutbal Amorrites, Mashkan-shapir, and Larsa (Fig. 33) suggests a division of rule similar to Samsi-Addu and his sons (contra Steinkeller 2004: 36; cf. Van de Mieroop 1993b: 50–51). After Kudur-mabuk took over first Mashkan-shapir, and then Larsa, he remained the paramount of the Yamutbal and their holdings, including these two key cities, for as long as he was in evidence. His was the larger and, contrary to modern opinion, the far more prestigious entity, while his sons were allowed to control only the smaller entities. Warad-Sin ruled Larsa,

96 Or demonstrate other ties to Yamutbal.
97 The meaning of titles here – the differences between *rabian Amurru* and *abu amurru* – is important, however those differences cannot be understood until the meaning of Amurru is really established, and that cannot happen until the place of pastoralism in social and political organization as well as economic operation is resolved.

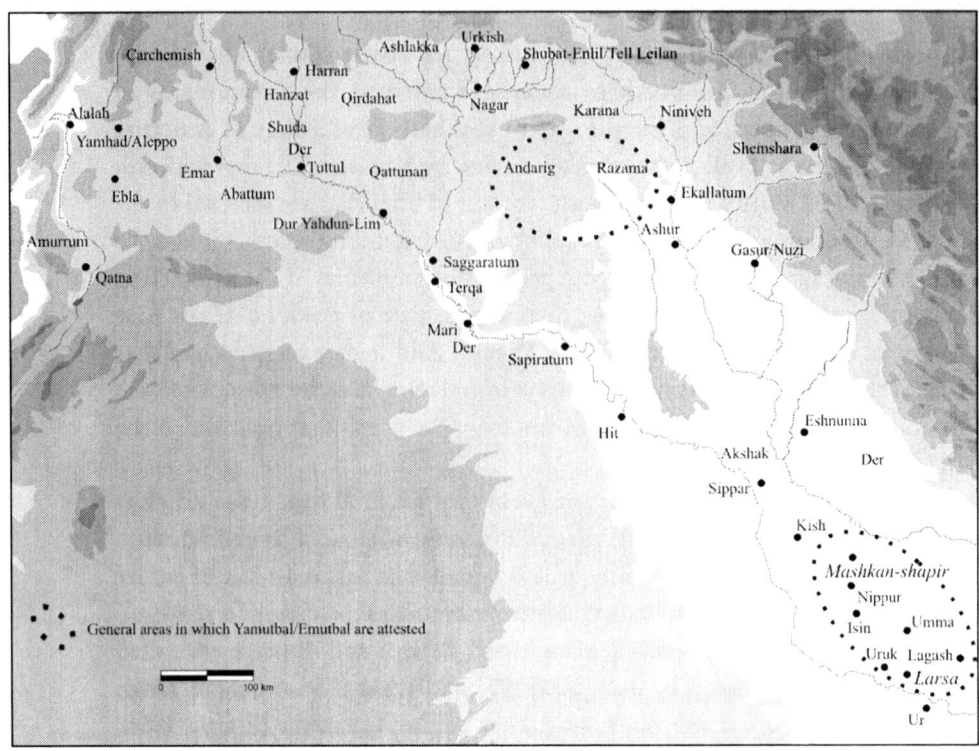

33. Map of Yamutbal/Emutbal regions.

succeeded by Rim-Sin, while Sin-muballit[98] was leader of Mashkan-shapir in the last years of Rim-Sin's reign (Charpin et al. 1988: 146–8; Steinkeller 2004: 29); and even though Warad-Sin is said to have recaptured Mashkan-shapir after Kudur-mabuk temporarily lost it, he remained subordinate to his father. This make sense of the use of attributes in Kudur-mabuk's titulary that are the prerogative of royalty only, while at the same time Kudur-mabuk never ruled Larsa directly (cf. Brisch 2007: 52–3). Therefore none of Kudur-mabuk's three sons could in fact be operative leaders of the Emutbal until his death, which according to Steinkeller (2004) is most likely to have taken place in Warad-Sin's reign – although he is still mentioned in the early years of Rim-Sin, leading Frayne (1990: 270) to assume that it was not until Year Eight of Rim-Sin's reign that Kudur-mabuk's death occurred. Thereafter, neither Kudur-mabuk nor the Emutbal nor the Amorrites are mentioned, indicating perhaps that the association no longer existed for Rim-Sin. Why then did Rim-Sin not become leader of the Emutbal? First, we cannot be sure that he did not; titles too often reflect only the situation in which they are invoked to be certain that their

98   Steinkeller (2004: 41, n. 77) wonders if Kudur-mabuk married a daughter of Sin-iddinam. The breaking of pattern in naming the third son Sin-muballit in the manner of Sin-iddinam and his successors, and not XXX-Sin like Kudur-mabuk's other two sons, suggests that perhaps he did.

absence is meaningful,[99] and much of Rim-Sin's titulary is concerned with his conquests and the expansion of the kingdom (Charpin 2004a). In fact, after the conquest of Isin there were no new year names, with Isin the subject of the next thirty (Van de Mieroop 1993b: 47, 55). Second, it is possible that succession among the Emutbal was not direct from father to son. It is also possible that the Emutbal were no longer so closely associated with the southern region. As Rim-Sin's geopolitical reality changed, perhaps so too did his titulary.

There is another explanation, however: that the role of leader was simply taken by someone else. Kudur-mabuk himself may have usurped power over the Emutbal in the first place, thereby rendering both Warad-Sin's and Rim-Sin's potential to rule – once he was gone – tenuous at best, especially if they lacked the personal attributes and connections that had enabled their father to maintain control. There are only three extant inscriptions that do not mention Warad-Sin and are most probably Kudur-mabuk's rather than his son's – although because one of these three invokes the title *abu Emutbala* it is thought in fact to date to after Year Eight of Warad-Sin's reign. Larsa and the Emutbal are also mentioned in this inscription, in a somewhat apologetic, or self-justificatory, tone, where Kudur-mabuk "did no wrong to Larsa and Yamutbal, did not do anything that was not pleasing to the god Šamaš" (Frayne 1990: 267),[100] surely suggestive of an accusation from someone that he did! But in an inscription on a pendant dedicated to a goddess and found at Terqa (Frayne 1990), Kudur-mabuk identifies himself only as the son of Simti-shilhak, invoking his Elamite provenance and no other.[101] The fact that Kudur-mabuk's personal name is Elamite, indicating that ethnically he may not have been an Amorrite, has long been one of the very confusing issues here (Steinkeller 2004: 30; cf. Brisch 2007: 51),[102] and I would hesitate to interpret this too literally. Nevertheless, the history of titulary suggests that Warad-Sin was justifying both his own position and Kudur-mabuk's in his constant reference to his father's association with the role of *abu Amurrim*, which might be understood not as a generic title (Steinkeller 2004: 35) but as claiming true Amorriteness for the Elamite usurper, masking his otherness at the same time. In the same vein, *abu Emutbala* might then be an attempt to keep the identification of both father and son with that specific group uppermost, suggesting that the identification was

---

99 See also Seri 2005: 55.
100 And here Larsa and Yamutbal are identified as virtually synonymous because the same offense would harm both.
101 In general, the title *abu Amurrim* or *abu Emutbala* comes before Simti-shilhak's name in the inscriptions of all three.
102 This, and the fact that there is an attestation of the reverse situation – that is, someone who bears an Amorrite name is nevertheless designated as an Elamite – is very important for understanding what the term "Amorrite" means. In brief, however, the role of the Elamites in the downfall of Ur suggests that there is more than a close association between what is meant by "Amorrite" and the region of Elam at this time.

contested. The cessation of such titulary in Year Seven of Rim-Sin would indicate, therefore, not that he did not *wish* to be identified with the Emutbal, but that the Emutbal no longer *allowed* him to be.

But while Fleming (2004: 124) reads Rim-Sin's titulary as indicative of his dropping the family's tribal connections and Steinkeller (2004: 41) reads it as insisting on them (indicating the essential ambiguity of such materials), the fact remains that Larsa and the Emutbal were, for a very long time, intimately connected. What then of Yamutbal in the north? Along with the Numha, its neighbor in the Sinjar and oft-time enemy (Durand 2004: 135), as territory between them was contested (Durand 2004: 136), the Yamutbal of the north had embedded towns – of which Andarig and Razama were key (it was Kurda for the Numha) – and also resident Babylonian diplomatic missions (Durand 2004: 138). Yamutbal of the north participated in interregional affairs, such as the war against Eshnunna (Durand 2004: 140).

Since northern Yamutbal and southern Emutbal were concurrent, active political entities, it would seem that the Yamutbal originated in one of these two places and then went to the other, leaving some members behind. Or perhaps they were two parts of the same entity, two ends of a territorial range. Emutbal is located in the heartland of the southern Mesopotamian zone of irrigated agriculture, where pastoralism would be limited. While the assumption, then, might be that Emutbal were no longer pastoralists, there is no a priori reason why this should be the case; certainly the invocation of kinship would give access to pasturage in the north if there were no adverse conditions that would tend to exclusionary kinship practices. The absence of any documentation of a continued polity is not really surprising, in that by the time of our sources for the northern Yamutbal, the Mari texts, a political connection is unlikely to exist any longer; Kudur-mabuk's usurpation of Emutbal rule might have brought such a connection to an end, and this seems to have taken place before the time of Samsi-Addu. Such postulated political continuity may be imagined in several ways – as a split rule as we see for Kudur-mabuk himself and also for Samsi-Addu, or as two independent leaderships nevertheless linked by idioms of kinship. Here is where the mirrored toponyms assume another dimension; as I have argued in detail (Porter 2009a), they themselves may be thought of as geographic representations of kinship, intended to maintain bonds stretched by time and space.

In the early second millennium, the Yamutbal are well attested as located between the Habur and the Tigris (Fig. 33). If Yamuti, the Mardu king of the Ebla texts (Archi 1985), may perhaps be Yamutbal, and since Steinkeller (2004: 40) has suggested that the former name is a shortened version of the latter (in which case, one may ask why the specific ancestral group of which he was king is not mentioned, even though he himself may be the Yamutbal's eponymous ancestor), does this suggest that the Yamutbal are located elsewhere in the mid-third millennium?

This does not need to be the case on several grounds. That Mardu, or even Tidnu, are known to Ebla and associated on occasion with Tuttul or Emar does not establish their origin or even their current location, only their occasional political affiliations – and political affiliation is always fluid, if not volatile, as the Mari texts show so clearly. Pastoralists *move*. They move over the short term, obviously, in order to find pasture, but also over the long term, through a variety of processes. Traditional grazing lands can give way to new ones that themselves become traditional as political and environmental conditions change; the group can become distributed over landscapes differently than was the case before. But the fundamental relationships to the sedentary members of the social group, to the urban centers and other settlements that constitute part of the political and social identities of the mobile group, may easily remain unchanged. Wholesale migration is not a necessary outcome therefore of changes in grazing territories, and textual geographies can only be understood as a function of the situation at the moment in time when the text was written, and this would include any consciousness of historical location.

There is another explanation altogether for the divergent geographies invoked in various sources, an explanation evident in the listing at Ebla. That Mardu, Dadanu, and Ibal of the steppe are mentioned in conjunction with each other indicates that there is an association between them in the minds of the record-keepers that may not be spatial but conceptual – namely that all three groups were associated with pastoralism.

This seems rather self-evident, given the deep historical connection between Amorrites and pastoralism, in contemporary academic terms if not ancient ones, but, in fact, if the strict control of sources over time and space is maintained, it is not. It cannot be assumed but must be argued. This is because, with the single exception of the Mari reference, there is no indication until the Ur III period of who the Mardu are, or what they might be – it was unusual to identify people by their homeland or language (Sallaberger 2007: 445) – and Mardu, taken this way, would prove a significant exception. But people are also designated in antiquity by professions, and it is in this light that we should start to think of the meaning of Mardu/Amurru. It is not who the Mardu *are* that is significant, so much as what they *do* – and what they do is practice a different way of life: mobile pastoralism. Under this scenario, many of the supposed contradictions that have dogged this discussion disappear.

I do not mean that Mardu is a term meaning a profession like "priest" or "overseer." It does not stand for "shepherd" or "animal herder" (although Mardu often are these), but instead that the Mardu are people who define themselves as mobile pastoralists – whatever they actually do and wherever they are actually located. The term says nothing about their ethnicity, political affiliation, occupation, or even point of origin, but its deployment in distinction to other mobile groups suggests that it may carry, in much the same way as Fleming (2004: 47) proposes for the name "Hana" in the Mari texts,[103] a sense of "our mobile groups." The only reason this was not an acceptable resolution to the problem in the past (as Kamp and Yoffee 1980) was because of the evidence that pastoralists were both intrinsic to the Mesopotamian system and living in cities, which in traditional views of pastoralism is simply impossible. In those views, nomads are mutually exclusive, indeed outright hostile, to all that Mesopotamia stands for in the modern world – civilization. Situations where the son is designated as Mardu but not the father, for example, are therefore not a mistake, as commonly assumed (Buccellati 1966: 55), but moments where one member of the family has simply shifted to a different part of the familial enterprise or way of life. If Mardu/*Amurru* should in fact be read as "mobile pastoralist," then the "Amorrites" are hardly a monolithic group, but are constituted only by the point of reference of any of the texts that mention them.

The same is surely true, in two ways, of geographic indications: one, they mean simply those pastoralists who are in the area of Emar, Tuttul, Lagash, or Elam at that time or with whom that polity has a relationship, no matter the distance between them;[104] two, the Ebla geography of the Mardu is not the geography of Ur III and neither has anything to do with a largely imagined geography supposedly apparent in Akkadian references. As for the linguistic argument, that personal names contain traces of a different language that correlates with the designation Mardu and, ergo, renders those so-labeled a separate ethnic group, the writing of names is a secondary derivation of the function of the label. Those practicing pastoralism in the steppe or mountains, who are indicated as such by the designation Mardu, share a ruralized version of Akkadian (which is what, in my view, this "language" called Amorrite is). The name is recognized as a marker of that position or location. This may be simple acculturation or a conscious claim of identity.

This brings us back to the question of the frequent association of Mardu with **kur** – both as a generic designation and in reference to a specific mountain, Jebel Bishri in particular. The focus on Bishri comes, first, from the assumed need for an Amorrite locale in proximity to Ebla, and second, from Akkadian references to repeated problems with the Amorrites there – at least, as presented by contemporary discussion of these sources. In reality, Naram-Sin's inscription records a battle at Jebel Bishri midway through his reign, but that battle was not against the Amorrites – it was part of the great rebellion against him by a coalition of southern kings, including Ur, Uruk, Umma, and Lagash, who flee or

---

103 Cf. Anbar 2005.
104 Similarly when "an inhabitant of Tuttul is called a 'resident' of Mardu" (Archi 1985: 8).

are chased to Jebel Bishri, where Naram-Sin defeats them (Frayne 1993: 90–94, 103–8). In the long list of senior officials captured there, the two Amorrite captains are the very last and most minor.

The second attestation of a battle between Akkadians and Amorrites at Bishri (Frayne 1993) is simply a claim by Sharkalisharri of his famous ancestor's accomplishments. That Jebel Bishri is referred to as the Mardu mountain reflects only the understanding that this is a traditional grazing land for pastoralists, not that it belongs to a particular pastoralist entity. Jebel Hamrin, Jebel Bishri, and the mountains of the Gudea inscription (Marchesi 2006: 16) may all therefore qualify as **kur** Mardu, whether grazed by Mardu of Ebla or Mardu of Lagash or Mardu of Anshan. This is not a competition between possible contenders for the homeland of the Amorrites; the evidence shows the three generalized geographies are different locations for pastoral territories, at different points in time, and for different groups. The fluidity in these sources is the product of the mobility of their subjects.

A precise, bounded meaning to the term "Mardu" is not to be expected, therefore, because our need for categories is not the same as that of the ancients. The concept embodied by Mardu means more and less than "nomad" (Sallaberger 2007: 445) – if nomad means that one is either mobile or has stopped being mobile and is now sedentarized, because this renders an either/or situation which is not how pastoralist peoples in antiquity (or today) think of the situation or themselves. If a man lives in a city but his parents live in the steppe, in tents that are dismantled and reassembled perhaps regularly, perhaps every now and then, or if he lives in the mountains moving steadily in search of forage, but his brother lives in a small hamlet next to his barley field, a field given to him by the king, is he a nomad or not? If he and his family live in the steppe and the highlands and the urban center at various points of the year, while part of his extended kin-group lives only in the city and has always done so, is *he* a nomad or not? And what if it is the other way around? One may devise a range of terms on a continuum that attempt to classify a way of life or a subsistence practice, slotting each of these scenarios into one or the other, but in the end such an exercise completely misses the point and thus lacks analytical utility; people do not think of themselves in terms of classification, and thus they do not make choices and decisions and take action according to those categories, be they scribes of Ur trying to keep tabs on who owes what, and who is due what, from the storehouses, or be they mobile groups seeking adequate pasture. In a way, it is no more complicated than saying, "my brother's family are cattle ranchers, they live in the country" – except that "my brother's family are sheep farmers and they move through the country" means that a number of many different elements come into play in a world where those social ties (and economic ones too) are critical to the perpetuation of society in both actuality and ideology.

Mardu, then, are mobile components of various polities attested first in the heartlands of Mesopotamia, in places such as Shurrupak and Lagash, and they are no different from their sedentary relations, in terms of their belonging to the polity. The same is true in the northwest, at Ebla. Specific ancestral groups become evident at different times and places, usually, I would suggest, because issues of identity are in question (cf. Wossink 2009). This is the case with the Tidnu, since we are not dealing with a generic name but a particular ancestral group. One possibility, as Marchesi (2006: 16–17) suggests, is simply that Tidnu moved from the Syrian steppe where they were located in the mid-third millennium, to the Transtigridian steppe toward the end of the millennium; this is perfectly possible. But it is not necessary, as already argued. They may well have originated in the Hamrin and for a period of time grazed in the steppe west of the Euphrates or west of Ebla. Tidnu may not in fact be the same entity in any way as Didanu. In the Ebla texts, the Tidnu are distinguished from Mardu who are part of Ebla itself (the fact that there is an **en** of Martu not withstanding), but they are not considered particularly special. Their prominence later is something else again, however – it is under the Third Dynasty of Ur that they are attributed an identity that renders them, quite literally, beyond the pale. This is seen in the inscription of Shu-Sin, an "historical text" that gives particular weight to the status of the Tidnu – and Mardu – as enemies.

But we cannot take historical texts at face value, as forthright descriptions of a real situation, any more than we can take other kinds of text that are regularly viewed with a skeptical eye; many factors shape the perception of what that reality could be, just as – at the same time – perceptions of reality are deliberately manipulated by the production of text. Such is certainly the case in the Ur III documentation, where literary works and historical documents invoke each other in creating a past – a process that, I would argue, is an intrinsic part of Mesopotamian political culture, at least in the post-Akkadian world. But it is more than only legitimation, it is also the creation of political identity, a political identity defined by who is embraced by this new rule and who is not and by what the nature of that rule will be. In some instances, a conscious inclusion is created, a statement of the multiple political networks and perhaps social contexts to which this or that leader belongs. Sometimes it is exclusionary. And while it may be mobility that warrants genealogy (as a device carried in the social knowledge of the person and as the structure of bonds that may stretch), it is history, materialized and codified in tablets, that is rooted in place. A correlation between approach or form and desired outcome is also possible: it is genealogy that renders inclusion, and it is history – in one guise or another – that is used to render exclusion. This does not mean that there is no historical information to be gleaned from sources such as year names and building inscriptions – on the contrary – but that these records can be constructed and manipulated, just as fiction can be embedded in history.

It is, I suggest, the fall of Akkad that ultimately stimulates this past-making in so fervid a way. A number of successors must surely have staked their claims, and competition for control was intense. Indeed, as scholars often note, the Sumerian King List declaims: "Who was king? Who was not king?" (Jacobsen 1939: vii.a). The eventual winners, however, were unquestionably the dynasty founded by Ur-Nammu, and yet it is clear that challenges to Ur III authority were ongoing because Shulgi and Shu-Sin are equally the subjects of parts of this discourse. Thus a propaganda campaign was instigated, resulting in the great floruit of "literary" and pseudo-historical texts that, on the one hand, established the legitimacy of the victors and, on the other, the illegitimacy of the losers. If this constitutes an "invention of tradition" (Brisch 2007: 28, quoting Hobsbawm and Ranger 1983), it is not so much the fiction of a unified Sumer in a contentious reality that is at stake (as Michalowski 1983) as it is the establishment of the idea of a single, all-encompassing power in the face of a complex network of political players, opportunists, and dissenters that crisscrossed Mesopotamia.

Among the contenders were the eventual inheritors of Ur, the Isin dynasty. The heated dispute contained in certain Ur III and Isin materials demonstrates how intense was the need, not just for political dominance, but also for societal – and divine – acceptance, and a recorded one at that. Political power was certainly vested in divine approval, as any number of texts, including the *Curse of Agade* (Cooper 1983) and the *Lamentation over the Destruction of Sumer and Ur* (Michalowski 1989), show – indeed, it is to be seen in the transformation of the Ur III version of the Sumerian King List (Steinkeller 2003) under Isin rule (Michalowski 1983, 2005a: 205). The act of writing itself has an implicit element of sanctification. The battle for "hearts and minds," whether of gods and/or people, was as important as any military encounter. Isin sources also show an equal concern for succession and legitimacy, emphasizing the weakness of former rulers (Michalowski 2005a).

In any case, a multitude of groups converge at this point in time – and diverge – to meet up with other groups in different places, so that there is not a constant and consistent body of people pressing on the edges of civilization, but a fairly fluid opposition to this particular polity. Mardu are the enemy of choice in these texts not, I suggest, because they are outsiders, marauders from the fringe, but because they are the very opposite: direct, *internal* competition for control of the four riverbanks, competition because the actions of Shulgi in wresting control of the pastoralist lands and pastoralist products wrought their own response. It is the status of the Mardu as part of the Mesopotamian heartlands that gave rise to this particular juxtaposition of the production of a past with the creation of a literary "other."

If "Mardu" came to represent outsiders when used by Ur to describe a group rather than an individual, it symbolized "resistance" when appropriated by those connected not necessarily by blood or type of organization (Wossink 2009) but by their common position. This resistance is not any innate nature of pastoralists in relationship to sedentary authorities, no rejection of order and culture, but instead it is historically contingent on the conflict arising from the redesign of economy in the Ur III and, specifically, of the place and organization of pastoralism within it. The Tidnu, in particular, would have been disenfranchised by the rearrangement of the management of animal husbandry, but they were by no means the only such group. The autonomy of family and/or household pastoral production was reduced in this great process of centralization under Shulgi of Ur, routes and movements controlled and, I suspect, taxes on pastoralist producers sharply increased. The distribution of and exercise of power are also likely to have changed. It is not hard to predict resistance in such circumstances, especially when the state's monopoly of force and its control of its own territory are questionable. But we know that the Third Dynasty of Ur in fact tried something very specific to this problem – the great "wall." Whether erected against mobile populations who moved voluntarily from under the control of Ur, in which their position was vastly diminished, or against those forcibly expelled, the wall was intended to define the limits of political control.

This, then, is the debate between the Old Babylonian and neo-Sumerian stories of Gilgamesh. The more contested one's claim, the more elaborate one's construction of a past. The location of the contest, too, must surely play a part in the venue through which that created past is disseminated. If Sumerian was the language of the literary propaganda wars between Ur III and Isin, Akkadian now becomes the locus of the Amorrite reaction for several reasons: it was their base language in any case; its use in formal discourse was a rejection of the previous regimes; and, more than this, it was also the language of the populace. The fact that so much of this discussion appears in stories of the broadest appeal, attached to well-known characters, raises the specter of popular discontent. If these texts *are* situated in a larger debate, it is one not only within/between the texts themselves, or as representative of a ruling elite, but within society as a whole. If, as I suggest, it is a moment in time when the Third Dynasty of Ur pushed out those who would not submit to their control, we can imagine great social fragmentation occurring, as families and households engaged in multiple resource extraction become sundered.

Until we have family archives for this period, we shall never see this directly in the texts, because the administrative archives from Ur III and even the Mari letters derive from the public sector and are about an entirely other set of concerns. But we can see the outcome of it in the organization and geographic distribution of Amorrite political entities across the land of the four riverbanks, which *is* discernible from texts. With an anthropological sensibility brought to this evidence, it becomes clear that fragmentation is again both a concern and a dynamic – not, however, in the standard way, resulting in a split between pastoralist and farmer, but in its very opposite – as giving rise to mechanisms that defeat it. In this case, it is the consolidation of group identities – identities expressed especially as ancestral groups, in opposition to the hegemony of the center – that results in new political entities, but not new populations, emerging in the land of the four riverbanks, from Ur to Mari and beyond.

CONCLUSION: BEYOND "TRIBE" AND "STATE"

Although organized in not just different but diametrically opposed ways, the geographies of expansion in both the Uruk period and Ur III period are remarkably similar, proceeding in successive bands, sweeping the line of the Euphrates and Tigris rivers, and extending progressively northeastward. Key reasons behind the expansion are also remarkably similar: the integration and control of mobile pastoralists in support of the dominant industry of greater Mesopotamia, woolen textile production. If the family-based, decentralized approach practiced in the fourth millennium did not work (or rather, worked too well), the highly centralized, militaristic extension of control exercised at the end of the third millennium, in this instance clearly calculated to achieve its ends, also failed to accomplish its goals. Yet for two and a half thousand years, two fundamental relationships, with dynamics of their own, remained in play: one, the relationship between mobile and sedentary members of the ancestral group; two, the relationship between ancestral groups and the polity.

These relationships did not, however, remain unchanged. The organization of and means taken to accomplish these relationships shifted considerably over time and space. Sometimes, social and political boundaries stretched; sometimes, they retracted. Sometimes, social interactions were inclusive, transcending multiple kinds of difference, while at other times they were exclusive or reified and there is no necessary correlation between any of these situations. In any combination of conditions, though, an interlocking complex of structure, discourse, and practice vested, in part, in kinship, religion, and the dead, allowed communities comprised of pastoralists and sedentarists dispersed over time and space to maintain cohesion and identity, both within themselves and as parts of larger communities.

To delineate this historically (and at the largest of scales): in the second half of the fourth millennium, during the Uruk expansion, there was a progressive extension of social relationships over considerable space, social relationships

that were construed through time – that is, through descent. Those social relationships, however, were simultaneously becoming increasingly reified, resulting
at the beginning of the third millennium in their severe contraction in spatial
as well as social dimensions. As ancestral groups in the north grew increasingly
segregated from ties to the larger community, they became increasingly bound
to a single and delineated space in ways that shaped the nature of the polity that
was to come there. Meanwhile, in the south, the reorientation of pastoralist
movement from far north and east to the near west, east, and southwest led to,
on the one hand, a new set of ties with the arid lands of the Arabian Peninsula
and, on the other, a more restricted and contested territorial base, bound by the
powerful new polities, each with their own mobile constituents, that claimed
Mesopotamia's margins for themselves.

That individual ancestral groups, within or external to larger political
entities, are not as obvious in the mid- to late third millennium is a testament, not to their irrelevance, but to the stability of their integration within
the polity – both vertically, in terms of their connection to institutions that
transcended individual groups and that took their defining shape at this time,
and horizontally, between the multiple ancestral groups that comprised the
political entities that now covered the landscape, north and south. Nor does
this lack of visibility speak to the irrelevance/separation of mobile pastoralists,
but rather to the stability of their interaction with the urban component of
the community, and, perhaps, to durable relationships with grazing territories.
That stability was severely and deliberately disrupted at the end of the third
millennium, though, when a new way of organizing the economy was insti-
tuted, with dramatic and unintended consequences. The depredations enacted
by neo-Sumerian policies to connections between mobile and sedentary members of the ancestral group led to complementary, and sometimes contradictory, reactions as those connections were reasserted. Just as at the beginning
of the third millennium, individual ancestral identities came into focus,[1] with
ancestral names invoked to create distinctions between, and allegiances to, different groups. Many of these names do not appear in the extant records until
the second to fourth centuries of the second millennium, because this is when
people with those names start writing the texts. And, too, identity formation
is an ongoing process – in response, in this instance, to increasing social and
spatial dislocations and competition.

At the same time, a larger political identity is simultaneously created by,
and in reaction to, the exclusionary practices of neo-Sumerian rulers, an identity ultimately appropriated by those excluded, who came to call themselves
"Amorrites." The notion of "Amorrite" is increasingly reified, yet is not necessarily exclusionary, as can be seen in the confusion – or, better, conflation – between

---

1   And cf. Buccellati 2008: 148.

Amorrites and Elamites (among others) that is occasionally attested, where key Amorrite players have Elamite names or vice versa.

Another feature that has proved puzzling in Mesopotamian history of this time is the fact that, despite the rise to power of a newly apparent group, there is, after all, little disruption of settlement in the south – and probably, despite current consensus, in the north too (Porter 2007a). This is because, in the final analysis, no new people appeared. Foreign ethnicities did not take over; nomads did not sweep in from the desert. Rather, those members of ancestral groups within the urban centers who rejected Sumerian policies and who maintained, despite those policies, their integration with mobile kin, rose, through processes that remain obscure to us, to power. Again, however, and just as happened toward the end of the fourth millennium, horizontal connections between multiple ancestral groups were disrupted when individual social identities, at least in some contexts, trumped civic ties, leading to considerable instability in the second millennium as these groups jostled for territory and power.

It is this duality between social and political function and identity – a duality that emerges, splits, and merges again – that is often mistaken for two political forms, tribe and state. The conflation between social interactions, and social identities, and political organization under the rubric "tribe" has too long muddied the waters. Extract the political from the construct, finally, and many of the anomalies that have persistently dogged archaeological and historical reconstructions readily disappear. Yet political organization and operation are not entirely divorced from the social; in the ancient world, the polity was, to varying degrees, configured through actual and philosophical/ideological concepts of kinship. Kinship remains in evidence as a dominant ideology of interaction in early Near Eastern polities; it is not lost to class as the basis of social organization. Even if clear differentials are manifest in social position and wealth holdings, kinship cuts across such divisions; social allegiances on the basis of wealth may coexist with allegiances based on ideas of family. That this is increasingly recognized has led to attempts to develop intermediary terminologies, such as "complex chiefdom" or "segmentary states." These terms, however, are simply typological variations within the same framework and do not come to grips with the fundamental issues at stake. In the time and place under consideration here, both in societies called tribes and in societies called states, social structure is constructed similarly and operates similarly, in order to achieve similar ends. Significant variation is nevertheless found in the way social structure is perpetuated across society. That variation should be a major object of study.

At the same time, other sets of dualities – in the actual histories and academic interpretations of the political organization of northern and southern regions – become much more interestingly inflected. Traditionally seen as following varying – indeed, opposite – trajectories, with secular institutions of authority originating in the north and religious ones in the south, institutions in both north and south are born out of the same processes, processes initiated in the Uruk period. This is not to say that subsequent outcomes were the same in both areas, but it does mean that the kinds of contrasts currently reemerging in the literature, where the north is seen as tribal in organization – at its most developed, a complex chiefdom or segmentary state – while the south is seen as a true state, are not vested in understandings of the complicated set of relationships that really comprise the terms as they are currently treated in anthropological discourse. The terms, then, should be set aside in favor of the relationships.

One of the processes that proved so dynamic in what took place next was the deployment of religion in the integration of the group. I did not set out to write a book about the impact of religion on the dynamics of urbanization or state formation, but to my surprise it emerged from this study that religious practices are a significant factor in shaping ancient society and polity in the land of the four riverbanks, both north and south, in large part because daily life, social interactions, and political organization are imbued with, and predicated upon, indigenous understandings of how the world works. We would classify those understandings as religious, but I think that ancient peoples would not. "Religion" should be understood as an umbrella term covering public and familial practices and beliefs. I would not argue, however, that political authority originated in either a theocracy or a temple economy. Although I have not much discussed the nature of secular authority, whether authoritarian, communitarian, or heterarchical, I understand it – again, in both north and south – to be a product of kinship systems and the ways in which they are both structured and practiced, as well as the way individual kin-groups are interdigitated – or not – with each other. Variation in social interactions and political practices are not regionally determined, but a compound product of contingent situations.

In the end, perhaps the most salient point to emerge from this delineation of how mobility changed the world is that the archaeological evidence is as much the product of practices that people perform in order to perpetuate their existences and the sociopolitical environments of those existences as it is the reflection of social hierarchy, economic function, and political organization. Those practices are often ritualized and, equally, often sanctioned within a religious context. They shape the nature of existence, with intended and unintended consequences. They are embodied. They are the outcome of ideologies and structures. This is certainly not a new idea in much of archaeology, although it has yet to make sufficient impact on that of the Near East. It was not a point I intended to demonstrate, nor was it a foundational theoretical premise. But that is the story the evidence tells.

APPENDIX

ETCSL Title	ETCSL	GROUPS
Letter from Shulgi to Puzur-Shulgi about waterways	t.3.1.10	A
Letter from Aradmu to Shulgi about irrigation work	t.3.1.03	A
Letter from Shulgi to Aradmu about Apillasha	t.3.1.02	A
Letter from Aradmu (?) to Shulgi about bandits and Apillasha	t.3.1.11	A
Letter from Ur-DUN to Shulgi about Apillasha	t.3.1.11.1	A
Letter from Shulgi to Puzur-Shulgi about the fortress Igi-hursaga	t.3.1.08	A
Letter from Aradmu to Shulgi about Apillasha	c.3.1.01	A
Letter from Shulgi to Aradmu about Aba-indasa's letter	t.3.1.06.1	A1
Letter from Shulgi (?) to Aradmu about troops	t.3.1.13.1	A1
Letter from Aba-indasa to Shulgi about his neglect	t.3.1.21	A1
Letter from Aradmu to Shulgi about Aba-indasa's missing troops	t.3.1.05	A1
Letter from Sharrum-bani to Shu-Sin about keeping the Mardu at bay	c.3.1.15	B
Letter from Puzur-Shulgi to Shulgi about the advance of the enemy	t.3.1.07	B
Letter from Aradmu to Shulgi about the country	t.3.1.04	B
Letter from Sin-illat to Iddin-Dagan about confronting the Mardu	c.3.2.01	B
Letter from Aradmu to Shulgi about the fortress Igi-hursaga	c.3.1.06	B
Letter from Shulgi to Ishbi-Erra about the purchase of grain	c.3.1.13.2	C
Letter from Ishbi-Erra to Ibbi-Sin about the purchase of grain	c.3.1.17	C
Letter from Ibbi-Sin to Ishbi-Erra about his bad conduct	c.3.1.18	C
Letter from Ibbi-Sin to Puzur-Shulgi hoping for Ishbi-Erra's downfall	c.3.1.20	C

BIBLIOGRAPHY

Abdi, K. 1999. The Beveled-Rim Bowl: Function and Distribution (Farsi, English summary). In *The Iranian World. Essays on Iranian Art and Archaeology Presented to Ezat O. Negahban*, edited by A. Alizadeh, M. Majidzadeh, and S. Shahmirzadi, 222-3. Tehran: Iran University Press.

    2003. The Early Development of Pastoralism in the Central Zagros Mountains. *Journal of World Prehistory* 17/4:395-448.

Adams, R. McC. 1970. The Study of Ancient Mesopotamian Settlement Patterns and the Problem of Urban Origins. *Sumer* 25:111-24.

    1974. The Mesopotamian Social Landscape: A View from the Frontier. In *Reconstructing Complex Societies*, edited by C. Moore, 1-20. Supplement to the Bulletin of the American Schools of Oriental Research No. 20. Santa Fe, NM: ASOR.

    1978. Strategies of Maximization, Stability, and Resilience in Mesopotamian Society, Settlement and Agriculture. *Proceedings of the American Philosophical Society* 122:329-35.

    1981. Heartland of Cities: Surveys of Ancient Settlement and Land Use on the Central Floodplain of the Euphrates. Chicago: University of Chicago Press.

    2006a. Shepherds at Umma in the Third Dynasty of Ur: Interlocutors with a World beyond the Scribal Field of Ordered Vision. *Journal of Economic and Social History of the Orient* 49/2:133-69.

    2006b. Intensified Large-Scale Irrigation as an Aspect of Imperial Power. In *Agricultural Strategies*, edited by J. Marcus and C. Stanish, 17-37. Cotsen Advanced Seminar Series, vol. 2. University of California, Los Angeles. Los Angeles: Cotsen Institute of Archaeology Press.

    2007. The Limits of State Power on the Mesopotamian Plain. *Cuneiform Digital Library Bulletin* 2007/1-3. http://cdli.ucla.edu/pubs/cdlb/2007/cdlb2007_001.html.

    2008. An Interdisciplinary Overview of a Mesopotamian City and Its Hinterlands. *Cuneiform Digital Library Journal* 2008/1. http://www.cdli.ucla.edu/pubs/cdlj/2008/cdlj2008_001.html.

Ahluwalia, D. 2001. Politics and Post-colonial Theory: African Inflections. London: Routledge.

Akkermans, P., and K. Duistermaat. 1997. Of Storage and Nomads: The Sealings from Late Neoltihic Sabi Abyad, Syria. *Paléorient* 22:17–44.

Akkermans, P., and G. Schwartz. 2003. *The Archaeology of Syria.* Cambridge: Cambridge University Press.

Algaze, G. 1989. The Uruk Expansion: Cross-Cultural Exchange in Early Mesopotamian Civilization. *Current Anthropology* 30:571–608.

2001. The Prehistory of Imperialism: The Case of Uruk Period Mesopotamia. In *Uruk Mesopotamia and Its Neighbors. Cross-Cultural Interactions in the Era of State Formation,* edited by M. Rothman, 27–84. School of American Research Advanced Seminar Series. Santa Fe, NM: School of American Research Press.

2005. *The Uruk World System: The Dynamics of Expansion of Early Mesopotamian Civilization.* First published 1993. Chicago: University of Chicago Press.

2008. Ancient Mesopotamia at the Dawn of Civilization: The Evolution of an Urban Landscape. Chicago: University of Chicago Press.

Alizadeh, A. 2008. Archaeology and the Question of Mobile Pastoralism in Late Prehistory. In *The Archaeology of Mobility: Old World and New World Nomadism,* edited by H. Barnard and W. Wendrich, 78–114. Cotsen Advanced Seminars 4. Los Angeles: Cotsen Institute of Archaeology Press.

2009. Prehistoric Mobile Pastoralists in South-Central and Southwestern Iran. In *Nomads, Tribes, and the State in the Ancient Near East: Cross-Disciplinary Perspectives,* edited by J. Szuchman, 129–45. Oriental Institute Seminars 5. Chicago: The Oriental Institute of the University of Chicago.

Allred, L. 2006. Cooks and Kitchens: Centralized Food Production in Late Third Millennium Mesopotamia. PhD diss., The Johns Hopkins University.

Alster, B. 1990. Sumerian Literary Dialogues and Debates and Their Place in Near Eastern Literature. In *Living Waters. Scandinavian Orientalistic Studies Presented to Professor Dr. Frede Løkkegaard on his Seventy-Fifth Birthday, January 27th 1990,* edited by E. Keck, S. Sondergaard, and E. Wulff, 1–16. Copenhagen: Museum Tusculanum Press.

1991. Contributions to the Sumerian Lexicon. *Revue d'assyriologie* 85:1–2.

1996. Inanna Repenting: The Conclusion of Inanna's Descent. *Acta Sumerologica* 18:1–18.

2002. *ilū awīlum: we-e i-la,* « Gods: Men » versus « Man: God.» Punning and the Reversal of Patterns in the Atrahasis Epic. In *Riches Hidden in Secret Places: Ancient Near Eastern Studies in Memory of Thorkild Jacobsen,* edited by T. Abusch. Winona Lake, IN: Eisenbrauns.

Amselle, J.-L. 1990. *Logique métisses: Anthropologie de l'identité en Afrique et ailleurs.* Paris: Payot.

Anbar, M. 2005. Hanum: nom ethnique ou nom générique? In *An Experienced Scribe Who Neglects Nothing: Ancient Near Eastern Studies in Honor of Jacob Klein,* edited by Y. Sefati, P. Artzi, C. Cohen, B. Eichler, and V. Hurowitz, 446–61. Bethesda, MD: CDL Press.

Anderson, B. 1991. *Imagined Communities: Reflections on the Origin and Spread of Nationalism.* First published 1983. New York: Verso.

Anderson, P. 1974a. *Passages from Antiquity to Feudalism.* London: New Left Books.

1974b. *Lineages of the Absolutist State.* London: New Left Books.

Archi, A. 1981. Notes on Eblaite Geography II. *Studi Eblaiti* 4:1–17.

1982. About the Organization of the Eblaite State. *Studi Eblaiti* 5:201–20.

1985. Mardu in the Ebla texts. *Orientalia* 54:7–13.

1986. Die ersten zehn Könige von Ebla. *Zeitschrift für Assyriologie* 76:213–17.

1988a. Cult of the Ancestors and Tutelary God at Ebla. In *FUCUS: A Semitic/Afrasian Gathering in Remembrance of Albert Ehrman*, edited by Y. Arbeitmen, 109–10. Amsterdam Studies in the Theory and History of Linguistic Science, Series 4: Current Issues in Linguistic Theory. Amsterdam: John Benjamins.

1988b. ARET VII: Testi amministrativi: Registrazioni di metalli e tessuti (L.2769). Rome: Università degli Studi di Roma "La Sapienza."

1990. Agricultural Production in the Ebla Region. *Les annals archeologiques Arabes Syriennes* 40:51–5.

1992. The City of Ebla and the Organization of Its Rural Territory. *Altorientalische Forschungen* 19/1:24–8.

1993. *Five Tablets from the Southern Wing of Palace G-Ebla*. Syro-Mesopotamian Studies 5/2. Malibu, CA: Undena.

1995. La religione del culto nel periodo Protosiriano. In *Ebla: Alle origini della civiltà urbana*, edited by P. Matthiae, F. Pinnock, and G. Scandone Matthiae, 134–9. Milan: Mondadori Electa.

1996a. Chronologie relative des archives d'Ebla. In *Amurru I: Mari, Ebla et les Hourrites. Dix ans de travaux*, edited by J.-M. Durand, 11–28. Paris: Éditions Recherche sur les Civilisations.

1996b. Les comptes rendus annuels de métaux. In *Amurru I: Mari, Ebla et les Hourrites. Dix ans de travaux*, edited by J.-M. Durand, 73–99. Paris: Éditions Recherche sur les Civilisations.

1998. The Regional State of Nagar According to the Texts of Ebla. In *About Subartu: Studies Devoted to Upper Mesopotamia*, edited by M. Lebeau, 1–15. Turnhout: Brepols.

1999. The Steward and His Jar. *Iraq* 61:147–58.

2001. The King-Lists from Ebla. In *Historiography in the Cuneiform World*, edited by T. Abusch, P.-A. Beaulieu, J. Huehnergard, P. Machinist, and P. Steinkeller, 1–14. Proceedings of the XLVe Rencontre Assyriologique Internationale Part I. Bethesda, MD: CDL Press.

2002a. Jewels for the Ladies of Ebla. *Zeitschrift für Assyriologie* 92/2:161–99.

2002b. ŠEŠ-II-IB: A Religious Confraternity. In *Eblaitica: Essays on the Ebla Archives and Eblaite Language*, vol. 4, edited by C. H. Gordon and G. A. Rendsburg, 23–56. Winona Lake, IN: Eisenbrauns.

2004. Translation of Gods: Kumarpi, Enlil, Dagan/NISABA, Ḫalki. *Orientalia* 73/4:319–36.

2005. The Head of Kura – the Head of 'Adabal. *Journal of Near Eastern Studies* 64/2:81–100.

2006. Eblaite in Its Geographical and Historical Context. In *The Akkadian Language in Its Semitic Context. Studies in the Akkadian of the Third and Second Millennium BC*, edited by G. Deutscher and N. Kouwenberg, 96–112. Leiden: Nederlands Institute for the Near East.

Archi, A., and M.-G. Biga. 2003. A Victory over Mari and the Fall of Ebla. *Journal of Cuneiform Studies* 55:1–44.

Archi, A., M. Biga, and L. Milano. 1988. Studies in Eblaite Prosopography. In *Eblaite Personal Names and Semitic Name-Giving: Papers of a Symposium Held in Rome, July 15–17, 1985*, edited by A. Archi, 205–85. Archivi Reali di Ebla – Studi 1. Rome: Università degli Studi di Roma "La Sapienza."

Aruz, J., ed., with R. Wallenfels. 2003. *The Art of the First Cities*. New Haven: Yale University Press.

Asad, T. 1979. Equality in Nomadic Social Systems? Notes toward the Dissolution of an Anthropological Category. In *Pastoral Production and Society*, edited by L'Equipe ecologie et anthropologie des sociétiés pastorals, 419–28. Proceedings of the International Meeting on Nomadic Pastoralism - Paris 1-3 Dec. 1976. Paris: Éditions de la Maison des Sciences de l'Homme.

Astour, M. 1992. An Outline of the History of Ebla (Part I). In *Eblaitica: Essays on the Ebla Archives and Eblaite Language*, vol. 3, edited by C. Gordon, 3–82. Winona Lake, IN: Eisenbrauns.

Baadsgaard, A., J. Monge, and R. Zettler. N.d. Bludgeoned, Burned, and Beautified: Re-evaluating Mortuary Practices in the Royal Cemetery of Ur. In *Sacred Killing: The Archaeology of Sacrifice in the Ancient Near East*, edited by A. Porter and G. Schwartz. Winona Lake, IN: Eisenbrauns.

Badler, V. 2002. A Chronology of Uruk Artifacts from Godin Tepe in Central Western Iran and Implications for the Interrelationships between Local and Foreign Cultures. In *Artefacts of Complexity: Tracking the Uruk in the Near East*, edited by J. N. Postgate, 79–111. Cambridge: British School of Archaeology in Iraq.

Bahrani, Z. 2002. Performativity and the Image: Narrative, Representation and the Uruk Vase. In *Leaving No Stones Unturned: Essays on the Ancient Near East and Egypt in Honor of Donald P. Hansen*, edited by E. Ehrenberg, 15–22. Winona Lake, IN: Eisenbrauns.

2003. *The Graven Image. Representation in Babylonia and Assyria*. Philadelphia: University of Pennsylvania Press.

Baines, J., and N. Yoffee. 1998. Order, Legitimacy, and Wealth in Ancient Egypt and Mesopotamia. In *Archaic States*, edited by G. Feinman and J. Marcus, 199–260. Santa Fe, NM: School of American Research Press.

Baltali, S. 2006. Culture Contact, Integration and Architectural Style: Archaeological Evidence from Northern Mesopotamia. Paper presented at the Conference on Cultures of Contact, Stanford Archaeology Center, February 2006. *http://traumwerk.stanford.edu:3455/CulturesofContact/admin/download.html?attachid=51689*.

2007. Culture Contact, Integration and Architectural Style: Archaeological Evidence from Northern Mesopotamia. *Stanford Journal of Archaeology* 5:1–17.

Barnard, H., and W. Wendrich, eds. 2008. *The Archaeology of Mobility: Old World and New World Nomadism*. Cotsen Advanced Seminars 4. Los Angeles: Cotsen Institute of Archaeology Press.

Baştuğ, S. 1998. The Segmentary Lineage System: A Reappraisal. In *Changing Nomads in a Changing World*, edited by J. Ginat and A. M. Khazanov, 94–123. Portland, OR: Sussex Academic Press.

Bates, D., and S. Lees. 1977. The Role of Exchange in Productive Specialization. *American Anthropologist* 79:824–41.

Beale, T. 1978. Bevelled-rim Bowls and Their Implications for Change and Economic Organization in the Later Fourth Millennium. *Journal of Near Eastern Studies* 37:289–313.

Beck, L. 1986. *The Qashqa'i of Iran*. New Haven, CT: Yale University Press.

Berelov, I. 2006. Signs of Sedentism and Mobility in an Agro-Pastoral Community during the Levantine Middle Bronze Age: Interpreting Site Function and Occupation Strategy at Zahrat adh-Dhra' 1 in Jordan. *Journal of Anthropological Archaeology* 25:117–43.

Berlejung, A. 1997. Washing the Mouth: The Consecration of Divine Images in Mesopotamia. In *The Image and the Book: Iconic Cults, Aniconism, and the Rise of*

Book Religion in Israel and the Ancient Near East, edited by K. van der Toorn, 45–72. Leuven: Peeters.

Berlin, A. 1983. Ethnopoetry and the Enmerkar Epics. *Journal of the American Oriental Society* 103/1:17–24.

Berman, J. C. 1989. Neutron Activation Analysis of Beveled Rim Bowls and Other Uruk Ceramics from the Susiana Plain, Southwestern Iran. *Paléorient* 15/1:289–90.

Bernbeck, R. 1992. Migratory Patterns in Early Nomadism: A Reconsideration of Tepe Tula'i. *Paléorient* 18/1:77–88.

    2008a. An Archaeology of Multi-Sited Communities. In *The Archaeology of Mobility: Old World and New World Nomadism*, edited by H. Barnard and W. Wendrich, 43–77. Cotsen Advanced Seminars 4. Los Angeles, CA: Cotsen Institute of Archaeology Press.

    2008b. Royal Deification: An Ambiguation Mechanism for the Creation of Courtier Subjectivities. In *Religion and Power: Divine Kingship in the Ancient World and Beyond*, edited by N. Brisch, 157–70. Oriental Institute Seminars 4. Chicago: The Oriental Institute.

Bernbeck, R., and S. Pollock. 2002. Reflections on the Historiography of 4th Millennium Mesopotamia. In *Material Culture and Mental Spheres: Rezeption archaeologischer Denkrichtungen in der Vorderasiatischen Alterumskunde*, edited by A. Hausleiter, S. Kerner, and B. Müller-Neuhof, 171–204. Münster: Ugarit Verlag.

Bettini, L. 2006. Permanent Values in a Changing World: Bedouin Women's Tales from North-East Syria. In *Nomadic Societies in the Middle East and North Africa: Entering the 21st Century*, edited by D. Chatty, 966–93. Leiden: Brill.

Bhabha, H. 1994. *The Location of Culture*. London: Routledge.

Bienkowski, P., and E. van der Steen. 2001. Tribes, Trade, and Towns: A New Framework for the Late Iron Age in Southern Jordan and the Negev. *Bulletin of the American Schools of Oriental Research* 323:21–47.

Biga, M.-G. 1988. Archive L. 2586, L.2875, L.2764. In *Eblaite Personal Names and Semitic Name-Giving*, edited by A. Archi, 285–7. Studies in Eblaite Prosopography. Archivi Reali di Ebla – Studi I. Rome: Università degli Studi di Roma "La Sapienza."

    1995. I rapport diplomatic nel Periodo protosiriano. In *Ebla: Alle origini civiltà urbano*, edited by P. Matthiae, F. Pinnock, and G. Scandone Matthiae, 140–47. Milan: Mondadori Electa.

    1998. The Marriage of the Eblaite Princess Tagrish-Darnu with the Son of Nagar's King. In *About Subartu: Studies Devoted to Upper Mesopotamia*, edited by M. Lebeau, 17–22. Subartu IV/1. Turnhout: Brepols.

    2007/8. Buried among the Living at Ebla? Funerary Practices and Rites in a XXIV Cent. B.C. Syrian Kingdom. In *Sepolti tra i vivi, Buried among the Living: Evidenza ed interpretazione di contesti funerari in abitato. Atti del Convegno Internazionale*, edited by G. Bartoloni and M.-G. Benedettini, 250–75. Scienze dell'Antichità 14/1, Rome: Università degli Studi di Roma "La Sapienza."

Biga, M.-G., and F. Pomponio. 1987. Iš'ar-Damu, roi d'Ebla. *Nouvelles Assyriologiques Bréves et Utilitaires* 4:60–61.

Black, J. 1998. *Reading Sumerian Poetry*. Ithaca, NY: Cornell University Press.

    2002. The Sumerians in Their Landscape. In *Riches Hidden in Secret Places: Ancient Near Eastern Studies in Memory of Thorkild Jacobsen*, edited by T. Abusch, 41–62. Winona Lake, IN: Eisenbrauns.

Black, J., G. Cunningham, E. Robson, and G. Zólyomi. 2004. *The Literature of Ancient Sumer*. Oxford: Oxford University Press.

Black, J., G. Cunningham, J. Ebeling, E. Flückiger-Hawker, E. Robson, J. Taylor, and G. Zólyomi. 1998-2006. *The Electronic Text Corpus of Sumerian Literature*. Oxford: http://etcsl.orinst.ox.ac.uk/

Bloch, M. 1971. *Placing the Dead. Tombs, Ancestral Villages and Kinship Organization in Madagascar*. Seminar Studies in Anthropology No. 1. London: Seminar Press.

    1986. *From Blessing to Violence: History and Ideology of the Circumcision Ritual of the Merina of Madagascar*. Cambridge: Cambridge University Press.

Boese, J., and W. Sallaberger. 1996. Apil-kin von Mari und der Konige der III. Dynastie von Ur. *Altorientalische Forschungen* 23: 24-39.

Boivin, N. 2008. *Material Cultures, Material Minds. The Impact of Things on Human Thought, Society and Evolution*. Cambridge: Cambridge University Press.

Bonechi, M. 1991. Onomastica dei testi di Ebla: Nomi propri come fossili-guida? *Studi epigrafici e linguistici sul Vicino Oriente antico* 8:59-79.

    1992. Relations amicales syro-palestiniennes: Mari et Hasor au XVIIIe siècle av. J.C. In *Recueil d'études en l'honneur de Michel Fleury*, edited by J.-M. Durand, 9-22. Florilegium marianum. Mémoires de Nouvelles Assyriologiques Brèves et Utilitaires 2. Paris: Société pour l'Étude du Proche-Orient Ancien.

    1993. *I nomi geografici di Ebla*. Répetoire Géographique des Textes Cunéiformes 12/1. Wiesbaden: Reichert Verlag.

    1997. Lexique et idéologie royale à l'époque proto-syrienne. *Mari Annales de Recherches Interdisciplinaires* 8:477-535.

    1998. Remarks on the III Millennium Geographical Names of the Syrian Upper Mesopotamia. In *About Subartu: Studies Devoted to Upper Mesopotamia*, edited by M. Lebeau, 219-43. Subartu 4/1. Turnhout: Brepols.

    1999. Lexique hydrographique à Ebla. In *Landscapes, Territories, Frontiers and Horizons in the Ancient Near East*, edited by L. Milano, S. de Martino, F. Fales, and G. Lanfranchi, 97-101. Compte rendu de la XLIV Rencontre Assyriologique Internationale, Venezia 1997. Padua: Sargon srl.

    2001. The Dynastic Past of the Rulers of Ebla. *Ugarit Forschungen* 33:53-64.

    N.d. Studies on the Architectonic and Topographic Terms in the Ebla Texts 2. In press *Revue d'Assyriologie*.

Bonechi, M., and J.-M. Durand. 1992. Oniromancie et magie à Mari à l'époque d'Ébla. In *Literature and Literary Language at Ebla*, edited by P. Fronzaroli, 151-61. Quaderni di Semistica 18. Florence: Università di Firenze.

Bonte, P. 1979. Pastoral Production, Territorial Organization and Kinship in Segmentary Lineage Societies. In *Social and Ecological Systems*, edited by P. Burnham and R. Ellen, 203-34. London: Academic Press.

Bösze, I. 2009. *Analysis of the Early Bronze Age Graves in Tell Bi'a (Syria)*. Oxford: British Archaeological Reports.

Bourdieu, P. 1990. *The Logic of Practice*. Translated by R. Nice. First published 1980. Cambridge: Polity Press.

    1995. *Outline of a Theory of Practice*. Translated by R. Nice. First published 1977. Cambridge: Cambridge University Press.

Bracci, S. 2009. Growth and Development of Ancient Near Eastern Towns of the Diyala Region. Some Topographical Considerations. *Zeitschrift für Orient-Archaeologie* 2:8-35.

Bradley, R. 2000. *An Archaeology of Natural Places*. London: Routledge.

Breniquet, C. 1996. Du Fil a retordre: Réflexions sur les "idoles aux yeux" et les fileuses de l'époque d'Uruk. In *Collectanea Orientalia: Histoire, arts de l'espace et industrie de la terre. Etudes offertes en homage à Agnès Spycket,* edited by H. Gasche and B. Hrouda, 31–53. Neuchâtel-Paris: Recherches et Publication.

Brentjes, B. 1989. Comment on G. Algaze, The Uruk Expansion: Cross-Cultural Exchange in Early Mesopotamian Civilization. *Current Anthropology* 30:591–92.

Bretschneider, J. 2007. The "Reception Palace" of Uruk and Its Architectural Origin. In *Power and Architecture: Monumental Public Architecture in the Bronze Age Near East and Aegean,* edited by J. Bretschneider, J. Driessen, and K. van Lerberghe, 11–22. Orientalia Lovaniensia Analecta 156. Leuven: Peeters.

Bretschneider, J., J. Driessen, and K. van Lerberghe, eds. 2007. *Power and Architecture: Monumental Public Architecture in the Bronze Age Near East and Aegean.* Orientalia Lovaniensia Analecta 156. Leuven: Peeters.

Brisch, N. 2006. In Praise of the Kings of Larsa. In *Approaches to Sumerian Literature: Studies in Honour of Stip (H. L. J. Vanstiphout),* edited by P. Michalowski and N. Veldhuis, 37–45. Leiden: Brill.

2007. *Tradition and Poetics of Innovation: Sumerian Court Literature of the Larsa Dynasty (c. 2003–1763 BCE).* Alter Orient und Altes Testament Band 339. Münster: Ugarit-Verlag.

Brown, J. 2003. The Cahokia mound 72-sub 1 burials as collective representations. *The Wisconsin Archaeologist* 84:83–99.

Buccellati, G. 1966. *The Amorites of the Ur III Period.* Pubblicazioni del Seminario di Semitistica 1. Naples: Istituto Orientale di Napoli.

1990a. "River Bank," "High Country," and "Pasture Land": The Growth of Nomadism on the Middle Euphrates and the Khabur. In *Tall al-Hamīdīya 2,* edited by S. Eichler, M. Wäfler, and D. Warburton, 89–117. Orbis Biblicus et Orientalis Series Archaeologica 6. Freibourg: Universitätsverlag and Göttingen: Vandenhoeck und Ruprecht.

1990b. Salt at the Dawn of History: The Case of the Bevelled-Rim Bowls. In *Resurrecting the Past. A Joint Tribute to Adnan Bounni,* edited by P. Matthiae, M. van Loon, and H. Weiss, 17–40. Leiden: Nederlands Historisch-Archaeologisch Instituut te Istanbul.

2008. The Origin of the Tribe and of "Industrial" Agropastoralism in Syro-Mesopotamia. In *The Archaeology of Mobility: Old World and New World Nomadism,* edited by H. Barnard and W. Wendrich, 141–59. Cotsen Advanced Seminars 4. Los Angeles: Cotsen Institute of Archaeology Press.

Buchli, V. 2004. Material Culture: Current Problems. In *A Companion to Social Archaeology,* edited by L. Meskell and R. Preucel, 179–94. Oxford: Blackwell.

Burnham, P. 1979. Spatial Mobility and Political Centralization in Pastoral Societies. In *Pastoral Production and Society,* edited by L'Equipe ecologie et anthropologie des sociétiés pastorals, 349–60. Proceedings of the International Meeting on Nomadic Pastoralism - Paris 1–3 Dec. 1976. Paris: Éditions de la Maison des Sciences de l'Homme.

Butterlin, P. 1999. Les modalités du contact: chronologie et espaces de l'expansion urukéenne dans le secteur de Birecik. *Paleorient* 25/1:128–40.

Butterlin, P. 2003. *Les temps Proto-Urbains de Mésopotamie. Contacts et acculturation à l'époque d'Uruk au Moyen-Orient.* Paris: CNRS.

2007. Mari, les Šakkanakkû et la crise de la fin du Troisième Millénaire. In *Sociétés humaines et changement climatique à la fin du Troisième Millénaire: Une crise a-t-elle eu lieu en Haute-Mésopotamie?* edited by C. Marro and C. Kuzucuoglu, 227–46. Varia Anatolica 18. Paris: De Boccard.

Carter, E. N.d. On Human and Animal Sacrifice in the Late Neolithic at Domuztepe. In *Sacred Killing: The Archaeology of Sacrifice in the Ancient Near East*, edited by A. Porter and G. Schwartz. Winona Lake, IN: Eisenbrauns.

Carter, E., and A. Parker. 1995. Pots, People and the Archaeology of Death in Northern Syria and Southern Anatolia in the Latter Half of the Third Millennium BC. In *The Archaeology of Death in the Ancient Near East*, edited by S. Campbell and A. Green, 96–115. Oxbow Monograph 51. Oxford: British Archaeology Reports.

Carsten, J. 1995. The Substance of Kinship and the Heat of the Hearth: Feeding, Personhood, and Relatedness among Malays in Pulau Langkawi. *American Ethnologist* 22/2:223–41.

2000. Introduction: Cultures of Relatedness. In *Cultures of Relatedness: New Approaches to the Study of Kinship*, edited by J. Carsten, 1–36. Cambridge: Cambridge University Press.

2004. *After Kinship*. Cambridge: Cambridge University Press.

Carsten, J., and S. Hugh-Jones, eds. 1995. *About the House: Lévi-Strauss and Beyond*. Cambridge: Cambridge University Press.

Casimir, M. J., and A. Rao. 2003. The Historical Framework of Nomadism in South Asia: A Brief Overview. In *Nomadism in South Asia*, edited by A. Rao and M. J. Casimir, 43–80. Oxford in India Readings in Sociology and Social Anthropology. New Delhi: Oxford University Press.

Castel, C., and E. Peltenburg. 2007. Urbanism on the Margins: Third Millennium BC Al-Rawda in the Arid Zone of Syria. *Antiquity* 81:601–16.

Caton, S. 1990. Anthropological Theories of Tribe and State Formation in the Middle East: Ideology and the Semiotics of Power. In *Tribes and State Formation in the Middle East*, edited by P. Khoury and J. Kostiner, 74–108. Berkeley: University of California Press.

Cavigneaux, A., and Al-Rawi, F. 1993. New Sumerian Literary Texts from Tell Haddad (Ancient Meturan): A First Survey. *Iraq* 55: 91–105.

Charpin, D. 1984. Inscriptions votives d'epoque assyrienne. *Mari Annales de Recherches Interdisciplinaires* 3:41–81.

2003. La "toponymie en miroir" dans le Proche-Orient Amorrite. *Revue d'Assyriologie* 97:3–34.

2004a. Histoire politique du Proche-Orient Amorrite (2002–1595). In *Mesopotamien: Die altbabylonische Zeit*, edited by P. Attinger, W. Sallaberger, and M. Wäfler, 23–480. Orbis Biblicus et Orientalis 160/4. Fribourg: Academic Press.

2004b. Nomades et sédentaires dans l'armée de Mari au temps de Yahdum-Lîm. In *Amurru 3: Nomades et sédentaires dans le Proche-Orient ancien*, edited by C. Nicolle, 83–94. Compte rendu de la XLVIe Rencontre Assyriologique Internationale, Paris, 2000. Paris: Éditions Recherche sur les Civilisations.

Charpin, D., and J.-M. Durand. 1985. La prise du pouvoir par Zimri-Lim. *Mari Annales de Recherches Interdisciplinaires* 4:293–343.

1986. "Fils de Sim'al": Les origines tribales des rois de Mari. *Revue d'Assyriolgique* 80:141–83.

Chatty, D. 2006a. Nomads of the Middle East and North Africa Facing the 21st Century. In *Nomadic Societies in the Middle East and North Africa: Entering the 21st Century*, edited by D. Chatty, 1–29. Leiden: Brill.

2006b. Assumptions of Degradation and Misuse: The Bedouin in the Syrian *Bādiya*. In *Nomadic Societies in the Middle East and North Africa: Entering the 21st Century*, edited by D. Chatty, 737–58. Leiden: Brill.

Chazan, M., and M. Lehner. 1990. An Ancient Analogy: Pot Baked Bread in Ancient Egypt and Mesopotamia. *Paléorient* 16/2:21–35.

Chesson, M. 2003. Households, Houses, Neighborhoods, and Corporate Villages: Modeling the Early Bronze Age as a House Society. *Journal of Mediterranean Archaeology* 16/1:79–102.

Childe, V. G. 1951. *Man Makes Himself.* Revised edition. New York: The New American Library.

Claudot-Hawad, H. 2006. A Nomadic Fight against Immobility: The Tuareg in the Modern State. In *Nomadic Societies in the Middle East and North Africa: Entering the 21st Century*, edited by D. Chatty, 654–81. Leiden: Brill.

Cole, D. 1981. Bedouin and Social Change in Saudi Arabia. *Journal of Asian and African Studies* 16/1–2:128–49.

Collins, P. 2000. *The Uruk Phenomenon: The Role of Social Ideology in the Expansion of the Uruk Culture during the Fourth Millennium BC*. BAR International Series 900. Oxford: Archaeopress.

Colson, E. 1986. Political Organizations in Tribal Societies: A Cross-Cultural Comparison. *American Indian Quarterly* 10:5–20.

Cooper, J. 1983. *The Curse of Akkad*. Baltimore: The Johns Hopkins University Press.

    1993a. Paradigm and Propaganda. The Dynasty of Akkade in the 21st Century. In *Akkad the First World Empire: Structure, Ideology, Traditions*, edited by M. Liverani, 11–23. Padua: Sargon srl.

    1993b. Sacred Marriage and Popular Cult in Early Mesopotamia. In *Official Cult and Popular Religion in the Ancient Near East*, edited by E. Matsushima, 81–96. Papers of the First Colloquium on the Ancient Near East – The City and Its Life, held at the Middle Eastern Culture Center in Japan March 20–22, 1992. Heidelberg: Universitätsverlag C. Winter.

    1996. Magic and M(is)use: Poetic Promiscuity in Mesopotamian Ritual. In *Proceedings of the Groningen Group for the Study of Mesopotamian Literature*, vol. 2: *Mesopotamian Poetic Language: Sumerian and Akkadian*, edited by M. E. Vogelzang and H. L. J. Vanstiphout, 47–57. Cuneiform Monographs 6. Groningen: Styx.

    2002. Buddies in Babylonia. Gilgamesh, Enkidu and Mesopotamian Homosexuality. In *Riches Hidden in Secret Places: Ancient Near Eastern Studies in Memory of Thorkild Jacobsen*, edited by T. Abusch, 73–86. Winona Lake, IN: Eisenbrauns.

    2006. Response for the First Sessions: Origins, Functions, Adaptation, Survival. In *Margins of Writing, Origins of Cultures: New Approaches to Writing and Reading in the Ancient Near East*, edited by S. Sanders, 83–7. Oriental Institute Symposia 2. Chicago: The Oriental Institute.

Cooper, L. 2006. *Early Urbanism on the Syrian Euphrates*. New York: Routledge.

    2010. Urban Elements in Early Bronze Age Settlements of the Northern Euphrates Valley of Syria. *Al-Rafidan 2010*. Special Issue: Formation of Tribal Communities: Integrated Research in the Middle Euphrates, Syria: 177–90.

Crawford, H. 2002. "Nearer My God to Thee?" The Relationship between Man and His Gods in Third-Millennium BC Mesopotamia. In *Of Pots and Pans. Papers on the Archaeology and History of Mesopotamia and Syria Presented to David Oates in Honour of his 75th Birthday*, edited by L. al-Gailani Werr, J. Curtis, H. Martin, A. McMahon, J. Oates, and J. Reade, 47–53. London: Nabu.

Cribb, R. 1991. *Nomads in Archaeology*. Cambridge: Cambridge University Press.

    2008. No Room to Move: Mobility, Settlement and Conflict among Mobile Peoples. In *The Archaeology of Mobility: Old World and New World Nomadism*, edited by

H. Barnard and W. Wendrich, 543–56. Cotsen Advanced Seminars 4. Los Angeles Cotsen Institute of Archaeology Press.

Cunningham, G. 2007. A Catalogue of Sumerian Literature. In *Analysing Literary Sumerian: Corpus-based Approaches*, edited by J. Ebeling and G. Cunningham, 351–412. London: Equinox.

Dahl, J. 2003. The Ruling Family of Ur III Umma: A Prosopographical Analysis of a Provincial Elite Family in Southern Iraq ca. 2100–2000 BC. PhD diss., University of California, Los Angeles.

Dalley, S. 1998. *Myths from Mesopotamia: Creation, the Flood, Gilgamesh, and Others*. Oxford: Oxford University Press.

Damerow, P. 2006. The Origins of Writing as a Problem of Historical Epistemology. Cuneiform Digital Library Journal 2006:1. http://cdli.ucla.edu/pubs/cdlj/2006/cdlj2006_001.html

Deimel, A. 1923. *Die Inschriften von Fara, II: Schultexte aus Fara*. Wissenschaftliche Veröffentlichungen der Deutschen Orient-Gesellschaft 43. Leipzig: J. C. Hinrichs'sche Buchhandlung.

deJong Ellis, M. 1989. Observations on Mesopotamian Oracles and Prophetic Texts: Literary and Historiographical Considerations. *Journal of Cuneiform Studies* 41:127–86.

Delnero, P. 2006. Variation in Sumerian Literary Compositions: A Case Study Based on the Decad. PhD diss., University of Pennsylvania.

   2007. Pre-verbal /n/: Function, Distribution, and Stability. In *Analysing Literary Sumerian: Corpus-based Approaches*, edited by J. Ebeling and G. Cunningham, 105–43. London: Equinox.

Delougaz, P. 1940. *The Temple Oval at Khafājah*. Oriental Institute Publications 53. Chicago: University of Chicago Press.

   1952. *Pottery from the Diyala Region*. Oriental Institute Publications 63. Chicago: University of Chicago Press.

Delougaz, P., H. Hill, and S. Lloyd. 1967. *Private Houses and Graves in the Diyala Region*. Oriental Institute Publications 88. Chicago: University of Chicago Press.

Delougaz, P., and H. Kantor. 1996. *Chogha Mish. Volume 1: The First Five Seasons of Excavations, 1961–1971*. Edited by A. Alizadeh. Oriental Institute Publications 101. Chicago: The Oriental Institute.

Delougaz, P., and S. Lloyd. 1942. *Pre-Sargonid Temples in the Diyala Region*. Oriental Institute Publications 58. Chicago: University of Chicago.

Dessine, F. 2008. Savoir-faire et transferts techniques en Mesopotamie, en Anatolie, et dans le Caucase au IVe et IIIe millennaire av. J.-C. *Anatolia Antiqua* XVI:13–22.

Dever, W. 1992. Pastoralism and the End of the Urban Early Bronze Age in Palestine. In *Pastoralism in the Levant: Archaeological Materials in Anthropological Perspectives*, edited by O. Bar-Yosef and A. Khazanov, 83–92. Monographs in World Archaeology, No 10. Madison, WI: Prehistory Press.

   1995. Social Structure in the Early Bronze IV Period in Palestine. In *The Archaeology of Society in the Holy Land*, edited by T. Levy, 282–96. New York: Continuum.

Dietler, M. 2005. The Archaeology of Colonization and the Colonization of Archaeology: Theoretical Challenges from an Ancient Mediterranean Colonial Encounter. In *The Archaeology of Colonial Encounters: Comparative Perspectives*, edited by G. Stein, 33–68. School of American Research Advanced Seminar Series. Santa Fe, NM: School of American Research Press.

Dietler, M., and I. Herbich. 1998. *Habitus*, Techniques, Style: An Integrated Approach to the Social Understanding of Material Culture and Boundaries. In *The Archaeology of Social Boundaries*, edited by M. Stark, 232-63. Washington, DC: Smithsonian Institution.

Digard, J.-P. 1990. Les relations nomades-sédentaires au Moyen Orient. Éléments d'une polémique. In *Nomades et sédentaires en Asie Centrale*, edited by H.-P. Francfort, 97-111. Actes du Colloque franco-soviétique d'Alma-Ata 1987. Paris: CNRS.

Dirlik, A. 1994. The Postcolonial Aura: Third World Criticism in the Age of Global Capitalism. *Critical Inquiry* 20/2:328-56.

Dobres, M.-A. 2000. *Technology and Social Agency*. Oxford: Blackwell.

Dobres, M.-A., and J. Robb, eds. 2000. *Agency in Archaeology*. London: Routledge.

Dolce, R. 1998. The Palatial Ebla Culture in the Context of North Mesopotamia and North Syrian Main Powers. In *About Subartu: Studies Devoted to Upper Mesopotamia*, edited by M. Lebeau, 67-82. Subartu IV/1. Turnhout: Brepols.

———. 2006. Ebla and Akkad: Clues of an Early Meeting. Another Look at the Artistic Culture of Palace G. In *Ina Kibrat Erbetti. Studi di Archeologia orientale dedicati a Paolo Matthiae*, edited by F. Baffi, R. Dolce, S. Mazzoni, and F. Pinnock, 127-206. Rome: Casa Editrice, Università degli Studi di Roma "La Sapienza."

———. 2008. Ebla before the Achievement of Palace G Culture: An Evaluation of the Early Syrian Archaic Period. In *Proceedings of the 4th International Congress of the Archaeology of the Ancient Near East: 29 March–3 April 2004, Freie Universität Berlin*. Vol. 2: *Social and Cultural Transformation: The Archaeology of Transitional Periods and Dark Ages; Excavation Reports*, edited by H. Kühne, R. M. Czichon, and F. J. Kreppner, 65-80. Wiesbaden: Harrasowitz Verlag.

Dunham, S. 1993. A Wall Painting from Tell al-Raqa'i, North-East Syria. *Levant* 25:127-43.

Durand, J.-M. 1992. Unité et diversités au Proche-Orient à l'époque Amorrite. In *La circulation des biens, des personnes et des idées dans le Proche-Orient ancien*, edited by D. Charpin and F. Joannès, 97-128. CRRAI 38. Paris: Éditions Recherche sur les Civilisations.

———. 1997. *Documents épistolaires du palais de Mari*. Tome I. Littératures anciennes du Proche-Orient. Paris: Les Éditions du Cerf.

———. 1998. *Documents épistolaires du palais de Mari*. Tome II. Littératures anciennes du Proche-Orient. Paris: Les Éditions du Cerf.

———. 2000. *Documents épistolaires du palais de Mari*. Tome III. Littératures anciennes du Proche-Orient. Paris: Les Éditions du Cerf.

———. 2004. Peuplement et sociétés à l'époque amorrite (I) Les clans bensim'alites. In *Amurru 3: Nomades et sédentaires dans le Proche-Orient ancien*, edited by C. Nicholle, 111-19. Compte rendu de la XLVIe Rencontre Assyriologique Internationale (Paris, 10-13 juillet 2000). Paris: Éditions Recherche sur les Civilisations.

———. 2005. *Le culte des pierres et les monuments commémoratifs en Syrie amorrite*. Florilegium marianum 8. Paris: Société pour l'Étude du Proche-Orient Ancien.

Durand, J.-M. 2010. The Banks of the Euphrates along the Bishri. In *Al-Rafidan 2010*. Special Issue: Formation of Tribal Communities: Integrated Research in the Middle Euphrates, Syria: 253-262.

Durand, J.-M., and M. Guichard. 1997. Les rituels de Mari (texts n° 2 à n° 5). In *Recueil d'études à la mémoire de Marie-Thérèse Barrelet*, edited by D. Charpin and J.-M. Durand, 19-78. Florilegium marianum 3. Paris: Société pour l'Étude du Proche-Orient Ancien.

Dyson-Hudson, N. 1972. The Study of Nomads. In *Perspectives on Nomadism*, edited by W. Irons and N. Dyson-Hudson, 2-29 Leiden: Brill.

Dyson-Hudson, R., and N. Dyson-Hudson. 1980. Nomadic Pastoralism. *Annual Review of Anthropology* 9:15-61.

Edwards, J., and M. Strathern. 2000. Including Our Own. In *Cultures of Relatedness: New Approaches to the Study of Kinship*, edited by J. Carsten, 149-67. Cambridge: Cambridge University Press.

Edzard, D. 1981. *ARET II. Verwaltungstexte verschieden Inhalts (aus dem archiv L.2769)*. Rome: Missione Archaeologica Italiana in Siria.

1997. *Gudea and His Dynasty. The Royal Inscriptions of Mesopotamia, Early Periods*, vol. 3.1. Toronto: University of Toronto Press.

Eickelman, D. 1998. Being Bedouin: Nomads and Tribes in the Arab Social Imagination. In *Changing Nomads in a Changing World*, edited by J. Ginat and A. Khazanov, 38-49. Brighton: Sussex Academic Press.

Eidem, J. 1994. Raiders of the Lost Treasure of Samsi-Addu. In *Recueil d'études à la mémoire de Maurice Birot*, edited by D. Charpin and J.-M. Durand, 201-8. Florilegium marianum 2. Paris: Société pour l'Étude du Proche-Orient Ancien.

2000. Northern Jazira in the 18th Century BC: Aspects of Geopolitical Patterns. Pp. 255-64 in *La Djéziré et l'Euphrate syriens de la protohistoire à la fin du second millénaire av. J. C. Tendances dans l'interprétation historique des données nouvelles*, edited by O. Rouault and M. Wäfler. Subartu VII. Turnhout: Brepols.

Einwag, B., T. McClellan, A. Otto, and A. Porter. N.d. The Banat-Bazi Complex in the Third Millennium: Past Perspectives, Future Prospects. In preparation.

Ekeh, P. 1990. Social Anthropology and Two Contrasting Uses of Tribalism in Africa. *Comparative Studies in Society and History* 32/4:660-700.

El-Haramein, F., and B. Adleh. 1994. Bread in Syria. *Food Reviews International* 10/4:419-36.

Emberling, G. 2002. Political Control in the Early State: The Eye Temple and the Uruk Expansion in Northern Mesopotamia. In *Of Pots and Pans. Papers on the Archaeology and History of Mesopotamia and Syria Presented to David Oates in Honour of his 75th Birthday*, edited by L. al-Gailani Werr, J. Curtis, H. Martin, A. McMahon, J. Oates, and J. Reade, 82-90. London: Nabu.

Emberling, G., and H. McDonald. 2001. Excavations at Tell Brak 2000: Preliminary Report. *Iraq* 63:21-54.

2003. Excavations at Tell Brak 2001-2002: Preliminary Report. *Iraq* 65:1-75.

Englund, R. 1991. Hard Work - Where Will It Get You? Labor Management in Ur III Mesopotamia. *Journal of Near Eastern Studies* 50/4:255-80.

1995. Regulating Dairy Productivity in the Ur III Period. *Orientalia* 64:377-429.

Evans-Pritchard, E. 1956. *Nuer Religion*. Oxford: Oxford University Press.

1969. *The Nuer*. First Published 1940. Oxford: Oxford University Press.

Falkowitz, R. 1983. Notes on "Lugalbanda and Enmerkar." *Journal of the American Oriental Society*, 103/1:103-14.

Falsone, G., and P. Sconzo. 2007. The "Champagne-Cup" Period at Carchemish: A Review of the Early Bronze Age Levels on the Acropolis Mound and the Problem of the Inner Town. In *Euphrates River Valley Settlement: The Carchemish Sector in the Third Millennium BC*, edited by E. Peltenburg, 73-93. Levant Supplementary Series 5. Oxford: Oxbow.

Featherstone, S. 2005. *Postcolonial Cultures*. Edinburgh: Edinburgh University Press.

Feinman, G., and J. Marcus, eds. 1998. *Archaic States*. Santa Fe, NM: School of American Research Press.

Feinman, G. M., and J. Neitzel. 1984. Too Many Types: An Overview of Sedentary Prestate Societies in the Americas. In *Advances in Archaeological Method and Theory*, vol. 7, edited by M. Shiffer, 39–102. New York: Academic Press.

Felli, C. 2000. Middle Uruk Pottery from Area HS1, Tell Brak. Aspects of Cultural Continuity and Change. In *Proceedings of the First International Congress on the Archaeology of the Ancient Near East: Rome, May 18th–23rd 1998*, vol. 1, edited by P. Matthiae, A. Enea, L. Peyronel, and F. Pinnock, 411–20. Rome: Dipartimento di Scienze Storiche, Archeologiche e Anthropologiche dell'Antichità.

    2003. Developing Complexity. Early to Mid-Fourth Millennium Investigations: The Northern Middle Uruk Period. In *Excavations at Tell Brak*. Vol. 4: *Exploring an Upper Mesopotamian Regional Centre, 1994–1996*, edited by R. Matthews, 53–95. Cambridge: McDonald Institute for Archaeological Research and British School of Archaeology in Iraq.

Ferraro, E. 2008. Kneading Life – Women and the Celebration of the Dead in the Ecuadorian Andes. *Journal of the Royal Anthropological Institute* 14/2:262–77.

Fiandra, E., and M. Frangipane. 2007. Arslantepe: A Complex Administrative System before Writing. In *Arslantepe* Cretulae. *An Early Centralized Administrative System Before Writing*, edited by M. Frangipane, 416–68. Rome: Università degli Studi di Roma "La Sapienza."

Finet, A. 1980. L'apport du Tell Kannas à l'histoire Proche-Oreintale, de la fin du 4e millénaire à la moitié du 2e. *Le Moyen Euphrate: Zone de contacts et d'échanges*, edited by J. C. Margueron, 107–15. Leiden: Brill.

Finkbeiner, U. 1991. *Uruk Kampagne 35–37 1982–84: Die archäologische Oberflächenuntersuchung (Survey)*. Ausgrabungen in Uruk-Warka Endberichte 4. Mainz: Phillipe von Zabern.

Finkelstein, J. 1966. The Genealogy of the Hammurabi Dynasty. *Journal of Cuneiform Studies* 20:95–118.

Fleming, D. 2004. *Democracy's Ancient Ancestors*. Cambridge: Cambridge University Press.

    2009. Kingship of City and Tribe Conjoined: Zimri-Lim at Mari. In *Nomads, Tribes, and the State in the Ancient Near East: Cross-Disciplinary Perspectives*, edited by J. Szuchman, 227–40. Oriental Institute Seminars 5. Chicago: The Oriental Institute of the University of Chicago.

Fleming, D., and S. Milstein. 2010. *The Buried Foundation of the Gilgamesh Epic: The Akkadian Huwawa Narrative*. Cuneiform Monograph Series, 39. Leiden: Brill.

Flückiger-Hawker, E. 1999. *Ur-Namma of Ur in Sumerian Literary Tradition*. Orbis Biblicus et Orientalis 166. Freibourg: Universitätsverlag; and Göttingen: Vandenhoeck und Ruprecht.

Forest, J.-D. 1987. La grande architecture obeidienne: Sa forme et sa function. In *Préhistoire de la Mésopotamie*, edited by J.-L. Huot, 385–423. Paris: CNRS.

    1999. L'expansion urukéene: Notes d'un voyageur. *Paléorient* 25/1:141–9.

Forest, J.-D., and N. Gallois. 2007. Mesopotamian Art from Its Origins to c. 2000 BC. In *The Art and Architecture of Mesopotamia*, edited by G. Curatola, J.-D. Forest, N. Gallois, C. Lippolis, and R. V. Ricciardi, 13–64. [English translation]. New York: Abbeville Press.

Fortes, M. 1945. *The Dynamics of Clanship among the Tallensi*. London: Oxford University Press.

1949. *The Web of Kinship among the Tallensi*. London: Oxford University Press.

1953. The Structure of Unilinear Descent Groups. *American Anthropologist* 55/1:17–41.

1969. *Kinship and the Social Order*. Chicago: Aldine.

1979. Preface. In *Segmentary Lineage Systems Reconsidered*, edited by L. Holy, vii–xii. The Queen's University Papers in Social Anthropology 4. Belfast: Department of Social Anthropology, Queen's University of Belfast.

Fortin, M. 1998a. New Horizons in Ancient Syria: The View from 'Atij. *Near Eastern Archaeology* 61/1:15–24.

1998b. Le quartier domestique de la station commerciale de Tell 'Atij sur le moyen Khabour, au IIIème millenaire av. J.-C. In *Espace natural, espace habité en Syrie du Nord (10e –2e millénaires av. J.-C.)*, edited by M. Fortin and O. Aurenche, 229–42. Toronto: The Canadian Society for Mesopotamian Studies.

Foster, B. 1981. A New Look at the Sumerian Temple State. *Journal of the Economic and Social History of the Orient* 24/3:225–41.

Fowles, S. 2002. From Social Type to Social Process: Placing "Tribe" in a Historical Framework. In *The Archaeology of Tribal Societies*, edited by W. Parkinson, 13–33. Ann Arbor, MI: International Monographs in Prehistory.

Foxvog, D. A. 1980. Funerary Furnishing in an Early Sumerian Text from Adab. In *Death in Mesopotamia: Papers Read at the XXVIe Rencontre Assyriologique Internationale*, edited by B. Alster, 67–75. Mesopotamia 8. Copenhagen: Akademisk.

Frachetti, M. D. 2008. *Pastoral Landscapes and Social Interaction in Bronze Age Eurasia*. Berkeley: University of California Press.

Frachetti, M., and A. Mar'yashev. 2007. Long-term Occupation and Seasonal Settlement of Eastern Eurasian Pastoralists at Begash, Kazakhstan. *Journal of Field Archaeology* 32/3:221–42.

Frangipane, M. 1992. Dipinti murale in un edificio "palaziale" di Arslantepe-Malatya: Aspetti ideologici nelle prime forme di centralizzazione economica. *Studi Micenei ed Egeo-Anatolici* 30:143–54.

1993a. Excavations at Arslantepe-Malatya, 1992. *Kazi Sonuçlari Toplantisi* XV:211–28.

1993b. Local Components in the Development of Centralized Societies in Syro-Anatolian Regions. In *Between the Rivers and Over the Mountains*, edited by M. Frangipane, H. Hauptmann, M. Liverani, P. Matthiae, and M. Mellink, 133–61. Rome: Università degli Studi di Roma "La Sapienza."

1997. A Fourth-Millennium Temple/Palace Complex at Arslantepe-Malatya. North-South Relations and the Formation of Early State Societies in the Northern Regions of Greater Mesopotamia. *Paléorient* 23:45–73.

2001. Centralization Processes in Greater Mesopotamia: Uruk Expansion as the Climax of Systemic Interactions among Areas of Greater Mesopotamian Region. In *Uruk Mesopotamia and Its Neighbors. Cross-Cultural Interactions in the Era of State Formation*, edited by M. Rothman, 307–49. School of American Research Advanced Seminar Series. Santa Fe, NM: School of American Research Press.

2002. "Non-Uruk" Developments and Uruk-Linked Features on the Northern Borders of Greater Mesopotamia. In *Artefacts of Complexity: Tracking the Uruk in the Near East*, edited by J. N. Postgate, 123–48. Cambridge: British School of Archaeology in Iraq.

2007a. Establishment of a Middle/Upper Euphrates Early Bronze I Culture from the Fragmentation of the Uruk World: New Data from Zeytinli Bahçe Höyük

(Urfa, Turkey). In *Euphrates River Valley Settlement: The Carchemish Sector in the Third Millennium BC*, edited by E. Peltenburg, 122-41. Levant Supplementary Series 5. Oxford: Oxbow.

2007b. Thousands of *Cretulae* in the Fourth Millennium "Palatial" Complex at Arslantepe (Period VIA, LC5): The Archaeological Contexts. In *Arslantepe Cretulae. An Early Centralized Administrative System before Writing*, edited by M. Frangipane, 25-60. Rome: Università degli Studi di Roma "La Sapienza."

2007/8. The Arslantepe "Royal Tomb": New Funerary Customs and Political Changes in the Upper Euphrates Valley at the Beginning of the Third Millennium BC. In *Sepolti tra i vivi/ Buried among the Living: Evidenza ed interpretazione di contesti funerari in abitato*. Atti del Convegno Internazionale, edited by G. Bartoloni and M.-G. Benedettini, 169-94. Scienze dell'Antichità 14/1, Rome: Università degli Studi di Roma "La Sapienza."

Frangipane, M., and A. Palmieri. 1983. A Protourban Center of the Late Uruk Period. *Origini* XII/2:287-455.

Frangipane M., E. Andersson Strand, R. Laurito, S. Möller-Wiering, M.-L. Nosch, A. Rast- Eicher, and A. Wisti Lasson. 2009. Arslantepe, Malatya (Turkey): Textiles, Tools and Imprints of Fabrics from the 4th to the 2nd Millennium BCE. *Paléorient* 35/1:5-29.

Frangipane, M., G. di Nocera, A. Hauptmann, P. Morbidelli, A. Palmieri, L. Sadori, M. Schultz, and T. Schmidt-Schultz. 2001. New Symbols of a New Power in a "Royal" Tomb from 3000 BC Arslantepe, Malatya (Turkey). *Paléorient* 27/2:105-39.

Frayne, D. 1990. *Old Babylonian Period (2003–1595). The Royal Inscriptions of Mesopotamia*, vol. 4. Toronto: University of Toronto Press.

1993. *Sargonic and Gutian Periods (2334–213 BC). The Royal Inscriptions of Mesopotamia. Early Periods*, vol. 2. Toronto: University of Toronto Press.

1997. *Ur III Period (2112–2004 BC). The Royal Inscriptions of Mesopotamia*, vol. 3/2. Toronto: University of Toronto Press.

Fried, M. 1957. The Classification of Corporate Unilineal Descent Groups. *Journal of the Royal Anthropological Institute* 87/1:1-29.

1968. On the Concepts of "Tribe" and "Tribal Society." In *Essays on the Problem of the Tribe*, edited by J. Helm, 3-20. Proceedings of the 1967 Annual Spring Meeting, the American Ethnological Society. Seattle: University of Washington Press.

1975. *The Notion of Tribe*. Menlo Park, CA: Cummings Publishing Company.

Friedman, J. 1975. Tribes, States and Transformations. In *Marxist Analyses and Social Anthropology*, edited by M. Bloch, 161-203. New York: Littlehampton Book Services.

1996. The Politics of De-Authentification: Escaping from Identity, a Response to "Beyond Authenticity" by Mark Rogers. *Identities* 3/1-2:127-36.

Fronzaroli, P. 1984. "Materiali per il lessico eblaita," *Studi Eblaiti* 7:145-90.

1992. The Ritual Texts of Ebla. In *Literature and Literary Language at Ebla*, edited by P. Fronzaroli, 163-85. Quaderni di Semitistica 18. Florence: Università di Firenze.

1993. ARET IX. Testi rituali della regalità (Archivio L.2769). Rome: Casa Editrice, Università degli Studi di Roma "La Sapienza."

1997. Divinazione ad Ebla (TM.76.G.86). *Miscellanea Eblaitica* 4:1-22.

1998. Kam$_4$mu in Ebla Letters. In *About Subartu: Studies Devoted to Upper Mesopotamia. Culture, Society and Image*, edited by M. Lebeau, 103-14. Subartu IV/2. Turnhout: Brepols.

Fuji, S., and T. Adachi. 2010. Archaeological Investigations of Bronze Age Cairn Fields on the Northwestern Flank of Mt. Bishri. *Al-Rafidan 2010.* Special Issue: Formation of Tribal Communities: Integrated Research in the Middle Euphrates, Syria: 61–78.

Gadotti, A. 2005. "Gilgameš, Enkidu and the Netherworld" and the Sumerian Gilgameš Cycle. PhD diss., The Johns Hopkins University.

Galaty, M. 2002. Modeling the Formation and Evolution of an Illyrian Tribal System: Ethnographic and Archaeological Analogs. In *The Archaeology of Tribal Societies,* edited by W. Parkinson, 109–22. International Monographs in Prehistory, Archaeological Series 15. Ann Arbor, MI: International Monographs in Prehistory.

Galvin K. 2008. Responses of Pastoralists to Land Fragmentation: Social Capital, Connectivity, and Resilience. In *Fragmentation of Semi-Arid and Arid Landscapes: Consequences for Human and Natural Systems,* edited by K. Galvin, R. Reid, R. Behnke, Jr., and N. Hobbs, 369–89. Dordrecht, Netherlands: Springer.

2009. Transitions: Pastoralists Living with Change. *Annual Review of Anthropology* 38:185–98.

Garrard, A., S. Colledge, and L. Martin. 1996. The Emergence of Crop Cultivation and Caprine Herding in the "Marginal Zone" of the Southern Levant. In *The Origins and Spread of Agriculture and Pastoralism in Eurasia,* edited by D. R. Harris, 204–26. Washington, DC: Smithsonian Institution.

Geertz, C. 1973. *The Interpretation of Cultures.* New York: Basic.

Gelb, I. 1954. Two Assyrian King Lists. *Journal of Near Eastern Studies* 13:209–30.

1972. The *Arua* Institution. *Révue d'Assyriologie* 66:1–32.

1979. Household and Family in Early Mesopotamia. In *State and Temple Economy in the Ancient Near East,* edited by E. Lipinski, 1–97. Orientalia Lovaniensia Analecta 5–6. Louvain: Peeters.

1980. A *Computer-Aided Analysis of Amorite.* Assyriological Studies 21. Chicago: Oriental Institute of the University of Chicago.

1986. Ebla and Lagash: Environmental Contrast. In *The Origin of Cities in Dry Farming Syria and Mesopotamia in the Third Millennium B.C.,* edited by H. Weiss, 157–67. Guilford, CT: Four Quarters.

Gelb, I., P. Steinkeller, and R. Whiting. 1991. *Earliest Land Tenure Systems in the Near East: Ancient Kudurrus.* Oriental Institute Publications 104. Chicago: Oriental Institute of the University of Chicago.

Gellner, E. 1969. *Saints of the Atlas.* London. Weidenfeld & Nicolson.

1984. Forword to *Nomads and the Outside World* by A. Khazanov. Madison: University of Wisconsin Press.

1990. Tribalism and the State in the Middle East. In *Tribes and State Formation in the Middle East,* edited by P. Khoury and J. Kostiner, 109–26. Berkeley: University of California Press.

George, A. 2003. *The Babylonian Gilgamesh Epic: Introduction, Critical Edition and Cuneiform Texts,* vol. 1. Oxford: Oxford University Press.

Geyer, B., and J. Monchambert. 1987. Prospection de la moyenne vallée de Euphrate: Rapport préliminaire, 1982–1985. *Mari Annales de Recherches Interdisciplinaires* 5:293–344.

Giddens, A. 1979. *Central problems in Social Theory: Action, Structure and Contradiction in Social Analysis.* Berkeley: University of California Press.

1981. *A Contemporary Critique of Historical Materialism*. Vol. 1: *Power, Property and the State*. Berkeley: University of California.

1984. *The Constitution of Society: Outline of the Theory of Structuration*. Berkeley: University of California Press.

1987. *A Contemporary Critique of Historical Materialism*. Vol. 2: *The Nation-State and Violence*. Berkeley: University of California.

Gilbert, A. 1975. Modern Nomads and Prehistoric Pastoralists: The Limits of Analogy. *Journal of the Ancient Eastern Society of Columbia University* 7:53–71.

Gillespie, S. 2000a. Beyond Kinship: An Introduction. In *Beyond Kinship: Social and Material Reproduction in House Societies*, edited by R. Joyce and S. Gillespie, 1–21. Philadelphia: University of Pennsylvania Press.

2000b. Lévi-Strauss: Maison and Société à Maisons. In *Beyond Kinship: Social and Material Reproduction in House Societies*, edited by R. Joyce and S. Gillespie, 22–52. Philadelphia: University of Pennsylvania Press.

Glassner, J.-J. 1986. *La chute d'Akkadé: Lévénement et sa mémoire*. Berlin: Dietrich Reimer Verlag.

2003. *The Invention of Cuneiform. Writing in Sumer*. Translated by Z. Bahrani and M. Van de Mieroop. Baltimore: The Johns Hopkins University Press.

Glatzer, B. 1983. Political Organization of Pashtun Nomads and the State. In *The Conflict of Tribe and State in Iran and Afghanistan*, edited by R. Tapper, 212–32. London: Croom Helm.

Glazier, J. 1984. Mbeere Ancestors and the Domestication of Death. *Man* 19/1:133–48.

Gledhill, J. 1988. Introduction: The Comparative Analysis of Social and Political Transitions. In *State and Society. The Emergence and Development of Social Hierarchy and Political Centralization*, edited by J. Gledhill, B. Bender, and M. Trolles Larsen, 1–29. One World Archaeology 4. London: Unwin Hyman.

2000. *Power and Its Disguises: Anthropological Perspectives on Politics*. London: Pluto.

Goetze, A. 1953. Four Ur Dynasty Tablets Mentioning Foreigners. *Journal of Cuneiform Studies* 7:103–7.

Goldenweiser, A. 1910. Totemism, an Analytical Study. *Journal of American Folklore* 23/88:179–293.

1914. The Social Organization of the Indians of North America. *Journal of American Folklore* 27/106:411–36.

Goldschmidt, W. 1979. A General Model for Pastoral Social Systems. In *Pastoral Production and Society*,15–29. Proceedings of the International Meeting on Nomadic Pastoralism, Paris 1–3 Dec. 1976. Cambridge.

Goody, J. 1961. The Classification of Double Descent Systems. *Current Anthropology* 2/1:3–25.

1969. *Comparative Studies in Kinship*. Stanford, CA: Stanford University Press.

1982. *Cooking, Cuisine and Class: A Case Study in Comparative Sociology*. Cambridge: Cambridge University Press.

González-Ruibal, A. 2006. House Societies vs. Kinship-Based Societies: An Archaeological Case from Iron Age Europe. *Journal of Anthropological Archaeology* 25/1:144–73.

Gosden, C. 2004. *Archaeology and Colonialism. Culture Contact from 5000 BC to the Present*. Cambridge: Cambridge University Press.

Gough, K. 1971. Nuer Kinship: A Re-examination. In *The Translation of Culture: Essays to E. E. Evans-Pritchard*, edited by T. Beidelman, 72–122. London: Tavistock Press.

Goulder, J. 2010. Administrator's Bread: An Experiment-based Re-assessment of the Functional and Cultural Role of the Uruk Bevel-Rim Bowl. *Antiquity* 84:351–62.

Green, M. 1980. Animal Husbandry at Uruk in the Archaic Period. *Journal of Near Eastern Studies* 39:1–35.

Guarino, P. 2008. Mass Produced Bowls in a Late Chalcolithic Ceremonial Building at Arslantepe. Evidence of a Centralized Economic System before the Spread of Uruk Culture. In *Proceedings of the 4th International Congress of the Archaeology of the Ancient Near East: 29 March–3 April 2004, Freie Universität Berlin. Vol. 2: Social and Cultural Transformation: The Archaeology of Transitional Periods and Dark Ages; Excavation Reports*, edited by H. Kühne, R. Czichon, and F. J. Kreppner, 147–54. Wiesbaden: Harrasowitz Verlag.

Gulliver, P. 1975. Nomadic Movements: Causes and Implications. In *Pastoralism in Tropical Africa*, edited by T. Monod, 369–84. London: Oxford University Press.

Hald, M.-M., and M. Charles. 2008. Storage of Crops during the Fourth and Third Millennia B.C. at the Settlement Mound of Tell Brak, Northeast Syria. *Vegetation History and Archaeobotany* 17 (Suppl. 1): S35–S41.

Hall, J., and G. Ikenberry. 1989. *The State*. Minneapolis: University of Minnesota Press.

Hallo, W. 1960. A Sumerian Amphictony. *Journal of Cuneiform Studies* 14:88–114.

1966. The Coronation of Ur-Nammu. *Journal of Cuneiform Studies* 20:133–41.

1987. The Birth of Kings. In *Love and Death in the Ancient Near East: Essays in Honor of Marvin H. Pope*, edited by J. Marks and R. Good, 46–52. Guilford, CT: Four Quarters.

2006. A Sumerian Apocryphon? The Royal Correspondence of Ur Reconsidered. In *Approaches to Sumerian Literature: Studies in Honour of Stip (H. L. J. Vanstiphout)*, edited by P. Michalowski and N. Veldhuis, 85–104. Leiden: Brill.

Hammade, H., and Y. Yamazake. 2006. *Tell al-'Abr (Syria). Ubaid and Uruk Periods*. Memoires 4, Association pour la Promotion de l'Histoire et de l'Archéologie Orient. Louvain: Peeters.

Hansen, K. 1999. The Cook, His Wife, the Madam, and Their Dinner: Cooking, Gender and Class in Zambia. In *Changing Food Habits. Case Studies from Africa, South America and Europe*, edited by C. Lentz, 73–89. Amsterdam: Harwood.

Hasegawa, A. 2010. Sondage at the Site of Tell Ghanem al-Ali. *Al-Rafidan 2010*. Special Issue: Formation of Tribal Communities: Integrated Research in the Middle Euphrates, Syria: 25–36.

Hegmon, M. 1998. Technology, Style and Social Practices: Archaeological Approaches. In *The Archaeology of Social Boundaries*, edited by M. Stark, 264–79. Washington, DC: Smithsonian Institution.

Heim, M. 2004. *Theories of the Gift in South Asia. Hindu, Budhhist and Jain reflections on Dana*. New York: Routledge.

Heimpel, W. 1992. Herrentum und Königtum im vor- und frühgeschichtlichen Alten Orient. *Zeitschrift für Assyriologie* 82:4–21.

2003. *Letters to the King of Mari: A New Translation, with Historical Introduction, Notes, and Commentary*. Winona Lake, IN: Eisenbrauns.

Helms, S. W. 1981. *Jawa: Lost City of the Black Desert*. Ithaca, NY: Cornell University Press.

Helwing, B. 1999. Cultural Interaction at Hassek Höyük, Turkey. New Evidence from Pottery Analysis. *Paléorient* 25/1:91–9.

2003. Feasts as a Social Dynamic in Prehistoric Western Asia – Three Case Studies from Syria and Anatolia. *Paléorient* 29/2:63–85.

2005. Early complexity in Highland Iran: Recent Archaeological Research into the Chalcolithic of Iran. *TÜBA-AR: Turkish Academy of Sciences Journal of Archaeology* 8:39–60.

Hempelmann, R. 2008. Kharab Sayyar: The Foundation of the Early Bronze Age Settlement. In *Proceedings of the 5th International Congress on the Archaeology of the Ancient Near East, Madrid, April 3–8 2006*, edited by J.-M. Córdoba, M. Molist, M. C. Pérez, I. Rubio, and S. Martínez, 153–64. Actas del V Congreso Internacional de Arqueología del Oriente Próximo Antiguo, vol. 2. Madrid: Centro Superior de Estudios sobre el Oriente Proximo y Egipto.

2010. Religion und Gesellschaft in Tell Chuēra während der Frühbronzezeit. In *Kulturlandschaft Syrien. Zentrum und Peripherie Festschrift für Jan-Waalke Meyer*, edited by J. Becker, R. Hempelmann, and E. Rehm. Münster: Ugarit-Verlag.

Hobsbawm, E., and T. Ranger, eds. 1983. *The Invention of Tradition*. Cambridge: Cambridge University Press.

Hodder, I., and S. Değerlendirmesi. N.d. 2007 Season Review. In *Çatalhöyük 2007 Archive Report, Çatalhöyük Research Project*, 1–7. http://www.catalhoyuk.com/downloads/Archive_Report_2007.pdf

Hole, F. 1991. Middle Habur Settlement and Agriculture in the Ninevite 5 Period. *Bulletin of the Canadian Society for Mesopotamian Studies* 21:17–29.

Holy, L. 1979a. Nuer Politics. In *Segmentary Lineage Systems Reconsidered*, edited by L. Holy, 23–48. The Queen's University Papers in Social Anthropology 4. Belfast: Department of Social Anthropology, Queen's University of Belfast.

1979b. The Segmentary Lineage Structure and Its Existential Status. In *Segmentary Lineage Systems Reconsidered*, edited by L. Holy, 1–22. The Queen's University Papers in Social Anthropology 4. Belfast: Department of Social Anthropology, Queen's University of Belfast.

1996. *Anthropological Perspectives on Kinship*. London: Pluto.

Honça, M., and G. Algaze. 1998. Preliminary Report on the Human Skeletal Remains at Titris Höyük: 1991–1996 Seasons. *Anatolica* 24:1–38.

Horowitz, W., and N. Wasserman. 2004. From Hazor to Mari and Ekallatum: A Recently Discovered Old-Babylonian Letter from Hazor. In *Amurru 3: Nomades et sedentaires dans le Proche-Orient ancient*, edited by C. Nicolle, 335–44. Compte rendu de la XLVIe Rencontre Assyriologique Internationale (Paris, 10–13 juillet 2000). Paris: Éditions Recherche sur les Civilisations.

Horwitz, L. K., E. Tchernov, P. Ducos, C. Becker, A. von den Driesch, L. Martin, and A. Garrad. 1999. Animal Domestication in the Southern Levant. *Paléorient* 25/2:63–80.

Huber, F. 2001. La Correspondence Royale d'Ur, un corpus apocryphe. *Zeitschrift für Assyriologie* 91:169–206.

Huehnergard, J. 1992. Languages: Introductory Survey. In *Anchor Bible Dictionary*, vol. 4, edited by D. N. Freedman, 155–70. New York: Doubleday.

1995. The Semitic Languages. In *Civilizations of the Ancient Near East*, vol. 4, edited by J. M. Sasson, 2117–34. New York: Charles Scribner's Sons.

Humphrey, C. 1979. The Uses of Genealogy: A Historical Study of the Nomadic and Sedentarised Buryat. In *Pastoral Production and Society*, edited by L'Equipe ecologie et anthropologie des sociétiés pastorals, 235–60. Proceedings of the International

Meeting on Nomadic Pastoralism – Paris 1–3 Dec. 1976. Paris: Éditions de la Maison des Sciences de l'Homme.

Humphrey, C., D. Sneath, and E. Allworth. 1999. *The End of Nomadism? Society, State, and the Environment in Inner Asia*. Durham, NC: Duke University Press.

Hurowitz, V. 2006. What Goes In Is What Comes Out – Materials for Creating Cult Statues. In *Text, Artifact and Image: Revealing Ancient Israelite Religion*, edited by G. Beckman and T. Lewis, 3–23. Brown Judaic Series 346. Providence, RI: SBL.

Hutchinson, S. 1996. *Nuer Dilemmas. Coping with Money, War and the State*. Berkeley: University of California Press.

    2000. Identity and Substance: The Broadening Bases of Relatedness among the Nuer of Southern Sudan. In *Cultures of Relatedness: New Approaches to the Study of Kinship*, edited by J. Carsten, 55–72. Cambridge: Cambridge University Press.

Ingham, B. 2006. Language and Identity: The Perpetuation of Dialects. In *Nomadic Societies in the Middle East and North Africa. Entering the 21st Century*, edited by Dawn Chatty, 523–38. Leiden: Brill.

Irons, W. 1974. Nomadism as a Political Adaptation: The Case of the Yomut Turkmen. *American Ethnologist* 1:635–58.

Ismail, F., W. Sallaberger, P. Talon, and K. Lerberghe. 1996. *Administrative Documents from Tell Beydar (Seasons 1993–1995)*. Subartu II. Turnhout: Brepols.

Jacobsen, T. 1953. The Reign of Ibbi-Suen. *Journal of Cuneiform Studies* 7:36–47.

    1975. Religious Drama in Ancient Mesopotamia. In *Unity and Diversity: Essays in the History, Literature and Religion of the Ancient Near East*, edited by H. Goedicke and J. Roberts, 65–97. Baltimore: The Johns Hopkins University Press.

Jahn, B. 2007. The Migration and Sedentarization of the Amorites from the Point of View of the Settled Babylonian Population. In *Representation of Political Power: Case Histories from Times of Change and Dissolving Order in the Ancient Near East*, edited by M. Heinz and M. Feldman, 193–209. Winona Lake, IN: Eisenbrauns.

Jean-Marie, M. 1990. Les tombeaux en pierres de Mari. *Mari Annales de Recherches Interdisciplinaires* 6:303–36.

Jestin, R. 1937. *Tablettes sumériennes de Šuruppak au Musée de Stamboul (TSŠ)*. Paris: Boccard.

Joannès, F. 1996. Routes et voies de communication dans les archives de Mari. In *Amurru I: Mari, Ebla et le Hourrites: Dix ans de travaux*, edited by J.-M. Durand, 323–61. Paris: Éditions Recherche sur les Civilisations.

Joffe, A. 2000. Egypt and Syro-Mesopotamia in the 4th Millennium: Implications of the New Chronology. *Current Anthropology* 41/1:113–23.

Johnson, G. 1987. The Changing Organization of Uruk Administration on the Susiana Plain. In *The Archaeology of Western Iran: Settlement and Society from Prehistory to the Islamic Conquest*, edited by F. Hole, 107–39. Washington, DC: Smithsonian.

Johnson, A., and T. Earle. 1987. *The Evolution of Human Societies: from Foraging Group to Agrarian State*. Stanford, CA: Stanford University Press.

Jones, P. 2003. Embracing Inana: Legitimation and Mediation in the Ancient Mesopotamian Sacred Marriage Hymn Iddin-Dagan A. *Journal of the American Oriental Society* 123/2:291–302.

Joyce, R. 2000. Heirlooms and Houses: Materiality and Social Memory. In *Beyond Kinship: Social and Material Reproduction in House Societies*, edited by R. Joyce and S. Gillespie, 189–212. Philadelphia: University of Pennsylvania Press.

2008. Signs for the Future: Rethinking the Archaeology of Long-Term Things. Paper presented at the Theoretical Archaeology Group, Columbia University, NY, May 25th.

Joyce R., and S. Gillespie, eds. 2000. *Beyond Kinship: Social and Material Reproduction in House Societies*. Philadelphia: University of Pennsylvania Press.

Kaberry, P. 1967. The Plasticity of New Guinea Kinship. In *Social Organization: Essays Presented to Raymond Firth*, edited by M. Freedman, 105-23. Chicago: Aldine.

Kafadar, C. 1995. *Between Two Worlds: The Construction of the Ottoman State*. Berkeley: University of California Press.

Kamp, K., and N. Yoffee. 1980. Ethnicity in Ancient Western Asia during the Early Second Millennium BC. *Bulletin of the American Schools of Oriental Research* 237:85-103.

Kapchan, D., and P. Turner Strong. 1999. Theorizing the Hybrid. *The Journal of American Folklore* 112/445:239-53.

Katz, D. 2007. Sumerian Funerary Rituals in Context. In *Performing Death: Social Analysis of Funerary Tradition in the Ancient Near East and Mediterranean*, edited by N. Laneri, 167-87. Oriental Institute Seminar 3. Chicago: Oriental Institute.

Keegan, J. 1993. *A History of Warfare*. New York: Alfred A. Knopf.

Keesing, R. 1970. Shrines, Ancestors and Cognatic Descent: The Kwaio and Tallensi. *American Anthropologist* 72/4:755-75.

1971. Descent, Residence and Cultural Codes. In *Anthropology in Oceania*, edited by L. Hiatt and C. Jayawardena, 121-38. Sydney: Angus and Robertson.

1975. *Kin-groups and Social Structure*. New York: Harcourt.

Kelly, R. 1985. *The Nuer Conquest: The Structure and Development of an Expansionist System*. Ann Arbor: The University of Michigan Press.

Khazanov, A. 1978. Characteristic Features of Nomadic Communities in the Eurasian Steppes. In *The Nomadic Alternative: Modes and Models of Interaction in the African-Asian Desert and Steppes*, edited by W. Weissleder, 119-26. The Hague: Mouton.

1984. *Nomads and the Outside World*. Madison: University of Wisconsin Press.

2009. Specific Characteristics of Chalcolithic and Bronze Age Pastoralism in the Near East. In *Nomads, Tribes, and the State in the Ancient Near East: Cross-Disciplinary Perspectives*, edited by J. Szuchman, 119-27. Oriental Institute Seminars 5. Chicago: Oriental Institute Publications.

Khoury, P., and J. Kostiner. 1990. Introduction: Tribes and the Complexities of State Formation in the Middle East. In *Tribes and State Formation in the Middle East*, edited by P. Khoury and J. Kostiner, 1-24. Berkeley: University of California Press.

Klein, J. 1976. Šulgi and Gilgameš: Two Brother-Peers (Šulgi 0). *Kramer Anniversary Volume: Cuneiform Studies in Honor of Samuel Noah Kramer*, edited by B. Eichler, J. Heimerdinger, and A. Sjöberg, 271-92. Alter Orient und Altes Testament 25. Neukirchen-Vluyn: Neukirchener Verlag.

1981. The Royal Hymns of Shulgi King of Ur: Man's Quest for Immortal Fame. *Transactions of the American Philosophical Society*, n.s. 71/7:1-48.

1992 Sacred Marriage. In *The Anchor Bible Dictionary*, vol. 5, edited by D. N. Freedman, 866-70. New York: Doubleday.

1997. The God Martu in Sumerian Literature. In *Sumerian Gods and Their Representations*, edited by I. Finkel and M. Geller, 99-116. Cuneiform Monographs 7, Groningen: Styx.

Klengel, H. 1992. *Syria, 3000–300 B.C.: A Handbook of Political History*. Berlin: Akademie.

Kohl, P. 1989. Comment on G. Algaze, The Uruk Expansion: Cross-Cultural Exchange in Early Mesopotamian Civilization. *Current Anthropology* 30:593–94.

Kohlmeyer K. 1996: Houses in Habuba Kabira-South: Spatial Organisation and Planning of Late Uruk Residential Architecture. In *Houses and Households in Ancient Mesopotamia*, edited by K. Veenhof, 90–103. Leiden: Nederlands Instituut voor het Nabije Oosten.

Kopytoff, I. 1986. The Cultural Biography of Things: Commoditization as Process. In *The Social Life of Things: Commodities in Cultural Perspective*, edited by A. Appadurai, 64–91. New York: Cambridge University Press.

Kouchoukos, N. 1998. Landscape and Social Change in Late Prehistoric Mesopotamia. PhD diss., Yale University.

Kouchoukos, N., and T. Wilkinson. 2007. Landscape Archaeology in Mesopotamia: Past, Present and Future. In *Settlement and Society: Essays Dedicated to Robert McCormick Adams*, edited by E. Stone, 1–18. Los Angeles: Cotsen Institute of Archaeology; Chicago: Oriental Institute.

Kraus, W. 1998. Contestable Identities: Tribal structures in the Moroccan High Atlas. *Journal of the Royal Anthropological Institute* 4/1:1–22.

Kuper, A. 1973. *Anthropologists and Anthropology. The British School 1922–72*. New York: Penguin Books.

1982. Lineage Theory: A Critical Retrospect. *Annual Review of Anthropology* 11:71–95.

1988. *The Invention of Primitive Society: Transformations of an Illusion*. London: Routledge.

Kupper, J.-R. 1957. *Les nomades en Mesopotamie au temps des rois de Mari*. Paris: Société d'Édition Les Belle Lettres.

Kuznar, L., and R. Sedlmeyer. 2008. NOMAD: An Agent-Based Model (ABM) of Pastoralist-Agriculturalist Interaction. In *The Archaeology of Mobility: Old World and New World Nomadism*, edited by H. Barnard and W. Wendrich, 557–83. Cotsen Advanced Seminars 4. Los Angeles: Cotsen Institute of Archaeology Press.

Lafont, B. 2001. Relations internationals, alliances et dilplomatie au temps des rois de Mari. In *Amurru 2: Mari, Ébla et les Hourrites, dix ans de travaux*, edited by J.-M. Durand and D. Charpin, 213–328. Paris: Éditions Recherche sur les Civilisations.

La Fontaine, J. 1973. Descent in New Guinea: An Africanist View. In *The Character of Kinship*, edited by J. Goody, 35–51. Cambridge: Cambridge University Press.

Lambert, M. 1962. Deux termes techniques de l'économie sumérienne. *Revue d'Assyriologie* 56: 40–44.

Lambert, W. 1968. Another Look at Hammurabi's Ancestors. *Journal of Cuneiform Studies* 22:1–2.

1985. The Pantheon of Mari. *Mari Annales de Recherches Interdisciplinaires* 4:525–39.

Lambert, W., and A. Millard. 1999. *Atra-Ḫasis. The Babylonian Story of the Flood*. First published 1969, Oxford. Winona Lake, IN: Eisenbrauns.

Lamphere, L. 2005. Replacing Heternormative Views of Kinship and Marriage. *American Ethnologist* 32/1:34–6.

Lancaster, W. 1981. *The Rwala Bedouin Today*. Cambridge: Cambridge University Press.

Lancaster, W., and F. Lancaster. 1986. The Concept of Territory among the Rwala Bedouin. *Nomadic Peoples* 20:41–8.

1991. Limitations on Sheep and Goat Herding in the Eastern Badia of Jordan: An Ethno-archaeological Enquiry. *Levant* 23:125–38.

1998. Who are these Nomads? What do they do? Continuous Change or Changing Continuities? In *Changing Nomads in a Changing World*, edited by J. Ginat and A. Khazanov, 24–37. Brighton: Sussex Academic Press.

2006. Integration into Modernity: Some Tribal Rural Societies in the Bilad Ash-Sham. In *Nomadic Societies in the Middle East and North Africa. Entering the 21st Century*, edited by Dawn Chatty, 335–69. Leiden: Brill.

Landsberger, B. 1954. Assyrische Königsliste und "Dunkles Zeitalter." *Journal of Cuneiform Studies* 8/1:31–45.

Laneri, N. 2002. The Discovery of a Funerary Ritual. Inanna/Ishtar and Her Descent in the Nether World in Titriş Höyük, Turkey. *East and West* 1/4:9–52.

Lapidus, I. 1990. Tribes and State Formation in Islamic History. In *Tribes and State Formation in the Middle East*, edited by P. Khoury and J. Kostiner, 25–48. Berkeley: University of California Press.

Lattimore, O. 1962. *Inner Asian Frontiers of China*. First published in 1940. Boston: Beacon Press.

Latour, B. 1993. *We Have Never Been Modern*. Translated by C. Porter. London: Harvester Wheatsheaf.

Leach, E. 1954. *Political Systems of Highland Burma*. London: G. Bell and Sons.

1962. On Certain Unconsidered Aspects of Double Descent Systems. *Man* 62:130–34.

Lees, S., and D. Bates. 1974. The Origins of Specialized Nomadic Populations: A Systemic Model. *American Antiquity* 39:187–93.

Lefébure, C. 1979. Introduction: The Specificity of Nomadic Pastoral Societies. In *Pastoral Production and Society*, edited by l'Équipe ecologie et anthropologie des sociétiés pastorales, 1–14. Proceedings of the International Meeting on Nomadic Pastoralism – Paris 1–3 Dec. 1976. Paris: Éditions de la Maison des Sciences de l'Homme.

Lentz, C. 1995. "Tribalism" and Ethnicity in Africa: A Review of Four Decades of Anglophone Research. *Cahiers des Sciences Humaines* 31/2:303–28.

Lesser, A. 1961. Social Fields and the Evolution of Society. *South-western Journal of Anthropology* 17:40–48.

Lévi-Strauss, C. 1969. *The Elementary Structures of Kinship*. Edited by R. Needham, translated by J. Harle Bell and J. R. von Sturmer. Boston: Beacon Press.

Lewis, N. 1987. *Nomads and Settlers in Syria and Jordan 1800–1980*. Cambridge. Cambridge University Press.

Leys, C. 1994. Confronting the African Tragedy. *New Left Review* 204:33–47.

Liebermann, S. 1969. An Ur III Text from Drehem Recording "Booty from the Land of Mardu." *Journal of Cuneiform Studies* 22:53–62.

Lionnet, F. 1993. "Logiques métisses": Cultural Appropriation and Postcolonial Representations. *College Literature* 19–20/3–1:100–120.

Liverani, M. 1973. "The Amorites." In *Peoples of Old Testament Times*, edited by Donald J. Wiseman, 100–133. Oxford: Clarendon.

1993. Akkad: An introduction. In *Akkad, the First World Empire: Structure, Ideology, Traditions*, edited by M. Liverani, 1–10. Padua: Sargon srl.

2006. *Uruk. The First City*. Translated by Z. Bahrani and M. Van de Mieroop. First published 1998. London: Equinox.

Liverani, M., ed. 1993. *Akkad, The First World Empire: Structure, Ideology, Traditions.* History of the Ancient Near East/Studies-5. Padua: Sargon srl.

Liverani, M., and W. Heimpel. 1995. Observations on Livestock Management in Babylonia. *Acta Sumerolgica* 17:127–44.

Lönnqvist, M. 2008. Were Nomadic Amorites on the Move? Migration, Invasion and Gradual Infiltration as Mechanisms for Cultural Transitions. In *Proceedings of the 4th International Congress of the Archaeology of the Ancient Near East: 29 March–3 April 2004, Freie Universität Berlin.* Vol. 2: *Social and Cultural Transformation: The Archaeology of Transitional Periods and Dark Ages; Excavation Reports,* edited by H. Kühne, R. Czichon, and F. Kreppner, 195–215. Wiesbaden: Harrasowitz Verlag.

——— 2010. Tracing Tribal Implications among the Bronze Age Tomb Types in the Region of Jebel Bishri in Syria. *Al-Rafidan 2010.* Special Issue: Formation of Tribal Communities: Integrated Research in the Middle Euphrates, Syria: 165–73.

Lonsdale, J. 1977. When Did the Gusii (or any other group) Become a "Tribe"? *Kenya Historical Review* 5:122–33.

——— 1996. Moral Ethnicity, Ethnic Nationalism and Political Tribalism: The Case of the Kikuyu. In *Staat und gesellschaft in Afrika: Erosions- und Reforprozesse,* edited by Peter Meyns, 93–106. Münster: Lit.

Luke, J. 1965. Pastoralism and Politics in the Mari Period: A Re-examination of the Character and Political Significance of the Major West Semitic Tribal Groups on the Middle Euphrates, ca. 1828–1758 B.C. PhD diss., University of Michigan.

Lupton, A. 1996. *Stability and Change: Sociopolitical Development in North Mesopotamia and South-East Anatolia 4000–2700 B.C.* BAR International Series 627. Oxford: Tempvs Reparatvm.

Lynch, J. 2010. Gilgamesh's Ghosts: Textual Variation, the Dead, and the Mesopotamian Scribal Tradition. PhD diss., University of California, Los Angeles.

Lyonnet, B. 1998. Le peuplement de la Djéziré occidentale au début du 3e millénaire, villes circulaires et pastoralisme: Questions et hypothèses. In *About Subartu: Studies Devoted to Upper Mesopotamia,* edited by M. Lebeau, 179–95. Subartu IV/1. Turnhout: Brepols.

——— 2000. Objectifs de la prospection, mèthodologie et resultants gènèraux. In *Prospection archéologique Haut-Khabur Occidental (Syrie du N.E.),* vol. 1, edited by B. Lyonnet, 5–73. Beirut: Institut Français d´Archéologie du Proche-Orient.

——— 2009. Who Lived in the Third-millennium "Round Cities" of Northern Syria? In *Nomads, Tribes, and the State in the Ancient Near East: Cross-Disciplinary Perspectives,* edited by J. Szuchman, 179–200. Oriental Institute Seminars 5. Chicago: University of Chicago.

Maeda, T. 1994. Bal-ensí in the Drehem Texts. *Acta Sumerologica* 16:115–64.

Maekawa, K. 1980. Female Weavers and Their Children in Lagash: Pre-Sargonic and Ur III. *Acta Sumerologica* 2:81–125.

——— 1987. Collective Labor Service in Girsu-Lagash: The Pre-Sargonic and Ur III Periods. In *Labor in the Ancient Near East,* edited by M. Powell, 49–72. New Haven, CT: American Oriental Society.

——— 1996. Confiscation of Private Properties in the Ur III period. A Study of e_2-dul-la and nig_2-GA. *Acta Sumerologica* 18:103–68.

Mafeje, A. 1971. The Ideology of "Tribalism." *The Journal of Modern African Studies* 9/2:253–61.

——— 1991. *The Theory and Ethnography of African Social Formations: The Case of Interlacustrine Kingdoms.* London: Codesria Book Series.

Maine, H. 1986. *Ancient Law. Classics of Anthropology*. First published 1861. Tuscon: University of Arizona Press.

Maisels, C. 1990. *The Emergence of Civilization: From Hunting and Gathering to Agriculture, Cities and the State in the Near East*. London: Routledge.

Mallowan, M. 1947. Excavations at Brak and Chagar Bazar. *Iraq* 9:1–259.

Mann, M. 1986. *The Sources of Social Power: A History of Power from the Beginning to A.D. 1760*. Cambridge: Cambridge University Press.

Marchesi, G. 2006. *LUMMA in the Onomasticon and Literature of Ancient Mesopotamia*. History of the Ancient Near East Studies, vol. 10. Padua: Sargon srl.

Marfoe, L. 1979. The Integrative Transformation: Patterns of Sociopolitical Organization in Southern Syria. *Bulletin of the American Schools of Oriental Research* 234:1–43.

Margueron, J.-Cl. 1982. Mari: Originalité ou dépendance? *Studi Eblaiti* V:121–44.

2004. *Mari: Métropole de l'Euphrate au IIIe et au début du IIe millénaire av. J.-C.* Paris: Éditions A. et J. Picard.

Marro, C. 1997. *La culture du Haut-Euphrate au Bronze Ancien. Essai d'interpretation à partir de la céramique peinte de Keban (Turquie)*. Varia Anatolica VIII. Paris: De Boccard.

2007. Late Chalcolithic Ceramic Cultures in the Anatolian Highlands. In *Ceramics in Transitions: Chalcolithic through Iron Age in the Highlands of the Southern Caucasus and Anatolia*, edited by K. Rubinson and A. Sagona, 9–37. Louvain: Peeters.

Marx, E. 1977. The Tribe as a Unit of Subsistence: Nomadic Pastoralism in the Near East. *American Anthropologist* 79/2:343–63.

1978. Ecology and Politics of Middle Eastern Pastoralists. In *The Nomadic Alternative: Modes and Models of Interaction in the African-Asian Desert and Steppes*, edited by W. Weissleder, 41–74. The Hague: Mouton.

2005. Nomads and Cities: The Development of a Conception. In *Shifts and Drifts in Nomad-Sedentary Relations*, edited by S. Leder and B. Streck, 3–15. Nomaden und Sesshafte 2. Wiesbaden: Dr. Ludwig Reichert Verlag.

2006. The Political Economy of Middle Eastern and North African Pastoral Nomads. In *Nomadic Societies in the Middle East and North Africa. Entering the 21st Century*, edited by D. Chatty, 78–97. Leiden: Brill.

2007. Nomads and Cities: Changing Conceptions. In *On the Fringe of Society: Archaeological and Ethnoarchaeological Perspectives on Pastoral and Agricultural Societies*, edited by B. Saidel and E. van der Steen, 75–78. BAR International Series 1657. Oxford: Archaeopress.

Matthews, R. 2000. Sampling an Urban Centre: Tell Brak Excavations 1994–1996. Pp. 1005–12 in *Proceedings of the First International Congress on the Archaeology of the Ancient Near East: Rome, May 18th–23rd 1998*, vol. 2, edited by P. Matthiae, A. Enea, L. Peyronel, and F. Pinnock. Rome: Dipartimento di Scienze Storiche, Archeologiche e Anthropologiche dell'Antichità.

2002. Seven Shrines of Subartu. In *Of Pots and Pans. Papers on the Archaeology and History of Mesopotamia and Syria Presented to David Oates in Honour of his 75th Birthday*, edited by L. al-Gailani Werr, J. Curtis, H. Martin, A. McMahon, J. Oates, and J. Reade, 186–90. London: Nabu.

2003. A Chiefdom in the Northern Plains. In *Excavations at Tell Brak*. Vol. 4: *Exploring an Upper Mesopotamian Regional Centre, 1994–1996*, edited by R. Matthews, 97–193. London: British School of Archaeology in Iraq/Cambridge: McDonald Institute for Archaeological Research.

Matthews, R., and H. Fazeli. 2004. Copper and Complexity: Iran and Mesopotamia in the Fourth Millennium B.C. *Iran* 42:61–75.

Matthews, V. 1978. *Pastoral Nomadism in the Mari Kingdom (ca. 1839–1760 B.C.)*. American Schools of Oriental Research, Dissertation Series 3. Cambridge, MA: American School of Oriental Research.

Matthiae, P. 1980. Appunti di iconografia eblaita, II. La testa di Atareb. *Studi Eblaiti* 2:41–7.

1981. *Ebla: An Empire Rediscovered*. New York: Doubleday.

1988. On the Economic Foundations of the Early Syrian Culture of Ebla. In *Wirtschaft und Gesellschaft von Ebla: Akten der Internationalen Tagung, Heidelberg 4–7 November 1986*, edited by H. Hauptmann and H. Waetzoldt, 75–80. Heidelberg: Heidelberg Orientverlag.

1989. Masterpieces of Early and Old Syrian Art: Discoveries of the 1988 Ebla Excavations in a Historical Perspective. *Proceedings of the British Academy* 75:25–56.

1993. L'aire sacrée d'Ishtar à Ebla: Résultats des fouilles de 1990–1992. *Comptes rendus des séances de l'année-Académie des inscriptions et belles-lettres 1993*: 613–62.

1995. Fasi storiche e cronolgia archeologica. In *Ebla: Alle origini della civiltà urbana*, edited by P. Matthiae, F. Pinnock, and G. Scandone Matthiae, 86–95. Milan: Mondadori Electa.

1996. Tell Mardikh-Ebla (Siria), campagna di scavi 1995. *Orient Express* 1996/3: 84–7.

1997a. Where Were the Early Kings of Syria Buried? *Altorientalische Forschungen* 24:268–76.

1997b. Tell Mardikh, 1977–1996: Vingt ans de Fouilles et de Découvertes. La renaissance d'Ebla Amorrheenne. *Akkadica* 101:1–29.

2000. Nouvelles fouilles à Ébla (1998–1999): Forts et palais de l'enceinte urbaine. *Comptes-rendus de l'Académie des inscriptions et belles-lettres* 144/2:567–610.

2002. About the Formation of Old Syrian Architectural Tradition. In *Of Pots and Pans: Papers on the Archaeology and History of Mesopotamia and Syria Presented to David Oates in Honour of his 75th Birthday*, edited by L. al-Gailani Werr, J. Curtis, H. Martin, A. McMahon, J. Oates, and J. Reade, 191–209. London: Nabu.

2008. *Gli Archivi Reali di Ebla: La scoperta, i testi, il significato*. Roma: Mondadori/ Sapienza.

Matthiae, P., and G. Pettinato. 1976. Aspetti amministrativi e topografici di Ebla nel 111 millennio av. C. A. Documentazione epigrafica. *Rivista degli Studi Orientali* 50:1–15.

Mauss, M. 1990. *The Gift. The Form and Reason for Exchange in Archaic Societies*. First published 1922. Translation by W. Halls. New York: Norton.

Mauzé, M., ed. 1997. *Present Is Past. Some Uses of Tradition in Native Societies*. Lanham, MD: University Press of America.

Mazzoni, S. 1991. Ebla e la formazione della cultura urbana in Siria. *La Parola del Passato* 46:163–94.

1993. Cylinder Seal Impression on Jars at Ebla: New Evidence. In *Aspects of Art and Iconography: Anatolia and Its Neighbors. Studies in Honor of Nimet Özgüç*, edited by M. Mellink, E. Porada, and T. Özgüc, 399–416. Ankara: Türk Tarih Kurumu Basimevi.

1995. Le Origini della città protosiriana. In *Ebla: Alle origini della civiltà urbana*, edited by P. Matthiae, F. Pinnock, and G. Scandone Matthiae, 96–103. Milan: Mondadori Electa.

1999. On the Results of the Tell Brak Excavations. *Orientalistische Literaturzeitung* 94:605-24.

2003. Ebla: Crafts and Power in an Emergent State of Third Millennium BC Syria. *Journal of Mediterranean Archaeology* 16/2:173-91.

2006. Syria and the Emergence of Cultural Complexity. In *Ina Kibrat Erbetti. Studi di Archeologia orientale dedicati a Paolo Matthiae*, edited by F. Baffi, R. Dolce, S. Mazzoni, and F. Pinnock, 321-47. Rome: Casa Editrice, Università degli Studi di Roma "La Sapienza."

McAnany, P. 1995. *Living with the Ancestors: Kinship and Kingship in Ancient Maya Society.* Austin: University of Texas.

McClellan, T. 1998. Tell Banat North: The White Monument. In *About Subartu: Studies Devoted to Upper Mesopotamia*, edited by M. Lebeau, 243-71. Subartu IV/1. Turnhout: Brepols.

McClellan, T. 1999. Urbanism on the Upper Syrian Euphrates. In *Archaeology of the Upper Syrian Euphrates: The Tishrin Dam Area*, edited by G. del Olmo Lete and J.-L. Montero Fenollós, 413-25. Aula Orientalis-Supplementa 15. Barcelona: Universität de Barcelona.

McClellan, T., R. Grayson, and C. Ogleby. 2000. Bronze Age Water Harvesting in North Syria. In *La Djéziré et l'Euphrate syriens de la Protohistoire à la fin du IIe millénaire av. J.-C. Tendances dans l'interprétation historique des données nouvelles, Actes du colloque international organisé au Collège de France, 21–24 juin 1993*, edited by O. Rouault and M. Wäfler, 137-55. Subartu VII. Turnhout: Brepols.

McClellan, T., and A. Porter. 1995. Jawa and North Syria. *Studies in the History and Archaeology of Jordan* V:49-65.

McCorriston, J. 1997. The Fiber Revolution. Textile Intensification, Alienation and Social Stratification in Ancient Mesopotamia. *Current Anthropology* 38/4:517-49.

1998. Landscape and Human Interaction in the Middle Habur Drainage from the Neolithic Period to the Bronze Age. In *Espace naturel, espace habité en Syrie du Nord (10ᵉ-2ᵉ millénaires av. J.-C.)*, edited by M. Fortin and O. Aurenche, 43-54. Toronto: The Canadian Society for Mesopotamian Studies.

McGuire, R. 1992. *A Marxist Archaeology.* San Diego, CA: Academic Press.

McLennan, J. 1970. *Primitive Marriage.* First published 1865. Chicago: University of Chicago Press.

McMahon, A., and J. Oates. 2007. Excavations at Tell Brak 2006-2007. *Iraq* 69:145-71.

Meeker, M. 2005. Magritte on the Bedouins: *Ce n'est pas une société segmentaire.* In *Shifts and Drifts in Nomad–Sedentary Relations*, edited by S. Leder and B. Streck, 79-98. Nomaden und Sesshafte 2. Wiesbaden: Dr. Ludwig Reichert Verlag.

Meggitt, M. 1965. *The Lineage System of the Mae-Enga of New Guinea.* New York: Barnes and Noble.

Meijer, D. 2008. Cracking the Code? Aspect and Impact in Mesopotamian Architecture. In *4 ICAANE. Proceedings of the 4th International Congress of the Archaeology of the Ancient Near East.* Vol. 1: *The Reconstruction of Environment: Natural Resources and Human Interrelations through Time. Art History: Visual Communication*, edited by H. Kühne, R. Czichon, and F. Kreppner, 431-36. Weisbaden: Harrasowitz Verlag.

Meskell, L. 2002. The Intersections of Identity and Politics in Archaeology. *Annual Review of Anthropology* 31:279-302.

2005. Introduction: Object Orientations. In *Archaeologies of Materiality*, edited by L. Meskell, 1-17. Oxford: Blackwell.

Meyer, J.-W. 2007. Town Planning in 3rd Millennium Tell Chuera. In *Power and Architecture: Monumental Public Architecture in the Bronze Age Near East and Aegean*, edited by J. Bretschneider, J. Driessen, and K. van Lerberghe, 129–42. Orientalia Lovaniensia Analecta 156. Leuven: Peeters.

    2010a. Tribal Community and State: The Change of Settlements and Settlement Patterns in Upper Mesopotamia during the 3rd Millennium B.C. - a Re-evaluation. *Al-Rafidan 2010*. Special Issue: Formation of Tribal Communities: Integrated Research in the Middle Euphrates, Syria: 203–11.

    2010b. The Cemetery of Abu-Hamad: A Burial Place of Pastoral Groups? *Al-Rafidan 2010*. Special Issue: Formation of Tribal Communities: Integrated Research in the Middle Euphrates, Syria: 155–64.

Meyer, J.-W., M. al-Khalaf, I. Mussa, S. Doerner, R. Hempelmann, and M. Würz. 2003. Die 4. Grabungskampagne in Kharab Sayyar 2002. *Mitteilungen der Deutschen Orient-Gesellschaft zu Berlin* 135:81–102.

Meyer, J.-W., and R. Hempelmann. 2006. Bemerkungen zu Mari aus der Sicht von Tell Chuera - Ein Beitrag zur Geschichte der ersten Hälfte des 3. Jts. V. Chr. *Altorientalische Forschungen* 33/1:22–41.

Michalowski, P. 1976. The Royal Correspondence of Ur. PhD diss., Yale University.

    1983. History as Charter: Some Observations on the Sumerian King List. *Journal of the American Oriental Society* 103/1:237–38.

    1985. Third Millennium Contacts: Observations on the Relationships between Mari and Ebla. *Journal of the American Oriental Society* 105/2:293–302.

    1988. Thoughts about Ibrium. In *Wirtschaft und Gesellschaft von Ebla: Akten der Internationalen Tagung, Heidelberg, 4–7 November 1986*, edited by H. Hauptmann and H. Waetzoldt, 267–77. Heidelberg: Orientverlag.

    1989. *The Lamentation over the Destruction of Sumer and Ur*. Winona Lake, IN: Eisenbrauns.

    1993. *Letters from Early Mesopotamia*. Writings from the Ancient World, vol. 3. Society of Biblical Literature. Atlanta: Scholars Press.

    1995. The Men from Mari. In *Immigration and Emigration within the Ancient Near East, Festchrift Lipinski*, edited by K. van Lergerhe and A. Schoors, 181–88. Orientalia Lovaniensia Analecta 65. Leuven: Peeters.

    1996. Ancient Poetics. In *Proceedings of the Groningen Group for the Study of Mesopotamian Literature*, vol. 2: *Mesopotamian Poetic Language: Sumerian and Akkadian*, edited by M. Vogelzang and H. Vanstiphout, 141–53. Cuneiform Monographs 6. Groningen: Styx.

    2005a. Literary Works from the Court of King Ishbi-Erra of Isin. In *"An Experienced Scribe Who Neglects Nothing": Ancient Near Eastern Studies in Honor of Jacob Klein*, edited by Y. Sefat, P. Artzi, C. Cohen, B. Eichler, and V. Hurowitz, 199–211. Bethesda, MD: CDL Press.

    2005b. Iddin-Dagan and His Family. *Zeitschrift für Assyriologie* 95:65–76.

    2006a. The Lives of the Sumerian Language. In *Margins of Writing, Origins of Cultures: New Approaches to Writing and Reading in the Ancient Near East*, edited by S. Sanders, 159–84. Oriental Institute Symposia 2. Chicago: Oriental Institute Publications.

    2006b. The Strange History of Tumal. In *Approaches to Sumerian Literature. Studies in Honour of Stip (H. L. J. Vanstiphout)*, edited by P. Michalowski and N. Veldhuis, 145–66. Leiden: Brill.

2006c. Love or Death? Observations on the Role of the Gala in Ur III Ceremonial Life. *Journal of Cuneiform Studies* 58:49–62.

2008. The Mortal Kings of Ur: A Short Century of Divine Rule in Ancient Mesopotamia. In *Religion and Power. Divine Kingship in the Ancient World and Beyond*, edited by N. Brisch, 33–46. Oriental Institute Seminars 4. Chicago: University of Chicago.

Milano, L. 1990a. *ARET IX. Testi amministrativi: Assegnazioni di prodotti alimentari*. Rome: Università degli Studi di Roma "La Sapienza."

1990b. é-duru$_5$^{ki} = "One Score" (of People) in the Ebla Accounting. *Zeitschrift für Assyriologie* 80:9–14.

Milano, L., W. Sallaberger, P. Talon, and K. Van Lerberghe, eds. 2004. *Third Millennium Cuneiform Texts from Tell Beydar (Seasons 1996–2002)*. Subartu 12. Turnhout: Brepols.

Millard, A. 1988. The Bevelled-Rim Bowls: Their Purpose and Significance. *Iraq* 50:49–58.

Mintz, S., and C. Du Bois. 2002. The Anthropology of Food and Eating. *Annual Review of Anthropology* 31:99–119.

Moortgat, A. 1967. Tell Chuera in Nordost-Syrien. *Vorläufiger Bericht über die fünfte Grabungskampagne 1964*. Berlin: Mann.

Moortgat, A., and U. Moortgat-Correns. 1976. *Tell Chuera in Nordost-Syrien: Vorläufiger Bericht über die siebente Grabungskampagne 1974*. Berlin: Mann.

Morandi Bonacossi, D. 2000. The Beginning of the Early Bronze Age at Tell Shiukh Fawqani (Tishrin Dam Area) and in the Upper Syrian Euphrates Valley. In *Proceedings of the First International Congress on the Archaeology of the Ancient Near East: Rome, May 18th–23rd 1998*, vol. 2, edited by P. Matthiae, A. Enea, L. Peyronel, and F. Pinnock, 1105–23. Rome: Dipartimento di Scienze Storiche, Archeologiche e Anthropologiche dell'Antichità.

Morgan, L. 1966. *Systems of Consanguinity and Affinity of the Human Family*. First published 1871. Smithsonian Contributions to Knowledge 218. Washington, DC: Smithsonian Institution.

1985. *Ancient Society, or Researches in the Lines of Human Progress from Savagery through Barbarism to Civilization*. First published 1877. Classics of Anthropology. Tuscon: University of Arizona Press.

Munchaev, R., and N. Merpert. 2002. Twenty-Five Field Seasons of the Russian Mission in North Mesopotamia. In *Of Pots and Pans. Papers on the Archaeology and History of Mesopotamia and Syria Presented to David Oates in Honour of his 75th Birthday*, edited by L. al-Gailani Werr, J. Curtis, H. Martin, A. McMahon, J. Oates, and J. Reade, 240–58. London: Nabu.

Nakamura, C. 2005. Mastering Matters: Magical Sense and Apotropaic Figurine Worlds of Neo-Assyria. In *Archaeologies of Materiality*, edited by L. Meskell, 18–45. Oxford: Blackwell.

Nicholas, I. 1987. The Function of Bevelled-Rim Bowls: A Case Study at the TUV Mound, Tal-e-Malyan, Iran. *Paléorient* 13/2:61–72.

1990. *The Proto-Elamite Settlement at TUV*. Philadelphia: University Museum Monograph 69.

Nichols, J., and J. Weber. 2006. Amorites, Onagers, and Social Reorganization in Middle Bronze Age Syria. In *After Collapse: The Regeneration of Complex Societies*, edited by G. Schwartz and J. Nichols, 38–57. Tucson: University of Arizona Press.

Nishiaki, Y. 2010. Archaeological Evidence of the Early Bronze Age Communities in the Middle Euphrates Steppe, North Syria. *Al-Rafidan 2010.* Special Issue: Formation of Tribal Communities: Integrated Research in the Middle Euphrates, Syria: 37–48.

Nissen, H. 1970. Grabung in den Quadraten K/L XII in Uruk-Warka. *Baghdader Mitteilungen* 5:101–91.

———. 1980. The Mobility between Settled and Non-Settled in Early Babylonia: Theory and Evidence. In *L'archéologie de l'Iraq: Perspectives et limites de l'interprétation anthropologique des documents.* Colloques internationaux du CNRS 580, 285–90. Paris: CNRS.

———. 2001. Cultural and Political Networks in the Ancient Near East during the Fourth and Third Millennia B.C. In *Uruk Mesopotamia and Its Neighbors. Cross-Cultural Interactions in the Era of State Formation,* edited by M. Rothman, 149–80. School of American Research Advanced Seminar Series. Santa Fe, NM: School of American Research Press.

———. 2002. Uruk: Key Site of the Period and Key Site of the Problem. In *Artefacts of Complexity: Tracking the Uruk in the Near East,* edited by J. N. Postgate, 1–16. Cambridge: British School of Archaeology in Iraq.

Nissen, H., P. Damerow, and R. Englund. 1993. *Archaic Bookkeeping: Early Writing and Techniques of Economic Administration in the Ancient Near East.* Translated by P. Larsen. Chicago: University of Chicago.

Noegel, S. 1996. Wordplay in the Tale of the Poor Man of Nippur. *Acta Sumerologica* 18:169–86.

Oates, D., and J. Oates. 1993. Excavations at Tell Brak 1992–93. *Iraq* 55:155–99.

———. 2006a. Ebla and Nagar. In *Ina Kibrat Erbetti. Studi di Archeologia orientale dedicati a Paolo Matthiae,* edited by F. Baffi, R. Dolce, S. Mazzoni, and F. Pinnock, 399–423. Rome: Casa Editrice, Università degli Studi di Roma "La Sapienza."

———. 2006b. Tripartite Buildings and Early Urban Tell Brak. In *Les espaces Syro-Mésopotamiens. Dimensions de l'expérience humaine au Proche-Orient ancient. Volume d'hommage offert à Jean-Claude Margueron,* edited by P. Butterlin, M. Lebeau, J.-Y. Monchambert, J. Montero Fenollós, and B. Muller, 33–40. Subartu XVII. Turnhout: Brepols.

Oates, D., J. Oates, and H. McDonald. 2001. *Excavations at Tell Brak.* Vol. 2: *Nagar in the Third Millennium BC.* McDonald Institute Monographs. Oxford. British School of Archaeology in Iraq.

Oates, J. 1986. *Babylon.* Revised edition. London: Thames and Hudson.

———. 2002. Tell Brak: The 4th Millennium Sequence and Its Implications. In *Artefacts of Complexity. Tracking the Uruk in the Near East,* edited by J. Postgate, 111–22. Cambridge: British School of Archaeology in Iraq.

———. 2005. Archaeology in Mesopotamia: Digging Deeper at Tell Brak. *Proceedings of the British Academy* 131:1–39.

———. 2007. Monumental Public Architecture in Late Chalcolithic and Bronze Age Mesopotamia, with Particular Reference to Tell Brak and Tell al Rimah. In *Power and Architecture: Monumental Public Architecture in the Bronze Age Near East and Aegean,* edited by J. Bretschneider, J. Driessen, and K. van Lerberghe, 161–81. Orientalia Lovaniensia Analecta 156. Leuven: Peeters.

Oates, J., A. McMahon, P. Karsgaard, S. al-Quntar, and J. Ur. 2007. Early Mesopotamian Urbanism: A New View from the North. *Antiquity* 81:585–600.

Oates, J., and D. Oates. 1997. An Open Gate: Cities of the Fourth Millennium BC (Tell Brak 1997). *Cambridge Archaeological Journal* 7/2:287-307.

Obeid, M. 2006. Uncertain Livelihoods: Challenges Facing Herding in a Lebanese Village. In *Nomadic Societies in the Middle East and North Africa: Entering the 21st Century*, edited by D. Chatty, 463-95. Leiden: Brill.

Ochsenschlager, E. 2004. *Iraq's Marsh Arabs in the Garden of Eden*. Philadelphia: University of Pennsylvania Museum.

O'Connor, M. 2004. The Onomastic Evidence for Bronze-Age West Semitic. *Journal of the American Oriental Society* 124/3:439-70.

Ohnuma, K., and A. al-Khabour. 2010. Integrated Research in the Bishri Region. *Al-Rafidan 2010*. Special Issue: Formation of Tribal Communities: Integrated Research in the Middle Euphrates, Syria: 3-8.

Ökse, T. 2005. Early Bronze Age Chamber Tomb Complexes at Gre Virike (Period IIA) on the Middle Euphrates. *Bulletin of the American Schools of Oriental Research* 339:21-46.

Olávarri, E. 1995. Dos tumbas del Bronce Antiguo de Qara Qūzāq. *Aula Orientalis* 13:15-23.

Olávarri, E., and C. Valdés. 1996. Excavaciones en Tell Qara Qūzāq, Informe provisional: Campañas quinta y sexta (1993-1994), Misión Arqueológica de la Universidad de Barcelona en Siria. *Aula Orientalis* 14:45-54.

Olávarri, E., and C. Valdés Pereiro. 2001. Excavaciones en Tell Qara Qūzāq: Campañas IV-VI (1992-1994). In *Tell Qara Quzaq II. Campañas IV-VI (1992-1994)*, edited by G. Del Olmo lete, J.-L. Montero Fenellós, and C. Valdés, 13-76. Barcelona: Editorial Ausa.

Orthmann, W. 1981. *Halawa 1977 bis 1979, Vorlaufiger Bericht über die 1 bis 3 Grabungskampagne*. Bonn: Rudolph Habelt Verlag.

1989. *Halawa 1980 bis 1986, Vorlaufiger Bericht über die 4.-9. Grabungskampagne*. Bonn: Dr. Rudolph Habelt.

Otto, A. 2006. Archaeological Perspectives on the Localization of Naram-Sin's Armanum. *Journal of Cuneiform Studies* 58:1-26.

Otto, T., H. Thrane, and H. Vandkilde, eds. 2006. *Warfare and Society. Archaeological and Social Anthropological Perspectives*. Aarhus: Aarhus University.

Owen, D. 1993. Some New Evidence on Yahmadiu = Ahlamu. In *The Tablet and the Scroll. Near Eastern Studies in Honor of William Hallo*, edited by M. Cohen, D. Snell, and D. Eisberg, 181-4. Bethesda, MD: CDL Press.

Palmié, S. 2006. Creolization and Its Discontents. *Annual Review of Anthropology* 35:433-56.

Palumbi, G. 2007/8. From Collective Burials to Symbols of Power: The Translation of Role and Meanings of the Stone-Lined Cist Burial Tradition from Southern Caucasus to the Euphrates Valley. In *Sepolti tra i vivi/Buried among the Living: Evidenza ed interpretazione di contesti funerari in abitato*. Atti del Convegno Internazionale, edited by G. Bartoloni and M.-G. Benedettini, 141-67. Scienze dell'Antichità 14/1. Rome: Università degli Studi di Roma "La Sapienza."

2008. *The Red and the Black. Social and Cultural Interaction between the Upper Euphrates and Southern Caucasus Communities in the Fourth and Third Millennium BC*. Rome: Università degli Studi di Roma "La Sapienza."

Parker Pearson, M. 1997. Close Encounters of the Worst Kind: Malagasy Resistance and Colonial Disasters in Southern Madagascar. *World Archaeology* 28/3:393-417.

Parkes, P. 2003. Fostering Fealty: A Comparative Analysis of Tributary Allegiances of Adoptive Kinship. *Comparative Studies in Society and History* 45/4:741-82.

Parkinson, W. 2002. Introduction: Archaeology and Tribal Societies. In *The Archaeology of Tribal Societies*, edited by W. Parkinson, 1-12. Ann Arbor, MI: International Monographs in Prehistory.

Parry, B. 2002. Directions and Dead Ends in Postcolonial Studies. In *Relocating Postcolonialism*, edited by D. Goldberg and A. Quayson, 66-81. Oxford: Blackwell.

Patterson, T. 2008, A Brief History of Postcolonial Theory and Implications for Archaeology. In *Archaeology and the Postcolonial Critique*, edited by M. Liebmann and U. Rizvi, 21-34. New York: AltaMira Press.

Pauketat, T. 2007. *Chiefdoms and Other Archaeological Delusions*. New York: AltaMira Press.

Pearce, J. 1999. Investigating Ethnicity at Hacinebi: Ceramic Perspectives on Style and Behaviour in 4th Millennium Mesopotamian-Anatolian Interaction. *Paléorient* 25/1:35-42.

Peletz, M. 1995. Kinship Studies in Late Twentieth Century Anthropology. *Annual Review of Anthropology* 24:343-72.

Peltenburg, E. 1999. The Living and the Ancestors: Early Bronze Age Mortuary Practices at Jerablus Tahtani. In *Archaeology of the Upper Syrian Euphrates, the Tishrin Dam Area*, edited by G. del Olmo Lete and J.-L. Montero, 427-42. Aula Orientalis-Supplementa. Barcelona: Universität de Barcelona.

2007/8. Enclosing the Ancestors and the Growth of Socio-political Complexity in Early Bronze Age Syria. In *Sepolti tra i vivi/Buried among the Living: Evidenza ed interpretazione di contesti funerari in abitato*. Atti del Convegno Internazionale, edited by G. Bartoloni and M.-G. Benedettini, 215-47. Scienze dell'Antichità 14/1, Rome: Università degli Studi di Roma "La Sapienza."

Peltenburg, E., E. Eastaugh, M. Hewson, A. Jackson, A. McCarthy, and T. Rymer. 2000. Jerablus Tahtani, Syria, 1998-9: Preliminary Report. *Levant* 32:53-75.

Peregrine, P. 1996. Introduction: World-systems Theory and Archaeology. In *Pre-Columbian World Systems*, edited by P. Peregrine and G. Feinman, 1-10. Madison, WI: Prehistory Press.

Peters, E. 1967. Some Structural Aspects of the Feud among the Camel-Herding Bedouin of Cyrenaica. *Africa* 37:261-82.

Peters, J., D. Helmer, A. von den Driesch, and S. Segui. 1999. Early Animal Husbandry in the Northern Levant. *Paléorient* 25/2:27-47.

Pettinato, G. 1995. Il regno Mar-tu nella documentazione di Ebla, in *Immigration and Emigration within the Ancient Near East. Festschrift E. Lipinski*, edited by K. van Lerberghe and A. Schoors, 229-43. Orientalia Lovaniensia Analecta 65. Leuven: Peeters.

Peyronel, L. 2006. Sailing the Lower Sea. The Oldest Roots of the Lands of Dilmun and Magan. In *Ina Kibrat Erbetti. Studi di Archeologia orientale dedicati a Paolo Matthiae*, edited by F. Baffi, R. Dolce, S. Mazzoni, and F. Pinnock, 445-87. Rome: Casa Editrice, Università degli Studi di Roma "La Sapienza."

Pfälzner, P. 2001. *Haus und Haushalt: Wohnformen des dritten Jahrtausends vor Christus in Nordmesopotamien*. Mainz: Phillipe von Zabern.

2007. Archaeological Investigations in the Royal Palace of Qatna. In *Urban and Natural Landscapes of an Ancient Syrian Capital*, edited by D. Morandi Bonacossi, 29-64. Studi Archeologici su Qatna 1. Udine: Editrice Universitaria Udinese srl.

Pierson, C. 1996. *The Modern State*. London: Routledge.

Pittman, H. 2001. Mesopotamian Intraregional Relations Reflected through Glyptic Evidence in the Late Chalcolithic 1-5 periods. In *Uruk Mesopotamia and Its Neighbors. Cross-Cultural Interactions in the Era of State Formation*, edited by M. Rothman, 403-43. School of American Research Advanced Seminar Series. Santa Fe, NM: School of American Research Press.

2007. The Fourth Millennium Glyptics at Arslantepe. 2. The Corpus of Seal Designs, Descriptive Catalogue of Glyptic Imagery. In *Arslantepe* Cretulae. *An Early Centralized Administrative System before Writing*, edited by M. Frangipane, 182-242. Rome: Università degli Studi di Roma "La Sapienza."

Poebel, A. 1942. The Assyrian King List from Khorsabad. *Journal of Near Eastern Studies* 1/3:247-306; 1/4:460-92.

Pollock, S. 1990. Archaeological Investigations on the Uruk Mound, Abu Salabikh, Iraq. *Iraq* 52:85-93.

1992. Bureaucrats and Managers, Peasants and Pastoralists, Imperialists and Traders: Research on the Uruk and Jemdat Nasr Periods in Mesopotamia. *Journal of World Prehistory* 6/3:297-336.

1999. *Ancient Mesopotamia: The Eden That Never Was*. Cambridge: Cambridge University Press.

2001. The Uruk Period in Southern Mesopotamia. In *Uruk Mesopotamia and Its Neighbors: Cross-Cultural Interactions in the Era of State Formation*, edited by M. Rothman, 181-232. School of American Research Advanced Seminar Series. Santa Fe, NM: School of American Research Press.

2003. Feasts, Funerals and Fast Food in Early Mesopotamian States. In *The Archaeology and Politics of Food and Feasting in Early States and Empires*, edited by T. Bray, 17-38. New York: Kluwer Academic/Plenum.

Pollock, S., and R. Bernbeck. 2000. And They Said, Let Us Make Gods in Our Image: Gendered Ideologies in Ancient Mesopotamia. In *Reading the Body. Representations and Remains in the Archaeological Record*, edited by A. Rautman, 150-64. Philadelphia: University of Pennsylvania Press.

Pollock, S., and C. Coursey. 1995. Ceramics from Hacinebi Tepe: Chronology and Connections. *Anatolica* 21:101-41.

Pollock, S., M. Pope, and C. Coursey. 1996. Household Production at the Uruk Mound, Abu Salabikh, Iraq. *American Journal of Archaeology* 100/4:683-98.

Pomponio, F., and G. Visicato. 1994. *Early Dynastic Administrative Tablets of Šuruppak*. Naples: Istituto Universitario Orientale di Napoli.

Pomponio, F., and P. Xella. 1997. *Les dieux d'Ebla. Étude analytique des divinités éblaites à l'époque des archives royales du IIIe millénaire*. Münster: Ugarit-Verlag.

Pongratz-Leisten, B. 2011. Divine Agency and Astralization of the Gods in Ancient Mesopotamia. In *Reconsidering Revolutionary Monotheism*, edited by B. Pongratz-Leisten, 136-86. Winona Lake, IN: Eisenbrauns.

Porter, A. 1985. Jawa: An Adaptive Strategy in a Marginal Environment. MA thesis, University of Melbourne.

1995. Tell Banat - Tomb 1. *Damaszener Mitteilungen* 8:1-50.

1999. The Ceramic Horizon of the Early Bronze in the Upper Euphrates. In *Archaeology of the Upper Syrian Euphrates, the Tishrin Dam Area*, edited by G. del Olmo Lete and J.-L. Montero, 311-20. Aula Orientalis-Supplementa. Barcelona: Universität de Barcelona.

2000. Mortality, Monuments and Mobility: Ancestor Traditions and the Transcendence of Space. Ph.D. diss, University of Chicago.

2002a. The Dynamics of Death. Ancestors, Pastoralism and the Origins of a Third Millennium City in Syria. *Bulletin of American Schools of Oriental Research* 325:1–36.

2002b. Communities in Conflict: Death and the Contest for Social Order in the Euphrates River Valley. *Near Eastern Archaeology* 65/3:156–73.

2004. The Urban Nomad: Countering the Old Clichés. In *Amurru 3: Nomades et sédentaires dans le Proche-Orient ancien*, edited by C. Nicolle, 69–74. Compte rendu de la XLVIe Rencontre Assyriologique Internationale, Paris, 2000. Paris: Éditions Recherche sur les Civilisations.

2007a. You say Potato, I say ...: Typology, Chronology and the Origin of the Amorites. In *Sociétés humaines et changement climatique à la fin du Troisième Millénaire: Une crise a-t-elle eu lieu en Haute-Mésopotamie?* edited by C. Marro and C. Kuzucuoglu, 69–115. Varia Anatolica 18. Paris: De Boccard.

2007b. The Ceramic Assemblages of the Third Millennium in the Euphrates Region. In *Céramique de l'Âge du Bronze en Syrie II*, edited by M. Maqdissi, V. Matoïan, and C. Nicolle, 3–20. Beirut: Institut Français d'Archéologie du Proche-Orient.

2007/8. Evocative Topography: Experience, Time and Politics in a Landscape of Death. In *Sepolti tra i vivi/Buried among the Living: Evidenza ed interpretazione di contesti funerari in abitato.* Atti del Convegno Internazionale, edited by G. Bartoloni and M.-G. Benedettini, 195–214. Scienze dell'Antichità 14/1, Rome: Università degli Studi di Roma "La Sapienza."

2009a. Beyond Dimorphism: Ideologies and Materialities of Kinship as Time-Space Distantiation. In *Nomads, Tribes, and the State in the Ancient Near East: Cross-Disciplinary Perspectives*, edited by J. Szuchman, 199–223. Oriental Institute Seminars 5. Chicago: Oriental Institute.

2009b. When the Subject *Is* the Object: The Partible Person and the Stelae of Naram-Sin. Paper presented at the Annual Meetings of the European Association of Archaeologists, Riva del Garda, Italy, September 15–20.

2010a. From Kin to Class – and Back Again! Changing Paradigms of the Early Polity. In *The Development of Pre-state Communities in the Ancient Near East: Studies in Honour of Edgar Peltenburg*, edited by L. MacGuire and D. Bolger, 72–8. Oxford: Oxbow.

2010b. Akkad and Agency, Archaeology and Annals: Considering Power and Intent in Third Millennium BCE Mesopotamia. In *Agency and Identity in the Ancient Near East: New Paths Forward*, edited by S. Steadman and J. Ross. London: Equinox.

In press. Mortal Mirrors: Creating Kin through Human Sacrifice in Third Millennium Syro-Mesopotamia. In *Sacred Killing: The Archaeology of Sacrifice in the Ancient Near East*, edited by A. Porter and G. Schwartz. Winona Lake, IN: Eisenbrauns.

Porter, A., and T. McClellan. 1998. The Third Millennium Settlement Complex at Tell Banat: Results of the 1994 Excavations. *Damaszener Mitteilungen* 10:11–63.

Postgate, J. 1975. Some Old Babylonian Shepherds and Their Flocks. *Journal of Semitic Studies* 20/1:1–21.

1992. *Early Mesopotamia: Society and Economy at the Dawn of History.* London: Routledge.

Potts, D. 1984. On Salt and Salt Gathering in Ancient Mesopotamia. *Journal of the Economic and Social History of the Orient* 27/3:225–71.

1993. Rethinking Some Aspects of Trade in the Arabian Gulf. *World Archaeology* 24/3:423–40.

2009. Bevel-Rim Bowls and Bakeries: Evidence and Explanations from Iran and the Indo-Iranian Borderlands. *Journal of Cuneiform Studies* 61:1–23.

Quenet, P. 2007. Was There a Post-Uruk Collapse in the Carchemish Area? In *Euphrates River Valley Settlement: The Carchemish Sector in the Third Millennium BC*, edited by E. Peltenburg, 105–21. Levant Supplementary Series 5. Oxford: Oxbow.

Radcliffe-Brown, A. 1930/31. The Social Organization of Australian Tribes. *Oceania* 1: 34–63; 206–46; 322–41; 426–56.

1935. Patrilineal and Matrilineal Succession. *Iowa Law Review* 20:286–303.

Ranger, T. 1993. The Invention of Tradition Revisited: The Case of Colonial Africa. In *Legitimacy and the State in Twentieth Century Africa*, edited by T. Ranger and O. Vaughan, 201–5. London: Macmillan.

Reichel, C. 2002. Administrative Complexity in Syria during the 4th Millennium BC. The Seals and Sealings from Tell Hamoukar. *Akkadica* 123:35–56.

2009. Hamoukar. In *Oriental Institute 2008–2009 Annual Report*, edited by G. Stein, 77–87. Chicago: Oriental Institute.

Renfrew, C., and J. Cherry, eds. 1986. *Peer Polity Interaction and Socio-political Change*. Cambridge: Cambridge University Press.

Renger, J. 1995. Institutional, Communal, and Individual Ownership or Possession of Arable Land in Ancient Mesopotamia from the End of the Fourth to the End of the First Millennium B.C. *The Chicago-Kent Law Review* 71:269–313.

Richards, A. 1960. *East African Chiefs. A Study of Political Development in Some Uganda and Tanganyika Tribes*. London: Faber and Faber.

Richardson, S. 2007. Death and Dismemberment in Mesopotamia: Discorporation between the Body and the Body Politic. In *Performing Death: Social Analyses of Funerary Traditions in the Ancient near East and Mediterranean (OIS 3)*, edited by N. Laneri, 189–208. Chicago: Oriental Institute.

Ristvet, L. 2008. Legal and Archaeological Territories of the Second Millennium BC in Northern Mesopotamia. *Antiquity* 82:585–99.

Ristvet, L., and Weiss, H. 2005. The Hābūr Region in the Late Third and Early Second Millennium B.C. In *The History and Archaeology of Syria*, vol. 1, edited by W. Orthmann, 1–26. Saarbrucken: Saarbrucken Verlag.

Rivers, W. 1924. *Social Organization*. London: Kegan Paul, Trench, Trubner and Co.

Roaf, M. 1984. Ubaid Houses and Temples. *Sumer* 43:80–90.

Robertson, J. 1995. The Social and Economic Organization of Ancient Mesopotamian Temples. In *Civilizations of the Ancient Near East*, edited by J. M. Sasson. New York: Charles Scribner's Sons.

Rosen, S. 2009. History Does Not Repeat Itself: Cyclicity and Particularism in Nomad-Sedentary Relations in the Negev in the Long Term. In *Nomads, Tribes, and the State in the Ancient Near East: Cross-Disciplinary Perspectives*, edited by J. Szuchman, 57–86. Chicago: Oriental Institute Publications.

Ross, J. 2010. The Scribal Artifact: Technological Innovation in the Uruk Period. In *Agency and Identity in the Ancient Near East: New Paths Forward*, edited by S. Steadman and J. Ross, 80–98. London: Equinox.

Rothman, M. 2001. The Local and the Regional: An Introduction. In *Uruk Mesopotamia and Its Neighbors. Cross-Cultural Interactions in the Era of State Formation*, edited by M. Rothman, 3–26. School of American Research Advanced Seminar Series. Santa Fe, NM: School of American Research Press.

2002. Tepe Gawra: Chronology and Socio-Economic Change in the Foothills of Northern Iraq in the Era of State Formation. In *Artefacts of Complexity: Tracking the*

Uruk in the Near East, edited by J. N. Postgate, 49–77. Cambridge: British School of Archaeology in Iraq.

2003. Ripples in the Stream: Transcaucasia-Anatolian Interaction in the Murat/ Euphrates Basin at the beginning of the Third Millennium BC. In *Archaeology in the Borderlands: Investigations in Caucasia and Beyond*, edited by A. Smith and K. Rubinson, 95–110. Los Angeles: The Cotsen Institute of Archaeology.

2004. Studying the Development of Complex Society: Mesopotamia in the Late Fifth and Fourth Millennia BC. *Journal of Archaeological Research* 12/1:75–119.

2007. The Archaeology of Early Administrative Systems in Mesopotamia. In *Settlement and Society: Essays Dedicated to Robert McCormick Adams*, edited by E. Stone, 235–54. Los Angeles: Cotsen Institute of Archaeology; Chicago: Oriental Institute.

Rowton, M. 1965. The Topological Factor in the Hapiru Problem. *Assyriological Studies* 16:375–87.

1967a. The Woodlands of Ancient Western Asia. *Journal of Near Eastern Studies* 26:261–77.

1967b. The Physical Environment and the Problem of the Nomads. Recontre Assyriologique Internationale, *Comptes Rendus* 15:109–21.

1969a. The Abu Amurrim'. *Iraq* 31:68–73.

1969b. Watercourses and Water Rights in the Official Correspondance from Larsa and Isin. *Journal of Cuneiform Studies* 21:267–74.

1969c. The Role of Watercourses in the Growth of Mesopotamian Civilization. *Alter Orient and Altes Testament* 1:307–16.

1973a. Autonomy and Nomadism in Western Asia. *Orientalia* 42:247–58.

1973b. Urban Autonomy in a Nomadic Environment. *Journal of Near Eastern Studies* 32:201–15.

1974. Enclosed Nomadism. Journal of the Economic and Social History of the Orient 17/1:1–30.

1976a. Dimorphic Structure and Topology. *Oriens Antiquus* 15:17–31.

1976b. Dimorphic Structure and the Tribal Elite. *Studia Instituti Anthropos* 28:219–57.

1977. Dimorphic Structure and the Parasocial Element. *Journal of Near Eastern Studies* 36/3:181–98.

1980. Pastoralism and the Periphery in Evolutionary Perspective. In *L'Archéologie de l'Iraq du début de l'Époque Néolithique à 333 avant notre ère*, edited by M.-Th. Barrelet, 291–301. Paris: CNRS.

1981. Economic and Political Factors in Ancient Nomadism. In *Nomads and Sedentary Peoples*, edited by J. Castillo, 25–36. Mexico City: 30th International Congress of Human Sciences in Asia and North Africa.

1982a. War, Trade and the Emerging Power Center. In *Mesopotamien und seine Nachbarn*, edited by H. Nissen and J. Renger, 187–94. Berlin: Dietrich Reimer Verlag.

1982b. Sumer's Strategic Periphery in Topological Perspective. In *Zikir šumim: Assyriological Studies presented to F. R. Kraus on the Occasion of His Seventieth Birthday*, edited by G. van Driel et al., 318–25. Leiden: Nederlands Instituut voor het Nabije Oosten.

Rubio, G. 2006a. Writing in Another Tongue: Alloglottography in the Ancient Near East. In *Margins of Writing, Origins of Cultures: New Approaches to Writing and Reading in the Ancient Near East*, edited by S. Sanders, 33–66. Oriental Institute Symposia 2. Chicago: Oriental Institute Publications.

2006b. Shulgi and the Death of Sumerian. In *Studies in Sumerian Literature*, edited by P. Michałowski and N. Veldhuis, 167–79. Leiden: Brill/Styx.

In press. *Sumerian Literary Texts from the Ur III Period* (Mesopotamian Civilizations). Winona Lake, IN: Eisenbrauns.

Sagona, A. 1984. *The Caucasian Region in the Early Bronze Age*. Oxford: British Archaeological Reports.

Sagona, A., and P. Zimanksy. 2009. *Ancient Turkey*. New York: Routledge.

Sahlins, M. 1961. The Segmentary Lineage: An Organization of Predatory Expansion. *American Anthropologist* 80:53–70.

1968. *Tribesmen*. Englewood Cliffs, NJ: Prentice-Hall.

Said, E. 1978. *Orientalism*. New York: Vintage.

Saidel, Benjamin A., and Eveline J. van der Steen, eds. 2007. *On the Fringe of Society: Archaeological and Ethnoarchaeological Perspectives on Pastoral and Agricultural Societies*. BAR International Series1657. Oxford: Archaeopress.

Sallaberger, W. 1996. Calendar and Pantheon. In *Administrative Texts from Tell Beydar*, edited by F. Ismail, W. Sallaberger, P. Talon, and K. van Lerberghe, 85–7. Subartu II. Turnhout: Brepols.

2004. A Note on the Sheep and Goat Flocks, Introduction to texts 151–167. In *Third Millennium Cuneiform Texts from Tell Beydar (Seasons 1996–2002)*, edited by L. Milano, W. Sallaberger, P. Talon, and K. Van Lerberghe, 13–21. Subartu XII. Turnhout: Brepols.

2007. From Urban Culture to Nomadism: A History. In *Sociétés humaines et changement climatique à la fin du Troisième Millénaire: Une crise a-t-elle eu lieu en Haute-Mésopotamie?* edited by C. Marro and C. Kuzucuoglu, 417–56. Varia Anatolica 18. Paris: De Boccard.

Sallaberger, W., and A. Westenholz. 1999. *Mesopotamien. Akkade-Zeit und Ur III Zeit*. Orbis Biblicus et Orientalis 160/3. Freibourg Schweiz: Universitätsverlag and Göttingen: Vandenhoeck und Ruprecht.

Sallaberger, W., and J. Ur. 2004. Tell Beydar/Nabada in Its Regional Setting. In *Third Millennium Cuneiform Texts from Tell Beydar (Seasons 1996–2002.)*, edited by L. Milano, W. Sallaberger, P. Talon, and K. Van Lerberghe, 51–71. Subartu XII. Turnhout: Brepols.

Salzman, P. 1971. Introduction. *Anthropological Quarterly* 44/3:104–8.

1972. Multi-resource Nomadism in Iranian Baluchistan. In *Perspectives on Nomadism*, edited by W. Irons and N. Dyson-Hudson, 60–68. Leiden. Brill.

1978a. Ideology and Change in Middle Eastern Tribal Societies. *Man* 13/4:618–37.

1978b. Does Complementary Opposition Exist? *American Anthropologist* 80:53–70.

1978c. The Study of "Complex Society" in the Middle East: A Review Essay. *International Journal of Middle Eastern Studies* 9:539–57.

1980. Is Nomadism a Useful Concept? *Nomadic Peoples* 6:1–7.

1999. Is Inequality Universal? *Current Anthropology* 40/1:31–61.

2000. *Black Tents of Baluchistan*. Washington, DC: Smithsonian Institution Press.

2008a. *Culture and Conflict in the Middle East*. Amherst, NY: Humanity Books.

2008b. The Middle East's Tribal DNA. *Middle East Quarterly* 15/1:23–33.

Salzman, P., ed. 1980. *When Nomads Settle: Processes of Sedentarization as Adaptation and Response*. New York: Praeger.

Sanders, S. 2006. Margins of Writing, Origins of Cultures. In *Margins of Writing, Origins of Cultures: New Approaches to Writing and Reading in the Ancient Near East*, edited by S. Sanders, 3–11. Oriental Institute Symposia 2. Chicago: Oriental Institute Publications.

Sandstrom, A. 2000. Toponymic Groups and House Organization: The Nahuas of Northern Veracruz, Mexico. In *Beyond Kinship: Social and Material Reproduction in House Societies*, edited by R. Joyce and S. D. Gillespie, 53–72. Philadelphia: University of Pennsylvania Press.

Sasson, J. 1998. The King and I: A Mari King in Changing Perceptions. *Journal of the American Oriental Society* 118:453–70.

Scheffler, H. 1966. Ancestor Worship in Anthropology: Or, Observations on Descent and Descent Groups. *Current Anthropology* 7/5:541–51.

Schloen, J. 2001. *The House of the Father as Fact and Symbol: Patrimonialism in Ugarit and the Ancient Near East*. Winona Lake, IN: Eisenbrauns.

Schmandt-Besserat, D. 1992. *Before Writing. Vol. I, From Counting to Cuneiform*. Austin: University of Texas Press.

Schneider, D. 1967. Kinship and Culture: Descent and Filiation as Cultural Constructs. *Southwestern Journal of Anthropology* 23:65–109.

1980. *American Kinship: A Cultural Account*. 2nd ed. Chicago: University of Chicago Press.

1984. *A Critique of the Study of Kinship*. Ann Arbor: University of Michigan Press.

Schulting, R. 2009. Lex talionis, "An eye for an eye"? Contexts for Violence in Neolithic Europe. Paper Presented at the Second Visiting Scholar Spring Conference, *The Archaeology of Violence: An Integrated Approach to the Study of Violence and Conflict*. Institute for European and Mediterranean Archaeology. Buffalo, State University of New York, April 18–19.

Schwartz, G. 1988. Excavations at Karatut Mevkii and Perspectives on the Uruk/Jemdat Nasr Expansion. *Akkadica* 56:1–41.

1995. Pastoral Nomadism in Ancient Western Asia. In *Civilizations of the Ancient Near East*, edited by J. M. Sasson, 249–58. New York: Charles Scribner's Sons.

2000. Perspectives on Rural Ideologies: The Tell al-Raqa'i Temple. In *La Djéziré et l'Euphrate syriens de la protohistoire à la fin du second millénaire av. J.-C.: Tendances dans l'interprétation historique des données nouvelles*, edited by O. Rouault and M. Wäfler, 163–82. Subartu VII. Turnhout: Brepols.

2001. Syria and the Uruk Expansion. In *Uruk Mesopotamia and Its Neighbors: Cross-Cultural Interactions in the Era of State Formation*, edited by M. Rothman, 233–64. School of American Research Advanced Seminar Series. Santa Fe, NM: School of American Research Press.

2007. Status, Ideology, and Memory in Third Millennium Syria: "Royal" Tombs at Umm al Marra. In *Performing Death: Social Analysis of Funerary Tradition in the Ancient Near East and Mediterranean*, edited by N. Laneri, 39–68. Oriental Institute Seminar 3. Chicago: Oriental Institute.

Schwartz, G., and H. Curvers. 1992. Tell al-Raqa'i 1989 and 1990: Further Investigations at a Small Rural Site of Early Urban Northern Mesopotamia. *American Journal of Archaeology* 96:397–419.

Schwartz, G., and S. Falconer, eds. 1994. *Archaeological Views from the Countryside. Village Communities in Early Complex Societies*. Washington, DC: Smithsonian Institution Press.

Schwartz, G., and E. Klucas. 1998. Spatial Analysis and Social Structure at Tell al-Raqa'i. In *Espace natural, espace habité en Syrie du Nord (10ᵉ–2ᵉ millénaires av. J.-C.)*, edited by M. Fortin and O. Aurenche, 199–207. Toronto: The Canadian Society for Mesopotamian Studies.

Sconzo, P. 2010. *Tell el-Abd, Syria: A Study of the Third Millennium Pottery of a Small Settlement of the Middle Euphrates River Valley*. PhD diss., Eberhard Karls Universität Tübingen.

Seaman, G. 1991. Introduction: World Systems and State Formation on the Eurasian Periphery. In *Rulers from the Steppe: State Formation on the Eurasian Periphery*, edited by G. Seaman and D. Marks, 1–20. Los Angeles: University of Southern California.

Seri, A. 2005. *Local Power in Old Babylonian Mesopotamia*. London: Equinox.

Service, E. 1962. *Primitive Social Organization: An Evolutionary Perspective*. New York: Random House.

1975. *Origins of the State and Civilization: The Process of Cultural Evolution*. New York: W. W. Norton and Company.

Sharlach, T. 2004. *Provincial Taxation and the Ur III State*. Cuneiform Monographs 26. Leiden: Brill.

Shryock, A. 1997. *Nationalism and the Genealogical Imagination: Oral History and Textual Authority in Tribal Jordan*. Comparative Studies on Muslim Societies 23. Berkeley: University of California Press.

Sigrist, M. 1992. *Drehem*. Bethesda, MD: CDL Press.

1993. *Texts from the British Museum. Sumerian Archival Texts I*. Bethesda, MD: CDL Press.

Smith, A. 1991. *National Identity*. London: Penguin Books.

Smith, A. T. 2003. *The Political Landscape: Constellations of Authority in Early Complex Polities*. Berkeley: University of California Press.

2005. Prometheus Unbound: Southern Caucasia in Prehistory. *Journal of World Prehistory* 19:229–79.

Smith, L. 2004. *Archaeological Theory and the Politics of Cultural Heritage*. New York: Routledge.

Smith, M. 1956. On Segmentary Lineage Systems. *Journal of the Royal Anthropological Institute* 86:39–79.

Smith, S. 2003. *Wretched Kush: Ethnic Identities and Boundaries in Egypt's Nubian Empire*. London: Routledge.

Sommerfeld, W. 2000. Naram-Sin, die "Grosse Revolte" und MAR.TU^{ki}. In *Assyriologica et Semitica – Festschrift für Joachim Oelsner anlässlich seines 65. Geburtstages am 18. Februar 1997*, edited by J. Marzahn and H. Neumann, 419–36. Alter Orient und Altes Testament – AOAT 252. Münster: Ugarit-Verlag.

Southall, A. 1970. The Illusion of Tribe. In *The Passing of Tribal Man*, edited by P. Gutkind, 28–50. Leiden: Brill.

1988. The Segmentary State in Africa and Asia. *Comparative Studies in Society and History* 30/1:52–82.

Spivak, G. 1988. Can the Subaltern Speak? In *Marxism and the Interpretation of Culture*, edited by C. Nelson and L. Grossberg, 271–313. Urbana: University of Illinois Press.

Stein, G. 1987. Regional Economic Integration in Early State Societies: Third Millennium B.C. Pastoral Production at Gritille, Southeast Turkey. *Paléorient* 13/2:101–11.

1994a. Economy, Ritual, and Power in Ubaid Mesopotamia. In *Chiefdoms and Early States in the Near East: The Organizational Dynamics of Complexity*, edited by G. Stein and M. Rothman, 35–46. Monographs in World Prehistory 18. Madison, WI: Prehistory Press.

1994b. Segmentary States and Organizational Variation in Early Complex Societies: A Rural Perspective. In *Archaeological Views from the Countryside: Village Communities in Early Complex Societies*, edited by G. Schwartz and S. Falconer, 10–18. Smithsonian Series in Anthropological Inquiry. Washington, DC: Smithsonian Institution Press.

1998. Heterogeneity, Power, and Political Economy: Some Current Research Issues in the Archaeology of Old World Complex Societies. *Journal of Archaeological Research* 6/1:1–44.

1999a. Material Culture and Social Identities: The Evidence for a 4th Millennium BC Mesopotamian Uruk Colony at Hacinebi, Turkey. *Paléorient* 25/1:11–22.

1999b. *Rethinking World Systems: Diasporas, Colonies and Interaction in Uruk Mesopotamia*. Tuscon: University of Arizona Press.

2001a. Indigenous Social Complexity at Haçinebi (Turkey) and the Organization of Colonial Contact. In *Uruk Mesopotamia and Its Neighbors: Cross-Cultural Interactions in the Era of State Formation*, edited by M. Rothman, 265–306. School of American Research Advanced Seminar Series. Santa Fe, NM: School of American Research Press.

2001b. Understanding Ancient State Societies in the Old World. In *Archaeology at the Millennium: A Sourcebook*, edited by G. Feinman and T. D. Price, 353–79. New York: Klewer Academic Press.

2002. The Uruk Expansion in Anatolia: A Mesopotamian Colony and Its Indigenous Host Community at Hacinebi, Turkey. In *Artefacts of Complexity: Tracking the Uruk in the Near East*, edited by J. N. Postgate, 149–71. Cambridge: British School of Archaeology in Iraq.

2004. Structural Parameters and Sociocultural Factors in the Economic Organization of Northern Mesopotamian Urbanism in the Third Millennium B.C. In *Archaeological Perspectives on Political Economies*, edited by G. Feinman and L. Nichols, 61–79. Salt Lake City: University of Utah Press.

2005a. The Comparative Archaeology of Colonial Encounters. In *The Archaeology of Colonial Encounters: Comparative Perspectives*, edited by G. Stein, 3–31. School of American Research Advanced Seminar Series. Santa Fe, NM: School of American Research Press.

2005b. The Political Economy of Mesopotamian Colonial Encounters. In *The Archaeology of Colonial Encounters: Comparative Perspectives*, edited by G. Stein, 143–71. School of American Research Advanced Seminar Series. Santa Fe, NM: School of American Research Press.

Stein, G., R. Bernbeck, C. Coursey, A. McMahon, N. Miller, A. Misir, J. Nicola, H. Pittman, S. Pollock, and H. Wright. 1996. Uruk Colonies and Anatolian Communities: An Interim Report on the 1992–1993 Excavations at Hacinebi, Turkey. *American Journal of Archaeology* 100:205–60.

Stein, G., K. Boden, C. Edens, J. Edens, K. Keith, A. McMahon, and H. Özbal. 1997. Excavations at Hacinebi, Turkey – 1996. *Anatolica* 23:111–71.

Stein, G., and C. Edens. 1999. Hacinebi and the Uruk Expansion: Additional Comments. *Paléorient* 25/1:167–71.

Stein, G., and R. Özbal. 2007. A Tale of Two *Oikumenai*: Variation in the Expansionary Dynamics of 'Ubaid and Uruk Mesopotamia. In *Settlement and Society: Essays*

Dedicated to Robert McCormick Adams, edited by E. Stone, 329–42. Los Angeles: Cotsen Institute of Archaeology; Chicago: Oriental Institute.

Stein, G., and M. Rothman, eds. 1994. *Chiefdoms and Early States in the Near East: The Organizational Dynamics of Complexity*. Madison, WI: Prehistory Press.

Steinkeller, P. 1987a. The Foresters of Umma: Toward a Definition of Ur III Labor. In *Labor in the Ancient Near East*, edited by M. Powell, 73–115. American Oriental Series 68. New Haven, CT: American Oriental Society.

1987b. The Administrative and Economic Organization of the Ur III State: The Core and the Periphery. In *The Organization of Power: Aspects of Bureaucracy in the Ancient Near East*, edited by McG. Gibson and R. Biggs, 19–41. Studies in Ancient Oriental Civilization 46. Chicago: Oriental Institute.

1992. Early Semitic Literature and Third Millennium Seals with Mythological Motifs. In *Literature and Literary Language at Ebla*, edited by P. Fronzaroli, 243–84. Quaderni di Semistica 18. Florence: Università di Firenze.

1993. Early Political Development in Mesopotamia and the Origins of the Sargonic Empire. In *Akkad, The First World Empire: Structure, Ideology, Traditions*, edited by M. Liverani, 131–55. History of the Ancient Near East / Studies – 5. Padua: Sargon srl.

1999a. Land Tenure Conditions in Third Millennium Babylonia: The Problem of Regional Variation. In *Privatization in the Ancient Near East and Classical World*, vol. 1, edited by M. Hudson and B. Levine, 289–329. Bulletin No. 5. Peabody Museum of Archaeology and Ethnology. Cambridge, MA: Harvard University.

1999b. On Rulers, Priests and Sacred Marriage: Tracking the Evolution of Early Sumerian Kingship. In *Priests and Officials in the Ancient Near East: Papers of the Second Colloquium on the Ancient Near East: The City and Its Life Held at the Middle East Culture Center in Japan (Mitaka, Tokyo)*, edited by K. Watanabe, 103–37. Heidelberg: C. Winter.

2003. An Ur III Manuscript of the Sumerian King List. In *Literatur, Politik und Recht in Mesopotamien*, edited by W. Sallaberger, K. Volk, and A. Zgoll, 267–92. OBC 14. Weisbaden: Harrasowitz.

2004. A History of Mashkan-shapir and Its Role in the Kingdom of Larsa. In *The Anatomy of a Mesopotamian City: Survey and Soundings at Mashkan-shapir*, edited by E. Stone and P. Zimansky, 26–42. Winona Lake, IN: Eisenbrauns.

2007a. New Light on Šimaški and Its Rulers. *Zeitschrift für Assyriologie* 97:215–32.

2007b. On Sand Dunes, Mountain Ranges, and Mountain Peaks. In *Studies Presented to Robert D. Biggs, June 4, 2004*, edited by M. Roth, W. Farber, and M. Stolper, 219–32. From the Workshop of the Chicago Assyrian Dictionary, vol. 2. Chicago: Oriental Institute.

Stephen, F., and E. Peltenburg. 2002. Scientific Analyses of Uruk Ceramics from Jerablus Tahtani and other Middle-Upper Euphrates Sites. In *Artefacts of Complexity: Tracking the Uruk in the Near East*, edited by J. N. Postgate, 173–90. Iraq Archaeological Reports 5. Cambridge: British School of Archaeology in Iraq.

Stone, E. 2002. The Ur III-Old Babylonian Transition: An Archaeological Perspective. *Iraq* 64:79–84.

2007. The Mesopotamian Urban Experience. In *Settlement and Society: Essays Dedicated to Robert McCormick Adams*, edited by E. Stone, 213–34. Los Angeles: Cotsen Institute of Archaeology: Chicago: Oriental Institute.

Stone, E., and D. Owen. 1991. *Adoption in Old Babylonian Nippur and the Archive of Mannum-mešu-lişşur*. Mesopotamian Civilizations 5. Winona Lake, IN: Eisenbrauns.

Strathern, A. 1969. Descent and Alliance in the New Guinea Highlands: Some Problems of Comparison. *Proceedings of the Royal Anthropological Institute of Great Britain and Ireland* for 1968, 37–52.

———— 1973. Kinship, Descent and Locality: Some New Guinea Examples. In *The Character of Kinship*, edited by J. Goody, 21–33. Cambridge: Cambridge University Press.

Strathern, M. 1992a. *After Nature: English Kinship in the Late Twentieth Century*. Cambridge: Cambridge University Press.

———— 1992b. *Reproducing the Future: Essays on Anthropology, Kinship and the New Reproductive Technologies*. Manchester: Manchester University Press.

Streck, M. 2000. *Das amurritische Onomastikon der altbabylonischen Zeit*. Band 1. *Die Amurriter Die onomastische Forschung Othographie und Phonologie Nominalmorphologie*. Alter Orient und Altes Testament 271/1. Münster: Ugarit-Verlag.

Strommenger, E. 1980. *Habuba Kabira. Eine Stadt vor 5000 Jahren*. Mainz am Rhein: Philipp von Zabern.

Sudo, H. 2010. The Development of Wool Exploitation in Ubaid-Period Settlements of North Mesopotamia. In *Beyond the Ubaid: Transformation and Integration in the Late Prehistoric Societies of the Middle East*, edited by R. Carter and G. Philip, 169–79. Studies in Ancient Oriental Civilization 63. Chicago: Oriental Institute.

Suleiman, A., and A. Tarakji. 1995. Tell Kashkashouk III. *Syria* 72:172–83.

Sumner, W. 1986. Proto-Elamite Civilization in Fars. In *Gamdat Nasr: Period or Regional Style?* edited by U. Finkbeiner and W. Rollig, 199–211. Beihefte Zum Tübinger Atlas Des Vorderen Orients, Reihe B, Nr. 62.Weisbaden: Ludwig Reichert Verlag.

———— 1994. The Evolution of Tribal Society in the Southern Zagros Mountains, Iran. In *Chiefdoms and Early States in the Near East: The Organizational Dynamics of Complexity*, edited by G. Stein and M. Rothman, 47–65. Monographs in World Archaeology 18. Madison, WI: Prehistory Press.

Sürenhagen, D. 1978. *Untersuchungen zur Keramikproducktion innerhalb der Spät-Urukzeitichen Siedlung Ḥabuba Kabira-Süd in Nordsyrien*. Berlin: Verlag Bruno Hessling.

———— 1986. The Dry Farming Belt: The Uruk Period and Subsequent Developments. In *The Origins of Cities in Dry-Farming Syria and Mesopotamia in the Third Millennium B.C.*, edited by H. Weiss, 7–43. Guilford, CT: Four Corners.

Swanton, J. 1905. The Social Organization of American Tribes. *American Anthropologist* 7:663–73.

Sweet, R. 1994. A New Look at the "Sacred Marriage" in Ancient Mesopotamia. In *Corolla Tornontonensis: Studies in Honor of Ronald Morton Smith*, edited by E. Robbins and S. Sandahl, 85–104. Toronto: Tsar.

Swidler, N. 1972. The Development of the Kalat Khanate. In *Perspectives on Nomadism*, edited by W. Irons and N. Dyson-Hudson, 115–21. Leiden: Brill.

Szarzynska, K. 1993. Offerings for the Goddess Inana in Archaic Uruk. *Revue d'Assyriologie* 87/1:7–28.

Szuchman, J. 2009. Integrating Approaches to Nomads, Tribes, and the State in the Ancient Near East. In *Nomads, Tribes, and the State in the Ancient Near East: Cross-Disciplinary Perspectives*, edited by J. Szuchman, 1–13. Oriental Institute Seminars 5. Chicago: University of Chicago.

Talon, P. 1996. Personal Names. In *Administrative Texts from Tell Beydar*, edited by F. Ismail, W. Sallaberger, P. Talon, and K. van Lerberghe, 75–80. Subartu II. Turnhout: Brepols.

Tapper, R. 1979. The Organization of Nomadic Communities in Pastoral Societies of the Middle East. In *Pastoral Production and Society*, edited by L'Équipe ecologie et anthropologie des sociétiés pastorals, 43–66. Proceedings of the International Meeting on Nomadic Pastoralism – Paris 1–3 Dec. 1976. Paris: Éditions de la Maison des Sciences de l'Homme.

Thureau-Dangin, F. 1903. *Recueil des tablettes chaldéennes*. Paris: Ernest Leroux.

Tigay, J. 1982. *The Evolution of the Gilgamesh Epic*. Philadelphia: University of Pennsylvania Press.

Tilley, C. 1997. *A Phenomenology of Landscape: Places, Paths and Monuments*. Oxford: Berg.

    2004. *The Materiality of Stone: Explorations in Landscape Phenomenology*. Oxford: Berg.

    2006. Identity, Place, Landscape and Heritage. *Journal of Material Culture* 11/1:7–32.

    2007. Materiality in Materials. *Archaeological Dialogues* 14/1:16–20.

Tinney, S. 1999a. On the Curricular Setting of Sumerian Literature. *Iraq* 41:159–72.

    1999b. Ur-Namma the Canal-Digger: Context, Continuity and Change in Sumerian Literature. *Journal of Cuneiform Studies* 51:31–54.

Tonietti, M.-V. 2010. The Expedition of Ebla against Ašdar(um) and the Queen of Harran. *Zeitschrift für Assyriologie* 100: 56–85.

Trigger, B. 1996. Alternative Archaeologies: Nationalist, Colonialist, Imperialist. In *Contemporary Archaeology in Theory*, edited by R. Preucel and I. Hodder, 615–31. Oxford: Blackwell.

    2003. *Understanding Early Civilizations*. Cambridge: Cambridge University Press.

    2004. Writing Systems: A Case Study in Cultural Evolution. In *The First Writing: Script Invention as History and Process*, edited by S. Houston, 39–69. Cambridge: Cambridge University Press.

Trufelli, F. 2000. Andirons, Hut Symbols and Eye Idols. In *Proceedings of the First International Congress on the Archaeology of the Ancient Near East: Rome, May 18th–23rd 1998*, vol. 2, edited by P. Matthiae, A. Enea, L. Peyronel, and F. Pinnock, 1679–1689. Rome: Dipartimento di Scienze Storiche, Archeologiche e Anthropologiche dell'Antichità.

Tsukimoto, A. 1985. *Untersuchungen zur Totenpflege (kispum) im alten Mesopotamien*. Alter Orient und Altes Testament. Neukirchen-Vluyn: Neukirchener Verlag.

Ur, J. 2004. Urbanism and Society in the Third Millennium Upper Khabur Basin. PhD diss., University of Chicago.

    2010. Cycles of Civilization in Northern Mesopotamia, 4400–2000 BC. *Journal of Archaeological Research*. 18: 387–431.

Ur, J., P. Karsgaard, and J. Oates. 2007. Early Urban development in the Near East. *Science* 317:1188.

Valdés, C. 1995. La cerámic de las tumbas del *locus* 12 (Tell Qara Qūzāq, Siria, campaña de 1992). *Aula Orientalis* 13:31–58.

Valdés Pereiro, C. 1999. Tell Qara Quzak: A Summary of the First Results. In *Archaeology of the Upper Syrian Euphrates, the Tishrin Dam Area*, edited by G. del Olmo Lete and J.-L. Montero, 117–27. Aula Orientalis-Supplementa. Barcelona: Universität de Barcelona.

Van de Mieroop, M. 1993a. Sheep and Goat Herding According to Old Babylonian Texts from Ur. *Bulletin on Sumerian Agriculture* 7:161–82.

1993b. The Reign of Rim-Sin. *Revue d'Assyriologie* 87/1:47–69.

1999. Literature and Political Discourse in Ancient Mesopotamia: Sargon II of Assyria and Sargon of Agade. In *Munuscula Mesopotamia: Festschrift für Johannes Renger*, edited by B. Böck, E. Cangik-Kirschbaum, and T. Richter, 327–39. Alter Orient und Altes testament Band 267. Münster: Ugarit-Verlag.

2004. *A History of the Ancient Near East ca. 3000–323 BC*. Oxford: Blackwell.

Van der Steen, E. 2009. Tribal Societies in the Nineteenth Century: A Model. In *Nomads, Tribes, and the State in the Ancient Near East: Cross-Disciplinary Perspectives*, edited by J. Szuchman, 105–17. Oriental Institute Seminars 5. Chicago: Oriental Institute.

Van der Steen, E., and B. Saidel. 2007. On the Fringe of Society: Archaeological and Ethnoarchaeological Perspectives on Pastoral and Agricultural Societies: Introduction. In *On the Fringe of Society: Archaeological and Ethnoarchaeological Perspectives on Pastoral and Agricultural Societies*, edited by B. Saidel and E. van der Steen, 1–8. BAR International Series1657. Oxford: Archaeopress.

van der Toorn, K. 1994. Gods and Ancestors in Emar and Nuzi. *Zeitschrift für Assyriologie* 84:38–59.

1996. Domestic Religion in Ancient Mesopotamia. In *Houses and Households in Ancient Mesopotamia*, edited by K. Veenhof, 69–78. Leiden: Nederlands Instituut voor het Nabije Oosten.

van Driel, G. 2000. The Mesopotamian North: Land Use, An Attempt. In *Rainfall and Agriculture in Northern Mesopotamia (MOS Studies 3) Proceedings of the Third MOS Symposium (Leiden 1999)*, edited by R. M. Jas, 265–99. PIHANS 88. Leiden: Nederlands Historisch-Archaeologisch Instituut te Istanbul.

2002. Jebel Aruda: Variations on a Late Uruk Domestic Theme. In *Artefacts of Complexity: Tracking the Uruk in the Near East*, edited by J. Postgate, 191–205. Iraq Archaeological Reports 5. Cambridge: British School of Archaeology in Iraq.

van Driel, G., and C. van Driel-Murray. 1979. Jebel Aruda, 1977–78. *Akkadica* 12:2–33.

1983. Jebel Aruda, the 1982 Season of Excavation. *Akkadica* 33:1–26.

van Gennep, A. 1960. *The Rites of Passage*. First published 1909. Chicago: University of Chicago Press.

van Koppen, F. 2006. Old Babylonian Period Inscriptions and Miscellaneous Old Babylonian Period Documents. In *The Ancient Near East: Historical Sources in Translation*, edited by M. W. Chavalas, 88–133. Oxford: Blackwell.

Vanstiphout, H. 1996. Ambiguity as a Generative Force in Standard Sumerian Literature, or Empson in Nippur. In *Proceedings of the Groningen Group for the Study of Mesopotamian Literature*. Vol. 2, *Mesopotamian Poetic Language: Sumerian and Akkadian*, edited by M. Vogelzang and H. Vanstiphout, 155–66. Cuneiform Monographs 6. Groningen: Styx.

2000. A Meeting of Cultures? Rethinking the "Marriage of Martu." In *Languages and Cultures in Contact: At the Crossroads of Civilizations in the Syro-Mesopotamian Realm*, edited by K. van Lerberghe and G. Voet, 461–74. Orientalia Lovaniensia Analecta 96. Leuven: Peeters.

2002. Sanctus Lugalbanda. In *Riches Hidden in Secret Places: Ancient Near Eastern Studies in Memory of Thorkild Jacobsen*, edited by T. Abusch, 259–89. Winona Lake, IN: Eisenbrauns.

2004. *Epics of Sumerian Kings: The Matter of Aratta*. Leiden: Brill.

Veenhof, K. 1982. The Old Assyrian Merchants and Their Relations with the Native Population of Anatolia. In *Mesopotamien und seine Nachbarn*, edited by H. Nissen and J. Renger, 147–60. Berlin: Dietrich Reimer Verlag.

Veldhuis, N. 2001. The Solution of the Dream: A New Interpretation of Bilgames' Death. *Journal of Cuneiform Studies* 53:133–48.

2002. Review of Flückiger-Hawker 1999. *Journal of the American Oriental Society* 122:127–30.

2004. *Religion, Literature, and Scholarship: The Sumerian Composition "Nanše and the Birds," with a Catalogue of Sumerian Bird Names*. Cuneiform Monographs 22. Leiden: Brill

2006. How Did They Learn Cuneiform? Tribute/Word List C as an Elementary Exercise. In *Approaches to Sumerian Literature. Studies in Honour of Stip (H. L. J. Vanstiphout)*, edited by P. Michalowski and N. Veldhuis, 181–200. Leiden: Brill.

Verdon, M. 1980. Descent: An Operational View. *Man* 15:129–50.

Verhoeven, M. 1999. *An Archaeological Ethnography of a Neolithic Community: Space, Place and Social Relations in the Burnt Village at Tell Sabi Abyad, Syria*. PIHANS 83. Leiden: NINO-The Netherlands Institute for the Near East.

Viganò, L. 1995. Rituals at Ebla. *Journal of Near Eastern Studies* 54/3:215–22.

Waetzoldt, H. 1972. *Untersuchungen zur neusumerischen Textilindustrie*. Studi Economici e Tecnologici 1. Rome: Centro per le Antichità e la Storia dell'Arte Vicino Oriente.

1987. Compensation of Craft Workers and Officials in the Ur III Period. In *Labor in the Ancient Near East*, edited by M. Powell, 117–41. American Oriental Series 68. New Haven, CT: American Oriental Society.

Walls, N. 2001. *Desire, Discord and Death: Approaches to Near Eastern Myth*. Boston: American Schools of Oriental Research.

Wattenmaker, P. 1990. Comment on G. Algaze, The Uruk Expansion: Cross-Cultural Exchange in Early Mesopotamian Civilization. *Current Anthropology* 31:67–9.

1994. Political Fluctuations and Local Exchange Systems: Evidence from the Early Bronze Age Settlements at Kurban Höyük. In *Chiefdoms and Early States in the Near East: The Organizational Dynamics of Complexity*, edited by G. Stein and M. Rothman, 193–208. Madison, WI: Prehistory Press.

1998. *Household and State in Upper Mesopotamia*. Washington, DC: Smithsonian Institution.

Weber, J. 2008. Discarding Death and Burying Rubbish: Semantics and Agency in Practice. Paper Presented at the British Association for Near Eastern Archaeology, Liverpool, United Kingdom, February 29–March 2.

Weber, M. 1978. *Economy and Society: An Outline of Interpretive Sociology*, edited by G. Roth and C. Wittich. Berkeley: University of California Press.

Webster, J. 1997. Necessary Comparisons: A Post-Colonial Approach to Religious Syncretism in the Roman Provinces. *World Archaeology* 28/3:324–38.

Weismantel, M. 1995. Making Kin: Kinship Theory and Zumbagua Adoptions. *American Ethnologist* 22/4:685–704.

Weiss, B. 1996. *The Making and Unmaking of the Haya Lived World. Consumption, Commoditization, and Everyday Practice*. Durham, NC: Duke University Press.

Weiss, H. 1989. Comment on G. Algaze, The Uruk Expansion: Cross-Cultural Exchange in Early Mesopotamian Civilization. *Current Anthropology* 30:597–98.

1990. Tell Leilan 1989: New Data for Mid-Third Millennium Urbanization and State Formation. *Mitteilungen der Deutschen Orient-Gesellschaft zu Berlin* 122:193–218.

Weiss, H., and M.-A. Courty. 1993. The Genesis and Collapse of the Akkadian Empire: The Accidental Refraction of Historical Law. In *Akkad, The First World Empire: Structure, Ideology, Traditions*, edited by M. Liverani, 131–55. History of the Ancient Near East / Studies-5. Padua: Sargon srl.

Westenholz, J. 2007. The True Shepherd of Uruk. In *Studies Presented to Robert D. Biggs, June 4, 2004*, edited by M. Roth, W. Farber, and M. Stolper, 305–24. From the Workshop of the Chicago Assyrian Dictionary, vol. 2. Chicago: Oriental Institute.

Whiting, R. 1995. Amorite Tribes and Nations of Second-Millennium Western Asia. In *Civilizations of the Ancient Near East*, vols. 1–2, edited by J. M. Sasson, 1231–42. New York: Charles Scribner's Sons.

Wiggermann, F. 1996. Scenes from the Shadow Side. In *Proceedings of the Groningen Group for the Study of Mesopotamian Literature*, vol. 2: *Mesopotamian Poetic Language: Sumerian and Akkadian*, edited by M. E. Vogelzang and H. L. J. Vanstiphout, 207–30. Cuneiform Monographs 6. Groningen: Styx.

——— 2000. Agriculture in the Northern Balikh Valley. The Case of Middle Assyrian Tell Sabi Abyad. In *Rainfall and Agriculture in Northern Mesopotamia*, edited by R. Jas, 171–231. Istanbul: Nederlands Historisch-Archaeologisch Instituut.

Wilcke, C. 1987. Lugalbanda. *Reallexikon der Assyriologie* 7:117–32.

Wilkinson, T. A. 2002. Uruk into Egypt: Imports and Imitations. In *Artefacts of Complexity: Tracking the Uruk in the Near East*, edited by J. N. Postgate, 237–48. Cambridge: British School of Archaeology in Iraq.

Wilkinson, T. J. 1994. The Structure and Dynamics of Dry-Farming States in Upper Mesopotamia. *Current Anthropology* 35/5:483–520.

——— 2000. Settlement and Land Use in the Zone of Uncertainty in Upper Mesopotamia. In *Rainfall and Agriculture in Northern Mesopotamia (MOS Studies 3) Proceedings of the Third MOS Symposium (Leiden 1999)*, edited by R. M. Jas, 3–35. PIHANS 88. Leiden: Nederlands Historisch-Archaeologisch Instituut te Istanbul.

——— 2002. The Settlement Transition of the Second Millennium BC in the Western Khabur. In *Of Pots and Pans. Papers on the Archaeology and History of Mesopotamia and Syria Presented to David Oates in Honour of his 75th Birthday*, edited by L. al-Gailani Werr, J. Curtis, H. Martin, A. McMahon, J. Oates, and J. Reade, 361–72. London: Nabu.

——— 2003. *Archaeological Landscapes of the Near East*. Tucson: University of Arizona Press.

Wilkinson, T. J., J. H. Christiansen, J. Ur, M. Widell, and M. Altaweel. 2007. Urbanization within a Dynamic Environment: Modeling Bronze Age Communities in Upper Mesopotamia. *American Anthropologist* 109/1:52–68.

Williams, J. 2005. Picturing Food and Power at the Treaty Councils. *Oregon Historical Quarterly* 106/3:462–67.

Wolf, E. 1982. *Europe and the People without History*. Berkeley: University of California.

Woods, C. 2006. Bilingualism, Scribal Learning, and the Death of Sumerian. In *Margins of Writing, Origins of Cultures: New Approaches to Writing and Reading in the Ancient Near East*, edited by S. Sanders, 91–120. Oriental Institute Symposia 2. Chicago: Oriental Institute Publications.

Wossink, A. 2009. *Challenging Climate Change. Competition and Cooperation among Pastoralists and Agriculturalists in Northern Mesopotamia (c. 3000–1600 BC)*. Leiden: Sidestone.

Wright, H. 2001. Cultural Action in the Uruk World. In *Uruk Mesopotamia and Its Neighbors: Cross-Cultural Interactions in the Era of State Formation*, edited by M. Rothman, 123–48. School of American Research Advanced Seminar Series. Santa Fe, NM: School of American Research Press.

2002. Arrows and Arrowheads in the Uruk World. In *Of Pots and Pans. Papers on the Archaeology and History of Mesopotamia and Syria Presented to David Oates in Honour of his 75th Birthday*, edited by L. al-Gailani Werr, J. Curtis, H. Martin, A. McMahon, J. Oates, and J. Reade, 373–78. London: Nabu.

Wright, H., and G. Johnson. 1975. Population, Exchange, and Early State Formation in Southwestern Iran. *American Anthropologist* 77:267–89.

Wright, H., and E. Rupley. 2001. Calibrated Radiocarbon Age Determination of Uruk-Related Assemblages. In *Uruk Mesopotamia and Its Neighbors. Cross-Cultural Interactions in the Era of State Formation*, edited by M. Rothman, 85–122. School of American Research Advanced Seminar Series. Santa Fe, NM: School of American Research Press.

Wright, R. 1989. Comment on G. Algaze, The Uruk Expansion: Cross-Cultural Exchange in Early Mesopotamian Civilization. *Current Anthropology* 30:599–600.

1996. Technology, Gender and Class. Worlds of Difference in Ur III Mesopotamia. In *Gender and Archaeology*, edited by R. Wright, 79–104. Philadelphia: University of Pennsylvania Press.

1998. Crafting Social Identity in Ur III Southern Mesopotamia. *Archeological Papers of the American Anthropological Association* 8/1:57–69.

Xella, P. 1998. The Eblaite God Nidabal. In *"Und Mose schrieb dieses Lied auf," Studien zum Alten Testament und zum Alten Orient. Festschrift für Oswald Loretz*, edited by M. Dietrich and I. Kottsieper, 883–95. Alter Orient und Altes Testament 250. Münster: Ugarit-Verlag.

Yanagisako, S., and J. Collier. 1987. Toward a Unified Analysis of Gender and Kinship. In *Gender and Kinship: Essays toward a Unified Analysis*, edited by S. Yanagisako, and J. Collier, 14–50. Stanford, CA: Stanford University Press.

Yoffee, N. 1993. Two Many Chiefs? (or, Safe Texts for the '90s). In *Archaeological Theory. Who Sets the Agenda?* edited by N. Yoffee and A. Sherratt, 60–78. Cambridge: Cambridge University Press.

1995. Political Economy in Early Mesopotamian States. *Annual Review of Anthropology* 24:281–311.

1997. The Obvious and the Chimerical: City-States in Archaeological Perspective. In *The Archaeology of City-States: Cross-Cultural Approaches*, edited by D. Nichols and T. Charlton, 255–63. Washington, DC: Smithsonian Institution Press.

2005. *Myths of the Archaic State: Evolution of the Earliest Cities, States and Civilizations.* Cambridge: Cambridge University Press.

Young, R. 1995. *Colonial Desire.* London: Routledge.

Zagarell, A. 1986. Trade, Women, Class and Society in Ancient Western Asia. *Current Anthropology* 27:415–30.

Zarins, J. 1990. Early Pastoral Nomadism and the Settlement of Lower Mesopotamia. *Bulletin of the American Schools of Oriental Research* 280:31–67.

Zeder, M. 1991. *Feeding Cities: Specialized Animal Economy in the Ancient Near East.* Washington, DC: Smithsonian Institution Press.

1994. After the Revolution: Post-Neolithic Subsistence in Northern Mesopotamia. *American Anthropologist* 96/1:97–126.

1995. The Archaeobiology of the Khabur Basin. *Bulletin of the Canadian Society for Mesopotamian Studies* 29:21–32.

1998. Environment, Economy, and Subsistence on the Threshold of Urban Emergence in Northern Mesopotamia. In *Natural Space, Inhabited Space in Northern Syria (10ᵗʰ–2nd millennium B.C.)*, edited by M. Fortin and O. Aurenche, 55–67. Canadian Society for Mesopotamian Studies 33. Québec: Canadian Society for Mesopotamian Studies.

INDEX

Lightning Source UK Ltd.
Milton Keynes UK
UKOW02f0408010214

225696UK00006B/173/P